1982

CHOICE and ACTION

An Introduction to Ethics

CHOICE
AND
ACTION

An Introduction to Ethics

Charles L. Reid
Youngstown State University

Macmillan Publishing Co., Inc.
NEW YORK

Collier Macmillan Publishers
LONDON

Printed in the United States of America

Macmillan Publishing Co., Inc.
866 third avenue, new york, new york 10022

Collier Macmillan Canada, Ltd.

Library of Congress Cataloging in Publication Data

Reid, Charles L (date)
   Choice and action.

   1. Ethics—Addresses, essays, lectures. I. Title.
BJ1025.R44 170   80–12358
ISBN 0–02–399180–1

Printing: 1 2 3 4 5 6 7 8   Year: 1 2 3 4 5 6 7

To Frances

PREFACE

During the time in which this book has been in preparation and was being handed out in various forms to students in my Ethics course, "ethics" has undergone an enormous transformation. It has felt the impact of Rawls' *Theory of Justice,* demands for normative guidance in medicine and biomedical research, successive Supreme Court decisions (which often did as much to provoke debate as resolve it)—pornography, privacy, abortion, capital punishment, discrimination and reverse discrimination—there have been scandals in government throwing the glare of publicity on a "public life" that had not always been public, and there were demands by various groups for rights.

Yet, the classics in ethics retain their appeal and wisdom, and some are even more applicable than before. I have tried to bring forth from long discussion and testing of the materials in this book a text that would serve the dual purpose of providing a sound and decently comprehensive foundation in systematic ethics from the classical theories and at the same time a treatment of contemporary normative issues in ethics that would throw some light on the field and moderate the confusion that attends the popular debates by sharpening the issues and reducing the "fear of the unknown." Accordingly the book is divided into two Parts: Part One being a systematic treatment of the theoretical issues in ethics, and Part Two being a presentation of contemporary normative problems centering around rights, issues of life and death and human intervention in other sensitive and dangerous areas of people's life and mind.

I am happy to acknowledge the assistance of several persons who helped to make this book better: First, my classes in "Ethical Theories" who used and commented on several trial versions of the expository material; my colleague Professor Tom Shipka who offered helpful suggestions on an early draft of Chapter One; Professor Charles Kielkopf of Ohio State University for comments on an early draft of several chapters; Professors John Hudson of the University of Texas at Austin and Joseph Kupfer of Iowa State University of Science and Technology for comments on parts of the manuscript in a semi-final form and suggestions for readings; Professor Arthur Wheeler of Kent State University for the same; and especially grateful appreciation to Professor George E. Massey of California State University at Long Beach for enthusiastic, painstaking and expert criticism and helpful advice on the semi-final and final drafts. I must apologize to these people for any failure to make the most of their suggestions, since it was seldom that I seriously disagreed with them. In one case, another publisher's permissions policy severely restricted the scope of one reading selection. Otherwise, responsibility for the book remains mine.

At Macmillan, Ken Scott and Ellen Rope were patient and helpful. Youngstown State University gets credit for a sabbatical in which part of the work was done, for the services of Interlibrary Loan under Hildegard Schnuttgen and for Anna Ficocelli of the Department of Philosophy, who typed various parts of various drafts.

C.L.R.

Youngstown State University

CONTENTS

PART *TWO*

Contemporary Normative Ethical Problems   237

Contents

CHOICE and ACTION
An Introduction to Ethics

PART
ONE

Theoretical Issues
in Ethics

1
Ethics, Society, and Individuals

Cindy's college registration says she is a sophomore, nineteen, and single. She says she is in love. Her doctor says she's pregnant. In the age of "the Pill," IUD, and sex education, she suddenly finds herself statistically among those American "expectant mothers" who did not plan it that way.*

Some time ago, she made up her mind about "premarital sex" and now her problem is not the risk of pregnancy but how long to stay pregnant and what to do after the pregnancy ends, naturally or artificially. What is alive inside her grows daily and relentlessly. She cannot avoid some choices that will affect her future and the lives of an undetermined number of other persons. Even if she makes no plans, and willy-nilly gives birth one day on the subway, she will have chosen to do something for which she, and others, will take the consequences. Plenty of advice—all too much—is available to her and will no doubt be offered readily by her closest girl friend, her mother, "him," a clergyman, a social worker, or even the dean of women. She can get an abortion, or OD; she can marry the guy or move in with him, or put the baby out for adoption, raise it as a single parent, leave it on a doorstep, or smother it and hide the body. Some of these may be impossible actions for her to take, and none of the options may be easy.

Some General Problems and Types of Ethics

Cindy's is a moral problem since it concerns value issues about her welfare and that of other people. It is not an "academic" question for her, or for anyone who cares. It can, however, illustrate some of

* In the 1970s teenage pregnancies in the United States averaged about 1 million per year. About one sixth of the estimated 4 million sexually active American female teenagers would have an unwanted pregnancy in any given year (Richard Lincoln, "Is Pregnancy Good for Teenagers?", *U.S.A. Today,* **107:** 2398 [July, 1978], p. 36).

the main problems of ethics and some of the main answers that have been arrived at by some very brilliant and dedicated thinkers of the past and present. It can show the peculiarities of those issues called "moral" and what is involved in trying to meet them on the most favorable ground. And not least, it opens up the question of whether questions of right and wrong, good and evil are really rational questions at all and whether any solution to them can be arrived at solely by thinking about them. Although Cindy knew the risks, something happened to her that she did not want to happen; she is very unhappy and finds her future very uncertain. She wonders, as anyone does who thinks about morality, whether her decision about pregnancy will result in equal or worse predicaments than her decisions about "sex." In her turmoil she is likely to conclude that questions about what she *should* do, morally, are irrelevant, and that she *will* do simply whatever her heredity and environment *make* her do.

The first issue to be clarified is the difference between facts and values. *Questions of fact* are questions about what is true and what is false: "Am I pregnant?" was a question of fact. "Yes, my dear, you are" was the answer. Generally, questions of fact have the characteristic that their answers, e.g., in this case "Yes" or "No" are testable by some widely accepted method, such as the rabbit test.

A *question of value* actually divides into two parts: first, a question of *value* as such, including issues about what is most worthwhile, what is good or evil, desirable or undesirable; secondly, a question of *obligation,* including what actions are morally right or wrong, moral responsibility, what one ought to do, one's duty, and so on.

Cindy's values are the things she thinks most worthwhile, the kind of life she wants most, and the kind of person she wants to be. "Do I want to have a baby now, with all that the choice is likely to include?" is a question of value, and that includes questions of the best means of bringing those values about or protecting them. This and the question of obligation, "Should I remain pregnant?" contrast with the question of fact, "Am I pregnant?" (which will, so to speak, answer itself sooner or later). To ask, "Should I remain pregnant?" is to ask, "What ought I to do about this pregnancy?" or, "Which of the available options open to me should I take?"

Is there any expert on morality who can answer questions of "Should I?" as the doctor answered the question of "Am I?" That problem resolves into this: Is there any kind of test for right and wrong (such as the rabbit test) for questions of fact? There are all sorts of people of whom it is *said* that they are authorities on morality: sociologists, theologians, philosophy professors, and Mom. But their tests give conflicting answers, and we are thrown back to the question, Are they really experts; do they know? For surely a "Yes" from a social worker and a "No" from a priest on the question of abortion cannot both be "knowledge" any more than there can be two different answers to the same mathematics problem. The issue involved here is *how* to arrive at a "correct" answer to questions of value as one does in questions of fact. Widespread disagreement on morals may make us throw up our hands. But that could be a copout. I am, after all, responsible for my choices and must take the consequences. The very least that the study of ethics could hope to do would be to examine the peculiar nature of morality and if no sure-fire tests for good and evil, right and wrong, are available, at least to see why there are not.

We are likely to suffer from a premature sense of confusion and despair here and say, "It's all a matter of opinion." But even if so, is one opinion as good as another? And when I must act on my opinion, do I actually suppose that any opinion I follow will be as good as another? I have not said that solutions of moral problems are simple and easy. Patience is required. But neither are they baffling enigmas. A little thought here can sharpen the issue of facts and values: Solutions to moral problems, moral "answers," are only as good as the *reasons* on which they are based. Philosophy generally asks the question of what the difference is between good reasons and bad reasons for anything; and moral philosophy, or "ethics," concerns the reasons why anything is worthwhile and why one choice is better than another. When I spoke of tests for good and evil, right and wrong, that is what I meant: reasons why.

As a question of values, Cindy's problem is to do whatever will help her to have the kind of life she wants most. But that is not the only issue involved. For example, abortion will surely cross her mind as a possible way out of her predicament, of continuing in college, of preventing too early a marriage and responsibilities and disapproval of people whose respect she values. But some will tell her in horror that abortion is wrong in itself, regardless of the idealistic ends it might serve. They will say that it is not a question of what she values, but what God, or Nature, values and commands, and that God or Nature, or both, are dead set against it, and that she will act contrary to God and Nature if she has an abortion. No end could possibly justify this means, they will say.

We can notice in passing that a couple of questions of fact are essential to this issue. One is whether in fact God or Nature are set against abortion, indeed whether in fact such a thing as God or Nature exists. Again, the reason why God and Nature will be said to oppose abortion is that it is the taking of human life when everything is set up to bring about and further human life. The second question of fact here is whether abortion is indeed the taking of a human life or not. Answers to these questions of fact, yes or no, will surely be essential to the further moral question of "Ought I to have an abortion?"

But we must not get sidetracked from the main distinctions in ethics here, the issue raised by those who advise her against abortion because it is an act that is always wrong and never justified by any circumstances (except, perhaps, to save her life, which is not in danger at the moment) is one called a problem of *obligation.*

Those who say that there are some actions that are simply wrong in all circumstances try to separate questions of obligation from questions of values as much as possible, and make the issue of right and wrong actions decidable by some test other than the results of actions. Such theories of obligation are generally called deontological (from the Greek for "it is obligatory") theories, and are represented by Immanuel Kant in Chapter Six. The other theory of obligation—or family of theories, called result theories, teleological theories, or consequentialist theories—insists that the *results* of an action make it right or wrong; that is, that the issue of right and wrong hangs upon the issue of what is good or evil, and that to do *right* is simply to do what brings about the best possible *results.* Those who say that some acts, such as stealing, lying, and murder, are always wrong hold that whatever good result the act might have cannot possibly justify performing it. Do not tamper with human life, they will say; that is God's business. Let Him judge what will be best, and He has already said in the Bible and in Nature that it will be best not to take human life, to lie, or to steal.

There is a section of readings in this book in which different thinkers give their arguments for and against abortion. The point of this discussion is to show that questions about means and ends are central to moral problems, and that there is a fundamental division of theories based on the role of ends or values in deciding questions of right and wrong actions. Later I shall maintain that it is basically contrary to reason in general to say that an action of a certain kind is *always* wrong, regardless of the circumstances or the results of the act. For it is a part of what is meant by intelligence and reasoning that one considers the consequences and differs one's actions with differing circumstances. Besides, those who argue that questions of right and wrong are independent of the question of the good or bad results of actions usually smuggle in results, anyway—e.g., in terms of eternal punishment as a consequence of murder—and thus accept the theory they deny, after all. And again, I shall challenge the confused notion that God's or Nature's values are beyond human comprehension but nevertheless are known by theologians and others.

This may be a convenient place to review some of the things I have said before going on to different aspects of ethics. First, ethics is about choices and actions that affect human welfare, or what is right. (Later we shall have to add the welfare of all sentient beings, for such problems as cruelty to animals, preserving species, and so on.) Welfare, of course, is a matter of values. Questions in ethics or moral philosophy are questions about what is most worthwhile or good and about what ought to be done. A general answer to "What is worthwhile (or good)?" is a theory of value. A general answer to "What ought I to do (or what is right)?" is a theory of obligation. I have spoken of the difference between questions of fact and questions of value, and said that answers to questions of fact are tested by rules of evidence, especially experiment and observation, e.g., looking and seeing. But the answer to questions of value and obligation are not so easily agreed upon by using such direct empirical tests as looking and seeing that something is or is not the case. All sorts of people can agree that Cindy is pregnant, but will disagree as to whether she *ought* to be, whether it is right, and so forth. And this raised the question of whether moral and value judgments such as "Cindy ought to get an abortion" or "Cindy would do wrong if she put her baby out for adoption" could ever be *rational* judgments, as "Cindy is one month pregnant" is. Lastly, I have mentioned two general types of theories of obligation, one that says that what is right is to be defined in terms of what will bring about the most good, and this is called a *result-theory* or *teleological* theory of obligation. The other type of theory says that questions of right must be settled independently of good or bad results of actions. This kind of theory is called *deontological* and it holds that actions are right in themselves or wrong in themselves, just by virtue of being the kind of acts they are.

Three Kinds of Study of Ethics: Some Fact–Value Confusions, Red Herrings, and Blind Alleys

The phenomenon of widespread moral disagreement and the diversity of morals in different societies, times, and places is the greatest obstacle to any serious thinking about ethics. The growth of the sciences of psychology and sociology provide very tempting short circuits to an understanding of the nature of morality and what people are doing when they make moral or value judgments. It is particularly easy but grotesquely premature to say at the outset, "It's all a matter of opinion," "It's up to the individual," "Morals are relative," or "There are no universal, objective moral standards," or simply, "What's right for you may be wrong for me," or "Who's to say what's right?" It is tempting because one is very strongly lured to some quick and easy general formula that will cut through the maze of contradictions and controversies in morals. Such a formula that does not get down to the peculiar features of moral judgments and the institution of human morality is not a solution but a conclusion that there is no solution, or, which is much the same, that there are as many solutions as there are individuals or groups. When "the experts" disagree, as they do in ethics, it provides a perfect opportunity to say, "To hell with it, why should I bother my head?" Aristotle saw this when he confronted rampant relativism and skepticism in ancient Greece and said of ethics: It is the mark of an educated man that he does not seek more precision than the subject-matter permits. Ethics is not a science at all, much less an exact science. But much more has been done to clarify issues and arrive at tentative solutions than the beginner can imagine. You have seen that I have already argued that questions of value and obligation are different from questions of fact. You *may* or may not think that is sufficient reason to close the book if you believe that questions of fact are the only kinds of questions that can be answered, and thus moral questions are outside the pale of human intelligence or reason. But more, much more, can be done towards "answers."

It can at least be agreed beyond doubt that people do have values, because everyone thinks that some things are better than others and that some things are very bad indeed. People do offer justifications for their actions as to why they are right, or confess that they have done wrong at sometime or another in their lives and have reasons for thinking that they did wrong. One may object that they never *know* whether something is valuable or not, and that they never know whether they did right or not. That objection has to be met if one is to take ethics seriously. But at least everybody does have ideas about right and wrong, good and evil. That branch of ethics that is the study of what people do believe and practice with regard to values and right and wrong is called descriptive ethics.

More than anything else, descriptive ethical statements are a reporting or describing of moral beliefs and practices of individuals or groups, as contrasted with *evaluating* these. Many examples of descriptive ethics occur in sociology, anthropology, and psychology.

If you say that you believe that murder is always wrong and if your actions are consistent with this—e.g., if you refuse to kill someone whom you would like very much to be out of this world and whose murder you could commit without being punished for—these are surely *facts about* your values that can be observed and reported. So with the moral beliefs and practices of a group. If natives of a certain island practice infanticide, it can be observed and reported. Gallup polls may or may not be accurate but furnish some reasons for conclusions as to what Americans believe about the rightness or wrongness of smoking pot. The questions of whether infanticide or smoking pot are wrong or right are a different kind of question from the question of whether people *believe* that it is, and *act* as if it were.

If you *make* a moral judgment, that is different from *reporting* someone else's moral or value judgment. The making and justification of moral judgments is called normative ethics. If I say, "War is evil," that is making a normative judgment. If I go on to say, "It is evil because it destroys life and life is valuable," that, too, is a normative judgment. When I say or think that anything is good or evil, right or wrong, virtuous or vicious, that is engaging in normative ethics.

As distinguished from the reporting or describing function of descriptive statements in ethics, the task of statements in *normative* ethics is to make or justify moral judgments. I might in some sense "report" my *own* moral judgment in, say, answering "Yes" to the question asked of prospective jurors, "Do you oppose capital punishment?" But generally expressions of one's own moral judgments are normative, and to say that I think capital punishment is evil in so many words is a normative, not a descriptive, judgment.

If all making of moral judgments could be interpreted as statements of *fact* (which is not to imply that any could), many people might feel less puzzled about ethics. Suppose that the statement, "Capital punishment is evil," was always simply a "report" or description of one's own psychological state, a reading off of one's feelings as one might answer a physician's question when asked, "There, does that feel better now?" Then, "I feel that the death penalty is wrong" would be a literal telling of how one feels, telling what feelings one has, as it were, almost as symptoms might be reported to a psychiatrist. This has serious disadvantages that we shall discuss later under Subjectivism in Chapter Two, disadvantages that seem to be a high price for the simplification that it would accomplish. I can only indicate it is one thing to talk about one's *feelings* (describe them, and so on) and quite another to talk about capital punishment. In other words, to say that moral judgments are simply factual reports of the speaker's feelings is to state that they are not about, say, capital punishment at all. But it is about capital punishment and not my feelings I am talking about when I pronounce it evil. It may be an unjustified statement, but it is not one that is justified by asking whether I do in fact have that feeling.

The same sort of arguments apply against the notion that all moral judgments are simply reporting one's conscience or the beliefs of one's group. Suppose we should say "Well, 'war is evil' simply means 'My conscience is against war' or 'I have been taught to believe that war is evil.'" That is a confusion. I do one kind of thing to show you that my conscience is against war, or I offer you one kind of reason for you to believe that my conscience is against war, but I would never offer either as a reason why you should believe that war is evil. "War is evil because it is against my conscience" is very different from "War is evil because it destroys human life and human life is valuable." The same reason would apply against the notion that normative moral judgments are simply reports of one's group's beliefs.

"My church is against war on moral grounds" is a report about one's church, and is not a normative judgment about war. The following question would still be open: "Yes, I know your conscience is against war or your church is opposed to war as evil, but *is* war evil?" No one would say that thinking war was good makes war good, and the same sort of argument has to apply to thinking that war is evil. But for all this, some important points in ethics are made by the view that "nothing's either good or bad, but thinking makes it so." We shall have to await a fuller context to see these points, but for now the mere fact that I have a belief does not make the belief true.

I was engaging in *metaethics* in my discussion of what moral judgments are and what they mean, and what people are doing when they say or think that something is right or wrong, good or evil. The judgment, " 'Right' does not mean 'believed to be right,' " was a metaethical judgment. It consists not in reporting moral judgments and practices nor in making moral judgments, but in talking about what moral judgments are, what they mean, and how they work. So does the statement, "Facts are different from values." Metaethics is a *conceptual* activity, not a sociological observation or report about actual moral beliefs and practices of individuals or groups. What it is about is the meaning and function of moral concepts, and not about sociological, anthropological, or psychological facts. At the risk of some confusion, it can be said that there is a descriptive element in metaethics, and that this consists of getting the facts on how people do use their moral words. And there is very much a normative element in metaethics, and it consists of applying conceptual and epistemological norms, not moral norms. Suppose you say, "War is wrong but armed conquest of one nation by another is okay." I would have to answer with some sort of inquiry or remark about what you mean, such as, "I don't understand; you seem to be contradicting yourself. Isn't armed conquest war, and if war is wrong, isn't armed conquest wrong, too?" I would not be talking about war and its wrongness, but about your statement about war, and what it means. My reply would then be metaethics, not normative or descriptive ethics. The example is bizarre but the same sort of principle becomes more important when discussing such issues as whether all killing of human beings is murder or whether abortion is murder. I would be questioning the meaning of important moral words, and concepts. Disputes about killing and abortion can go on endlessly unless it is clear to both parties what they are saying. Simple as this seems, there is often an obvious sort of refusal to come to grips with these metaethical issues in just these debates about abortion, capital punishment, and war.

To summarize, reporting moral beliefs and practices is categorized as *descriptive ethics;* making moral judgments and attempting to justify them as *normative ethics;* and clarifying or explaining moral judgments as *metaethics.* They are different because they are about different things. A report is about what people actually think or actually do; a moral judgment is about what people ought to think or ought to do; a metaethical judgment is a judgment about moral judgments, not about people or actions.

The distinction helps to eliminate some dogging confusions. Suppose I say, "What was right twenty years ago is wrong today," or "What is right in Samoa is wrong in Timbuctoo." What am I talking about? It isn't clear. Am I reporting the difference between people's moral beliefs today and their beliefs twenty years ago, and am I giving a factual account of the differences between morals in Samoa and Timbuctoo? If so, that's one thing, descriptive ethics. But if I am agreeing with the people of twenty years ago and the people of today, or with the people of Samoa and the people of Timbuctoo (admittedly a very puzzling thing for me to do), then I am engaging in normative ethics, making moral judgments, not reporting them. Again, if I am saying something abut the meaning of right and wrong and the nature of morality as an institution, then I am engaging in metaethics. The distinction between the three kinds of talk about morality is essential to understanding the doctrine that "morals are relative," i.e., relativism. For to say, "Morals are relative" seems in many people's talk to be the same as to say, "Moral beliefs and practices vary from place to place and time to time." The latter is a judgment in descriptive ethics but it can easily be thought to be an open-and-shut case in metaethics, i.e., that it is of the very nature of morality that it is relative; or in normative ethics, e.g., that when one is in Rome he should do as the Romans do, or that whatever is thought to be right is right. These problems will be discussed further in Chapter Two and in the readings on relativism.

"Who's to Say What's Right?": A Question About Knowing Right from Wrong, or About Sticking Your Nose into Other People's Business

It is becoming clear that one's first systematic look into some of the technicalities of ethics is likely to be haunted by the deep suspicion that it is an impossible task; and that ethics is not even an academic subject, much less a branch of human knowledge. I have repeatedly tried to counteract that suspicion by showing some of the confusions that it is often based upon. The next issue we will examine in this chapter is another manifestation of this reaction, and one that is frequently heard. In light of all the moral disagreement that so much blood has been spilled over—and ink—down the centuries, it is a natural question; it is not necessarily an unanswerable one.

The first fact to note is that everyone does "say what is right." You say what is right every day, when you decide what you ought to do. The question is whether you can only say what is right for you and not for anyone else. And there is an obvious sense in which a person cannot say what is right for anyone else: He or she cannot make other people's moral decisions for them (unless, of course, they first decide to abide by these decisions, but that is their decision, not his or hers). For making a decision is rather like taking medicine: No one can take it for you; that is part of the meaning of "taking medicine" and "making a decision." But is this all that is meant by saying that no one can say what is right for anyone else?

No, for "saying what is right for someone else" also means "saying what would be right for someone else to do." I shall argue that if a person cannot say what is right for someone else, that person cannot say what is right for him or her, either. If "who's to say what's right?" and "who's to judge?" reflect a strong individualism, I can cite one of the most rugged individualists and subjectivists of all, Jean-Paul Sartre, who said that every choice made by an individual is a choice made for all individuals, for it is saying what any and every human being should do in circumstances.

Let's take a more down-to-earth example: Andy Sr. is a big brawny man in his early fifties. He is a union steward in a machine shop. In his youth he liked to drink beer every evening in the local taverns, and was quite a rugged individualist. He never allowed what he took to be a slight against his ethnic background, his favorite football team, his religion, or his current girl friend to go unchallenged. And he never lost a fight. If a guy's mouth was too big, it was reason enough for Andy to loosen his teeth. But now it's different. Andy regrets all those tavern brawls, and thinks that he was wrong. He drinks his beer at home and is active in his men's group at church. Andy Jr. is twenty-two. He comes home once or twice a week with a definite aroma of draft beer about him, skinned knuckles, and an occasional black eye, but always a winner's grin. Andy Sr. shakes his head. "That's me all over again when I was his age," he says. "The kid's got a lot to learn. He'll regret it when he gets arrested or marks somebody up the way I did old Stan down at the shop. I put a scar on his lip. It was over nothing. But I ain't gonna tell him what to do. He's got his own life to live. I ain't saying he's wrong. Who am I to tell a twenty-two-year-old what's right or wrong?"

So Andy Sr. is as good an example of "who's to say" as anybody. He thinks that it was wrong for him to be a tavern brawler in his youth and not just now that he's in his fifties. He isn't saying—exactly —that it is wrong for anybody else, even for his son. Now I said that Andy Sr. is also a union steward at the shop. His boss cuts all kinds of corners on safety devices and gets all the sweat out of the men that he can, and Andy Sr. is busy with grievances and hearings about working conditions and violations of the contract. He is an old union man from way back, and he will harangue you for hours about a living wage and decent human working conditions. The boss is driven by ambition to get ahead in the world and his wife is a social climber and hooked on credit cards. Andy Jr. has imbibed some of his father's individualism and has said on more than one occasion to his father, "Look, Dad, if you were ambitious and your wife never had enough money, you'd drive the men the same as Al (the boss) does. How do you know what you'd do if you were in his shoes?" Andy Sr. always turns a little red and says, "Hell, we're human beings, not animals!" and walks out of the room. He is saying what's right for somebody else: his boss, and any boss; his fellow workers, and any workers.

Let's look for a moment at "who's to say" in these three situations: Andy Sr.'s youthful tavern brawling, Andy Jr.'s youthful tavern brawling, and the working conditions at the shop. Andy Sr. is not saying that it was right for him to be a tavern brawler when he was young, but wrong now that he's too old; he is saying it was wrong for him when he was young, though at the time he thought it was a duty to take no guff from anybody. So he is judging himself as a young man and saying it was wrong for him then and not just wrong now. He's unwilling to say that it's wrong for Andy Jr., his spitting image. In fact, I can see no difference between the two men and the two cases except that Andy Sr. is one individual and Andy Jr. is another. Why would it not be wrong for Andy Jr. if it was wrong for Andy Sr.? What is the difference? Probably the really important factor here is that Andy Sr. confuses making a moral judgment about a situation with running somebody else's life, a very different thing.

His moral indignation at his boss is much more consistent. He is ready to say that it would be wrong for anybody to use any employee the way his boss does, and that it is right not just for him, but for all workers not to be "sweated" to have a living wage and reasonably safe working conditions. Here he not only "says what's right" in the sense of making a moral judgment about other people, but he "says what's right" when he stands up for the workers and tells the boss to back off, or they'll walk out. The boss complains at home, over martinis, that the union is trying to run his life for him, and his wife quite agrees.

Let's press this a little further. If Andy Jr. *asked* Andy Sr. if he thought it was wrong for Andy Jr. to throw a punch when somebody made a crack about his religion or his ethnic background, Andy Sr. would probably reluctantly say, "Yes, it's wrong. But that's just my opinion." It would appear that the real crux of the "who's to say what's right" query is that people don't like to be told that they are wrong and that other people are, therefore, reluctant to tell them. In-

consistently, they like to have the moral judgment passed on them
that they are right, not just because other people don't like to hear
criticism, but because they, too, don't want to open up any discussions by others of *their* conduct. "Keep your nose out of my private
affairs and I'll keep mine out of yours."

But that is not the issue in moral philosophy or ethics. That issue
is whether one individual's moral judgments in any sense apply to
any other individual. And I have argued that if my moral judgments
apply to my conduct, they apply to the conduct of everybody else who
is in the same circumstances that I am. Granted that everybody is an
individual and that no two individuals are alike, it would be a mistake to suppose that an individual judges his or her own case on the
basis of the totality of all his or her peculiarities and differences from
other people, and on the basis of all the minute details of the prevailing circumstances. What I am arguing is that there are no morally
important differences in the case of Andy Sr. and Andy Jr. as tavern
brawlers, just as there are no important moral differences between
Andy Sr.'s shop and other shops like it. A punch in the jaw is a punch
in the jaw, an injured workman is an injured workman, and a drop
of sweat is a drop of sweat. And the fact that it is not prudent to
go around offering moral advice that is not asked for does not in
the least invalidate the moral judgment that, say, Andy Jr. morally
ought to be more careful and keep his fists to himself.

If this example illustrates nothing else, it does at least show that
even when people seem to think very little of moral judgments by
saying, "Who's to say what's right? or "Who's to judge?" they nevertheless do consider other people's moral opinions of them very important, because they don't want to hear a negative moral judgment
passed on themselves by others.

Ethics and Society: The Moral Point of View

This importance of applying the same standards to other people
that one does to one's own decisions has been emphasized in several recent writings in ethics as fundamental to what is called the
moral point of view. It will hardly be questioned that ethics is primarily a social phenomenon concerning relationships between human beings and how they treat each other. If we take the example
of a hermit who has no family and whose acts do not affect other
people in any measurable way, it seems pointless to ask whether he
or she can be selfish or generous, deceitful or honest, and so forth.
We may, surely, ask whether a recluse has any moral obligations to
him- or herself, or duties to the animal creatures who share his or her
domain. Without society there is little that can be called morality, and
without morality, there is not much that could be called society. If an

infant could, like the fabled wolf boys or feral men, survive to adult-hood without human contacts, we would hardly say of such a person that he or she has any morals. He or she can't even talk or concep-tualize about right and wrong. And if, by some miracle, a group of infants so abandoned could grow to adulthood, there would be little in their mode of living that we could call social. (We don't, in fact, have any idea of what kind of group living they might practice, if any, but lacking even animal instincts, they would probably have less of a "society" than rabbits or wolves, much less ants or wasps.) If one argues that moral issues are relevant to such pitiful creatures, since there is a God who demands righteousness of people, it must be replied that such a God could hardly be thought to hold these virtual subhumans, or subanimals, responsible for their deeds, unless He has somehow managed to reveal His will to them.

Kurt Baier has been the most outstanding contemporary thinker on these issues. He has argued that to adopt "the moral point of view" at all, to operate in a moral framework at all, is to apply to other people the same standards that one applies to oneself. This would seem to be a fundamental requirement for any society in which all individuals are to reap the most benefits from their associations with others, and not just for "democratic" societies. It requires that not any and every impulse of the individual is to be followed, for he cannot have much sense of security or predictable life if others sim-ilarly follow all their impulses.

But can human beings apply to others the same standards that they apply to themselves—is it psychologically possible? If not, there is no point in urging them to do so and condemning or punishing them if they do not—no point, that is, except a very hypocritical one, ex-ploiting other people by preaching morality and all the while doing as one pleases. Meanwhile the other people are hoodwinked into being generous, self-sacrificing, and the like as the exploiter reaps all the advantages without any of the inconveniences. Astute psy-chologists such as Plato, Thomas Hobbes, and Friedrich Nietzsche explored the hypocrisy and exploitation of human beings by other human beings before Freud gave much more "scientific" though still highly speculative accounts of them. Plato has one of the characters in his dialogue, the *Republic,* argue that people support morality in public not because they want to be moral, but because they don't want to be treated immorally by others—killed, lied to, stolen from, or cruelly abused. In our present-day American society, this issue is very much alive as a basic question about institutions—the family, religion, the economic and political arenas—in which, it is often said, people preach one thing but practice quite another. There is no ques-tion but that morality is a means of social control; the question is who benefits most by it. Are all benefits to one gained at the expense of another person? If there are winners, must there always be losers, too? These issues are primarily psychological, sociological, and political, but there are important conceptual moral issues involved, too. They are treated in Chapter Three and in the readings on egoism.

Summary

I have discussed and given examples of the peculiar nature of moral questions and the main types of answers to them, how moral and value questions differ from questions of fact. I have shown that the fact of moral disagreement is the fundamental problem in ethics, and have raised the issue as to whether any rational solution to moral disagreement is possible, and have indicated that it is a matter of degree. Perhaps no sure-fire general method of settling moral disputes, and a method of knowing right from wrong and good from evil (which is the same thing), are on the horizon. Nevertheless much more is known and can be known than the often bloody but always confusing spectacle of moral controversy through the ages would seem to indicate. With this introduction completed, it is time to go into some of the particulars, beginning with the nature, extent, and significance of moral disagreement itself, in Chapter 2.

WHY SHOULD WE BE MORAL? °

KURT BAIER

The Supremacy of Moral Reasons

Are moral reasons really superior to reasons of self-interest as we all believe? Do we really have reason on our side when we follow moral reasons against self-interest? What reasons could there be for being moral? Can we really give an answer to 'Why should we be moral?' It is obvious that all these questions come to the same thing. When we ask, 'Should we be moral?' or 'Why should we be moral?' or 'Are moral reasons superior to all others?' we ask to be shown the reason for being moral. What is this reason?

Let us begin with a state of affairs in which reasons of self-interest are supreme. In such a state everyone keeps his impulses and inclinations in check when and only when they would lead him into behavior detrimental

° From Kurt Baier, *The Moral Point of View* (Ithaca, N.Y.: Cornell University Press, 1958), pp. 309–315. Reprinted by permission.

to his own interest. Everyone who follows reason will discipline himself to rise early, to do his exercises, to refrain from excessive drinking and smoking, to keep good company, to marry the right sort of girl, to work and study hard in order to get on, and so on. However, it will often happen that people's interests conflict. In such a case, they will have to resort to ruses or force to get their own way. As this becomes known, men will become suspicious, for they will regard one another as scheming competitors for the good things in life. The universal supremacy of the rules of self-interest must lead to what Hobbes called the state of nature. At the same time, it will be clear to everyone that universal obedience to certain rules overriding self-interest would produce a state of affairs which serves everyone's interest much better than his unaided pursuit of it in a state where everyone does the same. Moral rules are universal rules designed to override those of self-interest when following the latter is harmful to others. 'Thou shalt not kill,' 'Thou shalt not lie,' 'Thou shalt not steal' are rules which forbid the inflicting of harm on someone else even when this might be in one's interest.

The very *raison d'être* of a morality is to yield reasons which overrule the reasons of self-interest in those cases when everyone's following self-interest would be harmful to everyone. Hence moral reasons are superior to all others.

"But what does this mean?" it might be objected. "If it merely means that we do so regard them, then you are of course right, but your contention is useless, a mere point of usage. And how could it mean any more? If it means that we not only do so regard them, but *ought* so to regard them, then there must be *reasons* for saying this. But there could not be any reasons for it. If you offer reasons of self-interest, you are arguing in a circle. Moreover, it cannot be true that it is always in my interest to treat moral reasons as superior to reasons of self-interest. If it were, self-interest and morality could never conflict, but they notoriously do. It is equally circular to argue that there are moral reasons for saying that one ought to treat moral reasons as superior to reasons of self-interest. And what other reasons are there?"

The answer is that we are now looking at the world from the point of view of *anyone*. We are not examining particular alternative courses of action before this or that person; we are examining two alternative worlds, one in which moral reasons are always treated by everyone as superior to reasons of self-interest and one in which the reverse is the practice. And we can see that the first world is the better world, because we can see that the second world would be the sort which Hobbes describes as the state of nature.

This shows that I ought to be moral, for when I ask the question 'What ought I to do?' I am asking, 'Which is the course of action supported by the best reasons?' But since it has just been shown that moral reasons are superior to reasons of self-interest, I have been given a reason for being moral, for following moral reasons rather than any other, namely, they are better reasons than any other.

But is this always so? Do we have a reason for being moral whatever the conditions we find ourselves in? Could there not be situations in which it is not true that we have reasons for being moral, that, on the contrary, we have reasons for ignoring the demands of morality? Is not Hobbes right in saying that in a state of nature the laws of nature, that is, the rules of morality, bind only *in foro interno?*

Hobbes argues as follows.

(i) To live in a state of nature is to live outside society. It is to live in conditions in which there are no common ways of life and, therefore, no reliable expectations about other people's behavior other than that they will follow their inclination or their interest.

(ii) In such a state reason will be the enemy of co-operation and mutual trust. For it is too risky to hope that other people will refrain from protecting their own interests by the preventive elimination of probable or even possible dangers to them. Hence reason will counsel everyone to avoid these risks by preventive action. But this leads to war.

(iii) It is obvious that everyone's following self-interest leads to a state of affairs which is desirable from no one's point of view. It is, on the contrary, desirable that everybody should follow rules overriding self-interest whenever that is to the detriment of others. In other words, it is desirable to bring about a state of affairs in which all obey the rules of morality.

(iv) However, Hobbes claims that in the state of nature it helps nobody if a single person or a small group of persons begins to follow the rules of morality, for this could only lead to the extinction of such individuals or groups. In such a state, it is therefore contrary to reason to be moral.

(v) The situation can change, reason can support morality, only when the presumption about other people's behavior is reversed. Hobbes thought that this could be achieved only by the creation of an absolute ruler with absolute power to enforce his laws. We have already seen that this is not true and that it is quite different if people live in a society, that is, if they have common ways of life, which are taught to all members and somehow enforced by the group. Its members have reason to expect their fellows generally to obey its rules, that is, its religion, morality, customs, and law, even when doing so is not, on certain occasions, in their interest. Hence they too have reason to follow these rules.

Is this argument sound? One might, of course, object to step (i) on the grounds that this is an empirical proposition for which there is little or no evidence. For how can we know whether it is true that people in a state of nature would follow only their inclinations or, at best, reasons of self-interest, when nobody now lives in that state or has ever lived in it?

However, there is some empirical evidence to support this claim. For in the family of nations, individual states are placed very much like indi-

vidual persons in a state of nature. The doctrine of the sovereignty of
nations and the absence of an effective international law and police force
are a guarantee that nations live in a state of nature, without commonly
accepted rules that are somehow enforced. Hence it must be granted that
living in a state of nature leads to living in a state in which individuals
act either on impulse or as they think their interest dictates. For states pay
only lip service to morality. They attack their hated neighbors when the
opportunity arises. They start preventive wars in order to destroy the enemy before he can deliver his knockout blow. Where interests conflict, the
stronger party usually has his way, whether his claims are justified or not.
And where the relative strength of the parties is not obvious, they usually
resort to arms in order to determine "whose side God is on." Treaties are
frequently concluded but, morally speaking, they are not worth the paper
they are written on. Nor do the partners regard them as contracts binding
in the ordinary way, but rather as public expressions of the belief of the
governments concerned that for the time being their alliance is in the
interest of the allies. It is well understood that such treaties may be can-
celed before they reach their predetermined end or simply broken when it
suits one partner. In international affairs, there are very few examples of
Nibelungentreue, although statesmen whose countries have profited from
keeping their treaties usually make such high moral claims.

It is, moreover, difficult to justify morality in international affairs. For
suppose a highly moral statesman were to demand that his country adhere
to a treaty obligation even though this meant its ruin or possibly its extinction. Suppose he were to say that treaty obligations are sacred and
must be kept whatever the consequences. How could he defend such a
policy? Perhaps one might argue that someone has to make a start in order
to create mutual confidence in international affairs. Or one might say that
setting a good example is the best way of inducing others to follow suit.
But such a defense would hardly be sound. The less skeptical one is about
the genuineness of the cases in which nations have adhered to their treaties from a sense of moral obligation, the more skeptical one must be about
the effectiveness of such examples of virtue in effecting a change of international practice. Power politics still govern in international affairs.

We must, therefore, grant Hobbes the first step in his argument and
admit that in a state of nature people, as a matter of psychological fact,
would not follow the dictates of morality. But we might object to the next
step that knowing this psychological fact about other people's behavior
constitutes a reason for behaving in the same way. Would it not still be
immoral for anyone to ignore the demands of morality even though he
knows that others are likely or certain to do so, too? Can we offer as a
justification for morality the fact that no one is entitled to do wrong just
because someone else is doing wrong? This argument begs the question
whether it *is* wrong for anyone in this state to disregard the demands of
morality. It cannot be wrong to break a treaty or make preventive war

if we have no reason to obey the moral rules. For to say that it is wrong to do so is to say that we ought not to do so. But if we have no reason for obeying the moral rule, then we have no reason overruling self-interest, hence no reason for keeping the treaty when keeping it is not in our interest, hence it is not true that we have a reason for keeping it, hence not true that we ought to keep it, hence not true that it is wrong not to keep it.

I conclude that Hobbes's argument is sound. Moralities are systems of principles whose acceptance by everyone as overruling the dictates of self-interest is in the interest of everyone alike, though following the rules of a morality is not of course identical with following self-interest. If it were, there could be no conflict between a morality and self-interest and no point in having moral rules overriding self-interest. Hobbes is also right in saying that the application of this system of rules is in accordance with reason only in social conditions, that is, when there are well-established ways of behavior.

The answer to our question 'Why should we be moral?' is therefore as follows. We should be moral because being moral is following rules designed to overrule self-interest whenever it is in the interest of everyone alike that everyone should set aside his interest. It is not self-contradictory to say this, because it may be in one's interest *not* to follow one's interest at times. We have already seen that enlightened self-interest acknowledges this point. But while enlightened self-interest does not require any genuine sacrifice from anyone, morality does. In the interest of the possibility of the good life for everyone, voluntary sacrifices are sometimes required from everybody. Thus, a person might do better for himself by following enlightened self-interest rather than morality. It is not possible, however, that *everyone* should do better for himself by following enlightened self-interest rather than morality. The best possible life *for everyone* is possible only by everyone's following the rules of morality, that is, rules which quite frequently may require individuals to make genuine sacrifices.

It must be added to this, however, that such a system of rules has the support of reason only where people live in societies, that is, in conditions in which there are established common ways of behavior. Outside society, people have no reason for following such rules, that is, for being moral. In other words, outside society, the very distinction between right and wrong vanishes.

EXISTENTIALISM IS HUMANISM °

JEAN-PAUL SARTRE

... What is meant by the term *existentialism?*

Most people who use the word would be rather embarrassed if they had to explain it, since, now that the word is all the rage, even the work of a musician or painter is being called existentialist. A gossip columnist in *Clartés* signs himself *The Existentialist,* so that by this time the word has been so stretched and has taken on so broad a meaning, that it no longer means anything at all. It seems that for want of an advance-guard doctrine analogous to surrealism, the kind of people who are eager for scandal and flurry turn to this philosophy which in other respects does not at all serve their purposes in this sphere.

Actually, it is the least scandalous, the most austere of doctrines. It is intended strictly for specialists and philosophers. Yet it can be defined easily. What complicates matters is that there are two kinds of existentialist; first, those who are Christian, among whom I would include Jaspers and Gabriel Marcel, both Catholic; and on the other hand the atheistic existentialists, among whom I class Heidegger, and then the French existentialists and myself. What they have in common is that they think that existence precedes essence, or, if you prefer, that subjectivity must be the starting point.

Just what does that mean? Let us consider some object that is manufactured, for example, a book or a paper-cutter: here is an object which has been made by an artisan whose inspiration came from a concept. He referred to the concept of what a paper-cutter is and likewise to a known method of production, which is part of the concept, something which is, by and large, a routine. Thus, the paper-cutter is at once an object produced in a certain way and, on the other hand, one having a specific use; and one can not postulate a man who produces a paper-cutter but does not know what it is used for. Therefore, let us say that, for the paper-cutter, essence—that is, the ensemble of both the production routines and the properties which enable it to be both produced and defined—precedes existence. Thus, the presence of the paper-cutter or book in front of me is determined. Therefore, we have here a technical view of the world whereby it can be said that production precedes existence.

When we conceive God as the Creator, He is generally thought of as a superior sort of artisan. Whatever doctrine we may be considering, whether one like that of Descartes or that of Leibnitz, we always grant that will more or less follows understanding or, at the very least, accompanies it, and that when God creates He knows exactly what He is creating. Thus,

° From Jean-Paul Sartre, *Existentialism and Human Emotions* (New York: Philosophical Library, 1947), pp. 12–43, with omissions. Reprinted by permission of Philosophical Library and Editions Nagel, Paris.

the concept of man in the mind of God is comparable to the concept of paper-cutter in the mind of the manufacturer, and, following certain techniques and a conception, God produces man, just as the artisan, following a definition and a technique, makes a paper-cutter. Thus, the individual man is the realization of a certain concept in the divine intelligence.

In the eighteenth century, the atheism of the *philosophes* discarded the idea of God, but not so much for the notion that essence precedes existence. To a certain extent, this idea is found everywhere; we find it in Diderot, in Voltaire, and even in Kant. Man has a human nature; this human nature, which is the concept of the human, is found in all men, which means that each man is a particular example of a universal concept, man. In Kant, the result of this universality is that the wild-man, the natural man, as well as the bourgeois, are circumscribed by the same definition and have the same basic qualities. Thus, here too the essence of man precedes the historical existence that we find in nature.

Atheistic existentialism, which I represent, is more coherent. It states that if God does not exist, there is at least one being in whom existence precedes essence, a being who exists before he can be defined by any concept, and that this being is man, or, as Heidegger says, human reality. What is meant here by saying that existence precedes essence? It means that, first of all, man exists, turns up, appears on the scene, and, only afterwards, defines himself. If man, as the existentialist conceives him, is indefinable, it is because at first he is nothing. Only afterward will he be something, and he himself will have made what he will be. Thus, there is no human nature, since there is no God to conceive it. Not only is man what he conceives himself to be, but he is also only what he wills himself to be after this thrust toward existence.

Man is nothing else but what he makes of himself. Such is the first principle of existentialism. It is also what is called subjectivity, the name we are labeled with when charges are brought against us. But what do we mean by this, if not that man has a greater dignity than a stone or table? For we mean that man first exists, that is, that man first of all is the being who hurls himself toward a future and who is conscious of imagining himself as being in the future. Man is at the start a plan which is aware of itself, rather than a patch of moss, a piece of garbage, or a cauliflower; nothing exists prior to this plan; there is nothing in heaven; man will be what he will have planned to be. Not what he will want to be. Because by the word "will" we generally mean a conscious decision, which is subsequent to what we have already made of ourselves. I may want to belong to a political party, write a book, get married; but all that is only a manifestation of an earlier, more spontaneous choice that is called "will." But if existence really does precede essence, man is responsible for what he is. Thus, existentialism's first move is to make every man aware of what he is and to make the full responsibility of his existence rest on him. And when we say that a man is responsible for himself, we do not only mean that he is responsible for his own individuality, but that he is responsible for all men.

The word subjectivism has two meanings, and our opponents play on the two. Subjectivism means, on the one hand, that an individual chooses and makes himself; and, on the other, that it is impossible for man to transcend human subjectivity. The second of these is the essential meaning of existentialism. When we say that man chooses his own self, we mean that every one of us does likewise; but we also mean by that that in making this choice he also chooses all men. In fact, in creating the man that we want to be, there is not a single one of our acts which does not at the same time create an image of man as we think he ought to be. To choose to be this or that is to affirm at the same time the value of what we choose, because we can never choose evil. We always choose the good, and nothing can be good for us without being good for all.

If, on the other hand, existence precedes essence, and if we grant that we exist and fashion our image at one and the same time, the image is valid for everybody and for our whole age. Thus, our responsibility is much greater than we might have supposed, because it involves all mankind. If I am a workingman and choose to join a Christian trade-union rather than be a communist, and if by being a member I want to show that the best thing for man is resignation, that the kingdom of man is not of this world, I am not only involving my own case—I want to be resigned for everyone. As a result, my action has involved all humanity. To take a more individual matter, if I want to marry, to have children; even if this marriage depends solely on my own circumstances or passion or wish, I am involving all humanity in monogamy and not merely myself. Therefore, I am responsible for myself and for everyone else. I am creating a certain image of man of my own choosing. In choosing myself, I choose man.

This helps us understand what the actual content is of such rather grandiloquent words as anguish, forlornness, despair. As you will see, it's all quite simple.

First, what is meant by anguish? The existentialists say at once that man is anguish. What that means is this: the man who involves himself and who realizes that he is not only the person he chooses to be, but also a lawmaker who is, at the same time, choosing all mankind as well as himself, can not help escape the feeling of his total and deep responsibility. Of course, there are many people who are not anxious; but we claim that they are hiding their anxiety, that they are fleeing from it. Certainly, many people believe that when they do something, they themselves are the only ones involved, and when someone says to them, "What if everyone acted that way?" they shrug their shoulders and answer, "Everyone doesn't act that way." But really, one should always ask himself, "What would happen if everybody looked at things that way?" There is no escaping this disturbing thought except by a kind of double-dealing. A man who lies and makes excuses for himself by saying "not everybody does that," is someone with an uneasy conscience, because the act of lying implies that a universal value is conferred upon the lie.

Anguish is evident even when it conceals itself. This is the anguish that Kierkegaard called the anguish of Abraham. You know the story: an angel has ordered Abraham to sacrifice his son; if it really were an angel who has come and said, "You are Abraham, you shall sacrifice your son," everything would be all right. But everyone might first wonder, "Is it really an angel, and am I really Abraham? What proof do I have?"

There was a madwoman who had hallucinations; someone used to speak to her on the telephone and give her orders. Her doctor asked her, "Who is it who talks to you?" She answered, "He says it's God." What proof did she really have that it was God? If an angel comes to me, what proof is there that it's an angel? And if I hear voices, what proof is there that they come from heaven and not from hell, or from the subconscious, or a pathological condition? What proves that they are addressed to me? What proof is there that I have been appointed to impose my choice and my conception of man on humanity? I'll never find any proof or sign to convince me of that. If a voice addresses me, it is always for me to decide that this is the angel's voice; if I consider that such an act is a good one, it is I who will choose to say that it is good rather than bad.

Now, I'm not being singled out as an Abraham, and yet at every moment I'm obliged to perform exemplary acts. For every man, everything happens as if all mankind had its eyes fixed on him and were guiding itself by what he does. And every man ought to say to himself, "Am I really the kind of man who has the right to act in such a way that humanity might guide itself by my actions?" And if he does not say that to himself, he is masking his anguish.

There is no question here of the kind of anguish which would lead to quietism, to inaction. It is a matter of a simple sort of anguish that anybody who has had responsibilities is familiar with. For example, when a military officer takes the responsibility for an attack and sends a certain number of men to death, he chooses to do so, and in the main he alone makes the choice. Doubtless, orders come from above, but they are too broad; he interprets them, and on this interpretation depend the lives of ten or fourteen or twenty men. In making a decision he can not help having a certain anguish. All leaders know this anguish. That doesn't keep them from acting; on the contrary, it is the very condition of their action. For it implies that they envisage a number of possibilities, and when they choose one, they realize that it has value only because it is chosen. We shall see that this kind of anguish, which is the kind that existentialism describes, is explained, in addition, by a direct responsibility to the other men whom it involves. It is not a curtain separating us from action, but is part of action itself.

When we speak of forlornness, a term Heidegger was fond of, we mean only that God does not exist and that we have to face all the consequences of this. The existentialist is strongly opposed to a certain kind of secular ethics which would like to abolish God with the least possible expense. About 1880, some French teachers tried to set up a secular ethics which went something like this: God is a useless and costly hypothesis; we are discarding it; but, meanwhile, in order for there to be an ethics, a society, a civilization, it is essential that certain values be taken seriously and that they be considered as having an *a priori* existence. It must be obligatory, *a priori*, to be honest, not to lie, not to beat your wife, to have children, etc., etc. So we're going to try a little device which will make it possible to show that values exist all the same, inscribed in a heaven of ideas, though otherwise God does not exist. In other words—and this, I believe, is the tendency of everything called reformism in France—nothing will be changed if God does not exist. We shall find ourselves with the same norms of honesty, progress, and humanism, and we shall have made of God an outdated hypothesis which will peacefully die off by itself.

The existentialist, on the contrary, thinks it very distressing that God does not exist, because all possibility of finding values in a heaven of ideas disappears along with Him; there can no longer be an *a priori* Good, since there is no infinite and perfect consciousness to think it. Nowhere is it written that the Good exists, that we must be honest, that we must not lie; because the fact is we are on a plane where there are only men. Dostoievsky said, "If God didn't exist, everything would be possible." That is the very starting point of existentialism. Indeed, everything is permissible if God does not exist, and as a result man is forlorn, because neither within him nor without does he find anything to cling to. He can't start making excuses for himself.

If existence really does precede essence, there is no explaining things away by reference to a fixed and given human nature. In other words, there is no determinism, man is free, man is freedom. On the other hand, if God does not exist, we find no values or commands to turn to which legitimize our conduct. So, in the bright realm of values, we have no excuse behind us, nor justification before us. We are alone, with no excuses.

That is the idea I shall try to convey when I say that man is condemned to be free. Condemned, because he did not create himself, yet, in other respects is free; because, once thrown into the world, he is responsible for everything he does. The existentialist does not believe in the power of passion. He will never agree that a sweeping passion is a ravaging torrent which fatally leads a man to certain acts and is therefore an excuse. He thinks that man is responsible for his passion.

The existentialist does not think that man is going to help himself by finding in the world some omen by which to orient himself. Because he thinks that man will interpret the omen to suit himself. Therefore, he thinks that man, with no support and no aid, is condemned every moment to invent man. Ponge, in a very fine article, has said, "Man is the future of man." That's exactly it. But if it is taken to mean that this future is recorded in heaven, that God sees it, then it is false, because it would really no longer be a future. If it is taken to mean that, whatever a man may be, there is a future to be forged, a virgin future before him, then this remark is sound. But then we are forlorn.

To give you an example which will enable you to understand forlornness better, I shall cite the case of one of my students who came to see me under the following circumstances: his father was on bad terms with his mother, and, moreover, was inclined to be a collaborationist; his older brother had been killed in the German offensive of 1940, and the young man, with somewhat immature but generous feelings, wanted to avenge him. His mother lived alone with him, very much upset by the half-treason of her husband and the death of her older son; the boy was her only consolation.

The boy was faced with the choice of leaving for England and joining the Free French Forces—that is, leaving his mother behind—or remaining with his mother and helping her to carry on. He was fully aware that the woman lived only for him and that his going-off—and perhaps his death—would plunge her into despair. He was also aware that every act that he did for his mother's sake was a sure thing, in the sense that it was helping her to carry on, whereas every effort he made toward going off and fighting was an uncertain move which might run aground and prove completely useless; for example, on his way to England he might, while passing through Spain, be detained indefinitely in a Spanish camp; he might reach England or Algiers and be stuck in an office at a desk job. As a result, he was faced with two very different kinds of action: one, concrete, immediate, but concerning only one individual; the other concerned an incomparably vaster group, a national collectivity, but for that very reason was dubious, and might be interrupted en route. And, at the same time, he was wavering between two kinds of ethics. On the one hand, an ethics of sympathy, of personal devotion; on the other, a broader ethics, but one whose efficacy was more dubious. He had to choose between the two.

Who could help him choose? Christian doctrine? No. Christian doctrine says, "Be charitable, love your neighbor, take the more rugged path, etc., etc." But which is the more rugged path? Whom should he love as a brother? The fighting man or his mother? Which does the greater good, the vague act of fighting in a group, or the concrete one of helping a particular human being to go on living? Who can decide a priori? Nobody. No book of ethics can tell him. The Kantian ethics says, "Never treat any person as a means, but as an end." Very well, if I stay with my mother, I'll treat her as an end and not as a means; but by virtue of this very fact, I'm running the risk of treating the people around me who are fighting, as means; and, conversely, if I go to join those who are fighting, I'll be treating them as an end, and, by doing that, I run the risk of treating my mother as a means.

If values are vague, and if they are always too broad for the concrete and specific case that we are considering, the only thing left for us is to trust our instincts. That's what this young man tried to do; and when I saw him, he said, "In the end, feeling is what counts. I ought to choose whichever pushes me in one direction. If I feel that I love my mother enough to sacrifice everything else for her—my desire for vengeance, for action, for adventure—then I'll stay with her. If, on the contrary, I feel that my love for my mother isn't enough, I'll leave."

. . . Forlornness implies that we ourselves choose our being. Forlornness and anguish go together.

As for despair, the term has a very simple meaning. It means that we shall confine ourselves to reckoning only with what depends upon our will, or on the ensemble of probabilities which make our action possible. When we want something, we always have to reckon with probabilities. I may be counting on the arrival of a friend. The friend is coming by rail or streetcar; this supposes that the train will arrive on schedule, or that the streetcar will not jump the track. I am left in the realm of possibility; but possibilities are to be reckoned with only to the point where my action comports with the ensemble of these possibilities, and no further. The moment the possibilities I am considering are not rigorously involved by my action, I ought to disengage myself from them, because no God, no scheme, can adapt the world and its possibilities to my will. When Descartes said, "Conquer yourself rather than the world," he meant essentially the same thing. . . .

Actually, things will be as man will have decided they are to be. Does that mean that I should abandon myself to quietism? No. First, I should involve myself; then, act on the old saw, "Nothing ventured, nothing gained." Nor does it mean that I shouldn't belong to a party, but rather that I shall have no illusions and shall do what I can. For example, suppose I ask myself, "Will socialization, as such, ever come about?" I know nothing about it. All I know is that I'm going to do everything in my power to bring it about. Beyond that, I can't count on anything. Quietism is the attitude of people who say, "Let others do what I can't do." The doctrine I am presenting is the very opposite of quietism, since it declares, "There is no reality except in action." Moreover, it goes further, since it adds, "Man is nothing else than his plan; he exists only to the extent that he fulfills himself; he is therefore nothing else than the ensemble of his acts, nothing else than his life."

According to this, we can understand why our doctrine horrifies certain people. Because often the only way they can bear their wretchedness is to think, "Circumstances have been against me. What I've been and done doesn't show my true worth. To be sure, I've had no great love, no great friendship, but that's because I haven't met a man or woman who was worthy. The books I've written haven't been very good because I haven't had the proper leisure. I haven't had children to devote myself to because I didn't find a man with whom I could have spent my life. So there remains within me, unused and quite viable, a host of propensities, inclinations, possibilities, that one wouldn't guess from the mere series of things I've done."

Now, for the existentialist there is really no love other than one which manifests itself in a person's being in love. There is no genius other than one which is expressed in works of art; the genius of Proust is the sum of Proust's works; the genius of Racine is his series of tragedies. Outside of that, there is nothing. Why say that Racine could have written another tragedy, when he didn't write it? A man is involved in life, leaves his impress on it, and outside of that there is nothing. To be sure, this may seem a harsh thought to someone whose life hasn't been a success. But, on the other hand, it prompts people to understand that reality alone is what counts, that dreams, expectations, and hopes warrant no more than to define a man as a disappointed dream, as miscarried hopes, as vain expectations. In other words, to define him negatively and not positively. However, when we say, "You are nothing else than your life," that does not imply that the artist will be judged solely on the basis of his works of art; a thousand other things will contribute toward summing him up. What we mean is that a man is nothing else than a series of undertakings, that he is the sum, the organization, the ensemble of the relationships which make up these undertakings . . .

Besides, if it is impossible to find in every man some universal essence which would be human nature, yet there does exist a universal human condition. It's not by chance that today's thinkers speak more readily of man's condition than of his nature. By condition they mean, more or less definitely, the *a priori* limits which outline man's fundamental situation in the universe. Historical situations vary; a man may be born a slave in a pagan society or a feudal lord or a proletarian. What does not vary is the necessity for him to exist in the world, to be at work there, to be there in the midst of other people, and to be mortal there. The limits are neither subjective nor objective, or, rather, they have an objective and a subjective side. Objective because they are to be found everywhere and are recognizable everywhere; subjective because they are *lived* and are nothing if man does not live them, that is, freely determine his existence with reference to them. And though the configurations may differ, at least none of them are completely strange to me, because they all appear as attempts either to pass beyond these limits or recede from them or deny them or adapt to them. Consequently, every configuration, however individual it may be, has a universal value.

Every configuration, even the Chinese, the Indian, or the Negro, can be understood by a Westerner. "Can be understood" means that by virtue of a situation that he can imagine, a European of 1945 can, in like manner, push himself to his limits and reconstitute within himself the configuration of the Chinese, the Indian, or the African. Every configuration has universality in the sense that every configuration can be understood by every man. This does not at all mean that this configuration defines man forever, but that it can be met with again. There is always a way to understand the idiot, the child, the savage, the foreigner, provided one has the necessary information . . .

If anybody thinks that he recognizes here Gide's theory of the arbitrary act, he fails to see the enormous difference between this doctrine and Gide's. Gide does not know what a situation is. He acts out of pure caprice. For us, on the contrary, man is in an organized situation in which he himself is involved. Through his choice, he involves all mankind, and he can not avoid making a choice: either he will remain chaste, or he will marry without having children, or he will marry and have children; anyhow, whatever he may do, it is impossible for him not to take full responsibility for the way he handles this problem. Doubtless, he chooses without referring to preestablished values, but it is unfair to accuse him of caprice. Instead, let us say that moral choice is to be compared to the making of a work of art. And before going any further, let it be said at once that we are not dealing here with an aesthetic ethics, because our opponents are so dishonest that they even accuse us of that. The example I've chosen is a comparison only.

Having said that, may I ask whether anyone has ever accused an artist who has painted a picture of not having drawn his inspiration from rules set up *a priori?* Has anyone ever asked, "What painting ought he to make?" It is clearly understood that there is no definite painting to be made, that the artist is engaged in the making of his painting, and that the painting to be made is precisely the painting he will have made. It is clearly understood that there are no *a priori* aesthetic values, but that there are values which appear subsequently in the coherence of the painting, in the correspondence between what the artist intended and the result. Nobody can tell what the painting of tomorrow will be like. Painting can be judged only after it has once been made. What connection does that have with ethics? We are in the same creative situation. We never say that a work of art is arbitrary. When we speak of a canvas of Picasso, we never say that it is arbitrary; we understand quite well that he was making himself what he is at the very time he was painting, that the ensemble of his work is embodied in his life.

The same holds on the ethical plane. What art and ethics have in common is that we have creation and invention in both cases. We can not decide *a priori* what there is to be done. I think that I pointed that out quite sufficiently when I mentioned the case of the student who came to see me, and who might have applied to all the ethical systems, Kantian or otherwise, without getting any sort of guidance. He was obliged to devise his law himself. Never let it be said by us that this man—who, taking affection, individual action, and kind-heartedness toward a specific person as his ethical first principle, chooses to remain with his mother, or who, preferring to make a sacrifice, chooses to go to England—has made an arbitrary choice. Man makes himself. He isn't ready made at the start. In choosing his ethics, he makes himself, and force of circumstances is such that he can not abstain from choosing one. We define man only in relationship to involvement. It is therefore absurd to charge us with arbitrariness of choice . . .

2

Relativism and Subjectivism

Moral disagreement and other value conflicts between people have an important meaning for ethics, if for no other reason than that people think they have. They have thought so at least since the time of the Greeks, who were among the first to record an awareness of the diversity of morals, and speculate about its significance. But it is quite another matter to try to clear up just what its importance, meaning, or significance *are* and just what the facts of moral disagreement imply for ethics. This chapter examines two theories of ethics that some philosophers and social scientists have thought they imply. The first of these, relativism, has several forms, while the second, subjectivism, is somewhat easier to give a single description of, though it, too, has varied expressions.

Both theories have had a primarily negative character, and have had their greatest strength as criticisms of the claims, or supposed claims, of traditional normative ethics, especially those theories that seemed to be based on the will of an absolute being, or an unchanging order of things called Nature, or any kind of knowledge of good and evil that was supposed to be innate, or inborn, or any kind of human faculty for such knowledge, such as intuition or conscience. The facts of moral disagreement and other value conflicts show, these theories argue, that something is amiss with such traditional ideas. These two theories seem to presuppose that if moral beliefs cannot elicit agreement from a wide spectrum of individuals in all times and places of human society, they are in a poor position as compared with scientific beliefs or beliefs about everyday matters of fact. In considering these two theories, we get a further look at how moral ideas arise and how they are accepted, and how confusions arise in interpreting people's ethics.

Relativism

Part One: Sociological and Anthropological Data on Which Relativism Is Often Based

Subjectivism might seem to be the theory we should take up first, for it is accepted by many people, at least in part, and to some it seems undebatable. Subjectivism, as we shall see in more detail at the end of the chapter, theorizes that when a person says something such as "War is evil," or "Lying is sometimes necessary," the person is not talking about war or lying at all, but about that person's feelings about war and lying. The theory continues that war and lying produce different feelings in different people, and that we cannot therefore say that the evil is in the war or the goodness or badness in the lying, but is a feeling in the person, its being good to some, and bad to others. For two reasons, however, we will take up relativism first, despite the familiarity of the other theory. First, relativism is based more on disagreements and differences between groups, eras, and parts of the world, and puts the diversity of morals in the largest "writing" and in the longest perspective. Secondly, looking at the differences between societies and eras points up the fact that individuals, the subjects in subjectivism, always reflect the influence of a group or a larger social reality in their own morality. Another way this has been put is that relativism leads to subjectivism. So, even though we recognize that in modern society a person can see plenty of moral and other value conflicts within his or her own society and need not go back in time or cross oceans to reflect upon the diversity of morals, we will nevertheless start with such diversity as it is "writ large" in groups, times, and places.

The sociological and anthropological data on which relativism is based are well known. After a brief recital of some of the most striking instances of moral diversity, we will formulate the first of the versions of relativism that have been distinguished. As to differences in epochs, the Christian Middle Ages in Europe will do as well as any, and especially the monastic, ascetic ideals of that time. Compare that within the same religious tradition with contemporary Christianity's official abandonment of long-standing ideas on premarital sex, birth control, and divorce. However much one might quibble about differences between contemporary Protestant and Catholic views on these issues, even Catholic views of today and, say, before the beginning of World War II are certainly more liberal or relaxed than before 1945. If we leave the realm of sex and compare medieval Christianity with the worldliness espoused by the Kwakiutls described by Ruth Benedict, we observe a tremendous variation on the value attached to material goods, the Kwakiutls' main goal the amassing of the latter, so abominable to the medieval monk. Another cross-cultural comparison shows a contrast between the groups that have throughout history practiced infanticide, cannibalism, and geronticide (the killing of the aged) with Judeo–Christian moral views. To avoid the complicated issues involved in war and abortion, we can get a clear contrast by limiting ourselves to these three kinds of killing of human beings. Geronticide is especially a vivid disparity: One society will expose its aged to weather and starvation, another will bury its old people alive, another will proclaim, "Honor thy father and mother," and "Thou shalt not kill," and call some deliberate withdrawal of life-support machinery from aged patients murder. Or, take the custom of the widow in India destroying herself that was so foreign to the British who took over India. In marriage customs, right and wrong present a dazzling array: monogamy, polygamy, polyandry. In addition to infanticide ("because it was summer," a missionary reported the natives as saying) and geronticide, the Eskimos have provided still another practice at once titillating and shocking to Americans: the hospitality of lending one's wife to a male guest for the night. In dress and modesty, contrast the rare sight of the Victorian female ankle with the Amazonian Indian women who wear only a G-string of sorts. Burial customs present still another realm of variety: What does and does not dishonor a corpse differs greatly from society to society.

We could multiply the data manyfold by sifting through anthropology books and the accounts of missionaries and travelers, but it becomes repetitious after a time. That point is reached at the time that we are ready to consider the first type of relativism, called by Frankena and Brandt descriptive relativism and by Paul Taylor sociological relativism. These three writers accept a threefold classification of relativisms, and even among the ethicists mentioned there are differences of description of the three kinds. But a general characterization of descriptive or sociological relativism reveals a doctrine that cultures vary greatly in moral beliefs and practices, and the differences between them are not just on the surface; when, for instance, medieval monks and Kwakiutls dispute about values there is a vast gulf between them. The importance of surface disagreement versus fundamental differences brings us to the more important issue about the relationship of relativism as a theory in ethics to the data on which it is based.

Part Two: Interpretation of the Data

Descriptive or sociological relativism's interpretation of the scientific study of moral and other value differences takes it to be genuine and fundamental, as opposed to those who might say that all societies have basically the same values or standards. If we take a *moral rule* to be a rule for or against a certain practice such as deliberate and malicious taking of human life or kindness to guests, and take a *moral principle* to be the general rule or statement of value justifying certain moral rules, we might argue against sociological or descriptive relativism that different societies might disagree in moral rules but that they do agree in the moral principles that they accept. This accounts for the significance of the issue as to whether moral disagreement is fundamental or not. Also, an argument against this first type of relativism could be that when we look closely at different societies we might even find general agreement not only on a few moral principles but on some moral rules as well; this is the view that has gained in popularity among anthropologists of, say, post-World II days as compared with relativists such as Ruth Benedict. Readings by Kroeber and Kluckhohn reflect this stress on cultural similarities rather than differences, as do some of the writings of Linton and Redfield.

One argument against sociological or descriptive relativism is that the appearance of dissimilarities is diminished by noticing how some apparent disagreements in values are really disagreements over questions of fact. For instance, Duncker and others have pointed out that groups that insist that children should put parents to death before they become old and decrepit are not callously following some arbitrary custom, but base the practice on the belief that it is a fact about physiology and death that if a person dies in a senile, decrepit condition, they continue to live in that manner forever, and thus cannot enjoy eternal life as well as they could if they had, physiologically, "quit while they were ahead." It makes no difference that this is a religious belief, it is as much a belief about facts as any contemporary Western idea about the physiology of death. It is rather like people who disagree over whether tomatoes are poisonous: The behavior of the person who thinks they are will be quite different from the actions of a person toward tomatoes who thinks they are not poisonous, though an outsider might suppose from the difference that it was not about poison but a disagreement about values. In fact, one person's eating tomatoes because he or she thought they were lifegiving and another's not eating them because he or she thought they were fatal would ordinarily be said to indicate strong agreement on values and actions: the value of life and actions to survive. The same would apply to the foregoing practice of parricide, parent killing.

But despite efforts to minimize cultural dissimilarities in values, the argument of Taylor must be the most fundamental one as against both relativism and its deniers, and that is simply that the issue of value agreement or disagreement is largely irrelevant to the question of whether values are absolute or relative, or standards are universally applicable or not. We can reinforce Taylor's point by remembering something that we learn in thinking about knowledge and truth: If two people know something, then they agree, as when, say, they both know the answer to a mathematics problem. But the fact that they agree is not what makes the answer true; rather it is the truth of both their answers that produces the agreement. If they disagree it means only that not both of them can be right and, of course, both can be wrong. It surely does not mean, in mathematics, that there is no right answer to a problem, or that one answer that is found is as right as any other answer that is found, or that the mathematician's circumstances affect the answer.

This point from the theory of knowledge cannot be overemphasized in discussing relativism. Surely, however, value disagreement is not exactly like mathematical disagreement. For, whatever the nature of mathematics, there is much plausibility in the view that truths of mathematics are a matter of definition: that the proposition "$2 + 2 = 4$" is always true because of the meaning of the terms in it. And surely, few, if any, theories of ethics have suggested that such is the nature of moral truths or propositions in ethics. Rather, relativisms take moral propositions as being the kind of thing that sound like, and really should be like, propositions stating facts: "The apple is good" or "Stealing is wrong" sound like and should be in the same classification with "The apple is a Winesap" and "Stealing has increased 5 per cent over last year in this neighborhood," but not "An apple is a fruit," and "Stealing is taking something that does not belong to you"; the former are factual propositions and the latter, mere statements of definitions, which are true whatever the facts may be. But different kinds of relativism hold that moral propositions do not turn out to be what they sound like or should be, and that is one big problem they present. We cannot, it might be continued, tell the value of an apple the way we can tell the classification of its kind, or the wrongness of robbery the way we tell the number of robberies in a neighborhood for a given period. What we do have to go on, the theory might continue further, is the fact that people believe that stealing is wrong, and that Smith believes that this apple is good, and so forth. People in another society might approve stealing and another person, or even Smith at a different time (when he has a cold) might believe that the same apple is not good. So, what is the conclusion? One form of relativism says the conclusion is that the apple is good and not good, stealing is wrong and not wrong, or, in any case, a person could not *show* that the one view was more true or false than the other in the case of the apple and of stealing. This view is called by Brandt, Frankena, and Taylor metaethical relativism. (We shall wait until our exploration of subjectivism to see what we think about the possibility that some moral statements might be true but could not be shown to be true.)

Metaethics, you will remember, is neither the reporting nor the making of normative ethical judgments, but the explaining of them. Metaethical relativism explains moral judgments as either meaning different things in different societies, or else as being something that each society has a properly different method of validating. Thus, the typical expression of metaethical relativism is that a moral judgment can be true in one society and false in another. But this is a rather dry, philosophical, and analytical presentation. Anthropologists, and the older ideas of Herodotus on the subject, have a more lively and appealing way of putting it:

> Darius . . . called . . . certain Greeks . . . and asked—"What he should pay them to eat the bodies of their fathers when they died?" To which they answered that there was no sum that would tempt them to do such a thing. He then sent for certain Indians . . . called Callatians, men who eat their fathers, and asked them, while the Greeks stood by, and knew by the help of an interpreter all that was said—"What he should give them to burn the bodies of their fathers at their decease?" The Indians exclaimed aloud and bade him forebear such language . . . Pindar was right . . . "Custom is king o'er all." (*The History of Herodotus*)

Sumner's selection at the end of the chapter agrees. Von Fritz puts it as baldly as anyone could, in a virtual satire of the view:

> Science has proved that there exists no ethical principle which is even theoretically acknowledged by all human societies. Hence ethical values are nothing but functions of the societies in which they originate. The question of what is morally good or morally evil has no meaning except in reference to the moral value system of a given society. There are therefore, no "absolute" criteria by which the value system of a given society can be judged objectively. It may, of course, be judged on the basis of the value system of another society. But there is no possibility of deciding "objectively" which . . . is morally better.*

I will argue later that this is a treasure trove of jumping to conclusions but, for the moment, just by looking at what the satire says we can see that it qualifies as a statement of metaethical relativism.

Herskovits is probably the most recent and most famous of relativists among anthropologists. He expressed it in many works and in 1947 his colleagues, the governing board of the American Anthropo-

---

* Kurt von Fritz, "Relative and Absolute Values," *Moral Principles of Action,* ed. by Nanda Ruth Anshen (New York: Harper and Brothers, 1952), p. 94. Von Fritz is "quoting" an imaginary relativist.

logical Association, had him write a statement of the importance of tolerance that was sent to the fledgling United Nations Organization. It embodied his concept of cultural relativism as the basis for tolerance. In his 1955 book entitled *Cultural Anthropology* he wrote:

> The principle of cultural relativism, briefly stated, is as follows: *Judgments are based on experience, and experience is interpreted by each individual in terms of his own enculturation.* Those who hold for the existence of fixed values will find materials in other societies that necessitate reinvestigation of their assumptions. (Herskovits's italics) †

Notice that Herskovits's plea for tolerance of the moral practices of one society by another follows lines made familiar by John Locke in 1690 in his epoch-making *Essay Concerning Human Understanding.* Locke argued there that there are "no innate practical (i.e., moral) principles" because none are universally agreed upon. All knowledge comes from without, from experience, and different people's experience is different, having different circumstances, and so on. Here we can see that Herskovits goes somewhat beyond Locke and argues that experience is not only the content of our knowledge, the materials out of which it is made, but also that the interpretation of experience varies with the difference in cultural experience. We are faced here primarily with a view of moral knowledge as something that is caused; and, given different cultural causes, one inevitably gets different cultural effects, i.e., different values.

Part Three: The Relative and the Nonrelative in Relativist Theories: Normative Relativism

Herskovits's plea for tolerance on the basis of metaethical relativism brings us to the third and last of the three kinds of moral relativism. You recall that normative ethics is the area in which people make moral and other value judgments, and justify them. A relativist in the normative area of ethics holds that people should do whatever their society or group thinks is right, that it is wrong to judge people's actions in one society by the standards of another society, one's own, for instance. Let us look at Herskovits's plea for tolerance in his own words:

> *Cultural* relativism, in all cases, must be sharply distinguished from concepts of the relativity of individual behavior, which would negate all social controls over conduct. Conformity to the code of the group is a requirement for all regularity in life. Yet to say that we have a right to expect conformity to the code of our day for ourselves does not imply that we need expect, much less impose, conformity to our code on persons who

† Published by Alfred A. Knopf, Inc., p. 351. Quoted by permission.

live by other codes. The very core of cultural relativism is the social discipline that comes of respect for differences—of mutual respect.*

Thus, he would reject those versions of normative relativism that, according to Brandt, hold that a person should always do whatever that individual thinks is right, and that that is what *is* right.

The criticisms that I will briefly level against relativism will follow. I want first to acknowledge that pleas for tolerance, and even a certain amount of "show-me" skepticism are healthy if there is anything at all to the frequent observation that people are ethnocentric and egotistical; all other things being equal, people surely are prone to foist their own standards onto other people. That alone would not show that anyone is ever wrong in doing so, however. It does show that a basically negative outlook such as relativism provides needed reminders of the proneness, and of the need for justification in attempting to get others to accept one's own standards. The criticisms I have against relativism center around a confusion of various other kinds of ethics with metaethics and vice versa.

The relativist depicted by Von Fritz even seems to be unaware of the distinction between metaethics and other kinds of judgments in ethics. In the preceding quotation he says that there is no objective criterion for judging any society's value system. I grant that if there are no standards but normative ethical standards involved, the judging of one society's code is always by standards of another society's code (unless we are talking about the judging of a society's code by itself, i.e., the code judging itself.) In that case, it's a simple issue of one society's word against another's, mine against yours. But if we ask one simple question, the whole scene alters: Does a moral code have any function whatever; is a moral code anything at all? Herskovits regarded conformity to a code as the basis of regularity and thus stability in a group's life. Let's apply that to Von Fritz's relativist: How well or how poorly a code works to do this social job (not denying that it might do other very important jobs, also) is a nonmoral, metaethical standard for judging that code. We need not get into discussion of judging it to be primitive or advanced or anything of that kind at all. What we are doing is judging it as a moral code. A code that is so self-contradictory in what it tells you to do that it says you should and you should not pay back the same debt to the same lender at the same time is not just a poor code for me, it's a poor code, period. A code that, if followed, gets a society "wiped out," made extinct, isn't just bad for a society that doesn't happen to like being exterminated, it's bad for any society and thus just plainly a bad code, if it is a code at all.

* *Ibid.*, p. 365. Quoted by permission.

You see what relativism as depicted by Von Fritz has neglected: The standards described for judging different codes of different societies are epistemological standards, basically. They are called meta-ethical because they are concerned with understanding a moral code, its meaning, its content, its function, how it does its job (in the sense of the means it employs and in another sense, how well it does it). And here, "understand" is not used in the sense of "approve" though sympathetic insight is essential to knowing a code as in knowing most if not all sorts of other things about human beings. But the standards we are discussing are specifically not normative ethical standards, though they are norms and implement values, the value of *having* a moral code as against not having one. A code of ethics could be better or worse in these terms very much as a code of laws might: A code giving self-contradictory advice or a vague or an immensely complex or a socially suicidal code of laws is bound to be regarded as worse than one that lacks these qualities. And so with a moral code.

Von Fritz's relativist would be right if he were talking only about judging one society's normative standards by another society's normative moral standards. But we aren't limited to that option; there are and must be metaethical standards, too. Must be? Why? That can be answered by asking, How does a society or an individual change moral standards? We can say it is a case of coming to dislike a standard that has been followed and looking about for one that will be liked better, but that still leaves the question of whether this is a matter of chance, and arbitrary, in the way that fads and styles come and go. Suppose that an individual gets fed up with one society and leaves it for another. If he or she leaves it for *moral* reasons, some kind of metaethical standard is being applied by that person. He or she is surely *not* doing what Von Fritz would object to: judging one society by the standards of another. Or, suppose that same person does not decide to leave the society in which he or she was born, but having come to disapprove of its moral principles and/or moral rules (either the ones it professes or the ones it does not profess in words but follows in deeds), the person decides to stay and change the society, i.e., to become a moral reformer. Let's say the person meets with success; others listen and slowly the society's code or parts thereof are changed. On what basis do people listen and change their minds? Insofar as the reasons are broadly moral reasons they are metaethical, and are the application of metaethical standards. To say, "Normative standard B is better than normative standard A," is to apply something other than a normative moral standard, say, C. It is to apply a norm, yes, a standard, surely, but a standard for judging normative moral standards. And that is something that people do whenever they consciously *adopt* a normative standard, as the person and society above did. Whether this qualifies as what Von Fritz calls an objective criterion can be judged from his own implied meaning of "objective," i.e., nonethnocentric.

All of this is not to say that there are standards that would enable a judge of normative moral codes of all societies to award first, second, and third prizes to societies X, Y, and Z! What I mean here is that two moral codes might be equally consistent, applicable to their people's everyday concerns (i.e., feasible), equally clear, and equal on the score of being nonsuicidal, and yet be different, and, let us even suppose, conflicting with each other in their moral advice or commands. We are, here, as in many other places in philosophy, at the point where philosophical judgment can eliminate some ideas, but cannot eliminate all but one, the "true," "best," and the like. But Von Fritz is simply and demonstrably mistaken in supposing that there are no standards for judging normative ethical standards except other normative ethical standards.

The very adoption of any viewpoint as a point of vantage for looking at all moral codes would seem to involve the use of some metaethical standards. If an anthropologist or philosopher is to tell me that I and all other individuals except those who share his views am immersed in ethnocentrism but that he has somehow escaped it and found a pinnacle from which to look at all of us in the lowlands, I can only smile at that, though the smile will soon fade if he does not see why I smile. Let us suppose, however, that metaethical relativism is an intellectually respectable viewpoint. Something more ordinarily goes with it, and Von Fritz has hinted at it and Herskovits has spelled that out: tolerance, nonintervention, and possibly, no proselyting or missionary activity for one's own moral code among other peoples, and at home, no condemnation of other people's codes. "You ought not condemn or try to wipe out the moral code of any other society" is plainly an out-and-out normative moral standard. And what's more, it is claimed to be nonrelative, if anything at all is meant by Herskovits's plea.

This is disturbing. Suppose that I am told that I am not to interfere with a society that has an intolerant, imperialistic, aggressive, and so on moral code? To adopt that bit of normative advice would in some cases be suicide, depending on whether that society found it tempting or convenient or not to move in against me, and my society. Tolerance, as critics of liberalism have often pointed out, cannot tolerate intolerance. It has, of course, been a frequent ploy of an expansive nation to claim that it had to attack the other in self-defense, but I am not talking about that. I am talking about the inconsistency of, first, a normative code that includes a prohibition against intervention in an interventionistic society, and second, the inconsistency of a relativism that says that "all moral norms are relative except the moral norm that says tolerance, nonintervention, and the like are not relative." A further point against relativism might be argued, but I shall not take the time for the complexities it involves: Relativism would seem to imply not only that violent intervention in the moral affairs of another society is wrong, but that even benevolent peaceful, rational, and similar attempts to change the moral views of another people to coincide with one's own views is wrong. Yet, of course, such attempts within a society by its own reformers or revolutionists are probably more frequent than external interference. That activity by one's own people is, according to Herskovits, harmful to the "regularity," i.e., order, of life. So the paradox of relativism once more arises: the fact of change in societies is an argument for relativism, but deliberate initiation of change, e.g., by reform or cultural imperialism, is judged wrong by relativists of Herskovits's kind. It is not a mere word play to argue that relativism seems to have its absolutes: (1) Tolerance is a nonrelative value; and (2) the actual, in-force standards of a society are absolute in that society, or for that society. Perhaps another way of putting it would be that regularity of life, or order, seems to be an absolute.

Brenda Cohen's article notes some of the failings of the general relativistic point of view as seeking "toleration" under her heading of False Liberalism as against a "true" liberalism, which she advocates.

Arguments about relativism usually become enmeshed in confusions about the role of acceptance of standards, or belief in standards. Von Fritz's relativist can discover no moral standards except those that are in force, i.e., accepted and practiced. We can call these positive or actual or historical, but the notion of being accepted by someone, somewhere and at sometime, is common to all these descriptions. Debates about relativism usually involve an emphasis on the importance of saying things such as "for them" or "for us"; for instance, relativists would usually accept the idea that a person ought strictly to say not that something is right, but that it is right for someone, at sometime, and at some place. But such additions do not add any new information about standards, or the nature of right and wrong; they do endanger the distinction between thinking that something is right, and something's being right. In other areas this distinction is recognized by relativists. If I think I can fly without wings or other mechanical assistance, that does not make it true. Only the most staunch believer in "Right you are if you think you are" in physical matters would hold that view. But with morals it is different, the relativist says. If a society thinks it's right to fly, it's right for its members to fly. But what does that mean above and beyond that they think it's right? In morals, it appears, the relativist thinks that thinking it's right makes it right, whereas in physics thinking it's true doesn't make it true—something else does. It is not entirely facetious or wholly a cheap shot to reply that if a person thinks the relativist is wrong, then the relativist's theory admits that it is wrong. That would be not so much a word play as a reminder that the relativist does not keep it clearly in mind that there is such a thing as metaethics, and it's one thing to make normative judgments and another to explain them and to talk about what people are doing when they do so. But whatever the subtleties and complexities of this issue, any theory that says that the only evidence for a belief that is available and the only evidence that is needed is the fact that the belief is held is implausible on the very face of it.

Finally, it ought to be noted that the logical relations between the three kinds of relativism accepted by different kinds of relativists are possibly confusing. But it should not be supposed that the three kinds of relativism are mutually exclusive, that is, a person can hold all three forms at the same time and not be obviously inconsistent. In fact, descriptive, or sociological, relativism is usually regarded as the main basis for holding one or both of the other two kinds. Thus, the fact that morals vary considerably from group to group, time to time, and place to place, is taken as the main reason for supposing that morals are relative in the metaethical sense, as Von Fritz illustrates. Many ethicists would object, however, to making descriptive relativism the basis of normative relativism on the grounds that an "is" cannot be the justification of an "ought," e.g., the fact that polygamy is believed to be right by your group could not by itself place you under obligation to go out and find a second wife, nor can monogamy be justification for shoving all your spouses out of your tent except one. My main problem is seeing how a person who holds metaethical relativism could seriously and reflectively embrace normative relativism, too. This criticism comes in conjunction with previous criticisms of the apparent inconsistencies of holding that all moral norms are relative, but that the obligation to obey those of one's group is not, and that the obligation to be tolerant of other people's norms (which are relative) is a nonrelative obligation. If I belong to Tribe A and you belong to Tribe B, and your norms are so intolerant as to say, "O, members of Tribe B, hearken! It is thy solemn duty to exterminate all members of Tribe A!" I am naturally going to find it a little difficult to be tolerant of you, and to say, "O, member of Tribe B, if that is thy tribe's belief, that is what thou oughtest to do, even though it may cost me my life!" But if I am a rational and reflective person, it is not merely the instinct for survival that will give me trouble in being a normative relativist, though that would be enough to cause me not to be a relativist of that kind in the circumstances. I am going to have very serious intellectual difficulties; talking about whether morals are relative is an intellectual enterprise, if it is anything at all, and espousing relativism or nonrelativism is an intellectual activity. My intellectual problem is going to be that I just cannot seriously see how I can be very much committed to a morality that my group thinks is right when I am consciously committed to the metaethical idea that any other and opposing morality has as much chance of being shown to be right as mine. To compound the muddle I would be in, if my tribe believes it the greatest moral sin to be done in by a member of Tribe B, I would be holding both that all B tribespeople ought to try their best to kill me, and, at the very least, that it would be wrong to let them do their duty. Thus, I would be seriously and conscientiously believing that it would be both right and wrong if I should die at the hands of a B tribesperson. "Right for them" and "wrong for me" does not help me out of the muddle at all.

There is one way that has been suggested of solving the problem of how something can be right for me and wrong for you, and vice versa, and that is relativism's fairly close kin, subjectivism. We now turn to that theory.

Subjectivism

This is a metaethical theory about the meaning of moral and other value judgments. It has already been suggested as a solution to the problem of the face-off between a person of Tribe A and one of Tribe B. In the situation described we might say that the confusions can all be cleared up by looking at it from the standpoint of the two individuals involved: Tribesman A thinks its wrong for Tribesman B to kill him; Tribesman B thinks its right for him to kill Tribesman A, or, as people often put it, "For him, it's right; for you, it's wrong." Subjectivism's solution to this problem is somewhat like resolving the differences between a person who is color-blind and one who is not, or between a person who is jaundiced and "sees yellow" and one who is not. To the color-blind person the "red" apple looks gray; to the noncolor-blind person, the "red" apple looks red. "To," or "for" the first, it *is* gray; "to" or "for" the second, it *is* red. To the one, for all practical purposes it is gray and to the other, for all practical purposes, red, and, we sometimes say, it might as well be gray, so far as the first person is concerned.

But subjectivism does something more in explaining moral judgments than simply translating a color-perception situation into its appropriate moral counterpart. Subjectivism says that what you are really saying in a moral situation is that you have certain feelings or attitudes. Thus, "It is right for Tribesman B to kill Tribesman A" is not really about tribesmen at all; it is about the feelings of the person who is making this normative judgment, and a more accurate version of it would read, "When I think about Tribesman B killing Tribesman A, I have a positive, or approving, feeling." This would resolve the problems I would have in being both a metaethical and normative relativist, the subjectivist would assure me, by saying that it cuts the Gordian knot of saying something is both right and wrong at the same time. The problem, we might be further assured, is in attributing the possession of the property of rightness and denying that the action has it, both at the same time. The apple could not be both red and gray (all over, and at the same time), but it could surely cause the sensation of gray in one person and the sensation of red in another. An act could not be both right and wrong at the same time, but it surely could cause one person to have feelings of approval and another to have feelings of disapproval.

The difference between these two situations—the killing and the apple—is that, though in physics and psychology we do not say that the apple really is red, we do say that normal observers perceive it as red, have sensations of redness and the like under standard conditions (e.g., sunlight, no jaundice or color-blindness, and so on). And even more than this, with regard to weight, we do say that the apple really does have such and such weight, or weigh so much, whether it be put in grams or ounces, whether it feels light to a person who has just been throwing the discus, or heavy to a person who has been powdering her nose for the past ten minutes. Now, different subjectivists might hold different further ideas on the matter of whether acts such as killing really are right or wrong in themselves, but they would agree that if these acts are in themselves right or wrong you, I, and no other observer can know that they have such a property of rightness or wrongness in them, as apples have the property of weight in them. All we can know is how we feel about them, and that is, according to the subjectivist, what we are really expressing when we make moral judgments about killing or other actions.

In criticism of this viewpoint, we should note in fairness to the theory that the subjectivist does not claim to be subjective in making moral judgments or in explaining them. The subjectivist would, if anything, deny that and say that when we admit that all we know of right and wrong is how we feel, what attitudes or emotions come to us when we see killing or think about it, we are being *objective!* Beyond that, we should also admit that recognition of the influence of subjective elements in our moral judgments is likely to be blinded by such things as ethnocentrism and egotism in us. We can often catch ourselves in such rationalizations.

But in trying to solve the problem of moral disagreement the theory pays too high a price, and it is the price of changing the subject. It does not so much solve the problem as dissolve it, when solution, not dissolution, is needed; for subjectivism is a denial that there is any such thing as moral disagreement. "I have positive, approving feelings about B killing A" and "I, on the other hand, have strongly negative and disapproving feelings about B killing A" are not in conflict at all, so far as the truth of the first statement and the truth of the second are concerned. Both can be true at the same time and are, if the two persons are correctly or accurately reporting their feelings, or reading off their psychology at the moment. I said that the subjectivist position changes the subject of ethics. One would ordinarily suppose we are talking about killing and not our feelings about killing when we say that it is right or that it is wrong. It requires a great wrenching of the concept of right and wrong to say that all statements about it ought to be translated into statements about feelings. It would lack even more plausibility if there were not times when we do substitute "feel" for "think" in such expressions as "I feel that tomorrow will be better" or "Here's how I feel about it . . ."

The last objection I make to subjectivism is that feelings themselves are subject to moral judgments. If you are afraid of the dark when you are three years old, that is one thing. But to be afraid of the dark when you are thirty is another. The person who is callous and has no feelings about the misfortunes of even close relatives, the thin-skinned person, the person who "flies off the handle" at the least provocation—all these are examples of moral judgments passed upon people's feelings. Sometimes a person will say, "I know I shouldn't feel that way, but I can't help it." This also indicates a person sometimes makes moral judgments about his or her own feelings. What account must subjectivism make of this? It can only say that "It's wrong for me to feel glad at your misfortune" really means something like "I feel disapproval of my feeling of approval at your misfortune." I am not arguing against subjectivism that it could not go very far toward making such translations, and even such translations as explain other people's moral judgments about one's feelings. For instance, it is not senseless to say, "I feel strong negative feelings about your strong negative feelings about your father," instead of "It's wrong to hate your father." And as Ruth Benedict's famous article suggests, it may well be that the determination of whether a feeling is justified or not, or whether a feeling is the kind a person should or should not have in a certain situation, is relative to the society in which the judgment is being made. Yet, there is hardly any evidence that there is no limit on what people in different societies can be conditioned to feel about the same circumstance, say, violent death, suffering of a friend, or the emaciation of one's own body by hunger.

Conclusion

One way of understanding relativism and subjectivism in ethics is to notice how strongly both substitute the category of causes for reasons. Some versions of relativism frame their ideas in those terms more than others so that morals are always an effect and, given a different set of causes, one has a set of effects that differs. Thus, a society will have as its values whatever happens to have been available as a thing to value and whatever, among alternative things that might have been valued, those things that someone, a long time ago perhaps, did happen to like, i.e., to value. What were their reasons for coming to believe that these things are good, and these actions concerning them were right or wrong? Sumner's reading tells us that the origin of the mores is always unconscious, and always located in the dim, dark past, beyond our present-day knowledge; that is, there were no reasons of any conscious sort, there were only causes. Subjectivism also stresses what things cause people to feel. They vary and perhaps this is one reason why subjectivism has been frequently confused with relativism and vice versa. But if the newer anthropology has not shown that agreement would disprove relativism, it has shown some probable limit to the variation in people's ability to value just any and every kind of thing.

The main problem that I have found with relativism has been its hasty conclusions about moral agreement and disagreement. It may be that it has also maximized disagreements and minimized agreements, though agreement that X is true does not make it true, nor does disagreement as to whether X is true mean that it can never be known whether X is true or false, and, least of all, does it show, as relativism sometimes suggests, that there isn't anything of the kind that the statement X is talking about.

Both relativism and subjectivism have difficulty accounting for the very change that both of them are concerned about, the variability of ethics. When an individual or a society changes its mind as to the rightness or wrongness of war, or of capital punishment or abortion, relativism and subjectivism do not give us any clear account of the change or justifications that have been given for it or as to whether any could or should be given. Subjectivism, for instance, has me saying instead of "I used to believe that capital punishment was wrong, but now I think it's right," something like this: "In times past when I thought of capital punishment I had negative, disapproving feelings, but now when I think of it, I have positive, approving feelings about it."

Variability and change, moral disagreement, and value conflict are confusing, but they are among the most instructive things about morals and values generally. On that aspect, relativists and subjectivists are correct. For reasons I have given, however (and others that come out of them) they draw badly mistaken conclusions. That does not make me an absolutist, only a nonrelativist.

FOLKWAYS *

WILLIAM GRAHAM SUMNER

1. Definition and mode of origin of the folkways. If we put together all that we have learned from anthropology and ethnography about primitive men and primitive society, we perceive that the first task of life is to live. Men begin with acts, not with thoughts. Every moment brings necessities which must be satisfied at once. Need was the first experience, and it was followed at once by a blundering effort to satisfy it. It is generally taken for granted that men inherited some guiding instincts from their beast ancestry, and it may be true, although it has never been proved. If there were such inheritances, they controlled and aided the first efforts to satisfy needs. Analogy makes it easy to assume that the ways of beasts had produced channels of habit and predisposition along which dexterities and other psychophysical activities would run easily. Experiments with new-born animals show that in the absence of any experience of the relation of means to ends, efforts to satisfy needs are clumsy and blundering. The method is that of trial and failure, which produces repeated pain, loss, and disappointments. Nevertheless, it is a method of rude experiment and selection. The earliest efforts of men were of this kind. Need was the impelling force. Pleasure and pain, on the one side and the other, were the rude constraints which defined the line on which efforts must proceed. The ability to distinguish between pleasure and pain is the only psychical power which is to be assumed. Thus ways of doing things were selected, which were expedient. They answered the purpose better than other ways, or with less toil and pain. Along the course on which efforts were compelled to go, habit, routine, and skill were developed. The struggle to maintain existence was carried on, not individually, but in groups. Each profited by the other's experience; hence there was concurrence towards that which proved to be most expedient. All at last adopted the same way for the same purpose; hence the ways turned into customs and became mass phenomena. Instincts were developed in connection with them. In this way folkways arise. The young learn them by tradition, imitation, and authority. The folkways, at a time, provide for all the needs of life then and there. They are uniform, universal in the group, imperative, and invariable. As time goes on, the folkways become more and more arbitrary, positive, and imperative. If asked why they act in a certain way in certain cases, primitive people always answer that it is because they and their ancestors always have done so. A sanction also arises from ghost fear. The ghosts of ancestors would be angry if the living should change the ancient folkways.

* From William Graham Sumner, *Folkways* (Chicago: Ginn and Company, 1906), Sections 1, 3, 28, 29, 30, 31, 15, 16, 17, 18, 34, 42, 43, 44, 61, 62, 63, 83, 232, 494, 438, and 439.

3. *Folkways are made unconsciously.* It is of the first importance to notice that, from the first acts by which men try to satisfy needs, each act stands by itself, and looks no further than the immediate satisfaction. From recurrent needs arise habits for the individual and customs for the group, but these results are consequences which were never conscious, and never foreseen or intended. They are not noticed until they have long existed, and it is still longer before they are appreciated. Another long time must pass, and a higher stage of mental development must be reached, before they can be used as a basis from which to deduce rules for meeting, in the future, problems whose pressure can be foreseen. The folkways, therefore, are not creations of human purpose and wit. They are like products of natural forces which men unconsciously set in operation, or they are like the instinctive ways of animals, which are developed out of experience, which reach a final form of maximum adaptation to an interest, which are handed down by tradition and admit of no exception or variation, yet change to meet new conditions, still within the same limited methods, and without rational reflection or purpose. From this it results that all the life of human beings, in all ages and stages of culture, is primarily controlled by a vast mass of folkways handed down from the earliest existence of the race, having the nature of the ways of other animals, only the topmost layers of which are subject to change and control, and have been somewhat modified by human philosophy, ethics, and religion, or by other acts of intelligent reflection. . . .

28. *Folkways due to false inference.* Furthermore, folkways have been formed by accident, that is, by irrational and incongruous action, based on pseudo-knowledge. In Molembo a pestilence broke out soon after a Portuguese had died there. After that the natives took all possible measures not to allow any white man to die in their country. On the Nicobar islands some natives who had just begun to make pottery died. The art was given up and never again attempted. White men gave to one Bushman in a kraal a stick ornamented with buttons as a symbol of authority. The recipient died leaving the stick to his son. The son soon died. Then the bushmen brought back the stick lest all should die. Until recently no building of incombustible materials could be built in any big town of the central province of Madagascar, on account of some ancient prejudice. . . . Soon after the Yakuts saw a camel for the first time smallpox broke out amongst them. They thought the camel to be the agent of the disease. A woman amongst the same people contracted an endogamous marriage. She soon afterwards became blind. This was thought to be on account of the violation of ancient customs. A very great number of such cases could be collected. In fact they represent the current mode of reasoning of nature people. It is their custom to reason that, if one thing follows another, it is due to it. A great number of customs are traceable to the notion of the evil eye, many more to ritual notions of uncleanness. No scientific investigation could discover the origin of

the folkways mentioned, if the origin had not chanced to become known to civilized men. We must believe that the known cases illustrate the irrational and incongruous origin of many folkways. In civilized history also we know that customs have owed their origin to "historical accident"—the vanity of a princess, the deformity of a king, the whim of a democracy, the love intrigue of a statesman or prelate. By the institutions of another age it may be provided that no one of these things can affect decisions, acts, or interests, but then the power to decide the ways may have passed to clubs, trades unions, trust, commercial rivals, wire-pullers, politicians, and political fanatics. In these cases also the causes and origins may escape investigation.

29. *Harmful folkways.* There are folkways which are positively harmful. Very often these are just the ones for which a definite reason can be given. The destruction of a man's goods at his death is a direct deduction from other-worldliness; the dead man is supposed to want in the other world just what he wanted here. The destruction of a man's goods at his death was a great waste of capital, and it must have had a disastrous effect on the interests of the living, and must have very seriously hindered the development of civilization. With this custom we must class all the expenditure of labor and capital on graves, temples, pyramids, rites, sacrifices, and support of priests, so far as these were supposed to benefit the dead. The faith in goblinism produced other-worldly interests which overruled ordinary worldly interests. Foods have often been forbidden which were plentiful, the prohibition of which injuriously lessened the food supply. There is a tribe of Bushmen who will eat no goat's flesh, although goats are the most numerous domestic animals in the district. Where totemism exists it is regularly accompanied by a taboo on eating the totem animal. Whatever may be the real principle in totemism, it overrules the interest in an abundant food supply. "The origin of the sacred regard paid to the cow must be sought in the primitive nomadic life of the Indo-European race," because it is common to Iranians and Indians of Hindostan. The Libyans ate oxen but not cows. The same was true of the Phoenicians and Egyptians. In some cases the sense of a food taboo is not to be learned. It may have been entirely capricious. Mohammed would not eat lizards, because he thought them the offspring of a metamorphosed clan of Israelites. On the other hand, the protective taboo which forebade killing crocodiles, pythons, cobras, and other animals enemies of man was harmful to his interests, whatever the motive. "It seems to be a fixed article of belief throughout southern India, that all who have willfully or accidentally killed a snake, especially a cobra, will certainly be punished, either in this life or the next, in one of three ways: either by childlessness, or by leprosy, or by ophthalmia." Where this faith exists man has a greater interest to spare a cobra than to kill it. India furnishes a great number of cases of harmful mores. "In India every tendency of humanity seems intensified and exaggerated. No country in the

world is so conservative in its traditions, yet no country has undergone so many religious changes and vicissitudes." "Every year thousands perish of disease that might recover if they would take proper nourishment, and drink the medicine that science prescribes, but which they imagine that their religion forbids them to touch.". . .

30. How "truth" and "right" are found. If a savage puts his hand too near the fire, he suffers pain and draws it back. He knows nothing of the laws of the radiation of heat, but his instinctive action conforms to that law as if he did know it. If he wants to catch an animal for food, he must study its habits and prepare a device adjusted to those habits. If it fails, he must try again, until his observation is "true" and his device is "right." All the practical and direct element in the folkways seems to be due to common sense, natural reason, intuition, or some other original mental endowment. It seems rational (or rationalistic) and utilitarian. Often in the mythologies his ultimate rational element was ascribed to the teaching of a god or a culture hero. In modern mythology it is accounted for as "natural."

Although the ways adopted must always be really "true" and "right" in relation to facts, for otherwise they could not answer their purpose, such is not the primitive notion of true and right.

31. The folkways are "right." Rights. Morals. The folkways are the "right" ways to satisfy all interests, because they are traditional, and exist in fact. They extend over the whole of life. There is a right way to catch game, to win a wife, to make one's self appear, to cure disease, to honor ghosts, to treat comrades or strangers, to behave when a child is born, on the warpath, in council, and so on in all cases which can arise. The ways are defined on the negative side, that is, by taboos. The "right" way is the way which the ancestors used and which has been handed down. The tradition is its own warrant. It is not held subject to verification by experience. The notion of right is in the folkways. It is not outside of them, of independent origin, and brought to them to test them. In the folkways, whatever is, is right. This is because they are traditional, and therefore contain in themselves the authority of the ancestral ghosts. When we come to the folkways we are at the end of our analysis. The notion of right and ought is the same in regard to all the folkways, but the degree of its varies with the importance of the interest at stake. The obligation of conformable and coöperative action is far greater under ghost fear and war than in other matters, and the social sanctions are severer, because group interests are supposed to be at stake. Some usages contain only a slight element of right and ought. It may well be believed that notions of right and duty, and of social welfare, were first developed in connection with ghost fear and other-worldliness, and therefore that, in that field also, folkways were first raised to mores. "Rights" are the rules of mutual give and take in the competition of life which are imposed on comrades in the in-group, in order that the peace may prevail there which is essential to the group strength. Therefore rights can never be "natural" or "God-given," or absolute in any sense. The morality of a group at a time is the sum of the taboos and prescriptions in the folkways by which right conduct is defined. Therefore morals can never be intuitive. They are historical, institutional, and empirical.

World philosophy, life policy, right, rights, and morality are all products of the folkways. They are reflections on, and generalizations from, the experience of pleasure and pain which is won in efforts to carry on the struggle for existence under actual life conditions. The generalizations are very crude and vague in their germinal forms. They are all embodied in folklore, and all our philosophy and science have been developed out of them.

15. *Ethnocentrism* is the technical name for this view of things in which one's own group is the center of everything, and all others are scaled and rated with reference to it. Folkways correspond to it to cover both the inner and the outer relation. Each group nourishes its own pride and vanity, boasts itself superior, exalts its own divinities, and looks with contempt on outsiders. Each group thinks its own folkways the only right ones, and if it observes that other groups have other folkways, these excite its scorn. Opprobrious epithets are derived from these differences. "Pig-eater," "cow-eater," "uncircumcised," "jabberers," are epithets of contempt and abomination. The Tupis called the Portuguese by a derisive epithet descriptive of birds which have feathers around their feet, on account of trousers. For our present purpose the most important fact is that ethnocentrism leads a people to exaggerate and intensify everything in their own folkways which is peculiar and which differentiates them from others. It therefore strengthens the folkways.

16. *Illustrations of ethnocentrism.* The Papuans on New Guinea are broken up into village units which are kept separate by hostility, cannibalism, head hunting, and divergences of language and religion. Each village is integrated by its own language, religion, and interests. A group of villages is sometimes united into a limited unity by connubium. A wife taken inside of this group unit has full status; one taken outside of it has not. The petty group units are peace groups within and are hostile to all outsiders. The Mbayas of South America believed that their deity had bidden them live by making war on others, taking their wives and property, and killing their men.

17. When Caribs were asked whence they came, they answered, "We alone are people." The meaning of the name Kiowa is "real or principal people." The Lapps call themselves "men," or "human beings." The Greenland Eskimo think that Europeans have been sent to Greenland to learn virtue and good manners from the Greenlanders. Their highest form of praise for a European is that he is, or soon will be, as good as a Greenlander. The Tunguses call themselves "men." As a rule it is found that na-

ture peoples call themselves "men." Others are something else—perhaps not defined—but not real men. In myths the origin of their own tribe is that of the real human race. They do not account for the others. The Ainos derive their name from that of the first man, whom they worship as a god. Evidently the name of the god is derived from the tribe name. When the tribal name has another sense, it is always boastful or proud. The Ovambo name is a corruption of the name of the tribe for themselves, which means "the wealthy." Amongst the most remarkable people in the world for ethnocentrism are the Seri of Lower California. They observe an attitude of suspicion and hostility to all outsiders, and strictly forbid marriage with outsiders.

18. The Jews divided all mankind into themselves and Gentiles. They were the "chosen people." The Greeks and Romans called all outsiders "barbarians." In Euripides' tragedy of *Iphigenia in Aulis* Iphigenia says that it is fitting the Greeks should rule over barbarians, but not contrariwise, because Greeks are free, and barbarians are slaves. The Arabs regarded themselves as the noblest nation and all others as more or less barbarous. In 1896, the Chinese minister of education and his counselors edited a manual in which this statement occurs: "How grand and glorious is the Empire of China, the middle kingdom! She is the largest and richest in the world. The grandest men in the world have all come from the middle empire." In all the literature of all the states equivalent statements occur, although they are not so naïvely expressed. In Russian books and newspapers the civilizing mission of Russia it talked about, just as, in the book and journals of France, Germany, and the United States, the civilizing mission of those countries is assumed and referred to as well understood. Each state now regards itself as the leader of civilization, the best, the freest, and the wisest, and all others as inferior. Within a few years our own man-on-the-curbstone has learned to class all foreigners of the Latin peoples as "dagos," and "dago" has become an epithet of contempt. These are all cases of ethnocentrism.

34. Definition of the mores. When the elements of truth and right are developed into doctrines of welfare, the folkways are raised to another plane. They then become capable of producing inferences, developing into new forms, and extending their constructive influence over men and society. Then we call them the mores. The mores are the folkways, including the philosophical and ethical generalizations as to societal welfare which are suggested by them, and inherent in them, as they grow.

42. Purpose of the present work. "Ethology" would be a convenient term for the study of manners, customs, usages, and mores, including the study of the way in which they are formed, how they grow or decay, and how they affect the interests which it is their purpose to serve. The Greeks applied the term "ethos" to the sum of the characteristic usages, ideas, standards, and codes by which a group was differentiated and individualized in character from other groups. "Ethics" were things which pertained to the ethos and therefore the things which were the standard of right. The Romans used "mores" for customs in the broadest and richest sense of the word, including the notion that customs served welfare, and had traditional and mystic sanction, so that they were properly authoritative and sacred. It is a very surprising fact that modern nations should have lost these words and the significant suggestions which inhere in them. The English language has no derivative noun from "mores," and no equivalent for it. The French *moeurs* is trivial compared with "mores." The German *Sitte* renders "mores" but very imperfectly. The modern peoples have made morals and morality a separate domain, by the side of religion, philosophy, and politics. In that sense, morals is an impossible and unreal category. It has no existence, and can have none. The word "moral" means what belongs or appertains to the mores. Therefore the category of morals can never be defined without reference to something outside of itself. Ethics, having lost connection with the ethos of a people, is an attempt to systematize the current notions of right and wrong upon some basic principle, generally with the purpose of establishing moral on an absolute doctrine, so that it shall be universal, absolute, and everlasting. In a general way also, whenever a thing can be called moral, or connected with some ethical generality, it is thought to be "raised," and disputants whose method is to employ ethical generalities assume especial authority for themselves and their views. These methods of discussion are most employed in treating of social topics, and they are disastrous to sound study of facts. They help to hold the social sciences under the dominion of metaphysics. The abuse has been most developed in connection with political economy, which has been almost robbed of the character of a serious discipline by converting its discussions into ethical disquisitions.

43. *Why use the word mores.* "Ethica," in the Greek sense, or "ethology," as above defined, would be good names for our present work. We aim to study the ethos of groups, in order to see how it arises, its power and influence, the modes of its operation on members of the group, and the various attributes of it (ethica). "Ethology" is a very unfamiliar word. It has been used for the mode of setting forth manners, customs, and mores in satirical comedy. The Latin word "mores" seems to be, on the whole, more practically convenient and available than any other for our purpose, as a name for the folkways with the connotations of right and truth in respect to welfare, embodied in them. The analysis and definition above given show that in the mores we must recognize a dominating force in history, constituting a condition as to what can be done, and as to the methods which can be employed.

44. *Mores are a directive force.* Of course the view which has been stated is antagonistic to the view that philosophy and ethics furnish creative and determining forces in society and history. That view comes down to us from

the Greek philosophy and it has now prevailed so long that all current discussion conforms to it. Philosophy and ethics are pursued as independent disciplines, and the results are brought to the science of society and to statesmanship and legislation as authoritative dicta. . . . It can be seen also that philosophy and ethics are products of the folkways. They are taken out of the mores, but are never original and creative; they are secondary and derived. They often interfere in the second stage of the sequence—act, thought, act. Then they produce harm, but some ground is furnished for the claim that they are creative or at least regulative. In fact, the real process in great bodies of men is not one of deduction from any great principle of philosophy or ethics. It is one of minute efforts to live well under existing conditions, which efforts are repeated indefinitely by great numbers, getting strength from habit and from the fellowship of united action. The resultant folkways become coercive. All are forced to conform, and the folkways dominate the societal life. Then they seem true and right, and arise into mores as the norm of welfare. Thence are produced faiths, ideas, doctrines, religions, and philosophies, according to the stage of civilization and the fashions of reflection and generalization.

61. *The mores and institutions.* Institutions and laws are produced out of mores. An institution consists of a concept (idea, notion, doctrine, interest) and a structure. The structure is a framework, or apparatus, or perhaps only a number of functionaries set to coöperate in prescribed ways at a certain conjuncture. The structure holds the concept and furnishes instrumentalities for bringing it into the world of facts and action in a way to serve the interests of men in society. Institutions are either crescive or enacted. They are crescive when they take shape in the mores, growing by the instinctive efforts by which the mores are produced. Then the efforts, through long use, become definite and specific. Property, marriage, and religion are the most primary institutions. They began in folkways. They became customs. They developed into mores by the addition of some philosophy of welfare, however crude. Then they were made more definite and specific as regards the rules, the prescribed acts, and the apparatus to be employed. This produced a structure and the institution was complete. Enacted institutions are products of rational invention and intention. They belong to high civilization. Banks are institutions of credit founded on usages which can be traced back to barbarism. There came a time when, guided by rational reflection on experience, men systematized and regulated the usages which had become current, and thus created positive institutions of credit, defined by law and sanctioned by the force of the state. Pure enacted institutions which are strong and prosperous are hard to find. It is too difficult to invent and create an institution, for a purpose, out of nothing. The electoral college in the constitution of the United States is an example. In that case the democratic mores of the people have seized upon the device and made of it something quite different from what the inventors planned. All institutions have come

out of mores, although the rational element in them is sometimes so large that their origin in the mores is not to be ascertained except by an historical investigation (legislatures, courts, juries, joint stock companies, the stock exchange). Property, marriage, and religion are still almost entirely in the mores. Amongst nature men any man might capture and hold a woman at any time, if he could. He did it by superior force which was its own supreme justification. But his act brought his group and her group into war, and produced harm to his comrades. They forbade capture, or set conditions for it. Beyond the limits, the individual might still use force, but his comrades were no longer responsible. The glory to him, if he succeeded, might be all the greater. His control over his captive was absolute. Within the prescribed conditions, "capture" became technical and institutional, and rights grew out of it. The woman had a status which was defined by custom, and was very different from the status of a real captive. Marriage was the institutional relation, in the society and under its sanction, of a woman to a man, where the woman had been obtained in a prescribed way. She was then a "wife." What her rights and duties were was defined by the mores, as they are to-day in all civilized society.

62. *Laws.* Acts of legislation come out of the mores. In low civilization all societal regulations are customs and taboos, the origin of which is unknown. Positive laws are impossible until the stage of verification, reflection, and criticism is reached. Until that point is reached there is only customary law, or common law. The customary law may be codified and systematized with respect to some philosophical principles, and yet remain customary. The codes of Manu and Justinian are examples. Enactment is not possible until reverence for ancestors has been so much weakened that it is no longer thought wrong to interfere with traditional customs by positive enactment. Even then there is reluctance to make enactments, and there is a stage of transition during which traditional customs are extended by interpretation to cover new cases and to prevent evils. Legislation, however, has to seek standing ground on the existing mores, and it soon becomes apparent that legislation, to be strong, must be consistent with the mores. Things which have been in the mores are put under police regulation and later under positive law. It is sometimes said that "public opinion" must ratify and approve police regulations, but this statement rests on an imperfect analysis. The regulations must conform to the mores, so that the public will not think them too lax or too strict. The mores of our urban and rural populations are not the same; consequently legislation about intoxicants which is made by one of these sections of the population does not succeed when applied to the other. The regulation of drinking places, gambling places, and disorderly houses has passed through the above-mentioned stages. It is always a question of expediency whether to leave a subject under the mores, or to make a police regulation for it, or to put it into criminal law. Betting, horse racing, dangerous sports, electric cars, and vehicles are cases now of things

which seem to be passing under positive enactment and out of the unfor-mulated control of the mores. When an enactment is made there is a sacri-fice of the elasticity and automatic self-adaptation of custom, but an enact-ment is specific and is provided with sanctions. Enactments come into use when conscious purposes are formed, and it is believed that specific devices can be framed by which to realize such purposes in the society. Then also prohibitions take the place of taboos, and punishments are planned to be deterrent rather than revengeful. The mores of different societies, or of different ages, are characterized by greater or less readiness and confidence in regard to the use of positive enactments for the realization of societal purposes.

63. *How laws and institutions differ from mores.* When folkways have be-come institutions or laws they have changed their character and are to be distinguished from the mores. The element of sentiment and faith inheres in the mores. Laws and institutions have a rational and practical character, and are more mechanical and utilitarian. The great difference is that institu-tions and laws have a positive character, while mores are unformulated and undefined. There is a philosophy implicit in the folkways; when it is made explicit it becomes technical philosophy. Objectively regarded, the mores are the customs which actually conduce to welfare under existing life con-ditions. Acts under the laws and institutions are conscious and voluntary; under the folkways they are always unconscious and involuntary, so that they have the character of natural necessity. Educated reflection and skepti-cism can disturb this spontaneous relation. The laws, being positive prescrip-tions, supersede the mores so far as they are adopted. It follows that the mores come into operation where laws and tribunals fail. The mores cover the great field of common life where there are no laws or police regulations. They cover an immense and undefined domain, and they break the way in new domains, not yet controlled at all. The mores, therefore, build up new laws and police regulations in time.

83. *Inertia and rigidity of the mores.* We see that we must conceive of the mores as a vast system of usages, covering the whole of life, and serv-ing all its interests; also containing in themselves their own justification by tradition and use and wont, and approved by mystic sanctions until, by ra-tional reflection, they develop their own philosophical and ethical generali-zations, which are elevated into "principles" of truth and right. They coerce and restrict the newborn generation. They do not stimulate to thought, but the contrary. The thinking is already done and is embodied in the mores. They never contain any provision for their own amendment. They are not questions, but answers, to the problem of life. They present themselves as final and unchangeable, because they present answers which are offered as "the truth." No world philosophy, until the modern scientific world philos-ophy, and that only within a generation or two, has ever presented itself as

perhaps transitory, certainly incomplete, and liable to be set aside to-morrow by more knowledge. No popular world philosophy or life policy ever can present itself in that light. It would cost too great a mental strain. All the groups whose mores we consider far inferior to our own are quite as well satisfied with theirs as we are with ours. The goodness or badness of mores consists entirely in their adjustment to the life conditions and the interests of the time and place. . . . Therefore it is a sign of ease and welfare when no thought is given to the mores, but all coöperate in them instinctively. The nations of southeastern Asia show us the persistency of the mores, when the element of stability and rigidity in them becomes predominant. Ghost fear and ancestor worship tend to establish the persistency of the mores by dogmatic authority, strict taboo, and weighty sanctions. The mores then lose their naturalness and vitality. They are stereotyped. They lose all relation to expediency. They become an end in themselves. They are imposed by imperative authority without regard to interests or conditions (caste, child marriage, widows). When any society falls under the dominion of this disease in the mores it must disintegrate before it can live again. In that diseased state of the mores all learning consists in committing to memory the words of the sages of the past who established the formulae of the mores. Such words are "sacred writings," a sentence of which is a rule of conduct to be obeyed quite independently of present interests, or of any rational considerations.

232. *Mores and morals; social code.* For every one the mores give the notion of what ought to be. This includes the notion of what ought to be done, for all should coöperate to bring to pass, in the order of life, what ought to be. All notions of propriety, decency, chastity, politeness, order, duty, right, rights, discipline, respect, reverence, coöperation, and fellowship, especially all things in regard to which good and ill depend entirely on the point at which the line is drawn, are in the mores. The mores can make things seem right and good to one group or one age which to another seem antagonistic to every instinct of human nature. The thirteenth century bred in every heart such a sentiment in regard to heretics that inquisitors had no more misgivings in their proceedings than men would have now if they should attempt to exterminate rattlesnakes. The sixteenth century gave to all such notions about witches that witch persecutors thought they were waging war on enemies of God and man. Of course the inquisitors and witch persecutors constantly developed the notions of heretics and witches. They exaggerated the notions and then gave them back again to the mores, in their expanded form, to inflame the hearts of men with terror and hate and to become, in the next stage, so much more fantastic and ferocious motives. Such is the reaction between the mores and the acts of the living generation. The world philosophy of the age is never anything but the reflection on the mental horizon, which is formed out of the mores, of the ruling ideas which are in the mores themselves. It is from a failure to recognize

the to and fro in this reaction that the current notion arises that mores are produced by doctrines. The "morals" of an age are never anything but the consonance between what is done and what the mores of the age require. The whole revolves on itself, in the relation of the specific to the general, within the horizon formed by the mores. Every attempt to win an outside standpoint from which to reduce the whole to an absolute philosophy of truth and right, based on an unalterable principle, is a delusion. New elements are brought in only by new conquests of nature through science and art. The new conquests change the conditions of life and the interests of the members of the society. Then the mores change by adaptation to new conditions and interests. The philosophy and ethics then follow to account for and justify the changes in the mores; often, also, to claim that they have caused the changes. They never do anything but draw new lines of bearing between the parts of the mores and the horizon of thought within which they are inclosed, and which is a deduction from the mores. The horizon is widened by more knowledge, but for one age it is just as much a generalization from the mores as for another. It is always unreal. It is only a product of thought. The ethical philosophers select points on this horizon from which to take their bearings, and they think that they have won some authority for their systems when they travel back again from the generalization to the specific custom out of which it was deduced. The cases of the inquisitors and witch persecutors who toiled arduously and continually for their chosen ends, for little or no reward, show us the relation between mores on the one side and philosophy, ethics, and religion on the other.

494. Honor, seemliness, common sense, conscience. Honor, common sense, seemliness, and conscience seem to belong to the individual domain. They are reactions produced in the individual by the societal environment. Honor is the sentiment of what one owes to one's self. It is an individual prerogative, and an ultimate individual standard. Seemliness is conduct which befits one's character and standards. Common sense, in the current view, is a natural gift and universal outfit. As to honor and seemliness, the popular view seems to be that each one has a fountain of inspiration in himself to furnish him with guidance. Conscience might be added as another natural or supernatural "voice," intuition, and part of the original outfit of all human beings as such. If these notions could be verified, and if they proved true, no discussion of them would be in place here, but as to honor it is a well-known and undisputed fact that societies have set codes dividually and standards of it which were arbitrary, irrational, and both individually and socially inexpedient, as ample experiment has proved. These codes have been and are imperative, and they have been accepted and obeyed by great groups of men who, in their own judgment, did not believe them sound. These codes came out of the folkways of the time and place. Then comes the question whether it is not always so. Is honor, in any case, anything but the code of one's duty to himself which he has accepted from the group in which he was educated? Family, class, religious sect, school, occupation, enter into the social environment. In every environment there is a standard of honor. When a man thinks that he is acting most independently, on his personal prerogative, he is at best only balancing against each other the different codes in which he has been educated, e.g., that of the trades union against that of the Sunday school, or of the school against that of the family. What we think "natural" and universal, and to which we attribute an objective reality, is the sum of traits whose origin is so remote, and which we share with so many, that we do not know when or how we took them up, and we can remember no rational selection by which we adopted them. The same is true of common sense. It is the stock of ways of looking at things which we acquired unconsciously by suggestion from the environment in which we grew up. Some have more common sense than others, because they are more docile to suggestion, or have been taught to make judgments by people who were strong and wise. Conscience also seems best explained as a sum of principles of action which have in one's character the most original, remote, undisputed, and authoritative position, and to which questions of doubt are habitually referred. If these views are accepted, we have in honor, common sense, and conscience other phenomena of the folkways, and the notions of eternal truths of philosophy or ethics, derived from somewhere outside of men and their struggles to live well under the conditions of earth, must be abandoned as myths.

438. *Specification of the subject.* The ethnographers write of a tribe that the "morality" in it, especially of the women, is low or high, etc. This is the technical use of morality—as a thing pertaining to the sex relation only or especially, and the ethnographers make their propositions by applying our standards of sex behavior, and our form of the sex taboo, to judge the folkways of all people. All that they can properly say is that they find a great range and variety of usages, ideas, standards, and ideals, which differ greatly from ours. Some of them are far stricter than ours. Those we do not consider nobler than ours. We do not feel that we ought to adopt any ways because they are more strict than our traditional ones. We consider many to be excessive, silly, and harmful. A Roman senator was censured for impropriety because he kissed his wife in the presence of his daughter.

439. *Meaning of "immoral."* When, therefore, the ethnographers apply condemnatory or depreciatory adjectives to the people whom they study, they beg the most important question which we want to investigate; that is, What are standards, codes, and ideas of chastity, decency, propriety, modesty, etc., and whence do they arise? The ethnographical facts contain the answer to this question. . . . "Immoral" never means anything but contrary to the mores of the time and place. Therefore the mores and the morality may move together, and there is no permanent or universal stan-

dard by which right and truth in regard to these matters can be established and different folkways compared and criticised.

CULTURE °

ALFRED LOUIS KROEBER AND CLYDE KLUCKHOHN

We know by experience that sincere comparison of cultures leads quickly to recognition of their "relativity." What this means is that cultures are differently weighted in their values, hence are differently structured, and differ both in part-functioning and in total-functioning; and that true understanding of cultures therefore involves recognition of their particular value systems. Comparisons of cultures must not be simplistic in terms of an arbitrary or preconceived universal value system, but must be multiple, with each culture first understood in terms of its own particular value system and therefore its own idiosyncratic structure. After that, comparison can with gradually increasing reliability reveal to what degrees values, significances, and qualities are common to the compared cultures, and to what degree distinctive. In proportion as common structures and qualities are discovered, the uniquenesses will mean more. And as the range of variability of differentiations become better known, it will add to the significance of more universal or common features—somewhat as knowledge of variability deepens significance of a statistical mean. . . .

The inescapable fact of cultural relativism does not justify the conclusion that cultures are in all respects utterly disparate monads and hence strictly noncomparable entities. If this were literally true, a comparative science of culture would be *ex hypothesi* impossible. It is unfortunately the case that up to this point anthropology has not solved very satisfactorily the problem of describing cultures in such a way that objective comparison is possible. . . .

In principle, however, there is a generalized framework that underlies the more apparent and striking facts of cultural relativity. All cultures constitute so many somewhat distinct answers to essentially the same questions posed by human biology and by the generalities of the human situation. These are the considerations explored by Wissler under the heading of "the universal culture pattern" and by Murdock under the rubric of "the least common denominators of cultures." Every society's patterns for living must provide approved and sanctioned ways for dealing with such universal circumstances as the existence of two sexes; the helplessness of in-

° From Alfred Louis Kroeber and Clyde Kluckhohn, *Culture: A Critical Review of Concepts and Definitions,* Papers of the Peabody Museum of Archaeology and Ethnology, **47**: 1. Copyright 1952 by the President and Fellows of Harvard College. Reprinted by permission.

fants; the need for satisfaction of the elementary biological requirements such as food, warmth, and sex; the presence of individuals of different ages and of differing physical and other capacities. The basic similarities in human biology the world over are vastly more massive than the variations. Equally, there are certain necessities in social life for this kind of animal regardless of where that life is carried on or in what culture. Cooperation to obtain subsistence and for other ends requires a certain minimum of reciprocal behavior, of a standard system of communication, and indeed of mutually accepted values. The facts of human biology and of human group living supply, therefore, certain invariant points of reference from which cross-cultural comparison can start without begging questions that are themselves at issue. As Wissler pointed out, the broad outlines of the ground plan of all cultures is and has to be about the same because men always and everywhere are faced with certain unavoidable problems which arise out of the situation "given" by nature. Since most of the patterns of all cultures crystallize around the same foci, there are significant respects in which each culture is not wholly isolated, self-contained, disparate but rather related to and comparable with all other cultures.

Nor is the similarity between cultures, which in some ways transcends the fact of relativity, limited to the sheer forms of the universal culture pattern. There are at least some broad resemblances in content and specifically in value content. Considering the exuberant variation of cultures in most respects, the circumstance that in some particulars almost identical values prevail throughout mankind is most arresting. No culture tolerates indiscriminate lying, stealing, or violence within the in-group. The essential universality of the incest taboo is well-known. No culture places a value upon suffering as an end in itself; as a means to the ends of the society (punishment, discipline, etc.), yes; as a means to the ends of the individual (purification, mystical exaltation, etc.), yes; but of and for itself, never. We know of no culture in either space or time, including the Soviet Russian, where the official ideology denies an after-life, where the fact of death is not ceremonialized. Yet the more superficial conception of cultural relativity would suggest that at least one culture would have adopted the simple expedient of disposing of corpses in the same way most cultures do dispose of dead animals—i.e., just throwing the body out far enough from habitations so that the odor is not troubling. When one first looks rather carefully at the astonishing variety of cultural detail over the world one is tempted to conclude: human individuals have tried almost everything that is physically possible and nearly every individual habit has somewhere at some time been institutionalized in at least one culture. To a considerable degree this is a valid generalization—but not completely. In spite of loose talk (based upon an uncritical acceptance of an immature theory of cultural relativity) to the effect that the symptoms of mental disorder are completely relative to culture, the fact of the matter is that all cultures define as abnormal individuals who are permanently inaccessible to communication or who fail to maintain some degree of control over their impulse life. Social life is impossible without communication, without some measure of order: the behavior of any "normal" individual must be predictable—within a certain range—by his fellows and interpretable by them.

To look freshly at values of the order just discussed is very difficult because they are commonplaces. And yet it is precisely because they are *common*places that they are interesting and important. Their vast theoretical significance rests in the fact that despite all the influences that predispose toward cultural variation (biological variation, difference in physical environments, and the processes of history) all of the very many different cultures known to us have converged upon these universals. It is perfectly true (and for certain types of enquiry important) that the value "thou shalt not kill thy fellow tribesman" is not concretely identical either in its cognitive or in its affective aspects for a Navaho, an Ashanti, and a Chukchee. Nevertheless the central conception is the same, and there is understanding between representatives of different cultures as to the general intent of the prohibition. . . .

There is nothing supernatural or even mysterious about the existences of these universalities in culture content. Human life is—and has to be—a moral life (up to a point) because it is a social life. It may safely be presumed that human groups which failed to incorporate certain values into their nascent cultures or which abrogated these values from their older tradition dissolved as societies or perished without record. Similarly, the biological sameness of the human animal (needs and potentialities) has also contributed to convergences.

The fact that a value is a universal does not, of course, make it an absolute. It is possible that changed circumstances in the human situation may lead to the gradual disappearance of some of the present universals. However, the mere existence of universals after so many millennia of culture history and in such diverse environments suggests that they correspond to something extremely deep in man's nature and/or are necessary conditions to social life.

When one moves from the universals or virtual universals to values which merely are quite widespread, one would be on most shaky ground to infer "rightness" or "wrongness," "better" or "worse" from relative incidence. A value may have a very wide distribution in the world at a particular time just because of historical accidents such as the political and economic power of one nation at that time. Nations diffuse their culture into the areas their power reaches. Nevertheless this does not mean one must take all cultural values except universals as of necessarily equal validity. Slavery or cannibalism may have a place in certain cultures that is not evident to the ethnocentric Christian. Yet even if these culture patterns play an important part in the smooth functioning of these societies, they are still subject to a judgment which is alike moral and scientific. This judgment is not just a projection of values, local in time and space, that are associated with

Western culture. Rather, it rests upon a *consensus gentium* and the best scientific evidence as to the nature of raw human nature—i.e., that human nature which all cultures mold and channel but never entirely remake. To say that certain aspects of Naziism were morally wrong, is not parochial arrogance. It is—or can be—an assertion based both upon cross-cultural evidence as to the universalities in human needs, potentialities, and fulfillments and upon natural science knowledge with which the basic assumptions of any philosophy must be congruent.

Any science must be adequate to explain both the similarities and the differences in the phenomena with which it deals. Recent anthropology has focussed its attention preponderantly upon the differences. They are there; they are very real and very important. Cultural relativism has been completely established and there must be no attempt to explain it away or to depreciate its importance because it is inconvenient, hard to take, hard to live with. Some values are almost purely cultural and draw their significance only from the matrix of that culture. Even the universal values have their special phrasings and emphases in accord with each distinct culture. . . .

At the same time one must never forget that cultural differences, real and important though they are, are still so many variations on themes supplied by raw human nature and by the limits and conditions of social life. In some ways culturally altered human nature is a comparatively superficial veneer. The common understandings between men of different cultures are very broad, very general, very easily obscured by language and many other observable symbols. True universals or near universals are apparently few in number. But they seem to be as deep-going as they are rare. Relativity exists only within a universal framework. Anthropology's facts attest that the phrase "a common humanity" is in no sense meaningless. This is also important. . . .

In sum, cultures are distinct yet similar and comparable. As Steward has pointed out, the features that lend uniqueness are the secondary or variable ones. Two or more cultures can have a great deal of content—and even of patterning—in common and still there is distinctness; there are universals, but relativistic autonomy remains a valid principle. Both perspectives are true and important, and no false either-or antinomy must be posed between them. Once again there is a proper analogy between cultures and personalities. Each human being is unique in his concrete totality, and yet he resembles all other human beings in certain respects and some particular human beings a great deal. It is no more correct to limit each culture to its distinctive features and organization, abstracting out as "pre-cultural" or as "conditions of culture" the likenesses that are universal, than to deny to each personality those aspects that derive from its cultural heritage and from participation in common humanity.

SOCIAL SCIENCE AND ETHICAL RELATIVISM °
PAUL TAYLOR

Social Science and Ethical Relativism

As a participant in the American Philosophical Association (Eastern Division) symposium on "Ethical Relativity in the Light of Recent Developments in Social Science," Professor Clyde Kluckhohn published a summary of recent studies in anthropology, sociology, and psychology concerning universal elements to be found in all human cultures.[1] "For at least a generation," he says, "American anthropology (and to a considerable degree, anthropology in the world in general) concentrated its attention upon the differences between peoples, neglecting the similarities. Recently, the balance has been righted somewhat." [2] He then goes on to give an account of these similarities as they have been set forth in recent published work by psychologists and sociologists as well as by anthropologists. Throughout this discussion Professor Kluckhohn appears to believe that such universal elements or similarities among different cultures are evidence against, or somehow provide the basis for an argument against, or at least justify a qualification of, ethical relativism. (By "ethical relativism" he means, and I shall mean, the assertion that two people or groups of people may hold contradictory ethical views without either being mistaken.[3]) I want to argue that these recent findings of the social scientists do not disprove or provide evidence against ethical relativism, and that they are not even relevant to the relativism-absolutism controversy in ethics.[4]

It has long been the opinion of moral philosophers that the facts about the *differences* among the ethical judgments of different societies do not give support to ethical relativism. A person who denies relativism and claims that moral standards validly apply to all men everywhere and in every age may accept the scientific evidence of the contradictions among moral opinions of different cultures. He simply says some opinions are true (i.e., good reasons can be given for them) and some opinions are false (i.e., good reasons can be given against them). He might not know which

---

° From Paul Taylor, "Social Science and Ethical Relativism," *The Journal of Philosophy,* 55 (1958), pp. 32–44. Reprinted by permission of the author and *The Journal of Philosophy.*

[1] Clyde Kluckhohn, "Ethical Relativity: Sic et Non," this JOURNAL, VOL. LII (Nov. 10, 1955), pp. 663–677.

[2] *Ibid.,* p. 664.

[3] If "holding contradictory ethical views" is interpreted as "disagreement in attitude" and not as a contradiction in the usual sense, then relativism is the view that there are no better reasons for taking one attitude rather than another, while absolutism is the view that such reasons can be given.

[4] At the A.P.A. meeting on this topic, very few members raised this point, which was crucial to the whole discussion, and it was not considered at any length by the participants in the symposium.

are true and which are false. It might be *empirically* impossible for him at the time to give good reasons for or against certain opinions. But he believes that at least it makes sense to say that some are true and others are false, which is precisely what the ethical relativist denies. The ethical relativist claims it is *logically* impossible to give good reasons (reasons which are not culture-bound) for or against moral judgments.

Now just as the facts of cultural differences do not argue for ethical relativism, so the facts of cultural similarities do not argue against ethical relativism. Let us first examine the principle behind this statement and then consider the particular facts of cultural similarities pointed out by Professor Kluckhohn and see why they do not affect the argument for or against ethical relativism. Suppose that there were no differences in the ethical views of different societies. Indeed we can imagine without very much difficulty that a totalitarian power has conquered the world and has subjected everyone to a particular ethical code. By means of indoctrination, propaganda, censorship, brainwashing, and other techniques, the totalitarian power has made everyone in the world come to accept identical moral views. Would this make those moral views true? Of course not. Would this universal concurrence of moral opinion have any bearing on whether any moral view was true or false? I think we must again answer in the negative. Whether a given moral opinion is true or false depends not on who believes it or how many believe it, but on whether reasons can be given to justify it. And such reasons will not include counting the number of people who believe it. One can say that it is true if *rational* people believe it. But again what makes a person rational has nothing to do with how many people he agrees with in his moral opinions. Therefore, even if there were universal concurrence of moral opinion throughout the world, the ethical relativist would not be refuted and the ethical absolutist would not be vindicated. For the relativist would simply say: What is right in such a world is right because people believe it is right, or because they approve of it. If in another world, or in some future age, people (even one person) came to believe otherwise, then that which is right now, for everyone, would become wrong for those who disagreed. And neither person or group could be said to have a more valid opinion than the other. The absolutist would say: The fact that all people now agree about what is right and wrong does not make their beliefs true. They may be correct or they may be mistaken. To decide this we must examine their beliefs to see whether good reasons can be given for or against them.

But it may still be objected that the universal concurrence of moral opinion was imagined to be artificially forced on people, and this is what makes it irrelevant to the relativism-absolutism controversy. If everyone in the world came to have the same opinion naturally, without any interference from despots or thought controllers, then the relativist's position would be invalidated. The crux of this argument lies in the meaning of the word "naturally." If this means spontaneously and emotionally, without the discipline of rational thought, then relativism remains untouched. But if "naturally" means by the free exercise of reason and intelligence, then relativism would indeed be invalidated, but it would not be invalidated just because everyone agreed about morals.

If people came to agree about moral matters spontaneously and emotionally, the relativist would point out that a person's emotional life is conditioned in part by his social environment, and therefore whatever ethical opinions he arrived at through the spontaneous expression and development of his emotions would be relative to his social conditioning. And the fact that everyone had similar emotional reactions in ethical matters would merely imply that they had been subjected to similar environmental conditioning (though a conditioning which had not been deliberately controlled by human agents). Furthermore we would infer that *if* people had been subjected to *other* conditioning their moral opinions would be just as valid as the opinions of those who all agree under the same conditioning.

If, on the other hand, we accept the second meaning of "naturally," then relativism would be disproved and absolutism proved. For in this case rational beings would come to agree about what is right and wrong, and their opinions would be morally justifiable. But what would justify them is not their agreement but their rationality. (Being rational *means* being able to justify, to give good reasons for, one's opinions.) Even if rational beings did not agree, ethical relativism would not by that fact be shown to be true. For this would be a case of honest disagreement among enlightened and competent judges, whose disagreement must leave the correct moral judgment in doubt until further enlightenment brings about agreement. Ethical relativism would be proven only if two or more completely rational and enlightened judges disagreed. We cannot be sure that such a hypothetical eventuality would not happen, of course, and this is one of the reasons why we cannot be sure that ethical relativism is a mistaken view. But whether relativism or absolutism be true, it is sufficient for our argument that this question is not settled by pointing out either that everyone agrees or that no one agrees in their ethical judgments.

Let us now turn to Professor Kluckhohn's exposition of the specific findings of social scientists concerning the similarities among different societies, and let us see if anything can be inferred from them as to whether ethical relativism or ethical absolutism is true. Although Professor Kluckhohn does not classify the findings he discusses, I think they can be arranged into five major groups, according to the kind of factor whose universality is asserted: (1) the universality of morality in general, (2) the universality of certain human needs, (3) the universality of certain human capacities, (4) the universality of "basic field conditions," of social structures and psychological functions, and (5) the universality of certain sentiments, emotions, and attitudes.

(1) Professor Kluckhohn refers to "the universality of moral standards in general," [5] and to the fact that even very different types of society "affirm the same moral value: allegiance to the norms of one's culture." [6] Examples given for universal moral standards in general are: a concept of murder as distinguished from "justifiable homicides," regulations upon sexual behavior, prohibitions upon untruth, and mutual obligations between parents and children. Variation occurs, however, "as to details of prescribed behavior, instrumentalities, and sanctions." [7] And at one point Professor Kluckhohn declares: "To be sure, there must be room left for relativity as regards specific moral rules." [8]

Now let us grant that in every culture there is a set of moral principles or rules of conduct to which the members of the society owe allegiance. If these principles or rules differ on such matters as what types of homicide are justified and what are to be considered murder, what types of sexual behavior are permissible, what circumstances exempt a person from the obligation to tell the truth, and what kinds of acts are obligatory with regard to one's parents or one's children, this variation will make almost all moral judgments culture-bound. What an ethical absolutist wants to know is not so much whether morality in general is good for society, but whether it is right to let a person die of neglect when he can no longer contribute to a society's economic production, whether it is right to kill unwanted infants, whether monogamy is the best sexual institution, whether a person ought to tell the truth under specified circumstances, and so on. No justification, however valid, of morality in general will be relevant to his problem. But aside from this there is still a more important point, and this is that the justification of morality in general cannot consist in, nor be derived from, the fact that morality in general is to be found in all societies. It is true that if a person demanded reasons for having moral rules *at all*, one could point to the necessity for morality in order to carry on community life, and then ask the person whether he would not want to have community life and all the good things which result from it. And anthropological and sociological data concerning the function of morality in human society would indeed give factual evidence in support of the claim that morality is necessary for the carrying on of community life. But there have been people (such as hermits) who have approved of isolated existence, in which obligations to others would have no place. What would be the point, then, in showing such people the necessity of morality in all societies? The absolutist's concern would be to show that isolated existence really is worse than social existence, if he wants to justify morality in general. But he could not use the data concerning the universality of morality in all societies to support this value judgment. This first set of facts, then, will be

[5] Kluckhohn, *loc. cit.*, p. 671.
[6] *Ibid.*, p. 673.
[7] *Ibid.*, p. 672.
[8] *Ibid.*, p. 673.

of no help to a person (1) who wants to know what specific moral rules are justifiable, or (2) who wants to know whether a person is making a mistake in committing himself to a life of isolation. To the relativist who says that no specific moral rules are more justifiable than any others, and who says that no reasons can be given to argue the rightness or wrongness of the hermit's way of life, this first set of facts is irrelevant. And it is also irrelevant to the absolutist, who takes the opposite point of view.

(2) After presenting certain recent findings in psychology, Professor Kluckhohn concludes that there is a "growing trend toward agreement" that "there are pan-human universals as regards needs and capacities that shape, or could rightly shape, at least the broad outlines of a morality that transcends cultural difference." [9] I wish to distinguish "needs" and "capacities," so I shall discuss only the former at this point. No doubt it is the case that human beings have certain fundamental needs which are present no matter what kind of society exists. But two ethical questions must be asked with reference to these needs: (1) Why ought these needs to be satisfied? (2) If some needs are not inborn (unlearned) and depend for their emergence and development on a certain type of physical and social environment, it is then at least theoretically within human capacity to control their emergence and development, and one must ask, What needs ought to be allowed to emerge and develop? Neither of these questions can be answered by indicating the universality of a certain number of needs in all existing cultures. One might say that at least the needs for survival of the individual ought to be satisfied. But this is to assume that survival is desirable, and there is not universal agreement on this, as the existence of people who want to commit suicide testifies. The relativist claims that no arguments can be given to show that committing suicide is wrong (or right), while the absolutist says there are such arguments. But their dispute clearly will not be resolved by pointing out universal or near-universal needs for the preservation of life, unless it is also shown why such needs ought to be fulfilled.

If reference is made to universal "drives," "motives," or "dynamic forces" among all men, the same reasoning applies, since the question to be answered is: *Ought* these drives or motives or dynamic forces to be satisfied, to be allowed to guide human behavior, whether in a pure or in a "sublimated" form? Professor Kluckhohn quotes Franz Boas: "The dynamic forces that mould social life are the same now as those that moulded life thousands of years ago." [10] But this common element cannot provide a basis for ethical absolutism unless reasons are given which justify the channeling of these dynamic forces in particular ways, rather than trying to repress, frustrate, or block them to whatever degree man is capable.

(3) The appeal to universal human capacities or potentialities in sup-

[9] *Ibid.*, p. 666.
[10] *Ibid.*, p. 669.

port of ethical absolutism is certainly not new with Professor Kluckhohn. It is becoming a very widespread idea among contemporary social scientists and psychologists who are interested in ethics. Perhaps the most prominent example is Erich Fromm, who in *Man for Himself* interprets human existence as "the unfolding of the specific powers of an organism." [11] He goes on to say that "all organisms have an inherent tendency to actualize their specific potentialities. *The aim of man's life,* therefore, is to be understood as *the unfolding of his powers according to the laws of his nature.*" [12] At another point he states, "There is no meaning to life except the meaning man gives his life by the unfolding of his powers, by living productively." [13] Now it has often been said that man is potentially anything he can become. He has the potentiality for sainthood or sadism, for benevolence or bigotry. The ethical question, of course, is concerned with *which* potentialities ought to be actualized. Fromm's answer to this is that those potentialities ought to be actualized which are peculiarly human.[14] But certainly there are many ways of behaving, thinking, and feeling which only man is capable of, yet which no psychologist or social scientist would want to judge as morally right. Fromm himself recognizes this difficulty and tries to get around it by making a distinction between "primary" and "secondary" potentialities. The former are actualized if "proper" or "normal" conditions are present, the latter are actualized under "abnormal, pathogenic" conditions which are "in contrast to existential needs." [15] It is clear that this distinction assumes the moral criterion which, according to Fromm, the "science of man" is supposed to provide. Suppose someone wishes to actualize his "secondary" potentialities. To claim he is making a mistake or is doing what is morally wrong requires a justification on grounds other than the pointing out of other potentialities the person is capable of realizing, and other than asserting that his life is "abnormal" or "pathogenic." And clearly the fact that certain potentialities are common to all men, in all cultures, is not a good reason for the ethical judgment that they are the potentialities which ought to be actualized. For this is simply to say that a person ought to do what other people can do, given the environmental conditions of their cultures. This rule is ambiguous, since part of man's potentiality is the ability to change his culture and this rule gives no guidance as to the morally proper or obligatory direction of change. Enough has been said, I think, to show that no reasonable or intelligent person would accept such a rule, and that the relativist and absolutist positions regarding moral standards are not affected by citing universal potentialities in man.

(4) The fourth category of universal elements which Professor Kluckhohn

[11] Erich Fromm, *Man for Himself* (New York, 1947), p. 19.
[12] *Ibid.,* p. 20. Italics are Fromm's.
[13] *Ibid.,* p. 45.
[14] *Ibid.,* p. 45.
[15] *Ibid.,* p. 218.

discusses includes a rather wide variety of "formal similarities" which may be suggested by the following very incomplete list: "basic field conditions" such as society, culture, and symbolic interaction (p. 666); "the experience of intimate association with the 'primary group' upon whom [the individual] was emotionally and otherwise dependent" (p. 667); having two parents of opposite sex and facing the emotional problems of being in competition with one's siblings (p. 668); possessing basically similar neurological mechanisms for dealing with problems (p. 668); the existence of music graphic arts, dancing, parallels in linguistic structure, standards of personal excellence, kinship terminology, and age grading (p. 670); such "cultural constants" as family, religion, war, and communication (p. 670); "the notion of integration of individual to the group" (p. 671); and "the fundamental idea of reciprocity" (p. 671). These relationships, social structures, psychological functions, environmental conditions, etc., which are common to all human societies are no more relevant to the issue between relativism and absolutism in ethics than are the previous types of universals we have considered. To give evidence that everyone competes with his siblings or that everyone grows up in intimate association with two parents of opposite sex is not to give evidence that any particular set of family relations is better than any other. Nor is it to give evidence that one can or cannot make reasonable judgments about the proper way of living with one's siblings, parents, or children. Similarly, that there are such "cultural constants" as war and religion does not imply that wars are ethically right or that religion ought to continue to be a part of human culture. Of course if one has already given reasons for adopting a set of moral rules or for seeking a set of ideals in life, and if it is then demonstrated that wars violate these rules and prevent the realization of these ideals, and that religion gives dramatic symbolization of and emotional orientation toward the rules and ideals, then one may deduce the wrongness of war and the rightness of religion. But the relativist and absolutist are disputing over the first point: whether reasons can be given for adopting a set of moral rules or for seeking certain ideals in life, and whether, if such reasons can be found, those reasons are not entirely culture-bound. And this dispute cannot be resolved by pointing out cultural universals of the sort mentioned above.

(5) The last group of universals are sentiments, emotions, and attitudes common to all human beings in all societies. Professor Kluckhohn speaks of the "universal sentiments" of "love, jealousy, respect, need for respect, and the like." [16] Even if we expand this to include a wide range of emotions and attitudes, which I think Professor Kluckhohn and many other social scientists would be willing to do, the relativism-absolutism controversy is not logically involved. For the ethical issues concern such questions as, Whom ought we to love, and in what way? Under what circumstances, if any, is it proper or permissible to feel jealousy? Why should a person

[16] Kluckhohn, *op. cit.*, p. 667.

respect others? To acknowledge the universality of love, jealousy, and respect has nothing to do with answering these questions. It may be thought, however, that under the "emotive" theory of ethics, according to which ethical terms are expressive of attitudes (liking, disliking, approval, disapproval, etc.), these facts about the universality of certain attitudes would become relevant. But I do not think this is so, since the beliefs about which the relativist and absolutist disagree are concerned with what ought to be the objects of positive attitudes and what ought to be the objects of negative attitudes, as well as with what reasons, if any, can be cited to justify the taking of one attitude rather than another about a given object. It may be the case that in all human societies people have the experience of approving and disapproving of different things, but if they do not agree on what to approve of and what to disapprove of, the mere fact that they all have the experience of approving and disapproving is of no consequence for the truth or falsity, verifiability or unverifiability, reasonableness or unreasonableness, of moral utterances.

In all fairness to Professor Kluckhohn I want to make it clear that, although the general tenor of his article (as of many other recent writings of social scientists) is that the facts of pan-human universals do somehow imply or support or confirm ethical absolutism, he nevertheless makes at least two remarks which indicate his doubt about this. After emphasizing that the universals he has discussed are "primarily conceptual and that variation rages rampant as to details of prescribed behavior, instrumentalities, and sanctions," he goes on to say that equally important is "the fact that universality as such is not transmutable into a categorical imperative." [17] This explicitly denies that the universality of actual needs, capacities, structures, and attitudes is itself sufficient to establish absolute, cross-cultural moral norms. It is, however, not as strong as the assertion which I wish to make in this paper: that such universality is entirely irrelevant to the dispute about whether there are absolute, cross-cultural moral norms, and if there are, what they could be. Another statement revealing Professor Kluckhohn's doubt is his warning that "we must not glibly equate universals with absolutes." [18] But he then proceeds to make vague and confusing statements about the relation between universals and absolutes. He says:

> If, in spite of biological variation and historical and environmental diversities, we find these congruences, is there not a presumptive likelihood that these moral principles somehow correspond to inevitabilities, given the nature of the human organism and of the human situation? They may at any rate lead us to "conditional absolutes" or "moving absolutes," not in the metaphysical but in the empirical sense.[19]

[17] *Ibid.*, p. 672.
[18] *Ibid.*, p. 673.
[19] *Ibid.*, p. 673.

Since the relation between factual universals and moral absolutes is the very crux of the issue, I shall try to analyze briefly this relation, with special reference to the end of Professor Kluckhohn's article where he draws some tentative conclusions about ethical absolutes. These absolutes, I take it, are the "conditional" or "moving" sort of absolutes he mentions in the quoted passage. My point will be to show that in drawing his conclusions Professor Kluckhohn commits himself to an absolutist ethical viewpoint which neither presupposes his previous discussion of universals nor is confirmed by evidence derivable from that discussion.

Allowing for "relativity as regards specific moral rules," Professor Kluckhohn "provisionally accepts" three cross-cultural absolutes: (1) the "common conscience" which science as an international or nonnational social institution requires,[20] (2) that way of life which admits of being extended to mankind as a whole and which recognizes the right persons to be treated as persons,[21] and (3) use of the scientific study of culture as a corrective to ethnocentrism and as a way to the discovery of invariant values as regards "the broad issues of principle, especially those at a higher level of generality."[22] There is also added the following point: "Some needs and motives are so deep and so generic that they are beyond the reach of argument: pan-human morality expresses and supports them."[23] Perhpas Professor Kluckhohn intends by this that no reasonable, intelligent, and sane human being would disapprove of the fulfillment of such needs and motives, in which case he follows through the theme of rationality which we shall see unifies and underlies his other three absolutes.

Now the *adoption* of the ethical position outlined in the preceding paragraph is not logically dependent on and is not justified by facts about universal elements in human cultures, though these facts do have an important function in the *systematic development* and *application* of that ethical position. The ethical absolutism to which Professor Kluckhohn tentatively commits himself is actually a *methodological* absolutism. The first and third absolutes are a commitment to scientific method as a way to discover cross-cultural moral norms which are rationally justifiable. The second (Kantian) absolute is the principle of impartiality or disinterestedness (which is the same as the principle of equality of treatment, or the principle of the supreme value of persons as persons) which can be justified as a necessary condition for the reasonableness of a judge in ethical disputes.[24] I think what Professor Kluckhohn does here is to set up conditions which define a rationally justifiable decision regarding the adoption of moral rules,

20 *Ibid.*, p. 674.
21 *Ibid.*, p. 675.
22 *Ibid.*, p. 675.
23 *Ibid.*, p. 676.
24 See W. M. Sibley, "The Rational versus the Reasonable," *Philosophical Review*, Vol. LXII (Oct., 1953), pp. 554–560; and M. G. Singer, "Generalization in Ethics," *Mind*, Vol. LXIV (July, 1955), pp. 361–375.

norms, or ideals. These conditions would have to include enlightenment concerning the relevant facts, intelligence in the making of inferences, fairness or impartiality in the consideration of conflicting interests (each interest being given an equal *prima facie* claim to satisfaction), and a fundamental sanity in the life of the decision-maker or judge. And this is quite different from deducing a moral ought from statements about cultural similarities or pan-human universals. We have already seen that no deduction of this sort is valid. Yet there is an important place for the findings of social science and psychology in ethics. What social scientists and psychologists can do in the attempt to work out a rationally justifiable decision or judgment concerning rules of conduct, objectives worth striving for, etc., is (1) to give us facts to help us to predict with greater probability the consequences of adopting various rules or objectives; (2) to widen our horizon of knowledge so that we can envisage alternatives we might not have thought of before; (3) to show us the origin of our attitudes and customs, their causes and effects in social history and in the individual psyche, so that we may understand how they influence our present judgments and how they might be changed; and (4) in general to make us well informed about all empirical knowledge that bears on the situation of choice or judgment. Now the pointing out of universal elements in all cultures will be relevant only so far as the knowledge of such universals contributes to these four tasks. But there would be nothing special about the fact that pan-human universals rather than peculiarities of societies were being pointed out. They would simply comprise further facts which, in the forming of a rational decision or judgment, would be helpful in varying degrees according to the situation.

Finally, the absolute, cross-cultural *method* here proposed for arriving at rationally justifiable judgments of absolute, cross-cultural *moral norms* is neither itself universally used (or professed to be used) throughout all cultures nor is its use justified by appeal to elements that are universally present in all cultures. What is and what is not universal is entirely irrelevant to the question of whether one has good reasons for adopting the method. That question is the question whether it is reasonable to be reasonable, since the proposed method is simply what is meant by being rational or reasonable in ethical matters in the first place. It is not necessary to discuss this question here.[25] All that is necessary is to see that the attempt to derive absolute moral norms from pan-human universals and the adoption of an absolute method (that is, a method valid for all human beings in all societies) for the rational justification of absolute moral norms are two entirely different things, and that the second enterprise does not logically depend on scientific knowledge of pan-human universals. The scientific knowledge of pan-human universals is relevant not to the question

25 For a discussion of this question see my "Four Types of Ethical Relativism," *Philosophical Review*, Vol. LXIII (Oct., 1954), pp. 506–510.

of whether the method can justifiably be adopted in the first place, but to the use of the method once it has been adopted. Such knowledge enters the method whenever it is helpful in increasing the factual enlightenment necessary for arriving at a given moral decision or judgment in an informed, impartial, and intelligent manner. As such it is no different from any other kind of factual knowledge.

The controversy between ethical relativism and ethical absolutism concerns (1) whether there are absolute, cross-cultural moral norms, and (2) whether there is a rational, cross-cultural method for arriving at justifiable moral decisions and judgments. The scientific knowledge of pan-human universals has been shown to be irrelevant to (1) in our foregoing discussion of universals, and it is here shown to be irrelevant to (2), since (2) concerns the justification for adopting a method, not the use of the method once it has been adopted.

THE PSYCHOLOGICAL BASIS
OF CULTURAL RELATIVISM °

SOLOMON ASCH

The Psychological Basis of Cultural Relativism

Cultural relativism finds a strict psychological foundation in the propositions of stimulus-response psychology about needs and learning. In particular they offer an apparently cogent explanation of the formation of different reactions to identical conditions. Stimulus-response theory asserts that one can at will attach to a given situation S_1 any of a number of acts, feelings, and evaluations, depending on the consequences that follow. To situation S_1 any of responses R_x, R_y, R_z are possible. Which of the responses will become connected to the situation S_1 depends on which response will be followed by reward. It follows that we can, by the manipulation of rewards and punishments, attach to the *same* situation either of two *opposed* responses. There are situations that approximate outwardly to this interpretation. A signal in a conditioning experiment can be connected with food or with shock; a word can designate one object or another wholly unlike it. In an earlier discussion we questioned this interpretation and its general applicability. There we noted that the stimulus-response account presupposes a thoroughgoing relation of arbitrariness between situation and action and between action and consequence. Let us now see how this interpretation is applied to practices and convictions.

° From Solomon Asch, *Social Psychology* (Englewood Cliffs: Prentice-Hall, 1952), Chapter 13, with omissions. Reprinted by permission of Solomon Asch, copyright owner.

The extension is accomplished simply by the assertion that beliefs, customs, and values are also "responses," learned in precisely the same way as one learns the connection between a person and his name or between a person and his telephone number. We learn to believe that which rewards and to disbelieve that which incurs pain. Therefore the manipulation of rewards and punishments can determine us to judge the same action as good or bad, true or false. For an organism governed by rewards and punishments these are the only possible and necessary "proofs." The laws of learning grind out truth and falsehood indifferently; rewards and punishments are the sole content and criterion of right and wrong. It follows that our ideas of right and wrong, beautiful or ugly are decided by social sanctions and that identical actions can be made desirable or despicable. It is on this basis that we are said to learn that gangsters are bad and that democracy is desirable. These are standards that we have "accepted"; nothing in the nature of democracy and crime points to their value.* Life in society is therefore likened to the running of a maze in which the paths are arbitrarily fixed and which one learns to run in the search for satisfaction and avoidance of pain. "Culture, as conceived by social scientists, is a statement of the design of the human maze, of the type of reward involved, and of what responses are to be rewarded. It is in this sense a recipe for learning." When to-day we encounter the statement that culture is "learned" it often refers not only to the necessity of past experience but also to the arbitrary effect of experience described here.

Deeply embedded in this view is the assumption that aside from a few biological needs there are no other forces or tendencies in men. All else is "plasticity," the capacity to be shaped in almost indefinitely different ways by rewards and punishments. The temper of this position was clearly expressed in the following well-known statement of J. B. Watson:

> Give me a dozen healthy infants, well-formed, and my own specific world to bring them up in and I'll guarantee to take any one at random and train him to become any type of specialist I might select—doctor, lawyer, artist, merchant-chief, and yes, even beggar-man and thief, regardless of his talents, penchants, tendencies, abilities, vocations, and race of his ancestors.

The core of the same thought has been expressed more recently in the following statement:

> Man's biological nature is neither good nor bad, aggressive nor submissive, warlike nor peaceful, but neutral in these respects. He is capable of developing in either direction depending on what he is compelled to learn by his environment and by his culture. It is a mistake to assume that he can learn war more

---

* "We 'believe in' democracy, as we have been brought up in it, or we do not. If we do, we accept its mythology. The reason is because we have grown up in it, are familiar with it, and like it. Argument would not touch this faith."

easily than peace. His learning machinery is not prejudiced, as is sometimes thought, toward the acquirement of bad habits. The bias is in his social environment. [M. May: *Social Psychology of War and Peace.* Yale, 1944, p. 20.]

This position presupposes a dynamically empty organism, lacking autonomous tendencies beyond primary needs and lacking directed forces toward nature or society, which can therefore be turned with equal ease in opposed directions. To be sure, men can learn. But the fact of learning has the peculiar property of not altering them in any way that is significant for a conception of their character, since the habits they form contain nothing of comprehension or insight. Stimulus-response theory excluded the direct perception of social necessities or the guidance of sociological events by conscious direction. The following may serve as an illustration. We find that people react in one way when they find that someone has been untruthful and in a quite different way when he has been truthful. How is this to be understood? The stimulus-response answer is that such actions have in the past been connected with different consequences. What is of interest about the answer is not that it emphasizes the results of action, but its disregard of the idea that truthfulness and untruthfulness are comprehended in terms of their structure—in terms of what they signify for the relation between one person and another—and that they are evaluated on that basis. Instead of concluding that the requirement of truthfulness grows out of a grasp of the causal relation between act and consequence, it treats of truthfulness as a habit that has survived in the course of a trial and error process. This view is responsible for the conclusion that human nature is like water, which takes on whatever shape is imparted to it.

It is not difficult to see how this starting point decides the general interpretation of social action. If convictions and decisions are exclusively the outcome of arbitrary forces upon people who believe what they are made to believe, then one must not deceive oneself into holding that they are other than an expression of bias. In the sense of cultural relativism your values are not yours; they are those of the *Times*, or the *Tribune*, or whatever source of special pleading has succeeded in gaining access to you. You are a mouthpiece with society pulling the strings. At the center of these formulations is a definite assumption about the kind of dependence that prevails between individuals and groups. A plastic individual meets an established social order; the relation is that of hammer and anvil. Such views recommend themselves to many because of their objectivistic character; they appear to assume so much less than other psychologies. It remains to be seen whether they do not contain large assumptions.

Earlier we noted some difficulties in this mode of thinking; here we may simply repeat them. (1) It fails to describe the concrete cognitive and emotional operations one encounters in the social setting. In the present context it simply ignores the fact that people make ethical discriminations and that they sense requirements, and assumes that they are initially blank as far

as these distinctions are concerned. In effect, stimulus-response theory denies what we have attempted to state in the preceding chapter about the
basis of norms and values in cognitive and emotional dynamics. It is in these
terms that we have to understand the insistence that norms and values are
first "external" to the individual and are then "internalized." In the context
of the theory, "external" means action alien to the individual's character,
tendencies, and capacities; "internal" refers to the blind adoption of these
ways. The process of "socialization" is, according to this view, the uncritical
adoption of beliefs and values. (2) As we have seen in the preceding chapters, the stimulus-response account of human needs and rewards is more
restricted than observation leads us to conclude. Even if one could assume
that the constructs "drive," "reward," "response" were adequate to the actions of infra-human organisms (from the observation of which they are
largely derived), it would remain highly questionable whether they apply
without modification to social action. In their first intention these terms
refer to very particular phenomena, such as deprivation of food, turning a
corner, avoiding a shock. It would seem necessary to show that they are
relevant to social phenomena. But this is assumed, not proven. Therefore
the assertions that society may be likened to a maze and that culture is
learned are little more than reiterations of a belief that the rat's learning of
a maze (or a particular interpretation of it) is all we need for the understanding of customs and institutions.

Relational Determination Versus Relativism

The insufficiencies of an absolutist psychological theory of ethical judgments are obvious. It has no means for dealing with cultural diversity (or,
for that matter, with intra-individual diversity). On the other hand, although the observations to which relativism refers have greatly widened
the horizon of the social sciences, the psychological interpretation they
have received poses equally serious difficulties. It is often assumed that
these positions are the sole alternatives. Is there not, however, a way to
understand the diversities of human practices and convictions without at
the same time denying the authentic role of ethical discrimination? We will
attempt to show that there is an alternative that fits the facts more closely.

It is now necessary to consider a point about value-judgments that was
only adumbrated in the preceding chapter. When we evaluate an act as
right or wrong we do so with reference to its place and setting. We evaluate acts always as parts of given conditions. We consider it wrong to take
food away from a hungry child, but not if he is overeating. We consider it
right to fulfill a promise, but not if it is a promise to commit a crime. Each
of these examples is evidence that requiredness is not a property that belongs to an action irrespective of its setting and relations. Every judgment
of the value of an act takes into account the particular circumstances under
which it occurs. There follows the important consequence that the *same*

act may be evaluated as right because it is fitting under one set of conditions and as wrong because it violates the requirements of another set of conditions. (Whether there are some acts that we evaluate as right or wrong under all circumstances is a difficult question that we may leave open in an elementary discussion.)

It has been customary to hold that diverse evaluations of the same act are automatic evidence for the presence of different principles of evaluation. The preceding examples point to an error in this interpretation and to the need for a distinction between relational determination and relativism. Indeed, an examination of the relational factors that determine the demands we sense may point to the operation of constant principles in situations that differ in concrete details. We shall explore now the bearing of the fact of relational determination upon the culturally determined diversities of evaluation.

The essential proposition of ethical relativism states that one can connect to the identical situation different and even opposed evaluations. Comparative observations of cultures seem to support this view abundantly. Infanticide, as we have seen, receives different evaluations, as do numerous other practices. It seems to follow that the content of our most basic convictions is variable and that there is hardly a principle that, cherished under one social climate, is not violated in another. These observations apparently contradict the conclusion that we sense the demands of conditions. Relativism asserts this contradiction, claiming that evaluations are subjective habits and preferences.

Some years ago Duncker and Wertheimer examined this problem and called attention to a fundamental oversight in the relativistic position. Duncker showed that the conclusion of relativism rests exclusively on the diverse connections observed between outer conditions and practices. But psychological analysis requires that we take cognizance of certain intermediate steps. We act toward a given situation in terms of its meaning—what we understand of it and what experience has taught us about it. On this basis we make evaluations and sense requirements that guide action. The terms of which we must take cognizance in the analysis of actions that have value-character are: (a) the externally given conditions; (b) the meaning they have for the actor; (c) the evaluations and requirements that available knowledge and understanding produce; and (d) the resulting actions. Now the thesis of relativism points to a lack of constancy in the relation between (a) and (d). It fails however to deal with the intervening terms. In particular, it does not consider the relation of evaluation (c) to the given cognitive conditions (b). But relativism, if it is to be psychologically valid, must assert that one can attach different evaluations to situations that have the same cognitive and emotional content. If, for example, we are to speak of relativism with reference to infanticide we must assume that the *same* action which is tolerated under one set of conditions is outlawed under other conditions. This assumption is as a rule dubious. The character of the object "infant" may not be the same under all conditions. In the first few days of life, an infant may be regarded as not yet human, in the way that many regard the embryo. (It should be noted that infanticide, when practiced, occurs only during the first few days following birth.) Therefore, the act of killing will not have the same meaning under all conditions. Precisely the same issue arises in connection with the killing of parents. In the society that follows this practice there prevails the belief that people continue to lead in the next world the same existence as in the present and that they maintain forever the condition of health and vigor they had at the time of death. It is therefore a filial duty of the son to dispatch his parents, an act that has the full endorsement of the parent and of the community.

Duncker suggests that different and apparently opposed practices and values are frequently not the consequence of diversity in ethical principles but of differences in the comprehension of a situation—differences in "situational meaning." The same external situation may possess quite varied meanings, depending upon the existing level of knowledge and upon other conditions. The resulting differences of action may therefore not be due to a diversity of principle. The meaning of a situation is usually a dependent part of a wider context. In a society in which supernatural beings are part of the cognitive scene, it will be plausible and convincing to impute illness to a purposeful, human-like agency. Consequently, the exorcising of illness by prayer and incantation will, under the given conditions, have a marked relevance. It will not signify that the persons in question are employing novel principles of causation or that they possess different modes of perceiving causation. Similarly, the concept of "stranger" may vary greatly; it may decide whether we shall slay him or treat him essentially like ourselves. The relativistic argument, by failing to take into account the psychological content of the situation, equates things that are psychologically different and only externally the same. It seeks for a mechanical regularity between external situation and action instead of a structural identity between the psychological content of a situation and the act. If we consider the psychological content, we have to conclude that the same action may represent psychologically different contents and that different actions may be functionally identical. To establish whether human beings actually possess contradictory values, it would be necessary to show that the relations between situational meaning and evaluation, or between the terms (b) and (c) above, can vary. This relativism has decidedly failed to do.

Implicit in the preceding discussion is the conclusion that the fact of cultural differences cannot be automatically converted into an argument for a relativism of values. Cultural differences are compatible with identity in values. Indeed, the assumption of invariance dictates the conclusion that practices will differ with circumstances. If action and experience are a function of given conditions, we must expect that the former will vary with the latter. To expect uniform practices among societies is as reasonable as to expect all those with poor eyesight to wear identical lenses or for a person to face all situations with the same emotion. This point is well understood when the facts of material culture are under discussion. We consider it reasonable that the Bantu do not build igloos and that Eskimos do not live in thatched huts. Instead of stating conclusions about the relativism of building practices we quite properly take into account the climate, the materials available, and the level of knowledge. The same mode of thinking is indicated when we speak of values, if we do not assume in advance that they are arbitrary. When an Eskimo family permits an old person to expose himself to death this must be viewed in relation to their situation, their problems, and the alternatives open to them. The act does not have the same meaning for them that it would have for us today; Eskimos do not have homes for the aged or retirement pensions. If we take the given circumstances into account the possibility is present for understanding diverse actions in terms of the same operations of valuing.

What can we say about the relation between "situational meaning" and evaluation? In general, anthropological evidence does not furnish proof of relativism in the relation between the meaning of situations and their evaluation. We do not know of societies in which bravery is despised and cowardice held up to honor, in which generosity is considered a vice and ingratitude a virtue.* It seems rather, as Duncker proposed, that the relations between valuation and meaning are invariant. It is not usual to find groups placing a different valuation upon, or experiencing different obligations toward, a situation that they understand in an identical way. It seems rather that certain ethical discriminations are universally known. We still have to hear of a society to which modesty, courage, and hospitality are not known.

Throughout the preceding discussion we have assumed one far-reaching form of "relativism" to be present: that pertaining to knowledge and understanding. Historical conditions determine the extent and level of knowledge and therefore the content and evaluation of given conditions. We may illustrate the general fact with a simple instance. A need, such as hunger, does not innately refer to its adequate object. It is only when the hungry infant is fed that he can form a craving for milk or sweets and search for them subsequently. Obviously the object must be experienced (or heard about) if it is to become relevant to one's needs. One cannot crave an

---

* It may seem that this argument is one unassailable truism. The quality of goodness, one might object, is already included by definition in the acts we call just or courageous; to discover then that acts called just and courageous are positively valued is a tautology. This is, it seems to me, an erroneous conclusion. There is no difficulty in principle in describing the properties of actions independently of the evaluations they receive. To establish an invariance between meaning and evaluation presupposes that we have first described each independently. Investigation has not generally followed this path because the need for it was not evident. It is the merit of Duncker's discussion that it clarifies the need to determine the properties of action men consider right and wrong.

object one has not experienced. It will necessarily happen that in different societies there will be quite different food preferences. Here we have a concrete, if simple, instance of what many call relativism, although it is more properly an example of relational determination. What can it teach us? First, the variation is not unlimited; however different in quality and in adequacy, an article of food will generally become an object of craving because it has food-value. When two groups come in contact, each will continue to prefer its diet; here we have a difference that is to a degree arbitrary. But again we find that the differences are not as unlimited as a sketchy analysis suggests. To the extent that different diets are equally nutritious, a preference for the one that is familiar is a fact upon which one cannot place undue importance. It is more significant to ask about the changes in diet that follow increased knowledge. The answer is fairly obvious.

In the sense described there is a considerable relativism as a result of differences in level of knowledge. One cannot be intelligent about things one does not know; one cannot long for the sea or for mountains if one is not aware of their existence. One can have no desire for fame if one has no historical perspective; one cannot be fired with zeal to contribute to knowledge if science is unknown. Do not these facts commit us to a new relativism with the same practical consequences as the old? It seems to me that they do not. They demonstrate what no one questions—that knowledge and action change in accordance with material and social conditions.

A serious appraisal of the role of cognitive factors permits us to clarify an important problem about values. It may have seemed that to emphasize the probability of invariance between evaluation and action and the presence of certain universal ethical discriminations leaves no place for the growth or change of values. But it should be evident that changes of knowledge and understanding make necessary the evolution of values. When knowledge spreads that men have basic qualities in common, it becomes more difficult to oppress them. When we find that differences between races are chiefly socially determined, it becomes less easy to practice segregation and colonialism. When we learn that criminals have emotions and strong social tendencies we can no longer sustain a purely punitive attitude toward them. With an increased appreciation of the role of reflection and knowledge some come to feel the obligation to be intelligent. Increasing knowledge of human characteristics teaches us the value of the human person. As we learn more of the conditions that affect the development of persons we feel the obligation to improve the material conditions of mankind. In this way alone can we understand the more humane treatment of mental patients, the feeble-minded, and other disadvantaged groups. In this sense there can be a development in the notions of justice and the emergence of novel moral insight. There is reason to say that ideas have an immense effect on evaluation and action.

Many of the most significant changes in human relations have had, it must be added, a relatively expedient basis. Slaves have not usually been freed by an outburst of pity in their owners, nor has the improvement in the conditions of workers been due primarily to a more humane attitude among owners of wealth. There was no ethical impulse back of the industrial revolution, which made possible for the first time in history the freeing of mankind from want and oppression. These changes took place because they coincided with narrower interests. Yet it would not be right to hold this explanation as wholly adequate. Improvements in working conditions, the growth of public education and universal suffrage did, to be sure, wait upon definite technical developments. But these changes would not have come about if not for the tremendous role of the feeling of injustice by those who were oppressed and even by some who profited from existing exploitation. The demand for a shorter working day and for higher wages derives its strength not only from the force workers command when they unite; their force has its source to a profound degree in considerations of value. Under new conditions people perceive opportunities to improve their lot and to achieve values that earlier they could not realize or perhaps clearly conceive. These aspirations must be present and must function to take advantage of existing conditions. If we look closely we find that technical conditions and new relations of power do not alone account for social changes. Technical changes can work to give those concerned with justice an advantage, can win over those who are not zealous, and can weaken the position of those who are determined to maintain their advantage at all costs.

What are the consequences of these ideas for understanding cultural differences in evaluation? Perhaps the main effect is to make the practices of peoples more comprehensible by divesting them, not of interest, but of bizarreness and grotesqueness. Once we abandon certain assumptions about the externality of man's relation to the surroundings, a wholly different view of cultural differences unfolds before us. These need no longer appear as responses to manipulation by social conditions or as the final signs of limitation and subjectivity. We can now see them also as the necessary consequence of permanent human tendencies coming to expression under particular conditions. It also becomes clear that the first step in understanding action or conviction is to establish the way in which it appears to the actor and the reason it appears to him to be right. This is the way to proceed if we take seriously human capacities for comprehension and for formulating explanations within the limitations of knowledge and experience. We need to establish the core of relevance that action or belief has for its practitioners; to do so we need to see action in its context.

Considered from the standpoint of method, relativism deals with social data in a piecemeal way. The impressiveness of its conclusions rests almost entirely on the divorce of data from their context. It lists the diversity of practices in response to the same external conditions, tearing them out of their context. In consequence it obscures their concrete content and dynamics. It should also be mentioned here that an adequate examination must include a reference to the repercussions that standards and values have upon those who are under their sway. The reactions to regulations, the problems they solve, and the conflicts they generate are as pertinent as is their existence and observance. Those views that stress the almost unlimited malleability of human character tend to overlook the inevitable concomitants of conditions, which it would be hard to understand relativistically. Unless we look at interrelations we remove the possibility of understanding either cultural differences or similarities.*

In general, it is not enough to catalogue existing similarities and differences; these are only the starting point of inquiry. It is more important to show that cultural variations are facts having direction. To consider cultural differences in terms of change and direction is immediately to transcend the static position of relativism. It is not enough to say that some societies observe rules of cleanliness and others do not. It would be more consequential to ask whether one can as readily teach one group to adopt the habits of cleanliness as another to surrender them; whether one can as readily convert an American community to curing illness by sorcery as persuade a primitive group to adopt modern medical practices. It is not enough to say for example that the musical tastes of Japanese and Europeans differ. It is more significant to ask what the reactions of Japanese and Europeans would be to both forms of music when they have mastered each. If we proceed in this way we are likely to find that changes have a direction and that often the direction is irreversible because of the sensible character of some psychological processes. Instead of comparing men and societies as they are, it is more fruitful to study the tendencies they show in the course of change.

This discussion has not attempted to settle the extent to which values are invariant, but rather to suggest a way of thinking about their identities and differences. In particular, it has described an alternative to the positions of absolutism and relativism. In contrast to the former, we have taken into account the facts of cultural diversity. At the same time we have tried to go beyond the sheer factual demonstration of diversity. The first two positions, although entirely opposed in their conclusions, are at one on an essential point of theory. They reach opposed conclusions on the basis of the same technical assumption of elementarism; therefore they agree that the

---

* Nowhere is this better exemplified than in the mode of dealing with "irrational" beliefs and practices or those based on inadequate or distorted knowledge. When one considers them without reference to the conditions out of which they arise, they have a character of grotesqueness. It is easy to reach the view that the corresponding psychological processes are equally deficient and unreasonable, on the ground that the effect is similar to the cause. This also fits the conception that these practices are adopted uncritically under social pressure. Relativism accepts this mode of thinking and extends it; it assures us that our ways of acting and feeling too are no less outlandish. To proceed in this way is, however, to surrender the task of psychological analysis.

sole alternatives are between them. Indeed, it would be right to say that each rests its case on the failure of the other. Relativism argues that if there are valid standards they must everywhere be the same and that the variability of standards is evidence that they are arbitrary. Absolutism, on the other hand, seeks to preserve the validity of standards at the cost of ignoring observed differences. If, however, we take into account the structural properties of experience and action we can understand that standards are relative without abandoning the concept of a human nature. It is necessary to acknowledge that science, art, and moral convictions at no time express completely the facts of the world or human needs; in this general sense there is relativism. But we need also to see these achievements as part of the history of human development, as the strivings of an authentic human nature. If we follow this path we will not treat all social facts as equally arbitrary or identify what is with what is right. Instead we will consider what societies do to realize human possibilities or to stunt them.

THREE ETHICAL FALLACIES °

BRENDA COHEN

The aim of establishing systems of ethics on the basis of logic has long been abandoned as a project for moral philosophy. Practical conclusions about what to do, it is generally agreed, cannot be arrived at by mere armchair calculation—they are the prerogative of participating agents operating with a context of practical situations, consequences and other interacting agents. Nevertheless, while logic may be unable to delimit a positive path, it may yet be of use, it will be argued here, in providing negative guidance by indicating certain pitfalls or logical incoherences which can distort a person's approach to morality—particularly if that person sees himself as adopting a liberal stance on matters of morality.

Three fallacies in particular stand out as currently popular views—views which have been adopted in popular as well as philosophical reasoning—and which, in their acceptance, undermine the moral position of the individual who allows himself to be influenced by them. The term 'fallacy' is one which may be much abused, particularly in relation to ethical reasoning, but it will be used here in the informal sense in which inadequate reasoning leading to incorrect conclusions may be called fallacious, rather than in the formal sense in which some kind of error of syllogistic reasoning is detected. The three fallacies, then, which are to be investigated here are, respectively: first, a fallacy connected with individualism; secondly, a fallacy connected

° From Brenda Cohen, "Three Ethical Fallacies," *Mind,* **86** (Jan., 1977), pp. 78–87. Reprinted by permission of the author and *Mind.*

with relativism; and thirdly, a fallacy which I should like to call a fallacy of false liberalism. It will be argued that, whilst clearly being linked with each other, both in the sense that consideration of one leads naturally to consideration of another, and also in the sense that all are fallacies generated by a liberal approach to morality, these are separate and essentially independent ethical fallacies, and each will therefore be considered separately.

The Individualist Fallacy

One of the defendants at the Manson murder trial in California is reported to have said, 'What I did was right for me'. This statement is interesting in a number of ways. First, it is surprising to find morality invoked at all in connection with a peculiarly brutal multiple murder. But secondly, the concept of morality implied is itself an unusual one. It represents the most extreme form that subjectivism can take—a concept of right which is of singular application only, restricted only to the individual and relevant only to a particular occasion and instance. Nevertheless, it is distinguishable from (what it approaches) a complete repudiation of morality and a decision simply to please oneself about one's actions, in that a clear imperative element is also implied. Having decided on this very particular and individual right or obligation it is obviously felt both that it is as binding as more conventionally accepted moral dictates, and also that to some extent at least it can be used as a defence for action taken in order to comply with this intuited individual morality.

If this were an isolated case of the adoption of what might be called a private morality as a determinant of action, then perhaps one might be justified in regarding it as the aberration of a small group of individuals who have never felt the need to subject their concept of morality to the searching light of logical analysis. But if we can bring ourselves to step back from our contemporary scene and see ourselves for a moment as some future historian might see us, then it may well be that, on the contrary, this is the new and distinctive viewpoint of our generation. Its not always conscious similarity to European Existentialism, together with its relation to the widespread youth ideal expressed in the slogan 'doing one's thing' make of this concept of morality something much more generally accepted than the professional discussions of philosophers would lead one to suppose. Nevertheless, it must be said that a basic logical inconsistency lies at the root of this way of thinking, and whilst a mere cult of irrationality devoid of all reference to moral obligation is invulnerable to logical attack, there are strong arguments to show that morality, having essential logical characteristics, cannot be conjoined with this cult except by misunderstanding. Indeed it may be argued that the very idea of a private, unique-instance, morality is self-contradictory and incoherent; that a moral claim must have some wider reference than the individual and the moment, either in the sense that what is claimed about oneself must be taken to apply to others too (must, in other words, be generalisable or universalisable) or at least in the sense that it is of general application to potential future situations in the individual's own life.

Nevertheless, although this form of association may be most strikingly associated with esoteric cults such as the Manson 'family', it is also at the same time arguably much more central to Western thought than these particular associations would imply. In the notion of the sacrosanct status of the dictates of individual conscience, another and more generally accepted version of ethical individualism may be found.

The fallacy that lies at the root of such reasoning, however, is the fallacy of confusing two distinct and very different notions:

1. The view that the dictates of the individual conscience are always right, and
2. The view that no individual should be forced to act against the dictates of conscience.

These become conflated in:

3. The view that what a man's conscience dictates is *for him,* always right, with the corollary that it is morally wrong to act against conscience.

But View 1, once stated, can be seen to be inherently self-contradictory, in that it implies that a range of mutually incompatible propositions must all be judged to be right. In the case of ethical propositions, moreover, to assert that they are right is to endorse them. And to endorse simultaneously a range of mutually incompatible statements is to engage in an incoherent and self-nullifying procedure. View I, then, is logically incoherent and unlikely to be intentionally adopted by anyone who has a clear understanding of what holding it involves.

View 2, on the other hand, is not logically incoherent, nor is there any *a priori* reason why it should not be held by a considerable number of people, whatever their other moral convictions. It is, however, a practical and political principle—a ground-level moral principle—rather than an ethical assertion about the meaning of 'right' or the nature of duty, or the ultimate ground of moral obligation. Nevertheless, even as a practical principle, it is unlikely to be held in an absolute sense, or without any qualification. Whilst it will be admitted that only with extreme reluctance should anyone (and usually this will mean the state) force anyone else to act against their own conscience, it will on the whole tend to be held that this must in the last resort depend upon what an individual's conscience dictates to him. If, for instance, the Moors murderers, Ian Bradley and Myra Hindley, had claimed that for them the ritual torture and murder of young children was a matter of conscience (and they did indeed have some philosophical background to their activities) would this have been a reason for noninterference on the part of others? If it seems unlikely that a conscientious justification would be offered of this nature, then it may be pointed out that as a matter of fact many wartime atrocities which are at least comparable in terms of suffering caused, are indeed defended by those responsible, on the basis of a conscientious obligation to obey without question the orders of superior officers.

Even the practical principle expressed by View 2, then, is not without difficulty. The important point, however, is that both it, and View 1, are entirely distinct both from each other and from View 3, with which they may be jointly confused.

View 3, then, which is the view that what a man's conscience dictates is for him always right, derives its plausibility from its resemblance to Views 1 and 2. The addition of 'for him', however, which is what distinguishes View 3 from View 1, is strictly meaningless—there is no clear way in which such a phrase can be understood. It cannot, therefore, entail such a proposition as that it is always morally wrong to act against conscience, and while the example of the Nuremberg trials could be held to show that there is a widely accepted view that conscience must be supreme, they can equally and more correctly be taken to show that following one's own view of conscience (that for a soldier obedience is the highest value) does not exonerate one from moral responsibility or exempt one from moral condemnation.

A totally personal and individualistic ethic, then, is inevitably grounded on the shifting sands of some version of the individualist fallacy as described here. Moral judgment has a breadth of application built into its form and structure, which cannot be avoided by extreme versions of even conscientious individualism, and certainly not by the instinct-guided or idiosyncratic individualism implied in the phrase 'Right for me'.

The Relativist Fallacy

The Relativist Fallacy is the fallacy of supposing that the existence of different moral codes in different societies and in different sub-groups within a given society, together with an understanding of the psychological and sociological reasons accounting for these beliefs and variations on them, provides a reason for reducing the commitment one feels to one's own ethical beliefs. At least it may be thought that the existence of other beliefs provides a reason for holding one's own beliefs with less conviction, or for being more ready to make exceptions to the moral rules one has chosen to recognise. But to state this assumption is to see that the existence of alternative codes is strictly irrelevant to the degree of commitment which may be due to one's own.

Sir Isaiah Berlin quoted 'an admirable writer of our time', who well summed up the point I am trying to make here: 'To realise the relative validity of one's convictions' this writer is reported to have said, 'and yet stand for them unflinchingly, is what distinguishes a civilized man from a barbarian.'[1] To suppose otherwise is in effect to imply a version of the discredited ethical theory that majority opinion defines rightness, or that in the absence of universal consensus nothing can be held to be right, or that any view is equally right. But such a view could be held only by an external observer, operating from outside the human framework altogether —someone who is not himself a part of the world of which he judges that all views are equal. But of course, no one can possess this detachment, for we are all human-beings operating in a world of human-beings.

To some extent, such reasoning is based on a false antithesis: either moral values are objective, in which case they will be recognised by a special human faculty most usually characterised as intuition; in this case, no significant differences of moral opinion will be found to exist between honest and serious people who are at an equally advanced stage of development (itself a concept carrying its own set of difficulties); or, alternatively, moral values are subjective; there is no special way of arriving at them, and variations will be found in ethical practice and belief. The first case is thought to justify the strong holding of categorical beliefs and opinions, since I may hold that everyone who disagrees with me is wrong. The second is thought to entail that one should be extremely tentative in holding any moral opinion because anyone who disagrees with those opinions may be right.

Plainly, however, this is not what the subjective/objective dichotomy entails. For if moral values were objective, I would not be entitled to any particular degree of conviction as to the validity of my own particular beliefs, or even those of my social group or my society. The possibility of mistake must still loom large within an objectivist system. Conversely, if moral values are subjective, the mere fact that a belief is a belief of mine entails that it is one I do in fact hold. If I do not hold it with conviction, then it is simply not a particularly strong belief of mine, and only erroneous epistemological considerations could persuade me to put a whole category of beliefs into this limbo of doubtfulness.

It is a weakness of the sociology of knowledge that it starts up an elusive will-o'-the-wisp—a chain of what might be called meta-considerations. Not only ethics, but science, religion and philosophy are explained and relativised, and from the shifting sands of ordinary forms of knowledge, those who have been persuaded to adopt the sociological perspective, attempt to scramble to the firm ground of sociology itself—only to find, of course, that it is as relative as the sciences it appears to supersede. Neither recognition of variation in beliefs, then, nor recognition of the psycho-social origins of belief provide a ground for relativism in any sense that implies equality between one's own beliefs and those of others. Conviction is as appropriate for the anthropologist as for the intuitionist.

[1] Sir Isaiah Berlin, *Two Concepts of Liberty* (O.U.P., 1958), p. 57.

The Fallacy of False Liberalism

The Fallacy of False Liberalism is the fallacy of supposing that a liberal position in morality involves holding that everything is permitted. The Relativist Fallacy involved, by contrast, the view that everything is right, and the Individualist Fallacy that rightness is internal to the standards of the individual.

Liberalism, however, is especially associated with toleration, and it may be thought that it involves the lesser commitment of, whilst not *endorsing* every moral view, at least *permitting* the existence of all moral views as well as their practical expression in behaviour and action, subject to certain well-understood safeguards. In order to make it clear that it is *moral* liberalism that is in question here, rather than the political version of liberalism, something must be said about the way in which 'permission' is to be understood.

To begin with, it must be said that permitting people to act on their beliefs is a very different matter from permitting them to hold those beliefs, but given some stipulation about the necessity of allowing conscience a privileged position in determining action, the two may seem inextricably linked. The need to distinguish between action and belief has already been argued, however, in connection with the Individualist Fallacy. In this case, moreover, it is even more clear that action and belief must be treated separately. False liberalism appears to imply that no sanctions should be applied where any moral issue arises. The need to apply sanctions enforcing certain patterns of behaviour in matters where other people's interests are concerned may be accepted, but then set on one side as coming within the category of politics and social organisation rather than of pure morality. In order to see the issue purely as a moral issue it is necessary to assume, for the moment, that there is an area of purely self-regarding actions—moral matters whose outcome is of no reasonable interest to anyone other than the individual concerned.

The possible extent of such an area might, for illustrative purposes, be taken to include some of the areas discussed by Hart [1] and Devlin [2] with special reference to the Wolfenden Report—areas such as censorship, pornography and sexual behaviour, where the limits of public, as opposed to private interest, are a matter of controversy. The Wolfenden Report, in advocating the abolition of legal sanctions against prostitution as such, and against homosexual relationships between consenting adults, claimed that there must be an area of morality which is 'not the law's business'. Plainly, this opens up the question: if there is an area of human activity, in which there can be no legitimate public interest, perhaps because it is universally agreed that no consequences affecting other people ensue, would the liberal moralist, as opposed to the liberal legislator or judge, be obliged to say

[1] H. L. A. Hart, *Law, Liberty and Morality* (O.U.P., 1971). (Reprinted here.)
[2] P. Devlin, *The Enforcement of Morals* (O.U.P., 1965). (Reprinted here.)

that here, at least, everything is permitted? Is a liberal morality one which says (a) that in this area people are permitted to hold whatever moral view they choose, and (b) that they must be permitted to act on the basis of whatever view they have adopted?

As far as the first of these questions is concerned, a negative answer must be given. For a liberal morality is one which includes certain defined values, and not only the values of freedom and toleration.[3] Those whose proposals conflict with any of these values, and not merely the value of freedom, are not 'permitted' to hold their alternative values in a *moral* sense of the term, even though it may be wise that they should be permitted in a legal or political sense to hold them. Once again, the notion of moral permission, as opposed to practical permission, is in effect an endorsement of a contrary viewpoint, and as such, essentially fallacious. The second question, however, is ambiguous: the liberal legislator must allow people to act within this area on whatever view they have formed. The liberal moralist, however, whilst necessarily following suit, must be careful to avoid having his 'permission' interpreted as endorsement.

True as opposed to false liberalism, then, involves holding firmly to a particular set of principles, and inevitably, in holding these principles, the liberal becomes a proselytiser for his own point of view. He cannot, therefore, give his *moral* permission or endorsement to other positions, even though his espousal of the principle of individual freedom and toleration will entail a higher degree of permissiveness in practice than would be the case if he did not set a high value on these things.

The fallacy of False Liberalism, then, lies in equating practical permission with moral permission, toleration of a moral viewpoint with endorsement of that viewpoint, and the advocacy of freedom with a lack of commitment to any particular moral viewpoint.

The position that exposure of these three fallacies points to could well be called a theory of dogmatic or positive liberalism, and, in conclusion, some of the conclusions implicit in such a position will be indicated.

The Theory of Positive Liberalism

The notion of positive liberalism involves reference to a pluralistic value-system which includes some familiar, not to say traditional values (at least in Western culture), and there are other descriptions therefore, which might be equally appropriate. Some Christian ethical viewpoints, for instance, would not differ drastically from the view described here as liberalism, and other religions, too, would possibly be found to have much in common

---

[3] It would be hard to understand the claim that someone was a liberal, for instance, if humanity and benevolence were not amongst his values. There would also seem to be a requirement that he should favour truth and openness. On the other hand, justice, fairness and egalitarianism do not seem to be an essential part of the definition of a (moral) liberal. Cf. the term 'white liberal' as used in the United States.

with such a value-system. Essentially, however, a secular viewpoint is of wider interest, and while a variety of alternative names might be at least as appropriate—some might prefer, for instance, the term liberal humanism —the concept of liberalism does convey a certain well-understood range of values.

But to speak of *positive* liberalism, with the over-tones of dogmatism that this conveys, may seem to be unduly paradoxical. Indeed, it may be argued, it is liberalism's essentially nondogmatic nature that has led to the general deterioration in its standing as a reasonable and acceptable approach, and its replacement with firmer, more uncompromising approaches to the problems of society and of personal life. This, however, is precisely the reason for the juxtaposition of the terms: to reject liberal values as a result of recognising the need for firmness and commitment, is to open the door to acceptance of illiberal value-systems which, whilst supplying the firm ground essential for morality, can furnish considerably less nourishment for the human spirit than the system which is being rejected. In seeing firmness of purpose and attitude as an essential aspect of liberalism, the temptation to opt for a totally different value-system is so much diminished.

In considering such a liberal system of values, it can be seen that the three fallacies which have been described here are significant insofar as they each tend to affect the degree of conviction with which the liberal will hold to his values, and individually or collectively, they make of liberalism a value-system with a permanent tendency to slip into the extreme form of individualism described in relation to the first fallacy. If this tendency can be avoided, through the application of the logical arguments produced here, there is no reason why the values traditionally associated with the term 'liberalism' should not be re-asserted more forcefully and decisively than ever. These values will be chosen however, not because they seem to represent neutrality, or because they avoid the need for commitment, but simply because in the perennial conflict between the light and the dark they are judged to represent the former rather than the latter.

The practical consequences of such a view will be seen in a greater unwillingness, on the part of those who profess to share liberal values, to accommodate opposed viewpoints. If they believe in free speech, for instance, they will not be willing to adopt a position which appears to endorse its suppression. They will appreciate, in an unambiguous way, the inevitability of conflict on fundamental moral matters, and the impossibility, as well as inadvisability, of adopting a stance of sympathetic partial agreement with each and every alternative moral viewpoint. In favouring the plurality of liberal values, they will not feel at a disadvantage when confronted, for instance, with the utilitarian assumption of happiness as the only ultimate value, because they will have recognised that in the last analysis no value is supported, defended or proved—but simply chosen because of its intrinsic nature. Those who recognise only one such value will thus be seen to be in fundamental opposition to those who prefer the plurality of liberal or humanist values, but their case will be based on no firmer ground.

Instead of seeking compromise between his own views and those of others, or between the principles he espouses and the consequences of applying them in particular situations, the liberal who has avoided the fallacies which have been described here will, in his own self-recognition, become a figure of consequence on the moral scene—a figure of some definition, rather than a chameleon, which takes on the colour of whatever object lies nearest at the time of viewing. It is this chameleon characteristic of liberalism which has been most destructive of the standing of the liberal system of values; and it is this concept which, followed through to its conclusion, produces on the one hand the aberration of the extreme individualistic ethic summed up in the phrase 'Right for me', and on the other hand, the extreme of toleration and neutrality which an ill-defined relativism wrongly appears to entail.

3

Self-Interest

Heretofore the main interest has been in the relationships of facts to values, and of moral judgments to other kinds of judgments. In this chapter the first theory we take up is a continuation of that interest. It is a theory of human motivation called psychological egoism. The second theory that is discussed here moves into a new realm, normative ethics. It concerns a theory of obligation in which self-interest is the standard or moral principle, and is called ethical egoism, not because everyone regards it as right (far from it), but because it is a definition of what is right.

Psychological Egoism

In Chapter One I raised the question whether anyone can apply to other people the same moral principles and rules that he or she applies to him- or herself. Kurt Baier, we saw, insists that "the moral point of view" requires that people judge their own acts as they judge those of other people. We earlier discussed ("Who's to say what's right?") whether I can judge the acts of others by the same standards I apply to my own acts, and found thinkers as diverse as Sidgwick and Sartre saying I not only can but must. If Baier is right about the moral point of view and if no one can ever apply to his or her own acts the standards he or she applies to others, then the moral point of view is an impossible ideal, and a normative ethics is impossible. For there is no point in having a normative ethics if it cannot be followed (though some Christian ethicists have said that an impossible ideal is relevant to human life). Let's reflect upon a statement attributed to Immanuel Kant (see Ch. 6): "I ought implies I can," if I cannot, then I have no "ought" or obligation to do the thing in question. To say after I have done something that I could not possibly have avoided, "I ought not have done that," makes no sense, for it is to ascribe to myself a responsibility for which one of the main conditions is lacking: that I could have done it. In this light, it is important to ask whether the truth of certain theories makes ethics understandable or impossible.

Such a theory to ask about is "psychological egoism." It is a theory claiming that people do, as a matter of fact, always place their own self-interest first in every action. It seems to amount to the claim that there is a law of nature such that human beings do always act thus-and-so—specifically, always seek their own self-interest. Depending on your interpretation of "a law of nature," you will hold either that a person can or cannot disobey a law of nature. But if we hold that a person can defy the law of nature that says that one must always put his or her self-interest first in every action, we make it a matter of puzzlement just why, if psychological egoism is true, people always do put their self-interest first. It seems rather like the person who says he "can take it or leave it" but has never been known to leave it, only psychological egoism is ascribing the doctrine not to one person but to everyone who has ever lived, and seemingly is predicting that everyone who will ever live will conform to the same law.

The psychological egoist viewpoint is not peculiarly modern, but recognition of the problem for ethics has preoccupied modern philosophers and theologians. (In *Anna Karenina,* Tolstoy says that the *whole* of philosophy, not just moral philosophy, is concerned with reconciling public and private interests!) Modern economic theory has often assumed that human nature is indeed self-centered. Adam Smith believed it, but had "an invisible hand" reconciling the efforts of each person to look out for him- or herself with the good of all. Marxism has generally denied there is any built-in self-centeredness and held that it is society (e.g., capitalism) that gives to individuals whatever selfishness they may manifest.

Psychological egoism is best known in that form that says that pleasure is the main human "drive" and that each person always interprets his or her own self-interest in terms of pleasure and pain: Will the action bring pleasure or pain? If it will bring pleasure, the person considers it in his or her self-interest and does it; if pain, no. With some modifications Hobbes and Freud represent this viewpoint, and selections from Hobbes' contributions to the literature appear at the end of this chapter. It is from here on that our exposition of the doctrine will begin to be salted with large amounts of criticism.

First of all, as an explanation of this or that particular action, psychological egoism is too general. Its generality is what has probably been its greatest attraction, for it seems to be a theory that can explain everything we do. (Freud even once speculated as to whether human attraction in the libido and repulsion in *thanatos* or the "death wish" might not be continuous with attraction and repulsion of inorganic bodies as in gravitation and magnetism.) But explanations of facts must be responsible to the facts of which they are explanations, and any general explanation of so varied a body of facts as all human actions—past, present, and future—must indeed be very versatile. If it is self-interest that motivates all actions and if this self-interest is to be expressed in terms of pleasure, the theory has to account not only for kids stealing cars for joy rides, and for couples drinking their late-afternoon martinis, but also for mothers who dash into the fire to save their children, the proverbial soldier who smothers a grenade to save his buddies, and all the saints and heroes of the history books and the daily newspapers. It would appear that, from a survey of all the actions of real live people, those actions are such a mixed bag that the meaning of pleasure and self-interest must be stretched very wide if it is to cover them all. But I am not accusing men of the wide experience and considerable acquaintance with history had by Hobbes and Freud of ignorance. Both claimed, indeed, that their theories were squarely based upon fact. But that they did stretch these words very far beyond ordinary usage is obvious. We have to ask what the advantage is of doing so. For Hobbes and Freud were both talking about the same world, the world that you and I also know, even if less expertly, or over a smaller range than they.

Let us look at the ordinary meaning of self-interest. It is not as commonly used in our daily judgments about actions as are selfish and unselfish. It is most frequently used of the actions taken by groups, especially nations. Now, Hobbes remarks that nations always maintain the egoistic posture toward each other that individuals would if they thought they could get away with it. A nation is, in his view, a "mortall God" with the power of life and death over its citizens and completely sovereign with regard to other nations. It is the funded egoism of all its citizens and knows no morality but self-preservation. A nation does much bigger and more dramatic things in the name of self-interest than an individual can do with that professed motive, because it has more power. It does not feel as strongly as the individual does the need for some moral justification for acts so undertaken. "It was a threat to our security" is usually sufficient. One may well suppose that an individual would do the same if he or she thought he or she had the power to back it up. But that is to suppose beforehand that psychological egoism is true and cannot be used as evidence for psychological egoism. For that one must show a fairly consistent correlation between a consciousness of power and actions in the self-interest of the individual who has such a feeling. There are many such correlations but by no means any one-to-one correspondence.

To the extent that self-interest is related to the individual, it is probably most frequently used in discussions of ethics in textbooks, articles, and lectures. In such discussions it usually means that when an action is done out of the motive of self-interest, it is done in order to secure some benefit to the person who does it. We will ask in a moment whether that benefit can always be called pleasure, but our purpose at the moment is to look at self-interest in relation to the more commonly used words, "selfish," or "selfish interest." I can think of at least one moral philosopher who rejects William James's definition of "selfishness" as "hoggishness" but it probably represents the most reasonable one. Consider whether it is in your own self-interest to eat enough food to keep you alive and healthy. Yet, we do not ordinarily say of a person who eats lunch when there is plenty for all about him or her that he or she is selfish. If that person eats someone else's lunch knowing, or at least not caring, that the other person will suffer, or that the other person has at least as equal a claim to the food as he or she does, then we ordinarily would say that he or she is selfish in his or her action. The point is that acts motivated by self-interest are not always the same as actions done selfishly. Only those that fulfill one's own self-interests while disregarding the self-interests of others who will be affected by the action are likely to be called selfish. You can fulfill your self-interests on a desert island but it would be hard to think of your being selfish there, unless it is in such actions as relate to the nonhuman population of the island, animals. "Selfish" is a word of condemnation, and self-interest is so only when disregard of the self-interests of others is implied: "He's just looking out for himself and doesn't care whom he hurts."

There are few of us who would suppose that there is anyone else as interested in our welfare as ourselves, or in a position to do as much about it as we are. At best it would be only one person, or two, e.g., a parent, a wife or husband, or a very close friend of one or the other sex. "If you don't look out for yourself, who is going to do it for you?" is an apt question. And, on the other hand, not many of the actions of most of us seriously affect other people in great quantities, and we usually do not do either a great deal of good or a great deal of harm to other people's self-interests, even when we think little of the consequences of our acts on others. Given these suppositions, the psychological egoist may well point out that most people have a great incentive to look out for themselves in all their actions and few incentives to be concerned with the welfare of other people. But sympathy and compassion also enter the picture here and give us pause. For though I may seldom be motivated to seek out opportunities to promote the self-interests of other people, being busy with my own, it is a different matter if I am fairly sure that my action will hurt someone else and, in addition to that, if I am convinced that I will also have to watch them being hurt. Sympathy is fairly widespread, and it occurs even in children sometimes more than adults, so there is some basis for calling it natural and as constituting some counter-evidence against psychological egoism.

But however we construe self-interest, it cannot always be equated with "selfish" unless we suppose that people only fail to be selfish when there is no "it's-either-you-or-me" kind of competition and conflict of interests. In addition to that, if self-interest is to be taken as the main motive for all acts done by all individuals, we shall have to say that, because acts are so varied, selfishness must be very broadly construed, indeed, to cover all those things that people thus supposedly thought to be primarily in their best interests. And that is simply all the things that all human beings primarily aimed at in all their actions, whether it is taking candy from a baby and eating it yourself, or taking it from yourself and giving it to the baby, whether it is rescuing the baby from the fire or throwing him into it.

Of all the possible goals of human action, and all the things that have been suggested that everyone values and that things called good have in common, the most frequently suggested and most plausible one is pleasure. Both Hobbes and Freud agree that "act done primarily from self-interest" is the same as "act done to secure pleasure for oneself." Freud notes that, because it is virtually impossible for anyone to have as much pleasure as he or she wants, the goal gets scaled down in practice and becomes primarily one of the avoidance of pain, but not to the exclusion of getting pleasure when it is available without too much counterbalancing pain involved. I have reserved the discussion of the merits of pleasure as the goal that everyone should aim toward for the next chapter. Here I discuss only the question of whether it is a fact that everyone does seek pleasure as the main goal of all his or her actions. That doctrine is called psychological hedonism—psychological because it is an attempt at a doctrine of human motivation, and hedonism from the Greek word for "pleasure."

Psychological Hedonism as a Type of Psychological Egoism

From the outset, it has to be kept in mind that psychological hedonism is a type of psychological egoism, for to say that everyone does seek pleasure as the main motive for his or her action does not mean that the primary aim of all acts is to simply cause pleasure, to spread it around, as it were, but to cause pleasure to one's self. Hobbes was asked why he, an egoist, gave money to a beggar. He immediately answered that it was to relieve the beggar's need and his own, the beggar's hunger and Hobbes's pain at seeing him hungry. Of course, it has to be noted that Hobbes would not have been motivated to do the act, and thus would not have done it at all had he not sought to relieve his own pain.

If we try to define "pleasure" we can see at least one reason why disputes as to its place in ethics continue. Epicurus says that it is the absence of pain in the body and trouble in the mind. This would apply to many kinds of mental and physical states, anesthesia, and even sleep, of course. The main problem in it might easily seem to be that it is negative, whereas we usually think of pleasure as John Stuart Mill did, as not only including Epicurus's tranquility but excitement as well, not just the absence of something but the presence of something. What that something is can only be supplied by some sort of procedure such as listing things that people usually regard as pleasant states of mind, or sensations of the body. It is a more or less arbitrary decision whether we will include in our notion of pleasure those sensations and states of mind enjoyed by sadists and masochists. In *Lawrence of Arabia* Lawrence seemed to derive as much pleasure from being burned by a match as most people do from smoking a cigarette, if not more. If we include them we may be inclined to say that pleasure is whatever anyone enjoys. If we exclude them, the tendency might be to say that pleasure is what so-called normal people enjoy. Yet, even this restriction would make the definition very broad, since different "normal" people enjoy different things from what other normal ones enjoy. It is certainly a very broad definition that will be required if we are to accept psychological hedonism, for it must include not only the things that everyone obviously enjoys but also something that everyone seeks as the primary goal of all their actions. The way we can narrow that down somewhat is by saying that pleasure is what any person (or any normal person) has when his or her actions turn out as he or she hoped they would, or intended them to. This may be the same as saying, "He is pleased with the results," but one might be pleased with the results of one's actions when they did not turn out as he or she hoped they would, as when the result is different from but better than one had expected or hoped. If I enter the sweepstakes and hope to win a camera and win a car instead, this would be an example. I do derive pleasure from the result, as I had hoped I would, but the pleasure of winning a car is rather different from the pleasure of winning a camera.

The point that the example brings up concerns the question of whether all my actions have some one general motivation called pleasure, or whether I really do want specific things, or at least some specific kind of pleasure and not just any kind. In any action it is part of the meaning of the action's being motivated at all that I would not perform the action unless I wanted something in some general sense. I either want to see something changed, or to keep it from being changed. That is what action is, making some change in something, somehow, somewhere, in order to change something directly or to change one thing so that another thing will remain the same. What psychological hedonism says is that all our interests in everything we do, voluntarily, include somewhere among them the primary interest in either changing our own state of mind or our sensations from less pleasant to more pleasant, or to assure the continuance of a present pleasurable sensation or state of mind, or to assure that pleasurable sensations or states of mind that we have been experiencing from certain things or states of affairs continue to occur in the future. This includes not only such things as going to a concert but "saving for a rainy day."

It is here that "pleasure," as the psychological egoist uses it, is a very tricky sort of concept. First, if psychological hedonism means that everyone in all actions consciously or unconsciously intends to bring pleasure to oneself or assure the continuance of past or present pleasures, the kinds of psychological states that this must include are very wide in their spectrum. For they include not only obvious sensuous pleasures, such as those derived from sex or alcohol, but much more subtle and less obvious pleasures, such as absence of annoyances, or a sense of security, or just a sense of relaxation from work or mental strain. One straightens a picture that hangs cockeyed; why? Perhaps it only annoys him or her, or offends a desire for orderliness and symmetry. Perhaps he or she doesn't really care how the picture hangs, but thinks that people seeing it will think he or she is a sloppy person to let pictures hang thus. And to call all these different and fairly subtle states pleasure seems to give the word a broader meaning than ordinary.

Now, if we are also going to call that primary thing that falling on a grenade to save one's buddies brings pleasure, that does not seem obviously an apt description. Is the grenade faller always a masochist, and thus enjoys what most people don't? He may be. But if he is not, we have to look for some other reason for saying that his primary motive is pleasure to himself. The psychological egoist has to assert that his action is primarily motivated by benefit to himself. The psychological hedonist has to say that this benefit is in terms of pleasure. If not masochism, what? Suppose we can find no evidence that he is a glory seeker; he has, let us suppose, turned down opportunities for cheaper glories in the past. We may still argue that he might be seeking big glory and such as he would have at least a few witnesses to, his buddies. But if he has also shied away from big, though reasonably cheap, glories in the past when witnesses were also available, we shall have to look for other kinds of pleasure that motivated him. If he has given no indications before that he was so unhappy that he wanted to end his unhappiness by ending his life, we shall have to look elsewhere. The point is that the psychological hedonist will always look elsewhere for a motive of pleasure for one's acts when one kind of pleasure is ruled out. And if he cannot find it, he will say that it is there nevertheless, if only we knew all about the person.

But this unobservable evidence may be as much against the psychological hedonist as the other evidence has been. To appeal to unobservable and unavailable evidence is a new move in the game. This is the second kind of problem the psychological hedonist faces. He or she is no longer arguing from the facts of human behavior that all acts are primarily motivated by a desire for pleasure; he or she seems to have shifted to the view that man always seeks pleasure because man is already known to be a predominantly pleasure-seeking creature. At first he or she seems definitely to have been trying to show that man is a pleasure-seeking animal because man does in fact always seek pleasure. But now, it appears that he or she has assumed the very conclusion that he or she was trying to prove. If so, the technique for assuming the conclusion has been primarily one of making it true by definition: merely, for anything to be a man's action means for it to be aimed primarily at the individual's own pleasure. If this is the procedure, it is a questionable redefinition of "action." It is not a requirement for anything to be called an action for it also and always to be called something that is aimed primarily at the actor's pleasure, not outside the theory in question, psychological hedonism.

The third problem with psychological hedonism is that it is very questionable whether people always, or even usually, consciously or unconsciously, have in mind when they do an action, or decide to do it, any resulting sensation or state of mind for themselves. The action ordinarily is thought of by the actor in terms of some other result than his or her own sensations or state of mind. And this result is usually some external state of affairs. It is, surely, something of which the actor can and will have sensations, but this does not mean that he or she aims at having those sensations and that they are sensations that he or she believes will be pleasurable. The same applies to states of mind, such as a feeling of security that results from deliberately removing a threat. Even if we always got pleasure from the act of eating, that would not mean that this pleasure is always, or even usually what we aim at as the primary result of eating. Now, if in facing this problem a psychological hedonist says, well, if you don't aim at pleasure during the eating, you aim at the pleasure of survival, health, and the like, which is pleasure, nevertheless, we have to revert to the previous question of whether one aims at these as sensations and states of mind, or directly at these states called survival and health—and, even if we should agree that they are aimed at as sensations or states of mind whether they should be called pleasure.

Now, with regard to psychological egoism generally and to that version of it that defines self-interest in terms of the actor's pleasure, psychological hedonism, we can say that neither is true by definition. There is nothing in the meaning of "action" that always includes "done from self-interest, primarily" or "something done to produce pleasure in the actor, primarily." But that seems to be the most plausible way to make it sound true while also sounding as if it were a description or a generalization about all actions that have ever been examined by the person who defends the view. Not all actions and motives of the past and present population of the world are available for observation by any given theorist. But if the theorist wants to use as evidence all the actions recorded by other people, as well as those he or she has observed personally, and if at the same time he or she wants to call all this vast range of actions in a vast range of circumstances something motivated primarily by self-interest (or pleasure), he or she has stretched the meaning of "self-interest" or "pleasure" out of recognizable shape so that it will cover all actions. He or she has the very greatest difficulty saying what criterion he or she has for calling anything self-interest or pleasure if he or she calls all the primary motivations for all actions self-interest or pleasure. If he or she claims to know that the primary motivation for every action is self-interest or pleasure, he or she is claiming that one can tell the difference between an action primarily motivated by these and an action that is not primarily motivated by these. The odd thing is that on his or her own theory he or she would not be able to tell the difference from having seen examples of some acts that were thus motivated and having seen some acts that were not thus motivated. The theory asserts that no human could ever have seen an action that is not motivated primarily by self-interest or pleasure for there have never been any such actions to see. Then if he or she does not know of any negative instance by his or her own experience or by the experience of anyone else, how does he or she know that all those he or she has seen have been the opposite of an action not done from self-interest or motivated primarily by pleasure? If none of the vast range of human actions qualify, what imaginable actions could? This, I argue, he or she cannot tell us. And if he or she cannot tell us what it would be like for an action not to be motivated primarily by self-interest or pleasure, he or she cannot tell us what it would be like, specifically, for an action to be motivated primarily by self-interest or pleasure.

A last problem arises from psychological egoism and psychological hedonism. If the theory that all acts are motivated primarily by self-interest is true, there is no point in saying that an action is so motivated. There would be no point in saying it to another person who also knew it to be true (or even believed it to be true, without proof). "Act based primarily on self-interest" loses all its usefulness for distinguishing between actions if psychological egoism is true. The same applies to psychological hedonism and pleasure. It does not distinguish one action from another to say that it is motivated primarily by pleasure when all actions are primarily motivated by pleasure. As now ordinarily used, "self-interest" and "pleasure" do serve as means of classifying actions and distinguishing between some acts and other acts. What the psychological egoist and psychological hedonist propose is that we change this way of talking. Now, when someone proposes any change, it is always relevant to ask, "What would be the advantages?" Because of the confusions and vacuities I have argued that psychological egoism and psychological hedonism involve, I have to admit that I cannot find any clear advantage and that I do find a lot of disadvantages in the new way of talking that they propose. Granted that no one would do anything if he or she did not in some sense want something. It is either a misuse of words to say that what the individual always wants most of all is to benefit him- or herself or to get pleasure, for if words are used in some strict sense, with some clear criterion for self-interested action or action aimed primarily at one's own pleasure, these doctrines are simply false, and not an accurate description of the facts that they pretend to describe, or at least purport to—the facts of human actions and human motives.*

Ethical Egoism

The psychological egoist and psychological hedonist are doing psychology. Ethical egoism is a normative doctrine, saying not what is done but what ought to be done. Since it has been generally supposed that one does not have a moral obligation to do what one *cannot* do, if psychological egoism holds true, any normative doctrine that says one should sometimes act contrary to one's own self-interest would thus be telling one to do something that one does not have an obligation to do. But if psychological egoism is true, also, it follows that telling anyone that he or she should pursue his or her self-interest in every action would also be pointless, since he or she must do so, anyway, because it is everyone's nature to pursue his or her own self-interest as the primary goal of every action. Only if it is possible for a person to fail to do something is it relevant to tell him or her that

---

* An argument sometimes used for psychological hedonism is that a person does some things to avoid the pain of a hurting conscience. This argument has not been considered here, but the main objection to it centers around the question, But why would your conscience hurt if you did not do a certain thing, or if you did something else? The answer has to be, Because I think it is wrong. But if right and wrong are to be defined in terms of pleasure and pain, as in psychological hedonism, one should apparently think something is wrong because it causes pain, and not that it causes pain because one thinks it wrong.

he or she should. Thus, psychological egoism cannot be a basis for ethical egoism. Rather, it is a presupposition of ethical egoism that psychological egoism is false.

Two versions of the doctrine of ethical egoism have been distinguished in the literature. The first is one about which little can be said, mostly because it says little. It is called individual ethical egoism and it consists of one person making it his or her policy always to put his or her self-interest first in every action, but not advising others one way or the other, or publicly advocating or privately caring much one way or the other what other people should do. If this person engages in any discussion of ethics at all, presumably all his or her statements would be in the first person, "I intend to pursue my own self-interest," and so on. Since this person takes no position on what others should do, not much needs to be said about his or her position, for he or she applies it only to him- or herself. Presumably it would be to his or her advantage if everyone else were to be altruists and thus helped him or her along with his or her self-interests. But if competition is ever to the mutual advantage of people pursuing their own self-interests, this would not always be the case.

The doctrine that has been of more interest in ethics has been one in which it is held that everyone ought always to pursue his or her own self-interest, i.e., in every action. A person holding this doctrine does not confine it to the first person, but holds, "I ought to pursue my self-interest in every action, you ought to pursue yours, and he ought to pursue his." And since this is a theory of obligation, it holds not only that everyone is morally obligated to pursue his or her own self-interests, but also that a person is morally wrong, or his or her acts are morally wrong, if they do not. Thus, an immoral person would be precisely the habitual altruist, if his or her altruism were not so designed that promoting the self-interests of others was a secondary concern, and promoting his or her own self-interests always the primary one. The doctrine does not say that altruism is always wrong, it is wrong only if it fails to promote one's own self-interests, or at least if it is not intended to.

In favor of the doctrine, called universal ethical egoism because it applies to everyone, it can be said first, that usually no one is in a better position to promote one's self-interests than that person, and usually no one knows one's self-interests better than oneself. Also, it can be admitted that even if each person were so inclined to put the self-interests of others first, the human race might well be a jumble of confusion or else it might soon become extinct. For people would constantly be asking those around them what they needed now, or making guesses as to what others needed that might often be mistaken. I am not saying that a society of altruists would be a society of martyrs, but it might well be that many individuals would literally perish if their self-interests depended primarily upon others. Nor am I saying that if you don't look out for yourself, nobody else can or will, for that is not always true, and many times it is false. The ethical egoist has on his or her side a very basic presupposition of society, and that is that a person is primarily responsible for supplying his or her own self-interests, and especially in those situations where no one else is around and where no one else could know what his or her needs are at the moment.

Ethical egoism is a moral principle. It has been criticized on two main counts. One is that it is not morality at all, since it runs contrary to what has come to be called the moral point of view. If it very rightly emphasizes one social fact, that is that each individual ordinarily is that person on whom primary responsibility rests for looking out for him- or herself; it has been held to run contrary to another presupposition of society and morality, and that is that under some circumstances, a person must forego some self-interests so that a maximum or optimum of the self-interests of everyone in the society can be achieved. I as an individual member of society have an abundance of self-interests, but every other member of society can say the same. What is there about my case that would give me the right to say that mine must always be promoted even when in so promoting them I defeat the self-interests of others? And if each member of society has the right to make an exception of him- or herself, what happens to equality? Morality asks something difficult of us, and that is that each of us voluntarily forego some self-interests. The alternative is that we shall be forced by others to forego them when there is a conflict of interests. In such examples as voluntary price and wage controls, voluntary rationing, and so forth, we can see that some strong incentive is the only thing that can cause us to voluntarily sacrifice what we think will benefit us. It is more often the case that some more tangible penalty than public opinion or some more tangible reward than knowing that you have done right are needed to control prices, wages, and the distribution of goods or the use of purchasing power. Perhaps this is an argument in favor of psychological egoism, but as I have said, if psychological egoism is true, ethical egoism is beside the point.

The second criticism of ethical egoism is that it fails to function as an ethical principle in failing to give clear and practicable advice as to what it is right to do. W. K. Frankena and especially Brian Medlin have argued thus against it. Medlin holds that an ethical egoist is saying that he or she is morally obligated to seek his or her self-interest even when it conflicts with the self-interests of others, and that all others have a moral obligation to seek their self-interests even when they conflict with his or her own. So far this sounds as if it meets the criterion that a person should apply to others the same standards he or she applies to him- or herself. But that is not the issue at question in this criticism. The criticism is rather that when I say that everyone should observe his or her own self-interests, I seem to imply that I do and that I do not want to see my own self-interests accomplished or achieved, for I am telling others that they are morally bound to seek the defeat of my self-interests whenever their own conflict with mine, even while in the same breath I am affirming that I am morally bound to pursue my own self-interests.

For many years Western philosophers were usually opposed to ethical egoism (Nietzsche being a notable exception) and few, if any, widely respected written defenses of it could be found. That may no longer be so, for recently Jesse Kalin has been able to meet, at least part of the way, the critics of the doctrine. Kalin replies to Medlin that it is not the achievement or accomplishment of the self-interests of all that the ethical egoist is in favor of, for when two are in competition for one thing that both cannot have, one must lose. Rather, he says, it is the pursuit of the self-interests of everyone by everyone that the ethical egoist proclaims and advises; each person should pursue his or her own self-interests, even when they conflict with those of other people. As examples of how a person can consistently hold that everyone should, Kalin cites athletic and other competitions: Everyone connected with the game wants one side or the other to win, perhaps. But even the players recognize it as an obligation of the opposing players to try to beat them; otherwise a player would not be much of a player. This does not mean that a player for the Eagles will help a player for the Steelers or vice versa by slacking off in his own efforts, not if he is a good player. Kalin could also have cited Jefferson's statement in the Declaration of Independence that everyone has a right to the "pursuit of happiness" (though not necessarily its capture).

While giving Kalin an A for effort, I think I would have to make two counterobjections. One is that life is not a game, and when we are talking about such conflicts of self-interest as those in which one person's achieving his or her results in the injury or death of the other, we are talking about something different from a football game in which a player is injured or killed by the opposing side. At least in a football game it is also part of the things a player knows when he puts on his uniform that people have been injured in the game and people have even been killed in it. We could not say this of the competition between two persons off the playing field when the stakes are not to all intents and purposes high. But ethical egoism does not rule out the morality of killing another person in the pursuit of one's own self-interests except when to do so would threaten one's other self-interests, e.g., one's own freedom or life, limb, and so on. That puts a different face on it. It nowhere explicitly or implicitly forbids any means except those that will endanger one's self-interests or defeat them. How can anyone hold that others should pursue their self-interests with no exceptions but those? For that means when you say that everyone else is morally obligated to pursue his or her own self-interests even when they conflict with your own, you are saying that they are obligated to use any and every means they think will be successful, even when the self-interests at stake are petty by other standards and the means of achieving them are morally ghastly by other standards. This means, of course, that you acquiesce in your own demise if the competitor shall think it expedient, whether you see the blow coming and attempt to ward it off in your own self-interest or whether you "get it" in the back all unawares. For you may not even be aware that the other person is competing with you, much less of the means he or she has in mind. At least in football you know that you are competing and that a certain amount of rough stuff is permitted by the rules, and that in the permissible rough stuff there may be an accident.

If we carry ethical egoism even further and say, "Very well, murder, even when a person can get away with it, is ghastly by other moral standards, but we egoists are not bound by other standards," what is the logical consequence? It is, as Medlin says, that you seem to be saying that you both do and do not want to see your own self-interests triumph, even the interest in staying alive until old age inevitably kills you. If an ethical egoist preaches his or her doctrine as what is morally right, and if those around him or her or those who read his or her books and articles take it seriously and conscientiously follow it, the egoist has no complaint coming when someone does him or her in while pursuing his or her self-interests in competition with the egoist's own. A consistent preacher of egoism, then, would have to avoid all the ambushes he or she could think of, take precautions against his or her food being poisoned, and so forth. Such possibilities as this lead Kalin to admit in print that a person who believes in egoism would be defeating his or her own self-interests if he or she publicly proclaimed the doctrine. Paradoxically, Kalin does proclaim the doctrine!

Proclaiming ethical egoism, or arguing against nonethical egoist doctrines, leaving only egoism as the doctrine to be accepted by default, then has, on Kalin's own admission, dangers of all sorts to the self-interests of the proclaimer. The logical thing to do, says Kalin, is for the ethical egoist to keep his or her mouth shut on all moral topics. This has resulted in a controversial and problematic issue: Is it not immoral not to oppose immorality? And this would include opposing nonegoist teachings for, according to egoism, it is morally wrong not to be an egoist and to follow nonegoist doctrine. And yet, if you may be signing your own death warrant by proclaiming moral truth, it is admittedly not in your self-interest to proclaim moral truth, i.e., egoism. In any case, if your proclamation did not cause others to do you in when they are in competition with you, it would at least be saying that it would not be wrong for them to do so, and that you had no moral right to complain if they seriously injured you or killed you in a competition of self-interests. The paradox is this, regarding moral truth: If you think it is wrong for people not to be egoists and think it is wrong (because it may endanger your self-interests) to tell them it is wrong, are you really serious in saying that everyone should pursue his or her own self-interests, and are you not really qualifying it, after all, and holding a very restricted version of it?

Other than these somewhat involuted problems of being an ethical egoist, there are, of course, other and more traditional objections to ethical egoism, but they are similar to it in that they argue that it is difficult, if not impossible, to be a consistent ethical egoist in practice. If a consistent egoist would not tell others in words that egoism is his or her own policy in his or her actions, it is difficult, if not impossible, to keep from telling others by one's actions. The egoist who is not a hermit does things that other people can see. Even if those around him or her are not egoists in their actions, some of them may be encouraged to give him or her a dose of his or her own medicine when they get an abrupt shock from some means he or she has used against them in pursuit of his or her own self-interests. But let's suppose that he or she takes extreme or even reasonable care never to tip his or her hand that egoism is his or her policy. Let's even give him or her a marvelous computer by which he or she can always plan his or her actions so as to avoid suspicion that when it comes to a crunch, he or she is going to pursue his or her self-interests and yield to no one else's. The question is, Would he or she not end up denying him- or herself about as many of his or her self-interests as a person would who follows some other, nonegoist policy consistently and with a computer that enabled him or her to follow his or her nonegoist policy as consistently as the egoist follows his or hers? The whole question is purely theoretical and hypothetical, of course, but that is what we are discussing: theories of ethics, and their justification. Every view has its difficulties, but egoism seems to impose more on itself than other classical views, and seems to have at least as many as they from external sources.

I have presented the doctrines of psychological egoism and one form of it called psychological hedonism, and criticized both as radically altering ordinary ways of talking about self-interest and pleasure with no compensating benefits and with more drawbacks. I have also presented the doctrine called ethical egoism, a normative doctrine, and criticized it as being logically inconsistent and as being difficult, if not impossible, to practice consistently. As logically inconsistent advice, of course, it would fall as a moral principle by failing to give practicable advice.

LEVIATHAN *

THOMAS HOBBES

Of the Interior Beginnings of Voluntary Motions; Commonly Called the Passions; and the Speeches by Which They Are Expressed.

There be in animals, two sorts of *motions* peculiar to them: one called *vital;* begun in generation, and continued without interruption through their whole life; such as are the *course* of the *blood,* the *pulse,* the *breathing,* the *concoction, nutrition, excretion,* &c. to which motions there needs no help of imagination: the other is *animal motion,* otherwise called *voluntary motion;* as to *go,* to *speak,* to *move* any of our limbs, in such manner as is first fancied in our minds. That sense is motion in the organs and interior parts of man's body, caused by the action of the things we see, hear, &c.; and that fancy is but the relics of the same motion, remaining after sense, has been already said in the first and second chapters. And because *going, speaking,* and the like voluntary motions, depend always upon a precedent thought of *whither, which way,* and *what;* it is evident, that the imagination is the first internal beginning of all voluntary motion. And although un-studied men do not conceive any motion at all to be there, where the thing moved is invisible; or the space it is moved in is, for the shortness of it, insensible; yet that doth not hinder, but that such motions are. For let a space be never so little, that which is moved over a greater space, whereof that little one is part, must first be moved over that. These small beginnings of motion, within the body of man, before they appear in walking, speaking, striking, and other visible actions, are commonly called ENDEAVOUR.

This endeavour, when it is toward something which causes it, is called APPETITE, or DESIRE; the latter, being the general name; and the other often-times restrained to signify the desire of food, namely *hunger* and *thirst.* And when the endeavour is fromward something, it is generally called AVERSION. These words, *appetite* and *aversion,* we have from the Latins; and they both of them signify the motions, one of approaching, the other of retiring. So also do the Greek words for the same, which are ὁρμὴ and ἀφορμὴ. For

---

* From Thomas Hobbes, *Leviathan,* first published in 1651. Part One, Chapters 6, 13, 14, 15, 19, and 30, with omissions. Reprinted from *The English Works of Thomas Hobbes,* ed. by Sir Thomas Molesworth (London: John Bohn, 1839), Vol. 3.

nature itself does often press upon men those truths, which afterwards, when they look for somewhat beyond nature, they stumble at. For the Schools find in mere appetite to go, or move, no actual motion at all: but because some motion they must acknowledge, they call it metaphorical motion; which is but an absurd speech: for though words may be called metaphorical; bodies and motions can not.

That which men desire, they are also said to LOVE: and to HATE those things for which they have aversion. So that desire and love are the same thing; save that by desire, we always signify the absence of the object; by love, most commonly the presence of the same. So also by aversion, we signify the absence; and by hate, the presence of the object.

Of appetites and aversions, some are born with men; as appetite of food, appetite of excretion, and exoneration, which may also and more properly be called aversions, from somewhat they feel in their bodies; and some other appetites, not many. The rest, which are appetites of particular things, proceed from experience, and trial of their effects upon themselves or other men. For of things we know not at all, or believe not to be, we can have no further desire, than to taste and try. But aversion we have for things, not only which we know have hurt us, but also that we do not know whether they will hurt us, or not.

Those things which we neither desire, nor hate, we are said to *contemn:* CONTEMPT being nothing else but an immobility, or contumacy of the heart, in resisting the action of certain things; and proceeding from that the heart is already moved otherwise, by other more potent objects; or from want of experience of them.

And because the constitution of a man's body is in continual mutation, it is impossible that all the same things should always cause in him the same appetites, and aversions: much less can all men consent, in the desire of almost any one and the same object.

But whatsoever is the object of any man's appetite or desire, that is it which he for his part calleth *good:* and the object of his hate and aversion, *evil;* and of his contempt, *vile* and *inconsiderable.* For these words of good, evil, and contemptible, are ever used with relation to the person that useth them: there being nothing simply and absolutely so; nor any common rule of good and evil, to be taken from the nature of the objects themselves; but from the person of the man, where there is no commonwealth; or, in a commonwealth, from the person that representeth it; or from an arbitrator or judge, whom men disagreeing shall by consent set up, and make his sentence the rule thereof.

Of the Natural Condition of Mankind as Concerning Their Felicity, and Misery.

Nature hath made men so equal, in the faculties of the body, and mind; as that though there be found one man sometimes manifestly stronger in body, or of quicker mind than another; yet when all is reckoned together, the difference between man, and man, is not so considerable, as that one man can thereupon claim to himself any benefit, to which another may not pretend, as well as he. For as to the strength of body, the weakest has strength enough to kill the strongest, either by secret machination, or by confederacy with others, that are in the same danger with himself.

And as to the faculties of the mind, setting aside the arts grounded upon words, and especially that skill of proceeding upon general, and infallible rules, called science; which very few have, and but in few things; as being not a native faculty, born with us; nor attained, as prudence, while we look after somewhat else, I find yet a greater equality amongst men, than that of strength. For prudence, is but experience; which equal time, equally bestows on all men, in those things they equally apply themselves unto. That which may perhaps make such equality incredible, is but a vain conceit of one's own wisdom, which almost all men think they have in a greater degree, than the vulgar; that is, than all men but themselves, and a few others, whom by fame, or for concurring with themselves, they approve. For such is the nature of men, that howsoever they may acknowledge many others to be more witty, or more eloquent, or more learned; yet they will hardly believe there be many so wise as themselves; for they see their own wit at hand, and other men's at a distance. But this proveth rather that men are in that point equal, than unequal. For there is not ordinarily a greater sign of the equal distribution of any thing, than that every man is contented with his share.

From this equality of ability, ariseth equality of hope in the attaining of our ends. And therefore if any two men desire the same thing, which nevertheless they cannot both enjoy, they become enemies; and in the way to their end, which is principally their own conservation, and sometimes their delectation only, endeavour to destroy, or subdue one another. And from hence it comes to pass, that where an invader hath no more to fear, than another man's single power; if one plant, sow, build, or possess a convenient seat, others may probably be expected to come prepared with forces united, to dispossess, and deprive him, not only of the fruit of his labour, but also of his life, or liberty. And the invader again is in the like danger of another.

And from this diffidence of one another, there is no way for any man to secure himself, so reasonable, as anticipation; that is, by force, or wiles, to master the persons of all men he can, so long, till he see no other power great enough to endanger him: and this is no more than his own conservation requireth, and is generally allowed. Also because there be some, that taking pleasure in contemplating their own power in the acts of conquest, which they pursue farther than their security requires; if others, that otherwise would be glad to be at ease within modest bounds, should not by invasion increase their power, they would not be able, long time, by standing only on their defence, to subsist. And by consequence, such augmentation of dominion over men being necessary to a man's conservation, it ought to be allowed him.

Again, men have no pleasure, but on the contrary a great deal of grief, in keeping company, where there is no power able to over-awe them all. For every man looketh that his companion should value him, at the same rate he sets upon himself: and upon all signs of contempt, or undervaluing, naturally endeavours, as far as he dares, (which amongst them that have no common power to keep them in quiet, is far enough to make them destroy each other), to extort a greater value from his contemners, by damage; and from others, by the example.

So that in the nature of man, we find three principal causes of quarrel. First, competition; secondly, diffidence; thirdly, glory.

The first, maketh men invade for gain; the second, for safety; and the third, for reputation. The first use violence, to make themselves masters of other men's persons, wives, children, and cattle; the second, to defend them; the third, for trifles, as a word, a smile, a different opinion, and any other sign of undervalue, either direct in their persons, or by reflection in their kindred, their friends, their nation, their profession, or their name.

Hereby it is manifest; that during the time men live without a common power to keep them all in awe, they are in that condition which is called war; and such a war, as is of every man, against every man. For WAR, consisteth not in battle only, or the act of fighting; but in a tract of time, wherein the will to contend by battle is sufficiently known: and therefore the notion of *time*, is to be considered in the nature of war; as it is in the nature of weather. For as the nature of foul weather, lieth not in a shower or two of rain; but in an inclination thereto of many days together: so the nature of war, consisteth not in actual fighting; but in the known disposition thereto, during all the time there is no assurance to the contrary. All other time is PEACE.

Whatsoever therefore is consequent to a time of war, where every man is enemy to every man; the same is consequent to the time, wherein men live without other security, than what their own strength, and their own invention shall furnish them withal. In such condition, there is no place for industry; because the fruit thereof is uncertain: and consequently no culture of the earth; no navigation, nor use of the commodities that may be imported by sea; no commodious building; no instruments of moving, and removing, such things as require much force; no knowledge of the face of the earth; no account of time; no arts; no letters; no society; and which is worst of all, continual fear, and danger of violent death; and the life of man, solitary, poor, nasty, brutish, and short.

It may seem strange to some man, that has not well weighed these things; that nature should thus dissociate, and render men apt to invade, and destroy one another: and he may therefore, not trusting to this inference, made from the passions, desire perhaps to have the same confirmed by experience. Let him therefore consider with himself, when taking a journey, he arms himself, and seeks to go well accompanied; when going to sleep, he locks his doors; when even in his house he locks his chests; and this when he knows there be laws, and public officers, armed, to revenge all injuries shall be done him; what opinion he has of his fellow-subjects, when he rides armed; of his fellow citizens, when he locks his doors; and of his children, and servants, when he locks his chests. Does he not there as much accuse mankind by his actions, as I do by my words? But neither of us accuse man's nature in it. The desires, and other passions of man, are in themselves no sin. No more are the actions, that proceed from those passions, till they know a law that forbids them: which till laws be made they cannot know: nor can any law be made, till they have agreed upon the person that shall make it.

It may peradventure be thought, there was never such a time, nor condition of war as this; and I believe it was never generally so, over all the world: but there are many places, where they live so now. For the savage people in many places of America, except the government of small families, the concord whereof dependeth on natural lust, have no government at all; and live at this day in that brutish manner, as I said before. Howsoever, it may be perceived what manner of life there would be, where there were no common power to fear, by the manner of life, which men that have formerly lived under a peaceful government, use to degenerate into, in a civil war.

But though there had never been any time, wherein particular men were in a condition of war one against another; yet in all times, kings, and persons of sovereign authority, because of their independency, are in continual jealousies, and in the state and posture of gladiators; having their weapons pointing, and their eyes fixed on one another; that is, their forts, garrisons, and guns upon the frontiers of their kingdoms; and continual spies upon their neighbours; which is a posture of war. But because they uphold thereby, the industry of their subjects; there does not follow from it, that misery, which accompanies the liberty of particular men.

To this war of every man, against every man, this also is consequent; that nothing can be unjust. The notions of right and wrong, justice and injustice have there no place. Where there is no common power, there is no law: where no law, no injustice. Force, and fraud, are in war the two cardinal virtues. Justice, and injustice are none of the faculties neither of the body, nor mind. If they were, they might be in a man that were alone in the world, as well as his senses, and passions. They are qualities, that relate to men in society, not in solitude. It is consequent also to the same condition, that there be no propriety, no dominion, no *mine* and *thine* distinct; but only that to be every man's, that he can get; and for so long, as he can keep it. And thus much for the ill condition, which man by mere nature is actually placed in; though with a possibility to come out of it, consisting partly in the passions, partly in his reason.

The passions that incline men to peace, are fear of death; desire of such things as are necessary to commodious living; and a hope by their industry to obtain them. And reason suggesteth convenient articles of peace, upon which men may be drawn to agreement. These articles, are they, which otherwise are called the Laws of Nature: whereof I shall speak more particularly, in the two following chapters.

Of the First and Second Natural Laws, and of Contracts.

The RIGHT OF NATURE, which writers commonly call *jus naturale*, is the liberty each man hath, to use his own power, as he will himself, for the preservation of his own nature; that is to say, of his own life; and consequently, of doing any thing, which in his own judgment, and reason, he shall conceive to be the aptest means thereunto.

By LIBERTY, is understood, according to the proper signification of the word, the absence of external impediments: which impediments, may oft take away part of a man's power to do what he would; but cannot hinder him from using the power left him, according as his judgment, and reason shall dictate to him.

A LAW OF NATURE, *lex naturalis*, is a precept or general rule, found out by reason, by which a man is forbidden to do that, which is destructive of his life, or taketh away the means of preserving the same; and to omit that, by which he thinketh it may be best preserved. For though they that speak of this subject, use to confound *jus*, and *lex*, *right* and *law*: yet they ought to be distinguished; because RIGHT, consisteth in liberty to do, or to forbear; whereas LAW, determineth, and bindeth to one of them: so that law, and right, differ as much, as obligation, and liberty; which in one and the same matter are inconsistent.

And because the condition of man, as hath been declared in the precedent chapter, is a condition of war of every one against every one: in which case every one is governed by his own reason; and there is nothing he can make use of, that may not be a help unto him, in preserving his life against his enemies; it followeth, that in such a condition, every man has a right to every thing; even to one another's body. And therefore, as long as this natural right of every man to every thing endureth, there can be no security to any man, how strong or wise soever he be, of living out the time, which nature ordinarily alloweth men to live. And consequently it is a precept, or general rule of reason, *that every man, ought to endeavour peace, as far as he has hope of obtaining it; and when he cannot obtain it, that he may seek, and use, all helps, and advantages of war.* The first branch of which rule, containeth the first, and fundamental law of nature; which is, *to seek peace, and follow it.* The second, the sum of the right of nature; which is, *by all means we can, to defend ourselves.*

From this fundamental law of nature, by which men are commanded to endeavour peace, is derived this second law; *that a man be willing, when others are so too, as far-forth, as for peace, and defence of himself he shall think it necessary, to lay down this right to all things; and be contented with so much liberty against other men, as he would allow other men against himself.* For as long as every man holdeth this right, of doing any thing he liketh; so long are all men in the condition of war. But if other men will not lay down their right, as well as he; then there is no reason for any one, to divest himself of his: for that were to expose himself to prey, which no man is bound to, rather than to dispose himself to peace. This is that law of the Gospel; *whatsoever you require that others should do to you, that do ye to them.* And that law of all men, *quod tibi fieri non vis, alteri ne feceris.*

To *lay down* a man's *right* to any thing, is to *divest* himself of the *liberty,* of hindering another of the benefit of his own right to the same. For he that renounceth, or passeth away his right, giveth not to any other man a right which he had not before; because there is nothing to which every man had not right by nature: but only standeth out of his way, that he may enjoy his own original right, without hindrance from him; not without hindrance from another. So that the effect which redoundeth to one man, by another man's defect of right, is but so much diminution of impediments to the use of his own right original.

Right is laid aside, either by simply renouncing it; or by transferring it to another. By *simply* RENOUNCING; when he cares not to whom the benefit thereof redoundeth. By TRANSFERRING; when he intendeth the benefit thereof to some certain person, or persons. And when a man hath in either manner abandoned, or granted away his right; then is he said to be OBLIGED, or BOUND, not to hinder those, to whom such right is granted or abandoned, from the benefit of it: and that he *ought,* and it is his DUTY, not to make void that voluntary act of his own: and that such hindrance is INJUSTICE, and INJURY, as being *sine jure;* the right being before renounced, or transferred. So that *injury,* or *injustice,* in the controversies of the world, is somewhat like to that, which in the disputations of scholars is called *absurdity.* For as it is there called an absurdity, to contradict what one maintained in the beginning; so in the world, it is called injustice, and injury, voluntarily to undo that, which from the beginning he had voluntarily done. The way by which a man either simply renounceth, or transferreth his right, is a declaration, or signification, by some voluntary and sufficient sign, or signs, that he doth so renounce, or transfer; or hath so renounced, or transferred the same, to him that accepteth it. And these signs are either words only, or actions only; or, as it happeneth most often, both words, and actions. And the same are the BONDS, by which men are bound, and obliged: bonds, that have their strength, not from their own nature, for nothing is more easily broken than a man's word, but from fear of some evil consequence upon the rupture.

Whensoever a man transferreth his right, or renounceth it; it is either in consideration of some right reciprocally transferred to himself; or for some other good he hopeth for thereby. For it is a voluntary act: and of the voluntary acts of every man, the object is some *good to himself.* And therefore there be some rights, which no man can be understood by any words, or other signs, to have abandoned, or transferred. As first a man cannot lay down the right of resisting them, that assault him by force, to take away his life; because he cannot be understood to aim thereby, at any good to himself. The same may be said of wounds, and chains, and imprisonment; both because there is no benefit consequent to such patience; as there is to the patience of suffering another to be wounded, or imprisoned: as also because a man cannot tell, when he seeth men proceed against him by violence, whether they intend his death or not. And lastly the motive, and end for which this renouncing, and transferring of right is introduced, is nothing else but the security of a man's person, in his life, and in the means of so preserving life, as not to be weary of it. And therefore if a man by words, or other signs, seem to despoil himself of the end, for which those signs were intended; he is not to be understood as if he meant it, or that it was his will; but that he was ignorant of how such words and actions were to be interpreted.

The mutual transferring of right, is that which men call CONTRACT.

Of Other Laws of Nature.

From that law of nature, by which we are obliged to transfer to another, such rights, as being retained, hinder the peace of mankind, there followeth a third; which is this, *that men perform their covenants made:* without which, covenants are in vain, and but empty words; and the right of all men to all things remaining, we are still in the condition of war.

And in this law of nature, consisteth the fountain and original of JUSTICE. For where no covenant hath preceded, there hath no right been transferred, and every man has right to every thing; and consequently, no action can be unjust. But when a covenant is made, then to break it is *unjust:* and the definition of INJUSTICE, is no other than *the not performance of covenant.* And whatsoever is not unjust, is *just.*

But because covenants of mutual trust, where there is a fear of not performance on either part, as hath been said in the former chapter, are invalid; though the original of justice be the making of covenants; yet injustice actually there can be none, till the cause of such fear be taken away; which while men are in the natural condition of war, cannot be done. Therefore before the names of just, and unjust can have place, there must be some coercive power, to compel men equally to the performance of their covenants, by the terror of some punishment, greater than the benefit they expect by the breach of their covenant; and to make good that propriety, which by mutual contract men acquire, in recompense of the universal right they abandon: and such power there is none before the erection of a commonwealth. And this is also to be gathered out of the ordinary definition of justice in the Schools: for they say, that *justice is the constant will of giving to every man his own.* And therefore where there is no *own,* that is no propriety, there is no injustice; and where there is no coercive power erected, that is, where there is no commonwealth, there is no propriety; all men having right to all things: therefore where there is no commonwealth, there nothing is unjust. So that the nature of justice, consisteth in keeping of valid covenants: but the validity of covenants begins not but with the constitution of a civil power, sufficient to compel men to keep them: and then it is also that propriety begins.

These are the laws of nature, dictating peace, for a means of the conservation of men in multitudes; and which only concern the doctrine of civil society. There be other things tending to the destruction of particular men; as drunkenness, and all other parts of intemperance; which may therefore also be reckoned amongst those things which the law of nature hath forbidden; but are not necessary to be mentioned, nor are pertinent enough to this place.

And though this may seem too subtle a deduction of the laws of nature, to be taken notice of by all men; whereof the most part are too busy in getting food, and the rest too negligent to understand; yet to leave all men inexcusable, they have been contracted into one easy sum, intelligible even to the meanest capacity; and that is, *Do not that to another, which thou wouldest not have done to thyself;* which sheweth him, that he has no more to do in learning the laws of nature, but, when weighing the actions of other men with his own, they seem too heavy, to put them into the other part of the balance, and his own into their place, that his own passions, and self-love, may add nothing to the weight; and then there is none of these laws of nature that will not appear unto him very reasonable.

I observe the *diseases* of a commonwealth, that proceed from the poison of seditious doctrines, whereof one is, *That every private man is judge of good and evil actions.* This is true in the condition of mere nature, where there are no civil laws; and also under civil government, in such cases as are not determined by the law. But otherwise, it is manifest, that the measure of good and evil actions, is the civil law; and the judge the legislator, who is always representative of the commonwealth. From this false doctrine, men are disposed to debate with themselves, and dispute the commands of the commonwealth; and afterwards to obey, or disobey them, as in their private judgments they shall think fit; whereby the commonwealth is distracted and *weakened.*

Another doctrine repugnant to civil society, is, that *whatsoever a man does against his conscience, is sin;* and it dependeth on the presumption of making himself judge of good and evil. For a man's conscience, and his judgment is the same thing, and as the judgment, so also the conscience may be erroneous. Therefore, though he that is subject to no civil law, sinneth in all he does against his conscience, because he has no other rule to follow but his own reason; yet it is not so with him that lives in a commonwealth; because the law is the public conscience, by which he hath already undertaken to be guided. Otherwise in such diversity, as there is of private consciences, which are but private opinions, the commonwealth must needs be distracted, and no man dare to obey the sovereign power, further than it shall seem good in his own eyes.

It hath been also commonly taught, *that faith and sanctity, are not to be attained by study and reason, but by supernatural inspiration, or infusion.* Which granted, I see not why any man should render a reason of his faith; or why every Christian should not be also a prophet; or why any man should take the law of his country, rather than his own inspiration, for the rule of his action. And thus we fall again in the fault of taking upon us to judge of good and evil; or to make judges of it, such private men as pretend to be supernaturally inspired, to the dissolution of all civil government. Faith comes by hearing, and hearing by those accidents, which guide us into the presence of them that speak to us; which accidents are all contrived by God Almighty; and yet are not supernatural, but only, for the great number of them that concur to every effect, unobservable. Faith and sanctity, are indeed not very frequent; but yet they are not miracles, but brought to pass by education, discipline, correction, and other natural ways, by which God worketh them in his elect, at such times as he thinketh fit. And these three opinions, pernicious to peace and government, have in this part of the world, proceeded chiefly from the tongues, and pens of unlearned divines, who joining the words of Holy Scripture together, otherwise than is agreeable to reason, do what they can, to make men think, that sanctity and natural reason, cannot stand together.

A fourth opinion, repugnant to the nature of a commonwealth, is this, *that he that hath the sovereign power is subject to the civil laws.* It is true, that sovereigns are all subject to the laws of nature; because such laws be divine, and cannot by any man, or commonwealth be abrogated. But to those laws which the sovereign himself, that is, which the commonwealth maketh, he is not subject. For to be subject to laws, is to be subject to the commonwealth, that is to the sovereign representative, that is to himself; which is not subjection, but freedom from the laws. Which error, because it setteth the laws above the sovereign, setteth also a judge above him, and a power to punish him; which is to make a new sovereign; and again for the same reason a third, to punish the second; and so continually without end, to the confusion, and dissolution of the commonwealth.

A fifth doctrine, that tendeth to the dissolution of a commonwealth, is, *that every private man has an absolute propriety in his goods; such, as excludeth the right of the sovereign.* Every man has indeed a propriety that excludes the right of every other subject: and he has it only from the sovereign power; without the protection whereof, every other man should have equal right to the same. But if the right of the sovereign also be excluded, he cannot perform the office they have put him into; which is, to defend them both from foreign enemies, and from the injuries of one another; and consequently there is no longer a commonwealth.

And if the propriety of subjects, exclude not the right of the sovereign representative to their goods; much less to their offices of judicature, or execution, in which they represent the sovereign himself.

There is a sixth doctrine, plainly, and directly against the essence of a commonwealth; and it is this, *that the sovereign power may be divided.* For what is it to divide the power of a commonwealth, but to dissolve it; for powers divided mutually destroy each other. And for these doctrines, men are chiefly beholding to some of those, that making profession of the laws, endeavour to make them depend upon their own learning, and not upon the legislative power.

ULTIMATE PRINCIPLES AND ETHICAL EGOISM °

BRIAN MEDLIN

I believe that it is now pretty generally accepted by professional philosophers that ultimate ethical principles must be arbitrary. One cannot derive conclusions about what should be merely from accounts of what is the case; one cannot decide how people ought to behave merely from one's knowledge of how they do behave. To arrive at a conclusion in ethics one must have at least one ethical premiss. This premiss, if it be in turn a conclusion, must be the conclusion of an argument containing at least one ethical premiss. And so we can go back, indefinitely but not forever. Sooner or later, we must come to at least one ethical premiss which is not deduced but baldly asserted. Here we must be a-rational; neither rational nor irrational, for here there is no room for reason even to go wrong.

But the triumph of Hume in ethics has been a limited one. What appears quite natural to a handful of specialists appears quite monstrous to the majority of decent intelligent men. At any rate, it has been my experience that people who are normally rational resist the above account of the logic of moral language, not by argument—for that can't be done—but by tooth and nail. And they resist from the best motives. They see the philosopher wantonly unravelling the whole fabric of morality. If our ultimate principles are arbitrary, they say, if those principles came out of thin air, then anyone can hold any principle he pleases. Unless moral assertions are statements of fact about the world and either true or false, we can't claim that any man is wrong, whatever his principles may be, whatever his behaviour. We have to surrender the luxury of calling one another scoundrels. That this anxiety flourishes because its roots are in confusion is evi-

° From Brian Medlin, "Ultimate Principles and Ethical Egoism," *Australasian Journal of Philosophy,* 35 (1957), pp. 111–118. Reprinted by permission of the *Australasian Journal of Philosophy.*

dent when we consider that we don't call people scoundrels, anyhow, for being mistaken about their facts. Fools, perhaps, but that's another matter. Nevertheless, it doesn't become us to be high-up. The layman's uneasiness, however irrational it may be, is very natural and he must be reassured.

People cling to objectivist theories of morality from moral motives. It's a very queer thing that by doing so they often thwart their own purposes. There are evil opinions abroad, as anyone who walks abroad knows. The one we meet with most often, whether in pub or parlour, is the doctrine that everyone should look after himself. However refreshing he may find it after the high-minded pomposities of this morning's editorial, the good fellow knows this doctrine is wrong and he wants to knock it down. But while he believes that moral language is used to make statements either true or false, the best he can do is to claim that what the egoist says is false. Unfortunately, the egoist can claim that it's true. And since the supposed fact in question between them is not a public ascertainable one, their disagreement can never be resolved. And it is here that even good fellows waver, when they find they have no refutation available. The egoist's word seems as reliable as their own. Some begin half to believe that perhaps it is possible to supply an egoistic basis for conventional morality, some that it may be impossible to supply any other basis. I'm not going to try to prop up our conventional morality, which I fear to be a task beyond my strength, but in what follows I do want to refute the doctrine of ethical egoism. I want to resolve this disagreement by showing that what the egoist says is inconsistent. It is true that there are moral disagreements which can never be resolved, but this isn't one of them. The proper objection to the man who says "Everyone should look after his own interests regardless of the interests of others" is not that he isn't speaking the truth, but simply that he isn't speaking.

We should first make two distinctions. This done, ethical egoism will lose much of its plausibility.

1. Universal and Individual Egoism

Universal egoism maintains that everyone (including the speaker) ought to look after his own interests and to disregard those of other people except in so far as their interests contribute towards his own.

Individual egoism is the attitude that the egoist is going to look after himself and no one else. The egoist cannot promulgate that he is going to look after himself. He can't even preach that he *should* look after himself and preach this alone. When he tries to convince me that he should look after himself, he is attempting so to dispose me that I shall approve when he drinks my beer and steals Tom's wife. I cannot approve of his looking after himself and himself alone without so far approving of his achieving his happiness, regardless of the happiness of myself and others. So that when he sets out to persuade me that he should look after himself regardless of others, he must also set out to persuade me that I should look after him regardless of myself and others. Very small chance he has! And if the individual egoist cannot promulgate his doctrine without enlarging it, what he has is no doctrine at all.

A person enjoying such an attitude may believe that other people are fools not to look after themselves. Yet he himself would be a fool to tell them so. If he did tell them, though, he wouldn't consider that he was giving them *moral* advice. Persuasion to the effect that one should ignore the claims of morality because morality doesn't pay, to the effect that one has insufficient selfish motive and, therefore, insufficient motive for moral behaviour is not moral persuasion. For this reason I doubt that we should call the individual egoist's attitude an ethical one. And I don't doubt this in the way someone may doubt whether to call the ethical standards of Satan "ethical" standards. A malign morality is none the less a morality for being malign. But the attitude we're considering is one of mere contempt for all moral considerations whatsoever. An indifference to morals may be wicked, but it is not a perverse morality. So far as I am aware, most egoists imagine that they are putting forward a doctrine in ethics, though there may be a few who are prepared to proclaim themselves individual egoists. If the good fellow wants to know how he should justify conventional morality to an individual egoist, the answer is that he shouldn't and can't. Buy your car elsewhere, blackguard him whenever you meet, and let it go at that.

2. Categorical and Hypothetical Egoism

Categorical egoism is the doctrine that we all ought to observe our own interests, *because that is what we ought to do.* For the categorical egoist the egoistic dogma is the ultimate principle in ethics.

The hypothetical egoist, on the other hand, maintains that we all ought to observe our own interests, because. . . . If we want such and such an end, we must do so and so (look after ourselves). The hypothetical egoist is not a real egoist at all. He is very likely an unwitting utilitarian who believes mistakenly that the general happiness will be increased if each man looks wisely to his own. Of course, a man may believe that egoism is enjoined on us by God and he may therefore promulgate the doctrine and observe it in his conduct, not in the hope of achieving thereby a remote end, but simply in order to obey God. But neither is *he* a real egoist. He believes, ultimately, that we should obey God, even should God command us to altruism.

An ethical egoist will have to maintain the doctrine in both its universal and categorical forms. Should he retreat to hypothetical egoism he is no longer an egoist. Should he retreat to individual egoism his doctrine, while logically impregnable, is no longer ethical, no longer even a doctrine. He may wish to quarrel with this and if so, I submit peacefully. Let him call himself what he will, it makes no difference. I'm a philosopher, not a rat-catcher, and I don't see it as my job to dig vermin out of such burrows as individual egoism.

Obviously something strange goes on as soon as the ethical egoist tries to promulgate his doctrine. What is he doing when he urges upon his audience that they should each observe his own interests and those interests alone? Is he not acting contrary to the egoistic principle? It cannot be to his advantage to convince them, for seizing always their own advantage they will impair his. Surely if he does believe what he says, he should try to persuade them otherwise. Not perhaps that they should devote themselves to his interests, for they'd hardly swallow that; but that everyone should devote himself to the service of others. But is not to believe that someone should act in a certain way to try to persuade him to do so? Of course, we don't always try to persuade people to act as we think they should act. We may be lazy, for instance. But in so far as we believe that Tom should do so and so, we have a tendency to induce him to do so and so. Does it make sense to say: "Of course you should do this, but for goodness' sake don't"? Only where we mean: "You should do this for certain reasons, but here are even more persuasive reasons for not doing it." If the egoist believes ultimately that others should mind themselves alone, then, he must persuade them accordingly. If he doesn't persuade them, he is no universal egoist. It certainly makes sense to say: "I know very well that Tom should act in such and such a way. But I know also that it's not to my advantage that he should so act. So I'd better dissuade him from it." And this is just what the egoist must say, if he is to consider his own advantage and disregard everyone else's. That is, he must behave as an individual egoist, if he is to be an egoist at all.

He may want to make two kinds of objection here:

(1) That it will not be to his disadvantage to promulgate the doctrine, provided that his audience fully understand what is to their ultimate advantage. This objection can be developed in a number of ways, but I think that it will always be possible to push the egoist into either individual or hypothetical egoism.

(2) That it is to the egoist's advantage to preach the doctrine if the pleasure he gets out of doing this more than pays for the injuries he must endure at the hands of his converts. It is hard to believe that many people would be satisfied with a doctrine which they could only consistently promulgate in very special circumstances. Besides, this looks suspiciously like individual egoism in disguise.

I shall say no more on these two points because I want to advance a further criticism which seems to me at once fatal and irrefutable.

Now it is time to show the anxious layman that we have means of dealing with ethical egoism which are denied him; and denied him by just that objectivism which he thinks essential to morality. For the very fact that our ultimate principles must be arbitrary means they can't be anything we please. Just because they come out of thin air they can't come out of hot air. Because these principles are not propositions about matters of fact and cannot be deduced from propositions about matters of fact, they must be the fruit of our own attitudes. We assert them largely to modify the attitudes of our fellows but by asserting them we express our own desires and purposes. This means that we cannot use moral language cavalierly. Evidently, we cannot say something like "All human desires and purposes are bad." This would be to express our own desires and purposes, thereby committing a kind of absurdity. Nor, I shall argue, can we say "Everyone should observe his own interests regardless of the interests of others."

Remembering that the principle is meant to be both universal and categorical, let us ask what kind of attitude the egoist is expressing. Wouldn't that attitude be equally well expressed by the conjunction of an infinite number of avowals thus?

I want myself to come out on top		I don't care about Tom, Dick, Harry . . .
	and	and
and		
I want Tom to come out on top		I don't care about myself, Dick, Harry . . .
	and	and
and		
I want Dick to come out on top		I don't care about myself, Tom, Harry . . .
	and	and
and		
I want Harry to come out on top		I don't care about myself, Dick, Tom . . .
	and	
etc.		etc.

From this analysis it is obvious that the principle expressing such an attitude must be inconsistent.

But now the egoist may claim that he hasn't been properly understood. When he says "Everyone should look after himself and himself alone," he means "Let each man do what he wants regardless of what anyone else wants." The egoist may claim that what he values is merely that he and Tom and Dick and Harry should each do what he wants and not care about what anyone else may want and that this doesn't involve his principle in any inconsistency. Nor need it. But even if it doesn't, he's no better off. Just what does he value? Is it the well-being of himself, Tom, Dick and Harry or merely their going on in a certain way regardless of whether or not this is going to promote their well-being? When he urges Tom, say, to do what he wants, is he appealing to Tom's self-interest? If so, his attitude can be expressed thus:

I want myself to be happy		I want myself not to care about Tom, Dick,
and	and	Harry . . .
I want Tom to be happy		

We need go no further to see that the principle expressing such an attitude must be inconsistent. I have made this kind of move already. What concerns me now is the alternative position the egoist must take up to be safe from it. If the egoist values merely that people should go on in a certain way, regardless of whether or not this is going to promote their well-being, then he is not appealing to the self-interest of his audience when he urges them to regard their own interests. If Tom has any regard for himself at all, the egoist's blandishments will leave him cold. Further, the egoist doesn't even have his own interest in mind when he says that, like everyone else, he should look after himself. A funny kind of egoism this turns out to be.

Perhaps now, claiming that he is indeed appealing to the self-interest of his audience, the egoist may attempt to counter the objection of the previous paragraph. He may move into "Let each man do what he wants and let each man disregard what others want when their desires clash with his own." Now his attitude may be expressed thus:

I want everyone to be happy	and	I want everyone to disregard the happiness of others when their happiness clashes with their own.

The egoist may claim justly that a man can have such an attitude and also that in a certain kind of world such a man could get what he wanted. Our objection to the egoist has been that his desires are incompatible. And this is still so. If he and Tom and Dick and Harry did go on as he recommends by saying "Let each man disregard the happiness of others, when their happiness conflicts with his own," then assuredly they'd all be completely miserable. Yet he wants them to be happy. He is attempting to counter this by saying that it is merely a fact about the world that they'd made one another miserable by going on as he recommends. The world could conceivably have been different. For this reason, he says, this principle is not inconsistent. This argument may not seem very compelling, but I advance it on the egoist's behalf because I'm interested in the reply to it. For now we don't even need to tell him that the world isn't in fact like that. (What it's like makes no difference.) Now we can point out to him that he is arguing not as an egoist but as a utilitarian. He has slipped into hypothetical egoism to save his principle from inconsistency. If the world were such that we always made ourselves and others happy by doing one another down, then we could find good utilitarian reasons for urging that we should do one another down.

If, then, he is to save his principle, the egoist must do one of two things. He must give up the claim that he is appealing to the self-interest of his audience, that he has even his own interest in mind. Or he must admit that, in the conjunction above, although "I want everyone to be happy" refers to ends, nevertheless "I want everyone to disregard the happiness of others when their happiness conflicts with his own" can refer only to means. That is, his so-called ultimate principle is really compounded of a principle and a moral rule subordinate to that principle. That is, he is really a utilitarian who is urging everyone to go on in a certain way so that everyone may be happy. A utilitarian, what's more, who is ludicrously mistaken about the nature of the world. Things being as they are, his moral rule is a very bad one. Things being as they are, it can only be deduced from his principle by means of an empirical premiss which is manifestly false. Good fellows don't need to fear him. They may rest easy that the world is and must be on their side and the best thing they can do is be good.

It may be worth pointing out that objections similar to those I have brought against the egoist can be made to the altruist. The man who holds that the principle "Let everyone observe the interests of others" is both universal and categorical can be compelled to choose between two alternatives, equally repugnant. He must give up the claim that he is concerned for the well-being of himself and others. Or he must admit that, though "I want everyone to be happy" refers to ends, nevertheless "I want everyone to disregard his own happiness when it conflicts with the happiness of others" can refer only to means.

I have said from time to time that the egoistic principle is inconsistent. I have not said it is contradictory. This for the reason that we can, without contradiction, express inconsistent desires and purposes. To do so is not to say anything like "Goliath was ten feet tall and not ten feet tall." Don't we all want to eat our cake and have it too? And when we say we do we aren't asserting a contradiction. We are not asserting a contradiction whether we be making an avowal of our attitudes or stating a fact about them. We all have conflicting motives. As a utilitarian exuding benevolence I want the man who mows my landlord's grass to be happy, but as a slugabed I should like to see him scourged. None of this, however, can do the egoist any good. For we assert our ultimate principles not only to express our own attitudes but also to induce similar attitudes in others, to dispose them to conduct themselves as we wish. In so far as their desires conflict, people don't know what to do. And, therefore, no expression of incompatible desires can ever serve for an ultimate principle of human conduct.

IN DEFENSE OF EGOISM *

JESSE KALIN

I

Ethical egoism is the view that it is morally right—that is, morally permissible, indeed, morally obligatory—for a person to act in his own self-interest, even when his self-interest conflicts or is irreconcilable with the self-interest of another. The point people normally have in mind in accepting and advocating this ethical principle is that of justifying or excusing their own self-interested actions by giving them a moral sanction.

This position is sometimes construed as saying that selfishness is moral, but such an interpretation is not quite correct. "Self-interest" is a general term usually used as a synonym for "personal happiness" and "personal welfare," and what would pass as selfish behavior frequently would not pass as self-interested behavior in this sense. Indeed, we have the suspicion that selfish people are characteristically, if not always, unhappy. Thus, in cases where selfishness tends to a person's unhappiness it is not in his self-interest, and as an egoist he ought not to be selfish. As a consequence, ethical egoism does not preclude other-interested, nonselfish, or altruistic behavior, as long as such behavior also leads to the individual's own welfare.

That the egoist may reasonably find himself taking an interest in others and promoting their welfare perhaps sounds nonegoistic, but it is not. Ethical egoism's justification of such behavior differs from other accounts in the following way: The ethical egoist acknowledges no general obligation to help people in need. Benevolence is never justified unconditionally or "categorically." The egoist has an obligation to promote the welfare only of those whom he likes, loves, needs, or can use. The source of this obligation is his interest in them. No interest, no obligation. And when his interest conflicts or is irreconcilable with theirs, he will reasonably pursue his own well-being at their expense, even when this other person is his wife, child, mother, or friend, as well as when it is a stranger or enemy.

Such a pursuit of one's own self-interest is considered *enlightened*. The name Butler provides for ethical egoism so interpreted is "cool self-love." [1]

* From Jesse Kalin, "In Defense of Egoism," *Morality and Rational Self-Interest* ed. by D. P. Gauthier (Englewood Cliffs, N.J.: Prentice-Hall, 1970), pp. 64–87. Reprinted by permission of Jesse Kalin, copyright owner.

[1] Butler, Joseph, *Fifteen Sermons Preached at the Rolls Chapel,* 1726. Standard anthologies of moral philosophy include the most important of these sermons; or see the Library of Liberal Arts Selection, *Five Sermons* (New York: The Bobbs-Merrill Company, Inc., 1950). See particularly Sermons I and XI. In XI, Butler says of rational self-love that "the object the former pursues is something internal—our own happiness, enjoyment, satisfaction . . . The principle we call "self-love" never seeks anything external for the sake of the thing, but only as a means of happiness or good." Butler is not, however, an egoist for there is also in man conscience and "a natural principle of benevolence" (see Sermon I).

On this view, a person is to harmonize his natural interests, perhaps cultivate some new interests, and optimize their satisfaction. Usually among
these interests will be such things as friendships and families (or perhaps
one gets his greatest kicks from working for UNICEF). And, of course, it is
a part of such enlightenment to consider the "long run" rather than just the
present and immediate future.

Given this account of ethical egoism plus the proper circumstances, a person could be morally justified in cheating on tests, padding expense accounts, swindling a business partner, being a slum landlord, draft-dodging,
lying, and breaking promises, as well as in contributing to charity, helping
friends, being generous or civic minded, and even undergoing hardship to
put his children through college. Judged from inside "standard morality," the
first actions would clearly be immoral, while the preceding paragraphs suggest the latter actions would be immoral as well, being done from a vicious
or improper motive.

With this informal account as background, I shall now introduce a formal
definition of ethical egoism, whose coherence will be the topic of the subsequent discussion:

(i) $(x)(y)(x$ ought to do y if and only if y is in x's overall self-interest)

In this formalization, "x" ranges over persons and "y" over particular actions, no kinds of action; "ought" has the sense "ought, all things considered."
(i) may be translated as: "A person ought to do a specific action, all
things considered, if and only if that action is in that person's overall (enlightened) self-interest."

(i) represents what Medlin calls "universal egoism." [2] The majority of
philosophers have considered universalization to be necessary for a sound
moral theory, though few have considered it sufficient. This requirement
may be expressed as follows: If it is reasonable for A to do s in C, it is
also reasonable for any similar person to do similar things in similar circumstances. Since everyone has a self-interest and since the egoist is arguing
that his actions are right simply because they are self-interested, it is intuitively plausible to hold that he is committed to regarding everyone as
morally similar and as morally entitled (or even morally obligated) to be
egoists. His claim that his own self-interested actions are right thus entails
the claim that all self-interested actions are right. If the egoist is to reject
this universalization, he must show that there are considerations in addition
to self-interest justifying his action, considerations making him relevantly
different from all others such that his self-interested behavior is justified

---

[2] Medlin, Brian, "Ultimate Principles and Ethical Egoism," *Australasian Journal of Philosophy*, XXXV (1957), 111–18; reprinted in this volume.

while theirs is not. I can't imagine what such considerations would be. In any case, egoism has usually been advanced and defended in its universalized form, and it is in this form that it will most repay careful examination. Thus, for the purposes of this paper, I shall assume without further defense the correctness of the universalization requirement.

It has also been the case that the major objections to ethical egoism have been derived from this requirement. Opponents have argued that once egoism is universalized, it can readily be seen to be incoherent. Frankena [3] and Medlin each advance an argument of this sort. In discussing their positions, I shall argue that the universalization of egoism given by (i) is coherent, that there is more than one type of "universalization," and that egoism can, in fact, be universalized in both senses. More importantly, I shall argue that the form of universalization presenting the most problems for the egoist is a form based upon a certain conception of value which the egoist can coherently reject. The result will be that egoism can with some plausibility be defended as an ultimate practical principle. At the least, if egoism is incorrect, this is not due to any incoherence arising from the universalization requirement.

II

One purpose of a moral theory is to provide criteria for first person moral judgments (such as "I ought to do *s* in C"); another purpose is to provide criteria for second and third person moral judgments (such as "Jones ought to do *s* in C"). Any theory which cannot coherently provide such criteria must be rejected as a moral theory. Can ethical egoism do this? Frankena argues that it cannot.

Frankena formulates egoism as consisting of two principles:

(a) If A is judging about himself, then A is to use this criterion: A ought to do *y* if and only if *y* is in A's overall self-interest.
(b) If A is a spectator judging about anyone else, B, then A is to use this criterion: B ought to do *y* if and only if *y* is in A's overall self-interest.

Frankena thinks that [(a) & (b)] is the only interpretation of (i) "consistent with the spirit of ethical egoism."

But isn't it the case that (a) and (b) taken together produce contradictory moral judgments about an important subset of cases, namely, those where people's self-interests conflict or are irreconcilable? If this is so, egoism as formulated by Frankena is incoherent and must be rejected.

To illustrate, let us suppose that B does *s*, and that *s* is in B's overall self-interest, but not in A's. Is *s* right or wrong? Ought, or ought not B do *s*? The answer depends on who is making the judgment. If A is making the

[3] Frankena, William, *Ethics* (Englewood Cliffs, New Jersey; Prentice-Hall, Inc., 1963), pp. 16–18. References to Frankena in sections II and V are to this book.

judgment, then "B ought not to do *s*" is correct. If B is making the judgment, then "B ought to do *s*" is correct. And, of course, when both make judgments, both "B ought to do *s*" and "B ought not to do *s*" are correct. Surely any principle which has this result as a possibility is incoherent.

This objection may be put another way. The ethical egoist claims that there is one ultimate moral principle applicable to everyone. This is to claim that (i) is adequate for all moral issues, and that all applications of it can fit into a logically coherent system. Given the above illustration, "B ought to do *s*" does follow from (a), and "B ought not to do *s*" does follow from (b), but the fact that they cannot coherently be included in a set of judgments shows that (a) and (b) are not parts of the same ultimate moral principle. Indeed, these respective judgments can be said to follow from a moral principle at all only if they follow from *different* moral principles. Apparently, the ethical egoist must choose between (i)'s parts if he is to have a coherent ethical system, but he can make no satisfactory choice. If (a) is chosen, second and third person judgments become impossible. If (b) is chosen, first person judgments become impossible. His moral theory, however, must provide for both kinds of judgment. Ethical egoism needs what it logically cannot have. Therefore, it can only be rejected.

The incompatibility between (a) and (b) and the consequent incoherence of (i) manifests itself in still a third way. Interpreted as a system of judgments, [(a) & (b)] is equivalent to: Everyone ought to pursue A's self-interest, and everyone ought to pursue B's self-interest, and everyone ought to pursue C's self-interest, and. . . .[4] When the interests of A and B are incompatible, one must pursue both of these incompatible goals, which, of course, is impossible. On this interpretation, ethical egoism must fail in its function of guiding conduct (one of the most important uses of moral judgments). In particular, it must fail with respect to just those

---

[4] This can be shown as follows:

i. Suppose A is the evaluator, then
What ought A to do? A ought to do what's in A's interest. (by (a))
What ought B to do? B ought to do   "   (by (b))
What ought C to do? C ought to do   "   (by (b))
etc. ·
Therefore, everyone ought to do what's in A's interest. (by (a) & (b))
ii. Suppose B is the evaluator, then
What ought A to do? A ought to do what's in B's interest. (by (b))
What ought B to do? B ought to do   "   (by (a))
What ought C to do? C ought to do   "   (by (b))
etc.
Therefore, everyone ought to do what's in B's interest. (by (a) & (b))
iii. Suppose C is the evaluator, then
.
.
.
etc.
Conclusion: Everyone ought to do what's in A's interest, and everyone ought to do what's in B's interest, and . . . *etc.*

cases for which the guidance is most wanted—conflicts of interests. In such situations, the theory implies that one must both do and not do a certain thing. Therefore, since ethical egoism cannot guide conduct in these crucial cases, it is inadequate as a moral theory and must be rejected.

Ethical egoism suffers from three serious defects if it is interpreted as [(a) & (b)]. These defects are closely related. The first is that the theory implies a contradiction, namely, that some actions are both right *and* wrong. The second defect is that the theory, if altered and made coherent by rejecting one of its parts, cannot fulfill one of its essential tasks: Altered, it can provide for first person moral judgments *or* for second and third person moral judgments, but not for both. The third defect is that the theory cannot guide conduct and must fail in its advice-giving function because it advises (remember: advises, all things considered) a person to do what it advises him not to do.

Any one of these defects would be sufficient to refute the theory, and indeed they do refute ethical egoism when it is defined as [(a) & (b)]. The only plausible way to escape these arguments is to abandon Frankena's definition and reformulate egoism so that they are no longer applicable. Clearly, (a) must remain, for it seems central to any egoistic position. However, we can replace (b) with the following:

(c) If A is a spectator judging about anyone else, B, then A is to use this criterion: B ought to do *y* if and only if *y* is in B's overall self-interest.

The objections to [(a) & (b)] given above do not apply to [(a) & (c)]. [(a) & (c)] yields no contradictions, even in cases where self-interests conflict or are irreconcilable. When we suppose that B is the agent, that *s* is in B's overall self-interest, and that *s* is against A's overall self-interest, both B and A will agree in their moral judgments about this case, that is, both will agree that B ought to do *s*. And, of course, the theory provides for all moral judgments, whether first, second, or third person; since it yields no contradictions, there is no need to make it coherent by choosing between its parts and thereby making it inadequate.

Finally, this interpretation avoids the charge that ethical egoism cannot adequately fulfill its conduct guiding function. Given [(a & (c)], it will never truly be the case that an agent ought to pursue anyone's self-interest except his own. Any judgment of the form "A ought to pursue B's self-interest" will be false, unless it is understood to mean that pursuit of B's self-interest is a part of the pursuit of A's self-interest (and this, of course, would not contribute to any incoherence in the theory). Thus, the theory will have no difficulty in being an effective practical theory; it will not give contradictory advice, even in situations where interests conflict. True, it will not remove such conflicts—indeed, in practice it might well encourage them; but a conflict is not a contradiction. The theory tells A to pursue a certain goal, and it tells B to pursue another goal, and does this unequivocally.

That both cannot succeed in their pursuits is irrelevant to the coherence of the theory and its capacity to guide conduct, since both *can* do what they are advised to do, all things considered—pursue their own self-interests.

(i), when interpreted as [(a) & (c)], is a fully objective moral theory. Therefore, in defending ethical egoism, one need not be driven into the kind of subjectivism which holds that "right," "wrong," "morally justified," and even "true" when used in a moral argument or judgment always mean "right for A," or "right for B," or "wrong for A," or "true for B," or perhaps "right from A's point of view," "wrong from B's point of view," etc.[5] Such usage would be exceedingly peculiar, for in what sense can a judgment or action be said to be justified, all things considered, if it is justified for me and unjustified for you? Thus, interpreting ethical egoism as [(a) & (c)] rather than as [(a) & (b)] has the great merit of making it possible to avoid the temptation to subjectivism.

There remains the question whether [(a) & (c)] is a plausible interpretation of (i), that is, whether it is "consistent with the spirit of ethical egoism." It is certainly consistent with the "spirit" behind the "ethical" part of egoism in its willingness to universalize the doctrine. It is also consistent with the "egoistic" part of the theory in that if a person does faithfully follow (a) he will behave as an egoist. Adding the fact that [(a) & (c)] is a coherent theory adequate to the special ethical chores so far discussed, do we have any reason for rejecting it as an interpretation of (i) and ethical egoism? So far, I think not. Therefore, I conclude that Frankena has failed to refute egoism. It has thus far survived the test of universalization and still remains as a candidate for "the one true moral theory."

III

In his article, "Ultimate Principles and Ethical Egoism," Brian Medlin maintains that ethical egoism cannot be an ultimate moral principle because it fails to guide our actions, tell us what to do, or determine our choice between alternatives.[6] He bases this charge on his view that because ethical egoism is the expression of inconsistent desires, it will always tell people to do incompatible things. Thus:

I have said from time to time that the egoistic principle is inconsistent. I have not said it is contradictory. This for the reason that we can, without contradiction, express inconsistent desires and purposes. To do so is not to say anything like "Goliath was ten feet tall and not ten feet tall." Don't we all want to have our cake and eat it too? And when we say we do we aren't asserting a contradiction whether we be making an avowal of our attitudes or stating a fact about them. We all have conflicting motives. None of this, however, can do the egoist

---

[5] As is Gardner Williams in his *Humanistic Ethics* (New York: Philosophical Library, 1951), see Chapter III, particularly pp. 29–31.
[6] All references to Medlin are to the reprint in this volume.

any good. For we assert our ultimate principles not only to express our own attitudes but also to induce similar attitudes in others, to dispose them to conduct themselves as we wish. In so far as their desires conflict, people don't know what to do. And, therefore, no expression of incompatible desires can ever serve for an ultimate principle of human conduct.

That egoism could not successfully guide one's conduct was a criticism discussed and rebutted in section II. There, it rested upon Frankena's formulation of egoism as equal to [(a) & (b)] and was easily circumvented by replacing principle (b) with principle (c). Medlin's charge is significant, however, because it appears to be applicable to [(a) & (c)] as well [7] and therefore must be directly refuted if egoism is to be maintained.

The heart of Medlin's argument is his position that to affirm a moral principle is to express approval of any and all actions following from that principle. This means for Medlin not only that the egoist is committed to approving all egoistic actions but also that such approval will involve wanting those actions to occur and trying to bring them about, even when they would be to one's own detriment.

But is not to believe that someone should act in a certain way to try to persuade him to do so? Of course, we don't always try to persuade people to act as we think they should act. We may be lazy, for instance. But insofar as we believe that Tom should do so and so, we have a tendency to induce him to do so and so. Does it make sense to say: "Of course you should do this, but for goodness' sake don't"? Only where we mean: "You should do this for certain reasons, but here are even more persuasive reasons for not doing it." If the egoist believes ultimately that others should mind themselves alone, then, he must persuade them accordingly. If he doesn't persuade them, he is no universal egoist.

---

[7] Medlin himself does not distinguish between (b) and (c). Some of his remarks suggest (c). Thus, at one point he says:

When he [the egoist] tries to convince me that he should look after himself, he is attempting so to dispose me that I shall approve when he drinks my beer and steals Tom's wife. I cannot approve of his looking after himself and himself alone without so far approving of his achieving his happiness, regardless of the happiness of myself and others.

This passage implies that as a spectator assessing another's conduct, I should employ principle (c) and approve of A's doing y whenever y promotes A's interest, even if this is at the expense of my welfare.

But other of his remarks suggest (b). Thus, the above passage continues:

So that when he sets out to persuade me that he should look after himself regardless of others, he must also set out to persuade me that I should look after him regardless of myself and others. Very small chance he has!

Here, the implication is that the egoist as spectator and judge of another should assess the other's behavior according to his own interests, not the other's, which would be in accordance with (b).

Perhaps Medlin is arguing that the egoist is committed to accepting both (b) and (c), as well as (a). This interpretation is consistent with his analysis of "approval."

According to Medlin, if I adopt ethical egoism and am thereby led to approve of A's egoistic actions (as would follow from (c)), I must also *want* A to behave in that way and must want him to be happy, to come out on top, and so forth where wanting is interpreted as setting an end for my own actions and where it tends (according to the intensity of the want, presumably) to issue in my "looking after him."

Of course, I will also approve of my pursuing my own welfare (as would follow from (a)) and will want myself to be happy, to come out on top, and so forth. Since I want my own success, I will want A's noninterference. Indeed, what I will want A to do, and will therefore approve of A's doing, is to pursue my welfare, rather than his own.

It is thus the case that whenever my interest conflicts with A's interest, I will approve of inconsistent ends and will want incompatible things ("I want myself to come out on top and I want Tom to come out on top," . . .). Since I approve of incompatible ends, I will be motivated in contrary directions—both away from and toward my own welfare, for instance. However, this incompatibility of desires is not sufficient to produce inaction and does not itself prove Medlin's point, for one desire may be stronger than the other. If the egoist's approval of his own well-being were always greater than his approval of anyone else's well-being, the inconsistent desires constituting egoism would not prevent (i) from decisively guiding conduct. Unfortunately for the egoist, his principle will in fact lead him to inaction, for in being universal (i) expresses equal approval of each person's pursuing his own self-interest, and therefore, insofar as his desires follow from this principle, none will be stronger than another.

We can now explain Medlin's conclusion that "the proper objection to the man who says 'Everyone should look after his own interests regardless of the interests of others' is not that he isn't speaking the truth, but simply that he isn't speaking." . . . Upon analysis, it is clear that the egoist is "saying" that others should act so that he himself comes out on top and should not care about Tom, Dick, *et al.*, but they should also act so that Tom comes out on top and should not care about himself, Dick, the others, and so forth. . . . This person *appears* to be saying how people should act, and that they should act in a definite way. But his "directions" can guide no one. They give one nothing to do. Therefore, such a man has in fact said nothing.

I think Medlin's argument can be shown to be unsuccessful without a discussion of the emotivism in which it is framed. The egoist can grant that there is a correct sense in which affirmation of a moral principle is the expression of approval. The crux of the issue is Medlin's particular analysis of approbation, and this can be shown to be incorrect.

We may grant that the egoist is committed to approving of anyone's egoistic behavior at least to the extent of believing that the person ought so to behave. Such approval will hold of all egoistic actions, even those that endanger his own welfare. But does believing that A ought to do *y* commit one to wanting A to do y? Surely not. This is made clear by the analogy with competitive games. Team A has no difficulty in believing that team B ought to make or try to make a field goal while not wanting team B to succeed, while hoping that team B fails, and, indeed, while trying to prevent team B's success. Or consider this example: I may see how my chess opponent can put my king in check. That is how he ought to move. But believing that he ought to move his bishop and check my king does not commit me to wanting him to do that, nor to persuading him to do so. What I ought to do is sit there quietly, hoping he does not move as he ought.

Medlin's mistake is to think that believing that A ought to do y commits one to *wanting* A to do y and hence to encouraging or otherwise helping A to do y. The examples from competitive games show that this needn't be so. The egoist's reply to Medlin is that just as team A's belief that team B ought to do so and so is compatible with their not wanting team B to do so and so, so the egoist's belief that A ought to do y is compatible with the egoist's not wanting A to do y. Once this is understood, egoism has no difficulty in decisively guiding conduct, for insofar as (i) commits the egoist to wanting anything, it only commits him to wanting his own welfare. Since he does not want incompatible goals, he has no trouble in deciding what to do according to (a) and in judging what others ought to do according to (c).

IV

There is in Medlin's paper confusion concerning what the egoist wants or values and why he believes in ethical egoism. The egoist does not believe that everyone ought to pursue their own self-interest merely because *he* wants to get *his* goodies out of life. If this were all there were to his position, the egoist would not bother with (i) or with moral concepts at all. He would simply go about doing what he wants. What reason, then, does he have to go beyond wanting his own welfare to ethical egoism? On Medlin's emotivist account, his reason must be that he also wants B to have B's goodies, and wants D to have his, and so forth, even when it is impossible that everybody be satisfied. But I argued in the preceding section that the egoist is not committed to wanting such states, and that it is not nonsense for him to affirm (i) and desire his own welfare yet not desire the welfare of others. Therefore, the question remains—why affirm egoism at all?

The egoist's affirmation of (i) rests upon both teleological and deontological elements. What *he* finds to be of ultimate value is his own welfare. He needn't be selfish or egocentric in the ordinary sense (as Medlin sometimes suggests by such paraphrases as "Let each man do what he wants regardless of what anyone else wants," . . .), but he will value his own interest above that of others. Such an egoist would share Sidgwick's view that when "the painful necessity comes for another man to choose between his own happiness and the general happiness, he must as a reasonable being prefer his own." [8] When this occasion does arise, the egoist will want the other's welfare less than he wants his own, and this will have the practical effect of not wanting the other's welfare at all. It is in terms of this personal value that he guides his actions, judging that he ought to do y if and only if y is in his overall self-interest. This is the teleological element in his position.

However, there is no reason that others should find his well-being to be of value to them, less more to be of ultimate value; and it is much more likely that each will find his own welfare to be his own ultimate value. But if it is reasonable for the egoist to justify his behavior in terms of what he finds to be of ultimate value, then it is also reasonable for others to justify their behavior in terms of what they find to be of ultimate value. This follows from the requirement of universalization and provides the deontological element. Interpreted as "Similar things are right for similar people in similar circumstances," the universalization principle seems undeniable. Failing to find any relevant difference between himself and others, the egoist must admit that it can be morally permissible for him to pursue his self-interest only if it is morally permissible for each person to pursue his self-interest. He therefore finds himself committed to (i), even though he does not *want* others to compete with him for life's goods.

Medlin and others have not construed egoism in this way. While they have acknowledged the role of deontological considerations in the production of (i) by noting the universalization requirement, they have given more emphasis to its teleological aspects. In particular, they have thought that at the least (i) states that a certain state of affairs is intrinsically valuable and *therefore* ought to be brought about. If this is so, to affirm the principle is to accept this set of values. Medlin then argues that an egoist cannot accept these values and remain a consistent egoist. He asks of the ethical egoist: "Just what does he value? Is it the well-being of himself, Tom, Dick, and Harry or merely their going on in a certain way regardless of whether or not this is going to promote their well-being?"

Consider this latter alternative and the result if everyone were to follow (i) and behave as the egoist claims it is most reasonable for them to do. We would have a state wherein everyone disregarded the happiness of others when their happiness clashed with one's own. . . . Given the normal condition of the world in which the major goods requisite for well-being (food, clothing, sex, glory, *etc.*) are not in overabundance, we would have a state of competition, struggle, and probably much avoidable misery. Hobbes' overstatement is that it would be a "war of everyman against everyman" in which life is "solitary, poor, nasty, brutish, and short."

---

[8] Henry Sidgwick, *The Methods of Ethics,* 7th ed. (London: Macmillan and Co., 1907), preface to the 6th edition, p. xvii.

Since Medlin holds that acceptance of a moral principle such as (i) rests on valuing that state of affairs which compliance to the principle would bring about, and that acceptance of this principle as ultimate rests on placing ultimate value on that state of affairs (on wanting that state more than any other), it is understandable that ethical egoism should appear to him to be "a funny kind of egoism."

Medlin's point is that a person valuing such a state of affairs is no longer an egoist in any natural sense of that term. An egoist values his own welfare. But the Hobbesian conditions described above include this value only incidentally, if at all. To make his position consistent, therefore, he must choose between the following alternatives. He can accept the actual values promoted by his theory. Since these are not egoistic values (confirmed by the fact that he could not convince others to value and promote such a state of affairs by appealing solely to their self-interest, . . .), this is to abandon egoism. Or he can accept self-interest as the ultimate value which, because of the universalization requirement, will involve accepting each person's self-interest as of equal value. This will be to abandon egoism and (i) for a form of utilitarianism.

Medlin's crucial charge against ethical egoism is not that it is incoherent or unable to fulfill the necessary functions of a moral theory such as decisively guiding conduct in cases where interests conflict, but that principle (i) is simply not an expression of egoism. Egoism is an unformulable moral theory, and hence *no* moral theory.[9] This charge rests, however, on what I shall call the material conception of value. Medlin's criticism rests on the assumption that ethical egoism (*i.e.*, principle (i)) is saying that there is something of intrinsic value which everyone ought to pursue—that there is one specific state of affairs everyone ought to pursue. This is false, and is the result of not distinguishing *material* valuations from what I shall call *formal* valuations.

In analyzing the teleological basis of (i), Medlin and others have been misled by imposing on the egoist a conception of intrinsic or ultimate value which he does not hold. They suppose that there is *one* value or set of values which is or ought to be *common* to everyone (or they suppose that principles like (i) express the desire that such a set of values be common to everyone). It is characteristic of this position that these values are of such a nature that everyone ought to promote them; they are objective and binding upon everyone. It is in terms of this common goal that each person's actions are to be guided and justified. Furthermore, these values demand and establish a harmony and concert among men's actions. There is some each, some state of affairs, perhaps quite complex, the establishment of which is the goal of all moral actions. The task of a moral theory, and par-

---

[9] The egoist "must behave as an individual egoist, if he is to be an egoist at all," but since "the individual egoist cannot promulgate his doctrine without enlarging it, what he has is no doctrine at all."

ticularly of any ultimate moral principle, is to direct one to such a goal. I call this view the *material conception of value*.

In utilitarianism, the single, though hardly simple, material value is the state of maximum social welfare—"the greatest happiness of the greatest number," "people being as happy as it is possible to make them," or some such variant. For Moore, it is a state in which there is a maximum of intrinsic goods—that is, of pleasure, knowledge, love, the enjoyment of beauty, moral qualities, and so forth.[10] On his view, Jones' pleasure is as valuable as my pleasure, and I have the same obligation to bring about that pleasure as Jones does. Supremacy of the state views are further instances of this conception, as is the view that each man is an end in himself and as such entitled to one's respent, where one sign of this respect is acting always so that any other being could share the ends of one's actions.

The egoist would replace this standard view with the *formal conception of value*. On this account, that which is to have ultimate value for different people will usually be the same only in the sense that it is the same *kind* of good but not the same particular instance of it. What is valued will be similar but normally not identical. In the statement, "Self-interest is the ultimate good," "self-interest" is used in a generic sense. What is specifically valued—the various contents of these self-interests—is quite different from person to person and sometimes mutually incompatible. What the egoist is saying, of course, is that his welfare has ultimate (or intrinsic) value to himself, though not to anyone else, and that Tom's welfare has ultimate (or intrinsic) value to Tom, but not to himself or others, and that Harry's welfare has ultimate value to Harry, but not. . . , and so forth. He is saying that his interests give him a reason for acting but give Tom and Harry none, and that Tom's interests give Tom a reason for acting but give him and Harry none, and that. . . , and so forth. Here, there is no common value shared by the egoist, Tom, Harry, *et al.*, unless by accident.

According to a teleological moral theory, what a person ought to do is maximize the good or ultimate value, whatever that might be. If ultimate value is understood in the material sense, one will naturally believe that everyone has an obligation to bring about the same particular state of affairs. And since the egoist says everyone ought to act in a certain way, one will assume that this is because there is something ultimately valuable about everyone acting in that way. This would be a mistake. A moral theory may be teleological in terms of merely formal values. Nothing stronger is necessary. One can agree that people ought to maximize the good, but maintain that there is nothing which is good to everyone. Thus, people will be justified in pursuing somewhat different states, and possibly come into conflict. Moral principles will not have the objective of establishing a concert and harmony among men's actions nor of expressing a common goal.

---

[10] Moore, G. E., *Ethics* (London: Oxford University Press, 1912), Chapter VII, "Intrinsic Value," see especially pp. 140, 146–47, 152–53.

(i), in particular, will not have as its purpose the promotion of material values. If everyone does follow (i), states highly disvaluable to some will result, and there is no assurance that the egoist will succeed in maximizing value for himself.

In the previous section, I argued that the egoist's belief that other egoists ought to act in a way harmful to himself could be understood by noting similar beliefs in competitive games. We can likewise understand how the egoist can construct a coherent moral system not essentially dependent on material values by noting that practical systems such as professional football can be explained and justified without assuming a set of ultimate values common to all the parties encompassed by them. Thus, the player's ultimate values are, let us say, winning and being superior, money (for themselves), the satisfaction of playing the game, and glory; the owner's values are money (for *themselves*), promotion of civic or business enterprises, and winning and being superior; the spectator's values are the pleasures of watching the game and being a fan, both aesthetic and more visceral; the official's values are money (for themselves), and perhaps other goods such as superiority or "love of the game." These values are virtually all only formally the same; but their pursuit by the respective parties is sufficient to produce the game. The players' interests, for instance, do not have to be shared or even mutually compatible—only one team can win, glory is a scarce good requiring the defeat of others, and so forth. One player need not care about the others, or the spectators, except in so far as they figure *as means* necessary to his ends. Since he cannot win, or make a fortune, or even play football without others playing too, he must get together with them to form a league with all its paraphernalia. But even with such cooperation, the ultimate values Tom the football player is pursuing are quite different materially from those pursued by Harry the football player, though probably of the same kind. Similarly, acceptance of the egoist principle requires no more of a commitment to common material values than acceptance of the competitive game does, that is, none.

We began this section with a question suggested by Medlin: Why does the egoist believe that everyone ought to pursue his own self-interest rather than believe that everyone ought to pursue *his* self-interest or simply going off to get his own? Medlin thought that the egoist could not coherently maintain (i) and remain an egoist—that he must in fact simply go off to get his own. I have argued that he can, and have tried to answer Medlin's question as follows: The egoist finds that his own self-interest gives him a reason to act in certain ways, but he does not think that this self-interest *per se* gives any other person a reason to act. Self-interest is an ultimate good in the formal but not the material sense. He therefore holds that what *he* ought to do, all things considered (what it would be most reasonable for him to do), is pursue his own self-interest, even to the harming of others when necessary. But he further acknowledges that if this form of reasoning is sufficient to justify his egoistic behavior, it is sufficient to justify anyone's, or everyone's egoistic behavior. Consequently, he will accept the universalization of his position to "For each person, it is most reasonable for him to pursue his own self-interest, even to the harming of others if necessary," or to "(x) (y) (x ought to do y if and only if y is in x's overall self-interest)." While this is a teleological moral principle because it states that a person ought to maximize value, it is a mistake to think that it points to one particular state of affairs which is valuable and which *therefore* ought to be promoted by everyone. Such a mistake is based on the failure to distinguish between material and formal valuations. Because (i) establishes other's welfare as valuable only in the formal sense, the egoist can affirm (i) without being committed to accepting either their welfare or Hobbesian-like conditions of competition as valuable, thus avoiding Medlin's dilemma.

V

Medlin remarks that the egoist would be a fool to tell other people they should "look after themselves and no one else." . . . He goes on to say:

> Obviously something strange goes on as soon as the ethical egoist tries to promulgate his doctrine. What is he doing when he urges upon his audience that they should each observe his own interests and those interests alone? Is he not acting contrary to the egoistic principle? It cannot be to his advantage to convince them, for seizing always their own advantage they will impair his.

So far as Medlin is concerned, I discussed this "strange" aspect of egoism when I argued that it was not necessary either to want or to urge another to do what he ought to do in order to believe that he ought to do it. Behind Medlin's requirement of promulgation was seen to be a commitment to the material conception of value. The difficulties such a commitment entail for the egoist can be avoided if he uses only formal valuations. Thus, Medlin has failed to show that the egoist must violate his principle in the very holding of it because he has failed to show that the egoist *must* promulgate that principle *if* he holds it.

At this point, many philosophers would argue that ethical egoism is an even stranger doctrine than Medlin supposes if it can be consistently held only when it is silently held. In this section, I shall examine their argument. We shall first look at what the egoist must abandon along with the requirement of promulgation. It appears as though this must include most of the activities and emotions characterizing morality as such. According to its critics, this would mean that ethical egoism was not a moral theory. We shall then consider the egoist's reply to this criticism.

Taking the long run fully into account, the egoist must hold his position silently if he is to remain prudent. This restriction is more serious than might be suspected, for it means the egoist must refrain not only from advocating his doctrine, but also from a wide range of behavior typical of any morality. For instance, he will not be able to enter into moral discussions, at least not sincerely or as an egoist, for to debate a moral issue will ultimately require him to argue for (i). This will not be to his interest for at least the reason that others will become suspicious of him and cease to trust him. They will learn he is an egoist and treat him accordingly. It would be even worse if he should win the debate and convince them.

Nor will he be able to give or receive moral advice. If it is objected that he can advise others as long as interests do not conflict, it will do to note that it is not to his interest to have his egoistic views known. Giving of advice involves giving reasons for certain actions; inquiries about the moral principle upon which that advice is based are therefore appropriate. Of course, the egoist can lie. When Harry comes to Tom about his affair with Dick's wife, Tom can approve, professing enlightened views about marriage, noting that there are no children, that both are adults, and so forth, although he knows Harry's behavior will soon lead to a scandal ruining Harry's career—all to Tom's advantage. Tom has advised Harry, but not sincerely; he has not told Harry *what he thinks Harry really ought to do*—what would be most in Harry's overall self-interest. And Tom ought not, since he himself is following (i). This all goes to make the point; the egoist is not sincerely advising Harry, but rather pretending to sincerely advise him while really deceiving and manipulating him.

This use of advice—to manipulate others—is limited, and perhaps bought at a price too great for the egoist to pay. Since advising is a public activity, urging others to be benevolent (in order to benefit from their actions) gives them grounds to require one to be benevolent toward them, and thus to create sanctions restricting the scope of his self-interested behavior.

Worst of all, it will do the egoist himself no good to *ask* for moral advice for he is bound not to get what he wants. If he asks nonegoists, he will be told to do things which might be in his self-interest, but usually won't be. What sort of help could he get from a Kantian or a utilitarian? Their advice will follow from the wrong moral principle. If he asks another egoist, he is no better off, since he cannot be trusted. Knowing that he is an egoist, he knows that he is following (a), acting in his own self-interest, and lying if he can benefit from it. The egoist is truly isolated from any moral community, and must always decide and act alone, without the help of others.

It will not be to the egoist's self-interest to support his moral principle with sanctions. He will be unable to praise those who do what they ought, unable to blame those who flagrantly shirk their moral tasks. Nor will he be able to establish institutions of rewards and punishments founded on his principle. The egoist cannot sincerely engage in any of these activities. He will punish or blame people for doing what they ought not to do (for doing what is not in their self-interests) only by coincidence and then under some other rubric than violation of (i). To punish people for not being egoists is to encourage them to be egoists, and this is not to his interest. Similarly, the egoist, if he engages in such an activity at all, will praise people for doing what they ought to do only by chance, and always under a different, nonegoistic label.

A corollary to this is the egoist's inability to teach (i) to his children (while himself following it). It is imprudent to raise egoistic children, since among other things, the probability of being abandoned in old age is greatly increased. Therefore, the egoist can give his children no sincere moral instruction, and most likely will be advised to teach them to disapprove of his actions and his character, should they become aware of their true nature.

Finally, one of the points of appealing to a moral principle is to justify one's behavior *to others*—to convince them that their (sometimes forcible) opposition to this behavior is unwarranted and ought to be withdrawn. When we do convince someone of the rightness of our actions, he normally comes onto our side, even if reluctantly. Thus, the teenage daughter tries to convince her father that it is right and proper for sixteen year old girls to stay out until 12:30 (rather than 11:00) because if she is successful and he agrees with her, he then has *no excuse* (other things being equal) for still withholding his permission. For an ethical egoist, this point is doomed to frustration for two reasons: first, because justifying one's behavior in terms of (i) gives an opponent no reason to cease his opposition if maintaining it would be in his own interest; and second, because it will not be to the egoist's interest to publicly justify his behavior to others on egoistic grounds, thereby running the risk of converting them to egoism. Therefore, the egoist is unable to engage in *interpersonal reasoning* with his moral principle as its basis—he can neither justify nor excuse his egoistic actions as such in the interpersonal sense of "justify" and "excuse."

Adherence to the egoistic principle makes it impossible, because imprudent, for one to sincerely engage in any of these moral activities. There are also typical moral attitudes and emotions which, while perhaps not impossible for an egoist to sincerely have, it is impossible for him to sincerely express. I have in mind remorse, regret, resentment, repentance, forgiveness, revenge, outrage and indignation, and the form of sympathy known as moral support. Let us take forgiveness. When can the egoist forgive another, and for what? One forgives the other's wrongs, wrongs which are normally done against oneself. First, it is hard to see how someone could wrong someone else given ethical egoism, for (i) gives one no obligations to others, and hence no way of shirking those obligations. At least, one has no such obligations directly. Second, what is the nature of the wrong action which is to be forgiven? It must be a failure to properly pursue self-interest. Suppose Harry makes this lapse. Can Tom forgive him? In so far as such forgiveness involves nonexpressed beliefs and attitudes, yes. But Tom would be unwise to express this attitude or to forgive Harry in the fuller, public sense. Partly because if their interests conflict, Tom's good will involve Harry's harm; Tom does not want Harry to do what he ought, and Tom ought not to encourage him to do so, which would be involved in overtly forgiving him. And partly because of the general imprudence of making it known that one is an egoist, which would be involved in expressing forgiveness of nonegoistic behavior. If the egoist is to forgive people where this involves the expression of forgiveness, his doing so must be basically insincere.

Similar considerations hold for the expression of the other emotions and attitudes mentioned. As for those which are not so clearly dependent upon some manner of public expression, such as resentment and remorse, it is perhaps not impossible for the egoist to have them (or to be capable of having them), but it is clear that their objects and occasion will be quite different from what they are in the standard morality. Resentment as a moral attitude involves taking offense at someone's failure to do what they ought. But why should the egoist be offended if other people don't look after their interests, at least when their interests are not connected with his own? And when their interests are connected, the offense does not arise from the fact that the other did something wrong—failed to properly pursue his own interests—but because of the further and undesirable consequences of this failure, but consequences for which that person was not liable. Resentment here is very strange, all the more so because of the formal rather than material commitment of the egoist to the obligation to pursue one's own self-interest. Since he doesn't value others' doing what they ought, any resentment he feels must be slight and rather abstract, amounting to little more than the belief that they ought not to behave that way.

Granting that it would not be in his overall self-interest for others to be egoists too, the ethical egoist has compelling reasons not to engage sincerely in any of the activities mentioned above, as well as not to give expression to various typical moral attitudes and emotions. This is strange not because the egoist is in some sense required to promulgate his doctrine while at the same time faithfully follow it, for we saw above that he can coherently reject this demand, but strange because his position seems to have lost most of the features characterizing a morality. When put into practice, ethical egoism discards the moral activities of advocacy, moral discussion, giving and asking of advice, using sanctions to reward and punish, praising and blaming, moral instruction and training, and interpersonal excusing and justification, as well as the expressing of many moral attitudes and emotions. With these features gone, what remains that constitutes a morality? The egoist may, indeed, have a coherent practical system, but since it lacks certain major structural features of a morality, it is not a *moral theory*. Consider a legal theory which, when put into practice, turns out to have neither trials, nor judges, nor juries, nor sentencing, nor penal institutions, nor legislating bodies. Could it still be a legal theory and lack all of these? Isn't the case similar with ethical egoism?

If the above account is correct, its conclusion would be that egoism is a coherent practical theory, able to guide behavior and provide for the critical assessment of the actions of others without contradiction, but simply not a moral theory of conduct. Many philosophers would agree to the basis of this conclusion—that a theory lacking the wide range of typical moral activities and expressions that egoism lacks is not a moral theory—among them Frankena and Medlin. On their views, a morality must be interpersonal in character—if it is not interpersonal through a commitment to material values, at least interpersonal through a commitment to the various public activities mentioned, and perhaps to methods of carrying them out which will tend toward producing harmonious, if not common, values. Since the egoist is committed to a noninterpersonal morality, a private not public morality, and to only formal values, his position is in their view a nonmoral position, many of whose conclusions will be judged immoral by any legitimate moral theory.

Frankena and Medlin agree that a silent theory is not a moral theory. A moral theory requires publicity, and cannot be private. Thus, Frankena says:

> Here we must understand that the ethical egoist is not just taking the egoistic principle of acting and judging as his own private maxim. One could do this, and at the same time keep silent about it or even advocate altruism to everyone else, which might well be to one's advantage. But if one does this, one is not adopting a moral principle, for as we shall see, if one takes a maxim as a moral principle, one must be ready to universalize it.   (p. 17)

Here, Frankena connects nonuniversalization with silence, and thereby universalization with promulgation. This is a very strong sense of "universalize" which goes well beyond the principle "What's right for one person is right for similar people in similar circumstances." One can satisfy the universalization requirement in this latter sense by acknowledging that everyone would be justified in behaving as you are. As we have seen, this can be done without either wanting or urging others to do what they ought. But Frankena takes universalization to be much more, as is made clear by this earlier passage:

> Now morality in the sense indicated is, in one aspect, a social enterprise, not just a discovery or invention of the individual for his own guidance . . . it is not social merely in the sense of being a system governing the relations of one individual to others . . . it is also social in its origins, sanctions, and functions. It is an instrument of society as a whole for the guidance of individuals and smaller groups. It makes demands on individuals which are, initially at least, external to them. . . . As a social institution, morality must be contrasted with prudence.   (pp. 5–6)

What it is important to note about this conception of universalization and morality is that it can coherently be rejected.[11] Universalization in this strong sense is not a rational requirement (not analytic) as it appears to be in the weak sense. Our extended analogy between ethical egoism and competitive games shows just how coherently these strong conditions can be abandoned. At the most, this strong sense (in part explicated in terms of the various moral activities discussed above) may be part of the notion of "morality"; if so, egoism could not correctly label itself "ethical" or claim to be a moral theory. But this fact does not show that egoism as defined by (i) is mistaken, unreasonable, or inferior to any moral theory.

I personally think that it makes sense to speak of egoism as a morality, since I think it makes sense to speak of a "private morality" and of its being superior to "public moralities." The egoist's basic question is "What ought I to do; what is most reasonable for me to do?" This question seems to me a moral question through and through, and any coherent answer to it thereby deserves to be regarded as a moral theory. What is central here is the rational justification of a certain course of behavior. Such behavior will be justified in the sense that its reasonableness follows from a coherent and plausible set of premises. This kind of justification and moral reasoning can be carried out on the desert island and is not necessarily interpersonal— it does not have as one of its goals the minimal cooperation of some second party. Whether one *calls* the result a "morality" or not is of no matter, for its opponents must show it to be a poor competitor to the other alternatives. With respect to egoism, they cannot do this by arguing that (i) is logically incoherent or is incapable of being a practical system or violates any "principles of reason," such as universalization. I have tried to show how all these attempts would fail. I have even suggested in sections III and IV the way the egoist can argue for the reasonableness of his position (and it has, of course, seemed eminently reasonable to innumerable men, the "com-

---

[11] This sense of universalization needn't be rejected. One can coherently promulgate (i), but as we saw in section IV, doing so would make one something other than an egoist in the fullest sense. At the least, such a person would appear to value the state wherein everyone pursues their own welfare, wherein everyone tries to come out on top; this is a material, not formal value. ("But perhaps neither gain nor loss. For us, there is only the trying. The rest is not our business." T. S. Eliot.) The more one stresses the "moral" aspects of adopting (i) which seem to require sincere participation in the various public activities mentioned above, the more the "egoist" will be committed to the other than egoistic values which will result if everyone heeds him, such as: conflict, struggle, and competition, strength, craft, and strategic ability, excitement, danger, and insecurity. While it is true that strictly speaking these values are not egoistic even so (i) retains its egoistic "flavor." This is evident when it is applied to situations of irreconcilable conflict. The issue is to be settled by force or craft, or whatever, just in the way that it would be settled under the full-fledged, nonpromulgated egoism. It is perhaps difficult to imagine someone having the outlook needed in order to publicly promulgate (i) in such inhospitable conditions; nonetheless, it seems a possibility, and perhaps the professional soldier or gambler, or Zorba the Greek are approximations. Certainly, he would not be Medlin's misguided utilitarian.

mon man" not being the least among these). I therefore conclude that ethical egoism is a possible moral theory, not to be lightly dismissed. Its challenge to standard moralities is great, and not easily overcome.

If one insists that egoism is without the pale of morality, the obvious question one must face is: "Why be moral?" It is not at all easy to convincingly show that the egoist should (that it would be most reasonable for him to) abandon his position for one which could require him to sacrifice his self-interest, even to the point of death. What must be shown is not simply that it is to the egoist's interests to *be in* a society structured by various social, moral, and legal institutions, all of which limit categorically certain expressions of self-interest (as do the penalty rules in football), which is Hobbes' point, but that the egoist also has compelling reasons (always) to abide by its rules, to continue to be moral, social, or legal when "the painful necessity comes for a man to choose between his own happiness and the general happiness."

The egoist can acknowledge that it is in his long range self-interest to be in a moral system and thus that there should be categorical public rules restricting his egoistic behavior. Publicly, these rules will be superior to self-interest, and will be enforced as such. But according to his private morality, they will not be superior. Rather, they will be interpreted as hypotheticals setting prices (sometimes very dear) upon certain forms of conduct. Thus, the egoist will believe that, while it is always reasonable to be in a moral system, it is not always reasonable to act morally while within that system (just as it is not always reasonable to obey the rules of football). The opponent of egoism, in order to soundly discredit it, must show that moral behavior is always reasonable.[12] If the conception of "formal value" is admitted as sound, and if the egoist is correct in his claim that there are no material values, I do not see how such attempts could be successful.

---

[12] This brief discussion of the question "Why be moral?" has Baier's attempt to show that egoism is ultimately unreasonable as its specific background, and is formulated in terms most appropriate to his treatment of the problem. See Kurt Baier, *The Moral Point of View* (New York; Random House, 1965), Chapter 7, especially sections 3 and 4. Section 3 reprinted in this volume.

4

"Happiness" Is Self-Realization: Aristotle

The fact of moral disagreement makes the importance of a viable test of right and wrong one of the greatest questions in ethics. In Chapter Three we looked at the first of several such tests or standards in normative ethics: self-interest, a result-theory of obligation. The standard (or standards) in this chapter are also result-theories. Here the good results of acts that are made the standard are spelled out as happiness.

The view that happiness or pleasure is the test of a right action has more of a moral ring to it for most people than at least open egoism has. It seems to do more justice to individual human nature and to the social nature of the human animal than egoism. Along with its competitor, the view that some things are right or wrong independently of their results, hedonism has been one of the two main contenders in Western ethics as a theory of obligation. But Aristotle is no hedonist.

Happiness and Pleasure

If we think that "the search for happiness" was invented by the writer of the Declaration of Independence and immortalized by afternoon TV soap operas, we may be surprised that it was a quest that was already proverbial in the time of Aristotle and Epicurus. Aristotle said that it was a matter of general agreement in his time that everyone was seeking happiness, but that people did not agree on what it is. Later, Epicurus, whose name has become attached to a very different doctrine from the one he taught in his writings, came up with a different theory of happiness from that one that Aristotle gave in his answer to the question. This is typical of persistent philosophical problems: They are important to people as people, but there is no widespread agreement on how the problems are to be solved or even how they are to be stated. It is too easy to suppose that problems about the meaning of a question is a mere matter of semantics, i.e., quibbles. But in view of the fact that these philosophical questions persist for so long, it has been a growing conviction among many twentleth-century philosophers that they, and other people, ought to be clear in their own minds as to what question they are trying to answer. Consideration of pleasure in the previous chapter has already shown some of the difficulty we are in for, if we interpret happiness as pleasure. Not all philosophers have by any means equated the two, and those who have exhibit turns of thought on the subject that we have not yet examined. Let us first look at one historical theory that happiness is not pleasure, and then see some of the factors that an attempt at distinguishing between the two will have to take into account. Then we shall devote the next chapter to pleasure as the standard of right and wrong.

In the *Nicomachean Ethics* Aristotle said that everyone agrees that happiness is what we are all looking for, and noted, at the same time, that we do not agree on what it is. The idea that happiness is simply the sensuous pleasures of the body had been expressed by one school of Greek philosophical thought. Aristotle rejected this equation, while agreeing that pleasure is important. His own view emphasized the relevance of the concept of human nature to the meaning of happiness. His concept of man is, in turn, heavily dependent upon the central place which he gives to purposes in his philosophy. For him the nature of a thing is defined in terms of the thing's purpose. Without maintaining that there is a personal, spiritual being of the kind that Western religions usually call God, he argued nevertheless that the universe is through and through a purposeful one. We need not, for present purposes, get hung up on the problem of whether purposes presuppose a purposer, some intelligent being who plans a world and creates it. Though Aristotle believed that there is a divine principle that the world somehow depends upon, it is sufficient for an understanding of his ethics to see that he thought of the universe as one in which the very stuff of which things are made strives for a goal, and, as it were, tries to make of itself all that it is capable of becoming. If one were to object that this view attributes to supposedly nonliving and nonintelligent matter qualities of life and mind, Aristotle can still defend the view by saying: Look and see how things usually turn out in the world of living things, at least; something makes an acorn grow into an oak and not become an eggplant.

The particular features of human nature that Aristotle singled out and his reasons for saying these constitute the human purpose are determinative for his ethics. He went by the principle that a thing's purpose is manifested in its peculiar traits. And here lies one reason why he did not identify happiness with pleasure and did not say that it is the purpose of man to seek or enjoy pleasure in all his actions. Man's purpose cannot lie in his possession of and manifestation of sense-perception and the use of the senses in general, nor in the possession and manifestation of the abilities to grow and reproduce his kind. All these things are not peculiar to man, for they are shared by the animals, and some, even by plants. What is peculiar to human beings, Aristotle claimed, is the possession of reason. Today we would fault his knowledge of psychology of animals, as we would many other scientific points, but in any case it must be admitted that if man is not alone in having reason, he has it to such a degree that he has no close competitors in the animal kingdom, on this score. Reason, in turn, said Aristotle, has a dual function in human life: the control of man's animal nature, and the exercise of reason apart from its application to some practical purpose.

The nature of happiness in connection with the purpose of man in Aristotle's theory takes a somewhat surprising turn now. For Aristotle says that it consists of an individual fulfilling his or her human function. First one must maintain rational control over a lower, animal makeup, and especially over the emotions. This self-control is called moral virtue and it is instilled by habit from one's childhood onward. The more distinctive and higher virtue, however, is intellectual virtue, which is the exercise of reason for its own sake in the pursuit of theoretical knowledge, especially the knowledge of eternal truths. The good person, then, is one who is a good specimen of humanity, one who fulfills the human function well. Where does happiness enter the picture? In the "well" aspect of human life, in well-being of the human animal, or one might almost say, in one's being in a "well kind of way." The emphasis is on activity of the soul (i.e., the total human personality) in accordance with virtue. Such virtue is indeed its own reward, and the characteristic sorts of psychological states of mind or feelings, e.g., of joy or contentment, which we moderns associate with happiness, were for Aristotle mostly incidental, and if they were present at all, he insisted that they should be present in moderation, for moderation of the emotions is a part of moral virtue. As for pleasure, Aristotle recognized its importance to human beings, but warned specifically against identifying it with happiness. He said that the life of virtue generates pleasure, and that one enjoys doing virtuous actions. But the pleasure is, as it were, a bonus, a by-product, and not the main thing about happiness.

This account of happiness is very remote from modern conceptions. One might, indeed, be willing to concede that it is more likely than not that the person who feels that he or she is fulfilling the human race's function in his or her individual life would be happy, i.e., have the psychological feelings that we associate with happiness. But one is likely to feel also that there is no guarantee of its being thus and of the inner feelings rewarding the outward effort. In fact, the only modern expressions that coincide with Aristotle's idea of happiness are some that perhaps go back almost to his own day and to the language he spoke. "Happy is the bride that the sun shines on" is a line from an Andrews Sisters' tune that is revived from time to time: lucky, fortunate, blessed? And the Beatitudes in the Sermon on the Mount have for the Latin word from which their title comes the original Greek, *makarios* for "blessed" or "happy." But if that is the main link that the modern conception of happiness has with Aristotle's, it is a very weak and obscure one.

Nor is Aristotle's emphasis upon intellectual virtue as the most important aspect of happiness any more likely to strike a responsive chord. Granted, some people are, in the modern sense, happy in the pursuit of truth, regardless of where it leads, but it isn't everybody's "cup of tea." And it is a part of modern criteria of happiness as a goal that it should be something open to all, not just to intellectuals or scientists of one sort or another. Nor, lastly, is the notion that happiness is to be found in fulfilling the purpose of human life likely to be helpful, even if we agreed that it is a laudable goal, for it is a very questionable assumption that there is a generic human function, over and above the purposes that individuals set themselves as their goals, and toward which native endowment and talent may direct them. Aristotle's argument that if a carpenter or a tailor or a jockey has a function and the human race does not, it would be a sorry state of affairs looks suspiciously like a fallacy of composition. But he is certainly not alone in expressing horror at the possibility that life, per se, might not have a purpose, and in supposing, apparently, that if life has no purpose it is meaningless, and so forth. The confused reasoning here, of course, lies in supposing that there is some reason why life should have a purpose over and above my purposes and yours.

But if Aristotle is in some ways a puzzling museum piece on the subject, in other ways he is very much to the point in discussing the relation of pleasure to happiness. For if he argued that happiness is not so much a state of consciousness as a state of well-being of the personality, and of self-realization, he did mark it off somewhat from pleasure as a psychological state of consciousness, and gave it a certain amount of independence from pleasure, which it does, in fact, have. For whatever else happiness is, it is a favorable verdict that a person renders about his or her own life situation and one's circumstances. Such a favorable verdict may be rendered, indeed, in the face of a great deal of pain, or when not much pleasure is evident in one's life at the time. If we ask a young mother if she is happy, she may well reply that she is, despite the fact that her daily routine is demanding, and that diaper pails and pre-dawn feedings are not exactly her idea of pleasure. When a person looks back over a period of his or her life and asks which were the happiest times, it often is not those times in which pleasures came one on top of another—

even though there may have been such periods, briefly—but times in which there were obstacles to something one thought worthwhile, and times in which one managed, more or less successfully, to cope with them and overcome them. They may often be times of struggle, and when they are, it runs counter to the notion that happiness is primarily satisfaction of desires or some master-stroke of success. Some theories of happiness say that it is more likely to lie in the anticipation of something worthwhile than in the actual achievement of such a goal.

As we think of them, happiness and pleasure have some things in common: First, they are states of mind, or psychological in nature. They can be produced by causes, e.g., electrodes inserted in the brain, or chemicals introduced into the bloodstream. The moral or ethical importance of such artificially induced happiness or pleasure is debatable. One might be inclined to say that these are mere physiological states, and do not have that traditional association with deliberation and choice that we demand of things that pertain to morality. "Ignorance is bliss" is countered by some remark about "a fool's paradise," as far as true happiness is concerned. But, on the other hand, if pleasure or happiness are things that can be produced on demand by tinkering with the individual's physiology, perhaps chance, cause and effect, and generally, things beyond the control of conscious deliberation and choice may be more important to the question of whether one will be happy or not, and may render some of the debate about happiness and morality beside the point.

The issues raised here are ones that go beyond the present context and involve many difficulties about free will, causes, and reasons. In any case, it must be agreed that whatever psychological states or events exist or occur, some cause is supposed necessary to produce them. But this does not mean that the mathematician's brain-thought processes in which he or she correctly does an equation are the sole explanation of correctly doing an equation any more than its physiology is a complete account of a successful football play, which also is within the scope of the rules of the game, or "legal." Nor would physiology or psychology be able to provide us with a complete account of the morality or immorality or amorality of a certain person's pleasure or happiness. That does not mean that these matters are therefore spiritual or that, say, theology is left, by default, to supply the rest of the story. For the status and function of moral discourse is not by any means an opaque mystery to us, the users of moral concepts, in our thought and talk about happiness and pleasure in connection with morality, a mystery to be dispelled only by some transcendent authority. We do meaningfully and successfully talk about these matters, and not by accident, but by having learned the language from users of the concepts, and having learned them not in a vacuum, but in the context of actions and emotions to which we were first-hand participants in or witnesses. What is essential here is that there are rules that we learn for using these words "happiness" (and especially "happy") and "pleasure," and that these rules are of as much importance in giving an account of the morality of happiness and pleasure as the rules of algebra or of football are in explaining what a mathematician or a halfback is doing and whether he's doing it right.

Thus, just as two sorts of things are going on when a mathematics problem is solved, or a football play is being executed—first, a set of cause-and-effect sequences within the body of the individual concerned, and in relation to the immediate environment, and the application of rules to a problem at hand—so in happiness and pleasure as an issue in morality, two things are going on: the physiology and psychology of pleasure or happiness, and all the complex set of causes and effects, but also the application of rules to the solution of a problem by the individual whose happiness or pleasure is the topic of discussion. For instance, it is essential not only to look at how happiness may as a matter of fact be produced as an effect within the human skin, but at the means by which one chooses to produce it, at the objects about which one feels pleasure or happiness, and so forth. If the high point of my day is always my two five-thirty martinis, I may be regarded as no great moral hero, but at least no great villain, either. But if my greatest pleasure is in putting other people down, that can hardly be regarded as a more moral way of enjoying life than the daily cocktail or two. It is part of the rules for discussing the morality of happiness or pleasure that moral approval is contingent very much on the question of what a person is happy about, or what he or she gets pleasure from.

NICOMACHEAN ETHICS °

ARISTOTLE

Every art and every inquiry, and similarly every action and pursuit, is thought to aim at some good; and for this reason the good has rightly been declared to be that at which all things aim. But a certain difference is found among ends; some are activities, others are products apart from the activities that produce them. Where there are ends apart from the actions, it is the nature of the products to be better than the activities. Now, as there

° From "Ethica Nicomachea" translated by W. D. Ross from *The Oxford Translation of Aristotle* edited by W. D. Ross, vol. 9 (1925). Reprinted by permission of Oxford University Press. Bks. One and Two with omissions.

are many actions, arts, and sciences, their ends also are many; the end of the medical art is health, that of shipbuilding a vessel, that of strategy victory, that of economics wealth. But where such arts fall under a single capacity—as bridle-making and the other arts concerned with the equipment of horses fall under the art of riding, and this and every military action under strategy, in the same way other arts fall under yet others— in all of these the ends of the master arts are to be preferred to all the subordinate ends; for it is for the sake of the former that the latter are pursued. It makes no difference whether the activities themselves are the ends of the actions, or something else apart from the activities, as in the case of the sciences just mentioned.

If, then, there is some end of the things we do, which we desire for its own sake (everything else being desired for the sake of this), and if we do not choose everything for the sake of something else (for at that rate the process would go on to infinity, so that our desire would be empty and vain), clearly this must be the good and the chief good. Will not the knowledge of it, then, have a great influence on life? Shall we not, like archers who have a mark to aim at, be more likely to hit upon what is right? If so, we must try, in outline at least, to determine what it is, and of which of the sciences or capacities it is the object. It would seem to belong to the most authoritative art and that which is most truly the master art. And politics appears to be of this nature; for it is this that ordains which of the sciences should be studied in a state, and which each class of citizens should learn and up to what point they should learn them; and we see even the most highly esteemed of capacities to fall under this, e.g. strategy, economics, rhetoric; now, since politics uses the rest of the sciences, and since, again, it legislates as to what we are to do and what we are to abstain from, the end of this science must include those of the others, so that this end must be the good for man. For even if the end is the same for a single man and for a state, that of the state seems at all events something greater and more complete whether to attain or to preserve; though it is worth while to attain the end merely for one man, it is finer and more godlike to attain it for a nation or for city-states. These, then, are the ends at which our inquiry aims, since it is political science, in one sense of that term.

Our discussion will be adequate if it has as much clearness as the subject-matter admits of, for precision is not to be sought for alike in all discussions, any more than in all the products of the crafts. Now fine and just actions, which political science investigates, admit of much variety and fluctuation of opinion, so that they may be thought to exist only by convention, and not by nature. And goods also give rise to a similar fluctuation because they bring harm to many people; for before now men have been undone by reason of their wealth, and others by reason of their courage. We must be content, then, in speaking of such subjects and with such premisses to indicate the truth roughly and in outline, and in speaking about things which are only for the most part true and with premisses of the same kind to reach conclusions that are no better. In the same spirit, therefore, should each type of statement be *received;* for it is the mark of an educated man to look for precision in each class of things just so far as the nature of the subject admits; it is evidently equally foolish to accept probable reasoning from a mathematician and to demand from a rhetorician scientific proofs.

Now each man judges well the things he knows, and of these he is a good judge. And so the man who has been educated in a subject is a good judge of that subject, and the man who has received an all-round education is a good judge in general. Hence a young man is not a proper hearer of lectures on political science; for he is inexperienced in the actions that occur in life, but its discussions start from these and are about these; and, further, since he tends to follow his passions, his study will be vain and unprofitable because the end aimed at is not knowledge but action. And it makes no difference whether he is young in years or youthful in character; the defect does not depend on time, but on his living, and pursuing each successive object, as passion directs. For to such persons, as to the incontinent, knowledge brings no profit; but to those who desire and act in accordance with a rational principle knowledge about such matters will be of great benefit.

These remarks about the student, the sort of treatment to be expected, and the purpose of the inquiry, may be taken as our preface.

Let us resume our inquiry and state, in view of the fact that all knowledge and every pursuit aims at some good, what it is that we say political science aims at and what is the highest of all goods achievable by action. Verbally there is very general agreement; for both the general run of men and people of superior refinement say that it is happiness, and identify living well and doing well with being happy; but with regard to what happiness is they differ, and the many do not give the same account as the wise. For the former think it is some plain and obvious thing, like pleasure, wealth, or honour; they differ, however, from one another—and often even the same man identifies it with different things, with health when he is ill, with wealth when he is poor; but, conscious of their ignorance, they admire those who proclaim some great ideal that is above their comprehension. Now some thought that apart from these many goods there is another which is self-subsistent and causes the goodness of all these as well. To examine all the opinions that have been held were perhaps somewhat fruitless; enough to examine those that are most prevalent or that seem to be arguable.

To judge from the lives that men lead, most men, and men of the most vulgar type, seem (not without some ground) to identify the good, or happiness, with pleasure; which is the reason why they love the life of enjoyment and of active disposition identify happiness with honour; [3] for this mentioned, the political, and thirdly the contemplative life. Now the mass of mankind are evidently quite slavish in their tastes, preferring a life suitable to beasts, but they get some ground for their view from the fact that many of those in high places share the tastes of Sardanapallus. A consideration of the prominent types of life shows that people of superior refinement. For there are, we may say, three prominent types of life—that just is, roughly speaking, the end of the political life. But it seems too superficial to be what we are looking for, since it is thought to depend on those who bestow honour rather than on him who receives it, but the good we divine to be something proper to a man and not easily taken from him. Further, men seem to pursue honour in order that they may be assured of their goodness; at least it is by men of practical wisdom that they seek to be honoured, and among those who know them, and on the ground of their virtue; clearly, then, according to them, at any rate, virtue is better. And perhaps one might even suppose this to be, rather than honour, the end of the political life. But even this appears somewhat incomplete; for possession of virtue seems actually compatible with being asleep, or with lifelong inactivity, and, further, with the greatest sufferings and misfortunes; but a man who was living so no one would call happy, unless he were maintaining a thesis at all costs. But enough of this; for the subject has been sufficiently treated even in the current discussions. Third comes the contemplative life, which we shall consider later.

The life of money-making is one undertaken under compulsion, and wealth is evidently not the good we are seeking; for it is merely useful and for the sake of something else. And so one might rather take the aforenamed objects to be ends; for they are loved for themselves. But it is evident that not even these are ends; yet many arguments have been thrown away in support of them. Let us leave this subject, then.

Let us again return to the good we are seeking, and ask what it can be. It seems different in different actions and arts; it is different in medicine, in strategy, and in the other arts likewise. What then is the good of each? Surely that for whose sake everything else is done. In medicine this is health, in strategy victory, in architecture a house, in any other sphere something else, and in every action and pursuit the end; for it is for the sake of this that all men do whatever else they do. Therefore, if there is an end for all that we do, this will be the good achievable by action, and if there are more than one, these will be the goods achievable by action.

So the argument has by a different course reached the same point; but we must try to state this even more clearly. Since there are evidently more than one end, and we choose some of these (e.g. wealth, flutes, and in general instruments) for the sake of something else, clearly not all ends are final ends; but the chief good is evidently something final. Therefore, if there is only one final end, this will be what we are seeking, and if there are more than one, the most final of these will be what we are seeking. Now we call that which is in itself worthy of pursuit more final than that which is worthy of pursuit for the sake of something else, and that which is never desirable for the sake of something else more final than the things that are desirable both in themselves and for the sake of that other thing, and therefore we call final without qualification that which is always desirable in itself and never for the sake of something else.

Now such a thing happiness, above all else, is held to be; for this we choose always for itself and never for the sake of something else, but honour, pleasure, reason, and every virtue we choose indeed for themselves (for if nothing resulted from them we should still choose each of them), but we choose them also for the sake of happiness, judging that by means of them we shall be happy. Happiness, on the other hand, no one chooses for the sake of these, nor, in general, for anything other than itself.

From the point of view of self-sufficiency the same result seems to follow; for the final good is thought to be self-sufficient. Now by self-sufficient we do not mean that which is sufficient for a man by himself, for one who lives a solitary life, but also for parents, children, wife, and in general for his friends and fellow citizens, since man is born for citizenship. But some limit must be set to this; for if we extend our requirement to ancestors and descendants and friends' friends we are in for an infinite series. Let us examine this question, however, on another occasion; the self-sufficient we now define as that which when isolated makes life desirable and lacking in nothing; and such we think happiness to be; and further we think it most desirable of all things, without being counted it would clearly be made more desirable by the addition of even the least of goods; for that which is added becomes an excess of goods, and of goods the greater is always more desirable. Happiness, then, is something final and self-sufficient, and is the end of action.

Presumably, however, to say that happiness is the chief good seems a platitude, and a clearer account of what it is is still desired. This might perhaps be given, if we could first ascertain the function of man. For just as for a fluteplayer, a sculptor, or any artist, and, in general, for all things that have a function or activity, the good and the 'well' is thought to reside in the function, so would it seem to be for man, if he has a function. Have the carpenter, then, and the tanner certain functions or activities, and has man none? Is he born without a function? Or as eye, hand, foot, and in general each of the parts evidently has a function, may one lay it down that man similarly has a function apart from all these? What then can this be? Life seems to be common even to plants, but we are seeking what is peculiar to man. Let us exclude, therefore, the life of nutrition and growth. Next there would be a life of perception, but *it* also seems to be common even to the horse, the ox, and every animal. There remains, then, an active life of the element that has a rational principle; of this, one part has such a principle in the sense of being obedient to one, the other in the sense of possessing one and exercising thought. And, as 'life of the rational element' also has two meanings, we must state that life in the sense of activity is what we mean; for this seems to be the more proper sense of the term.

Now if the function of man is an activity of soul which follows or implies a rational principle, and if we say 'a so-and-so' and 'a good so-and-so' have a function which is the same in kind, e.g. a lyre-player and a good lyre-player, and so without qualification in all cases, eminence in respect of goodness being added to the name of the function (for the function of a lyre-player is to play the lyre, and that of a good lyre-player is to do so well): if this is the case, [and we state the function of man to be a certain kind of life, and this to be an activity or actions of the soul implying a rational principle, and the function of a good man to be the good and noble performance of these, and if any action is well performed when it is performed in accordance with the appropriate excellence: if this is the case,] human good turns out to be activity of soul in accordance with virtue, and if there are more than one virtue, in accordance with the best and most complete.

But we must add 'in a complete life'. For one swallow does not make a summer, nor does one day; and so too one day, or a short time, does not make a man blessed and happy.

Yet evidently, as we said, [happiness] needs the external goods as well; for it is impossible, or not easy, to do noble acts without the proper equipment. In many actions we use friends and riches and political power as instruments; and there are some things the lack of which takes the lustre from happiness, as good birth, goodly children, beauty; for the man who is very ugly in appearance or ill-born or solitary and child-less is not very likely to be happy, and perhaps a man would be still less likely if he had thoroughly bad children or friends or had lost good children or friends by death. As we said, then, happiness seems to need this sort of prosperity in addition; for which reason some identify happiness with good fortune, though others identify it with virtue.

Virtue, then, being of two kinds, intellectual and moral, intellectual virtue in the main owes both its birth and its growth to teaching (for which reason it requires experience and time), while moral virtue comes about as a result of habit, whence also its name ($\dot{\eta}\theta\iota\kappa\dot{\eta}$) is one that is formed by a slight variation from the word $\check{\epsilon}\theta os$ (habit). From this it is also plain that none of the moral virtues arises in us by nature; for nothing that exists by nature can form a habit contrary to its nature. For instance the stone which by nature moves downwards cannot be habituated to move upwards, not even if one tries to train it by throwing it up ten thousand times; nor can fire be habituated to move downwards, nor can anything else that by nature behaves in one way be trained to behave in another. Neither by nature, then, nor contrary to nature do the virtues arise in us; rather we are adapted by nature to receive them, and are made perfect by habit.

Again, of all the things that come to us by nature we first acquire the potentiality and later exhibit the activity (this is plain in the case of the senses; for it was not by often seeing or often hearing that we got these senses, but on the contrary we had them before we used them, and did not come to have them by using them); but the virtues we get by first exercising them, as also happens in the case of the arts as well. For the things we have to learn before we can do them, we learn by doing them, e.g. men become builders by building and lyre-players by playing the lyre; so too we become just by doing just acts, temperate by doing temperate acts, brave by doing brave acts.

This is confirmed by what happens in states for legislators make the citizens good by forming habits in them, and this is the wish of every legislator, and those who do not effect it miss their mark, and it is in this that a good constitution differs from a bad one.

Again, it is from the same causes and by the same means that every virtue is both produced and destroyed, and similarly every art; for it is from playing the lyre that both good and bad lyre-players are produced. And the corresponding statement is true of builders and of all the rest; men will be good or bad builders as a result of building well or badly. For if this were not so, there would have been no need of a teacher, but all men would have been born good or bad at their craft. This, then, is the case with the virtues also; by doing the acts that we do in our transactions with other men we become just or unjust, and by doing the acts that we do in the presence of danger, and being habituated to feel fear or confidence, we become brave or cowardly. The same is true of appetites and feelings of anger; some men become temperate and good-tempered, others self-indulgent and irascible, by behaving in one way or the other in the appropriate circumstances. Thus, in one word, states of character arise out of like activities. This is why the activities we exhibit must be of a certain kind; it is because the states of character correspond to the differences between these. It makes no small difference, then, whether we form habits of one kind or of another from our very youth; it makes a very great difference, or rather *all* the difference.

Since, then, the present inquiry does not aim at theoretical knowledge like the others (for we are inquiring not in order to know what virtue is, but in order to become good, since otherwise our inquiry would have been of no use), we must examine the nature of actions, namely how we ought to do them; for these determine also the nature of the states of character that are produced, as we have said. Now, that we must act according to the right rule is a common principle and must be assumed—it will be discussed later, i.e. both what the right rule is, and how it is related to the other virtues. But this must be agreed upon beforehand, that the whole account of matters of conduct must be given in outline and not precisely, as we said at the very beginning that the accounts we demand must be in accordance with the subject-matter; matters concerned with conduct and questions of what is good for us have no fixity, any more than matters of health. The general account being of this nature, the account of particular cases is yet more lacking in exactness; for they do not fall under any art or precept but the agents themselves must in each case consider what is appropriate to the occasion, as happens also in the art of medicine or of navigation.

But though our present account is of this nature we must give what help we can. First, then, let us consider this, that it is the nature of such things to be destroyed by defect and excess, as we see in the case of strength and of health (for to gain light on things imperceptible we must use the evidence of sensible things); both excessive and defective exercise destroys the strength, and similarly drink or food which is above or below a certain amount destroys the health, while that which is proportionate both produces and increases and preserves it. So too is it, then, in the case of temperance and courage and the other virtues. For the man who flies from and fears everything and does not stand his ground against anything becomes a coward, and the man who fears nothing at all but goes to meet every danger becomes rash; and similarly the man who indulges in every pleasure and abstains from none becomes self-indulgent, while the man who shuns every pleasure, as boors do, becomes in a way insensible; temperance and courage, then, are destroyed by excess and defect, and preserved by the mean.

But not only are the sources and causes of their origination and growth the same as those of their destruction, but also the sphere of their actualization will be the same; for this is also true of the things which are more evident to sense, e.g. of strength; it is produced by taking much food and undergoing much exertion, and it is the strong man that will be most able to do these things. So too is it with the virtues; by abstaining from pleasures we become temperate, and it is when we have become so that we are most able to abstain from them; and similarly too in the case of courage; for by being habituated to despise things that are terrible and to stand our ground against them we become brave, and it is when we have become so that we shall be most able to stand our ground against them.

We must take as a sign of states of character the pleasure or pain that ensues on acts; for the man who abstains from bodily pleasures and delights in this very fact is temperate, while the man who is annoyed at it is self-indulgent, and he who stands his ground against things that are terrible and delights in this or at least is not pained is brave, while the man who is pained is a coward. For moral excellence is concerned with pleasures and pains; it is on account of the pleasure that we do bad things, and on account of the pain that we abstain from noble ones. Hence we ought to have been brought up in a particular way from our very youth, as Plato says, so as both to delight in and to be pained by the things that we ought; for this is the right education.

Next we must consider what virtue is. Since things that are found in the soul are of three kinds—passions, faculties, states of character, virtue must be one of these. By passions I mean appetite, anger, fear, confidence, envy, joy, friendly feeling, hatred, longing, emulation, pity, and in general the feelings that are accompanied by pleasure or pain; by faculties the things in virtue of which we are said to be capable of feeling these, e.g. of becoming angry or being pained or feeling pity; by states of character the things in virtue of which we stand well or badly with reference to the passions, e.g. with reference to anger we stand badly if we feel it violently or too weakly, and well if we feel it moderately; and similarly with reference to the other passions.

Now neither the virtues nor the vices are *passions*, because we are not called good or bad on the ground of our passions, but are so called on the ground of our virtues and our vices, and because we are neither praised nor blamed for our passions (for the man who feels fear or anger is not praised, nor is the man who simply feels anger blamed, but the man who feels it in a certain way), but for our virtues and our vices we *are* praised or blamed.

Again, we feel anger and fear without choice, but the virtues are modes of choice or involve choice. Further, in respect of the passions we are said to be moved, but in respect of the virtues and the vices we are said not to be moved but to be disposed in a particular way.

For these reasons also they are not *faculties;* for we are neither called good nor bad, nor praised nor blamed, for the simple capacity of feeling the passions; again, we have the faculties by nature, but we are not made good or bad by nature; we have spoken of this before.

If, then, the virtues are neither passions nor faculties, all that remains is that they should be *states of character.*

Thus we have stated what virtue is in respect of its genus.

We must, however, not only describe virtue as a state of character, but also say what sort of state it is. We may remark, then, that every virtue or excellence both brings into good condition the thing of which it is the excellence and makes the work of that thing be done well; e.g. the excellence of the eye makes both the eye and its work good; for it is by the excellence of the eye that we see well. Similarly the excellence of the horse makes a horse both good in itself and good at running and at carrying its rider and at awaiting the attack of the enemy. Therefore, if this is true in every case, the virtue of man also will be the state of character which makes a man good and which makes him do his own work well.

How this is to happen we have stated already, but it will be made plain also by the following consideration of the specific nature of virtue. In everything that is continuous and divisible it is possible to take more, less, or an equal amount, and that either in terms of the thing itself or relatively to us; and the equal is an intermediate between excess and defect. By the intermediate in the object I mean that which is equidistant from each of the extremes, which is one and the same for all men; by the intermediate relatively to us that which is neither too much nor too little—and this is not one, nor the same for all. For instance, if ten is many and two is few, six is the intermediate, taken in terms of the object; for it exceeds and is exceeded by an equal amount; this is intermediate according to arithmetical proportion. But the intermediate relatively to us is not to be taken so; if ten pounds are too much for a particular person to eat and two too little, it does not follow that the trainer will order six pounds; for this also is perhaps too much for the person who is to take it, or too little—too little for Milo, too much for the beginner in athletic exercises. The same is true of running and wrestling. Thus a master of any art avoids excess and defect, but seeks the intermediate and chooses this—the intermediate not in the object but relatively to us.

If it is thus, then, that every art does its work well—by looking to the intermediate and judging its works by this standard (so that we often say of good works of art that it is not possible either to take away or to add anything, implying that excess and defect destroy the goodness of works of art, while the mean preserves it; and good artists, as we say, look to this in their work), and if, further, virtue is more exact and better than any art, as nature also is, then virtue must have the quality of aiming at the intermediate. I mean moral virtue; for it is this that is concerned with passions and actions, and in these there is excess, defect, and the intermediate. For instance, both fear and confidence and appetite and anger and pity and in general pleasure and pain may be felt both too much and too little, and in both cases not well; but to feel them at the right times, with reference to the right objects, towards the right people, with the right motive, and in the right way, is what is both intermediate and best, and this is characteristic of virtue. Similarly with regard to actions also there is excess, defect, and the intermediate. Now virtue is concerned with passions and actions, in which excess is a form of failure, and so is defect, while the intermediate is praised and is a form of success; and being praised and being successful are both characteristics of virtue. Therefore virtue is a kind of mean, since, as we have seen, it aims at what is intermediate.

Again, it is possible to fail in many ways (for evil belongs to the class of the unlimited, as the Pythagoreans conjectured, and good to that of the limited), while to succeed is possible only in one way (for which reason also one is easy and the other difficult—to miss the mark easy, to hit it difficult); for these reasons also, then, excess and defect are characteristic of vice, and the mean of virtue;

For men are good in but one way, but bad in many.

Virtue, then, is a state of character concerned with choice, lying in a mean, i.e. the mean relative to us, this being determined by a rational principle, and by that principle by which the man of practical wisdom would determine it. Now it is a mean between two vices, that which depends on excess and that which depends on defect; and again it is a mean because the vices respectively fall short of or exceed what is right in both passions and actions, while virtue both finds and chooses that which is intermediate. Hence in respect of its substance and the definition which states its essence virtue is a mean, with regard to what is best and right an extreme.

But not every action nor every passion admits of a mean; for some have names that already imply badness, e.g. spite, shamelessness, envy, and in the case of actions adultery, theft, murder; for all of these and suchlike things imply by their names that they are themselves bad, and not the excesses or deficiencies of them. It is not possible, then, ever to be right with regard to them; one must always be wrong. Nor does goodness or badness with regard to such things depend on committing adultery with the right woman, at the right time, and in the right way, but simply to do any of them is to go wrong. It would be equally absurd, then, to expect that in unjust, cowardly, and voluptuous action there should be a mean, an excess, and a deficiency; for at that rate there would be a mean of excess and of deficiency, an excess of excess, and a deficiency of deficiency. But as there is no excess and deficiency of temperance and courage because what is intermediate is in a sense an extreme, so too of the actions we have mentioned there is no mean nor any excess and deficiency, but however they are done they are wrong; for in general there is neither a mean of excess and deficiency, nor excess and deficiency of a mean.

5

"Happiness" Is Pleasure: Hedonistic Utilitarianism

Egoistic Hedonism

We have already examined egoism and hedonism as psychological doctrines, or as purported descriptions of human motivation and action. Also, we have discussed egoism as a normative doctrine. You will recall that "hedonism" is from the Greek word for "pleasure." Thus, egoistic hedonism as a normative doctrine, as a theory of obligation, asserts that everyone ought to seek his or her pleasure as the main goal of every action.

If it is asked why it is obligatory or a duty, or always the right thing to do, the advocates of this doctrine do not usually have any justification that goes beyond simple psychological hedonism: Observation of other people and of oneself should convince you, they will say, that pleasure is worthwhile, and that it is, if not the only thing that is worthwhile in its own right, at least the most worthwhile of all things. It is valuable, as Mill states (speaking not as an egoistic hedonist but as a psychological hedonist), because it is valued and no further reason could be given, if that is not convincing. We have looked at the pro's and con's of psychological hedonism, and seen that it is doubtful that all the things that people do value could be lumped together and called pleasure, or that they value pleasure most, of several things, judging by the sacrifices they are willing to make for some goals that it seems a stretch of language to call pleasure.

We have also criticized egoism, and the same arguments apply against the hedonistic version of egoism as an ethical theory. One representative of egoistic hedonism will get some attention, however, and this is as much to correct some injustices to him as to criticize his inadequacies as an egoist.

Epicurus is popularly thought to have said, "Eat, drink and be merry, for tomorrow we die," or at least to have taught something like that. The quotation is not from him but from a statement quoted with disapproval by a biblical writer. Epicurus was not even an Epicurean in the popular sense of the word. He did not regard pleasure as the thrills or "kicks" that jaded libertines seek, but as the absence of pain in the body and trouble in the mind. Thus, pleasure, though he does regard it as the chief goal of mankind, is described as something negative, almost a state to be effected more by a "downer" than by an "upper." To eat, drink, and be merry in the usual sense of carousing would bring pain in terms of hangovers and stomach troubles. True, Epicurus did not believe in immortality, and even thought it a pernicious doctrine because it produced all sorts of anxieties in people's minds about punishment after death. This did not, however, have the consequence for him that people should burn the candle at both ends and hasten the day of death, and add miseries produced by dissipation to a reduction of the time in which one might enjoy oneself upon the earth.

Epicurus believed that such enjoyment as one could have should consist of a modest diet that would give the blessings of good digestion, keeping out of competitive activities such as politics, and cultivating the intellect with philosophy in the company of a few friends. The latter activity was the pastime in the famous Garden of Epicurus. Epicurus observed that some of the desires that Nature has given to us are such that if they are not fulfilled, we will die, and such is the desire for food and drink. Others, such as the desire for sex, are natural, but we will not die if they are not fulfilled (though we may think we're going to die!). The most dangerous of all desires are those that people cultivate artificially, and then burden themselves with cravings for their fulfillment, which are borrowed troubles. All in all, then, Epicurus offered a very modest program and as a believer in ethical egoism seems to be a veritable saint, nevertheless. He was not surely, a social reformer, or one who espoused programs of uplift. The times in which he lived would, of themselves, discourage anyone from such sanguine undertakings, for they were times in which social undertakings seemed to offer little of value to the individual.

In criticism of Epicurus we have to attack a weakness of all hedonism, and that is that pleasure, whether defined negatively as the absence of pain and worry or positively as stimulation and excitement, is far from making out its case as the sole intrinsic good. Epicurus's life of pleasure could be well within the capabilities of modern medicine and pharmacology; tranquilizers and sedatives can go far toward giving one an absence of trouble in the mind and pain in the body. Epicurus himself, to his credit, shied away from making this the be-all and end-all of life, for he emphasized the importance of intellectual pleasures, the joys of philosophy and of understanding life. That, at least, does seem to give some place to the human being as a creature who consciously and responsibly puts his or her hand to control of his or her own destiny, with all the risks involved. If pleasure were the main or only thing in life that was worthwhile, and if it could be guaranteed for life that a person would never feel pain, but only pleasant, or at least not unpleasant, sensations and emotions, we have to ask ourselves whether this would be a truly human life or not. For it would take a lot of restriction of human freedom to guarantee such lifelong freedom from pain and worry. Quite probably, in the bargain one would have to give up his or her proverbial right to make his or her own mistakes, for mistakes do often bring with them pain and worry.

Universal Hedonism

If ancient hedonism lacked a "social message" modern times certainly made up for it. The bad odor that the centuries of the intellectual domination of the Church attributed to hedonism did not evaporate with the Renaissance, but things were never quite the same. Hobbes's egoistic hedonism, for all its similarities to Epicureanism—especially that of Lucretius, the materialist poet- philosopher—had social overtones that belonged to the modern age, and not to the ancient. Hobbes had seen and worked for the "Renaissance man," Francis Bacon, in his ambitious climb to power and in his sudden fall and retirement to a life of writing and research. He lived in the time when free enterprise was still a new doctrine and yet to be established against the monopolies of government, and in the time of emerging nationalism. All these motifs found a place in Hobbes's political and ethical theories. But it remained for two reformers of nineteenth-century England to give to hedonism a certain respectability as a program and as an apology for statesmen and legislators. Those men were Jeremy Bentham and John Stuart Mill, who supported the reform legislation that was supposed to correct many of the social and political abuses of the Industrial Revolution.

Bentham's hedonism was one that emphasized quantity. That was natural in an age in which there were great expectations that the application of scientific methods to the study and improvement of society would bring, if not the Millennium, at least a sounder social order and better life for all. It was he who popularized the expression, "the greatest happiness for the greatest number," and in a little poem in the mode of "Thirty Days Hath September," gave a hedonistic calculus that he hoped could be easily committed to memory and applied directly to the average citizen's daily decisions affecting his fellowman. Bentham argued that Nature has placed man under the governance of two sovereign masters, pain and pleasure, and that these are at once the measure of right and wrong and the motivation or sanction for seeking the right and avoiding the wrong. He declared that the "principle of utility" is the principle by which "ought, right, and wrong" are interpreted and actions judged. The utility of an action is its tendency to promote the greatest happiness, i.e., "benefit, advantage, pleasure, good" of the greatest number of people whose interests are affected by the action. His hedonistic calculus, or moral arithmetic, was designed to compute the probable quantity of pleasure to be derived from two actions and to enable one to choose the one that would yield the greatest. If there is any question that he firmly believed that the most pleasure was of most importance, he is often cited as having said that, all other things being equal, "Pushpin is as good as poetry," that is, if it is enjoyed as much.

John Stuart Mill's father, James Mill, educated his son from the age of three, and, being a follower of Bentham, saw to it that John Stuart imbibed much of his doctrine. There was one feature of hedonism in Bentham with which Mill made a famous break and that was the quantitative emphasis. Mill praised Bentham's "greatest happiness" principle, but, for various reasons, among them a sensitivity to the question of public respectability of hedonism, argued that the quality of pleasure is as important a criterion for choosing between two actions as the quantity. Now, the doctrine of hedonism is regarded by a long tradition of English philosophers who supported it as being very much supported by the facts of common sense and a close, empirical scrutiny of human thought and action. Mill thought of it also as being very much a support for liberal democratic political doctrine. How can one solve the apparently difficult matter of judging which of two pleasures is higher in quality? Empirically and democratically; "the only competent judges" as to which of two pleasures is the better are people who have tried both. If, in addition to this consideration, there is disagreement between those who have tried both take the majority opinion; that is the higher-quality pleasure and the one you should choose.

That happiness is not only the main, but the only, intrinsic good Mill argues emphatically. And equally clear is he that happiness is the same as pleasure or the absence of pain, and unhappiness is pain and the privation of pleasure. He goes to some lengths to argue that objections to hedonism are based upon assumptions that some of the things that are a means to pleasure have come to be regarded as ends in themselves, e.g., virtue and justice. In a sense, he agrees, they are ends in that they have become parts of that complex, concrete whole that we call happiness. (He curiously speaks more of happiness than of pleasure after he has identified the two.) As with many social entities, he argues, man forgets the original and continuing point, their raison d'être, and virtue and justice would never have become important to us had they not played a vital role in man's happiness, nor would they continue long if they lost this utility. If you want to call his ethics a doctrine of "expedience" it agrees with the term that he himself uses, but he insists that many things that people regard as expedients, e.g., cutting corners and giving others a raw deal, are not expedience as far as society is concerned, for expedience is roughly equivalent to "social benefit," or "the good of society."

Mill takes it as his special project in *Utilitarianism* to provide a justification of the principle of utility, i.e., the greatest-happiness principle. In part this consists of rebutting criticisms of it from religious sources, but in part also of trying to show why you and I and all of us should promote the greatest happiness of the greatest number in all our actions. He does not claim that the principle can be proved deductively but, then, neither can the "first principles" of any subject, he says. But it should be clear from astute observation of others and studied and honest introspection of our own motives that the happiness of each person is a good to that person, and the general happiness is a good to the aggregate of people (society). This is the only proof that is available, he says, and all that could be desired, that each should promote the greatest happiness of the greatest number and not just of himself. There is, Mill argues, no proof that anything is desirable except as it is in fact desired, and the fact that each of us desires happiness is such.

Mill has been subjected to a tremendous amount of criticism for these two arguments, the one going from the fact that my happiness is a good to me and yours is a good to you, to the conclusion that therefore your happiness and the happiness of all people is a good to me, and vice versa; and the other going from the fact that something is desired (a descriptive judgment) to the normative judgment that it is desirable (i.e., should be desired). If these are fallacies, as some say, they are not obvious to the average English-speaking person brought up in a society that stresses cooperation and competition in the curious blend that has come down to us from early capitalism; and that has often had the blessing of such religious training as we might have been exposed to, and since the New Deal has not been wiped out by a much more leftist kind of economics and politics. There are logical difficulties, surely, and they appear when one looks closely at Mill's apparently oversimplified "proofs." It is not so clear how, from the fact that I like my happiness and you like yours, that you and I have a mutual obligation to promote each other's happiness when the occasion arises. How do we get that "ought" from that "is"? Similarly, there are problems about how I can go from the fact that I desire something to the value judgment that it is desirable. But a close reading of *Utilitarianism,* especially in the context of Mill's times and the causes to which he was committed, helps make his arguments more plausible if not logically airtight.

Briefly, Mill can be defended as holding that much of the point of *Utilitarianism* was an exhortation for political and social reform based on a less selfish and more politically astute attitude toward oneself and society. It comes through in several passages that Mill is arguing that each person's happiness is intricately tied up with the happiness of others and that my promoting your happiness when the occasion arises is a means to promotion of my own happiness, not just in the good feeling I might get from it, but more literally. The political liberal's point that where freedom is threatened anywhere it is not secure everywhere else can be translated here using "happiness" for "freedom": Wherever there are unhappy people around, it endangers the happiness of those who are more fortunate. Mill repeatedly emphasizes the importance of each person seeing that his or her own interests are inextricably bound up with the interests of other people in his or her society, and that social progress has largely consisted of larger and fuller recognition of this fact. Perhaps Mill's doctrine is saved from being egoism in disguise, or roundabout egoism by a genuine conviction on his part that it is quite possible and indeed necessary to inculcate in individuals an unfeigned concern for their fellow human beings. Mill may be overoptimistic on this point, but he is no Pollyanna. He argued that it is seldom necessary for us to consider the remote consequences of our actions, i.e., their effects upon someone half way around the world or upon our great-grandchildren.

Mill can also be defended against the charge that ethical hedonism cannot be based upon psychological hedonism. This charge must be double-barreled in Mill's case, for (1) if psychological hedonism is ipso facto psychological egoism, then the difficulties of deriving a nonegoist normative doctrine from it are apparent; and (2) if psychological egoism is a supposed law of nature or in any sense deterministic, it is hard to see how any normative ethics could be held on that basis. Now, it is clear that Mill certainly professes to accept psychological hedonism and, by implication, psychological egoism. However, it can be argued on his behalf that so far as determinism is concerned, he holds a sophisticated theory of cause and effect in human motives and actions, to the extent that free will and responsibility are perfectly compatible with them. As to the normative thrust of his ethics, it is toward convincing people that they should channel their efforts toward their own happiness in such a way that they promote the happiness of others, so far as their actions affect others, for the happiness of all is instrumental to the happiness of each. One can be asked to give up something that it is a law of his nature to seek, only if it is in exchange for something else that is in the same case. It must be admitted that Mill never argued any *quid pro quo* or tit-for-tat, nor claimed that each sacrifice of some certainly attainable, selfish pleasure would yield an even greater pleasure for oneself in the long run. Yet, he did exhort people to do so, and urged a "proper" moral upbringing for everyone in which the ability and tendency to gain such pleasures as come from seeing others benefited even at the cost of some creature comforts for oneself would be inculcated. Mill professedly hoped to load the dice in favor of a utilitarian outlook by directing man's natural self-interests into social channels by education, and legislation.

There are other issues that are of some importance in discussing Mill's hedonism as a classical presentation of the doctrine. Not the least is the notion of expedience or social good that served as the criterion for the rightness of actions done by the individual. It might be supposed that on this basis anything can be justified, but Mill took pains to rebut this as well as he could. We have to remember that if we are considering the principle of utility, it is claimed by its supporters to be the sole and soverign criterion of right and wrong. So we cannot say to a utilitarian that his or her ethics is terrible if it sometimes justifies murder, say, for the public good, or the greatest happiness of the greatest number. For he or she can ask us how we can justify the sparing of the life of a cruel tyrant who is waging a campaign of genocide or a global war, or both, in defiance of the public good and the interests of humanity. What is at issue here is that one cannot simply oppose the greatest happiness principle with a competing or alternative principle without arguments for the pro's and con's of both principles. If we apply the utilitarian principle directly to each question of right and wrong (what is called act utilitarianism or extreme utilitarianism), some of the acts regarded by other systems as always wrong and never right will not only sometimes be condoned, but obligatory, such as the assassination of the tyrant in the foregoing example. A somewhat different face is put on the matter and the gap between utilitarianism and other systems of ethics closes somewhat if we think of the greatest-happiness principle as generating moral rules from its applications in the past, somewhat as the past experience of competent judges of pleasure makes it unnecessary for us to experiment to find which is the best. Mill argues that mankind does not have to calculate the consequences of each action when past experience of his long history has given him moral rules as to which kinds of actions generally tend to produce the greatest happiness for the greatest number and which do not. If we follow this line of thought in interpreting the application of the greatest happiness principle we then have rule ultilitarianism, the view that, as a rule act A produces the greatest happiness, we can see that Mill would probably oppose many of the practices that other systems of ethics oppose and favor many that they do, and certainly Mill, in *On Liberty,* does exactly that. If an action might indeed in this particular case promote the greatest happiness for the greatest number but in all other known cases would not, a person might well hesitate to do it, or at least might want to check his or her calculations very carefully, regardless of how enthusiastic a utilitarian he or she might be.

On the other hand, if it were something that this person wanted very much to do for his or her own personal pleasure, he or she might suddenly switch from being a rule utilitarian who does not do what is as a rule not in accordance with the greatest happiness of the greatest number, and become an act (or extreme) utilitarian, if he could fudge a little and say it was really for the good of all. Kant, whom we shall discuss in the next chapter, has a horror for such people who make an exception of themselves, and thinks that he avoids that problem in his theory. Mill never claimed to have a foolproof theory, he said, and he argued that no other system was proof against those who were bent upon rationalizing their own predilections, anyway. For all this, it is apparent that utilitarianism, especially act utilitarianism, seems especially open to this kind of abuse.

Lastly, Mill can hardly be correct in his identification of happiness with pleasure. His better instincts opted for higher over lower pleasures and may be indicated by his preference (or deference?) in the latter part of *Utilitarianism* for happiness over pleasure. If our arguments on this in the chapter on Aristotle are of any value, the two are not the same. Nor can it be agreed readily that either pleasure or happiness is the sole intrinsic good. We can only say that if we redefine the words and make the doctrine true by (stipulative) definition.

UTILITARIANISM *

JOHN STUART MILL

What Utilitarianism Is

A passing remark is all that needs be given to the ignorant blunder of supposing that those who stand up for utility as the test of right and wrong use the term in that restricted and merely colloquial sense in which utility is opposed to pleasure. An apology is due to the philosophical opponents of utilitarianism for even the momentary appearance of confounding them with anyone capable of so absurd a misconception; which is the more extraordinary, inasmuch as the contrary accusation, of referring everything to

* From John Stuart Mill: UTILITARIANISM, ed. Oskar Piest, Copyright © 1957 by The Bobbs-Merrill Co. Inc. Reprinted with permission. (Chs. 2, 3 and 4, with omissions.)

pleasure, and that, too, in its grossest form, is another of the common charges against utilitarianism: and, as has been pointedly remarked by an able writer, the same sort of persons, and often the very same persons, denounce the theory "as impracticably dry when the word 'utility' precedes the word 'pleasure,' and as too practicably voluptuous when the word 'pleasure' precedes the word 'utility.'" Those who know anything about the matter are aware that every writer, from Epicurus to Bentham, who maintained the theory of utility meant by it, not something to be contradistinguished from pleasure, but pleasure itself, together with exemption from pain; and instead of opposing the useful to the agreeable or the ornamental, have always declared that the useful means these, among other things. Yet the common herd, including the herd of writers, not only in newspapers and periodicals, but in books of weight and pretension, are perpetually falling into this shallow mistake. Having caught up the word "utilitarian," while knowing nothing whatever about it but its sound, they habitually express by it the rejection or the neglect of pleasure in some of its forms: of beauty, of ornament, or of amusement. Nor is the term thus ignorantly misapplied solely in disparagement, but occasionally in compliment, as though it implied superiority to frivolity and the mere pleasures of the moment. And this perverted use is the only one in which the word is popularly known, and the one from which the new generation are acquiring their sole notion of its meaning. Those who introduced the word, but who had for many years discontinued it as a distinctive appellation, may well feel themselves called upon to resume it if by doing so they can hope to contribute anything toward rescuing it from this utter degradation.[1]

The creed which accepts as the foundation of morals "utility" or the "greatest happiness principle" holds that actions are right in proportion as they tend to promote happiness; wrong as they tend to produce the reverse of happiness. By happiness is intended pleasure and the absence of pain; by unhappiness, pain and the privation of pleasure. To give a clear view of the moral standard set up by the theory, much more requires to be said; in particular, what things it includes in the ideas of pain and pleasure, and to what extent this is left an open question. But these supplementary explanations do not affect the theory of life on which this theory of morality is grounded—namely, that pleasure and freedom from pain are the only things desirable as ends; and that all desirable things (which are as numerous in the utilitarian as in any other scheme) are desirable either for

[1] The author of this essay has reason for believing himself to be the first person who brought the word "utilitarian" into use. He did not invent it, but adopted it from a passing expression in Mr. Galt's *Annals of the Parish*. After using it as a designation for several years, he and others abandoned it from a growing dislike to anything resembling a badge or watchword of sectarian distinction. But as a name for one single opinion, not a set of opinions—to denote the recognition of utility as a standard, not any particular way of applying it—the term supplies a want in the language, and offers, in many cases, a convenient mode of avoiding tiresome circumlocution.

pleasure inherent in themselves or as means to the promotion of pleasure and the prevention of pain.

Now such a theory of life excites in many minds, and among them in some of the most estimable in feeling and purpose, inveterate dislike. To suppose that life has (as they express it) no higher end than pleasure—no better and nobler object of desire and pursuit—they designate as utterly mean and groveling, as a doctrine worthy only of swine, to whom the followers of Epicurus were, at a very early period, contemptuously likened; and modern holders of the doctrine are occasionally made the subject of equally polite comparisons by its German, French, and English assailants.

When thus attacked, the Epicureans have always answered that it is not they, but their accusers, who represent human nature in a degrading light, since the accusation supposes human beings to be capable of no pleasures except those of which swine are capable. If this supposition were true, the charge could not be gainsaid, but would then be no longer an imputation; for if the sources of pleasure were precisely the same to human beings and to swine, the rule of life which is good enough for the one would be good enough for the other. The comparison of the Epicurean life to that of beasts is felt as degrading, precisely because a beast's pleasures do not satisfy a human being's conceptions of happiness. Human beings have faculties more elevated than the animal appetites and, when once made conscious of them, do not regard anything as happiness which does not include their gratification. I do not, indeed, consider the Epicureans to have been by any means faultless in drawing out their scheme of consequences from the utilitarian principle. To do this in any sufficient manner, many Stoic, as well as Christian, elements require to be included. But there is no known Epicurean theory of life which does not assign to the pleasures of the intellect, of the feelings and imagination, and of the moral sentiments a much higher value as pleasures than to those of mere sensation. It must be admitted, however, that utilitarian writers in general have placed the superiority of mental over bodily pleasures chiefly in the greater permanency, safety, uncostliness, etc., of the former—that is, in their circumstantial advantages rather than in their intrinsic nature. And on all these points utilitarians have fully proved their case; but they might have taken the other and, as it may be called, higher ground with entire consistency. It is quite compatible with the principle of utility to recognize the fact that some kinds of pleasure are more desirable and more valuable than others. It would be absurd that, while in estimating all other things quality is considered as well as quantity, the estimation of pleasure should be supposed to depend on quantity alone.

If I am asked what I mean by difference of quality in pleasures, or what makes one pleasure more valuable than another, merely as a pleasure, except its being greater in amount, there is but one possible answer. Of two pleasures, if there be one to which all or almost all who have experience of both give a decided preference, irrespective of any feeling of moral obligation to prefer it, that is the more desirable pleasure. If one of the two is, by those who are competently acquainted with both, placed so far above the other that they prefer it, even though knowing it to be attended with a greater amount of discontent, and would not resign if for any quantity of the other pleasure which their nature is capable of, we are justified in ascribing to the preferred enjoyment a superiority in quality so far outweighing quantity as to render it, in comparison, of small account.

Now it is an unquestionable fact that those who are equally acquainted with and equally capable of appreciating and enjoying both do give a most marked preference to the manner of existence which employs their higher faculties. Few human creatures would consent to be changed into any of the lower animals for a promise of the fullest allowance of a beast's pleasures; no intelligent human being would consent to be a fool, no instructed person would be an ignoramus, no person of feeling and conscience would be selfish and base, even though they should be persuaded that the fool, the dunce, or the rascal is better satisfied with his lot than they are with theirs. They would not resign what they possess more than he for the most complete satisfaction of all the desires which they have in common with him. If they ever fancy they would, it is only in cases of unhappiness so extreme that to escape from it they would exchange their lot for almost any other, however undesirable in their own eyes. A being of higher faculties requires more to make him happy, is capable probably of more acute suffering, and certainly accessible to it at more points, than one of an inferior type; but in spite of these liabilities, he can never really wish to sink into what he feels to be a lower grade of existence. We may give what explanation we please of this unwillingness; we may attribute it to pride, a name which is given indiscriminately to some of the most and to some of the least estimable feelings of which mankind are capable; we may refer it to the love of liberty and personal independence, an appeal to which was with the Stoics one of the most effective means for the inculcation of it; to the love of power or to the love of excitement, both of which do really enter into and contribute to it; but its most appropriate appellation is a sense of dignity, which all human beings possess in one form or other, and in some, though by no means in exact, proportion to their higher faculties, and which is so essential a part of the happiness of those in whom it is strong that nothing which conflicts with it could be otherwise than momentarily an object of desire to them. Whoever supposes that this preference takes place at a sacrifice of happiness—that the superior being, in anything like equal circumstances, is not happier than the inferior—confounds the two very different ideas of happiness and content. It is indisputable that the being whose capacities of enjoyment are low has the greatest chance of having them fully satisfied; and a highly endowed being will always feel that any happiness which he can look for, as the world is constituted, is imperfect. But he can learn to bear its imperfections, if they are at all bearable; and they will not make him envy the being who is indeed unconscious of the imperfections, but only because he feels not at all the good which those imperfections qualify. It is better to be a human being dissatisfied than a pig satisfied; better to be Socrates dissatisfied than a fool satisfied. And if the fool, or the pig, are of a different opinion, it is because they only know their own side of the question. The other party to the comparison knows both sides.

It may be objected that many who are capable of the higher pleasures occasionally, under the influence of temptation, postpone them to the lower. But this is quite compatible with a full appreciation of the intrinsic superiority of the higher. Men often, from infirmity of character, make their election for the nearer good, though they know it to be the less valuable; and this no less when the choice is between two bodily pleasures than when it is between bodily and mental. They pursue sensual indulgences to the injury of health, though perfectly aware that health is the greater good. It may be further objected that many who begin with youthful enthusiasm for everything noble, as they advance in years, sink into indolence and selfishness. But I do not believe that those who undergo this very common change voluntarily choose the lower description of pleasures in preference to the higher. I believe that, before they devote themselves exclusively to the one, they have already become incapable of the other. Capacity for the nobler feelings is in most natures a very tender plant, easily killed, not only by hostile influences, but by mere want of sustenance; and in the majority of young persons it speedily dies away if the occupations to which their position in life has devoted them, and the society into which it has thrown them, are not favorable to keeping that higher capacity in exercise. Men lose their high aspirations as they lose their intellectual tastes, because they have not time or opportunity for indulging them; and they addict themselves to inferior pleasures, not because they deliberately prefer them, but because they are either the only ones to which they have access or the only ones which they are any longer capable of enjoying. It may be questioned whether anyone who has remained equally susceptible to both classes of pleasures ever knowingly and calmly preferred the lower, though many, in all ages, have broken down in an ineffectual attempt to combine both.

From this verdict of the only competent judges, I apprehend there can be no appeal. On a question which is the best worth having of two pleasures, or which of two modes of existence is the most grateful to the feelings, apart from its moral attributes and from its consequences, the judgment of those who are qualified by knowledge of both, or, if they differ, that of the majority among them, must be admitted as final. And there needs be the less hesitation to accept this judgment respecting the quality of pleasures, since there is no other tribunal to be referred to even on the question of quantity. What means are there of determining which is the acutest of two pains, or the intensest of two pleasurable sensations, except the general suffrage of those who are familiar with both? Neither pains nor pleasures are homogeneous, and pain is always heterogeneous with pleasure. What is there to decide whether a particular pleasure is worth purchasing at the cost of a particular pain, except the feelings and judgment of the experienced? When, therefore, those feelings and judgment declare the pleasures derived from the higher faculties to be preferable *in kind,* apart from the question of intensity, to those of which the animal nature, disjoined from the higher faculties, is susceptible, they are entitled on this subject to the same regard.

I have dwelt on this point as being a necessary part of a perfectly just conception of utility or happiness considered as the directive rule of human conduct. But it is by no means an indispensable condition to the acceptance of the utilitarian standard; for that standard is not the agent's own greatest happiness, but the greatest amount of happiness altogether; and if it may possibly be doubted whether a noble character is always the happier for its nobleness, there can be no doubt that it makes other people happier, and that the world in general is immensely a gainer by it. Utilitarianism, therefore, could only attain its end by the general cultivation of nobleness of character, even if each individual were only benefited by the nobleness of others, and his own, so far as happiness is concerned, were a sheer deduction from the benefit. But the bare enunciation of such an absurdity as this last renders refutation superfluous.

According to the greatest happiness principle, as above explained, the ultimate end, with reference to and for the sake of which all other things are desirable—whether we are considering our own good or that of other people—is an existence exempt as far as possible from pain, and as rich as possible in enjoyments, both in point of quantity and quality; the test of quality and the rule for measuring it against quantity being the preference felt by those who, in their opportunities of experience, to which must be added their habits of self-consciousness and self-observation, are best furnished with the means of comparison. This, being according to the utilitarian opinion the end of human action, is necessarily also the standard of morality, which may accordingly be defined "the rules and precepts for human conduct," by the observance of which an existence such as has been described might be, to the greatest extent possible, secured to all mankind; and not to them only, but, so far as the nature of things admits, to the whole sentient creation.

When, however, it is thus positively asserted to be impossible that human life should be happy, the assertion, if not something like a verbal quibble, is at least an exaggeration. If by happiness be meant a continuity of highly pleasurable excitement, it is evident enough that this is impossible. A state of exalted pleasure lasts only moments or in some cases, and with some intermissions, hours or days, and is the occasional brilliant flash of enjoyment, not its permanent and steady flame. Of this the philosophers who have taught that happiness is the end of life were as fully aware as those who taunt them. The happiness which they meant was not a life of rapture, but moments of such, in an existence made up of few and transitory pains, many and various pleasures, with a decided predominance of the active over the passive, and having as the foundation of the whole not to expect more from life than it is capable of bestowing. A life thus composed, to those who have been fortunate enough to obtain it, has always appeared worthy of the name of happiness. And such an existence is even now the lot of many during some considerable portion of their lives. The present wretched education and wretched social arrangements are the only real hindrance to its being attainable by almost all.

The objectors perhaps may doubt whether human beings, if taught to consider happiness as the end of life, would be satisfied with such a moderate share of it. But great numbers of mankind have been satisfied with much less. The main constituents of a satisfied life appear to be two, either of which by itself is often found sufficient for the purpose: tranquillity and excitement. With much tranquillity, many find that they can be content with very little pleasure; with much excitement, many can reconcile themselves to a considerable quantity of pain. There is assuredly no inherent impossibility of enabling even the mass of mankind to unite both, since the two are so far from being incompatible that they are in natural alliance, the prolongation of either being a preparation for, and exciting a wish for, the other. It is only those in whom indolence amounts to a vice that do not desire excitement after an interval of repose; it is only those in whom the need of excitement is a disease that feel the tranquillity which follows excitement dull and insipid, instead of pleasurable in direct proportion to the excitement which preceded it. When people who are tolerably fortunate in their outward lot do not find in life sufficient enjoyment to make it valuable to them, the cause generally is caring for nobody but themselves. To those who have neither public nor private affections, the excitements of life are much curtailed, and in any case dwindle in value as the time approaches when all selfish interests must be terminated by death; while those who leave after them objects of personal affection, and especially those who have also cultivated a fellow-feeling with the collective interests of mankind, retain as lively an interest in life on the eve of death as in the vigor of youth and health. Next to selfishness, the principal cause which makes life unsatisfactory is want of mental cultivation. A cultivated mind—I do not mean that of a philosopher, but any mind to which the fountains of knowledge have been opened, and which has been taught, in any tolerable degree, to exercise its faculties—finds sources of inexhaustible interest in all that surrounds it: in the objects of nature, the achievements of art, the imaginations of poetry, the incidents of history, the ways of mankind, past and present, and their prospects in the future.

Meanwhile, let utilitarians never cease to claim the morality of self-devotion as a possession which belongs by as good a right to them as either to the Stoic or to the Transcendentalist. The utilitarian morality does recognize in human beings the power of sacrificing their own greatest good for the good of others. It only refuses to admit that the sacrifice is itself a good. A sacrifice which does not increase or tend to increase the sum total of happiness, it considers as wasted. The only self-renunciation which it applauds is devotion to the happiness, or to some of the means of happiness, of others, either of mankind collectively or of individuals within the limits imposed by the collective interests of mankind.

I must again repeat what the assailants of utilitarianism seldom have the justice to acknowledge, that the happiness which forms the utilitarian standard of what is right in conduct is not the agent's own happiness but that of all concerned. As between his own happiness and that of others, utilitarianism requires him to be as strictly impartial as a disinterested and benevolent spectator. In the golden rule of Jesus of Nazareth, we read the complete spirit of the ethics of utility. "To do as you would be done by," and "to love your neighbor as yourself," constitute the ideal perfection of utilitarian morality. As the means of making the nearest approach to this ideal, utility would enjoin, first, that laws and social arrangements should place the happiness or (as, speaking practically, it may be called) the interest of every individual as nearly as possible in harmony with the interest of the whole; and, secondly, that education and opinion, which have so vast a power over human character, should so use that power as to establish in the mind of every individual an indissoluble association between his own happiness and the good of the whole, especially between his own happiness and the practice of such modes of conduct, negative and positive, as regard for the universal happiness prescribes; so that not only he may be unable to conceive the possibility of happiness to himself, consistently with conduct opposed to the general good, but also that a direct impulse to promote the general good may be in every individual one of the habitual motives of action, and the sentiments connected therewith may fill a large and prominent place in every human being's sentient existence. If the impugners of the utilitarian morality represented it to their own minds in this its true character, I know not what recommendation possessed by any other morality they could possibly affirm to be wanting to it; what more beautiful or more exalted developments of human nature any other ethical system can be supposed to foster, or what springs of action, not accessible to the utilitarian, such systems rely on for giving effect to their mandates.

The objectors to utilitarianism cannot always be charged with representing it in a discreditable light. On the contrary, those among them who entertain anything like a just idea of its disinterested character sometimes find fault with its standard as being too high for humanity. They say it is exacting too much to require that people shall always act from the inducement of promoting the general interests of society. But this is to mistake the very meaning of a standard of morals and confound the rule of action with the motive of it. It is the business of ethics to tell us what are our duties, or by what test we may know them; but no system of ethics requires that the sole motive of all we do shall be a feeling of duty; on the contrary, ninety-nine hundredths of all our actions are done from other motives, and rightly so done if the rule of duty does not condemn them. It is the more unjust to utilitarianism that this particular misapprehension should be made a ground of objection to it, inasmuch as utilitarian moralists have gone beyond almost all others in affirming that the motive has nothing to do with the morality of the action, though much with the worth of the agent. He who saves a fellow creature from drowning does what is morally right, whether his motive be duty or the hope of being paid for his trouble; he who betrays the friend that trusts him is guilty of a crime, even if his object be to serve another friend to whom he is under greater obligations. But to speak only of actions done from the motive of duty, and in direct obedience to principle: it is a misapprehension of the utilitarian mode of thought to conceive it as implying that people should fix their minds upon so wide a generality as the world, or society at large. The great majority of good actions are intended not for the benefit of the world, but for that of individuals, of which the good of the world is made up; and the thoughts of the most virtuous man need not on these occasions travel beyond the particular persons concerned, except so far as is necessary to assure himself that in benefiting them he is not violating the rights, that is, the legitimate and authorized expectations, of anyone else. The multiplication of happiness is, according to the utilitarian ethics, the object of virtue: the occasions on which any person (except one in a thousand) has it in his power to do this on an extended scale—in other words, to be a public benefactor— are but exceptional; and on these occasions alone is he called on to consider public utility; in every other case, private utility, the interest or happiness of some few persons, is all he has to attend to. Those alone the influence of whose actions extends to society in general need concern themselves habitually about so large an object. In the case of abstinences indeed —of things which people forbear to do from moral considerations, though the consequences in the particular case might be beneficial—it would be unworthy of an intelligent agent not to be consciously aware that the action is of a class which, if practiced generally, would be generally injurious, and that this is the ground of the obligation to abstain from it. The amount of regard for the public interest implied in this recognition is no greater than is demanded by every system of morals, for they all enjoin to abstain from whatever is manifestly pernicious to society.

Of the Ultimate Sanction of the Principle of Utility

The question is often asked, and properly so, in regard to any supposed moral standard—what is its sanction? what are the motives to obey? or, more specifically, what is the source of its obligation? whence does it derive its binding force? It is a necessary part of moral philosophy to provide the answer to this question, which, though frequently assuming the shape of an objection to the utilitarian morality, as if it had some special applicability to that above others, really arises in regard to all standards. It arises, in fact, whenever a person is called on to *adopt* a standard, or refer morality to any basis on which he has not been accustomed to rest it. For the customary morality, that which education and opinion have consecrated, is the only one which presents itself to the mind with the feeling of being *in itself* obligatory; and when a person is asked to believe that this morality *derives* its obligation from some general principle round which custom has not thrown the same halo, the assertion is to him a paradox; the supposed corollaries seem to have a more binding force than the original theorem; the superstructure seems to stand better without than with what is represented as its foundation. He says to himself, I feel that I am bound not to rob or murder, betray or deceive; but why am I bound to promote the general happiness? If my own happiness lies in something else, why may I not give that the preference?

The principle of utility either has, or there is no reason why it might not have, all the sanctions which belong to any other system of morals. Those sanctions are either external or internal. Of the external sanctions it is not necessary to speak at any length. They are the hope of favor and the fear of displeasure from our fellow creatures or from the Ruler of the universe, along with whatever we may have of sympathy or affection for them, or of love and awe of Him, inclining us to do His will independently of selfish consequences. There is evidently no reason why all these motives for observance should not attach themselves to the utilitarian morality as completely and as powerfully as to any other. Indeed, those of them which refer to our fellow creatures are sure to do so, in proportion to the amount of general intelligence; for whether there be any other ground of moral obligation than the general happiness or not, men do desire happiness; and however imperfect may be their own practice, they desire and commend all conduct in others toward themselves by which they think their happiness is promoted. With regard to the religious motive, if men believe, as most profess to do, in the goodness of God, those who think that conduciveness to the general happiness is the essence or even only the criterion of good must necessarily believe that it is also that which God approves. The whole force therefore of external reward and punishment, whether physical or moral, and whether proceeding from God or from our fellow men, together with all that the capacities of human nature admit of disinterested devotion to either, become available to enforce the utilitarian morality, in proportion as that morality is recognized; and the more powerfully, the more the appliances of education and general cultivation are bent to the purpose.

So far as to external sanctions. The internal sanction of duty, whatever our standard of duty may be, is one and the same—a feeling in our own mind; a pain, more or less intense, attendant on violation of duty, which in properly cultivated moral natures rises, in the more serious cases, into shrinking from it as an impossibility. This feeling, when disinterested and connecting itself with the pure idea of duty, and not with some particular form of it, or with any of the merely accessory circumstances, is the essence of conscience; though in that complex phenomenon as it actually exists, the simple fact is in general all encrusted over with collateral associations derived from sympathy, from love, and still more from fear; from all the forms of religious feeling; from the recollections of childhood and of all our past life; from self-esteem, desire of the esteem of others, and occasionally even self-abasement. This extreme complication is, I apprehend, the origin of the sort of mystical character which, by a tendency of the human mind of which there are many other examples, is apt to be attributed to the idea of moral obligation, and which leads people to believe that the idea cannot possibly attach itself to any other objects than those which, by a supposed mysterious law, are found in our present experience to excite it. Its binding force, however, consists in the existence of a mass of feeling which must be broken through in order to do what violates our standard of right, and which, if we do nevertheless violate that standard, will probably have to be encountered afterwards in the form of remorse. Whatever theory we have of the nature of origin of conscience, this is what essentially constitutes it.

The ultimate sanction, therefore, of all morality (external motives apart) being a subjective feeling in our own minds, I see nothing embarrassing to those whose standard is utility in the question, What is the sanction of that particular standard? We may answer, the same as of all other moral standards—the conscientious feelings of mankind. Undoubtedly this sanction has no binding efficacy on those who do not possess the feelings it appeals to; but neither will these persons be more obedient to any other moral principle than to the utilitarian one. On them morality of any kind has no hold but through the external sanctions. Meanwhile the feelings exist, a fact in human nature, the reality of which, and the great power with which they are capable of acting on those in whom they have been duly cultivated, are proved by experience. No reason has ever been shown why they may not be cultivated to as great intensity in connection with the utilitarian as with any other rule of morals.

It is not necessary, for the present purpose, to decide whether the feeling of duty is innate or implanted. Assuming it to be innate, it is an open question to what objects it naturally attaches itself; for the philosophic supporters of that theory are now agreed that the intuitive perception is of principles of morality and not of the details. If there be anything innate in the matter, I see no reason why the feeling which is innate should not be that of regard to the pleasures and pains of others. If there is any principle of morals which is intuitively obligatory, I should say it must be that. If so, the intuitive ethics would coincide with the utilitarian, and there would be no further quarrel between them. Even as it is, the intuitive moralists, though they believe that there are other intuitive moral obligations, do already believe this to be one; for they unanimously hold that a large *portion* of morality turns upon the consideration due to the interests of our fellow creatures. Therefore, if the belief in the transcendental origin of moral obligation gives any additional efficacy to the internal sanction, it appears to me that the utilitarian principle has already the benefit of it.

On the other hand, if, as is my own belief, the moral feelings are not innate but acquired, they are not for that reason the less natural. It is natural to man to speak, to reason, to build cities, to cultivate the ground, though these are acquired faculties. The moral feelings are not indeed a part of our nature in the sense of being in any perceptible degree present in all of us; but this, unhappily, is a fact admitted by those who believe the most strenuously in their transcendental origin. Like the other acquired capacities above referred to, the moral faculty, if not a part of our nature, is a natural outgrowth from it; capable, like them, in a certain small degree, of springing up spontaneously; and susceptible of being brought by cultivation to a high degree of development. Unhappily it is also susceptible, by a sufficient use of the external sanctions and of the force of early impressions, of being cultivated in almost any direction, so that there is hardly anything so absurd or so mischievous that it may not, by means of these influences, be made to act on the human mind with all the authority of conscience. To doubt that the same potency might be given by the same means to the principle of utility, even if it had no foundation in human nature, would be flying in the face of all experience.

But moral associations which are wholly of artificial creation, when the intellectual culture goes on, yield by degrees to the dissolving force of analysis; and if the feeling of duty, when associated with utility, would appear equally arbitrary; if there were no leading department of our nature, no powerful class of sentiments, with which that association would harmonize, which would make us feel it congenial and incline us not only to foster it in others (for which we have abundant interested motives), but also to cherish it in ourselves—if there were not, in short, a natural basis of sentiment for utilitarian morality, it might well happen that this association also, even after it had been implanted by education, might be analyzed away.

But there *is* this basis of powerful natural sentiment; and this it is which, when once the general happiness is recognized as the ethical standard, will constitute the strength of the utilitarian morality. This firm foundation is that of the social feelings of mankind—the desire to be in unity with our fellow creatures, which is already a powerful principle in human nature, and happily one of those which tend to become stronger, even without express inculcation, from the influences of advancing civilization.

. . . Neither is it necessary to the feeling which constitutes the binding force of the utilitarian morality on those who recognize it to wait for those social influences which would make its obligation felt by mankind at large. In the comparatively early state of human advancement in which we now live, a person cannot, indeed, feel that entireness of sympathy with all others which would make any real discordance in the general direction of their conduct in life impossible, but already a person in whom the social feeling is at all developed cannot bring himself to think of the rest of his fellow creatures as struggling rivals with him for the means of happiness, whom he must desire to see defeated in their object in order that he may succeed in his. The deeply rooted conception which every individual even now has of himself as a social being tends to make him feel it one of his natural wants that there should be harmony between his feelings and aims and those of his fellow creatures. If differences of opinion and of mental culture make it impossible for him to share many of their actual feelings —perhaps make him denounce and defy those feelings—he still needs to be conscious that his real aim and theirs do not conflict; that he is not opposing himself to what they really wish for, namely, their own good, but is, on the contrary, promoting it. This feeling in most individuals is much inferior in strength to their selfish feelings, and is often wanting altogether. But to those who have it, it possesses all the characters of a natural feeling. It does not present itself to their minds as a superstition of education or a law despotically imposed by the power of society, but as an attribute which it would not be well for them to be without. This conviction is the ultimate sanction of the greatest happiness morality. This it is which makes any mind of well-developed feelings work with, and not against, the outward motives to care for others, afforded by what I have called the external sanctions; and, when those sanctions are wanting or act in an opposite direction, constitutes in itself a powerful internal binding force, in proportion to the sensitiveness and thoughtfulness of the character, since few but those whose mind is a moral blank could bear to lay out their course of life on the plan of paying no regard to others except so far as their own private interest compels.

Of What Sort of Proof the Principle of Utility Is Susceptible

. . . The utilitarian doctrine is that happiness is desirable, and the only thing desirable as an end; all other things being only desirable as means to that end. What ought to be required of this doctrine, what conditions is it requisite that the doctrine should fulfil—to make good its claim to be believed?

The only proof capable of being given that an object is visible is that people actually see it. The only proof that a sound is audible is that people hear it; and so of the other sources of our experience. In like manner, I apprehend, the sole evidence it is possible to produce that anything is desirable is that people do actually desire it. If the end which the utilitarian doctrine proposes to itself were not, in theory and in practice, acknowledged to be an end, nothing could ever convince any person that it was so. No reason can be given why the general happiness is desirable, except that each person, so far as he believes it to be attainable, desires his own happiness. This, however, being a fact, we have not only all the proof which the case admits of, but which it is possible to require, that happiness is a good, that each person's happiness is a good to that person, and the general happiness, therefore, a good to the aggregate of all persons . . .

. . . there is in reality nothing desired except happiness. Whatever is desired otherwise than as a means to some end beyond itself, and ultimately to happiness, is desired as itself a part of happiness, and is not desired for itself until it has become so. Those who desire virtue for its own sake desire it either because the consciousness of it is a pleasure, or because the consciousness of being without it is a pain, or for both reasons united; as in truth the pleasure and pain seldom exist separately, but almost always together—the same person feeling pleasure in the degree of virtue attained, and pain in not having attained more . . .

6
Deontological Ethics: Kant

The theories of obligation we have looked at thus far have been teleological. Aristotle's was what is called self-realization; ethical egoism and hedonism round out the result theories. In presenting deontological ethics we are at last treating ethical theories that are similar to traditional religious ethics in the West, and the reader will quickly notice a similarity in Kant and the Golden Rule, though there are some occasionally startling differences.

Right and Good

In recent ethics it has become conventional to restrict right to a description of actions, and good to other things on which a positive value is placed. If we apply this distinction to the difference between teleological (result) and deontological ethics, the rather neat kind of distinction can be made that result theories base their theory of obligation (what is right) on their theory of value (what is good), whereas deontological theories have a theory of obligation that tries to "go it alone" without any help from a theory of value. Probably this is much too neat, as the average reader may have felt about the "good–right" distinction all along. (One might ask, e.g., is there no such thing as good conduct, doing good, and the like?) And especially if we suppose that a deontological theory will ignore results in a "damn-the-torpedoes-full-speed-ahead" attitude, we are going to be puzzled, or at least intrigued by just how a neat trick of that kind can be pulled off. Well, the prime example of deontological theories, Kant's, does some impressive things, and may do that, but some scholars of his ethics, e.g., Paton, do not think he makes the radical "good–right" distinction, and that he seriously talks about good actions, not simply doing right.

181

Some Background

Kant died two years before Mill was born, but he makes an excellent rebuttal to Mill before the fact in that many of the things Mill said, other hedonists had claimed before him, and many of the problems Mill tried to solve were those that Kant (with some credit to Hume) had pointed out earlier. Aside from that, Kant's distinctions in ethics are sometimes unavoidable, and here, as has been said about the rest of his philosophy by others, a person might not agree with Kant, but one can hardly avoid or ignore him and the problems he dealt with. Some of these distinctions will be pointed out as they arise and their connections with previous chapters will be noted.

Immanuel Kant is famous for his Copernican Revolution in philosophy, as he called it, the theory that in knowledge the mind does not conform itself to the world, the world conforms itself to the knowing mind. In terms of computers (which eighteenth-century theories of mind lend themselves to, because they emphasize machinery so much) nothing can get into the mind but what is programmed into it, and no output can be expected from it that it is not structured to deliver. Or, in terms of optics, just as the person who wears blue-tinted eyeglasses will see the world blue, one who views the world through his or her mind will see it tinted in the colors the mind puts on it. Thus, for instance, Kant accounted for the impressiveness of Newton's Laws of Physics: Our minds are Newtonian, they cannot make sense of the world in any other way except as governed by rigid laws of cause and effect, action and reaction, and mathematically, our minds are Euclidean: We cannot perceive space otherwise than in terms of Euclid's geometry, and so on; put on Newtonian and Euclidean spectacles and you will swear the world is Newtonian and Euclidean. Only, of course, it is Nature itself that has made our minds the way they are, and there is no taking off of the "glasses"; the price would be to have no mind, to perceive nothing.

Now, Kant may have hoped that the famous book in which he set forth the above theory, *Critique of Pure Reason,* would be long enough and systematic enough to cover not only knowledge of the world through science and mathematics, but also give an account of human action in the realm of right and wrong, good and evil. But if so, he found that the subject was too large or too difficult to fit into that book and had to wait for other publications, his *Fundamental Principles of the Metaphysics of Morals* (hereafter, *Grundlegung,* after the first word in its German title), *Critique of Practical Reason,* and *The Metaphysics of Ethics.* Our account here is based on his most widely read and most influential little book on ethics, the *Grundlegung.*

Good Will, Duty, Autonomy,
and the Categorical Imperative

In orienting himself in the world of action and morality, Kant sticks closely to the emphasis upon laws that characterizes his philosophy of knowledge. But if human choice and action are purely a matter of cause-and-effect laws, Kant is quick to say, there cannot be any such thing as right and wrong, or of what a person ought or ought not to do, since a person would only do what he or she is caused to do by "heredity," "environment," and the like. Kant is supposed to have said, "I ought implies I can," that is, if doing what I ought to do is as impossible as floating on air without help when I am thrown out the window (defying the law of gravity), there is no ought. So morality presupposes free will or, as he conceived it, self-determination. Man stands above nature in the sense that he is a being who not simply obeys the laws of nature (physiological, psychological, and so on) but acts in accordance with his idea of laws, and indeed, as the political realm suggests, makes his own laws for acting. Man is, as Kant puts it, a being who can be autonomous, self-governing, including self-legislating. But every individual who is normal has the same ability and whatever right one person has to live by one set of laws, the next person would have the same right to live by another set of his or her own making. This does not, as we might at first suppose, lead to the conclusion that everybody should be permitted to make his or her own rules in any way he or she happens to please, and by whatever principles, be they aesthetic or economic or political. Rather, in Kant's hands, this doctrine gets a very different kind of expression, since he does not regard freedom as doing whatever one happens to please.

Being free—or at least, if he is not free, morality makes no sense —is man then simply in a chaos, a natural anarchy in which each person may seek whatever values he or she happens to acquire along the way? Not at all. Kant's first move here is to find some absolute, some guidepost. It is the concept of the good will that he selects. All goods that people might seek can be bad if used by a person with a bad will—all goods except a good will that uses them. Only that is good without exception or qualification. But a good will is not the result of actions (except, of course, the actions of training or raising children, and the like); it is the cause of actions. So Kant has shut off result theories immediately, by saying they (result theories, like hedonism) are all about qualified and conditional goods.

What is a will? As applied to choices about right and wrong, surely, Kant says that it is practical reason, that is, seeing an end and finding means to it is a business that falls under the province of reason, reason being practical or applied to practice. Kant attacks hedonism on the ground that reason itself is poorly adapted to securing pleasure, or even happiness in some other sense, perhaps. And, as in other areas, human faculties are well adapted to their ends, so we must suppose that reason has some end other than happiness. Instinct would have done a better job if Nature had meant for us to seek happiness as the primary goal of life. No, reason is adapted to creating a good will, says Kant.

A good will is one that acts from duty, or the reverence (*achtung*) for law (moral law, or at least the general idea of law). Kant reminds us time and again that any motive that springs primarily from inclination or interest (self-interest) will be one that belongs to the realm of heteronomy of the will and not freedom. That is a point we must examine if we are to get the often subtle reasoning in Kant's ethics. It is easy to suppose that freedom is doing as you please, whatever you please. Not so in Kant. Pleasing, in the sense of following one's impulses or emotions (inclinations), be they ever so generous, is not being self-governed, but being governed by them, and they are in turn effects of something in heredity and environment. Choosing between one's own inclinations, and choosing to follow one, rather than another, is more on the order of freedom, but it does not consist simply of one inclination choosing itself over another inclination, but of something other than inclination, reason, or will. We might dispute Kant on this point, and argue that they are our inclinations, after all, and that we came by them honestly, but he will have none of that; insofar as they are in the cause-and-effect order of things, it is not morality but—cause and effect—nature.

What, then, is a worthy motive for doing right? The mere fact that it is right, says Kant. This requires explanation, so that it is not mere dogmatism. The idea of doing one's duty for the sake of duty is the only one that steers clear of self-interest and inclination, which yield no absolute sense of duty, or absolute right or wrong. The best they yield is: "If you want happiness, and the like, do this (some act, x)." But if you don't want happiness, you can shrug your shoulders and say, "I don't have to." Kant did not think that of this as the voice of duty, this "if" kind of advice, and he called them hypothetical imperatives. Duty rather says that something is right or something is wrong, no "if's," "and's," or "but's." "Do your duty, whatever it might be" is the formal kind of command that we get from looking closely at the very idea of morality, he claims, and a commitment to that is the thing we look for when we look for a person with a good will, and when we look for a good will in ourselves.

"Do your duty, whatever it might be" might not seem to take us anywhere. But what is my duty? Should I promote the greatest happiness for the greatest number, or what? Kant says this is only a formal principle; it does not, in itself, spell out any particular action to perform under any particular circumstances. It is, rather, a principle for judging all other principles a person may act upon, the supreme principle of morality. It is a test for any moral rule that is put forth as one to act upon. Kant calls these lesser principles maxims. For instance, a person sees that he or she needs money desperately to get out of a serious bind and the only way to get it is to borrow it, even though he or she can never pay it back, but the money will not be lent unless he or she promises to pay it back. A person who decides to make a lying promise of this kind is acting on the maxim that one should lie whenever this seems to be the only way to get out of a bind.

At this point the notion of acting from a sense of duty for duty's sake needs further clarification. How could it test the maxim that a person should lie if that is the only way to get out of a bind? Kant now spells out the idea of morality more clearly. If we really are free and self-governing, if we really take the notion seriously that reason is the means or faculty by which we are self-governing, and especially, if you and he and she and all other normal people have the same faculty of reason that I have and the same right to use it to govern their own actions, what happens? We see that if I have a right to lie to you when I'm in a pinch, you have a right to lie to me when you're in one, and so forth. But the very maxim should say that this is what anybody should do in these circumstances, for it is only incidental, as far as reason is concerned, that I happen to be the one. I could not generalize (or universalize) this maxim and want everyone to do as I find myself wanting to do here and now. So the basic ground rule for this whole business of morality becomes more recognizable, and sounds a little like the Golden Rule. The ground rule is simply that I cannot, morally, do what I could not in all consistency want everybody else to do in the same circumstances. Kant calls this the categorical imperative, that is, a command with no if's, an unconditional command. He has several—at least three—ways of stating it but this is the first.

Kant gives examples of the difference between a will that acts as duty requires, and a will that acts because duty requires. A business might always give the correct change, but one might do it because it is "good for business" while another does it because it is right. We could add a third type, one who does it because honesty has been beaten into him in childhood, or because he is acting under posthypnotic suggestion, or the like. Kant interprets all of these except the second as a will that is not autonomous, but heteronomous. The public is well served by all these people, he admits, and the results are good in all these cases. And, given a choice, a person would much rather deal with a person who is honest because of posthypnotic suggestion or past beatings than a person who will cheat another every chance he or she gets. Yet, we are discussing morality, Kant reminds us, and the moral worth of an action is assured only by the motive of duty. If there are, as we often suppose, mixed motives in actions—e.g., if a person gives the right change partly because it's wrong to cheat another, and partly because it's bad for business if discovered—Paton interprets Kant as holding that if the motive of duty is sufficient alone to determine the action without the presence of self-interest, the act is morally good. Kant sometimes sounded as if medicine had to taste bad to be good, e.g., if a person detests his or her life and wants to die, but refuses to commit suicide because it would be wrong, there is the only kind of self-preservation that deserves praise as being morally good. The first law of nature so much touted by Hobbes, self-preservation, has nothing to do with morality, so far as Kant is concerned. Self-preservation because of the moral law, not some law of nature, is of moral worth.

There are three different forms at least of the categorical imperative: The first says that a person should not do anything that he or she could not consistently will others to have to do. As a test for maxims, e.g., one can will his or her own lie to get out of a difficulty, but everyone should not have to lie to get out of trouble, for as applied to lying promises to repay debts, it would be a maxim that would simply eliminate the reliability of promises. One might compare the maxim: "Whenever I am short of money, I will print up a batch." This maxim, if everyone followed it, would eliminate money. Oddly enough, it is the fact that the counterfeit is the undetected exception that gives it whatever worth it has. Kant has much to say of exception: To make an exception of oneself is the essence of irrationality and immorality. To say, "Well, I know that what I am about to do is immoral by most standards, but I am an exception and no one will ever know that I am making an exception of myself, e.g., if someone complains, I'll fast-talk him and make him think it's really right, after all," is indeed to do as many people do, but it is outside the pale of morality, rather like an undetected illegal punch is outside of boxing, or an undetected spitball is outside of baseball. This leads us to the third formula for the categorical imperative (we'll return to the second).

Now suppose that someone says, "Ah, but a person in a ball game or boxing match is under careful supervision, and thousands of people are watching. More players would cheat if they could." Kant can take two kinds of approach to that objection: One is simply an "It's not cricket" approach: Call it something, but don't call it baseball or boxing. Applied to morality, ulterior motives simply must be ruled out; we are speaking only of what one must do if one wants to do what is right, not of what one must do to get certain results that are desired. The other is the kingdom of ends approach suggested by the third formula for the categorical imperative: *Always act as if you were a member of a kingdom of ends.* Surely, I do not know whether most other people are going to play me for a sucker when I try to do what is right. But I have to act as if I were a member of a society of rational beings, not animals, if I am going to pretend to any moral principles, even to myself. If I do get the worst end of things when I try to play by the moral rules (not just the rules of a particular society, but by the rules I think they ought to have), that is the chance I take. And rational beings have the same right to make rules as I do, and the right to be treated as I would insist by my rules that they treat me, whatever the rules may be. Both they and I have the same status of being ruler and ruled by the laws that we make. That is a kingdom of ends (and it came through Rousseau from some concepts in historical religious thought, and went on through Kant to Hegel and Sartre to some very different conclusions).

The second categorical imperative formulation is: *Always treat human beings, whether yourself or others, as an end in itself and never as a means only.* Autonomous, rational beings are such, since they make their own laws. They are not given innate laws of nature, instincts, to direct them toward some end that Nature intends them to reach, as Kant reminded us when he said that if Nature had wanted us to be happy, she would have given us an unerring instinct for happiness, but instead she has given us reason as the highest faculty we have to govern our lives. Notice that Kant does not say that it is immoral to treat people as means, for we must in some sense use each other, but making mere tools of people is what the categorical imperative forbids.

Criticisms and Defenses of Kant

Currently there is great agreement among moral philosophers that Kant supplied an essential to ethics: the generalizability or universalizability test—could I really want everyone to have to do what I am wanting to do, in the same circumstances? (Again, it is irrelevant to the circumstances that I am individual A and they are individuals B, C, and D, and so on.) There has been almost equally widespread doubt, however, that this is sufficient, as Kant claims. For instance, what if two duties conflict? Suppose that I cannot both tell the truth and save someone's life, for telling the truth will bring about his or her death? Kant's answer was that although I am autonomous, I am not omniscient; I don't really know that telling the truth is going to kill anyone, e.g., when an apparent assassin is looking for his victim and asks me if I have seen him, or when a person with a weak heart or a survivor of an auto crash asks if a loved one is dead in the crash. Tell the truth, if you are asked, but don't go around blabbing everything you know without a reason; this is Kant's advice. This is pretty thin, for it seems to want to say that we never know that two duties really are in conflict, when all our experience seems to point in the opposite direction.

W. D. Ross, late of Oxford, tried to supplement or correct Kant here. Suppose that I do see two things that seem to be my duties and that I literally can't do both, so far as I can tell. Surely, it is a duty *prima facie,* or all other things being equal, to tell the truth, just as it's my prima facie duty to stop for a red light. But if a person steps up to my car and wields a knife while I'm sitting there, I'd be irrational to wait for the light to turn green. Get out of there! So, if telling the truth endangers a life, I'd be irrational to do it.

Finally, there is the challenging task of seeing how the three forms of the Categorical Imperative really are merely three different ways of saying the same thing (as Kant claims), or having to give up in despair and concluding that they are really more than one supposedly "supreme moral principle." Some may think it an indication of the greatness of a philosopher that his interpreters would occasionally find that their reach exceeds their grasp. In any case, Kant's greatness is not especially diminished by more than a few of just such occasions.

THE FUNDAMENTAL PRINCIPLES
OF THE METAPHYSICS OF MORALS °

IMMANUEL KANT

Transition From the Common Rational Knowledge of Morality to the Philosophical

Nothing can possibly be conceived in the world, or even out of it, which can be called good without qualification, except a *good will.* Intelligence, wit, judgment, and the other *talents* of the mind, however they may be named, or courage, resolution, perseverance, as qualities of temperament, are undoubtedly good and desirable in many respects; but these gifts of nature may also become extremely bad and mischievous if the will which is to make use of them, and which, therefore, constitutes what is called *character,* is not good. It is the same with the *gifts of fortune.* Power, riches, honor, even health, and the general well-being and contentment with one's condition which is called *happiness,* inspire pride, and often presumption, if there is not a good will to correct the influence of these on the mind, and with this also to rectify the whole principle of acting,

° From Immanuel Kant, THE FUNDAMENTAL PRINCIPLES OF THE META-PHYSICS OF MORALS, translated by Thomas K. Abbott, ed. by Marvin Fox, copyright © 1949 by The Bobbs-Merrill Co., Inc. Reprinted with permission. Sections 1 and 2.

and adapt it to its end. The sight of a being who is not adorned with a single feature of a pure and good will, enjoying unbroken prosperity, can never give pleasure to an impartial rational spectator. Thus a good will appears to constitute the indispensable condition even of being worthy of happiness.

There are even some qualities which are of service to this good will itself, and may facilitate its action, yet which have no intrinsic unconditional value, but always presuppose a good will, and this qualifies the esteem that we justly have for them, and does not permit us to regard them as absolutely good. Moderation in the affections and passions, self-control, and calm deliberation are not only good in many respects, but even seem to constitute part of the intrinsic worth of the person; but they are far from deserving to be called good without qualification, although they have been so unconditionally praised by the ancients. For without the principles of a good will, they may become extremely bad; and the coolness of a villain not only makes him far more dangerous, but also directly makes him more abominable in our eyes than he would have been without it.

A good will is good not because of what it performs or effects, not by its aptness for the attainment of some proposed end, but simply by virtue of the volition—that is, it is good in itself, and considered by itself is to be esteemed much higher than all that can be brought about by it in favor of any inclination, nay, even of the sum-total of all inclinations. Even if it should happen that, owing to special disfavor of fortune, or the niggardly provision of a step-motherly nature, this will should wholly lack power to accomplish its purpose, if with its greatest efforts it should yet achieve nothing, and there should remain only the good will (not, to be sure, a mere wish, but the summoning of all means in our power), then, like a jewel, it would still shine by its own light, as a thing which has its whole value in itself. Its usefulness or fruitlessness can neither add to nor take away anything from this value. It would be, as it were, only the setting to enable us to handle it the more conveniently in common commerce, or to attract to it the attention of those who are not yet connoisseurs, but not to recommend it to true connoisseurs, or to determine its value.

There is, however, something so strange in this idea of the absolute value of the mere will, in which no account is taken of its utility, that notwithstanding the thorough assent of even common reason to the idea, yet a suspicion must arise that it may perhaps really be the product of mere high-flown fancy, and that we may have misunderstood the purpose of nature in assigning reason as the governor of our will. Therefore we will examine this idea from this point of view.

In the physical constitution of an organized being, that is, a being adapted suitably to the purposes of life, we assume it as a fundamental principle that no organ for any purpose will be found but what is also the fittest and best adapted for that purpose. Now in a being which has reason and a will, if the proper object of nature were its *conservation,* its *welfare,*

in a word, its *happiness,* then nature would have hit upon a very bad arrangement in selecting the reason of the creature to carry out this purpose.
For all the actions which the creature has to perform with a view to this
purpose, and the whole rule of its conduct, would be far more surely prescribed to it by instinct, and that end would have been attained thereby
much more certainly than it ever can be by reason. Should reason have
been communicated to this favored creature over and above, it must only
have served it to contemplate the happy constitution of its nature, to admire it, to congratulate itself thereon, and to feel thankful for it to the
beneficent cause, but not that it should subject its desires to that weak
and delusive guidance, and meddle bunglingly with the purpose of nature.
In a word, nature would have taken care that reason should not break
forth into *practical exercise,* nor have the presumption, with its weak insight, to think out for itself the plan of happiness and of the means of
attaining it. Nature would not only have taken on herself the choice of the
ends but also of the means, and with wise foresight would have entrusted
both to instinct.

And, in fact, we find that the more a cultivated reason applies itself
with deliberate purpose to the enjoyment of life and happiness, so much
the more does the man fail of true satisfaction. And from this circumstance
there arises in many, if they are candid enough to confess it, a certain
degree of *misology,* that is, hatred of reason, especially in the case of those
who are most experienced in the use of it, because after calculating all the
advantages they derive—I do not say from the invention of all the arts of
common luxury, but even from the sciences (which seem to them to be
after all only a luxury of the understanding)—they find that they have, in
fact, only brought more trouble on their shoulders rather than gained in
happiness; and they end by envying rather than despising the more common stamp of men who keep closer to the guidance of mere instinct, and
do not allow their reason much influence on their conduct. And this we
must admit, that the judgment of those who would very much lower the
lofty eulogies of the advantages which reason gives us in regard to the happiness and satisfaction of life, or who would even reduce them below zero,
is by no means morose or ungrateful to the goodness with which the world
is governed, but that there lies at the root of these judgments the idea that
our existence has a different and far nobler end, for which, and not for
happiness, reason is properly intended, and which must, therefore, be regarded as the supreme condition to which the private ends of man must,
for the most part, be postponed.

For as reason is not competent to guide the will with certainty in regard
to its objects and the satisfaction of all our wants (which it to some extent
even multiplies), this being an end to which an implanted instinct would
have led with much greater certainty; and since, nevertheless, reason is
imparted to us as a practical faculty, that is, as one which is to have in-

fluence on the *will*, therefore, admitting that nature generally in the distribution of her capacities has adapted the means to the end, its true destination must be to produce a *will*, not merely good as a *means* to something else, but *good in itself*, for which reason was absolutely necessary. This will then, though not indeed the sole and complete good, must be the supreme good and the condition of every other, even of the desire of happiness. Under these circumstances, there is nothing inconsistent with the wisdom of nature in the fact that the cultivation of the reason, which is requisite for the first and unconditional purpose, does in many ways interfere, at least in this life, with the attainment of the second, which is always conditional—namely, happiness. Nay, it may even reduce it to nothing, without nature thereby failing of her purpose. For reason recognizes the establishment of a good will as its highest practical destination, and in attaining this purpose is capable only of a satisfaction of its own proper kind, namely, that from the attainment of an end, which end again is determined by reason only, notwithstanding that this may involve many a disappointment to the ends of inclination.

We have then to develop the notion of a will which deserves to be highly esteemed for itself, and is good without a view to anything further, a notion which exists already in the sound natural understanding, requiring rather to be cleared up than to be taught, and which in estimating the value of our actions always takes the first place and constitutes the condition of all the rest. In order to do this, we will take the notion of duty, which includes that of a good will, although implying certain subjective restrictions and hindrances. These, however, far from concealing it or rendering it unrecognizable, rather bring it out by contrast and make it shine forth so much the brighter.

I omit here all actions which are already recognized as inconsistent with duty, although they may be useful for this or that purpose, for with these the question whether they are done *from duty* cannot arise at all, since they even conflict with it. I also set aside those actions which really conform to duty, but to which men have *no* direct *inclination*, performing them because they are impelled thereto by some other inclination. For in this case we can readily distinguish whether the action which agrees with duty is done *from duty* or from a selfish view. It is much harder to make this distinction when the action accords with duty, and the subject has besides a *direct* inclination to it. For example, it is always a matter of duty that a dealer should not overcharge an inexperienced purchaser; and wherever there is much commerce the prudent tradesman does not overcharge, but keeps a fixed price for everyone, so that a child buys of him as well as any other. Men are thus *honestly* served; but this is not enough to make us believe that the tradesman has so acted from duty and from principles of honesty; his own advantage required it; it is out of the question in this case to suppose that he might besides have a direct inclination in favor of the buyers, so that, as it were, from love he should give no advantage to one over another. Accordingly the action was done neither from duty nor from direct inclination, but merely with a selfish view.

On the other hand, it is a duty to maintain one's life; and, in addition, everyone has also a direct inclination to do so. But on this account the often anxious care which most men take for it has no intrinsic worth, and their maxim has no moral import. They preserve their life *as duty requires,* no doubt, but not *because duty requires.* On the other hand, if adversity and hopeless sorrow have completely taken away the relish for life, if the unfortunate one, strong in mind, indignant as his fate rather than desponding or dejected, wishes for death, and yet preserves his life without loving it—not from inclination or fear, but from duty—then his maxim has a moral worth.

To be beneficent when we can is a duty; and besides this, there are many minds so sympathetically constituted that, without any other motive of vanity or self-interest, they find a pleasure in spreading joy around them, and can take delight in the satisfaction of others so far as it is their own work. But I maintain that in such a case an action of this kind, however proper, however amiable it may be, has nevertheless no true moral worth, but is on a level with other inclinations, for example, the inclination to honor, which, if it is happily directed to that which is in fact of public utility and accordant with duty, and consequently honorable, deserves praise and encouragement, but not esteem. For the maxim lacks the moral import, namely, that such actions be done *from duty,* not from inclination. Put the case that the mind of that philanthropist was clouded by sorrow of his own, extinguishing all sympathy with the lot of others, and that while he still has the power to benefit others in distress, he is not touched by their trouble because he is absorbed with his own; and now suppose that he tears himself out of this dead insensibility and performs the action without any inclination to it, but simply from duty, then first has his action its genuine moral worth. Further still, if nature has put little sympathy in the heart of this or that man, if he, supposed to be an upright man, is by temperament cold and indifferent to the sufferings of others, perhaps because in respect of his own he is provided with the special gift of patience and fortitude, and supposes, or even requires, that others should have the same—and such a man would certainly not be the meanest product of nature—but if nature had not specially framed him for a philanthropist, would he not still find in himself a source from whence to give himself a far higher worth than that of a good-natured temperament could be? Unquestionably. It is just in this that the moral worth of the character is brought out which is incomparably the highest of all, namely, that he is beneficent, not from inclination, but from duty.

To secure one's own happiness is a duty, at least indirectly; for discontent with one's condition, under a pressure of many anxieties and amidst unsatisfied wants, might easily become a great *temptation to transgression of duty*. But here again, without looking to duty, all men have already the strongest and most intimate inclination to happiness, because it is just in this idea that all inclinations are combined in one total. But the precept of happiness is often of such a sort that it greatly interferes with some inclinations, and yet a man cannot form any definite and certain conception of the sum of satisfaction of all of them which is called happiness. It is not then to be wondered at that a single inclination, definite both as to what it promises and as to the time within which it can be gratified, is often able to overcome such a fluctuating idea, and that a gouty patient, for instance, can choose to enjoy what he likes, and to suffer what he may, since, according to his calculation, on this occasion at least, he has [only] not sacrificed the enjoyment of the present moment to a possibly mistaken expectation of a happiness which is supposed to be found in health. But even in this case, if the general desire for happiness did not influence his will, and supposing that in his particular case health was not a necessary element in this calculation, there yet remains in this, as in all other cases, this law—namely, that he should promote his happiness not from inclination but from duty, and by this would his conduct first acquire true moral worth.

It is in this manner, undoubtedly, that we are to understand those passages of Scripture also in which we are commanded to love our neighbor, even our enemy. For love, as an affection, cannot be commanded, but beneficence for duty's sake may, even though we are not impelled to it by any inclination—nay, are even repelled by a natural and unconquerable aversion. This is *practical* love, and not *pathological*—a love which is seated in the will, and not in the propensions of sense—in principles of action and not of tender sympathy; and it is this love alone which can be commanded.

The second proposition [1] is: That an action done from duty derives its moral worth, *not from the purpose* which is to be attained by it, but from the maxim by which it is determined, and therefore does not depend on the realization of the object of the action, but merely on the *principle of volition* by which the action has taken place, without regard to any object of desire. It is clear from what precedes that the purposes which we may have in view in our actions, or their effects regarded as ends and springs of the will, cannot give to actions any unconditional or moral worth. In what, then, can their worth lie if it is not to consist in the will and in reference to its expected effect? It cannot lie anywhere but in the *principle of the will* without regard to the ends which can be attained by the action. For the will stands between its *a priori* principle, which is formal, and its *a posteriori* spring, which is material, as between two roads, and as it must be deter-

[1] The first said that right acts are done from duty.

mined by something, it follows that it must be determined by the formal principle of volition when an action is done from duty, in which case every material principle has been withdrawn from it.

The third proposition, which is a consequence of the two preceding, I would express thus: *Duty is the necessity of acting from respect for the law.* I may have *inclination* for an object as the effect of my proposed action, but I cannot have *respect* for it just for this reason that it is an effect and not an energy of will. Similarly, I cannot have respect for inclination, whether my own or another's; I can at most, if my own, approve it; if another's, sometimes even love it, that is, look on it as favorable to my own interest. It is only what is connected with my will as a principle, by no means as an effect—what does not subserve my inclination, but overpowers it, or at least in case of choice excludes it from its calculation—in other words, simply the law of itself, which can be an object of respect, and hence a command. Now an action done from duty must wholly exclude the influence of inclination, and with it every object of the will, so that nothing remains which can determine the will except objectively the *law,* and subjectively *pure respect* for this practical law, and consequently the maxim [2] that I should follow this law even to the thwarting of all my inclinations.

Thus the moral worth of an action does not lie in the effect expected from it, nor in any principle of action which requires to borrow its motive from this expected effect. For all these effects—agreeableness of one's condition, and even the promotion of the happiness of others—could have been also brought about by other causes, so that for this there would have been no need of the will of a rational being; whereas it is in this alone that the supreme and unconditional good can be found. The pre-eminent good which we call moral can therefore consist in nothing else than *the conception of law* in itself, *which certainly is only possible in a rational being,* in so far as this conception, and not the expected effect, determines the will. This is a good which is already present in the person who acts accordingly, and we have not to wait for it to appear first in the result.[3]

[2] A *maxim* is the subjective principle of volition. The objective principle (*i.e.,* that which would also serve subjectively as a practical principle to all rational beings if reason had full power over the faculty of desire) is the practical *law.*

[3] It might be here objected to me that I take refuge behind the word *respect* in an obscure feeling, instead of giving a distinct solution of the question by a concept of the reason. But although respect is feeling, it is not a feeling *received* through influence, but is *self-wrought* by a rational concept, and, therefore, is specifically distinct from all feelings of the former kind, which may be referred either to inclination or fear. What I recognize immediately as a law for me, I recognize with respect. This merely signifies the consciousness that my will is *subordinate* to a law, without the intervention of other influences on my sense. The immediate determination of the will by the law, and the consciousness of this, is called *respect,* so that this is regarded as an *effect* of the law on the subject, and not as the *cause* of it. Respect is properly the . . . conception of a worth which thwarts my self-love. Accordingly it is something which is considered neither as an object of inclination nor of fear, although it has something analogous to both. The *object* of respect is the *law* only, that is, the law which we impose on *ourselves,* and yet recognize as necessary in itself. As a law, we are

But what sort of law can that be the conception of which must determine the will, even without paying any regard to the effect expected from it, in order that this will may be called good absolutely and without qualification? As I have deprived the will of every impulse which could arise to it from obedience to any law, there remains nothing but the universal conformity of its actions to law in general, which alone is to serve the will as a principle, that is, I am never to act otherwise than so *that I could also will that my maxim should become a universal law*. Here, now, it is the simple conformity to law in general, without assuming any particular law applicable to certain actions, that serves the will as its principle, and must so serve it if duty is not to be a vain delusion and a chimerical notion. The common reason of men in its practical judgments perfectly coincides with this, and always has in view the principle here suggested. Let the question be, for example: May I when in distress make a promise with the intention not to keep it? I readily distinguish here between the two significations which the question may have: whether it is prudent or whether it is right to make a false promise? The former may undoubtedly often be the case. I see clearly indeed that it is not enough to extricate myself from a present difficulty by means of this subterfuge, but it must be well considered whether there may not hereafter spring from this lie much greater inconvenience than that from which I now free myself, and as, with all my supposed *cunning*, the consequences cannot be so easily foreseen but the credit once lost may be much more injurious to me than any mischief which I seek to avoid at present, it should be considered whether it would not be more *prudent* to act herein according to a universal maxim, and to make it a habit to promise nothing except with the intention of keeping it. But it is soon clear to me that such a maxim will still only be based on the fear of consequences. Now it is a wholly different thing to be truthful from duty, and to be so from apprehension of injurious consequences. In the first case, the very notion of the action already implies a law for me; in the second case, I must first look about elsewhere to see what results may be combined with it which would affect myself. For to deviate from the principle of duty is beyond all doubt wicked; but to be unfaithful to my maxim of prudence may often be very advantageous to me, although to abide by it is certainly safer. The shortest way, however, and an unerring one, to discover the answer to this question whether a lying promise is consistent with duty, is to ask myself, Should I be content that my maxim (to extricate myself from difficulty by a false promise) should

---

subjected to it without consulting self-love as imposed by us on ourselves, it is a result of our will. In the former aspect it has an analogy to fear, in the latter to inclination. Respect for a person is properly only respect for the law (of honesty, etc.) of which he gives us an example. Since we also look on the improvement of our talents as a duty, we consider that we see in a person of talents, as it were, the *example of law* (viz. to become like him in this by exercise), and this constitutes our respect. All so-called moral *interest* consists simply in *respect* for the law.

hold good as a universal law, for myself as well as for others; and should I be able to say to myself, "Every one may make a deceitful promise when he finds himself in a difficulty from which he cannot otherwise extricate himself"? Then I presently become aware that, while I can will the lie, I can by no means will that lying should be a universal law. For with such a law there would be no promises at all, since it would be in vain to allege my intention in regard to my future actions to those who would not believe this allegation, or if they over-hastily did so, would pay me back in my own coin. Hence my maxim, as soon as it should be made a universal law, would necessarily destroy itself.

I do not, therefore, need any far-reaching penetration to discern what I have to do in order that my will may be morally good. Inexperienced in the course of the world, incapable of being prepared for all its contingencies, I only ask myself: Canst thou also will that thy maxim should be a universal law? If not, then it must be rejected, and that not because of a disadvantage accruing from it to myself or even to others, but because it cannot enter as a principle into a possible universal legislation, and I reason extorts from me immediate respect for such legislation. I do not indeed as yet *discern* on what this respect is based (this the philosopher may inquire), but at least I understand this—that it is an estimation of the worth which far outweighs all worth of what is recommended by inclination, and that the necessity of acting from *pure* respect for the practical law is what constitutes duty, to which every other motive must give place because it is the condition of a will being good *in itself,* and the worth of such a will is above everything. . . .

. . . There is therefore but one categorical imperative, namely, this: *Act only on that maxim whereby thou canst at the same time will that it should become a universal law.*[4]

Now if all imperatives of duty can be deduced from this one imperative as from their principle, then, although it should remain undecided whether what is called duty is not merely a vain notion, yet at least we shall be able to show what we understand by it and what this notion means.

Since the universality of the law according to which effects are produced constitutes what is properly called *nature* in the most general sense (as to form)—that is, the existence of things so far as it is determined by general laws—the imperative of duty may be expressed thus: *Act as if the maxim of thy action were to become by thy will a universal law of nature.*

We will now enumerate a few duties, adopting the usual division of

---

[4] A "maxim" is a subjective principle of action, and must be distinguished from the *objective principle,* namely, practical law. The former contains the practical rule set by reason according to the conditions of the subject (often its ignorance or its inclinations), so that it is the principle on which the subject *acts;* but the law is the objective . principle valid for every rational being, and is the principle on which it *ought to act—* that is an imperative.

them into duties to ourselves and to others, and into perfect and imperfect duties.[5]

1. A man reduced to despair by a series of misfortunes feels wearied of life, but is still so far in possession of his reason that he can ask himself whether it would not be contrary to his duty to himself to take his own life. Now he inquires whether the maxim of his action could become a universal law of nature. His maxim is: From self-love I adopt it as a principle to shorten my life when its longer duration is likely to bring more evil than satisfaction. It is asked then simply whether this principle founded on self-love can become a universal law of nature. Now we see at once that a system of nature of which it should be a law to destroy life by means of the very feeling whose special nature it is to impel to the improvement of life would contradict itself, and therefore could not exist as a system of nature; hence that maxim cannot possibly exist as a universal law of nature, and consequently would be wholly inconsistent with the supreme principle of all duty.

2. Another finds himself forced by necessity to borrow money. He knows that he will not be able to repay it, but sees also that nothing will be lent to him unless he promises stoutly to repay it in a definite time. He desires to make this promise, but he has still so much conscience as to ask himself: Is it not unlawful and inconsistent with duty to get out of a difficulty in this way? Suppose, however, that he resolves to do so, then the maxim of his action would be expressed thus: When I think myself in want of money, I will borrow money and promise to repay it, although I know that I never can do so. Now this principle of self-love or of one's own advantage may perhaps be consistent with my whole future welfare; but the question now is, Is it right? I change then the suggestion of self-love into a universal law, and state the question thus: How would it be if my maxim were a universal law? Then I see at once that it could never hold as a universal law of nature, but would necessarily contradict itself. For supposing it to be a universal law that everyone when he thinks himself in a difficulty should be able to promise whatever he pleases, with the purpose of not keeping his promise, the promise itself would become impossible, as well as the end that one might have in view in it, since no one would consider that anything was promised to him, but would ridicule all such statements as vain pretenses.

3. A third finds in himself a talent which with the help of some culture might make him a useful man in many respects. But he finds himself in comfortable circumstances and prefers to indulge in pleasure rather than

---

[5] It must be noted here that I reserve the division of duties for a future *metaphysic of morals*; so that I give it here only as an arbitrary one (in order to arrange my examples). For the rest, I understand by a perfect duty one that admits no exception in favor of inclination, and then I have not merely external but also internal perfect duties. This is contrary to the use of the word adopted in the schools; but I do not intend to justify it here, as it is all one for my purpose whether it is admitted or not.

to take pains in enlarging and improving his happy natural capacities. He asks, however, whether his maxim of neglect of his natural gifts, besides agreeing with his inclination to indulgence, agrees also with what is called duty. He sees then that a system of nature could indeed subsist with such a universal law, although men (like the South Sea islanders) should let their talents rest and resolve to devote their lives merely to idleness, amusement, and propagation of their species—in a word, to enjoyment; but he cannot possibly *will* that this should be a universal law of nature, or be implanted in us as such by a natural instinct. For, as a rational being, he necessarily wills that his faculties be developed, since they serve him, and have been given him, for all sorts of possible purposes.

4. A fourth, who is in prosperity, while he sees that others have to contend with great wretchedness and that he could help them, thinks: What concern is it of mine? Let everyone be as happy as Heaven pleases, or as he can make himself; I will take nothing from him nor even envy him, only I do not wish to contribute anything to his welfare or to his assistance in distress! Now no doubt, if such a mode of thinking were a universal law, the human race might very well subsist, and doubtless even better than in a state in which everyone talks of sympathy and good-will, or even takes care occasionally to put it into practice, but, on the other side, also cheats when he can, betrays the rights of men, or otherwise violates them. But although it is possible that a universal law of nature might exist in accordance with that maxim, it is impossible to *will* that such a principle should have the universal validity of a law of nature. For a will which resolved this would contradict itself, inasmuch as many cases might occur in which one would have need of the love and sympathy of others, and in which, by such a law of nature, sprung from his own will, he would deprive himself of all hope of the aid he desires.

These are a few of the many actual duties, or at least what we regard as such, which obviously fall into two classes on the one principle that we have laid down. We must be *able to will* that a maxim of our action should be a universal law. This is the canon of the moral appreciation of the action generally. Some actions are of such a character that their maxim cannot without contradiction be even *conceived* as a universal law of nature, far from it being possible that we should *will* that it *should* be so. In others, this intrinsic impossibility is not found, but still it is impossible to *will* that their maxim should be raised to the universality of a law of nature, since such a will would contradict itself. It is easily seen that the former violate strict or rigorous (inflexible) duty; the latter only laxer (meritorious) duty. Thus it has been completely shown by these examples how all duties depend as regards the nature of the obligation (not the object of the action) on the same principle.

If now we attend to ourselves on occasion of any transgression of duty, we shall find that we in fact do not will that our maxim should be a universal law, for that is impossible for us; on the contrary, we will that the opposite should remain a universal law, only we assume the liberty of making an *exception* in our own favor or (just for this time only) in favor of our inclination. Consequently, if we considered all cases from one and the same point of view, namely, that of reason, we should find a contradiction in our own will, namely, that a certain principle should be objectively necessary as a universal law, and yet subjectively should not be universal, but admit of exceptions. As, however, we at one moment regard our action from the point of view of a will wholly conformed to reason, and then again look at the same action from the point of view of a will affected by inclination, there is not really any contradiction, but an antagonism of inclination to the precept of reason, whereby the universality of the principle is changed into a mere generality, so that the practical principle of reason shall meet the maxim half way. Now, although this cannot be justified in our own impartial judgment, yet it proves that we do really recognize the validity of the categorical imperative and (with all respect for it) only allow ourselves a few exceptions which we think unimportant and forced from us.

7

Value and the Good

Thus far the question, "What is good?" has been subordinated to the question, "What is right and wrong?" As we have seen, those theories of right and wrong (i.e., of obligation) that are called variously result theories, consequentialist theories, or teleological theories say that what is right is determined by what is good and obligation depends upon value. Thus, if a definition of "good" were a mistaken one, the idea of right and wrong derived from it would go correspondingly awry. Theoretically, then, a case might be made that we should have considered good before right, not afterward. But to this two replies must be made. One is that not all those philosophers did say that right depends upon good, Kant especially. Secondly, those who made right dependent upon good offered arguments as to what is good.

In Chapter Four, Aristotle declared that the good is happiness, meaning, not pleasure (except incidentally), but self-realization. In Chapter Five, John Stuart Mill proclaimed that happiness is the only intrinsic good and that it is pleasure. Finally, in Chapter Six, Kant also discussed the good, declaring that the only unconditionally good thing there is consists of the good will. Yet, despite its prominent occurrence in the latter half of the text, there has been no really systematic and thoroughly critical examination of such important questions as, "How do we know what kinds of things are good (valuable, worthwhile)?" Nor will any exhaustive study be made of this now, for that is a realm in which the debate and literature of the past three quarters of a century are forbiddingly and exasperatingly large and technical. But not much will be done, either, by way of reviewing or retracing the steps we have taken regarding the knowledge of good and evil. Mostly, these will be taken for granted, and the discussion will proceed to issues about the nature of value and our knowledge of it.

First, it must be stressed that good is important in contexts other

than those in which we have seen it in operation. It is important independent of the issue as to whether or not right actions depend
somehow upon good results. That is so, if for no other reason than
that, as some have pointed out, in the language "good" is the most
general word of commendation. In learning a new language for conversation, the most general word in that language for commending or
showing approval will be one of the first learned, be it *"gut," "bon,"*
"dobra," or what-have-you. Further, it is at least conceivable that
good might be so much more important than right in ethics that one
would want to speak not only of good things but of actions themselves purely and simply in terms of good rather than right. But that
latter suggestion would complicate our study too much, and it will
not be followed up. Finally, good is important if for no other reason
than that it is often synonymous with "valuable," "beneficial," "worthwhile," and so forth.

This chapter is divided into discussion of the following topics:

1. Are there basically different kinds of classifications of value (even
more basic than, say, economic, religious, aesthetic, and so on)? The
answer to this will be: "Yes, moral value and nonmoral value, on the
one hand, and intrinsic value and extrinsic value, on the other."

2. Are there degrees of value, that is, a hierarchy of values? To
this the answer will be, once again, affirmative.

3. What is good? The answer to this question breaks down into
a. How is good known from nongood? Is this different, for instance,
from the way in which facts are known? b. What things are good?
That is, what is the denotation or reference of the word "good?"

Kinds of Value

1. *Moral and nonmoral value.* In Chapter Six, Kant wrote glowingly
of the good will as the only thing that is good without exception. It
happens that, as Kant describes it, the good will is a kind of goodness not to be found outside of rational beings, human or otherwise.
That tips us off not at all too subtly that Kant's good will is a moral
good, as contrasted with nonmoral goods. Kinds of moral goods reside in persons, or personal beings; they are attributes of, or tendencies of persons that are prized or valued by other persons. Such are
the virtues of honesty, fidelity, wisdom, bravery, justice, and so forth.
Not only does Kant's good will qualify, but Aristotle's moral virtues
are also moral values.

We must here avoid some easy errors: First, we are not to suppose
that right actions are moral goods simply because they proceed from
persons who are morally good. Here actions are the results of moral
good, not automatically, in any case, themselves moral goods. (We
still maintain the right–good distinction.) A second mistake would be

to suppose that nonmoral means the same as immoral. What is outside a class (say, of the class, moral things) may indeed be the opposite of what is in it, but it also may not be its opposite, but merely
different from it. That is the case generally with philosophical use
of the prefix "non-"; it does not mean "anti-" but merely "outside."
Most things outside of moral good would be value neutral, neither
good nor bad. On the distinction, note also that immoral good would
surely not be a synonym of nonmoral good.

Aristotle's and Kant's goods were moral goods. What of John Stuart
Mill's good, pleasure? That is not a moral good (again that does not
make it immoral!), as my having pleasure would not ordinarily seem
to be a basis for commending me as a good or virtuous person. This
is so, even though pleasure may be one of the most personal of
things, but so is pain, which in itself would not be either a moral or
a nonmoral good. In contrast, if a person were always inclined or
disposed to produce the "greatest happiness (pleasure) for the greatest number," in the eyes of Mill that person surely is virtuous, that is,
morally good. So also would the ethical egoist call a person always
disposed to promote his or her self-interest as the motive for every
action, though the enjoyment of the self-interest, whatever it might be
(e.g., pleasure, for the egoistic hedonist) is not itself a moral good
(though many other systems of normative ethics would call such an
egoistic tendency morally bad).

Intrinsic and Extrinsic Goods

The distinction between intrinsic and extrinsic goods has been
sketched in Aristotle, in Chapter Three. If anything is valued only as
a means to some other end it is an extrinsic good, or good only as
a means, or instrumentally good—all three being different ways of
saying the same thing. So, instruments, tools, or whatever you would
call them would be put in that class. But let us suppose that someone
values a pair of scissors or a pair of binoculars apart from their value
as a means of, say, cutting ribbons or checking up on his wife, or
any other. His so valuing them would be thinking of them or prizing
them as intrinsically good, even though they are instruments, in the
literal classification of instruments. Are they really intrinsically good?
We have not reached that point at which we are, like Aristotle, Mill,
or Kant, ready to make a definite answer to that question. Ours is,
for the moment the easier task of classifying goods, or values, in
terms of how this or that person regards them. (And we leave aside
the difficulty of whether it is the scissors or the man's feeling about
them that is or is not intrinsically valuable.) The example of literal
tools is chosen to show that a thing could have—for someone—both
intrinsic and extrinsic value at the same time. It is having value apart

from value as a tool or means to some end—though it may or may not have that, too—that makes something valued as intrinsically good. The miser by definition values money for its own sake, over and above any capacity it has for buying anything, and so takes money as an intrinsic good. And among those things that might be valued both for their usefulness as a means to an end and valued in themselves apart from any such use, there should be included health, a vacation, relaxation, and so forth.

Aristotle's reminder is often repeated. Not every good could be merely good as a means to some other good. In a moment this will lead into the discussion of hierarchies of values, but we must also notice something else important about instrumental goods, and that is few if any means to an end produce only that end as noticeable results. Whenever one looks at some crisis and its solution, or some new goal of a significant segment of society, there are important side effects or fallout incidental to it. For instance, cheap fuel may be "dirty" and result in high environmental cleanup costs to someone later. So, as Russell says, at least some means, some goods, can be evaluated by scientific methods as to whether they are efficient, cheap (in the long or short run), and generally not destructive of ends that are of comparable importance to the end they are designed to achieve, or even greater, such as health and safety.

Degrees of Value

A point about exchange value will illustrate how values in our lives get arranged in hierarchies. Consider the old expression, "selling your soul to the devil." Suppose that you have a soul and that somehow you are brought to a place in your life where you sell it for something, like Dr. Faustus. The Christian gospel asks, "What would a person give in exchange for his soul?" implying that nothing of comparable (or higher) value that a person has could be found. That would surely help to show about the highest of human values what we know from practice in economic life, that ordinarily we do not exchange something we value highly for something we do not. Similar points could be made by reference to one's "ruling passion" or "everyone has his price." And the question, "What would you give for . . . ?" asked repeatedly about a long list of things, if thoughtfully and honestly answered, would supposedly provide at least a sketch of one's hierarchy of values. One of the very important problems in such a procedure would be the question of whether the answer was honest and thoughtful enough; that is, would our answer be the same when the time actually came to make the choice, to strike the bargain? "Self-preservation is the first law of nature," it is said, and the taking of a person's life, not his or her eternal soul, is the foul deed most often and seriously depicted in fiction. Our response to the question, "Is this worth the risk of your life?" may be different in the comfort of an armchair, martini in hand, than at the beach where the cold, rough water has pulled a youngster farther out than he seems likely to be able to manage. Or, in more deceptive scenes our glands may pump juices into our brain and give us quite a different reply from what we had always thought. But so far as ethics is concerned, if we cannot reach a rational conclusion about values in the most ideal of circumstances, unhurried meditation or leisurely discussion with others, we cannot really expect to do so in emergencies. Now, if the problems seem more difficult than one thought, it can be argued that more thought, not less, should be given to them in calmer, less troubled times. Philosophy, of which ethics is a branch, does have something to say about the motto (often attributed to Socrates) inscribed on the Oracle at Delphi, "Know thyself."

As suggested by Aristotle, the connection between intrinsic good and hierarchies of value is that, ideally, the highest intrinsic good would be something that, if we possessed it, we would want for nothing else, certainly not desire to exchange it for anything else. But notice that Aristotle made the aside that the external goods are needed as well—food, clothing, shelter—and he, in fact, seemed to presuppose a larger number of things than that for the good life. Perhaps we can set self-preservation or survival in a clearer context here, then. Given little but food, clothing, and shelter, reasonable health, and so on, one who had not tasted of a variety of values, as John Stuart Mill's "competent judges" had, might not be dissatisfied with his or her lot. But mere survival, mere self-preservation in the most extreme deprivation and pain, is quite another matter than what we usually think of when we speak of self-preservation or survival as a high value. Later discussions of suicide and euthanasia go into this in more detail.

What Is Good?

Our question here is, How do you recognize or identify something that is good, and tell what is bad? A very practical answer has to be: "That depends on what it is; are you talking about good racehorses or good friends, or good steak?" But the turn that many philosophical discussions take is it depends on who you are, and that different people have different ideas of good or what "a good this" or "a good that" is. An in-between kind of approach may say, "Well, in shopping for steaks, I look for . . . , but other people might not agree." Complexities and difficulties and obscurities can pile up fast here, and being aware of that is perhaps the first move toward dealing with that fact.

Notice, if you will, another facet of the question about how to recognize good things. We would be less puzzled, in several ways, if we were asked: "What is red? How do you recognize or identify red things, or tell when something is red?" Or, "What is circularity, and how do you tell when something is circular?" There is not so much of a problem in these questions about who you are or what kinds of red or circular things as there is with telling what is good. We shall notice later that these problems are applicable to good things in a way that they are not applicable to red or circular but in a very different way than the conventional wisdom of widely accepted relativism suggests.

The contrast of good with red or circular as descriptive adjectives has been a focal point of much twentieth-century value theory, and has been one expression of the view coming down from Hume that you cannot derive an "ought" (value judgment) from an "is" (statement of fact.) One important way of putting the contrast is that the logical connection between factual statements and value judgments is "loose and separate," as Hume said in speaking of other matters, or simply that a value judgment might get connected to many very different, perhaps conflicting, statements of fact by different speakers or writers. Hence the philosophical discussion of values soon reaches the point at which it is said, "What's good depends on who's talking," in a way in which "what's red" or "what's circular" does not. It would be puzzling to hear someone say, "What's circular depends on who's talking," as it is not when speaking of good.

All of this is not to say that a lot of twentieth-century value theory has not supposed that as a respectable adjective good ought to function like red or circular, though the conclusion is soon reached that respectable is as respectable does, and good fails to serve as a properly descriptive and reliable carrier of precise information from one person to another. So much the worse for good was often the conclusion. If you could settle the question of whether a gigantic object like the earth is a sphere or egg shaped by scientific methods but could not settle the question of whether it was good by those methods, then values must be somehow subjective or relative or both. Spherical and circular were either in the gigantic object or they were not in it, but good was not; rather, it was in the eye of the beholder, the maker of value judgments. So you find Bertrand Russell arguing that values are subjective, and that value judgments expressed in language do not describe anything, nor assert or deny anything, and thus are neither true nor false. Value judgments are not about objects of knowledge, they are rather about, and express something about, objects of desire. And, as people's desires differ regarding the same object (one man's meat is another man's poison), we should not at all be surprised that people express very different evaluations of it.

Russell's view, as it was soon formulated by his countryman, A. J. Ayer, in *Language, Truth, and Logic* and later by the American, C. L. Stevenson, in *Ethics and Language,* was called emotivism or the emotive theory of ethics. (In Scandinavia, it sometimes went by the name "nihilism" for reasons that are perhaps already suggested.) Emotivism is not the subjectivism of Chapter Two, despite Russell's affirmation that values are subjective. Subjectivism, you recall, at least said that value judgments are at least true or false, since they assert that the speaker or writer has a certain kind of feeling or attitude. They are true if he or she has it, false if he or she does not. And they do describe something, do assert something. But emotivism denied that this is the case. Value judgments, rather, express or give vent to feelings; they do not describe them or even assert that the speaker or writer has them.

Much earlier on, Russell's Cambridge classmate G. E. Moore had maintained a quite different doctrine and it had, for at least a short time, been accepted by Russell. Nevertheless, though Moore's conclusions were quite different from the emotivists, his presuppositions were in important details similar: As a respectable adjective good (the main concept in ethics, Moore claimed) should refer to or denote something in reality, the property, good, or goodness. Moore concluded that it did indeed refer and describe as an adjective ought, but that what it referred to, the property good, was not a natural property, such as red or circular. You could see the latter pair. Goodness you could surely detect as a property of good things, but it could not be detected by the sense organs. Rather, it was known to be present in good things, Moore held, with a straight face, by means of a special kind of sense, the moral or value intuition that normal human beings have, and which may get educated or perverted or dulled, as our other mental or intellectual faculties might. In this, as in certain other typical theories he held, Moore went back to the eighteenth-century "Common Sense" Scottish philosopher Thomas Reid (no known kin to the present writer), a staunch opponent of Hume's skepticism. Reid had held that our moral sense (intuition of values and moral principles) detects the rightness of actions, when properly applied, just as our sense of sight detects the colors of things. Moore carried out the figure and said that good is like yellow; you can recognize yellow in yellow things, but you cannot do it from having yellow defined or yellowness described to you before you set eyes on a school bus or a caution light, or a canary or a lemon. Yellowness cannot be described in such a way that you could recognize it (at least, not without expensive and sophisticated physics equipment). It is not made up of parts, being a primary color. It is simple and unanalyzable, said Moore. But you know yellow, and you can tell when something is yellow and when it isn't, given proper conditions of observation. You know it by acquaintance with it, not description of it, as Russell's distinction in another context says. So it is with good. Good cannot be analyzed into parts; it is not a mixture of components by any formula. It is indescribable for the same reason. The word "good," he said, is "indefinable, simple, and unanalyzable," but nonetheless known by all sorts of people in all kinds of conditions, recognized by our moral or value intuition. So, value judgments do describe valuable things, and they do convey information, and assert something about reality that is either true or false. But value judgments could not be verified by the sense organs, as in science, but rather by focusing one's moral sense upon them.

To scientifically oriented philosophers such as Russell and the somewhat more narrowly science-minded school of thought called Logical Positivism or Logical Empiricism (containing Ayer and Stevenson, but not Russell), all such talk of some mysterious sense as this was anathema, as the supposedly nonnatural property, good. Moore's move in proclaiming such was a desperate attempt to shore up common sense and objectivity of values. They went in the direction of declaring an impassable divide between the world of facts known to science and the world of values clung to by the human psyche.

But there came a somewhat reconciliatory viewpoint in midcentury in the work of the relatively young Oxford philosopher, R. M. Hare. It put together in a kind of original synthesis a number of value theories, not simply Moore's and emotivism, but also the theory called Naturalism, the view that values are known to us by our "natural" faculties, i.e., those sense organs in which science has traditionally trusted; thus, the property good is either a property that might not be solely an object of valuation but, like redness or circularity, just "there" and value-neutral, or it might be a combination of such properties. For instance, a pear's degree of ripeness, its juiciness, its typical flavor, its texture, and its aroma might all be described in rather neutral terms, or the pear might be described as "delicious" or "scrumptious," or, bringing in its vitamins and food value, "good for you," "healthful," and so on. But it would not be some separate and peculiar property apart from these natural properties of ripeness, juiciness, and so forth that we were referring to when we called it scrumptious or simply a good pear. Some characterizations of naturalism also insist (as Asch did in Chapter Two's readings) that human nature is not so infinitely variable that people in one society might be capable of enjoying the kinds of pears that one supposes most people seek in the supermarket, whereas in another society pears that tasted like alum, were chewy to the teeth precisely like the ashes left from burnt coal, and always caused painful diarrhea, nosebleed, and such were the only ones the people prized. Hare's colleague, Philippa Foot, will present her naturalistic alternative to his contribution to value theory as the second and last reading for the present chapter (it will be discussed at the end of the chapter).

R. M. Hare's work, *The Language of Morals,* appeared some seven years after the end of the most destructive and horrible war of all time. The decline of emotivism could not be entirely coincidental with reflections upon the question of whether something more than conflicting attitudes, feelings, and desires, much less tastes, was needed to explain the ghastly inhumanities of that war, and yet, not something running toward the seemingly mystical features of the existentialism that followed that war as it had followed the First World War, also. In any event, Hare accepted some of the conclusions of Moore, some of the emotivists', and some of naturalism, without being a mere eclectic hodgepodge. With the naturalists and Moore, Hare argued that value judgments do make assertions or denials about reality; they do, at least a great part of the time, describe—that is, make statements that convey information, correct or incorrect—and are either true or false. They are thus the sort of thing about which evidence can be offered pro and con, quite often. As to whether "This is a good pear," for instance, is true and this *is* a good pear evidence can be offered not only from the individual's taste in pears, that is, his or her preference, but from the Department of Agriculture's grading of produce, if it is relevant to pears, e.g., the grade "Fancy" (assuming, of course, that these pears had not altered noticeably, except perhaps to ripen somewhat but not rot since the label was applied)! With that and other grading labels, as discussed in his colleague J. O. Urmson's paper "On Grading," labels such as "Grade A" in milk or "Choice" beef, the supposedly objective inspectors of meat, milk, and produce could agree within a fairly close degree, at least as much as, say, judges in the Olympic Games, about the quality of a product. Granted at the outset that even the value judgments of government inspectors sooner or later reflect the values of the consumers who pay their salaries from taxes, nevertheless, nothing much resembling the subjectivity of evaluating as Russell and the emotivists pictured it goes on in such grading. The inspectors have before them a set of fairly definite standards as to recognizable properties of pears, milk, or meat, and if the product has those properties the grade is given; if not, it is denied and a lower grade is used. But these are natural sense-recognizable properties.

We can expand somewhat, as Hare does, the lists of things and the variety of individual persons who make value judgments about them and much of what has been indicated about grading will still apply. If a car salesman, Honest John, tells you the used car he is trying to sell you has good brakes when the pedal will not even support itself and stand off the floor without an assist from your panicked toe, these are definitely not good brakes. They are not good brakes for the same reason that an alum-tasting, clinker-crunchy, nosebleed-inducing pear is not a good pear; they do not serve the purpose for which you want brakes on the car, or at least do not serve it well. So you tell Honest John that if you had wanted a coffin you would have gone to the undertaker, because that is what he is trying to sell you! If by some miracle you got the car off the lot, then totally demolished it in a wreck, you should be able to present a convincing case to a court that he had engaged in false or misleading representation of the product. That would be hard to do if Russell and the emotivists were correct in their theory of value judgments, though none of these ever were, to my knowledge, prone to express doubts as to whether some advertising might be so misleading as to deserve the label "false value judgment." Nonetheless, their theory denied that any such thing as a true or false value judgment exists or could exist. (We shall return to the possibility that on good a consensus is not the same as truth.) A device that lets a moving car continue with speed unchecked when applied is not what you choose as automobile brakes, as alum-tasting fruit is not what you choose as pears, so the two, respectively, could not qualify as good.

Hare offers a criticism of Moore that is along these lines: Suppose that Moore were right about the logical relation between the property good and natural properties, good being nonnatural. If that were true it would be entirely possible that a set of brakes could perform perfectly and at the same time not be good brakes, because the presence of these natural properties (stopping a car going forty miles per hour on dry concrete pavement in X seconds) would not at all assure the presence of that nonnatural property, good. Or, two sets of brakes of the kind just described could exist at the same time, yet one of them be good and the other not! Surely, Hare says, some mistake occurs in Moore's view, and there must be a more intimate, indissoluble connection between at least some natural properties and the application of the word "good."

Good functions at least sometimes to describe, says Hare, in opposition to emotivism. Thus, it does convey information, it does not merely express desire or approval. If you see a Lost and Found ad saying, "Lost, good penknife in Parker Park, night of June 12, Reward," you would not claim the reward if you picked up a knife with no blade and no indication that it had recently had a blade. A person calling the latter knife good would not be using good in the ordinary way, and it would be misleading and a waste of money for the ad, as few would be desperate or unintelligent enough to present such a knife as that for the reward. Communication in that case would call more for "Bladeless penknife, sentimental value, Reward." Granted, the ad as stated is not very descriptive. But the natural properties were left out deliberately to show that something is presented by way of information, in the mere use of the word "good" to describe the knife, contrary to emotivism.

Hare's agreement with Moore is in saying that good does describe, and that value judgments are typically true or false, and sometimes can be shown to be true or false. His agreement with the emotivists is in saying that, besides this describing use, good also has an evaluative use. Moore had made much of the dictionary's statement that "good" is "the most general word of commendation." The commending use of good Hare calls the evaluative use. Good is always used to commend or positively evaluate; it may or may not also have at the same time, the descriptive use Hare discusses. Thus, if the ad said, "Lost, one good thing, in Parker Park, night of June 12, Reward," it would sound like something out of a musical comedy, perhaps. We would not know what to look for, though it might not be entirely unreasonable if we found, say, a new penknife there, to call the number listed and ask whether that is the lost item. Suppose we did just that and were told, "No, what I lost was my innocence (my heart, and so forth). Thanks, anyway." Whatever all these very improbable examples might show or obfuscate, Hare nevertheless says that we would indeed know what the person was saying in one sense, and that is in calling it a good thing it was something he or she valued, that he or she would choose for some purpose, and so on. Thus, the emotivists were right in saying that good always commends, but wrong in saying that it never describes or informs.

Hare's accomplishment did not go far enough to satisfy Philippa Foot, his Oxford colleague, as we shall see momentarily, but it was much more formidable as against the subjectivism and relativism of a great number of well-educated and sophisticated people, not to mention the conventional wisdom of those who perhaps aspire to that group, or consider themselves at least honorary members thereof. I said much earlier that "What's good depends on who's talking" is to be examined more closely. It has been, by Hare. "Who's talking" was for Hare a circle of choosers and users of a certain kind of goods or services, and they talk to each other as people who have a mutual interest in those goods or services. It is not exactly "shop talk" but the idea is not very foreign to the case in point. Most of all, the use of good is not one without context, as some might suppose that philosophers would prefer, a sort of speaking to, or maybe for, the ages, and speaking ageless wisdom (i.e., contextless wisdom). If we stick to the context of choosers and users discussing matters of mutual interest, the kind of moral disagreement or relativity or subjectivity of values that is supposedly rampant at all times and places does not hinder communication between the speakers, writers, or readers to any particular degree. What are or are not good brakes, good gasoline, and so forth can be fairly well agreed on when that interest is fairly mutual. It may well not be what good gasoline or good brakes were twenty years ago when the states of the refiner's and brake-maker's arts were different. The supposed subjectivity of value judgment is dealt a heavy blow by the realization that language is inter-subjective, and words are public. Their meaning cannot be all that subjective, as is often supposed when it is assumed that we can never be sure, when we use words, that other people mean the same by them as we do. Words are learned from users, and by imitation. So much incentive to use them as others do is involved in the learning and use of them—use to do something for us—that invention of mystify-ing, private meanings is no part of everyday talk or writing; it would be self-defeating, unless we want to deceive or to play games.

The oft-supposed relativity of values is another matter, however. Surely what is or is not a good car or a good Frisbee is relative to something, depends upon something, and is not carved in stone or written in the stars. Surely it depends on the state of the art, and upon what we want the car or Frisbee to do. Why good should be con-textless and ageless here is once again a puzzle—what would be the point of such agelessness or lack of context? It does not seem that Hare finds any great value(!) is served by such, nor do I.

Ah, but there remains, to be sure, moral value. How does Hare's theory serve us with that? We can extend his points very well here. A friend who rapidly brings you to bankruptcy, or betrays confidences, or tries to seduce your spouse, or gives you herpes the first Tuesday of every month regularly as clockwork is hardly a friend, much less a good friend. "What are friends for?" has a point to it that is well taken when a friend is surprised by help in a disaster, but also when a friend causes a disaster through carelessness or maliciousness. "With friends like that, who needs enemies?" Hence Hare's point about choice. For what do you choose friends? (Omit for the moment the complication of asking whether it is selfish.) One does not choose them for the purpose of bringing sure disaster upon oneself unless one is pathological. Let us suppose that we chose friends to share many things, happy and unhappy, for companionship, perhaps for a certain amount of ego-boosting, and so forth. "Good friend" will not, then, be a wildly relative notion. We can as quickly agree that Jones is not describing a good friend when he speaks of a consistent back-stabber, as the want ad is not describing a bladeless instrument when it says, "good penknife."

But what of a good man or a good woman? Those are very general categories, and that is what is puzzling about them. It is to a large extent the absence of context that we are encountering again here as in many philosophical puzzlements about values. For what kinds of choices are connected with this good man or good woman?

Granted, one might want to point to someone who was "good all around" (as Aristotle might say) as an example or model for one's children. Yet, it is hardly realistic to want a child to become a carbon copy of someone else, to be like him or her in all details, even if all those details are regarded as good ones. The choice of a model for behavior, whether it is the choice made by the person whose behavior is to be altered or by another person, a third party, is not without context or specificity. In what ways is he or she a good model? What aspects of a person's behavior are the areas for improvement, and what aspects of the model's behavior seem most beneficial to emulate? "All around" is too unrealistic, when you think of it seriously.

Well, much remains to be said, however. If we think of child rearing and parenting, we must surely be aware of the great differences that exist in societies regarding those moral values, namely, good child and good parent. Assuming that the point has been made that it is important to ask, "Good in what way?" still much can be doubted as to whether good conveys much knowledge here, or whether one person can prove to another that someone is a good child or good parent (though we can still go the route of asking whether divorce courts and social workers know nothing of this good).

In any case, there are issues in which philosophers have expressed dissatisfaction with Hare regarding the more usual questions in ethics about the good or nonmoral goods such as we explored in Chapters Three through Six. Suppose that it is objected that when Hare is pressed hard, he is not able to deliver the objectivity that he seemed to promise, or that our presentation led us to hope for? On that he is among the first to admit that one can carry moral and other value challenges so far before the defenses of any moral theory break down. He is not prepared to give detailed advice on the settlement of disagreements in principle, for there cannot be proof of one principle or set of principles that a person might use to justify following certain moral rules (about lying, stealing, killing, and the like) as against another principle or set of principles used by another person to oppose those moral rules—or perhaps even defend the same moral rules but on those different grounds. This has been one of the features of Hare that has been most bothersome to his friends and foes. It is at that point that we must come to Philippa Foot's paper and the conclusion of this chapter and this first part of the book.

In a paper, "Moral Beliefs," read to the Aristotelian Society in 1958, Professor Foot went beyond Hare and defended naturalism (ironically, using the same techniques of linguistic analysis that had been used with such apparent devastating effect against it since the time of Moore's blast early in the century). Most of all, she wanted to reestablish the supposedly severed connection between is and ought or fact and value. This she tried to do in terms of showing that value statements can and do have factual statements used as evidence for them. Against Hare's assumption that almost any kind of evidence might be used for a reason why one believes this or that is morally right or obligatory, she says that antinaturalism has assumed that (1) a person may base moral beliefs on premises that no one else accepts; and (2) anyone might refuse any evidence for a value judgment because it was not evidence "for him." In the case of the first assumption, she insists that evaluations are not incidentally related to the things evaluated, but intimately connected with them. One could not be proud of just anything, for instance, say, that he or she has kept the sky from falling today, unless he or she were in a rather pathetic emotional or mental condition. Nor could just any and every practice be taught and accepted as virtuous or obligatory, say, clasping one's hand three times each hour or never facing north just after facing east. Surely, societies have enforced some very puzzling customs, but they do have a point to them, if nothing other than, say, that it's regarded as "bad luck." Such superstitions can, of course, be subjected to rational criticism: Jones comes to the village every day from the west and makes a left turn with no visible ill effects, defying the "no north just after east" ban. Such facts count against supposing that the connection between judgments about what is right and judgments about mundane events is loose or nonexistent.

Regarding the second assumption of critics of naturalism, Professor Foot admits that in some special cases a person might well say of some fact that supposedly clinches a value conclusion, "So what? That proves nothing; it is not even relevant to the value judgment in question." It is easy to suppose that factually true statements may leave us cold as regarding our attitude or commitment to the value judgment in question. But, ordinarily, "Doing that will physically injure you" is no irrelevant consideration to "You ought to do that," or "You ought not to do that."

The rest of Foot's paper is taken up with a consideration of the four cardinal virtues and showing that people have factual reasons for aiming at virtue and avoiding vice, moral goods, and evils, respectively.

Currently, the is and ought separation is in disarray. This could hardly be a mere coincidence, what with a return to pressing concern with very practical issues about life and death in a changing technology and volatile political climate. It is to those issues we turn in Part Two.

SCIENCE AND ETHICS *

BERTRAND RUSSELL

Those who maintain the insufficiency of science . . . appeal to the fact that science has nothing to say about "values." This I admit; but when it is inferred that ethics contains truths which cannot be proved or disproved by science, I disagree. The matter is one on which it is not altogether easy to think clearly, and my own views on it are quite different from what they were thirty years ago. But it is necessary to be clear about it if we are to appraise such arguments as those in support of Cosmic Purpose. As there is no consensus of opinion about ethics, it must be understood that what follows is my personal belief, not the dictum of science.

The study of ethics, traditionally, consists of two parts, one concerned with moral rules, the other with what is good on its own account. Rules of conduct, many of which have a ritual origin, play a great part in the lives of savages and primitive peoples. It is forbidden to eat out of the chief's dish, or to seethe the kid in its mother's milk; it is commanded to offer sacrifices to the gods, which, at a certain stage of development, are thought most acceptable if they are human beings. Other moral rules, such as the prohibition of murder and theft, have a more obvious social utility, and survive the decay of the primitive theological systems with which they were originally associated. But as men grow more reflective there is a tendency to lay less stress on rules and more on states of mind. This comes from two sources—philosophy and mystical religion. We are all familiar with passages in the prophets and the gospels, in which purity of heart is set above meticulous observance of the Law; and St. Paul's famous praise of charity, or love, teaches the same principle. The same thing will be found in all great mystics, Christian and non-Christian: what they value is a state of mind, out of which, as they hold, right conduct must ensue; rules seem to them external, and insufficiently adaptable to circumstances.

One of the ways in which the need of appealing to external rules of conduct has been avoided has been the belief in "conscience," which has been especially important in Protestant ethics. It has been supposed that God reveals to each human heart what is right and what is wrong, so that, in order to avoid sin, we have only to listen to the inner voice. There are, however, two difficulties in this theory: first, that conscience says different things to different people: secondly, that the study of the unconscious has given us an understanding of the mundane causes of conscientious feelings.

As to the different deliverances of conscience: George III's conscience told him that he must not grant Catholic Emancipation, as, if he did, he

* From *Religion and Science* by Bertrand Russell (1935). Reprinted by permission of Oxford University Press. Chapter IX, with omissions.

would have committed perjury in taking the Coronation Oath, but later monarchs have had no such scruples. Conscience leads some to condemn the spoliation of the rich by the poor, as advocated by communists; and others to condemn exploitation of the poor by the rich, as practised by capitalists. It tells one man that he ought to defend his country in case of invasion, while it tells another that all participation in warfare is wicked. During the War, the authorities, few of whom had studied ethics, found conscience very puzzling, and were led to some curious decisions, such as that a man might have conscientious scruples against fighting himself, but not against working on the fields so as to make possible the conscription of another man. They held also that, while conscience might disapprove of all war, it could not, failing that extreme position, disapprove of the war then in progress. Those who, for whatever reason, thought it wrong to fight, were compelled to state their position in terms of this somewhat primitive and unscientific conception of "conscience."

The diversity in the deliverances of conscience is what is to be expected when its origin is understood. In early youth, certain classes of acts meet with approval, and others with disapproval; and by the normal process of association, pleasure and discomfort gradually attach themselves to the acts, and not merely to the approval and disapproval respectively produced by them. As time goes on, we may forget all about our early moral training, but we shall still feel uncomfortable about certain kinds of actions, while others will give us a glow of virtue. To introspection, these feelings are mysterious, since we no longer remember the circumstances which originally caused them; and therefore it is natural to attribute them to the voice of God in the heart. But in fact conscience is a product of education, and can be trained to approve or disapprove, in the great majority of mankind, as educators may see fit. While, therefore, it is right to wish to liberate ethics from external moral rules, this can hardly be satisfactorily achieved by means of the notion of "conscience."

Philosophers, by a different road, have arrived at a different position in which, also, moral rules of conduct have a subordinate place. They have framed the concept of the Good, by which they mean (roughly speaking) that which, in itself and apart from its consequences, we should wish to see existing—or, if they are theists, that which is pleasing to God. Most people would agree that happiness is preferable to unhappiness, friendliness to unfriendliness, and so on. Moral rules, according to this view, are justified if they promote the existence of what is good on its own account, but not otherwise. The prohibition of murder, in the vast majority of cases, can be justified by its effects, but the practice of burning widows on their husband's funeral pyre cannot. The former rule, therefore, should be retained, but not the latter. Even the best moral rules, however, will have *some* exceptions, since no class of action *always* has bad results. We have thus three different senses in which an act may be ethically commendable: (1) it may be in accordance with the received moral code; (2) it may be sincerely intended to have good effects; (3) it may in fact have good effects. The third sense, however, is generally considered inadmissible in morals. According to orthodox theology, Judas Iscariot's act of betrayal had good consequences, since it was necessary for the Atonement; but it was not on this account laudable.

Different philosophers have formed different conceptions of the Good. Some hold that it consists in the knowledge and love of God; others in universal love; others in the enjoyment of beauty; and yet others in pleasure. The Good once defined, the rest of ethics follows: we ought to act in the way we believe most likely to create as much good as possible, and as little as possible of its correlative evil. The framing of moral rules, so long as the ultimate Good is supposed known, is a matter for science. For example: should capital punishment be inflicted for theft, or only for murder, or not at all? Jeremy Bentham, who considered pleasure to be the Good, devoted himself to working out what criminal code would most promote pleasure, and concluded that it ought to be much less severe than that prevailing in his day. All this, except the proposition that pleasure is the Good, comes within the sphere of science.

But when we try to be definite as to what we mean when we say that this or that is "the Good," we find ourselves involved in very great difficulties. Bentham's creed that pleasure is the Good roused furious opposition, and was said to be a pig's philosophy. Neither he nor his opponents could advance any argument. In a scientific question, evidence can be adduced on both sides, and in the end one side is seen to have the better case—or, if this does not happen, the question is left undecided. But in a question as to whether this or that is the ultimate Good, there is no evidence either way; each disputant can only appeal to his own emotions, and employs such rhetorical devices as shall rouse similar emotions in others.

Take, for example, a question which has come to be important in practical politics. Bentham held that one man's pleasure has the same ethical importance as another man's, provided the quantities are equal; and on this ground he was led to advocate democracy. Nietzsche, on the contrary, held that only the great man can be regarded as important on his own account, and that the bulk of mankind are only means to his well-being. He viewed ordinary men as many people view animals: he thought it justifiable to make use of them, not for their own good, but for that of the superman, and this view has since been adopted to justify the abandonment of democracy. We have here a sharp disagreement of great practical importance, but we have absolutely no means, of a scientific or intellectual kind, by which to persuade either party that the other is in the right. There are, it is true, ways of altering men's opinions on such subjects, but they are all emotional, not intellectual.

Questions as to "values"—that is to say, as to what is good or bad on its own account, independently of its effects—lie outside the domain of science, as the defenders of religion emphatically assert. I think that in this they are right, but I draw the further conclusion, which they do not draw, that questions as to "values" lie wholly outside the domain of knowledge. That is to say, when we assert that this or that has "value," we are giving expressions to our own emotions, not to a fact which would still be true if our personal feelings were different. To make this clear, we must try to analyze the conception of the Good.

It is obvious, to begin with, that the whole idea of good and bad has some connection with desire. *Prima facie,* anything that we all desire is "good," and anything that we all dread is "bad." If we all agreed in our desires, the matter could be left there, but unfortunately our desires conflict. If I say "what I want is good," my neighbor will say "No, what I want." Ethics is an attempt—though not, I think, a successful one—to escape from this subjectivity. I shall naturally try to show, in my dispute with my neighbor, that my desires have some quality which makes them more worthy of respect than his. If I want to preserve a right of way, I shall appeal to the landless inhabitants of the district; but he, on his side, will appeal to the landowners. I shall say: "What use is the beauty of the countryside if no one sees it?" He will retort: "What beauty will be left if trippers are allowed to spread devastation?" Each tries to enlist allies by showing that his own desires harmonize with those of other people. When this is obviously impossible, as in the case of a burglar, the man is condemned by public opinion, and his ethical status is that of a sinner.

Ethics is thus closely related to politics: it is an attempt to bring the collective desires of a group to bear upon individuals; or conversely, it is an attempt by an individual to cause his desires to become those of his group. This latter is, of course, only possible if his desires are not obviously opposed to the general interest: the burglar will hardly attempt to persuade people that he is doing them good, though plutocrats make similar attempts, and often succeed. When our desires are for things which all can enjoy in common, it seems not unreasonable to hope that others may concur; thus the philosopher who values Truth, Goodness and Beauty seems, to himself, to be not merely expressing his own desires, but pointing the way to the welfare of all mankind. Unlike the burglar, he is able to believe that his desires are for something that has value in an impersonal sense.

Ethics is an attempt to give universal, and not merely personal, importance to certain of our desires. I say "certain" of our desires, because in regard to some of them this is obviously impossible, as we saw in the case of the burglar. The man who makes money on the Stock Exchange by means of some secret knowledge does not wish others to be equally well informed: Truth (in so far as he values it) is for him a private possession, not the general human good that it is for the philosopher. The philosopher may, it is true, sink to the level of the stock-jobber, as when he claims priority for a discovery. But this is a lapse: in his purely philosophic capacity, he wants only to enjoy the contemplation of Truth in doing which he in no way interferes with others who wish to do likewise. . . .

. . . Every attempt to persuade people that something is good (or bad) in itself, and not merely in its effects, depends upon the art of rousing feelings, not upon an appeal to evidence. In every case the preacher's skill consists in creating in others emotions similar to his own—or dissimilar, if he is a hypocrite. I am not saying this as a criticism of the preacher, but as an analysis of the essential character of his activity.

When a man says "this is good in itself," he seems to be making a statement, just as much as if he said "this is square" or "this is sweet." I believe this to be a mistake. I think that what the man really means is: "I wish everybody to desire this," or rather "Would that everybody desired this." If what he says is interpreted as a statement, it is mrely an affirmation of his own personal wish; if, on the other hand, it is interpreted in a general way, it states nothing, but merely desires something. The wish, as an occurrence, is personal, but what it desires is universal. It is, I think, this curious interlocking of the particular and the universal which has caused so much confusion in ethics.

The matter may perhaps become clearer by contrasting an ethical sentence with one which makes a statement. If I say "all Chinese are Buddhists," I can be refuted by the production of a Chinese Christian or Mohammedan. If I say "I believe that all Chinese are Buddhists," I cannot be refuted by any evidence from China, but only by evidence that I do not believe what I say; for what I am asserting is only something about my own state of mind. If, now, a philosopher says "Beauty is Good," I may interpret him as meaning either "Would that everybody loved the beautiful" (which corresponds to "all Chinese are Buddhists") or "I wish that everybody loved the beautiful" (which corresponds to "I believe that all Chinese are Buddhists"). The first of these makes no assertion, but expresses a wish; since it affirms nothing, it is logically impossible that there should be evidence for or against it, or for it to possess either truth or falsehood. The second sentence, instead of being merely optative, does make a statement, but is one about the philosopher's state of mind, and it could only be refuted by evidence that he does not have the wish that he says he has. This second sentence does not belong to ethics, but to psychology or biography. The first sentence, which does belong to ethics, expresses a desire for something, but asserts nothing.

Ethics, if the above analysis is correct, contains no statements, whether true or false, but consists of desires of a certain general kind, namely such as are concerned with the desires of mankind in general—and of gods, angels, and devils, if they exist. Science can discuss the causes of desires, and the means for realizing them, but it cannot contain any genuinely ethical sentences, because it is concerned with what is true or false.

The theory which I have been advocating is a form of the doctrine which is called the "subjectivity" of values. This doctrine consists in maintaining that, if two men differ about values, there is not a disagreement as to any kind of truth, but a difference of taste. If one man says "oysters are good" and another says "I think they are bad," we recognize that there is nothing to argue about. The theory in question holds that all differences as to values are of this sort, although we do not naturally think them so when we are dealing with matters that seem to us more exalted than oysters. The chief ground for adopting this view is the complete impossibility of finding any arguments to prove that this or that has intrinsic value. If we all agreed, we might hold that we know values by intuition. We cannot prove, to a color-blind man, that grass is green and not red. But there are various ways of proving to him that he lacks a power of discrimination which most men possess, whereas in the case of values there are no such ways, and disagreements are much more frequent than in the case of colors. Since no way can be even imagined for deciding a difference as to values, the conclusion is forced upon us that the difference is one of tastes, not one as to any objective truth.

The consequences of this doctrine are considerable. In the first place, there can be no such thing as "sin" in any absolute sense; what one man calls "sin" another may call "virtue," and though they may dislike each other on account of this difference, neither can convict the other of intellectual error. Punishment cannot be justified on the ground that the criminal is "wicked," but only on the ground that he has behaved in a way which others wish to discourage. Hell, as a place of punishment for sinners, becomes quite irrational.

In the second place, it is impossible to uphold the way of speaking about values which is common among those who believe in Cosmic Purpose. Their argument is that certain things which have been evolved are "good," and therefore the world must have had a purpose which was ethically admirable. In the language of subjective values, this argument becomes: "Some things in the world are to our liking, and therefore they must have been created by a Being with our tastes, Whom, therefore, we also like, and Who, consequently, is good." Now it seems fairly evident that, if creatures having likes and dislikes were to exist at all, they were pretty sure to like some things in their environment, since otherwise they would find life intolerable. Our values have been evolved along with the rest of our constitution, and nothing as to any original purpose can be inferred from the fact that they are what they are.

Those who believe in "objective" values often contend that the view which I have been advocating has immoral consequences. This seems to me to be due to faulty reasoning. There are, as has already been said, certain ethical consequences of the doctrine of subjective values, of which the most important is the rejection of vindictive punishment and the notion of "sin." But the more general consequences which are feared, such as the decay of all sense of moral obligation, are not to be logically deduced. Moral obligation, if it is to influence conduct, must consist not merely of a belief, but of a desire. The desire, I may be told, is the desire to be "good" in a sense which I no longer allow. But when we analyze the desire to be "good" it generally resolves itself into a desire to be approved, or, alternatively, to act so as to bring about certain general consequences which we desire. We have wishes which are not purely personal, and, if we had not, no amount of ethical teaching would influence our conduct except through fear of disapproval. The sort of life that most of us admire is one which is guided by large impersonal desires; now such desires can, no doubt, be encouraged by example, education, and knowledge, but they can hardly be created by the mere abstract belief that they are good, nor discouraged by an analysis of what is meant by the word "good."

When we contemplate the human race, we may desire that it should be happy, or healthy, or intelligent, or warlike, and so on. Any one of these desires, if it is strong, will produce its own morality; but if we have no such general desires, our conduct, whatever our ethic may be, will only serve social purposes in so far as self-interest and the interests of society are in harmony. It is the business of wise institutions to create such harmony as far as possible, and for the rest, whatever may be our theoretical definition of value, we must depend upon the existence of impersonal desires. When you meet a man with whom you have a fundamental ethical disagreement—for example, if you think that all men count equally, while he selects a class as alone important—you will find yourself no better able to cope with him if you believe in objective values than if you do not. In either case, you can only influence his conduct through influencing his desires: if you succeed in that, his ethic will change, and if not, not.

Some people feel that if a general desire, say for the happiness of mankind, has not the sanction of absolute good, it is in some way "irrational." This is due to a lingering belief in objective values. A desire cannot, in itself, be either rational or irrational. It may conflict with other desires, and therefore lead to unhappiness; it may rouse opposition in others, and therefore be incapable of gratification. But it cannot be considered "irrational" merely because no reason can be given for feeling it. We may desire A because it is a means to B, but in the end, when we have done with mere means, we must come to something which we desire for no reason, but not on that account "irrationally." All systems of ethics embody the desires of those who advocate them, but this fact is concealed in a mist of words. Our desires are, in fact, more general and less purely selfish than most moralists imagine; if it were not so, no theory of ethics would make moral improvement possible. It is, in fact, not by ethical theory, but by the cultivation of large and generous desires through intelligence, happiness, and freedom from fear, that men can be brought to act more than they do at present in a manner that is consistent with the general happiness of mankind will not endeavor to further it, while those who desire it believe it to be subjective or objective, those who do not desire the happiness of mankind will not endeavor to further it, while those who desrie it will do what they can to bring it about.

I conclude that, while it is true that science cannot decide questions of

value, that is because they cannot be intellectually decided at all, and lie
outside the realm of truth and falsehood. Whatever knowledge is attainable, must be attained by scientific methods; and what science cannot discover, mankind cannot know.

MORAL BELIEFS *

PHILIPPA FOOT

I

To many people it seems that the most notable advance in moral philosophy during the past fifty years or so has been the refutation of naturalism; and they are a little shocked that at this late date such an issue
should be reopened. It is easy to understand their attitude: given certain
apparently unquestionable assumptions, it would be about as sensible to
try to reintroduce naturalism as to try to square the circle. Those who see
it like this have satisfied themselves that they know in advance that any
naturalistic theory must have a catch in it somewhere, and are put out at
having to waste more time exposing an old fallacy. This paper is an attempt to persuade them to look critically at the premises on which their
arguments are based.

It would not be an exaggeration to say that the whole of moral philosophy, as it is now widely taught, rests on a contrast between statements
of fact and evaluations, which runs something like this: 'The truth or falsity
of statements of fact is shewn by means of evidence; and what counts as
evidence is laid down in the meaning of the expressions occurring in the
statement of fact. (For instance, the meaning of "round" and "flat" made
Magellan's voyages evidence for the roundness rather than the flatness of
the Earth; someone who went on questioning whether the evidence was
evidence could eventually be shown to have made some linguistic mistake.)
It follows that no two people can make the same statement and count
completely different things as evidence; in the end one at least of them
could be convicted of linguistic ignorance. It also follows that if a man is
given good evidence for a factual conclusion he cannot just refuse to accept the conclusion on the ground that in his scheme of things this evidence
is not evidence at all. With evaluations, however, it is different. An evaluation is not connected logically with the factual statements on which it
is based. One man may say that a thing is good because of some fact
about it, and another may refuse to take that fact as any evidence at all,
for nothing is laid down in the meaning of "good" which connects it with

*From Philippa Foot, "Moral Beliefs," *Transactions of the Aristotelian Society,* 59
© (1959). Reprinted by courtesy of the editor of The Aristotelian Society. [Footnotes
omitted.]

one piece of "evidence" rather than another. It follows that a moral eccentric could argue to moral conclusions from quite idiosyncratic premises; he could say, for instance, that a man was a good man because he clasped and unclasped his hands and never turned N.N.E. after turning S.S.W. He could also reject someone else's evaluation simply by denying that his evidence was evidence at all.

'The fact about "good" which allows the eccentric still to use this term without falling into a morass of meaninglessness, is its "action-guiding" or "practical" function. This it retains; for like everyone else he considers himself bound to choose the things he calls "good" rather than those he calls "bad." Like the rest of the world he uses "good" in connexion only with a "pro-attitude"; it is only that he has pro-attitudes to quite different things, and therefore calls them good.'

There are here two assumptions about 'evaluations', which I will call assumption (1) and assumption (2).

Assumption (1) is that some individual may, without logical error, base his beliefs about matters of value entirely on premises which no one else would recognise as giving evidence at all. Assumption (2) is that, given the kind of statement which other people regard as evidence for an evaluative conclusion, he may refuse to draw the conclusion because *this* does not count as evidence for *him*.

Let us consider assumption (1). We might say that this depends on the possibility of keeping the meaning of 'good' steady through all changes in the facts about anything which are to count in favour of its goodness. (I do not mean, of course, that a man can make changes as fast as he chooses; only that, whatever he has chosen, it will not be possible to rule him out of order.) But there is a better formulation, which cuts out trivial disputes about the meaning which 'good' happens to have in some section of the community. Let us say that the assumption is that the evaluative function of 'good' can remain constant through changes in the evaluative principles; on this ground it could be said that even if no one can call a man *good* because he clasps and unclasps his hands, he can commend him or express his *pro-attitude* towards him, and if necessary can invent a new moral vocabulary to express his unusual moral code.

Those who hold such a theory will naturally add several qualifications. In the first place, most people now agree with Hare, against Stevenson, that such words as 'good' only apply to individual cases through the application of general principles, so that even the extreme moral eccentric must accept principles of commendation. In the second place 'commending', 'having a pro-attitude', and so on, are supposed to be connected with doing and choosing, so that it would be impossible to say, e.g., that a man was a good man only if he lived for a thousand years. The range of evaluation is supposed to be restricted to the range of possible action and choice. I am not here concerned to question these supposed restrictions on the use of evaluative terms, but only to argue that they are not enough.

The crucial question is this. Is it possible to extract from the meaning of words such as 'good' some element called 'evaluative meaning' which we can think of as externally related to its objects? Such an element would be represented, for instance, in the rule that when any action was 'commended' the speaker must hold himself bound to accept an imperative 'let me do these things'. This is externally related to its object because, within the limitation which we noticed earlier, to possible actions, it would make sense to think of anything as the subject of such 'commendation'. On this hypothesis a moral eccentric could be described as commending the clasping of hands as the action of a good man, and we should not have to look for some background to give the supposition sense. That is to say, on this hypothesis the clasping of hands could be commended without any explanation; it could be what those who hold such theories call 'an ultimate moral principle'.

I wish to say that this hypothesis is untenable, and that there is no describing the evaluative meaning of 'good', evaluation, commending, or anything of the sort, without fixing the object to which they are supposed to be attached. Without first laying hands on the proper object of such things as evaluation, we shall catch in our net either something quite different such as accepting an order or making a resolution, or else nothing at all.

Before I consider this question, I shall first discuss some other mental attitudes and beliefs which have this internal relation to their object. By this I hope to clarify the concept of internal relation to an object, and incidentally, if my examples arouse resistance, but are eventually accepted, to show how easy it is to overlook an internal relation where it exists.

Consider, for instance, pride.

People are often surprised at the suggestion that there are limits to the things a man can be proud of, about which indeed he can feel pride. I do not know quite what account they want to give of pride; perhaps something to do with smiling and walking with a jaunty air, and holding an object up where other people can see it; or perhaps they think that pride is a kind of internal sensation, so that one might naturally beat one's breast and say 'pride is something I feel *here*'. The difficulties of the second view are well known; the logically private object cannot be what a name in the public language is the name of. The first view is the more plausible, and it may seem reasonable to say that given certain behaviour a man can be described as showing that he is proud of something, whatever that something may be. In one sense this is true, and in another sense not. Given any description of an object, action, personal characteristic, etc., it is not possible to rule it out as an object of pride. Before we can do so we need to know what would be said about it by a man who is to be proud of it, or feels proud of it; but if he does not hold the right beliefs about it then whatever his attitude is it is not pride. Consider, for instance, the suggestion that someone might be proud of the sky or the sea: he looks at them and what he feels is *pride,* or he puffs out his chest and gestures with *pride* in their direction. This makes sense only if a special assumption is made about his beliefs, for instance that he is under some crazy delusion and believes that he has saved the sky from falling, or the sea from drying up. The characteristic object of pride is something seen (*a*) as in some way a man's own, and (*b*) as some sort of achievement or advantage; without this object pride cannot be described. To see that the second condition is necessary, one should try supposing that a man happens to feel proud because he has laid one of his hands on the other, three times in an hour. Here again the supposition that it is pride that he feels will make perfectly good sense if a special background is filled in. Perhaps he is ill, and it is an achievement even to do this; perhaps this gesture has some religious or political significance, and he is a brave man who will so defy the gods or the rulers. But with no special background there can be no pride, not because no one could psychologically speaking feel pride in such a case, but because whatever he did feel could not logically be pride. Of course, people can see strange things as achievements, though not just anything, and they can identify themselves with remote ancestors, and relations, and neighbours, and even on occasions with Mankind. I do not wish to deny there are many far-fetched and comic examples of pride.

We could have chosen many other examples of mental attitudes which are internally related to their object in a similar way. For instance, fear is not just trembling, and running, and turning pale; without the thought of some menacing evil no amount of this will add up to fear. Nor could anyone be said to feel dismay about something he did not see as bad; if his thoughts about it were that it was altogether a good thing, he could not say that (oddly enough) what he felt about it was dismay. 'How odd, I feel dismayed when I ought to be pleased' is the prelude to a hunt for the adverse aspect of the thing, thought of as lurking behind the pleasant façade. But someone may object that pride and fear and dismay are feelings or emotions and therefore not a proper analogy for 'commendation', and there will be an advantage in considering a different kind of example. We could discuss for instance, the belief that a certain thing is dangerous, and ask whether this could logically be held about anything whatsoever. Like 'this is good', 'this is dangerous' is an assertion, which we should naturally accept or reject by speaking of its truth or falsity; we seem to support such statements with evidence, and moreover there may seem to be a 'warning function' connected with the word 'dangerous' as there is supposed to be a 'commending function' connected with the word 'good'. For suppose that philosophers, puzzled about the property of dangerousness, decided that the word did not stand for a property at all, but was essentially a practical or action-guiding term, used for *warning*. Unless used in an 'inverted comma sense' the word 'dangerous' was used to warn, and this meant that anyone using it in such a sense committed himself to avoiding the things he called dangerous, to preventing other people from going near them, and perhaps to running in the opposite direction. If the conclusion were not obviously ridiculous, it would be easy to infer that a man whose application of the term was different from ours throughout might say that the oddest things were dangerous without fear of disproof; the idea would be that he could still be described as 'thinking them dangerous', or at least as 'warning', because by his attitude and actions he would have fulfilled the conditions for these things. This is nonsense because without its proper object *warning*, like *believing dangerous*, will not be there. It is logically impossible to warn about anything not thought of as threatening evil, and for danger we need a particular kind of serious evil such as injury or death.

There are, however, some differences between thinking a thing dangerous and feeling proud, frightened or dismayed. When a man says that something is dangerous he must support his statement with a special kind of evidence; but when he says that he feels proud or frightened or dismayed the description of the object of his pride or fright or dismay does not have quite this relation to his original statement. If he is shown that the thing he was proud of was not his after all, or was not after all anything very grand, he may have to say that his pride was not justified, but he will not have to take back the statement that he was proud. On the other hand, someone who says that a thing is dangerous, and later sees that he made a mistake in thinking that an injury might result from it, has to go back on his original statement and admit that he was wrong. In neither case, however, is the speaker able to go on as before. A man who discovered that it was not his pumpkin but someone else's which had won the prize could only say that he still felt proud if he could produce some other ground for pride. It is in this way that even feelings are logically vulnerable to facts.

It will probably be objected against these examples that for part of the way at least they beg the question. It will be said that indeed a man can be proud only of something he thinks a good action, or an achievement, or a sign of noble birth; as he can feel dismay only about something which he sees as bad, or frightened of some threatened evil; similarly he can warn only if he is also prepared to speak, for instance, of injury. But this will limit the range of possible objects of those attitudes and beliefs only if the range of these terms is limited in its turn. To meet this objection I shall discuss the meaning of 'injury' because this is the simplest case. Anyone who feels inclined to say that anything could be counted as an achievement, or as the evil of which people were afraid, or about which they felt dismayed, should just try this out. I wish to consider the proposition that anything could be thought of as dangerous, because if it causes injury it is dangerous, and anything could be counted as an injury. I shall consider bodily injury because this is the injury connected with danger; it is not correct to put up a notice by the roadside reading 'Danger!' on account of bushes which might scratch a car. Nor can a substance be labelled 'dangerous' on the ground that it can injure delicate fabrics; although we can speak of the danger that it may do so, that is not the use of the word which I am considering here.

When a body is injured it is changed for the worse in a special way, and we want to know which changes count as injuries. First of all, it matters how an injury comes about; e.g., it cannot be caused by natural decay. Then it seems clear that not just any kind of thing will do, for instance, any unusual mark on the body, however much trouble a man might take to have it removed. By far the most important class of injuries are injuries to a part of the body, counting as injuries because there is an interference with the function of that part; injury to a leg, an eye, an ear, a hand, a muscle, the heart, the brain, the spinal cord. An injury to an eye is one that affects, or is likely to affect, its sight; an injury to a hand one which makes it less well able to reach out and grasp, and perform other operations of this kind. A leg can be injured because its movements and supporting power can be affected; a lung because it can become too weak to draw in the proper amount of air. We are most ready to speak of an injury where the function of a part of the body is to perform a characteristic operation, as in these examples. We might hesitate to say that a skull can be injured, and might prefer to speak of damage to it, since although there is indeed a function (a protective function) there is no operation. But thinking of the protective function of the skull we may want to speak of injury here. In so far as the concept of *injury* depends on that of *function* it is narrowly limited, since not even every use to which a part of the body is put will count as its function. Why is it that, even if it is the means by which they earn their living, we would never consider the removal of the dwarf's hump or the bearded lady's beard as a bodily injury? It will be tempting to say that these things are disfigurements, but this is not the point; if we suppose that a man who had some invisible extra muscle made his living as a court jester by waggling his ears, the ear would not have been injured if this were made to disappear. If it were natural to men to communicate by movements of the ear, then ears would have the function of signalling (we have no word for this kind of 'speaking') and an impairment of this function would be an injury; but things are not like this. This court jester would use his ears to make people laugh, but this is not the function of ears.

No doubt many people will feel impatient when such facts are mentioned, because they think that it is quite unimportant that this or that *happens* to be the case, and it seems to them arbitrary that the loss of the beard, the hump, or the ear muscle would not be called an injury. Isn't the loss of that by which one makes one's living a pretty catastrophic loss? Yet it seems quite natural that these are not counted as injuries if one thinks about the conditions of human life, and contrasts the loss of a special ability to make people gape or laugh with the ability to see, hear, walk, or pick things up. The first is only needed for one very special way of living; the other in any foreseeable future for any man. This restriction seems all the more natural when we observe what other threats besides that of injury can constitute danger: of death, for instance, or mental derangement. A shock which could cause mental instability or impairment of memory would be called dangerous, because a man needs such things as intelligence, memory, and concentration as he needs sight or hearing or the use of hands. Here we do not speak of injury unless it is possible to connect the impairment with some physical change, but we speak of danger because there is the same loss of a capacity which any man needs.

There can be injury outside the range we have been considering; for a man may sometimes be said to have received injuries where no part of his body has had its functions interfered with. In general, I think that any blow which disarranged the body in such a way that there was lasting pain would inflict an injury, even if no other ill resulted, but I do not know of any other important extension of the concept.

It seems therefore that since the range of things which can be called injuries is quite narrowly restricted, the word 'dangerous' is restricted in so far as it is connected with injury. We have the right to say that a man cannot decide to call just anything dangerous, however much he puts up fences and shakes his head.

So far I have been arguing that such things as pride, fear, dismay, and the thought that something is dangerous have an internal relation to their object, and hope that what I mean is becoming clear. Now we must consider whether those attitudes or beliefs which are the moral philosopher's study are similar, or whether such things as 'evaluation' and 'thinking something good' and 'commendation' could logically be found in combination with any object whatsoever. All I can do here is to give an example which may make this suggestion seem implausible, and to knock away a few of its supports. The example will come from the range of trivial and pointless actions such as we were considering in speaking of the man who clasped his hands three times an hour, and we can point to the oddity of the suggestion that this can be called a good action. We are bound by the terms of our question to refrain from adding any special background, and it should be stated once more that the question is about what can count in favour of the goodness or badness of a man or an action, and not what could be, or be thought, good or bad with a special background. I believe that the view I am attacking often seems plausible only because the special background is surreptitiously introduced.

Someone who said that clasping the hands three times in an hour was a good action would first have to answer the question 'How do you mean?' For the sentence 'this is a good action' is not one which has a clear meaning. Presumably, since our subject is moral philosophy, it does not here mean 'that was a good thing to do' as this might be said of a man who had done something sensible in the course of any enterprise whatever; we are to confine our attention to 'the moral use of "good"'. I am not clear that it makes sense to speak of 'a moral use of "good"', but we can pick out a number of cases which raise moral issues. It is because these are so diverse and because 'this is a good action' does not pick out any one of them, that we must ask 'How do you mean?' For instance, some things that are done fulfil a duty, such as the duty of parents to children or children to parents. I suppose that when philosophers speak of good actions they would include these. Some come under the heading of a virtue such as charity, and they will be included too. Others again are actions which require the virtues of courage or temperance, and here the moral aspect is due to the fact that they are done in spite of fear or the temptation of pleasure; they must indeed be done for the sake of some real or fancied good, but not necessarily what philosophers would want to call a moral good. Courage is not *particularly* concerned with saving other people's lives, or temperance with leaving them their share of the food and drink, and the goodness of *what is done* may here be all kinds of usefulness. It is because there are these very diverse cases included (I suppose) under the expression 'a good action' that we should refuse to consider applying it without asking what is meant, and we should now ask what is intended when someone is supposed to say that 'clasping the hands three times in an hour is a good action'. Is it supposed that this action fulfils a duty? Then in virtue of what does a man have this duty, and to whom does he owe it? We have promised not to slip in a special background, but he cannot possibly have a *duty* to clasp his hands unless such a background exists. Nor could it be an act of charity, for it is not thought to do anyone any good, nor again a gesture of humility unless a special assumption turns it into this. The action could be courageous, but only if it were done both in the face of fear and for the sake of a good; and we are not allowed to put in special circumstances which could make this the case.

I am sure that the following objection will now be raised. 'Of course clasping one's hands three times in an hour cannot be brought under one of the virtues which we recognise, but that is only to say that it is not a good action by our current moral code. It is logically possible that in a quite different moral code quite different virtues should be recognised, for which we have not even got a name.' I cannot answer this objection properly, for that would need a satisfactory account of the concept of a virtue. But anyone who thinks it would be easy to describe a new virtue connected with clasping the hands three times in an hour should just try. I think he will find that he has to cheat, and suppose that in the community concerned the clasping of hands has been given some special significance, or is thought to have some special effect. The difficulty is obviously connected with the fact that without a special background there is no possibility of answering the question 'What's the point?' It is no good saying that there would be a point in doing the action because the action was a morally good action: the question is how it can be given any such description if we cannot first speak about the point. And it is just as crazy to suppose that we can call *anything* the point of doing something without having to say what the point of *that* is. In clasping one's hands one may make a slight sucking noise, but what is the point of that? It is surely clear that moral virtues must be connected with human good and harm, and that it is quite impossible to call anything you like good or harm. Consider, for instance, the suggestion that a man might say he had been harmed because a bucket of water had been taken out of the sea. As usual it would be possible to think up circumstances in which this remark would make sense; for instance, when coupled with a belief in magical influences; but then the harm would consist in what was done by the evil spirits, not in the taking of the water from the sea. It would be just as odd if someone were supposed to say that harm had been done to him because the hairs of his head had been reduced to an even number.

I conclude that assumption (1) is very dubious indeed, and that no one should be allowed to speak as if we can understand 'evaluation' 'commendation' or 'pro-attitude', whatever the actions concerned.

II

I propose now to consider what was called assumption (2), which said that a man might always refuse to accept the conclusion of an argument about values, because what counted as evidence for other people did not count for him. Assumption (2) could be true even if assumption (1) were false, for it might be that once a particular question of values—say a moral question—had been accepted, any disputant was bound to accept particular pieces of evidence as relevant, the same pieces as everyone else, but that he could always refuse to draw any moral conclusions whatsoever or to discuss any questions which introduced moral terms. Nor do we mean 'he might refuse to draw the conclusion' in the trivial sense in which anyone can perhaps refuse to draw *any* conclusion; the point is that any statement of value always seems to go beyond any statement of fact, so that he might have a reason for accepting the factual premises but refusing to accept the evaluative conclusion. That this is so seems to those who argue in this way to follow from the practical implication of evaluation. When a man uses a word such as 'good' in an 'evaluative' and not an 'inverted comma' sense, he is supposed to commit his will. From this it has seemed to follow inevitably that there is a logical gap between fact and value, for is it not one thing to say that a thing is so, and another to have a particular attitude towards its being so; one thing to see that certain effects will follow from a given action, and another to care? Whatever account was offered of the essential feature of evaluation—whether in terms of feelings, attitudes, the acceptance of imperatives or what not—the fact remained that with an evaluation there was a committal in a new dimension, and that this was not guaranteed by any acceptance of facts.

I shall argue that this view is mistaken; that the practical implication of the use of moral terms has been put in the wrong place, and that if it is described correctly the logical gap between factual premises and moral conclusion disappears.

In this argument it will be useful to have as a pattern the practical or 'action-guiding' force of the word 'injury', which is in some, though not all, ways similar to that of moral terms. It is clear I think that an injury is necessarily something bad and therefore something which as such anyone always has a reason to avoid, and philosophers will therefore be tempted to say that anyone who uses 'injury' in its full 'action-guiding' sense commits himself to avoiding the things he calls injuries. They will then be in the usual difficulties about the man who says he knows he ought to do something but does not intend to do it; perhaps also about weakness of the will. Suppose that instead we look again at the kinds of things which count as injuries, to see if the connexion with the will does not start here. As has been shown, a man is injured whenever some part of his body, in being damaged, has become less well able to fulfil its ordinary function. It follows that he suffers a disability, or is liable to do so; with an injured hand he will be less well able to pick things up, hold on to them, tie them together or chop them up, and so on. With defective eyes there will be a thousand other things he is unable to do, and in both cases we should naturally say that he will often be unable to get what he wants to get or avoid what he wants to avoid.

Philosophers will no doubt seize on the word 'want', and say that if we suppose that a man happens to want the things which an injury to his body prevents him from getting, we have slipped in a supposition about a 'pro-attitude' already; and that anyone who does not happen to have these wants can still refuse to use 'injury' in its prescriptive, or 'action-guiding' sense. And so it may seem that the only way to make a *necessary* connexion between 'injury' and the things that are to be avoided, is to say that it is used in an 'action-guiding sense' only when applied to something the speaker intends to avoid. But we should look carefully at the crucial move in that argument, and query the suggestion that someone might happen not to want anything for which he would need the use of hands or eyes. Hands and eyes, like ears and legs, play a part in so many operations that a man could only be said not to need them if he had no wants at all. That such people exist, in asylums, is not to the present purpose at all; the proper use of his limbs is something a man has reason to want if he wants anything.

I do not know just what someone who denies this proposition could have in mind. Perhaps he is thinking of changing the facts of human existence, so that merely wishing, or the sound of the voice, will bring the world to heel? More likely he is proposing to rig the circumstances of some individual's existence within the framework of the ordinary world, by supposing for instance that he is a prince whose servant will sow and reap and fetch and carry for him, and so use their hands and eyes in his service that he will not need the use of his. Let us suppose that such a story could be told about a man's life; it is wildly implausible, but let us pretend that it is not. It is clear that in spite of this we could say that any man had a reason to shun injury; for even if at the end of his life it could be said that by a strange set of circumstances he had never needed the use of his eyes, or his hands, this could not possibly be foreseen. Only by once more changing the facts of human existence, and supposing every vicissitude foreseeable, could such a supposition be made.

This is not to say that an injury might not bring more incidental gain than necessary harm; one has only to think of times when the order has gone out that able-bodied men are to be put to the sword. Such a gain might even, in some peculiar circumstances, be reliably foreseen, so that a man would have even better reason for seeking than for avoiding injury. In this respect the word 'injury' differs from terms such as 'injustice'; the practical force of 'injury' means only that anyone has *a* reason to avoid injuries, not that he has an overriding reason to do so.

It will be noticed that this account of the 'action-guiding' force of 'injury' links it with reasons for acting rather than with actually doing something. I do not think, however, that this makes it a less good pattern for the 'action-guiding' force of moral terms. Philosophers who have supposed that actual action was required if 'good' were to be used in a sincere evaluation have got into difficulties over weakness of will, and they should surely agree that enough has been done if we can show that any man has reason to aim at virtue and avoid vice. But is this impossibly difficult if we consider the kinds of things that count as virtue and vice? Consider, for instance, the cardinal virtues, prudence, temperance, courage and justice. Obviously any man needs prudence, but does he not also need to resist the temptation of pleasure when there is harm involved? And how could it be argued that he would never need to face what was fearful for the sake of some good? It is not obvious what someone would mean if he said that temperance or courage were not good qualities, and this not because of the 'praising' sense of these *words,* but because of the things that courage and temperance are.

I should like to use these examples to show the artificiality of the notions of 'commendation' and of 'pro-attitudes' as these are commonly employed. Philosophers who talk about these things will say that after the facts have been accepted—say that X is the kind of man who will climb a dangerous mountain, beard an irascible employer for a rise in pay, and in general face the fearful for the sake of something he thinks worth while—there remains the question of 'commendation' or 'evaluation'. If the word 'courage' is used they will ask whether or not the man who speaks of another as having courage is supposed to have commended him. If we say 'yes' they will insist that the judgement about courage *goes beyond the facts,* and might therefore be rejected by someone who refused to do so; if we say 'no' they will argue that 'courage' is being used in a purely descriptive or 'inverted comma sense', and that we have not got an example of the evaluative use of language which is the moral philosopher's special study. What sense can be made, however, of the question 'does he commend?' What is this extra element which is supposed to be present or absent after the facts have been settled? It is not a matter of liking the man who has courage, or of thinking him altogether good, but of 'commending him for his courage'. How are we supposed to do that? The answer that will be given is that we only commend someone else in speaking of him as courageous if we accept the imperative 'let me be courageous' for ourselves. But this is quite unnecessary. I can speak of someone else as having the virtue of courage, and of course recognise it as a virtue in the proper sense, while knowing that I am a complete coward, and making no resolution to reform. I know that I should be better off if I were courageous and so have a reason to cultivate courage, but I may also know that I will do nothing of the kind.

If someone were to say that courage was not a virtue he would have to say that it was not a quality by which a man came to act well. Perhaps he would be thinking that someone might be worse off for his courage, which is true, but only because an incidental harm might arise. For instance, the courageous man might have underestimated a risk, and run into some disaster which a cowardly man would have avoided because he was not prepared to take any risk at all. And his courage, like any other virtue, could be the cause of harm to him because possessing it he fell into some disastrous state of pride. Similarly, those who question the virtue of temperance are probably thinking not of the virtue itself but of men whose temperance has consisted in resisting pleasure for the sake of some illusory good, or those who have made this virtue their pride.

But what, it will be asked, of justice? For while prudence, courage and temperance are qualities which benefit the man who has them, justice seems rather to benefit others, and to work to the disadvantage of the just man himself. Justice as it is treated here, as one of the cardinal virtues, covers all those things owed to other people: it is under injustice that murder, theft and lying come, as well as the withholding of what is owed for instance by parents to children and by children to parents, as well as the dealings which would be called unjust in everyday speech. So the man who avoids injustice will find himself in need of things he has returned to their owner, unable to obtain an advantage by cheating and lying; involved in all those difficulties painted by Thrasymachus in the first book of the Republic, in order to show that injustice is more profitable than justice to a man of strength and wit. We will be asked how, on our theory, justice can be a virtue and injustice a vice, since it will surely be difficult to show that any man whatsoever must need to be just as he needs the use of his hands and eyes, or needs prudence, courage and temperance?

Before answering this question I shall argue that if it cannot be answered, then justice can no longer be recommended, as a virtue. The point of this is not to show that it must be answerable, since justice is a virtue, but rather to suggest that we should at least consider the possibility that justice is not a virtue. This suggestion was taken seriously by Socrates in the Republic, where it was assumed by everyone that if Thrasymachus could establish his premise—that injustice was more profitable than justice—his conclusion would follow: that a man who had strength to get away with injustice had reason to follow this as the best way of life. It is a striking fact about modern moral philosophy that no one sees any difficulty in accepting Thrasymachus' premise and rejecting his conclusion, and it is because Nietzsche's position is at this point much closer to that of Plato that he is remote from academic moralists of the present day.

In the Republic it is assumed that if justice is not a good to the just man, moralists who recommend it as a virtue are perpetrating a fraud. Agreeing with this, I shall be asked where exactly the fraud comes in; where the untruth that justice is profitable to the individual is supposed to be told. As a preliminary answer we might ask how many people are prepared to say frankly that injustice is more profitable than justice? Leaving aside, as elsewhere in this paper, religious beliefs which might complicate the matter, we will suppose that some tough atheistical character has asked 'Why should I be just?' (Those who believe that this question has something wrong with it can employ their favourite device for sieving out 'evaluative meaning', and suppose that the question is 'Why should I be "just"?') Are we prepared to reply 'As far as you are concerned you will be better off if you are unjust, but it matters to the rest of us that you should be just, so we are trying to get you to be just'? He would be likely to enquire into our methods, and then take care not to be found out, and I do not think that many of those who think that it is not necessary to show that justice is profitable to the just man would easily accept that there was nothing more they could say.

The crucial question is: 'Can we give anyone, strong or weak, a reason why he should be just?'—and it is no help at all to say that since 'just' and 'unjust' are 'action-guiding words' no one can even ask 'Why should I be just?' Confronted with that argument the man who wants to do things has only to be careful to avoid the *word*, and he has not been given a reason why he should not do the things which other people call 'unjust'. Probably it will be argued that he has been given a reason so far as anyone can ever be given a reason for doing or not doing anything, for the chain of reasons must always come to an end somewhere, and it may seem that one may always reject the reason which another man accepts. But this is a mistake; some answers to the question 'why should I?' bring the series to a close and some do not. Hume showed how *one* answer closed the series in the following passage:

> Ask a man *why he uses exercise;* he will answer, *because he desires to keep his health.* If you then enquire, *why he desires health,* he will readily reply,

because sickness is painful. If you push your enquiries farther, and desire a reason *why he hates pain,* it is impossible he can ever give any. This is an ultimate end, and is never referred to any other object. (*Enquiries,* Appendix I, V.)

Hume might just as well have ended this series with boredom: sickness often brings boredom, and no one is required to give a reason why he does not want to be bored, any more than he has to give reason why he does want to pursue what interests him. In general, anyone is given a reason for acting when he is shown the way to something he wants; but for some wants the question 'Why do you want that?' will make sense, and for others it will not. It seems clear that in this division justice falls on the opposite side from pleasure and interest and such things. 'Why shouldn't I do that?' is not answered by the words 'because it is unjust' as it is answered by showing that the action will bring boredom, loneliness, pain, discomfort or certain kinds of incapacity, and this is why it is not true to say that 'it's unjust' gives a reason in so far as any reasons can ever be given. 'It's unjust' gives a reason only if the nature of justice can be shown to be such that it is necessarily connected with what a man wants.

This shows why a great deal hangs on the question of whether justice is or is not a good to the just man, and why those who accept Thrasymachus' premise and reject his conclusion are in a dubious position. They recommend justice to each man, as something he has a reason to follow, but when challenged to show why he should do so they will not always be able to reply. This last assertion does not depend on any 'selfish theory of human nature' in the philosophical sense. It is often possible to give a man a reason for acting by showing him that someone else will suffer if he does not; someone else's good may really be more to him than his own. But the affection which mothers feel for children, and lovers for each other, and friends for friends, will not take us far when we are asked for reasons why a man should be just; partly because it will not extend far enough, and partly because the actions dictated by benevolence and justice are not always the same. Suppose that I owe someone money:

'. . . what if he be my enemy, and has given me just cause to hate him, What if he be a vicious man, and deserves the hatred of all mankind? What if he be a miser, and can make no use of what I would deprive him of? What if he be a profligate debauchee, and would rather receive harm than benefit from large possessions?'

Even if the general practice of justice could be brought under the motive of universal benevolence—the desire for the greatest happiness of the greatest number—many people certainly do not have any such desire. So that if justice is only to be recommended on these grounds a thousand tough characters will be able to say that they have been given no reason for practising justice, and many more would say the same if they were not too timid or too stupid to ask questions about the code of behaviour which they have been taught. Thus, given Thrasymachus' premise Thrasymachus' point of view is reasonable; we have no particular reason to admire those who practise justice through timidity or stupidity.

It seems to me, therefore, that if Thrasymachus' thesis is accepted things cannot go on as before; we shall have to admit that the belief on which the status of justice as a virtue was founded is mistaken, and if we still want to get people to be just we must recommend justice to them in a new way. We shall have to admit that injustice is more profitable than justice, at least for the strong, and then do our best to see that hardly anyone can get away with being unjust. We have, of course, the alternative of keeping quiet, hoping that for the most part people will follow convention into a kind of justice, and not ask awkward questions, but this policy might be overtaken by a vague scepticism even on the part of those who do not know just what is lacking; we should also be at the mercy of anyone who was able and willing to expose our fraud.

Is it true, however, to say that justice is not something a man needs in his dealings with his fellows, supposing only that he be strong? Those who think that he can get on perfectly well without being just should be asked to say exactly how such a man is supposed to live. We know that he is to practise injustice whenever the unjust act would bring him advantage; but what is he to say? Does he admit that he does not recognise the rights of other people, or does he pretend? In the first case even those who combine with him will know that on a change of fortune, or a shift of affection, he may turn to plunder them, and he must be as wary of their treachery as they are of his. Presumably the happy unjust man is supposed, as in Book II of the Republic, to be a very cunning liar and actor, combining complete injustice with the appearance of justice: he is prepared to treat others ruthlessly, but pretends that nothing is further from his mind. Philosophers often speak as if a man could thus hide himself even from those around him, but the supposition is doubtful, and in any case the price in vigilance would be colossal. If he lets even a few people see his true attitude he must guard himself against them; if he lets no one into the secret he must always be careful in case the least spontaneity betray him. Such facts are important because the need a man has for justice in dealings with other men depends on the fact that they are men and not inanimate objects or animals. If a man only needed other men as he needs household objects, and if men could be manipulated like household objects, or beaten into a reliable submission like donkeys, the case would be different. As things are, the supposition that injustice is more profitable than justice is very dubious, although like cowardice and intemperance it might turn out incidentally to be profitable.

The reason why it seems to some people so impossibly difficult to show that justice is more profitable than injustice is that they consider in isolation particular just acts. It is perfectly true that if a man is just it follows that he will be prepared, in the event of very evil circumstances, even to face death rather than to act unjustly—for instance, in getting an innocent man convicted of a crime of which he has been accused. For him it turns out that his justice brings disaster on him, and yet like anyone else he had good reason to be a just and not an unjust man. He could not have it both ways and while possessing the virtue of justice hold himself ready to be unjust should any great advantage accrue. The man who has the virtue of justice is not ready to do certain things, and if he is too easily tempted we shall say that he was ready after all.

PART
TWO

Contemporary Normative Ethical Problems

In this decade interest in normative, as distinct from descriptive and metaethical problems, has virtually mushroomed. Two main general areas can be pointed out: matters of life and death such as abortion, capital punishment, euthanasia, and new modes of bringing about conception and birth; and a heavy emphasis on rights. Some of these two general areas overlap.

Chapter Eight continues the debate between result, or consequentialist, theories of obligation and deontological theories in showing how Kant and utilitarians differ on punishment. The view of Kant is that no one can ever morally be treated as a means (e.g., made an example of), whereas theoretically utilitarians would allow this if it creates the greatest happiness for the greatest number (though John Rawls, a critic of that general theory, has defended it against that charge.) In Chapters Eleven and Twelve the deontological view that some acts are never justifiable is pitted against those who defend a woman's right to abortion on grounds less than risk to her own life. The right to life is a peculiarly frustrating issue when it revolves around the question, When is an embryo or fetus a human being, and abortion murder? Wertheimer gives an even-handed answer. In Chapter Fourteen once more the denial that some actions are ever justifiable conflicts with the views of those who argue that human life is no absolute value. Brandt defends the rationality and morality of suicide in some cases, while Fletcher argues for the morality of voluntary euthanasia. Beauchamp replies to Rachels's discussion of the difference between killing and letting die. On euthanasia both Rachels and Dyck refer to the principle of rule utilitarianism (see Chapter Five); actions that might be justifiable under act utilitarianism but that are, as a rule, wrong should be refrained from.

John Rawls's theory of justice gets expression in Chapter Nine in "Justice as Reciprocity," setting forth a view of just distribution in society. Feinberg's piece is on schemes for economic justice regarding income.

Devlin and Hart debate issues of morality and law that are germane to discussions of pornography, homosexuality, and prostitution in relation to the law and freedom. Thomas Nagel discusses the nature of sex by examining the nature of sexual perversion.

Finally, Leon Kass explores the developments in biology that steadily produce nagging challenge after nagging challenge to our thinking about the moral limits to tinkering with nature, as some might call it, or as others might say, the application of science to human needs. In June 1980, in *Diamond* v. *Chakrabarty*, the U.S. Supreme Court approved the patenting of new forms of life.

8

Punishment and
Capital Punishment

The concerns of social justice and criminal justice cannot be sep- arated, but the latter offers a more dramatic challenge, one that is often closer at hand than the reality of starving millions and surely easier to relate to. For there is the crowded prison, and in it the execution chamber. Its individual inhabitants never cease to be indi- viduals even when known by a number. The current rate in crime sta- tistics is that one out of five Americans have been touched by crime, have been robbed or assaulted, and that the poor and the minorities are more often the victims of crime than the rich or middle class. No quick or effective solution appears anywhere. It is not an exaggera- tion to say that not much seems to work, although scattered experi- ments offer some hopes.

But what is justice for the criminal and the victim? What is the purpose of punishment? And for those most serious of crimes, what punishment is appropriate? Westal Willoughby examines two theories justifying punishment: the retributive theory, looking to the past and the deed already done, seeking satisfaction, expiation, or vindication; and the utilitarian theory, looking to the future, to deterrence, to prevention of recidivism, and to the good of society, including that of the individual offender. Kant and Mill again square off.

Capital punishment has held attention through the seventies, even overshadowing debates about the rights of prisoners, prisoner riots, and county jails that were flaming death traps. In *Furman* v. *Georgia* the death penalty was put in mothballs because of the great differ- ences that existed in its use. The majority held this to be cruel and unusual punishment and administered unequally. The minority did not find it cruel or unusual, constitutionally, and reaffirmed its deterrent effect. Many states tried to bring their death-penalty laws into con- formity with the Court's ruling, and as the seventies closed executions resumed amid disagreements over laws and morals, as before.

Ernest van den Haag's article polishes rebuttals he has often given to arguments against capital punishment, offering criticism of the utilitarian theory of punishment on which decisions are usually reached by American courts and favoring a retributive approach. He accuses those who would abolish capital punishment of favoring its being made illegal despite any proof of its deterrent effects, and of favoring its abolition regardless of racial or economic conditions bearing upon its administration.

THEORIES OF PUNISHMENT °

WESTAL W. WILLOUGHBY

Thus far in our work we have been examining canons of justice as applicable to the distribution of rewards. We now turn to the questions of right involved in the apportionment of penalties or punishments. . . .

Examining the theories which have been brought forward by ethicists in justification of punishment, we find that they may be described as: (1) Retributive, (2) Deterrent, (3) Preventive, and (4) Reformatory, respectively. In determining the value of these theories it will be necessary, as was the case in reference to the theories of justice as applied to the distribution of rewards, to consider them not only from the standpoint of abstract justice, but as to the possibility of realizing them in practice.

The Retributive Theory. Beginning with the retributive, or as it may also be called, the vindictive, or expiative, theory, it is to be observed first of all that, in the strict sense of the word, only that pain may be spoken of as punishment which is imposed simply and solely for the sake of the pain to be felt by the one punished. According to the retributive theory, through punishment the offender expiates his offence, suffers retribution for the evil which has been done, and thus is vindicated the principle of justice which has been violated. Thus says Godwin, in his *Political Justice*, "Punishment is generally used to signify the voluntary infliction of evil upon a vicious being, not merely because the public good demands it, but because there is apprehended to be a certain fitness and propriety in the nature of things that render suffering abstractly, from the benefit to result, the suitable concomitant of vice." [1]

Accepting this definition which Godwin gives us as the true meaning of punishment, it is necessary to hold that, in so far as a penalty is imposed for any other than a vindictive object, as, for example, for the sake of

° From Westal W. Willoughby, *Social Justice* (New York: Macmillan, 1900), pp. 316–379 with many omissions.

[1] William Godwin, *Enquiry Concerning Political Justice*, London, 1793, p. 230.

deterrence, prevention, reformation, or social protection, it ceases to be punishment at all. For all of these other objects have a reference to some good that is to be secured in the future; whereas the retributive theory, by its very nature, looks wholly to the past. According to it, pain is inflicted, not in order that some advantage may accrue in the future, but because some wrong has been done in the past.

We have, then, to ascertain the circumstances, if any there be, under which it is ethically allowable for one not only to determine for another the propriety of his acts, but to visit upon such a one punishment in case he commits acts that have been arbitrarily prohibited.

The idea of retribution or expiation can apply only as between rational beings. It is true that Great Nature (*Natura Naturans*) is often spoken of as inflicting punishment and even as destroying those who violate her laws. But such language cannot be considered strictly correct. Indeed, the very idea of violating a law of nature is an improper one. The so-called laws of nature are but statements of uniformities of experience in the phenomenal world. As such they are not in any true sense commands, and are not possible of violation by men. Certain results, so far as our experience goes, are known to follow from certain causes. That is all. There is no law-giver to be offended. There is not necessarily present any idea of wickedness, nor do the elements of intention and moral responsibility necessarily play a part when, as a consequence of a certain state of facts, certain results, disagreeable or otherwise, are experienced by particular individuals or communities. But in order that the retributive theory may have standing at all, these elements must appear. According to the theory, one is punished because he is supposed to have done a moral wrong, that is, to have committed not simply a formal or legal wrong, but to have sinned in the sight of the power that punishes him. But only that one can be said to have sinned who has freely committed the reprobated act, and who, furthermore, at the time of its commission has been mentally qualified to judge regarding the character of the act committed and, being so qualified, actually intended to commit it.

Having defined now what is meant by punishment in its proper retributive or expiative sense, we come to the vital question whether a true system of ethics requires, or even permits, the existence of a right to inflict pain for this purpose. In short, can there be stated any rational ground for declaring that justice demands, under any conceivable conditions, that pain should be inflicted when no possible future good can result? If we answer "No," we of course deny that the idea of punishment, in its proper sense, should play any part whatsoever in our systems of ethics. . . .

That philosopher who, among modern writers, has defended most absolutely the retributive theory of punishment, is Kant. His views upon this point are to be found in his *Rechtslehre.*[2]

---

[2] Translated by W. Hastie: Immanuel Kant, *Kant's Philosophy of Law*, Edinburg, 1887.

"Judicial punishment," says Kant, "can never be administered merely as a means for promoting another good, either with regard to the criminal himself or to civil society, but must in all cases be imposed only because the individual on whom it is inflicted has committed some crime. For one man ought never to be dealt with merely as a means subservient to the purpose of another, nor be mixed up with the subjects of real right. Against such treatment his inborn personality has a right to protect him, even although he may be condemned to lose his civil personality. He must first be found guilty and punishable, before there can be any thought of drawing from his personality any benefit for himself or his fellow-citizens. The penal law is a categorical imperative; and woe to him who creeps through the serpent-windings of utilitarians to discover some advantage that may discharge him from the justice of punishment or even from the due measure of it according to the Pharisaic maxim: 'It is better that one man should die than that the whole people should perish.' For if Justice and Righteousness perish, human life would no longer have any value in the world. What, then, is to be said of such a proposal as to keep a criminal alive who has been condemned to death, on his being given to understand that if he agreed to certain dangerous experiments being performed upon him, he would be allowed to survive—if he come happily through them? It is argued that physicians might thus obtain new information that would be of value to the commonweal. But a court of justice would repudiate with scorn any proposal of this kind if made to it by the medical faculty; for justice would cease to be justice, if it were bartered away for any consideration whatever." [3]

Kant makes this repudiation of the utilitarian element still more emphatic, when he declares: "Even if a civil society resolved to dissolve itself with the consent of all its members,—as might be supposed in the case of a people inhabiting an island resolving to separate and scatter themselves throughout the whole world,—the last murderer living in prison ought to be executed before the resolution was carried out. This ought to be done in order that every one may realize the desert of his deeds, and that blood-guiltiness may not remain upon the people; for otherwise they might all be regarded as participators in the murder as a public violation of Justice." [4]

The vindictive theory is accepted by Kant not only as furnishing the motive for punishment, but as dictating the character of the penalty to be imposed in each case. The doctrine of *lex talionis* is to be applied without reservation. "This right," he says, "is the only principle which in regulating a public court, as distinguished from mere private judgment, can definitely assign both the quality and the quantity of a first penalty. All other stan-

[3] *Op. cit.*, p. 195. [Note the relevance to plea bargaining.—C.L.R.]
[4] *Idem*, p. 198.

dards are wavering and uncertain; and on account of other considerations involved in them, they contain no principle conformable to the sentence of pure and strict justice." [5]

Let us see now what theoretical justification Kant offers for his theory. It is, in short, that the criminal by the deliberate commission of his deed has, in effect, accepted as valid the principle involved in the deed. Therefore, says Kant, if that same principle be applied by society to him, he is in reality but subjected to a rule of conduct which, by his own conduct, he has declared to be a valid one. Thus, in answer to the argument made by Beccaria against the rightfulness of capital punishment, that it cannot be conceived that in the original civil compact the individual could or would have consented thus to dispose of his own life, Kant replies: "No one undergoes punishment because he has willed to be punished, but because he has willed a punishable action; for it is, in fact, no punishment when one experiences what he wills; and it is impossible for any one to will to be punished. To say, 'I will to be punished, if I murder any one,' can mean nothing more than, 'I submit myself along with all the other citizens to the laws': and if there are any criminals among the people, these laws will include criminal laws. The individual who, as a co-legislator, enacts penal law, cannot possibly be the same person who, as a subject, is punished according to the law; for, *quâ* criminal, he cannot possibly be regarded as having a voice in the legislation, the legislator being rationally viewed as just and holy. If any one, then, enact a penal law against himself as a criminal, it must be [as one person, as purely law-giving] which subjects him as one capable of crime, and consequently as another person . . . with all the others in the civil union, to this penal law. In other words, it is not the people taken distributively, but the tribunal of public justice as distinct from the criminal, that prescribes capital punishment; and it is not to be viewed as if the social compact contained the promise of all the individuals to allow themselves to be punished, thus disposing of themselves and their lives. For if the right to punish must be founded upon a promise to the wrong-doer, whereby he is to be regarded as being willing to be punished, it ought also to be left to him to find himself deserving of the punishment; and the criminal would thus be his own judge. The chief error, of this sophistry consists in regarding the judgment of the criminal himself, necessarily determined by his reason, that he is under obligation to undergo the loss of life, as a judgment that must be founded on a resolution of his will to take it away himself; and thus the execution of the right in question is represented as united in one and the same person with the adjudication of the right." [6]

What validity is there in this reasoning of Kant? Only this much, we

---

[5] *Op. cit.*, p. 196.
[6] Kant, *Op. cit., pp.* 201–202.

think. It furnishes a satisfactory answer to that school of thinkers who, having not yet thoroughly rid themselves of the social-compact and natural-right theories, declare that all social or political control over the individual, needs, for its justification, the consent of the individual. It is correct to say that in the commission of any given deed, the criminal logically accepts as a valid rule of conduct the principle involved in his act, and therefore that he cannot justly complain if society see fit to subject him to the operation of the same rule that he has already applied in his conduct toward others. But this is all. Kant's reasoning does not have any bearing upon the arguments of those who hold the views which we have accepted in this work. Kant says: "Man ought never to be dealt with merely as a means subservient to the purpose of another. . . . Against such treatment his inborn personality has a right to protect him" This principle is a very true one, and in fact constitutes, as we know, the fundamental fact of social justice, but it does not mean that the infliction of an evil upon a person, in order that some future social good may be achieved, is necessarily a contravention of it.

Kant says that a person should never be treated as a means. But a person is treated merely as a means only when his right to be considered as an end is wholly ignored. Now, when it becomes necessary in the interest of society to inflict an evil upon an individual, that individual is *quâ hoc* treated as a means; but he is also treated as an end, if in estimating the social good his individual good is considered, and in the selection of him for punishment the choice has been controlled by empiric facts which make it productive of more good that he, rather than any one or no one else, should be punished. Thus, just as, according to this interpretation of the sanctity of human personality, guiltiness of crime cannot of itself justify the infliction of pain; so, conversely, when the social good demands, innocence from wrong-doing cannot always relieve one from the duty of subjecting himself to, or release society from the obligation of imposing, an evil which in extreme cases may amount even to death. As Rashdall has well put it: "When a man is punished in the interest of society, he is indeed treated as a means, but his right to be treated as an end is not thereby violated, if his good is treated as of equal importance with the end of other human beings. Social life would not be possible without the constant subordination of the claims of individuals to the like claims of a greater number of individuals; and there may be occasions when in punishing a criminal we have to think more of the good of society generally than of the individual who is punished. . . . The retributive view of punishment, however, justifies the infliction of evil upon a living soul, even though it will do neither him nor any one else any good whatever. If it is to do anybody any good, punishment is not inflicted for the sake of retribution. It is the retributive theory, to my mind, which shows a disrespect for human personality by proposing to sacrifice human life and human well-being to a lifeless fetich styled the Moral Law, which apparently, though unconscious, has a sense of dignity, and demands the immolation of victims to avenge its injured *amour propre.*" [7]

The incorrectness of the retributive theory of punishment becomes manifest when we consider the results to which an attempt to apply it in practice would necessarily lead. In the first place, it would render impossible any penal law whatever, for it would never be possible for courts to gain that knowledge which the theory demands for the just apportioning of penalties. When reduced to their proper meaning, the words retribution, expiation, or vindication, mean the bringing home to the criminal the legitimate consequences of his conduct, that is, legitimate from the ethical standpoint. But this, of course, involves the determination of the degree of his moral responsibility, a task that is an impossibility for any legal tribunal. Conditions of knowledge, of heredity, of training, of opportunities for moral development, of social environment generally, and of motive have to be searched out, which are beyond even the ability of the criminal himself to determine,—far less of others,—before even an approximate estimate can be made of the simplest act. But even could this be done, there would be no possible standard by which to estimate the amount of physical pain to be imposed as a punishment for a given degree of moral guilt. For how measure a moral wrong by a physical suffering? Or, granting what is inconceivable, that such an equivalence could be fixed upon, how would it be possible to inflict upon the culprit just that amount of pain which he might deserve? Individuals differ physically and mentally, and these differences are widened by training and methods of life until it is impossible to determine the degree of discomfort or pain that a given penalty will cause a given individual. The fear of death itself varies widely with different individuals, and the same is true as to the estimation in which all other forms of evil are held. So far, therefore, from there being any certainty that two individuals will be equally punished who are subjected to the same penitential treatment, there is, in fact, almost a certainty that they will not be. . . .

The idea that . . . the State "avenges" the wrong done to itself and to individuals is, in fact, but a remnant of the old "natural rights" and "social compact" theories, according to which individuals originally had a "right" of self-protection and of vengeance which, when the body politic was formed, was handed over to it for exercise, and that thus the State obtained a just authority to exercise force and punitive power. . . .

Utilitarian Theories . . . utilitarian theories differ from each other according to the nature of the good sought. Thus we have: (1) The Deterrent Theory, according to which punishments are inflicted in order that other would-be law-breakers may be dissuaded from crime; (2) The Preventive Theory, the aim of which, as its name implies, is to prevent the repetition

---

[7] *International Journal of Ethics*, January, 1900, article, "The Ethics of Forgiveness."

of the offence by the surveillance, imprisonment, or execution of the criminal; (3) The Reformatory Theory, the object of which is the moral reformation of the delinquent; and (4) The Educative Theory, of which we have already spoken.

A point to be noticed about these theories is that they are not mutually exclusive. There is no reason why, the utilitarian idea being once accepted, we should not strive to reach in our penitential systems beneficial results in all four of the directions mentioned. It is therefore possible to speak of a given law being founded on one or the other of these ideas only in so far as deterrence, prevention, education, or reformation, as the case may be, is placed in the foreground as the chief end to be realized.

But we may go further than simply to declare that these theories are not mutually exclusive. We may assert that it is rationally impossible to select any one aim and to declare that in any system of penal justice that one should furnish the sole motive for its enactment and enforcement. It may be possible to pass particular laws the aim of which is solely in one or the other of these directions; but to attempt the establishment of an entire criminal code with but a single aim would inevitably lead to absurdities and injustices. If absolute prevention were the sole aim, capital punishment or lifelong imprisonment would be the normal punishment called for; for in no other way could there be furnished a guarantee against a repetition of the offence by the convicted one. If reformation were the sole aim sought, then, not to mention other absurdities, it would be necessary for a court to release from all punishment those hardened and habitual criminals regarding whom experience had demonstrated penal law to be without a reformatory influence. If deterrence were accepted as the absolute canon, we would be obliged to abandon all attempts at reformation, and by the strictness and severity of our punishments give ourselves up to an appeal simply to the fears of mankind. Finally, if the educative theory were to be solely relied upon, we would not be able to modify the character and severity of our punishments so as best to meet threatened invasions of social or political order. This would mean that in times of greatest need the State would find itself powerless. Thus, for example, should a grievous pestilence be threatened, necessity would demand that violations of quarantine and other health ordinances should be prevented at all hazards, and hence that extraordinarily severe penalties should be attached to their violation. Or, again, in a time of great political unrest and disorder, when the very life of the State is threatened, martial law would be demanded. But if we accept any but the deterrent theory as absolutely sufficient in itself, such measures would be unjustifiable.

As we have seen, the retributive theory rests under the embarrassment of predicating as a ground for the right to punish a motive which logically necessitates that the character and degree of the punishments which are inflicted should correspond with the degree of moral guilt of the offenders, whereas the determination of this degree of guilt is inherently beyond the power of any criminal court. From this difficulty the utilitarian theory is free. We have spoken of the ideas of deterrence, reformation, education, and prevention as distinct from one another, and so they are. Yet when viewed in their proper light, they are all out different phases of one supreme idea, the social welfare. The aim of the criminal law, like that of the civil law, and indeed of all laws and principles of conduct, is the general weal. Therefore, in passing upon the propriety of emphasizing in a given piece of legislation any one of these ideas, whether of reformation, education, prevention, or deterrence, it is ever necessary to consider the matter in its social and not in its individual light. There may thus be cases in which, as to the particular criminal or criminals concerned, a remission of punishment would exercise a more beneficial influence than its imposition, but in which social considerations demand a satisfaction of the law's full severity.

The bearing of this upon the question of justly apportioning penalties is that it makes it no longer necessary to attempt the impossible task of making the punishment correspond to the degree of the criminal's guilt, but leaves it open to the laws and to the courts to arrange their judgments according to the practical exigencies of each case as determined by the social need. . . .

Conclusion: [Surely] . . . the strenuous efforts which societies have made to check crime have at the most done little more than prevent its increase. This means, then, that little success has been reached either in the reformatory, educative, or deterrent directions. As a matter of fact, so far as regards the reformatory idea, there would probably be a consensus of opinion that, upon the whole, criminal law, as it has actually been administered in the past, has been far more corrupting than elevating to the individuals punished. And for the future the most sanguine are not inclined to believe that it will be possible, even with the most approved methods, to make the reformation obtained more than balance the inevitable corruption that punishment brings by the evil associations it necessitates, and the blow to pride and self-respect it gives. As for the educative value of punishment, this is in the highest degree problematical, and many there are who would reduce its possible influence to a very small maximum. How far penal laws have been deterrent it is impossible to say; but at the most, as we have seen, they have been efficient only to the extent of preventing an increase of crime. As regards, finally, the preventive idea, except where the punishment of death or imprisonment for life is imposed, little is accomplished.

The one lesson, then, which all these facts teach us is that, for a solution of the problem of crime, the real effort must be to abolish the causes of crime, in so far as they are dependent upon conditions within our control. This means, in truth, entire social regeneration; for wherever there is injustice, there will be crime. Not all crime, it is true, may be ascribed to social causes. Some of it is undoubtedly due to the deliberate choice of evil minds or to the promptings of the passions. But with social justice everywhere realized, with economic and social relations properly regulated, and with true education, mental and moral, technical and academic, adequately applied, a long step will have been taken towards the solution of the grave evil we have been discussing. . . . .

FURMAN V. GEORGIA *

MAJORITY OPINION

MR. JUSTICE MARSHALL, concurring.

These three cases present the question whether the death penalty is a cruel and unusual punishment prohibited by the Eighth Amendment to the United States Constitution. In No. 69–5003, Furman was convicted of murder for shooting the father of five children when he discovered that Furman had broken into his home early one morning. Nos. 69–5030 and 69–5031 involve state convictions for forcible rape. Jackson was found guilty of rape during the course of a robbery in the victim's home. The rape was accomplished as he held the pointed ends of scissors at the victim's throat. Branch also was convicted of rape committed in the victim's home. No weapon was utilized, but physical force and threats of physical force were employed.

The criminal acts with which we are confronted are ugly, vicious, reprehensible acts. Their sheer brutality cannot and should not be minimized. But, we are not called upon to condone the penalized conduct; we are asked only to examine the penalty imposed on each of the petitioners and to determine whether or not it violates the Eighth Amendment. The question then is not whether we condone rape or murder, for surely we do not; it is whether capital punishment is "a punishment no longer consistent with our own self-respect" and, therefore, violative of the Eighth Amendment.

* * *

MR. JUSTICE DOUGLAS, concurring.

In these three cases the death penalty was imposed, one of them for murder, and two for rape. In each the determination of whether the penalty should be death or a lighter punishment was left by the State to the discretion of the judge or of the jury. In each of the three cases the trial was to a jury. They are here on petitions for certiorari which we granted limited to the question whether the imposition and execution of the death penalty constitute "cruel and unusual punishment" within the meaning of

* United States Supreme Court Decision, 1972, majority opinion and dissenting opinion. The order of the descriptive excerpt from Mr. Justice Marshall is changed.

the Eighth Amendment as applied to the States by the Fourteenth.[1] I vote
to vacate each judgment, believing that the exaction of the death penalty
does violate the Eighth and Fourteenth Amendments. . . .

Whether the privileges and immunities route is followed, or the due
process route, the result is the same.

It has been assumed in our decisions that punishment by death is not
cruel, unless the manner of execution can be said to be inhuman and
barbarous. *In re Kemmler,* 135, U.S. 436, 447. It is also said in our opinions
that the proscription of cruel and unusual punishments "is not fastened to
the obsolete but may acquire meaning as public opinion becomes enlightened by a humane justice." *Weems* v. *United States, supra,* at 378. A like
statement was made in *Trop* v. *Dulles,* 356 U.S. 86, 101, that the Eighth
Amendment "must draw its meaning from the evolving standards of decency that mark the progress of a maturing society."

The generality of a law inflicting capital punishment is one thing. What
may be said of the validity of a law on the books and what may be done
with the law in its application do, or may, lead to quite different conclusions.

It would seem to be incontestable that the death penalty inflicted on one
defendant is "unusual" if it discriminates against him by reason of his race,
religion, wealth, social position, or class, or if it is imposed under a procedure that gives room for the play of such prejudices.

There is evidence that the provision of the English Bill of Rights of 1689,
from which the language of the Eighth Amendment was taken, was concerned primarily with selective or irregular application of harsh penalties
and that its aim was to forbid arbitrary and discriminatory penalties of a
severe nature: [2]

* * *

. . . [Goldberg and Dershowitz argue] that "[t]he extreme rarity with
which applicable death penalty provisions are put to use raises a strong
inference of arbitrariness." [3] The President's Commission on Law Enforcement and Administration of Justice recently concluded: [4]

Finally there is evidence that the imposition of the death sentence and the
exercise of dispensing power by the courts and the executive follow discrimina-

[1] The opinion of the Supreme Court of Georgia affirming Furman's conviction of
murder and sentence of death is reported in 225 Ga. 253, 167 S. E. 2d 628, and its
opinion affirming Jackson's conviction of rape and sentence of death is reported in 225
Ga. 790, 171 S. E. 2d 501. The conviction of Branch of rape and the sentence of
death were affirmed by the Court of Criminal Appeals of Texas and reported in 447
S. W. 2d. 932.

[2] Granucci, "Nor Cruel and Unusual," 57 Calif. L. Rev. 845–846.

[3] Goldberg & Dershowitz, Declaring the Death Penalty Unconstitutional, 83 Harv. L.
Rev. 1792.

[4] The Challenge of Crime in a Free Society 143 (1967).

tory patterns. The death sentence is disproportionately imposed and carried out on the poor, the Negro, and the members of unpopular groups.

A study of capital cases in Texas from 1924 to 1968 reached the following conclusions: [5]

Application of the death penalty is unequal: most of those executed were poor, young, and ignorant.

✿   ✿   ✿

Seventy-five of the 460 cases involved co-defendants, who, under Texas law, were given separate trials. In several instances where a white and a Negro were co-defendants, the white was sentenced to life imprisonment or a term of years, and the Negro was given the death penalty.

Another ethnic disparity is found in the type of sentence imposed for rape. The Negro convicted of rape is far more likely to get the death penalty than a term sentence, whereas whites and Latins are far more likely to get a term sentence than the death penalty.

Warden Lewis E. Lawes of Sing Sing said: [6]

[5] Koeninger, Capital Punishment in Texas, 1924–1968, 15 Crime & Delin. 132, 141 (1969).

In H. Bedau, The Death Penalty in America 474 (1967 rev. ed.), it is stated:

RACE OF THE OFFENDER BY FINAL DISPOSITION

Final Disposition	Negro		White		Total	
	N	%	N	%	N	%
Executed	130	88.4	210	79.8	340	82.9
Commuted	17	11.6	53	20.2	70	17.1
Total	147	100.0	263	100.0	410	100.0

$X^2 = 4.33$; P less than .05. (For discussion of statistical symbols, see Bedau, *supra*, at 469.)

"Although there may be a host of factors other than race involved in this frequency distribution, something more than chance has operated over the years to produce this racial difference. On the basis of this study it is not possible to indict the judicial and other public processes prior to the death row as responsible for the association between Negroes and higher frequency of executions; nor is it entirely correct to assume that from the time of their appearance on death row Negroes are discriminated against by the Pardon Board. Too many unknown or presently immeasurable factors prevent our making definitive statements about the relationship. Nevertheless, because the Negro/high-execution association is statistically present, some suspicion of racial discrimination can hardly be avoided. If such a relationship had not appeared, this kind of suspicion could have been allayed; the existence of the relationship, although not 'proving' differential bias by the Pardon Boards over the years since 1914, strongly suggests that such bias has existed."

The latter was a study in Pennsylvania of people on death row between 1914 and 1958, made by Wolfgang, Kelly, & Nolde and printed in 53 J. Crim. L. C. & P. S. 301 (1962). And see Hartung, Trends in the Use of Capital Punishment, 284 Annals 8, 14–17 (1952).

[6] *Life and Death in Sing Sing* 155–160 (1928).

Not only does capital punishment fail in its justification, but no punishment could be invented with so many inherent defects. It is an unequal punishment in the way it is applied to the rich and the poor. The defendant of wealth and position never goes to the electric chair or to the gallows. Juries do not intentionally favour the rich, the law is theoretically impartial, but the defendant with ample means is able to have his case presented with every favourable aspect, while the poor defendant often has a lawyer assigned by the court. Sometimes such assignment is considered part of political patronage; usually the lawyer assigned has had no experience whatever in a capital case.

Former Attorney General Ramsey Clark has said, "It is the poor, the sick, the ignorant, the powerless and the hated who are executed." [7] One searches our chronicles in vain for the execution of any member of the affluent strata of this society. The Leopolds and Loebs are given prison terms, not sentenced to death. . . .

We cannot say from facts disclosed in these records that these defendants were sentenced to death because they were black. Yet our task is not restricted to an effort to divine what motives impelled these death penalties. Rather, we deal with a system of law and of justice that leaves to the uncontrolled discretion of judges or juries the determination whether defendants committing these crimes should die or be imprisoned. Under these laws no standards govern the selection of the penalty. . . .

Those who wrote the Eighth Amendment knew what price their forebears had paid for a system based, not on equal justice, but on discrimination. In those days the target was not the blacks or the poor, but the dissenters, those who opposed absolutism in government, who struggled for a parliamentary regime, and who opposed governments' recurring efforts to foist a particular religion on the people. . . . But the tool of capital punishment was used with vengeance against the opposition and those unpopular with the regime. One cannot read this history without realizing that the desire for equality was reflected in the ban against "cruel and unusual punishments" contained in the Eighth Amendment.

[Our law has no place for castes].[8] . . . In ancient Hindu law a Brahman was exempt from capital punishment,[9] and under that law, "[g]enerally, in the law books, punishment increased in severity as social status diminished." [10] We have, I fear, taken in practice the same position, partially as a result of making the death penalty discretionary and partially as a result of the ability of the rich to purchase the services of the most respected and most resourceful legal talent in the Nation.

The high service rendered by the "cruel and unusual" punishment clause of the Eighth Amendment is to require legislatures to write penal laws

---

[7] Crime in America 335 (1970).

[8] See Johnson, The Negro and Crime, 217 Annals 93 (1941).

[9] See J. Spellman, Political Theory of Ancient India 112 (1964).

[10] C. Drekmeier, Kingship and Community in Early India 233 (1962).

that are even-handed, nonselective, and nonarbitrary, and to require judges
to see to it that general laws are not applied sparsely, selectively, and
spottily to unpopular groups.

A law that stated that anyone making more than $50,000 would be ex-
empt from the death penalty would plainly fall, as would a law that in
terms said that blacks, those who never went beyond the fifth grade in
school, those who made less than $3,000 a year, or those who were un-
popular or unstable should be the only people executed. A law which in
the overall view reaches that result in practice [11] has no more sanctity than
a law which in terms provides the same. . . .

Any law which is nondiscriminatory on its face may be applied in such
a way as to violate the Equal Protection Clause of the Fourteenth Amendment. *Yick Wo* v. *Hopkins,* 118 U.S. 356. Such conceivably might be the
fate of a mandatory death penalty, where equal or lesser sentences were
imposed on the elite, a harsher one on the minorities or members of the
lower castes. Whether a mandatory death penalty would otherwise be constitutional is a question I do not reach.

I concur in the judgments of the Court.

MR. JUSTICE BRENNAN, concurring.

The question presented in these cases is whether death is today a punishment for crime that is "cruel and unusual" and consequently, by virtue of
the Eighth and Fourteenth Amendments, beyond the power of the State
to inflict.

✦ ✦ ✦

The primary principle is that a punishment must not be so severe as to
be degrading to the dignity of human beings. Pain, certainly, may be a factor in the judgment. The infliction of an extremely severe punishment will

---

[11] Cf. B. Prettyman, Jr., Death and The Supreme Court 296–297 (1961)

"The disparity of representation in capital cases raises doubts about capital punishment itself, which has been abolished in only nine states. If a James Avery [345 U.S.
559] can be saved from electrocution because his attorney made timely objection
to the selection of a jury by the use of yellow and white tickets, while an Aubry
Williams [349 U.S. 375] can be sent to his death by a jury selected in precisely the
same manner, we are imposing our most extreme penalty in an uneven fashion.

"The problem of proper representation is not a problem of money, as some have
claimed, but of a lawyer's ability, and it is not true that only the rich have able
lawyers. Both the rich and the poor usually are well represented—the poor because
more often than not the best attorneys are appointed to defend them. It is the middle-
class defendant, who can afford to hire an attorney but not a very good one, who is
at a disadvantage. Certainly William Fikes [352 U.S. 191], despite the anomalous
position in which he finds himself today, received as effective and intelligent a defense
from his court-appointed attorneys as he would have received from an attorney his
family had scraped together enough money to hire.

"And it is not only a matter of ability. An attorney must be found who is prepared
to spend precious hours—the basic commodity he has to sell—on a case that seldom
fully compensates him and often brings him no fee at all. The public has no conception
of the time and effort devoted by attorneys to indigent cases. And in a first-degree case,
the added responsibility of having a man's life depend upon the outcome exacts a
heavy toll."

often entail physical suffering. See *Weems* v. *United States,* 217 U.S., at 366.[12] Yet the Framers also knew "that there could be exercises of cruelty by laws other than those which inflicted bodily pain or mutilation." *Id.,* at 372. Even though "[t]here may be involved no physical mistreatment, no primitive torture," *Trop* v. *Dulles, supra,* at 101, severe mental pain may be inherent in the infliction of a particular punishment. See *Weems* v. *United States, supra,* at 366.[13] That, indeed, was one of the conclusions underlying the holding of the plurality in *Trop* v. *Dulles* that the punishment of expatriation violates the Clause.[14] And the physical and mental suffering inherent in the punishment of *cadena temporal . . .* was an obvious basis for the Court's decision in *Weems* v. *United States* that the punishment was "cruel and unusual." [15]

More than the presence of pain, however, is comprehended in the judgment that the extreme severity of a punishment makes it degrading to the dignity of human beings. The barbaric punishments condemned by history, "punishments which inflict torture, such as the rack, the thumbscrew, the iron boot, the stretching of limbs and the like," are, of course, "attended with acute pain and suffering." *O'Neil* v. *Vermont,* 144 U.S. 323, 339 (1892)

[12] "It may be that even the cruelty of pain is not omitted. He must bear a chain night and day. He is condemned to painful as well as hard labor. What painful labor may mean we have no exact measure. It must be something more than hard labor. It may be hard labor pressed to the point of pain."

[13] "His prison bars and chains are removed, it is true, after twelve years, but he goes from them to a perpetual limitation of his liberty. He is forever kept under the shadow of his crime, forever kept within voice and view of the criminal magistrate, not being able to change his domicil without giving notice to the 'authority immediately in charge of his surveillance,' and without permission in writing. He may not seek, even in other scenes and among other people, to retrieve his fall from rectitude. Even that hope is taken from him and he is subject to tormenting regulations that, if not so tangible as iron bars and stone walls, oppress as much by their continuity, and deprive of essential liberty."

[14] "This punishment is offensive to cardinal principles for which the Constitution stands. It subjects the individual to a fate of ever-increasing fear and distress. He knows not what discriminations may be established against him, what proscriptions may be directed against him, and when and for what cause his existence in his native land may be terminated. He may be subject to banishment, a fate universally decried by civilized people. He is stateless, a condition deplored in the international community of democracies. It is no answer to suggest that all the disastrous consequences of this fate may not be brought to bear on a stateless person. The threat makes the punishment obnoxious." *Trop* v. *Dulles,* 356 U.S. 86, 102 (1958). Cf. *id.,* at 110–111 (BRENNAN, J., concurring):
"[I]t can be supposed that the consequences of greatest weight, in terms of ultimate impact on the petitioner, are unknown and unknowable. Indeed, in truth, he may live out his life with but minor inconvenience. . . . Nevertheless it cannot be denied that the impact of expatriation—especially where statelessness is the upshot—may be severe. Expatriation, in this respect, constitutes an especially demoralizing sanction. The uncertainty, and the consequent psychological hurt, which must accompany one who becomes an outcast in his own land must be reckoned a substantial factor in the ultimate judgment."

[15] "It is cruel in its excess of imprisonment and that which accompanies and follows imprisonment. It is unusual in its character. Its punishments come under the condemnation of the bill of rights, both on account of their degree and kind." *Weems* v. *United States,* 217 U.S., at 377.

(Field, J., dissenting). When we consider why they have been condemned, however, we realize that the pain involved is not the only reason. The true significance of these punishments is that they treat members of the human race as nonhumans, as objects to be toyed with and discarded. They are thus inconsistent with the fundamental premise of the Clause that even the vilest criminal remains a human being possessed of common human dignity.

The infliction of an extremely severe punishment, then, like the one before the Court in *Weems* v. *United States,* from which "[n]o circumstance of degradation [was] omitted," 217 U.S., at 366, may reflect the attitude that the person punished is not entitled to recognition as a fellow human being. That attitude may be apparent apart from the severity of the punishment itself. In *Louisiana ex rel. Francis* v. *Resweber,* 329 U.S. 459, 464 (1947), for example, the unsuccessful electrocution, although it caused "mental anguish and physical pain," was the result of "an unforeseeable accident." Had the failure been intentional, however, the punishment would have been, like torture, so degrading and indecent as to amount to a refusal to accord the criminal human status. Indeed, a punishment may be degrading to human dignity solely because it *is* a punishment. A State may not punish a person for being "mentally ill, or a leper, or . . . afflicted with a venereal disease," or for being addicted to narcotics. *Robinson* v. *California,* 370 U.S. 660, 666 (1962). To inflict punishment for having a disease is to treat the individual as a diseased thing rather than as a sick human being. That the punishment is not severe, "in the abstract," is irrelevant; "[e]ven one day in prison would be a cruel and unusual punishment for the 'crime' of having a common cold." *Id.,* at 667. Finally, of course, a punishment may be degrading simply by reason of its enormity. A prime example is expatriation, a "punishment more primitive than torture," *Trop* v. *Dulles,* 356 U.S., at 101, for it necessarily involves a denial by society of the individual's existence as a member of the human community.[16]

In determining whether a punishment comports with human dignity, we are aided also by a second principle inherent in the Clause—that the State must not arbitrarily inflict a severe punishment. This principle derives from the notion that the State does not respect human dignity when, with-

---

[16] "There may be involved no physical mistreatment, no primitive torture. There is instead the total destruction of the individual's status in organized society. It is a form of punishment more primitive than torture, for it destroys for the individual the political existence that was centuries in the development. The punishment strips the citizen of his status in the national and international political community. His very existence is at the sufferance of the country in which he happens to find himself. While any one country may accord him some rights, and presumably as long as he remained in this country he would enjoy the limited rights of an alien, no country need do so because he is stateless. Furthermore, his enjoyment of even the limited rights of an alien might be subject to termination at any time by reason of deportation. In short, the expatriate has lost the right to have rights." *Trop* v. *Dulles,* 356 U.S., at 101–102.

out reason, it inflicts upon some people a severe punishment that it does not inflict upon others. Indeed, the very words "cruel and unusual punishments" imply condemnation of the arbitrary infliction of severe punishments. And, as we now know, the English history of the Clause [17] reveals a particular concern with the establishment of a safeguard against arbitrary punishments.

* * *

A third principle inherent in the Clause is that a severe punishment must not be unacceptable to contemporary society. Rejection by society, of course, is a strong indication that a severe punishment does not comport with human dignity. In applying this principle, however, we must make certain that the judicial determination is as objective as possible.[18] Thus, for example, *Weems* v. *United States,* 217 U.S., at 380, and *Trop* v. *Dulles,* 356 U.S., at 102–103, suggest that one factor that may be considered is the existence of the punishment in jurisdictions other than those before the Court. *Wilkerson* v. *Utah, supra,* suggests that another factor to be considered is the historic usage of the punishment.[19] *Trop* v. *Dulles, supra,* at 99, combined present acceptance with past usage by observing that "the death penalty has been employed throughout our history, and, in a day when it is still widely accepted, it cannot be said to violate the constitutional concept of cruelty." In *Robinson* v. *California,* 370 U.S., at 666, which involved the infliction of punishment for narcotics addiction, the Court went a step further, concluding simply that "in the light of contemporary human knowledge, a law which made a criminal offense of such a disease would doubtless be universally thought to be an infliction of cruel and unusual punishment."

The question under this principle, then, is whether there are objective indicators from which a court can conclude that contemporary society con-

[17] "The phrase in our Constitution was taken directly from the English Declaration of Rights of [1689]. . . ." *Id.,* at 100.

[18] The danger of subjective judgment is acute if the question posed is whether a punishment "shocks the most fundamental instincts of civilized man," *Louisiana ex rel Francis* v. *Resweber, supra,* at 473 (Burton, J., dissenting), or whether "any man of right feeling and heart can refrain from shuddering," *O'Neil* v. *Vermont, supra,* at 340 (Field, J., dissenting), or whether "a cry of horror would rise from every civilized and Christian community of the country," *ibid.* Mr. Justice Frankfurter's concurring opinion in *Louisiana ex rel. Francis* v. *Resweber, supra,* is instructive. He warned "against finding in personal disapproval a reflection of more or less prevailing condemnation" and against "enforcing . . . private view[s] rather than that consensus of society's opinion which, for purposes of due process, is the standard enjoined by the Constitution." *Id.,* at 471. His conclusions were as follows: "I cannot bring myself to believe that [the State's procedure] . . . offends a principle of justice 'rooted in the traditions and conscience of our people.' " *Id.,* at 470. ". . . I cannot say that it would be 'repugnant to the conscience of mankind.' " *Id.,* at 471. Yet nowhere in the opinion is there any explanation of how he arrived at those conclusions.

[19] Cf. *Louisiana ex rel. Francis* v. *Resweber, supra,* at 463: "The traditional humanity of modern Anglo-American law forbids the infliction of unnecessary pain in the execution of the death sentence."

siders a severe punishment unacceptable. Accordingly, the judicial task is
to review the history of a challenged punishment and to examine society's
present practices with respect to its use. Legislative authorization, of course,
does not establish acceptance. The acceptability of a severe punishment
is measured, not by its availability, for it might become so offensive to
society as never to be inflicted, but by its use.

The final principle inherent in the Clause is that a severe punishment
must not be excessive. A punishment is excessive under this principle if it
is unnecessary: The infliction of a severe punishment by the State cannot
comport with human dignity when it is nothing more than the pointless
infliction of suffering. If there is a significantly less severe punishment
adequate to achieve the purposes for which the punishment is inflicted;
ef. *Robinson* v. *California, supra,* at 666; *id.,* at 677 (DOUGLAS J., concurring); *Trop* v. *Dulles, supra,* at 114 (BRENNAN, J., concurring), the punishment inflicted is unnecessary and therefore excessive.

✿   ✿   ✿

There are, then, four principles by which we may determine whether
a particular punishment is "cruel and unusual." The primary principle,
which I believe supplies the essential predicate for the application of the
others, is that a punishment must not by its severity be degrading to human
dignity. The paradigm violation of this principle would be the infliction of
a torturous punishment of the type that the Clause has always prohibited.
Yet "[i]t is unlikely that any State at this moment in history," *Robinson*
v. *California,* 370 U.S., at 666, would pass a law providing for the infliction
of such a punishment. Indeed, no such punishment has ever been before
this Court. The same may be said of the other principles. It is unlikely that
this Court will confront a severe punishment that is obviously inflicted in
wholly arbitrary fashion; no State would engage in a reign of blind terror.
Nor is it likely that this Court will be called upon to review a severe
punishment that is clearly and totally rejected throughout society; no legislature would be able even to authorize the infliction of such a punishment.
Nor, finally, is it likely that this Court will have to consider a severe
punishment that is patently unnecessary; no State today would inflict a
severe punishment knowing that there was no reason whatever for doing
so. In short, we are unlikely to have occasion to determine that a punishment is fatally offensive under any one principle.

Since the Bill of Rights was adopted, this Court had adjudged only three
punishments to be within the prohibition of the Clause. See *Weems* v.
United States, 217 U.S. 349 (1910) (12 years in chains at hard and painful labor); *Trop* v. *Dulles,* 356 U.S. 86 (1958) (expatriation); *Robinson*
v. *California,* 370 U.S. 660 (1962) (imprisonment for narcotics addiction).
Each punishment, of course, was degrading to human dignity, but of none
could it be said conclusively that it was fatally offensive under one or the

other of the principles. Rather, these "cruel and unusual punishments" seriously implicated several of the principles, and it was the application of the principles in combination that supported the judgment. That, indeed, is not surprising. The function of these principles, after all, is simply to provide means by which a court can determine whether a challenged punishment comports with human dignity. They are, therefore, interrelated, and in most cases it will be their convergence that will justify the conclusion that a punishment is "cruel and unusual." The test, then, will ordinarily be a cumulative one: If a punishment is unusually severe, if there is a strong probability that it is inflicted arbitrarily, if it is substantially rejected by contemporary society, and if there is no reason to believe that it serves any penal purpose more effectively than some less severe punishment, then the continued infliction of that punishment violates the command of the Clause that the State may not inflict inhuman and uncivilized punishments upon those convicted of crimes.

* * *

The question, then, is whether the deliberate infliction of death is today consistent with the command of the Clause that the State may not inflict punishments that do not comport with human dignity. I will analyze the punishment of death in terms of the principles set out above and the cumulative test to which they lead: It is a denial of human dignity for the State arbitrarily to subject a person to an unusually severe punishment that society has indicated it does not regard as acceptable, and that cannot be shown to serve any penal purpose more effectively than a significantly less drastic punishment. Under these principles and this test, death is today a "cruel and unusual" punishment.

Death is a unique punishment in the United States. In a society that so strongly affirms the sanctity of life, not surprisingly the common view is that death is the ultimate sanction. This natural human feeling appears all about us. There has been no national debate about punishment, in general or by imprisonment, comparable to the debate about the punishment of death. No other punishment has been so continuously restricted . . . nor has the State yet abolished prisons, as some have abolished this punishment. And those States that still inflict death reserve it for the most heinous crimes. Juries, of course, have always treated death cases differently, as have governors exercising their commutation powers. Criminal defendants are of the same view. "As all practicing lawyers know, who have defended persons charged with capital offenses, often the only goal possible is to avoid the death penalty." *Griffin* v. *Illinois*, 351 U.S. 12, 28 (1956) (Burton and Minton, JJ., dissenting). Some legislatures have required particular procedures, such as two-stage trials and automatic appeals, applicable only in death cases. "It is the universal experience in the administration of criminal justice that those charged with capital offenses are granted special considerations." *Ibid.* See *Williams* v. *Florida,* 399 U.S. 78, 103 (1970) (all States require juries of 12 in death cases). This Court, too, almost always treats death cases as a class apart.[20] And the unfortunate effect of this punishment upon the functioning of the judicial process is well known; no other punishment has a similar effect.

The only explanation for the uniqueness of death is its extreme severity. Death is today an unusually severe punishment, unusual in its pain, in its finality, and in its enormity. No other existing punishment is comparable to death in terms of physical and mental suffering. Although our information is not conclusive, it appears that there is no method available that guarantees an immediate and painless death.[21] Since the discontinuance of flogging as a constitutionally permissible punishment, *Jackson* v. *Bishop,* 404 F. 2d 571 (CA8 1968), death remains as the only punishment that may involve the conscious infliction of physical pain. In addition, we know that mental pain is an inseparable part of our practice of punishing criminals by death, for the prospect of pending execution exacts a frightful toll during the inevitable long wait between the imposition of sentence and the actual infliction of death. Cf. *Ex parte Medley,* 134 U.S. 160, 172 (1890). As the California Supreme Court pointed out, "the process of carrying out a verdict of death is often so degrading and brutalizing to the

---

[20] "That life is at stake is of course another important factor in creating the extraordinary situation. The difference between capital and non-capital offenses is the basis of differentiation in law in diverse ways in which the distinction becomes relevant." *Williams* v. *Georgia,* 349 U.S. 375, 391 (1955) (Frankfurter, J.). "When the penalty is death, we, like state court judges, are tempted to strain the evidence and even, in close cases, the law in order to give a doubtfully condemned man another chance." *Stein* v. *New York,* 346 U.S. 156, 196 (1953) (Jackson, J.). "In death cases doubts such as those presented here should be resolved in favor of the accused." *Andres* v. *United States,* 333 U.S. 740, 752 (1948) (Reed, J.). Mr. Justice Harlan expressed the point strongly: "I do not concede that whatever process is 'due' an offender faced with a fine or a prison sentence necessarily satisfies the requirements of the Constitution in a capital case. The distinction is by no means novel, . . . nor is it negligible, being literally that between life and death." *Reid* v. *Covert,* 354 U.S. 1, 77 (1957) (concurring in result). And, of course, for many years this Court distinguished death cases from all others for purposes of the constitutional right to counsel. See *Powell* v. *Alabama,* 287 U.S. 45 (1932); *Betts* v. *Brady,* 316 U.S. 455 (1942); *Bute* v. *Illinois,* 333 U.S. 640 (1948).

[21] See Report of Royal Commission on Capital Punishment 1949–1953, §§ 700–789, pp. 246–273 (1953); Hearings on S. 1760 before the Subcommittee on Criminal Laws and Procedures of the Senate Committee on the Judiciary, 90th Cong., 2d Sess., 19–21 (1968) (testimony of Clinton Duffy); H. Barnes & N. Teeters, New Horizons in Criminology 306–309 (3d ed. 1959); C. Chessman, Trial by Ordeal 195–202 (1955); M. DiSalle, The Power of Life and Death 84–85 (1965); C. Duffy & A. Hirschberg, 88 Men and 2 Women 13–14 (1962); B. Eshelman, Death Row Chaplain 26–29, 101–104, 159–164 (1962); R. Hammer, Between Life and Death 208–212 (1969); K. Lamott, Chronicles of San Quentin 228–231 (1961); L. Lawes, Life and Death in Sing Sing 170–171 (1928); Rubin, The Supreme Court, Cruel and Unusual Punishment, and the Death Penalty, 15 Crime & Delin. 121, 128–129 (1969); Comment, The Death Penalty Cases, 56 Calif. L. Rev. 1268, 1338–1341 (1968); Brief *amici curiae* filed by James V. Bennett, Clinton T. Duffy, Robert G. Sarver, Harry C. Tinsley, and Lawrence E. Wilson 12–14.

human spirit as to constitute psychological torture." *People* v. *Anderson,* 6 Cal. 3d 628, 649, 493 P. 2d 880, 894 (1972).[22] Indeed, as Mr. Justice Frankfurter noted, "the onset of insanity while awaiting execution of a death sentence is not a rare phenomenon." *Solesbee* v. *Balkcom,* 339 U.S. 9, 14 (1950) (dissenting opinion). The "fate of ever-increasing fear and distress" to which the expatriate is subjected, *Trop* v. *Dulles,* 356 U.S., at 102, can only exist to a greater degree for a person confined in prison awaiting death.[23]

The unusual severity of death is manifested most clearly in its finality and enormity. Death, in these respects, is in a class by itself. Expatriation, for example, is a punishment that "destroys for the individual the political existence that was centuries in the development," that "strips the citizen of his status in the national and international political community," and that puts "[h]is very existence" in jeopardy. Expatriation thus inherently entails "the total destruction of the individual's status in organized society." *Id.,* at 101. "In short, the expatriate has lost the right to have rights." *Id.,* at 102. Yet, demonstrably, expatriation is not "a fate worse than death." *Id.,* at 125 (Frankfurter, J., dissenting).[24] Although death, like expatriation, destroys the individual's "political existence" and his "status in organized society," it does more, for, unlike expatriation, death also destroys "[h]is very existence." There is, too, at least the possibility that the expatriate will in the future regain "the right to have rights." Death forecloses even that possibility.

Death is truly an awesome punishment. The calculated killing of a human being by the State involves, by its very nature, a denial of the executed person's humanity. The contrast with the plight of a person punished

---

[22] See Barnes & Teeters, *supra,* at 309–311 (3d ed., 1959); Camus, Reflections on the Guillotine, in A. Camus, Resistance, Rebellion, and Death 131, 151–156 (1960); C. Duffy & A. Hirschberg, *supra,* at 68–70, 254 (1962); Hammer, *supra,* at 222–235, 244–250, 269–272 (1969); S. Rubin, The Law of Criminal Correction 340 (1963); Bluestone & McGahee, Reaction to Extreme Stress: Impending Death by Execution, 119 Amer. J. Psychiatry 393 (1962); Gottlieb, Capital Punishment, 15 Crime & Delin. 1, 8–10 (1969); West, Medicine and Capital Punishment, in Hearings on S. 1760 before the Subcommittee on Criminal Laws and Procedures of the Senate Committee on the Judiciary, 90th Cong., 2d Sess., 124 (1968); Ziferstein, Crime and Punishment, The Center Magazine 84 (Jan. 1968); Comment, The Death Penalty Cases, 56 Calif. L. Rev. 1268, 1342 (1968); Note, Mental Suffering under Sentence of Death: A Cruel and Unusual Punishment, 57 Iowa L. Rev. 814 (1972).

[23] The State, of course, does not purposely impose the lengthy waiting period in order to inflict further suffering. The impact upon the individual is not the less severe on that account. It is no answer to assert that long delays exist only because condemned criminals avail themselves of their full panoply of legal rights. The right not to be subjected to inhuman treatment cannot, of course, be played off against the right to pursue due process of law, but, apart from that, the plain truth is that it is society that demands, even against the wishes of the criminal, that all legal avenues be explored before the execution is finally carried out.

[24] It was recognized in *Trop* itself that expatriation is a "punishment short of death." 356 U.S., at 99. Death, however, was distinguished on the ground that it was "still widely accepted." *Ibid.*

by imprisonment is evident. An individual in prison does not lose "the right to have rights." A prisoner retains, for example, the constitutional rights to the free exercise of religion, to be free of cruel and unusual punishments, and to treatment as a "person" for purposes of due process of law and the equal protection of the laws. A prisoner remains a member of the human family. Moreover, he retains the right of access to the courts. His punishment is not irrevocable. Apart from the common charge, grounded upon the recognition of human fallibility, that the punishment of death must inevitably be inflicted upon innocent men, we know that death has been the lot of men whose convictions were unconstitutionally secured in view of later, retroactively applied, holdings of this Court. The punishment itself may have been unconstitutionally inflicted, see *Witherspoon* v. *Illinois*, 391 U.S. 510 (1968), yet the finality of death precludes relief. An executed person has indeed "lost the right to have rights." As one 19th century proponent of punishing criminals by death declared, "When a man is hung, there is an end of our relations with him. His execution is a way of saying, 'You are not fit for this world, take your chance elsewhere.' " [25]

In comparison to all other punishments today, then, the deliberate extinguishment of human life by the State is uniquely degrading to human dignity. I would not hesitate to hold, on that ground alone, that death is today a "cruel and unusual" punishment, were it not that death is a punishment of longstanding usage and acceptance in this country. I therefore turn to the second principle—that the State may not arbitrarily inflict an unusually severe punishment.

The outstanding characteristic of our present practice of punishing criminals by death is the infrequency with which we resort to it. The evidence is conclusive that death is not the ordinary punishment for any crime.

*   *   *

Thus, although "the death penalty has been employed throughout our history," *Trop* v. *Dulles,* 356 U.S., at 99, in fact the history of this punishment is one of successive restriction. What was once a common punishment has become, in the context of a continuing moral debate, increasingly rare. The evolution of this punishment evidences, not that it is an inevitable part of the American scene, but that it has proved progressively more troublesome to the national conscience. The result of this movement is our current system of administering the punishment, under which death sentences are rarely imposed and death is even more rarely inflicted. It is, of course, "We, the People" who are responsible for the rarity both of the imposition and the carrying out of this punishment. Juries, "express[ing] the conscience of the community on the ultimate question of life or death," *Witherspoon* v. *Illinois*, 391 U.S., at 519. have been able to bring them-

[25] Stephen, Capital Punishments, 69 Fraser's Magazine 753, 763 (1864).

selves to vote for death in a mere 100 or so cases among the thousands tried each year where the punishment is available. Governors, elected by and acting for us, have regularly commuted a substantial number of those sentences. And it is our society that insists upon due process of law to the end that no person will be unjustly put to death, thus ensuring that many more of those sentences will not be carried out. In sum, we have made death a rare punishment today.

The progressive decline in, and the current rarity of, the infliction of death demonstrate that our society seriously questions the appropriateness of this punishment today. The States point out that many legislatures authorize death as the punishment for certain crimes and that substantial segments of the public, as reflected in opinion polls and referendum votes, continue to support it. Yet the availability of this punishment through statutory authorization, as well as the polls and referenda, which amount simply to approval of that authorization, simply underscores the extent to which our society has in fact rejected this punishment. When an unusually severe punishment is authorized for wide-scale application but not, because of society's refusal, inflicted save in a few instances, the inference is compelling that there is a deep-seated reluctance to inflict it. Indeed, the likelihood is great that the punishment is tolerated only because of its disuse. The objective indicator of society's view of an unusually severe punishment is what society does with it, and today society will inflict death upon only a small sample of the eligible criminals. Rejection could hardly be more complete without becoming absolute. At the very least, I must conclude that contemporary society views this punishment with substantial doubt.

The final principle to be considered is that an unusually severe and degrading punishment may not be excessive in view of the purposes for which it is inflicted. This principle, too, is related to the others. When there is a strong probability that the State is arbitrarily inflicting an unusually severe punishment that is subject to grave societal doubts, it is likely also that the punishment cannot be shown to be serving any penal purpose that could not be served equally well by some less severe punishment.

The States' primary claim is that death is a necessary punishment because it prevents the commission of capital crimes more effectively than any less severe punishment. The first part of this claim is that the infliction of death is necessary to stop the individuals executed from committing further crimes. The sufficient answer to this that if a criminal convicted of a capital crime poses a danger to society, effective administration of the State's pardon and parole laws can delay or deny his release from prison, and techniques of isolation can eliminate or minimize the danger while he remains confined.

The more significant argument is that the threat of death prevents the commission of capital crimes because it deters potential criminals who would not be deterred by the threat of imprisonment. The argument is not based upon evidence that the threat of death is a superior deterrent. Indeed, as my Brother MARSHALL establishes, the available evidence uniformly indicates, although it does not conclusively prove, that the threat of death has no greater deterrent effect than the threat of imprisonment. The States argue, however, that they are entitled to rely upon common human experience, and that experience, they say, supports the conclusion that death must be a more effective deterrent than any less severe punishment. Because people fear death the most, the argument runs, the threat of death must be the greatest deterrent.

It is important to focus upon the precise import of this argument. It is not denied that many, and probably most, capital crimes cannot be deterred by the threat of punishment. Thus the argument can apply only to those who think rationally about the commission of capital crimes. Particularly is that true when the potential criminal, under this argument, must not only consider the risk of punishment, but also distinguish between two possible punishments. The concern, then, is with a particular type of potential criminal, the rational person who will commit a capital crime knowing that the punishment is long-term imprisonment, which may well be for the rest of his life, but will not commit the crime knowing that the punishment is death. On the face of it, the assumption that such persons exist is implausible.

In any event, this argument cannot be appraised in the abstract. We are not presented with the theoretical question whether under any imaginable circumstances the threat of death might be a greater deterrent to the commission of capital crimes than the threat of imprisonment. We are concerned with the practice of punishing criminals by death as it exists in the United States today. Proponents of this argument necessarily admit that its validity depends upon the existence of a system in which the punishment of death is invariably and swiftly imposed. Our system, of course, satisfies neither condition. A rational person contemplating a murder or rape is confronted, not with the certainty of a speedy death, but with the slightest possibility that he will be executed in the distant future. The risk of death is remote and improbable; in contrast, the risk of long-term imprisonment is near and great. In short, whatever the speculative validity of the assumption that the threat of death is a superior deterrent, there is no reason to believe that as currently administered the punishment of death is necessary to deter the commission of capital crimes. Whatever might be the case were all or substantially all eligible criminals quickly put to death, unverifiable possibilities are an insufficient basis upon which to conclude that the threat of death today has any greater deterrent efficacy than the threat of imprisonment.[26]

---

[26] There is also the more limited argument that death is a necessary punishment when criminals are already serving or subject to a sentence of life imprisonment. If the only punishment available is further imprisonment, it is said those criminals will have nothing to lose by committing further crimes, and accordingly the threat of death

There is, however, another aspect to the argument that the punishment of death is necessary for the protection of society. The infliction of death, the States urge, serves to manifest the community's outrage at the commission of the crime. It is, they say, a concrete public expression of moral indignation that inculcates respect for the law and helps assure a more peaceful community. Moreover, we are told, not only does the punishment of death exert this widespread moralizing influence upon community values, it also satisfies the popular demand for grievous condemnation of abhorrent crimes and thus prevents disorder, lynching, and attempts by private citizens to take the law into their own hands.

The question, however, is not whether death serves these supposed purposes of punishment, but whether death serves them more effectively than imprisonment. There is no evidence whatever that utilization of imprisonment rather than death encourages private blood feuds and other disorders. Surely if there were such a danger, the execution of a handful of criminals each year would not prevent it. The assertion that death alone is a sufficiently emphatic denunication for capital crimes suffers from the same defect. If capital crimes require the punishment of death in order to provide moral reinforcement for the basic values of the community, those values can only be undermined when death is so rarely inflicted upon the criminals who commit the crimes. Furthermore, it is certainly doubtful that the infliction of death by the State does in fact strengthen the community's moral code; if the deliberate extinguishment of human life has any effect at all, it more likely tends to lower our respect for life and brutalize our values. That, after all, is why we no longer carry out public executions. In any event, this claim simply means that one purpose of punishment is to indicate social disapproval of crime. To serve that purpose our laws distribute punishments according to the gravity of crimes and punish more severely the crimes society regards as more serious. That purpose cannot justify any particular punishment as the upper limit of severity.

There is, then, no substantial reason to believe that the punishment of death, as currently administered, is necessary for the protection of society. The only other purpose suggested, one that is independent of protection for society, is retribution. Shortly stated, retribution in the context means that criminals are put to death because they deserve it.

Although it is difficult to believe that any State today wishes to proclaim adherence to "naked vengeance," *Trop* v. *Dulles,* 356 U.S., at 112 BRENNAN, J., concurring), the States claim, in reliance upon its statutory authorization, that death is the only fit punishment for capital crimes and

---

is the sole deterrent. But "life" imprisonment is a misnomer today. Rarely, if ever, do crimes carry a mandatory life sentence without possibility of parole. That possibility ensures that criminals do not reach the point where further crimes are free of consequences. Moreover, if this argument is simply an assertion that the threat of death is a more effective deterrent than the threat of increased imprisonment by denial of release on parole, then, as noted above, there is simply no evidence to support it.

that this retributive purpose justifies its infliction. In the past, judged by its statutory authorization, death was considered the only fit punishment for the crime of forgery, for the first federal criminal statute provided a mandatory death penalty for that crime, Act of April 30, 1790, § 14, 1 Stat. 115. Obviously, concepts of justice change; no immutable moral order requires death for murderers and rapists. The claim that death is a just punishment necessarily refers to the existence of certain public beliefs. The claim must be that for capital crimes death alone comports with society's notion of proper punishment. As administered today, however, the punishment of death cannot be justified as a necessary means of exacting retribution from criminals. When the overwhelming number of criminals who commit capital crimes go to prison, it cannot be concluded that death serves the purpose of retribution more effectively than imprisonment. The asserted public belief that murderers and rapists deserve to die is flatly inconsistent with the execution of a random few. As the history of the punishment of death in this country shows, our society wishes to prevent crime; we have no desire to kill criminals simply to get even with them.

In sum, the punishment of death is inconsistent with all four principles: Death is an unusually severe and degrading punishment; there is a strong probability that it is inflicted arbitrarily; its rejection by contemporary society is virtually total; and there is no reason to believe that it serves any penal purpose more effectively than the less severe punishment of imprisonment. The function of these principles is to enable a court to determine whether a punishment comports with human dignity. Death, quite simply, does not.

[DISSENTING OPINION]

∗ ∗ ∗

MR. CHIEF JUSTICE BURGER, with whom MR. JUSTICE BLACKMUN, MR. JUSTICE POWELL, and MR. JUSTICE REHNQUIST join, dissenting.

At the outset it is important to note that only two members of the Court, MR. JUSTICE BRENNAN and MR. JUSTICE MARSHALL, have concluded that the Eighth Amendment prohibits capital punishment for all crimes and under all circumstances. MR. JUSTICE DOUGLAS has also determined that the death penalty contravenes the Eighth Amendment, although I do not read his opinion as necessarily requiring final abolition of the penalty. For the reasons set forth in Parts I-IV of this opinion, I conclude that the constitutional prohibition against "cruel and unusual punishments" cannot be construed to bar the imposition of the punishment of death.

MR. JUSTICE STEWART and MR. JUSTICE WHITE have concluded that petitioners' death sentences must be set aside because prevailing sentencing practices do not comply with the Eighth Amendment. For the reasons set forth in Part V of this opinion, I believe this approach fundamentally misconceives the nature of the Eighth Amendment guarantee and flies directly in the face of controlling authority of extremely recent vintage.

I

If we were possessed of legislative power, I would either join with MR. JUSTICE BRENNAN *and* MR. JUSTICE MARSHALL or, at the very least, restrict the use of capital punishment to a small category of the most heinous crimes. Our constitutional inquiry, however, must be divorced from personal feelings as to the morality and efficacy of the death penalty, and be confined to the meaning and applicability of the uncertain language of the Eighth Amendment. There is no novelty in being called upon to interpret a constitutional provision that is less than self-defining, but, of all our fundamental guarantees, the ban on "cruel and unusual punishments" is one of the most difficult to translate into judicially manageable terms. The widely divergent views of the Amendment expressed in today's opinions reveal the haze that surrounds this constitutional command. Yet it is essential to our role as a court that we not seize upon the enigmatic character of the guarantee as an invitation to enact our personal predilections into law.

Although the Eighth Amendment literally reads as prohibiting only those punishments that are both "cruel" and "unusual," history compels the conclusion that the Constitution prohibits all punishments of extreme and barbarous cruelty, regardless of how frequently or infrequently imposed.

* * *

III

There are no obvious indications that capital punishment offends the conscience of society to such a degree that our traditional deference to the legislative judgment must be abandoned. It is not a punishment such as burning at the stake that everyone would ineffably find to be repugnant to all civilized standards. Nor is it a punishment so roundly condemned that only a few aberrant legislatures have retained it on the statute books. Capital punishment is authorized by statute in 40 States, the District of Columbia, and in the federal courts for the commission of certain crimes.[27] On four occasions in the last 11 years Congress had added to the list of federal crimes punishable by death.[28] In looking for reliable indicia of contemporary attitude, none more trustworthy has been advanced.

[27] See Department of Justice, National Prisoner Statistics No. 46, Capital Punishment 1930–1970, p. 50 (Aug. 1971). Since the publication of the Department of Justice report, capital punishment has been judicially abolished in California, *People* v. *Anderson,* 6 Cal. 3d 628, 493 P. 2d 880, cert. denied, 406 U.S. 958 (1972). The States where capital punishment is no longer authorized are Alaska, California, Hawaii, Iowa, Maine, Michigan, Oregon, West Virginia, and Wisconsin.

[28] See Act of Jan. 2, 1971, Pub. L. 91–644, Tit. IV, § 15, 84 Stat. 1891, 18 U. S. C. § 351; Act of Oct. 15, 1970, Pub. L. 91–452, Tit. XI, § 1102(a), 84 Stat. 956, 18 U. S. C. § 844(f) (i); Act of Aug. 28, 1965, 79 Stat. 580, 18 U. S. C. § 1751; Act of Sept. 5, 1961, § 1, 75 Stat. 466, 49 U. S. C. § 1472(i). See also opinion of MR. JUSTICE BLACKMUN, *post,* at 412–413.

One conceivable source of evidence that legislatures have abdicated their essentially barometric role with respect to community values would be public opinion polls, of which there have been many in the past decade addressed to the question of capital punishment. Without assessing the reliability of such polls, or intimating that any judicial reliance could ever be placed on them, it need only be noted that the reported results have shown nothing approximating the universal condemnation of capital punishment that might lead us to suspect that the legislatures in general have lost touch with current social values.[29]

Counsel for petitioners rely on a different body of empirical evidence. They argue, in effect, that the number of cases in which the death penalty is imposed, as compared with the number of cases in which it is statutorily available, reflects a general revulsion toward the penalty that would lead to its repeal if only it were more generally and widely enforced. It cannot be gainsaid that by the choice of juries—and sometimes judges [30]—the death penalty is imposed in far fewer than half the cases in which it is available.[31] To go further and characterize the rate of imposition as "freakishly rare," as petitioners insist, is unwarranted hyperbole. And regardless of its characterization, the rate of imposition does not impel the conclusion that capital punishment is now regarded as intolerably cruel or uncivilized.

It is argued that in those capital cases where juries have recommended mercy, they have given expression to civilized values and effectively renounced the legislative authorization for capital punishment. At the same time it is argued that where juries have made the awesome decision to send men to their deaths, they have acted arbitrarily and without sensitivity to prevailing standards of decency. This explanation for the infrequency of imposition of capital punishment is unsupported by known facts, and is

[29] A 1966 poll indicated that 42% of those polled favored capital punishment while 47% opposed it, and 11% had no opinion. A 1969 poll found 51% in favor, 40% opposed, and 9% with no opinion. See Erskine, The Polls: Capital Punishment, 34 Public Opinion Quarterly 290 (1970).

[30] The jury plays the predominant role in sentencing in capital cases in this country. Available evidence indicates that where the judge determines the sentence, the death penalty is imposed with a slightly greater frequency than where the jury makes the determination. H. Kalven & H. Zeisel, The American Jury 436 (1966).

[31] In the decade from 1961–1970, an average of 106 persons per year received the death sentence in the United States, ranging from a low of 85 in 1967 to a high of 140 in 1961; 127 persons received the death sentence in 1970. Department of Justice, National Prisoner Statistics No. 46, Capital Punishment 1930–1970, p. 9. See also Bedau, The Death Penalty in America, 35 Fed. Prob., No. 2, p. 32 (1971). Although accurate figures are difficult to obtain, it is thought that from 15% to 20% of those convicted of murder are sentenced to death in States where it is authorized. See, e.g., McGee, Capital Punishment as Seen by a Correctional Administrator, 28 Feb. Prob., No. 2, pp. 11, 12 (1964); Bedau, Death Sentences in New Jersey 1907–1960, 19 Rutgers L. Rev. 1, 30 (1964); Florida Division of Corrections, Seventh Biennial Report (July 1, 1968, to June 30, 1970) 82 (1970); H. Kalven & H. Zeisel, The American Jury 435–436 (1966). The rate of imposition for rape and the few other crimes made punishable by death in certain States is considerably lower. See, e.g., Florida Division of Corrections, Seventh Biennial Report, supra, at 83; Partington, The Incidence of the Death Penalty for Rape in Virginia, 22 Wash. & Lee L. Rev. 43–44, 71–73 (1965).

inconsistent in principle with everything this Court has ever said about the functioning of juries in capital cases.

In *McGautha* v. *California, supra,* decided only one year ago, the Court held that there was no mandate in the Due Process Clause of the Fourteenth Amendment that juries be given instructions as to when the death penalty should be imposed. After reviewing the autonomy that juries have traditionally exercised in capital cases and noting the practical difficulties of framing manageable instructions, this Court concluded that judicially articulated standards were not needed to insure a responsible decision as to penalty. Nothing in *McGautha* licenses capital juries to act arbitrarily or assumes that they have so acted in the past. On the contrary, the assumption underlying the *McGautha* ruling is that juries "will act with due regard for the consequences of their decision." 402 U.S., at 208.

The responsibility of juries deciding capital cases in our system of justice was nowhere better described than in *Witherspoon* v. *Illinois, supra:*

[A] jury that must choose between life imprisonment and capital punishment can do little more—and must do nothing less—than express *the conscience of the community* on the ultimate question of life or death.

And one of the most important functions any jury can perform in making such a selection is to maintain a link between contemporary community values and the penal system—a link without which the determination of punishment could hardly reflect 'the evolving standards of decency that mark the progress of a maturing society' 391 U.S., at 519 and n. 15 (emphasis added).

The selectivity of juries in imposing the punishment of death is properly viewed as a refinement on, rather than a repudiation of, the statutory authorization for that penalty. Legislatures prescribe the categories of crimes for which the death penalty should be available, and, acting as "the conscience of the community," juries are entrusted to determine in individual cases that the ultimate punishment is warranted. Juries are undoubtedly influenced in this judgment by myriad factors. The motive or lack of motive of the perpetrator, the degree of injury or suffering of the victim or victims, and the degree of brutality in the commission of the crime would seem to be prominent among these factors. Given the general awareness that death is no longer a routine punishment for the crimes for which it is made available, it is hardly surprising that juries have been increasingly meticulous in their imposition of the penalty. But to assume from the mere fact of relative infrequency that only a random assortment of pariahs are sentenced to death, is to cast grave doubt on the basic integrity of our jury system.

It would, of course, be unrealistic to assume that juries have been perfectly consistent in choosing the cases where the death penalty is to be imposed, for no human institution performs with perfect consistency. There are doubtless prisoners on death row who would not be there had they been tried before a different jury or in a different State. 'In this sense their fate has been controlled by a fortuitous circumstance. However, this element of fortuity does not stand as an indictment either of the general functioning of juries in capital cases or the integrity of jury decisions in individual cases. There is no empirical basis for concluding that juries have generally failed to discharge in good faith the responsibility described in *Witherspoon*—that of choosing between life and death in individual cases according to the dictates of community values.[32]

The rate of imposition of death sentences falls far short of providing the requisite unambiguous evidence that the legislatures of 40 States and the Congress have turned their backs on current or evolving standards of decency in continuing to make the death penalty available. For, if selective imposition evidences a rejection of capital punishment in those cases where it is not imposed, it surely evidences a correlative affirmation of the penalty in those cases where it is imposed. Absent some clear indication that the continued imposition of the death penalty on a selective basis is violative of prevailing standards of civilized conduct, the Eighth Amendment cannot be said to interdict its use.

---

[32] Counsel for petitioners make the conclusory statement that "[t]hose who are selected to die are the poor and powerless, personally ugly and socially unacceptable." Brief for Petitioner in No. 68–5027, p. 51. However, the sources cited contain no empirical findings to undermine the general premise that juries impose the death penalty in the most extreme cases. One study has discerned a statistically noticeable difference between the rate of imposition on blue collar and white collar defendants; the study otherwise concludes that juries do follow rational patterns in imposing the sentence of death. Note, A Study of the California Penalty Jury in First-Degree-Murder Cases, 21 Stan. L. Rev. 1297 (1969). See also H. Kalven & H. Zeisel, The American Jury 434–449 (1966).

Statistics are also cited to show that the death penalty has been imposed in a racially discriminatory manner. Such statistics suggest, at least as a historical matter, that Negroes have been sentenced to death with greater frequency than whites in several States, particularly for the crime of interracial rape. See, *e.g.*, Koeninger, Capital Punishment in Texas, 1924–1968, 15 Crime & Delin. 132 (1696); Note, Capital Punishment in Virginia, 58 Va. L. Rev. 97 (1972). If a statute that authorizes the discretionary imposition of a particular penalty for a particular crime is used primarily against defendants of a certain race, and if the pattern of use can be fairly explained only by reference to the race of the defendants, the Equal Protection Clause of the Fourteenth Amendment forbids continued enforcement of that statute in its existing form. Cf. *Yick Wo* v. *Hopkins,* 118 U.S. 356 (1886); *Gomillion* v. *Lightfoot,* 364 U.S. 339 (1960).

To establish that the statutory authorization for a particular penalty is inconsistent with the dictates of the Equal Protection Clause, it is not enough to show how it was applied in the distant past. The statistics that have been referred to us cover periods when Negroes were systematically excluded from jury service and when racial segregation was the official policy in many States. Data of more recent vintage are essential. See *Maxwell* v. *Bishop,* 398 F. 2d 138, 148 (CA8 1968), vacated, 398 U.S. 262 (1970). While no statistical survey could be expected to bring forth absolute and irrefutable proof of a discriminatory pattern of imposition, a strong showing would have to be made, taking all relevant factors into account.

It must be noted that any equal protection claim is totally distinct from the Eighth Amendment question to which our grant of certiorari was limited in these cases. Evidence of a discriminatory pattern of enforcement does not imply that any use of a particular punishment is so morally repugnant as to violate the Eighth Amendment.

* * *

Two of the several aims of punishment are generally associated with capital punishment—retribution and deterrence. It is argued that retribution can be discounted because that, after all, is what the Eighth Amendment seeks to eliminate. There is no authority suggesting that the Eighth Amendment was intended to purge the law of its retributive elements, and the Court has consistently assumed that retribution is a legitimate dimension of the punishment of crimes. See *Williams* v. *New York*, 337 U.S. 241, 248 (1949); *United States* v. *Lovett*, 328 U.S. 303, 324 (1946) (Frankfurter, J., concurring). Furthermore, responsible legal thinkers of widely varying persuasions have debated the sociological and philosophical aspects of the retribution question for generations, neither side being able to convince the other.[33] It would be reading a great deal into the Eighth Amendment to hold that the punishments authorized by legislatures cannot constitutionally reflect a retributive purpose.

The less esoteric but no less controversial question is whether the death penalty acts as a superior deterrent. Those favoring abolition find no evidence that it does.[34] Those favoring retention start from the intuitive notion that capital punishment should act as the most effective deterrent and note that there is no convincing evidence that it does not.[35] Escape from this empirical stalemate is sought by placing the burden of proof on the States and concluding that they have failed to demonstrate that capital punishment is a more effective deterrent than life imprisonment. Numerous justifications have been advanced for shifting the burden, and they are not without their rhetorical appeal. However, these arguments are not descended from established constitutional principles, but are born of the urge to bypass an unresolved factual question.[36] Comparative deterence is not a matter that lends itself to precise measurement; to shift the burden to the States is to provide an illusory solution to an enormously complex problem. If it were proper to put the States to the test of demonstrating the deterrent value of capital punishment, we could just as well ask them to prove the need for life imprisonment or any other punishment. Yet I know of no convincing evidence that life imprisonment is a more effective deterrent than 20 years' imprisonment, or even that a $10 parking ticket

---

[33] See Hart, The Aims of the Criminal Law, 23 Law & Contemp. Prob. 401 (1958); H. Packer, The Limits of the Criminal Sanction 37–39 (1968); M. Cohen, Reason and Law 41–44 (1950); Report of Royal Commission on Capital Punishment, 1949–1953, Cmd. 8932, § 52, pp. 17–18 (1953); Hart, Murder and the Principles of Punishment: England and the United States, 52 Nw. U. L. Rev. 433, 446–455 (1957); H. L. A. Hart, Law, Liberty and Morality 60–69 (1963).

[34] See, *e.g.*, Sellin, Homicides in Retentionist and Abolitionist States, in Capital Punishment 135 *et seq.* (T. Sellin ed. 1967); Schuessler, The Deterrent Influence of the Death Penalty, 284 Annals 54 (1952).

[35] See, *e.g.*, Hoover, Statements in Favor of the Death Penalty, in H. Bedau, The Death Penality in America 130 (1967 rev. ed.); Allen, Capital Punishment: Your Protection and Mine, in the Death Penalty in America, *supra*, at 135. See also Hart, 52 Nw. U. L. Rev. *supra*, at 457; Bedau, The Death Penalty in America, *supra*, at 265–266.

[36] See *Powell* v. *Texas*, 392 U.S. 514, 531 (1968) (Marshall, J.) (plurality opinion).

is a more effective deterrent than a $5 parking ticket. In fact, there are some who go so far as to challenge the notion that any punishments deter crime.[37] If the States are unable to adduce convincing proof rebutting such assertions, does it then follow that all punishments are suspect as being "cruel and unusual" within the meaning of the Constitution? On the contrary, I submit that the questions raised by the necessity approach are beyond the pale of judicial inquiry under the Eighth Amendment.

* * *

MR. JUSTICE POWELL, dissenting.

* * *

V

Petitioners seek to salvage their thesis by arguing that the infrequency and discriminatory nature of the actual resort to the ultimate penalty tend to diffuse public opposition. We are told that the penalty is imposed exclusively on uninfluential minorities—"the poor and powerless, personally ugly and socially unacceptable." [38] It is urged that this pattern of application assures that large segments of the public will be either uninformed or unconcerned and will have no reason to measure the punishment against prevailing moral standards.

Implicitly, this argument concedes the unsoundness of petitioners' contention, examined above under Part IV, that objective evidence shows a present and widespread community rejection of the death penalty. It is now said, in effect, not that capital punishment presently offends our citizenry, but that the public *would* be offended *if* the penalty were enforced in a nondiscriminatory manner against a significant percentage of those charged with capital crimes, and *if* the public were thereby made aware of the moral issues surrounding capital punishment. Rather than merely registering the objective indicators on a judicial balance, we are asked ultimately to rest a far-reaching constitutional determination on a prediction regarding the subjective judgments of the mass of our people under hypothetical assumptions that may or may not be realistic.

Apart from the impermissibility of basing a constitutional judgment of this magnitude on such speculative assumptions, the argument suffers from other defects. If, as petitioners urge, we are to engage in speculation, it is not at all certain that the public would experience deep-felt revulsion if the States were to execute as many sentenced capital offenders this year

[37] See, *e.g.*, K. Menninger, The Crime of Punishment 206–208 (1968).
[38] Brief of Petitioner in No. 68–5027, p. 51. Although the *Aikens* case is no longer before us . . . the petitioners in *Furman* and *Jackson* have incorporated petitioner's brief in *Aikens* by reference. See Brief for Petitioners in No. 69–5003, pp. 11–12; Brief for Petitioner in No. 69–5030, pp. 11–12.

as they executed in the mid-1930's.[39] It seems more likely that public reaction, rather than being characterized by undifferentiated rejection, would depend upon the facts and circumstances surrounding each particular case.

Members of this Court know, from the petitions and appeals that come before us regularly, that brutish and revolting murders continue to occur with disquieting frequency. Indeed, murders are so commonplace in our society that only the most sensational receive significant and sustained publicity. It could hardly be suggested that in any of these highly publicized murder cases—the several senseless assassinations or the too numerous shocking multiple murders that have stained this country's recent history— the public has exhibited any signs of "revulsion" at the thought of executing the convicted murderers. The public outcry, as we all know, has been quite to the contrary. Furthermore, there is little reason to suspect that the public's reaction would differ significantly in response to other less publicized murders. It is certainly arguable that many such murders, because of their senselessness or barbarousness, would evoke a public demand for the death penalty rather than a public rejection of that alternative. Nor is there any rational basis for arguing that the public reaction to any of these crimes would be muted if the murderer were "rich and powerful." The demand for the ultimate sanction might well be greater, as a wealthy killer is hardly a sympathetic figure. While there might be specific cases in which capital punishment would be regarded as excessive and shocking to the conscience of the community, it can hardly be argued that the public's dissatisfaction with the penalty in particular cases would translate into a demand for absolute abolition.

In pursuing the foregoing speculation, I do not suggest that it is relevant to the appropriate disposition of these cases. The purpose of the digression is to indicate that judicial decisions cannot be founded on such speculations and assumptions, however appealing they may seem.

But the discrimination argument does not rest alone on a projection of the assumed effect on public opinion of more frequent executions. Much also is made of the undeniable fact that the death penalty has a greater impact on the lower economic strata of society, which include a relatively higher percentage of persons of minority racial and ethnic group backgrounds. The argument drawn from this fact is two-pronged. In part it is merely an extension of the speculative approach pursued by petitioners, *i.e.*, that public revulsion is suppressed in callous apathy because the penalty does not affect persons from the white middle class which constitutes

---

[39] In 1935 available statistics indicate that 184 convicted murderers were executed. That is the highest annual total for any year since statistics have become available. NPS, *supra*, n. 18. The year 1935 is chosen by petitioners in stating their thesis: "If, in fact, 184 murderers were to be executed in this year 1971, we submit it is palpable that the public conscience of the Nation would be profoundly and fundamentally revolted, and that the death penalty for murder would be abolished forthwith as the atavistic horror that it is." Brief for Petitioner in No. 68–5027, p. 26. . . .

the majority in this country. This aspect, however, adds little to the infrequency rationalization for public apathy which I have found unpersuasive.

As MR. JUSTICE MARSHALL'S opinion today demonstrates, the argument does have a more troubling aspect. It is his contention that if the average citizen were aware of the disproportionate burden of capital punishment borne by the "poor, the ignorant, and the underprivileged," he would find the penalty "shocking to his conscience and sense of justice" and would not stand for its further use. *Ante*, at 365–366, 369. This argument, like the apathy rationale, calls for further speculation on the part of the Court. It also illuminates the quicksands upon which we are asked to base this decision. Indeed, the two contentions seem to require contradictory assumptions regarding the public's moral attitude toward capital punishment. The apathy argument is predicated on the assumption that the penalty is used against the less influential elements of society, that the public is fully aware of this, and that it tolerates uses of capital punishment only because of a callous indifference to the offenders who are sentenced. MR. JUSTICE MARSHALL'S argument, on the other hand, rests on the contrary assumption that the public does not know against whom the penalty is enforced and that if the public were educated to this fact it would find the punishment intolerable. *Ante*, at 369. Neither assumption can claim to be an entirely accurate portrayal of public attitude; for some acceptance of capital punishment might be a consequence of hardened apathy based on the knowledge of infrequent and uneven application, while for others acceptance may grow only out of ignorance. More significantly, however, neither supposition acknowledges what, for me, is a more basic flaw.

Certainly the claim is justified that this criminal sanction falls more heavily on the relatively impoverished and underprivileged elements of society. The "have-nots" in every society always have been subject to greater pressure to commit crimes and to fewer constraints than their more affluent fellow citizens. This is, indeed, a tragic byproduct of social and economic deprivation, but it is not an argument of constitutional proportions under the Eighth or Fourteenth Amendment. The same discriminatory impact argument could be made with equal force and logic with respect to those sentenced to prison terms. The Due Process Clause admits of no distinction between the deprivation of "life" and the deprivation of "liberty." If discriminatory impact renders capital punishment cruel and unusual, it likewise renders invalid most of the prescribed penalties for crimes of violence. The root causes of the higher incidence of criminal penalties on "minorities and the poor" will not be cured by abolishing the system of penalties. Nor, indeed, could any society have a viable system of criminal justice if sanctions were abolished or ameliorated because most of those who commit crimes happen to be underprivileged. The basic problem results not from the penalties imposed for criminal conduct but from social and economic factors that have plagued humanity since the beginning of recorded history, frustrating all efforts to create in any country at any time the perfect society in which there are no "poor," no "minorities" and no "underprivileged." The causes underlying this problem are unrelated to the constitutional issue before the Court.

THE COLLAPSE OF THE CASE AGAINST CAPITAL PUNISHMENT °

ERNEST VAN DEN HAAG

Three questions about the death penalty so overlap that they must each be answered. I shall ask seriatim: Is the death penalty constitutional? Is is useful? Is it morally justifiable? ° °

I. The Constitutional Question

The Fifth Amendment states that no one shall be "deprived of life, liberty, or property without due process of law," implying a "due process of law" to deprive persons of life. The Eighth Amendment prohibits "cruel and un-usual punishment." It is unlikely that this prohibition was meant to super-sede the Fifth Amendment, since the amendments were simultaneously enacted in 1791.[1]

The Fourteenth Amendment, enacted in 1868, reasserted and explicitly extended to the states the implied authority to "deprive of life, liberty, or property" by "due process of law." Thus, to regard the death penalty as unconstitutional one must believe that the standards which determine what is "cruel and unusual" have so evolved since 1868 as to prohibit now what was authorized then, and that the Constitution authorizes the courts to overrule laws in the light of *new* moral standards. What might these stan-

°From "The Collapse of the Case Against Capital Punishment" by Ernest van den Haag in *The National Review*, March 31, 1978, pp. 395–407. Reprinted by permission of the author.
° ° This is a greatly revised version of a paper first delivered at a symposium sponsored by the Graduate School of Criminal Justice and the Criminal Justice Research Center of Albany, N.Y., in April 1977.

[1] Apparently the punishment must be both—else cruel *or* unusual would have done. Historically it appears that punishments were prohibited if unusual in 1791 *and* cruel: the Framers did not want to prohibit punishments, even cruel ones, only if already unusual in 1791; they did prohibit new (unusual) punishments if cruel. The Eighth Amendment was not meant to apply to the death penalty in 1791 since it was not unusual then; nor was the Eighth Amendment intended to be used against capital punishment in the future, regardless of whether it may have come to be considered cruel: it is neither a new penalty nor one unusual in 1791.

dards be? And what shape must their evolution take to be constitutionally decisive?

Consensus. A moral consensus, intellectual or popular, could have evolved to find execution "cruel and unusual." It did not. Intellectual opinion is divided. Polls suggest that most people would vote for the death penalty. Congress recently has legislated the death penalty for skyjacking under certain conditions. The representative assemblies of two-thirds of the states did re-enact capital punishment when previous laws were found constitutionally defective.[2]

If, however, there were a consensus against the death penalty, the Constitution expects the political process, rather than judicial decisions, to reflect it. Courts are meant to interpret the laws made by the political process and to set constitutional limits to it—not to replace it by responding to a presumed moral consensus. Surely the "cruel and unusual" phrase was not meant to authorize the courts to become legislatures.[3] Thus, neither a consensus of moral opinion nor a moral discovery by judges is meant to be disguised as a constitutional interpretation. Even when revealed by a burning bush, new moral norms were not meant to become constitutional norms by means of court decisions.[4] To be sure, the courts in the past have occasionally done away with obsolete kinds of punishment—but never in the face of legislative and popular opposition and re-enactment. Abolitionists constantly press the courts now to create rather than to confirm obsolescence. That courts are urged to do what so clearly is for voters and lawmakers to decide suggests that the absence of consensus for abolition is recognized by the opponents of capital punishment. What then can the phrase "cruel and unusual punishment" mean today?

"Cruel" may be understood to mean excessive—punitive without, or beyond, a rational-utilitarian purpose. Since capital punishment excludes rehabilitation and is not needed for incapacitation, the remaining rational-utilitarian purpose would be deterrence, the reduction of the rate at which the crime punished is committed by others. I shall consider this reduction below. Here I wish to note that, if the criterion for the constitutionality of any punishment were an actual demonstration of its rational-utilitarian

---

[2] There may be a consensus against the death penalty among the college educated. If so, it demonstrates a) the power of indoctrination wielded by sociologists; b) the fact that those who are least threatened by violence are most inclined to do without the death penalty. College graduates are less often threatened by murder than the uneducated.

[3] See Chief Justice Burger dissenting in *Furman*: "In a democratic society legislatures not courts are constituted to respond to the will and consequently the moral values of the people."

[4] The First Amendment might be invoked against such sources of revelation. When specific laws do not suffice to decide a case, courts, to be sure, make decisions based on general legal principles. But the death penalty (as distinguished from applications) raises no serious legal problem.

effectiveness, all legal punishments would be in as much constitutional jeopardy as the death penalty. Are fines for corporations deterrent? rehabilitative? incapacitative? Is a jail term for marijuana possession? Has it ever been established that ten years in prison are doubly as deterrent as five, or at least sufficiently more deterrent? (I don't pretend to know what "sufficiently" might mean: whether 10 per cent or 80 per cent added deterrence would warrant 100 per cent added severity.)

The Constitution certainly does not require a demonstration of rational-utilitarian effects for any punishment. Such a demonstration so far has not been available. To demand it for one penalty—however grave—and not for others, when it is known that no such demonstration is available, or has been required hitherto for any punishment, seems unjustified. Penalties have always been regarded as constitutional if they can be plausibly intended (rather than demonstrated) to be effective (useful), and if they are not grossly excessive, i.e., unjust.

Justice, a rational but non-utilitarian purpose of punishment, requires that it be proportioned to the felt gravity of the crime. Thus, constitutional justice authorizes, even calls for, a higher penalty the graver the crime. One cannot demand that this constitutionally required escalation stop short of the death penalty unless one furnishes positive proof of its irrationality by showing injustice, i.e., disproportionality (to the felt gravity of the crime punished or to other punishments of similar crimes), as well as ineffectiveness, i.e., uselessness in reducing the crime rate. There is no proof of cruelty here in either sense.

"Unusual" is generally interpreted to mean either randomly capricious and therefore unconstitutional, or capricious in a biased, discriminatory way, so as particularly to burden specifiable groups, and therefore unconstitutional. (Random arbitrariness might violate the Eighth, biased arbitrariness the Fourteenth Amendment, which promises "the equal protection of the laws.") Apart from the historical interpretation noted above (Footnote 1), "unusual" seems to mean "unequal" then. The dictionary equivalent —"rare"—seems to be regarded as relevant only inasmuch as it implies "unequal." Indeed it is hard to see why rarity should be objectionable otherwise.

For the sake of argument, let me grant that either or both forms of capriciousness prevail [5] and that they are less tolerable with respect to the death penalty than with respect to milder penalties—which certainly are not meted out less capriciously. However prevalent, neither form of capriciousness would argue for abolishing the death penalty. Capriciousness is not inherent in that penalty, or in any penalty, but occurs in its distribution. Therefore, the remedy lies in changing the laws and procedures

[5] Attention should be drawn to John Hagan's "Extralegal Attributes and Criminal Sentencing" (*Law and Society Review*, Spring 1974), which throws doubt on much of the discrimination which sociologists have found.

which distribute the penalty. It is the process of distribution which is capable of discriminating, not that which it distributes.

Unavoidable Capriciousness. If capricious distribution places some convicts, or groups of convicts, at an unwarranted disadvantage,[6] can it be remedied enough to satisfy the Eighth and Fourteenth Amendments? Some capriciousness is unavoidable because decisions of the criminal justice system necessarily rest on accidental factors at many points, such as the presence or absence of witnesses to an act; or the cleverness or clumsiness of police officers who exercise their discretion in arresting suspects and seizing evidence. All court decisions must rest on the available and admissible evidence for, rather than the actuality of, guilt. Availability of evidence is necessarily accidental to the actuality of whatever it is that the evidence is needed for. Accident is the capriciousness of fate.

Now, if possible without loss of other desiderata, accident and human capriciousness should be minimized. But, obviously, discretionary judgments cannot be avoided altogether. The Framers of the Constitution were certainly aware of the unavoidable elements of discretion which affect all human decisions, including those of police officers, of prosecutors, and of the courts. Because it always was unavoidable, discretion no more speaks against the constitutionality of the criminal justice system or of any of its penalties now than it did when the Constitution was written—unless something has evolved since, to make unavoidable discretion, tolerable before, intolerable now, at least for the death penalty. I know of no such evolution; and I would think it was up to the legislative branch of government to register it had it occurred.

The Constitution, though it enjoins us to minimize capriciousness, does not enjoin a standard of unattainable perfection or exclude penalties because that standard has not been attained.[7] Actually, modern legislative trends hitherto have favored enlargement of discretion in the judicial process. I have always thought that enlargement to be excessive, immoral, irrational, and possibly unconstitutional—even when not abused for purposes of discrimination. Yet, though we should not enlarge it *praeter necessitatem* [beyond necessity], some discretion is unavoidable and even desirable, and no reason for giving up any punishment.

Avoidable Capriciousness. Capriciousness should be prevented by abolishing penalties capriciously distributed only in one case: when it is so un-

---

[6] I am referring throughout to discrimination among those already convicted of capital crimes. That discrimination can be tested. However, the fact that a higher proportion of blacks, or poor people, than of whites, or rich people, are found guilty of capital crimes does not *ipso facto* indicate discrimination, any more than does the fact that a comparatively high proportion of blacks or poor people become professional baseball players or boxers.

[7] Although this is the burden of Charles Black's *Capital Punishment: The Inevitability of Caprice and Mistake* (Norton, 1974). *Codex ipsus loquitur* [the book speaks for itself].

avoidable and so excessive that penalties are randomly distributed between the guilty and the innocent. When that is not the case, the abuses of discretion which lead to discrimination against particular groups of defendants or convicts certainly require correction, but not abolition of the penalty abused my maldistribution.

II. Preliminary Moral Issues

Justice and Equality. Regardless of constitutional interpretation, the morality and legitimacy of the abolitionist argument from capriciousness, or discretion, or discrimination, would be more persuasive if it were alleged that those selectively executed are not guilty. But the argument merely maintains that some other guilty but more favored persons, or groups, escape the death penalty. This is hardly sufficient for letting anyone else found guilty escape the penalty. On the contrary, that some guilty persons or groups elude it argues for extending the death penalty to them. Surely "due process of law" is meant to do justice; and "the equal protection of the law" is meant to extend justice equally to all. Nor do I read the Constitution to command us to prefer equality to justice. When we clamor for "equal justice for all" it is justice which is to be equalized and extended, and which therefore is the prior desideratum, not to be forsaken and replaced by equality but rather to be extended.

Justice requires punishing the guilty—as many of the guilty as possible, even if only some can be punished—and sparing the innocent—as many of the innocent as possible, even if not all are spared. Morally, justice must always be preferred to equality. It would surely be wrong to treat everybody with equal injustice in preference to meting out justice at least to some. Justice then cannot ever permit sparing some guilty persons, or punishing some innocent ones, for the sake of equality—because others have been unjustly spared or punished. In practice, penalties never could be applied if we insisted that they cannot be inflicted on any guilty person unless we can make sure that they are equally applied to all other guilty persons. Anyone familiar with law enforcement knows that punishments can be inflicted only on an unavoidably capricious, at best a random, selection of the guilty. I see no more merit in the attempt to persuade the courts to let all capital-crime defendants go free of capital punishment because some have wrongly escaped it than I see in an attempt to persuade the courts to let all burglars go because some have wrongly escaped imprisonment.

Although it hardly warrants serious discussion, the argument from capriciousness looms large in briefs and decisions because for the last seventy years courts have tried—unproductively—to prevent errors of procedure, or of evidence collection, or of decision-making, by the paradoxical method of letting defendants go free as a punishment, or warning, or deterrent, to errant law enforcers. The strategy admittedly never has prevented the errors it was designed to prevent—although it has released countless guilty persons. But however ineffective it be, the strategy had a rational purpose. The rationality, on the other hand, of arguing that a penalty must be abolished because of allegations that some guilty persons escape it, is hard to fathom—even though the argument was accepted by some Justices of the Supreme Court.

The Essential Moral Question. Is the death penalty morally just and/or useful? This is the essential moral, as distinguished from constitutional, question. Discrimination is irrelevant to this moral question. If the death penalty were distributed quite equally and uncapriciously and with super-human perfection to all the guilty, but was morally unjust, it would remain unjust in each case. Contrariwise, if the death penalty is morally just, how-ever discriminatorily applied to only some of the guilty, it does remain just in each case in which it is applied. Thus, if it were applied exclusively to guilty males, and never to guilty females, the death penalty, though unequally applied, would remain just. For justice consists in punishing the guilty and sparing the innocent, and its equal extension, though desirable, is not part of it. It is part of equality, not of justice (or injustice), which is what equality equalizes. The same consideration would apply if some benefit were distributed only to males but not equally to deserving females. The inequality would not argue against the benefit, or against distribution to deserving males, but rather for distribution to equally deserving females. Analogously, the nondistribution of the death penalty to guilty females would argue for applying it to them as well, and not against applying it to guilty males.

The utilitarian (political) effects of unequal justice may well be detri-mental to the social fabric because they outrage our passion for equality, particularly for equality before the law. Unequal justice is also morally repellent. Nonetheless unequal justice is justice still. What is repellent is the incompleteness, the inequality, not the justice. The guilty do not be-come innocent or less deserving of punishment because others escaped it. Nor does any innocent deserve punishment because others suffer it. Justice remains just, however unequal, while injustice remains unjust, however equal. However much each is desired, justice and equality are not identi-cal. Equality before the law should be extended and enforced, then—but not at the expense of justice.

Maldistribution Among the Guilty: A Sham Argument. Capriciousness, at any rate, is used as a sham argument against capital punishment by all abolitionists I have ever known. They would oppose the death penalty if it could be meted out without any discretion whatsoever. They would oppose the death penalty in a homogeneous country without racial discrim-ination. And they would oppose the death penalty if the incomes of those executed and of those spared were the same. Abolitionists oppose the death penalty, not its possible maldistribution. They should have the courage of their convictions.

Maldistribution Between the Guilty and the Innocent: Another Sham Argument. What about persons executed in error? The objection here is not that some of the guilty get away, but that some of the innocent do not —a matter far more serious than discrimination among the guilty. Yet, when urged by abolitionists, this too is a sham argument, as are all distributional arguments. For abolitionists are opposed to the death penalty for the guilty as much as for the innocent. Hence, the question of guilt, if at all relevant to their position, cannot be decisive for them. Guilt is decisive only to those who urge the death penalty for the guilty. They must worry about distribution—part of the justice they seek.

Miscarriages of Justice. The execution of innocents believed guilty is a miscarriage of justice which must be opposed whenever detected. But such miscarriages of justice do not warrant abolition of the death penalty. Unless the moral drawbacks of an activity or practice, which include the possible death of innocent bystanders, outweigh the moral advantages, which include the innocent lives that might be saved by it, the activity is warranted. Most human activities—construction, manufacturing, automobile and air traffic, sports, not to speak of wars and revolutions—cause the death of some innocent bystanders. Nevertheless, if the advantages sufficiently outweigh the disadvantages, human activities, including those of the penal system with all its punishments, are morally justified. Consider now the advantages in question.

III. Deterrence

New Evidence. Is there evidence for the usefulness of the death penalty in securing the life of the citizens? Researchers in the past found no statistical evidence for the effects sought: i.e., marginal deterrent effects, deterrent effects over and above those of alternative sanctions. However, in the last few years new and more sophisticated research has led, for instance, Professor Isaac Ehrlich to conclude that over the period 1933–1969, "an additional execution per year . . . may have resulted on the average in seven or eight fewer murders." [8] Other investigators have confirmed Ehrlich's tentative results. Not surprisingly, refutations have been attempted, and Professor Ehrlich has answered them. He has also published a new cross-sectional analysis of the data which confirms the conclusions of his original

[8] "The Deterrent Effect of Capital Punishment: A Question of Life and Death." *American Economic Review*, June 1975. In the period studied capital punishment was already infrequent and uncertain. Its deterrent effect might be greater when more frequently imposed for capital crimes, so that a prospective offender would feel more certain of it.

(time-series) study.[9] The matter will remain controversial for some time,[10] but two tentative conclusions can be drawn with some confidence by now. First, Ehrlich has shown that previous investigations, which did not find deterrent effects of the death penalty, suffer from fatal defects. Second, there is now some likelihood—much more than hitherto—of demonstrating marginal deterrent effects statistically.

The Choice. Thus, with respect to deterrence, we must choose 1) to trade the certain shortening of the life of a convicted murderer for the survival of between seven and eight innocent victims whose future murder by others may be less likely if the convicted murderer is executed. Or 2) to trade the certain lengthening of the life of a convicted murderer for the possible loss of the lives of between seven and eight innocent victims, who may be more likely to be murdered by others because of our failure to execute the convicted murderer.[11]

If we were certain that executions have a zero marginal effect, they could not be justified in deterrent terms. But even the pre-Ehrlich investigations never did demonstrate this. They merely found that an above-zero effect cannot be demonstrated statistically. While we do not know at present the degree of confidence with which we can assign an above-zero marginal deterrent effect to executions, we can be more confident than in the past. It seems morally indefensible to let convicted murderers survive at the probable—even at the merely possible—expense of the lives of innocent victims who might have been spared had the murderers been executed.

Non-deterrence as a Sham Argument. Most of the studies purporting to show that capital punishment produces no added deterrence, or that it cannot be shown to do so, were made by abolitionists, such as Professor Thorsten Sellin. They were used to show the futility of the death penalty. Relying on their intuition as well as on these studies, many abolitionists still are convinced that the death penalty is no more deterrent than life imprisonment. And they sincerely believe that the failure of capital pun-

---

[9] See *Journal of Legal Studies,* January 1977; *Journal of Political Economy,* June 1977; and (this is the cross-sectional analysis) *American Economic Review,* June 1977.

[10] *Per contra* see Brian Forst in *Minnesota Law Review,* May 1977, and *Deterrence and Incapacitation* (National Academy of Sciences, Washington, D.C., 1978). By now statistical analyses of the effects of the death penalty have become a veritable cottage industry. This has happened since Ehrlich found deterrent effects. No one much bothered when Thorsten Sellin found none. Still, it is too early for more than tentative conclusions. The two papers mentioned above are replied to, more than adequately in my view, in Isaac Ehrlich's "Fear of Deterrence," *Journal of Legal Studies,* June 1977.

[11] I thought that prudence as well as morality commanded us to choose the first alternative even when I believed that the degree of probability and the extent of deterrent effects might remain unknown. (See my "On Deterrence and the Death Penalty," *Journal of Criminal Law, Criminology, and Police Science,* June 1969.) That probability is more likely to become known now and to be greater than was apparent a few years ago.

ishment to produce additional deterrence argues for abolishing it. However, the more passionate and committed abolitionists use the asserted ineffectiveness of the death penalty as a deterrent as a sham argument—just as they use alleged capriciousness and maldistribution in application. They use the argument for debating purposes—but actually would abolish the death penalty even if it were an effective deterrent, just as they would abolish the death penalty if it were neither discriminatorily nor otherwise maldistributed.

Professors Charles Black (Yale Law School) and Hugo Adam Bedau (Tufts, Philosophy) are both well known for their public commitment to abolition of the death penalty, attested to by numerous writings. At a symposium held on October 15, 1977 at the Arizona State University at Tempe, Arizona, they were asked to entertain the hypothesis—whether or not contrary to fact—that the death penalty is strongly deterrent over and above alternative penalties: Would they favor abolition in the face of conclusive proof of a strong deterrent effect over and above that of alternative penalties? Both gentlemen answered affirmatively. They were asked whether they would still abolish the death penalty if they knew that abolition (and replacement by life imprisonment) would increase the homicide rate by 10 per cent, 20 per cent, 50 per cent, 100 per cent, or 1,000 per cent. Both gentlemen continued to answer affirmatively.

I am forced to conclude that Professors Black and Bedau think the lives of convicted murderers (however small their number) are more worth preserving than the lives of an indefinite number of innocent victims (however great their number). Or, the principle of abolition is more important to them than the lives of any number of innocent murder victims who would be spared if convicted murderers were executed.

I have had occasion subsequently to ask former Attorney General Ramsey Clark the same questions; he answered as Professors Black and Bedau did, stressing that nothing could persuade him to favor the death penalty—however deterrent it might be. (Mr. Clark has kindly permitted me to quote his view here.)

Now, Professors Black and Bedau and Mr. Clark do *not* believe that the death penalty adds deterrence. They do not believe therefore—regardless of the evidence—that abolition would cause an increase in the homicide rate. But the question they were asked, and which—after some dodging—they answered forthrightly, had nothing to do with the acceptance or rejection of the deterrent effect of the death penalty. It was a hypothetical question: If it were deterrent, would you still abolish the death penalty? Would you still abolish it if it were deterrent, so that abolition would lead to a quantum jump in the murder rate? They answered affirmatively.

These totally committed abolitionists, then, are not interested in deterrence. They claim that the death penalty does not add to deterrence only as a sham argument. Actually, whether or not the death penalty deters is, to them, irrelevant. The intransigence of these committed humanitarians is puzzling as well as inhumane. Passionate ideological commitments have been known to have such effects. These otherwise kind and occasionally reasonable persons do not want to see murderers executed ever—however many innocent lives can be saved thereby. *Fiat injustitia, pereat humanitas.*

Experiments? In principle one could experiment to test the deterrent effect of capital punishment. The most direct way would be to legislate the death penalty for certain kinds of murder if committed on weekdays, but never on Sunday. Or, on Monday, Wednesday, and Friday, and not on other days; on other days, life imprisonment would be the maximum sentence. (The days could be changed around every few years to avoid possible bias.) I am convinced there will be fewer murders on death-penalty than on life-imprisonment days. Unfortunately the experiment faces formidable obstacles.[12]

The Burden of Proof of Usefulness. Let me add a common-sense remark. Our penal system rests on the proposition that more severe penalties are more deterrent than less severe penalties. We assume, rightly, I believe, that a $5 fine deters rape less than a $500 fine, and that the threat of five years in prison will deter more than either fine.[13] This assumption of the penal system rests on the common experience that, once aware of them, people learn to avoid natural dangers the more likely these are to be injurious and the more severe the likely injuries. Else the survival of the human race would be hard to explain. People endowed with ordinary common sense (a class that includes a modest but significant number of sociologists) have found no reason why behavior with respect to legal dangers should differ from behavior with respect to natural dangers. Indeed, it doesn't. Hence, all legal systems proportion threatened penalties to the gravity of crimes, both to do justice and to achieve deterrence in proportion to that gravity.

But if, *ceteris paribus*, the more severe the penalty the greater the deterrent effect, then the most severe available penalty—the death penalty—would have the greatest deterrent effect. Arguments to the contrary assume either that capital crimes never are deterrable (sometimes merely because not all capital crimes have been deterred), or that, beyond life imprison-

[12] Though it would isolate deterrent effects of the punishment from incapacitating effects, and also from the effect of Durkheimian "normative validation" when it does not depend on threats. Still, it is not acceptable to our sense of justice that people guilty of the same crime would deliberately get different punishments and that the difference would be made to depend deliberately on a factor irrelevant to the nature of the crime or of the criminal.

[13] As indicated before, demonstrations are not available for the exact addition to deterrence of each added degree of severity in various circumstances, and with respect to various acts. We have coasted so far on a sea of plausible assumptions. (It is not contended, of course, that the degree of severity alone determines deterrent effects. Other factors may reinforce or offset the effect of severity, be it on the motivational [incentive] side, or as added costs and risks.)

ment, the deterrent effect of added severity is necessarily zero. Perhaps. But the burden of proof must be borne by those who presume to have located the point of zero marginal returns before the death penalty.

The Threat of Death Needed in Special Circumstances. Another common-sense observation. Without the death penalty, we necessarily confer immunity on just those persons most likely to be in need of deterrent threats: thus, prisoners serving life sentences can kill fellow prisoners or guards with impunity. Prison wardens are unlikely to be able to prevent violence in prisons as long as they give humane treatment to inmates and have no serious threats of additional punishment available for the murderers among them who are already serving life sentences. I cannot see the moral or utilitarian reasons for giving permanent immunity to homicidal life prisoners, thereby endangering the other prisoners and the guards, in effect preferring the life prisoners to their victims who *could* be punished if they murdered.

Outside prison an offender who expects a life sentence for his offense may murder his victim, or witnesses, or the arresting officer, to improve his chances of escaping. He could not be threatened with an additional penalty for his additional crime—an open invitation. Only the death penalty could deter in such cases.[14] If there is but a possibility that it will, we should retain it. But I believe there is a *probability* that the threat of the death penalty will deter.

Reserved for the Worst Crimes. However, effective deterrence requires that the threat of the ultimate penalty be reserved for the worst crime from which the offender may be deterred by that threat. Hence, the extreme punishment should not be prescribed when the offender, because already threatened by it, might feel he can add further crimes with impunity. Thus, rape, or kidnapping, should not incur the death penalty, while killing the victim of either crime should.[15] (The death penalty for rape may actually function as an incentive to murder the victim/witness.)

---

[14] Particularly since he, unlike the person already in custody, may have much to gain from his additional crime (see Footnote 18).

[15] The Supreme Court has decided that capital punishment for rape (at least of adults) is "cruel and unusual" (*Coker v. Georgia*, 1977). For the reasons stated in the text, I welcome the decision—but not the justification given by the Supreme Court. The penalty may indeed be as excessive as the court feels it is, but not in the constitutional sense of being irrationally or extravagantly so, and thus contrary to the Eighth Amendment. The seriousness of the crime of rape and the appropriateness of the death penalty for it are matters for political rather than judicial institutions to decide. I should vote against the death penalty for rape—and not only for the reasons stated in the text above; but the Court should have left the matter to the vote of the citizens.

The charge of racially discriminatory application was most often justified when the penalty was inflicted for rape. Yet I doubt that the charge will be dropped, or that the agitation against the death penalty will stop, once it is no longer inflicted for rape. Discrimination never was more than a pretext used by abolitionists.

This may not stop an Eichmann after his first murder; but it will stop most people before. To be sure, an offender not deterred from murdering one victim by the threat of execution is unlikely to be deterred from additional murders by further threats. The range of effective punishments is not infinite; on the contrary, it is necessarily more restricted than the range of possible crimes. Some offenders cannot be deterred by any threat. But most people can be; and most people respond to the size of the threat addressed to them. Since death is the ultimate penalty—the greatest threat available—it must be reserved for the ultimate crime even though it cannot always prevent it.

IV. Some Popular Arguments

Consider now some popular arguments against capital punishment.

Barbarization. According to Beccaria, with the death penalty the "laws which punish homicide . . . themselves commit it," thus giving "an example of barbarity." Those who speak of "legalized murder" use an oxymoronic phrase to echo this allegation. However, punishments—fines, incarcerations, or executions—although often physically identical to the crimes punished, are neither crimes, nor their moral equivalent. The difference between crimes and lawful acts, including punishments, is not physical, but legal: crimes differ from other acts of being unlawful. Driving a stolen car is a crime, though not physically distinguishable from driving a car lawfully owned. Unlawful imprisonment and kidnapping need not differ physically from the lawful arrest and incarceration used to punish unlawful imprisonment and kidnapping. Finally, whether a lawful punishment gives an "example of barbarity" depends on how the moral difference between crime and punishment is perceived. To suggest that its physical quality, *ipso facto,* morally disqualifies the punishment is to assume what is to be shown.

It is quite possible that all displays of violence, criminal or punitive, influence people to engage in unlawful imitations. This seems one good reason not to have public executions. But it does not argue against executions. Objections to displaying on TV the process of violently subduing a resistant offender do not argue against actually subduing him.[16] Arguments against the public display of vivisections, or of the effects of painful medications, do not argue against either. Arguments against the public display of sexual activity do not argue against sexual activity. Arguments against public executions, then, do not argue against executions.[17] The deterrent effect of punishments depends on their being known. But it does not depend on pun-

---

[16] There is a good argument here against unnecessary public displays of violence. (See my "What to Do about TV Violence," *The Alternative,* August/September 1976).

[17] It may be noted that in Beccaria's time executions were regarded as public entertainments. *Tempora mutantur et nos mutamur in illis.* [The times, and we, are changing.]

ishments' being carried out publicly. The threat of imprisonment deters, but incarcerated persons are not on public display.

Crimes of Passion. Abolitionists often maintain that most capital crimes are "acts of passion" which a) could not be restrained by the threat of the death penalty, and b) do not deserve it morally even if other crimes might. It is not clear to me why a crime motivated by, say, sexual passion is morally less deserving of punishment than one motivated by passion for money. Is the sexual passion morally more respectable than others? or more gripping? or, just more popular? Generally, is violence in personal conflicts morally more excusable than violence among people who do not know each other? A precarious case might be made for such a view, but I shall not attempt to make it.

Perhaps it is true, however, that many murders are irrational "acts of passion" which cannot be deterred by the threat of the death penalty. Either for this reason or because "crimes of passion" are throught less blameworthy than other homicides, most "crimes of passion" are not punishable by death now.[18]

But if most murders are irrational acts, it would therefore seem that the traditional threat of the death penalty has succeeded in deterring most rational people, or most people when rational, from committing murder, and that the fear of the penalty continues to deter all but those who are so irrational that they cannot be deterred by any threat. Hardly a reason for abolishing the death penalty. Indeed, that capital crimes are committed mostly by irrational persons and only by some rational ones would suggest that more rational persons might commit these crimes if the penalty were lower. This hardly argues against capital punishment. Else we would have to abolish penalties whenever they succeed in deterring people. Yet abolitionists urge that capital punishment be abolished because capital crimes are most often committed by the irrational—as though deterring the rational is not quite enough.

Samuel Johnson. Finally, some observations on an anecdote reported by Boswell and repeated ever since *ad nauseam.* Dr. Johnson found pickpockets active in a crowd assembled to see one of their number hanged. He concluded that executions do not deter. His conclusion does not follow from his observation.

1. Since the penalty Johnson witnessed was what pickpockets had ex-

---

[18] I have reservations on both these counts, being convinced that many crimes among relatives, friends, and associates are as blameworthy and as deterrable as crimes among strangers. Thus, major heroin dealers in New York are threatened with life imprisonment. In the absence of the death penalty they find it advantageous to have witnesses killed. Such murders surely are not acts of passion in the classical sense, though they occur among associates. They are, in practice, encouraged by the present penal law in New York.

pected all along, they had no reason to reduce their activities. Deterrence is expected to increase (i.e., crime is expected to decrease) only when penalties do. It is unreasonable to expect people who entered a criminal occupation—e.g., that of pickpocket—fully aware of the risks, to be subsequently deterred by those risks if they are not increased. They will not be deterred unless the penalty becomes more severe, or is inflicted more often.

2. At most, a public execution could have had the deterrent effect on pickpockets expected by Dr. Johnson because of its visibility. But visibility may also have had a contrary effect: the spectacle of execution was probably more fascinating to the crowd than other spectacles; it distracted attention from the activities of pickpockets and thereby increased their opportunities more than other spectacles would. Hence, an execution crowd might have been more inviting to pickpockets than other crowds. (As mentioned before, deterrence depends on knowledge, but does not require visibility.)

3. Even when the penalty is greatly increased, let alone when it is unchanged, the deterrent effect of penalties is usually slight with respect to those already engaged in criminal activities.[19] Deterrence is effective in the main by restraining people not as yet committed to a criminal occupation from entering it. This point bears some expansion.

The risk of penalty is the cost of crime offenders expect. When this cost (the penalty multiplied by the risk of suffering it) is high enough, relative to the benefit the crime is expected to yield, the cost will deter a considerable number of people who would have entered a criminal occupation had the cost been lower. When the net benefit is very low, only those who have no other opportunities at all, or are irrationally attracted to it, will want to engage in an illegal activity such as picking pockets. In this respect the effects of the cost of crime are not different from the effects of the cost of automobiles or movie tickets, or from the effects of the cost (effort, risks, and other disadvantages) of any activity relative to its benefits. When (comparative) net benefits decrease because of cost increases, so does the flow of new entrants. But those already in the occupation usually continue. *Habits, law-abiding or criminal, are less influenced by costs than habit formation is.* That is as true for the risk of penalties as for any other cost.

Most deterrence studies disregard the fact that the major effect of the legal threat system is on habit formation rather than on habits formed. It is a long- rather than a short-run effect. By measuring only the short-run effects (on habits already formed) rather than the far more important long-run (habit-forming) effects of the threat system, such studies underrate the effectiveness of the deterrence.

---

[19] The high degree of uncertainty and arbitrariness of penalization in Johnson's time may also have weakened deterrent effects. Witnessing and execution cannot correct this defect.

4. Finally, Dr. Johnson did not actually address the question of the deterrent effect of execution in any respect whatever. To do so he would have had to compare the number of pocket-picking episodes in the crowd assembled to witness the execution with the number of such episodes in a similar crowd assembled for some other purpose. He did not do so, probably because he thought that a deterrent effect occurs only if the crime is altogether eliminated. That is a common misunderstanding. But crime can only be reduced, not eliminated. However harsh the penalties there are always non-deterrables. Many, perhaps most, people can be deterred, but never all.

V. Final Moral Considerations

The Motive of Revenge. One objection to capital punishment is that it gratifies the desire for revenge, regarded as morally unworthy. The Bible has the Lord declare: "Vengeance is mine" (Romans 12:19). He thus legitimized vengeance and reserved it to Himself, probably because it would otherwise be disruptive. But He did not deprecate the desire for vengeance.

Indeed Romans 12:19 barely precedes Romans 13:4, which tells us that the ruler "beareth not the sword in vain: for he is the minister of God, a revenger to execute wrath upon him that doeth evil." It is not unreasonable to interpret Romans 12:19 to suggest that revenge is to be delegated by the injured to the ruler, "the minister of God" who is "to execute wrath." The Bible also enjoins, "the murderer shall surely be put to death" (Numbers 35:16–18), recognizing that the death penalty can be warranted—whatever the motive. Religious tradition certainly suggests no less. However, since religion expects justice and vengeance in the world to come, the faithful may dispense with either in this world, and with any particular penalties— though they seldom have. But a secular state must do justice here and now —it cannot assume that another power, elsewhere, will do justice where its courts did not.

The motives for the death penalty may indeed include vengeance. Vengeance is a compensatory and psychologically reparatory satisfaction for an injured party, group, or society. I do not see wherein it is morally blameworthy. When regulated and controlled by law, vengeance is also socially useful: legal vengeance solidifies social solidarity against lawbreakers and probably is the only alternative to the disruptive private revenge of those who feel harmed. Abolitionists want to promise murderers that what they did to their victims will never be done to them. That promise strikes most people as psychologically incongruous. It is.

At any rate, vengeance is irrelevant to the function of the death penalty. It must be justified independently, by its purpose, whatever the motive. An action, a rule, or a penalty cannot be justified or discredited by the motive for it. No rule should be discarded or regarded as morally wrong (or right) because of the motive of those who support it. Actions, rules, or penalties are justified not by the motives of supporters but by their purpose and by their effectiveness in achieving it without excessively impairing other objectives.[20] Capital punishment is warranted if it achieves its purpose—doing justice and deterring crime—regardless of whether or not it is motivated by vengeful feelings.

Characteristics. Before turning to its purely moral aspects, we must examine some specific characteristics of capital punishment. It is feared above all punishments because 1) it is not merely irreversible, as most other penalties are, but also irrevocable; 2) it hastens an event which, unlike pain, deprivation, or injury, is unique in every life and never has been reported on by anyone. Death is an experience that cannot actually be experienced and that ends all experience. Actually, being dead is no different from not being born—a (non) experience we all had before being born. But death is not so perceived. The process of dying, a quite different matter, is confused with it. In turn, dying is feared mainly because death is anticipated—even though death is feared because confused with dying. At any rate, the fear of death is universal and is often attached to the penalty that hastens it—as though without that penalty death would not come. 3) However, the penalty is feared for another reason as well. When death is imposed as a deliberate punishment by one's fellow men, it signifies a complete severing of human solidarity. The convict is explicitly and dramatically rejected by his fellow humans, found unworthy of their society, of sharing life with them. The rejection exacerbates the natural separation anxiety of those who expect imminent death, the fear of final annihilation. Inchoate as these characteristics are in most minds, the specific deterrent effect of executions depends on them, and the moral justification of the death penalty, above and beyond the deterrent effect, does no less.

Methodological Aside. Hitherto I have relied on logic and fact. Without relinquishing either, I must appeal to plausibility as well, as I turn to questions of morality unalloyed by other issues. For, whatever ancillary service facts and logic can render, what one is persuaded to accept as morally right or wrong depends on what appears to be plausible in the end. Outside the realm of morals one relies on plausibility only in the beginning.

The Value of Life. If there is nothing for the sake of which one may be put to death, can there ever be anything worth risking one's life for? If there is nothing worth dying for, is there any moral value worth living for? Is a life that cannot be transcended by—and given up, or taken, for—anything beyond itself more valuable than one that can be transcended? Can

---

[20] Different motives (the reason why something is done) may generate the same action (what is done), purpose, or intent, just as the same motive may lead to different actions.

it be that existence, life itself, is the highest moral value, never to be given up, or taken, for the sake of anything? And, psychologically, does a social value system in which life itself, however it is lived, becomes the highest of goods enhance the value of human life or cheapen it? I shall content myself here with raising these questions.[21]

Homo Homini Res Sacra. "The life of each man should be sacred to each other man," the ancients tell us. They unflinchingly executed murderers.[22] They realized it is not enough to proclaim the sacredness and inviolability of human life. It must be secured as well, by threatening with the loss of their own life those who violate what has been proclaimed as inviolable—the right of innocents to live. Else the inviolability of human life is neither credibly proclaimed nor actually protected. No society can profess that the lives of its members are secure if those who did not allow innocent others to continue living are themselves allowed to continue living—at the expense of the community. To punish a murderer by incarcerating him as one does a pickpocket cannot but cheapen human life. Murder differs in quality from other crimes and deserves, therefore, a punishment that differs in quality from other punishments. There is a discontinuity. It should be underlined, not blurred.

If it were shown that no punishment is more deterrent than a trivial fine, capital punishment for murder would remain just, even if not useful. For murder is not a trifling offense. Punishment must be proportioned to the gravity of the crime, if only to denounce it and to vindicate the importance of the norm violated. Wherefore all penal systems proportion punishments to crimes. The worse the crime the higher the penalty deserved. Why not then the highest penalty—death—for the worst crime—wanton murder? Those rejecting the death penalty have the burden of showing that no crime ever deserves capital punishment[23]—a burden which they have not so far been willing to bear.

Abolitionists insist that we all have an imprescriptible right to live to our natural term: if the innocent victim had a right to live, so does the murderer. That takes egalitarianism too far for my taste. The crime sets victim and murderer apart; if the vicitm did, the murderer does not deserve to live. If innocents are to be secure in their lives murderers cannot be. The thought

[21] Insofar as these questions are psychological, empirical evidence would not be irrelevant. But it is likely to be evaluated in terms depending on moral views.

[22] Not always. On the disastrous consequences of periodic failure to do so, Sir Henry Maine waxes eloquent with sorrow in his *Ancient Law* (pp. 408–9).

[23] One may argue that some crimes deserve more than execution and that the above reasoning would justify punitive torture as well. Perhaps. But torture, unlike death, is generally rejected. Therefore penalties have been reduced to a few kinds—fines, confinement, and execution. The issue is academic because, unlike the death penalty, torture has become repulsive to us. (Some reasons for this public revulsion are listed in Chapter 17 of my *Punishing Criminals*, Basic Books, 1975.) As was noted above (p. 404) the range of punishments is bound to be more limited than the range of crimes. We do not accept some punishments, however much deserved they may be.

that murderers are to be given as much right to live as their victims oppresses me. So does the thought that a Stalin, a Hitler, an Idi Amin should have as much right to live as their victims did.

Failure of Nerve. Never to execute a wrongdoer, regardless of how depraved his acts, is to proclaim that no act can be so irredeemably vicious as to deserve death—that no human being can be wicked enough to be deprived of life. Who actually can believe that? I find it easier to believe that those who affect such a view suffer from a failure of nerve. They do not think themselves—and therefore anyone else—competent to decide questions of life and death. Aware of human frailty, they shudder at the gravity of the decision and refuse to make it. The irrevocability of a verdict of death is contrary to the modern spirit that likes to pretend that nothing ever is definitive, that everything is open-ended, that doubts must always be entertained and revisions must always remain possible. Such an attitude may be helpful to the reflections of inquiring philosophers and scientists; but it is not proper for courts. They must make final judgments beyond a reasonable doubt. They must decide. They can evade decisions on life and death only by giving up their paramount duties: to do justice, to secure the lives of the citizens, and to vindicate the norms society holds inviolable.

One may object that the death penalty either cannot actually achieve the vindication of violated norms, or is not needed for it. If so, failure to inflict death on the criminal does not belittle the crime, or imply that the life of the criminal is of greater importance than the moral value he violated or the harm he did to his victim. But it is not so. In all societies the degree of social disapproval of wicked acts is expressed in the degree of punishment threatened.[24] Thus, punishments both proclaim and enforce social values according to the importance given to them. There is no other way for society to affirm its values. There is no other effective way of denouncing socially disapproved acts. To refuse to punish any crime with death is to suggest that the negative value of a crime can never exceed the positive value of the life of the person who committed it. I find that proposition quite implausible.

[24] Social approval is usually not unanimous, and the system of rewards reflects it less.

9
Social and
Economic Justice

John Rawls's *A Theory of Justice* has already acquired a reputation in the less than a decade since its appearance and is regarded as a book that will be a classic in its field. His "Justice as Fairness" preceded it and is the most famous of his papers. "Justice as Reciprocity" was circulated for some time before its publication in the same year as the book, and is reprinted here. Rawls sees justice as a virtue of social institutions or, as he calls them sometimes, practices. It is not identical with fairness. Justice concerns practices that people enter involuntarily; fairness, voluntary ones. Justice would apply to how taxes are administered or military service when one is drafted. But what justice and fairness share is the idea of reciprocity. Rawls sets forth two basic principles of justice: First, everyone participating in or affected by an institution should have as much liberty as is compatible with a maximum of liberty to everyone else. Second (the "difference" principle), inequalities are justifiable only if they work to the advantage of all and that everyone shall have access to participation in the offices and the like involved. He tries to derive these two principles from people's mutual self-interest and a community of needs and abilities. Rawls says that, all other considerations being equal, these are the principles people would voluntarily choose to live under. "All other things being equal" would be realized if people were divested of a knowledge of their own peculiar advantages and disadvantages, and a knowledge of their own strengths and weaknesses in relation to their fellow citizens; otherwise, self-interest would lead each person to propose rules that would favor him or her.

This "consent of the governed" is a return to some of the strengths of earlier "Social Contract" theories of society and government with a stress on rights that are not simply granted by rulers or dependent on social expedience and revocable. (See Hobbes in Chapter Three for one form of Social Contract theory). Rawls sees the superiority of his position over utilitarianism (see Bentham and Mill in Chapter Five) as illustrated by being able to show why slavery, for instance, is always wrong. Those utilitarians who tried to show why were much less successful in condemning it on their principles than he is on his, he claims.

Joel Feinberg discusses distributive justice in the modern context of economics, and asks what could justify differences of wealth or income among people in the United States, where a few have a lot and many have little. As most of us, he rejects sex, race, intelligence, or social position as justifications for the differences that may exist in income. He considers five other qualities as a basis for distribution: equality, need, merit, effort, and contribution to society. Feinberg concludes that equality, contribution, and effort should carry more weight than need as principles of distribution. Beyond the point at which basic economic needs are met, nonequalitarian principles of distribution come more into their own.

JUSTICE AS RECIPROCITY *

JOHN RAWLS

I

It might seem at first sight that the concepts of justice and fairness are the same, and that there is no reason to distinguish between them. To be sure, there may be occasions in ordinary speech when the phrases expressing these notions are not readily interchangeable, but it may appear that this is a matter of style and not a sign of important conceptual differences. I think that this impression is mistaken, yet there is, at the same time, some foundation for it. Justice and fairness are, indeed, different concepts, but they share a fundamental element in common, which I shall call the concept of reciprocity. They represent this concept as applied to two distinct cases: very roughly, justice to a practice in which there is no option whether to engage in it or not, and one must play; fairness to a practice in which there is such an option, and one may decline the invitation. In this paper I shall present an analytic construction of the concept of justice from this point of view, and I shall refer to this analysis as the analysis of justice as reciprocity.

Throughout I consider justice as a virtue of social institutions only, or of

* From John Stuart Mill: UTILITARIANISM WITH CRITICAL ESSAYS, ed. Samuel Gorovitz, copyright © 1971 by the Bobbs-Merrill Co., Inc. Reprinted with permission.

what I have called practices.[1] Justice as a virtue of particular actions or of persons comes in at but one place, where I discuss the prima facie duty of fair play (sec. 4). Further, the concept of justice is to be understood in its customary way as representing but one of the many virtues of social institutions; for these institutions may be antiquated, inefficient, or degrading, or any number of other things, without being unjust. Justice is not to be confused with an all-inclusive vision of a good society, or thought of as identical with the concept of right. It is only one part of any such conception, and it is but one species of right. I shall focus attention, then, on the usual sense of justice in which it means essentially the elimination of arbitrary distinctions and the establishment within the structure of a practice of a proper share, balance, or equilibrium between competing claims. The principles of justice serve to specify the application of "arbitrary" and "proper," and they do this by formulating restrictions as to how practices may define positions and offices, and assign thereto powers and liabilities, rights and duties. While the definition of the sense of justice is sufficient to distinguish justice as a virtue of institutions from other such virtues as efficiency and humanity, it does not provide a complete conception of justice. For this the associated principles are needed. The major problem in the analysis of the concept of justice is how these principles are derived and connected with this moral concept, and what is their logical basis; and further, what principles, if any, have a special place and may properly be called the principles of justice? The argument is designed to lay the groundwork for answering these questions.

I shall proceed in the following way. I section 2 I formulate a conception of justice by stating and commenting upon the two principles associated with it. While it is possible to argue that a case can be made for calling these principles *the* principles of justice, there is, for the moment, no need to regard them in this way. It is sufficient that they are typical of a family of principles which are normally associated with the concept of justice in the sense that a declaration that an institution is unjust would normally be supported, and would normally be expected to be supported, by reference to principles in this family. I am assuming, then, that an intuitive sense of the principles comprising this family is part of one's everyday understanding of the notion of justice. The way in which the principles of this family resemble one another, and the manner in which they are associated with the concept of justice, is shown by the background against which they may be thought to arise. How this is so the subsequent argument is designed to make clear.

---

[1] I use the word "practice" throughout as a sort of technical term meaning any form of activity specified by a system of rules which defines offices and roles, rights and duties, penalties and defenses, and so on, and which gives the activity its structure. As examples one may think of games and rituals, trials and parliaments, markets and systems of property.

In section 3 I attempt to demonstrate how the two principles of section 2, which are typical of those associated with the concept of justice, can be viewed as those principles which mutually self-interested and rational persons, when similarly situated and when required to make a firm commitment in advance, would acknowledge as restrictions governing the assignment of rights and duties in their common practices, and would thereby accept as limiting their rights against one another. The principles of justice are those required once the constraints of having a morality are applied to what can be mutually acknowledged on those occasions when questions of justice arise. One can say: The principles normally associated with the concept of justice are generated by applying these constraints to persons as situated on these occasions. In this fact the principles of justice find their philosophical derivation as part of a moral concept; and the manner in which they are associated with and complete the sense of justice is explained.

Sections 2 and 3 contain the main elements of the argument. In section 4 I have included a number of supplementary remarks to eliminate certain misunderstandings and to place the analysis of sections 2 and 3 in its proper perspective in relation to various other views to which it is in some ways related; and in section 5 the concept of reciprocity as the common element in the concepts of justice and fairness is isolated and discussed together with the prima facie duty of fair play. With these sections the main part of the analytic construction is completed.

In order, however, to bring out the special force of the analysis of justice as reciprocity, I shall argue in sections 6 and 7 that it is this aspect of justice for which utilitarianism, in its classical form as represented by Bentham and Sidgwick, is unable to account; but that this aspect is expressed, and allowed for, even if in a misleading way, by the idea of the social contract. There is, indeed, irony in this conclusion; for utilitarians attacked the notion of the social contract not only as a historical fiction, but as a superfluous hypothesis.[2] They thought that utility alone provides sufficient grounds for all social obligations, and that it is in any case the real basis of contractual obligations. But this is not so, I hope to show, unless one's conception of social utility embodies within it restrictions the basis of which can only be understood if one makes reference to those aspects of contractarian thought which express the concept of justice as reciprocity: namely, that persons must be regarded as possessing an original and equal liberty, and their common practices are unjust (or alternatively, unfair, depending on the options allowed) unless they accord with principles which persons so circumstanced and related could be reasonably expected to acknowledge and freely accept before one another. I hope that the comparison with classical utilitarianism will serve to bring out the distinctive features of the conception of justice as

[2] See Hume *Of the Original Contract* (1748), and Bentham *A Fragment of Government* (1776), ch. 1, pars. 36–48.

reciprocity, and thereby give substance and content to what is, I am afraid, a somewhat formal and abstract discussion.

II

The conception of justice which I want to consider as two principles associated with it. Both of them, and so the conception itself, are extremely familiar; and, indeed, this is as it should be, since one would hope eventually to make a case for regarding them as the principles of justice. It is unlikely that novel principles could be candidates for this position. It may be possible, however, by using the concept of reciprocity as a framework, to assemble these principles against a different background and to look at them in a new way. I shall now state them and then provide a brief commentary to clarify their meaning.

First, each person participating in a practice, or affected by it, has an equal right to the most extensive liberty compatible with a like liberty for all; and second, inequalities are arbitrary unless it is reasonable to expect that they will work out to everyone's advantage, and provided that the positions and offices to which they attach, or from which they may be gained, are open to all. These principles express justice as a complex of three ideas: liberty, equality, and reward for services contributing to the common good.[3]

A word about the term "person." This expression is to be construed variously depending on the circumstances. On some occasions it will mean human individuals, but in others it may refer to nations, provinces, business firms, churches, teams, and so on. The principles of justice apply to conflicting claims made by persons of all of these separate kinds. There is, perhaps, a certain logical priority to the case of human individuals: it may be possible to analyze the actions of so-called artificial persons as logical con-

---

[3] These principles are, of course, well known in one form or another. They are commonly appealed to in daily life to support judgments regarding social arrangements and they appear in many analyses of justice even where the writers differ widely on other matters. Thus if the principle of equal liberty is commonly associated with Kant (see *The Philosophy of Law*, W. Hastie, trans. [Edinburgh, 1887], pp. 56f), it can also be found in works so different as J. S. Mill's *On Liberty* (1859) and Herbert Spencer's *Justice* (pt. IV of *Principles of Ethics*) (London, 1891). Recently H. L. A. Hart has argued for something like it in his paper "Are There Any Natural Rights?" *Philosophical Review*, 64 (1955), 175–191. The injustice of inequalities which are not won in return for a contribution to the common advantage is, of course, a frequent topic in political writings of all sorts. If the conception of justice developed here is distinctive at all, it is only in selecting these two principles in this form; but for another similar analysis, see W. D. Lamont, *The Principles of Moral Judgment;* (Oxford: Clarendon Press, 1946), ch. V. Moreover, the essential elements could, I think, be found in St. Thomas Aquinas and other medieval writers, even though they failed to draw out the implicit equalitarianism of their premises. See Ewart Lewis *Medieval Political Ideas* (London: Routledge and Paul, 1954), vol. I, the introduction to ch. IV, especially pp. 220f. Obviously the important thing is not simply the announcement of these principles, but their interpretation and application, and the way they are related to one's conception of justice as a whole.

structions of the actions of human persons, and it is plausible to maintain that the world of institutions is derived solely from the benefits they bring to human individuals. Nevertheless an analysis of justice should not begin by making either of these assumptions, or by restricting itself to the case of human persons; and it can gain considerably from not doing so. As I shall use the term "person," then, it will be ambiguous in the manner indicated.

The first principle holds, of course, only if other things are equal: that is, while there must always be a justification for departing from the initial position of equal liberty (liberty being defined by reference to the pattern of rights and duties, powers and liabilities, established by a practice), and the burden of proof is placed on him who would depart from it, nevertheless, there can be, and often there is, a justification for doing so. Now, that similar particular cases, as defined by a practice, should be treated similarly as they arise, is part of the very concept of a practice; in accordance with the analysis of justice as regularity, it is involved in the notion of an activity in accordance with rules, and expresses the concept of equality in one of its forms: that is, equality as the impartial and equitable administration and application of the rules whatever they are, which define a practice. The first principle expresses the concept of equality in another form, namely, as applied to the definition and initial specification of the structure of practices themselves. It holds, for example, that there is a presumption against the distinctions and classifications made by legal systems and other practices to the extent that they infringe on the original and equal liberty of the persons participating in them, or affected by them. The second principle defines how this presumption may be rebutted.

It might be argued at this point that justice requires only that there be an equal liberty. If, however, a more extensive liberty were possible for all without loss or conflict, then it would be irrational to settle upon a lesser liberty. There is no reason for circumscribing rights unless their exercise would be incompatible, or would render the practice defining them less effective. Where such a limitation of liberty seems to have occurred, there must be some special explanation. It may have arisen from a mistake or misapprehension; or perhaps it persists from a time past when it had a rational basis, but does so no longer. Otherwise, such a limitation would be inexplicable; the acceptance of it would conflict with the premise that the persons engaged in the practice want the things which a more extensive liberty would make possible. Therefore no serious distortion of the concept of justice is likely to follow from associating with it a principle requiring the greatest equal liberty. This association is necessary once it is supposed, as I shall suppose, that the persons engaged in the practices to which the principles of justice apply are rational.

The second principle defines what sorts of inequalities are permissible; it specifies how the presumption laid down by the first principle may be put aside. Now by inequalities it is best to understand not any differences between offices and positions, but differences in the benefits and burdens attached to them either directly or indirectly, such as prestige and wealth, or liability to taxation and compulsory services. Players in a game do not protest against there being different positions, such as that of batter, pitcher, catcher, and the like, nor to there being various privileges and powers specified by the rules. Nor do citizens of a country object to there being the different offices of government such as that of president, senator, governor, judge, and so on, each with its special rights and duties. It is not differences of this kind that are normally thought of as inequalities, but differences in the resulting distribution established by a practice, or made possible by it, of the things men strive to attain or to avoid. Thus they may complain about the pattern of honors and rewards set up by a practice (e.g., the privileges and salaries of government officials) or they may object to the distribution of power and wealth which results from the various ways in which men avail themselves of the opportunities allowed by it (e.g., the concentration of wealth which may develop in a free price system allowing large entrepreneurial or speculative gains).

It should be noted that the second principle holds an inequality is allowed only if there is a reason to believe that the practice with the inequality, or resulting in it, will work for the advantage of *every* person engaging in it. Here it is important to stress that every person must gain from the inequality. Since the principle applies to practices, it implies then that the representative man in every office or position defined by a practice, when he views it as a going concern, must find it reasonable to prefer his condition and prospects with the inequality to what they would be under the practice without it. The principles exclude, therefore, the justification of inequalities on the grounds that the disadvantages of those in one position are outweighed by the greater advantages of those in another position. This rather simple restriction is the main modification I wish to make in the utilitarian principle as usually understood. When coupled with the notion of a practice, it is a restriction of consequence, and one which some utilitarians, notably Hume and Mill, have used in their discussions of justice without realizing apparently its significance, or at least without calling attention to it.[4]

Further, it is also necessary that the various offices to which special bene-

---

[4] It might seem as if J. S. Mill, in paragraph 36 of chapter V of *Utilitarianism,* expressed the utilitarian principle in this form, but in the remaining two paragraphs of the chapter, and elsewhere in the essay, he would appear not to grasp the significance of the change. Hume often emphasizes that every man must benefit. For example, in discussing the utility of general rules, he holds that they are requisite to the "well-being" of every individual; from a stable system of property "every individual person must find himself a gainer in balancing the account. . . ." "Every member of society is sensible of this interest; everyone expresses this sense to his fellows along with the resolution he has taken of squaring his actions by it, on the condition that others will do the same." (*A Treatise of Human Nature,* bk. III, pt. II, sect. II, par. 22.) Since in the discussion of the common good, I draw upon another aspect of Hume's account of justice, the logical importance of general rules, the conception of justice which I set out is perhaps closer to Hume's view than to any other. On the other hand, see footnote 27.

fits or burdens attach are open to all. It may be, for example, to the common advantage, as just defined, to attach special benefits to certain offices. Perhaps by doing so the requisite talent can be attracted to them and encouraged to give its best efforts. But any offices having special benefits must be won in a fair competition in which contestants are judged on their merits. If some offices were not open, those excluded would normally be justified in feeling unjustly treated, even if they benefited from the greater efforts of those who were allowed to compete for them. Moreover, they would be justified in their complaint not only because they were excluded from certain external emoluments of office, but because they were barred from attaining the great intrinsic goods which the skillful and devoted exercise of some offices represents, and so they would be deprived, from the start, of one of the leading ways to achieve a full human life.

Now if one can assume that offices are open, it is necessary only to consider the design and structure of practices themselves and how they jointly, as a system, work together. It will be a mistake to focus attention on the varying relative positions of particular persons, who may be known to us by their proper names, and to require that each such change, as a once and for all transaction viewed in isolation, must be in itself just. It is the practice, or the system of practices, which is to be judged, and judged from a general point of view: unless one is prepared to criticize it from the standpoint of a representative man holding some particular office, one has no complaint against it. Thus, as one watches players in a game and is moved by the changing fortunes of the teams one may be downcast by the final outcome; one may say to oneself that the losing team deserved to win on the basis of its skill, endurance, and pluck under adverse circumstances. But it will not follow from this that one thinks the game itself, as defined by its rules, is unfair. Again, as one observes the course of a free price system over time one witnesses the rise of one particular group of firms and the decline of another. Some entrepreneurs make profits, others have to take losses; and these profits and losses are not always correlated with their foresight and ability, or with their efforts to turn out worthwhile products. The fate of entrepreneurs is often the outcome of chance, or determined by changes in tastes and demand which no one could have foreseen; it is not always, by any means, founded on their deserts. But it does not follow from this that such an economic system is unjust. That the relative positions of particular entrepreneurs should be determined in this way is a consequence of the rules of the capitalist game. If one wishes to challenge it, one must do so, not from the changing relative positions of this or that entrepreneur, in this or that particular turn of fortune, but from the standpoint of the representative entrepreneur and his legitimate expectations in the system as a working institution, also, of course, keeping in mind the relation of this institution to the other practices of society.

Nothing is more natural than for those who suffer from the particular changes taking place in accordance with a practice to resent it as unjust, especially when there is no obvious correlation between these changes and ordinary conceptions of merit. This is as natural as that those who gain from inequities should overlook them, and even in time come to regard them as their due. Yet since the principles apply to the form and structure of practices as such, and not to particular transactions, the conception of justice they express requires one to appraise a practice from a general point of view, and thus from that of a representative man holding the various offices and positions defined by it. One is required to take a reasonably long view, and to ascertain how the practice will work out when regarded as a continuing system. At a later point I shall argue that unless persons are prepared to take up this standpoint in their social criticism, agreement on questions of justice is hardly possible; and that once they are prepared to do so, an argument can be given for taking these principles as the principles of justice.

III

Given these principles one might try to derive them from a priori principles of reason, or claim that they were known by intuition. These are familiar enough steps and, at least in the case of the first principle, might be made with some success. Of all principles of justice that of equality in its several forms is undoubtedly the one most susceptible to a priori argument. But it is obvious that the second principle, while certainly a common one, cannot be claimed as acceptable on these grounds. Indeed, to many persons it will surely seem overly restrictive; to others it may seem too weak. Some will want to hold that there are cases where it is just to balance the gains of some against the losses of others, and that the principle as stated contains an exaggerated bias in the direction of equality; while there are bound to be those to whom it will seem an insufficient basis upon which to found an account of justice. These opinions are certainly of considerable force, and it is only by a study of the background of the principle and by an examination of its intended applications that one can hope to establish its merits. In any case, a priori and intuitive arguments, made at this point, are unconvincing. They are not likely to lead to an understanding of the basis of the principles of justice, not at least as principles of justice: for what one wants to know is the way in which these principles complete the sense of justice, and why they are associated with this moral concept, and not with some other. I wish, therefore, to look at the principles in a different way; I want to bring out how they are generated by imposing the constraints of having a morality upon persons who confront one another on those occasions when questions of justice arise.

In order to do this, it seems simplest to present a conjectural account of the derivation of these principles as follows. Imagine a society of persons amongst whom a certain system of practices is already well established.

Now suppose that by and large they are mutually self-interested; their allegiance to their established practices is normally founded on the prospect of their own advantage. One need not, and indeed ought not, to assume that, in all senses of the term "person," the persons in this society are mutually self-interested. If this characterization holds when the line of division is the family, it is nevertheless likely to be true that members of families are bound by ties of sentiment and affection and willingly acknowledge duties in contradiction to self-interest. Mutual self-interestedness in the relations between families, nations, churches, and the like, is commonly associated with loyalty and devotion on the part of individual members. If this were not so the conflicts between these forms of association would not be pursued with such intensity and would not have such tragic consequences. If Hobbes' description of relations between persons seems unreal as applied to human individuals, it is often true enough of the relations between artificial persons; and these relations may assume their Hobbesian character largely in consequence of that element which that description professedly leaves out, the loyalty and devotion of individuals. Therefore, one can form a more realistic conception of this society if one thinks of it as consisting of mutually self-interested families, or some other association. Taking the term "person" widely from the start prepares one for doing this. It is not necessary to suppose, however, that these persons are mutually self-interested under all circumstances, but only in the usual situations in which they participate in their common practices concerning which the question of justice arises.

Now suppose further that these persons are rational: they know their own interests more or less accurately; they realize that the several ends they pursue may conflict with each other, and they are able to decide what level of attainment of one they are willing to sacrifice for a given level of attainment of another; they are capable of tracing out the likely consequences of adopting one practice rather than another, and of adhering to a course of action once they have decided upon it; they can resist present temptations and the enticements of immediate gain; and the bare knowledge or perception of the difference between their condition and that of others is not, within certain limits and in itself, a source of great dissatisfaction. Only the very last point adds anything to the standard definition of rationality as it appears say in the theory of price; and there is no need to question the propriety of this definition given the purposes for which it is customarily used. But the notion of rationality, if it is to play a part in the analysis of justice should allow, I think, that a rational man will resent or will be dejected by differences of condition between himself and others only where there is an accompanying explanation: that is, if they are thought to derive from injustice, or from some other fault of institutions, or to be the consequence of letting chance work itself out for no useful common purpose. At any rate, I shall include this trait of character in the notion of rationality for the purpose of analyzing the concept of justice. The legitimacy of doing so will, I think, become clear as the analysis proceeds. So if these persons strike us as unpleasantly egoistic in their relations with one another, they are at least free in some degree from the fault of envy.[5]

Finally, assume that these persons have roughly similar needs, interests, and capacities, or needs, interests, and capacities in various ways complementary, so that fruitful cooperation amongst them is possible; and suppose that they are sufficiently equal in power and the instruments thereof to guarantee that in normal circumstances none is able to dominate the others. This condition (as well as the other conditions) may seem excessively vague; but in view of the conception of justice to which the argument leads, there seems to be no reason for making it more exact at this point.[6]

Since these persons are conceived as engaging in their common practices, which are already established, there is no question of our supposing them to come together to deliberate as to how they will set up these practices for the first time. Yet we can imagine that from time to time they discuss with one another whether any of them has a legitimate complaint against their established institutions. This is only natural in any normal society. Now suppose that they have settled on doing this in the following way. They first try to arrive at the principles by which complaints and so practices themselves are to be judged. That is, they do not begin by complaining; they begin instead by establishing the criteria by which a complaint is to be counted legitimate. Their procedure for this is to let each person propose the principles upon which he wishes his complaints to be tried with the understanding that, if acknowledged, the complaints of others will be similarly tried; and moreover, that no complaints will be heard at all until everyone is roughly of one mind as to how complaints are to be judged. Thus while each person has a chance to propose the standards he wishes, these standards must prove acceptable to the others before his charges can be given a hearing. They all understand further that the principles proposed and acknowledged on this occasion are binding on future occasions. So each will be wary of proposing a principle which would give him a peculiar advantage in his present circumstances,

---

[5] There is no need to discuss here this addition to the usual conception of rationality. The reason for it will become clear as the argument proceeds, for it is analogous to, and is connected with, the modification of the utilitarian principle which the argument as a whole is designed to explain and to justify. In the same way that the satisfaction of interests, the representative claims of which violate the principles of justice, is not a reason for having a practice (see below, section 7), unfounded envy, within limits, need not be taken into account. One could, of course, have another reason for this addition, namely, to see what conception of justice results when it is made. This alone would not be without interest.

[6] In this description of the situation of the persons, I have drawn on Hume's account of the circumstances in which justice arises, see *A Treatise of Human Nature,* bk. III, pt. II, sec. II, and *An Enquiry Concerning the Principles of Morals,* sec. III, pt. I. It is, in particular, the scarcity of good things and the lack of mutual benevolence that leads to conflicting claims, and which gives rise to the "cautious, jealous virtue of justice," a phrase from the *Enquiry,* ibid., par. 3.

supposing it to be accepted (which is, perhaps, in most cases unlikely). Each person knows that he will be bound by it in future circumstances the peculiarities of which cannot be known, and which might well be such that the principle is then to his disadvantage. The basic idea in this procedure is that everyone should be required to make in advance a firm commitment to acknowledge certain principles as applying to his own case and such that others also may reasonably be expected to acknowledge them; and that no one be given the opportunity to tailor the canons of a legitimate complaint to fit his own special conditions, and then to discard them when they no longer suit his purpose.[7] Hence each person will propose principles of a general kind which will, to a large degree, gain their sense from the various applications to be made of them, the particular circumstances of these applications being as yet unknown. These principles will express the conditions in accordance with which each person is the least unwilling to have his interests limited in the design of practices, given the competing interests of the others, on the supposition that the interests of others will be limited likewise. The restriction which would so arise might be thought of as those a person would keep in mind if he were designing a practice in which his enemy were to assign him his place.

The elements of this conjectural account can be divided into two main parts so that each part has a definite significance. Thus the character and respective situations of the parties, that is, their rationality and mutual self-interestedness, and their being of roughly similar needs, interests and capacities, and their having needs, interests and capacities in various ways complementary, so that fruitful forms of cooperation are possible, can be taken to represent the typical circumstances in which questions of justice arise. For questions of justice are involved when conflicting claims are made upon the design of a practice and where it is taken for granted that each person will insist, so far as possible, on what he considers his rights. It is typical of cases of justice to involve persons who are pressing on one another their claims, between which a fair balance or equilibrium must be found. So much is expressed by the sense of the concept.

---

[7] Thus everyone is, so far as possible, prevented from acting on the kind of advice which Aristotle summarizes in the *Rhetoric*, k. I, ch. 15. There he describes a number of ways in which a man may argue his case, and which are, he observes, especially characteristic of forensic oratory. For example, if the written law tells against his case, a man must appeal to the universal law and insist on its greater equity and justice; he must argue that the juror's oath "I will give my verdict according to my honest opinion" means that one will not simply follow the letter of the unwritten law. On the other hand, if the law supports his case, he must argue that not to apply the law is as bad as to have no laws at all, or that less harm comes from an occasional mistake than from the growing habit of disobedience; and he must contend that the juror's oath is not meant to make the judges give a verdict contrary to law, but to save them from the guilt of perjury if they do not understand what the law really means. Cr. 1375a25–1372b25. Such tactics are, of course, common in arguments of all kinds; the notion of a considered judgment, and Adam Smith's and Hume's idea of an impartial spectator, is in part derived from the conception of a person so placed that he has no incentive to make these manoeuvers.

On the other hand, the procedure whereby principles are proposed and acknowledged can be taken to represent the constraints of having a morality; it is these constraints which require rational and mutually self-interested persons to act reasonably, in this case, to acknowledge familiar principles of justice. (The condition that the parties be sufficiently equal in power and the instruments thereof to guarantee that in normal circumstances none is able to dominate the others is to make the adoption of such a procedure seem more realistic; but the argument is not affected if we do without this condition, and imagine that the procedure is simply laid down.) Once the procedure is adopted and carried through each person is committed to acknowledge principles as impartially applying to his own conduct and claims as well as to another's, and he is committed moreover to principles which may constitute a constraint, or limitation, upon the pursuit of his own interests. Now a person's having a morality is analogous to having made a firm commitment in advance to acknowledge principles having these consequences for one's own conduct. A man whose moral judgments always coincided with his interests could be suspected of having no morality at all. There are, of course, other aspects to having a morality: the acknowledgment of moral principles must not only show itself in accepting a reference to them as reasons for limiting one's claims, but also in acknowledging the burden of providing a special explanation, or excuse, when one acts contrary to them, or else in showing shame and remorse (although not on purpose!), and (sincerely) indicating a desire to make amends, and so on. These aspects of having a morality and, more particularly, the place of moral feelings such as shame and remorse cannot be considered here. For the present it is sufficient to remark that the procedure of the conjectural account expresses an essential aspect of having a morality: namely, the acknowledgment of principles as impartially applying to one's own claims as well as to others, and the consequent constraint upon the pursuit of one's own interests.[8]

The two parts into which the foregoing account may be divided are intended, then, to represent the kinds of circumstances in which questions of justice arise (as expressed by the sense of the concept of justice) and the constraints which having a morality would impose upon persons so situated. By imposing these constraints on persons in the occasions of justice one can see how certain principles are generated, and one understands why these principles, and not others, come to be associated with the con-

---

[8] The idea that accepting a principle as a moral principle implies that one generally acts on it, failing a special explanation, has been stressed by R. M. Hare, *The Language of Morals* (Oxford: The University Press, 1952). His formulation of it needs to be modified, however, along the lines suggested by P. L. Gardiner, "On Assenting to a Moral Principle," *Proceedings of the Aristotelian Society*, n.s. 55 (1955), 23–44. See also C. K. Grant, "Akrasia and the Criteria of Assent to Practical Principles," *Mind* 65 (1956), 400–407, where the complexity of the criteria for assent is discussed. That having a morality at all involves acknowledging and acting on principles which may be contrary to one's self-interest is mentioned below, see section 5.

cept of justice; for given all the conditions as described in the conjectural account, it would be natural if the two principles of justice were to be jointly acknowledged. Since there is no way for anyone to win special advantages for himself, each would consider it reasonable to acknowledge equality as an initial principle. There is, however, no reason why they should regard this position as final. If there are inequalities which satisfy the conditions of the second principle, the immediate gain which equality would allow can be considered as intelligently invested in view of its future return. If, as is quite likely, these inequalities work as incentives to draw out better efforts, the members of this society may look upon them as concessions to human nature: they, like us, may think that people ideally should want to serve one another. But as they are mutually self-interested, their acceptance of these inequalities is merely the acceptance of the relations in which they actually stand, and a recognition of the motives which lead them to engage in their common practices. Being themselves self-interested, they have no title to complain of one another. And so provided the conditions of the principle are met, there is no reason why they should not allow such inequalities. Indeed, it would be short-sighted of them not to do so, and could result, in most cases, only from their being dejected by the bare knowledge, or perception, that others are better situated. Each person will, however, insist on an advantage to himself, and so on a common advantage, for none is willing to sacrifice anything for the others.[9]

These remarks are not offered as a rigorous proof that persons conceived and situated as the conjectural account supposes, and required to adopt the procedure described, would settle on the two principles of justice stated and commented upon in section 2. For this a much more elaborate and formal argument would have to be given. I shall not undertake a proof in this sense. In a weaker sense, however, the argument may be considered a proof, or as a sketch of a proof, although there still remain certain details to be filled in, and various alternatives to be ruled out. These I shall take up in later lectures. For the moment the essential point is simply that the proposition I seek to establish is a necessary one, or better, it is a kind of theorem: namely, that when mutually self-interested and rational persons confront one another in the typical circumstances of justice, and when they are required by a procedure expressing the constraints of having a morality to jointly acknowledge principles by which their claims on the design of their common practices are to be judged, they will settle upon these two principles as restrictions governing the assignment of rights and duties, and thereby accept them as limiting their rights against one another. It is this theorem which accounts for these principles as principles of justice, and ex-

---

[9] A similar argument is given by F. Y. Edgeworth in "The Pure Theory of Taxation," *Economic Journal* 7 (1897). Reprinted in *Classics in the Theory of Public Finance*, ed. Musgrave and Peacock (New York: St. Martin's, 1958), pp. 120f.

plains how they come to be associated with this moral concept. Moreover it is analogous to theorems about human conduct in other branches of social thought. That is, a simplified situation is described in which rational persons, pursuing certain ends and related to one another in a definite way, are required to act, subject to certain limitations. Then, given this situation, it is shown that they will act in a certain manner. The failure so to act would only mean that one or more of the conditions did not obtain. The proposition we are interested in is not, then, an empirical hypothesis. This is, of course, as it should be; for this proposition is to play a part in an analysis of the concept of justice. Its point is to bring out how the principles associated with the concept derive from its sense, and to show the basis for saying that the principles of justice may be regarded as those principles which arise when the constraints of having a morality are imposed upon persons in typical circumstances of justice.

IV

This conception of justice is, of course, connected with a familiar way of thinking which goes back at least to the Greek Sophists, and which regards the acceptance of the principles of justice as a compromise between persons of roughly equal power who would enforce their will on each other if they could, but who, in view of the equality of forces amongst them and for the sake of their own peace and security, acknowledge certain forms of conduct insofar as prudence seems to require. Justice is thought of as a pact between rational egoists, the stability of which pact is dependent on a balance of power and a similarity of circumstances.[10] While the analytic construction of the two previous sections is connected with this tradition, and with its most recent variant, the theory of games,[11] it differs from

---

[10] Perhaps the best known statement of this conception is that given by Glaucon at the beginning of book II of Plato's *Republic*. Presumably it was, in various forms, a common view among the Sophists; but that Plato gives a fair representation of it is doubtful. See K. R. Popper, *The Open Society and Its Enemies*, rev. ed. (Princeton, N.J.: Princeton University Press, 1950), pp. 112–118. Certainly Plato usually attributes to it a quality of manic egoism which one feels must be an exaggeration; on the other hand, see the Melian Debate in Thucydides, *The Peloponnesian War*, book V, ch. VII, although it is impossible to say to what extent the views expressed there reveal any current philosophical opinion. Also in this tradition are the remarks of Epicurus on justice in *Principal Doctrines*, XXXI–XXXVIII. In modern times elements of the conception appear in a more sophisticated form in Hobbes *The Leviathan* and in Hume *A Treatise of Human Nature*, book III, pt. II, as well as in the writings of the school of natural law such as Pufendorf's *De jure nature et gentium*. Hobbes and Hume are especially instructive. For Hobbes's argument see Howard Warrender's *The Political Philosophy of Hobbes* (Oxford: The University Press, 1957). W. J. Baumol's *Welfare Economics and the Theory of the State* (Cambridge, Mass.: Harvard University Press, 1952), is valuable in showing the wide applicability of Hobbes's fundamental idea (interpreting his natural law as principles of prudence), although in this book it is traced back only to Hume's *Treatise*.

[11] See J. von Neumann and O. Morgenstern, *The Theory of Games and Economic Behavior*, 2nd ed. (Princeton, N.J.: Princeton University Press, 1947). For a comprehensive and not too technical discussion of the developments since, see R. Duncan Luce and

it in several important respects. To forestall misinterpretations, and to help clarify the argument already given, I shall set out some of these differences at this point.

First, I wish to use the previous conjectural account of the derivation of the principles of justice as a way of analyzing the concept. Therefore I do not want to be interpreted as assuming a general theory of human motivation. When it is supposed that the parties are mutually self-interested, and are not willing to have their interests sacrificed to the others, I am referring to their conduct and motives as they are taken for granted in cases where questions of justice ordinarily arise. Justice is the virtue of practices where there are assumed to be competing interests and conflicting claims, and where it is supposed that persons will press their rights against one another. That persons are mutually self-interested in certain situations and for certain purposes, is what gives rise to the question of justice in practices covering those circumstances. Amongst an association of saints, if such a community could really exist, disputes about justice could hardly occur; for they would all work selflessly together for one end, the glory of God as defined by their common religion. Reference to this end would settle every question of right. The justice of practices does not arise until there are several different parties (whether we think of these as individuals, associations, or nations, and so on, makes no difference) who do press their claims on one another and who do regard themselves as representatives of interests which deserve to be considered. These conditions can obtain under the most varied circumstances and from any number of motives. The claims which nations press upon one another have mixed and various interests behind them. The same is true of social and personal conflicts in general. The conjectural account involves, then, no particular theory of human motivation; and it obviously does not imply that persons as human individuals are rational (or irrational) egoists. What it does is simply incorporate into the conception of justice the relations between persons which set the stage for questions of justice. This the conjectural account must do if it is to be a proper analysis. How wide or general these relations are and from what interests and motives they may be brought about on different occasions, are not matters that need to be discussed. They have no direct bearing on the analysis of justice.

Again, in contrast to the various conceptions of the social contract, the several parties do not establish any particular society or practice; nor do they covenant to obey a particular sovereign or to accept a given constitution.[12] They do not, as in the theory of games (in certain respects

---

Howard Raiffa, *Games and Decisions: Introduction and Critical Survey* (New York: John Wiley & Sons, 1957). Chapters VI and XIV discuss the developments most obviously related to the analysis of justice.

[12] For a general survey see Otto von Gierke, *The Development of Political Theory*, B. Freyd, trans. (London, 1939) pt. II, ch. II, and J. W. Gough, *Social Contract*, 2nd. edition (Oxford: The University Press, 1957).

a marvelously sophisticated development of this tradition), decide on individual strategies adjusted to their respective circumstances in the game. What the parties do is to jointly acknowledge certain principles of appraisal applicable to their common practices either as already established or as merely proposed. They accede to standards of judgment, not to a given practice; they do not make any specific agreement, or bargain, or adopt a particular strategy. The subject of their acknowledgment is then very general. It is simply the acknowledgment of certain principles of judgment, fulfilling certain conditions, to be used in criticizing the arrangement of their common affairs. Now, as we have seen, the relations of mutual self-interest between the parties who are similarly circumstanced mirror the condition under which questions of justice arise, and the procedure by which the principles of judgment are proposed and acknowledged reflects the constraints of having a morality. Each aspect, then, of the hypothetical description serves to emphasize a feature of the notion of justice. One could, if one liked, view the principles of justice as the "solution" of this highest order "game" of adopting, subject to the procedure described, principles of argument for all coming particular "games" the peculiarities of which one can in no way foresee. Or one could say the principles of justice represent the just or fair solution of this highest order "bargaining problem." The comparison is no doubt helpful; but it must not obscure the fact that this highest order "game," or "bargaining problem," is of a special sort.[13] Its

---

[13] The difficulty one gets into by a mechanical application of the theory of games to moral philosophy can be brought out by considering among several possible examples, R. B. Braithwaite's study, *Theory of Games as a Tool for the Moral Philosopher* (Cambridge: The University Press, 1955). On the analysis there given, it turns out that the fair division of playing time between Matthew and Luke depends on their preferences, and these in turn are connected with the instruments they wish to play. Since Matthew has a threat advantage over Luke, arising purely from the fact that Matthew, the trumpeter, prefers both of them playing at once to neither of them playing, whereas Luke, the pianist, prefers silence to cacophony, Matthew is allotted 26 evenings of play to Luke's 17. If the situation were reversed, the threat advantage would be with Luke. See pp. 36f. But now we have only to suppose that Matthew is a jazz enthusiast who plays the drums, and Luke a violinist who plays sonatas, in which case it will be fair, on this analysis, for Matthew to play whenever and as often as he likes, assuming, of course, as it is plausible to assume, that he does not care whether Luke plays or not. Certainly something has gone wrong. To each according to his threat advantage is hardly the principle of fairness. What is lacking is the concept of morality, and it must be brought into the conjectural account in some way or other. In the text this is done by the form of the procedure whereby principles are proposed and acknowledged (section 3). If one starts directly with the particular case as known, and if one accepts as given and definitive the preferences and relative positions of the parties, whatever they are, it is impossible to give an analysis of the moral concept of fairness. Braithwaite's use of the theory of games, insofar as it is intended to analyze the concept of fairness, is, I think, mistaken. This is not, of course, to criticize in any way the theory of games as a mathematical theory, to which Braithwaite's book certainly contributes, nor as an analysis of how rational (and amoral) egosists might behave (and so as an analysis of how people sometimes actually do behave). But it is to say that if the theory of games is to be used to analyze the concept of justice, its formal structure must be interpreted in a special and general manner as indicated in the text. Once we do this, though, we are in touch with a much older tradition.

significance is that its various pieces represent aspects of the concept of justice.

Finally, I do not, of course, conceive the several parties as necessarily coming together to establish their common practices for the first time. Some institutions may, to be sure, be set up de nuovo. But the hypothetical scheme has been so framed that it will apply when the full complement of social institutions already exists and represents the result of a long period of development. On the other hand, the account is not merely conjectural. In any society where people reflect upon their institutions (and this must include practically all societies), they will have some idea of what principles would be acknowledged under the conditions described, and there will be occasions when questions of justice are actually discussed in this way. Therefore if their practices do not accord with these principles, or better, if their practices grossly depart from them, there will be a noticeable effect seen in the quality of their social relations. For in this case there will be some recognized situations in which persons are mutually aware that one of them is being forced to accept what the other would concede is unjust, at least as applied to himself. One of them is, then, either claiming a special status for himself, or openly taking advantage of his position. He thus invites the other either to retaliate, when and in whatever way he can, or to acknowledge that he is inferior. But where persons mutually acknowledge the principles upon which their arrangements are founded as just or fair, the situation is necessarily different. For this mutual acknowledgment must show itself in an absence of resentment and in a sense of being fairly or justly treated. The conjectural account displays, then, the elements which determine the way in which participants in a practice will feel and react to one another. In this sense it is not simply a fiction, nor a purely abstract model. Since with due qualifications moral beliefs manifest themselves in conduct, an analysis of these, and of the concept of justice in particular, must connect up eventually with an explanation of human action and social institutions.

V

That the principles of justice may be regarded as associated with the sense of justice in the manner described illustrates some important facts about them. For one thing it suggests the thought that justice is the first moral virtue in the sense that it arises once the concept of morality is imposed on mutually self-interested persons who are similarly situated; it is the first moral concept to be generated when one steps outside the bounds of rational self-interest. More relevant at the moment, the conjectural derivation emphasizes that fundamental to both justice and fairness is the concept of reciprocity. In the sense in which I shall use this concept, the question of reciprocity arises when free persons, who have no moral authority over one another and who are engaging in or who find themselves participating in a joint activity, are amongst themselves settling upon or acknowledging the rules which define it and which determine their respective shares in its benefits and burdens. The principle of reciprocity requires of a practice that it satisfy those principles which the persons who participate in it could reasonably propose for mutual acceptance under the circumstances and conditions of the hypothetical account. Persons engaged in a practice meeting this principle can then face one another openly and support their respective positions, should they appear questionable, by reference to principles which it is reasonable to expect each to accept. A practice will strike the parties as conforming to the notion of reciprocity if none feels that, by participating in it, he or any of the others are taken advantage of or forced to give in to claims which they do not accept as legitimate. But if they are prepared to complain this implies that each has a conception of legitimate claims which he thinks it reasonable for all to acknowledge. If one thinks of the principles of justice as arising in the manner described, then they specify just this sort of conception.

It is this requirement of the possibility of mutual acknowledgment of principles by free and equal persons who have not authority over one another which makes the concept of reciprocity fundamental to both justice and fairness. Only if such acknowledgment is possible can there be true community between persons in their common practices; otherwise their relations will appear to them as founded to some degree on force and circumstance. Now, in ordinary speech, the concepts of justice and fairness are distinguished roughly in this way: Fairness applies to practices where persons are cooperating with or competing against one another and which allow a choice whether or not to do so. Thus one speaks of fair games, fair trade, and fair procedures of collective bargaining. No one has to play games, or to be in business in any particular industry; and if the rules of collective bargaining allow one party to demand certain things of the other, on any given occasion one of them must have taken the initiative. In the long run, the initiative is expected to be shared more or less evenly between them. On the other hand, justice applies to practices in which there is no choice whether or not to participate. It applies to those institutions which are either so pervasive that people find themselves enmeshed in them and made to conduct their affairs as they specify, as with systems of property and forms of government; or to those practices which, while limited to certain segments of society, nevertheless give no option to those caught in them, such as slaavery and serfdom, and exclusion from the franchise and subjection to special forms of taxation. The element of necessity in justice does not render the conception of mutual acknowledgment any less applicable than in cases where there is choice, although it does, other things being equal, make it more urgent to change unjust than unfair institutions. One activity in which persons participating in a practice can always engage is that of proposing and acknowledging principles to one another supposing each to be similarly circumstanced. To judge practices by the principles so arrived at is to apply to them the principle of reciprocity.

Now if the participants in a practice acknowledge that it satisfies the principle of reciprocity, and so accept its rules as just or fair (as the case requires), then, from the standpoint of justice, they have no complaint to lodge against it. Moreover, their engaging in it gives rise to a prima facie duty (and a corresponding prima facie right) of the parties to each other to act in accordance with the practice when it falls upon them to comply. When any number of persons engage in a practice or conduct a joint undertaking according to rules, and thereby restrict their liberty, those who have submitted to these restrictions when required have a right to a similar acquiescence on the part of those who have benefited by their submission. These conditions will obtain if a practice is correctly acknowledged to be just or fair, for in this case all who participate in it will benefit from it. The rights and duties so arising are special rights and duties in the sense that they depend on previous actions voluntarily undertaken, in this case in the parties having engaged in a common practice and knowingly accepted its benefits.[14] It is not, however, an obligation which presupposes a deliberate performative act in the sense of a promise, or contract, and the like.[15] An unfortunate mistake of the idea of the social contract was to suppose that political obligation does require some such act, or at least, to use language which suggests it.[16] It is sufficient that one has knowingly participated in and accepted the benefits of a practice acknowledged to be fair. This prima facie obligation may, of course, be overridden: it may

---

[14] For the definition of this prima facie duty, and for the idea that it is an important and distinct special duty, I am indebed to H. L. A. Hart. See his paper "Are There Any Natural Rights?", p. 185f. The concept of this duty has certain affinities to Hume's concept of convention, see the *Treatise*, bk. III, pt. II, sec. II, par. 9f, and the *Enquiry*, appendix III, pars. 7f, and 11; but Hume, concerned with origins, expressed the idea somewhat differently. For the relations with Locke's concept of tacit consent, see footnote 16 below.

[15] The sense of "performative" here is to be derived from J. L. Austin's paper in the symposium, "Other Minds," *Proceedings of the Aristotelian Society*, Supplementary Volume (1946), pp. 170–174.

[16] Thus Locke, in pars. 117–122 of *The Second Treatise of Government*, makes a distinction between express and tacit consent and asserts that it is only expressed consent which makes one fully a member of a commonwealth. He certainly means to refer to some explicit performative act, although I am unclear as to what act he has in mind. In contrast, he speaks of tacit consent which, while it does bind one to obeying the laws of a commonwealth, does not make one a full member of it. This is misleading since tacit consent, as ordinarily understood, is as much consent and binds as far as express consent. Its being tacit refers to the manner in which it is given. What Locke means by tacit consent is analogous to the duty of fair play, if not identical with it. This is shown by the definition of it in par. 119. (It may have other meanings, however, elsewhere in the *Treatise*). Even for Locke, then, an obligation to obey the rules laid down by a legitimate political authority can arise independently of a performative act, whether express or tacit, although not without a prior voluntary act. At least he mentions no such obligations, assuming a person possessed of full reason and without fail. The duty to honor one's parents, par. 66, for example, is not of this description.

happen, when it comes one's turn to follow a rule, that other considerations will justify not doing so. But one cannot, in general, be released from this obligation by denying the justice or fairness of the practice only when it falls upon one to obey. If a person rejects a practice, he should, so far as possible, declare his intention in advance and avoid participating in it or enjoying its benefits.

This duty I have called that of fair play, but it should be admitted that to refer to it in this way is, perhaps, to extend the ordinary notion of fairness. Usually acting unfairly is not so much the breaking of any particular rule, even if the infraction is difficult to detect (cheating), but taking advantage of loopholes or ambiguities in rules, availing oneself of unexpected or special circumstances which make it impossible to enforce them, insisting that rules be enforced to one's advantage when they should be suspended, and more generally, acting contrary to the intention of a practice. It is for this reason that one speaks of the sense of fair play: acting fairly requires more than simply being able to follow rules; what is fair must often be felt, or perceived, one wants to say. It is not, however, an unnataural extension of the duty of fair play to have it include the obligation which participants who have knowingly accepted the benefits of their common practice owe to each other to act in accordance with it when their performance falls due; for it is usually considered unfair if someone accepts the benefits of a practice but refuses to do his part in maintaining it. Thus one might say of the tax-dodger that he violates the duty of fair play: he accepts the benefits of government but will not do his part in releasing resources to it; and members of labor unions often say that fellow workers who refuse to join are being unfair: they refer to them as "free riders," as persons who enjoy what are the supposed benefits of unionism, higher wages, shorter hours, job security, and the like, but who refuse to share in its burdens in the form of paying dues, and so on.

The duty of fair play stands beside other prima facie duties such as fidelity and gratitude as a basic moral notion; yet it is not to be confused with them.[17] These duties are all clearly distinct, as would be obvious from their definitions. As with any moral duty, that of fair play implies a constraint on self-interest in particular cases; on occasion it enjoins conduct which a rational egoist strictly defined would not decide upon. So while justice does not require of anyone that he sacrifice his interests in

[17] This, however, commonly happens. Hobbes, for example, when invoking the notion of a "tacit covenant," appeals not to the natural law that promises should be kept but to his fourth law of nature, that of gratitude. On Hobbes's shift from fidelity to gratitude, see Warrender, op. cit., pp. 51–52, 233–237. While it is not a serious criticism of Hobbes, it would have improved his argument had he appealed to the duty of fair play. On his premises he is perfectly entitled to do so. Similarly Sidgwick thought that a principle of justice, such as every man ought to receive adequate requital for his labor, is like gratitude universalized. See *Methods of Ethics*, bk. III, ch. V, sec. 5. There is a gap in the stock of moral concepts used by philosophers into which the concept of the duty of fair play fits quite naturally.

that general position and procedure whereby the principles of justice are proposed and acknowledged, it may happen that in particular situations arising in the context of engaging in a practice, the duty of fair play will often cross his interests in the sense that he will be required to forego particular advantages which the peculiarities of his circumstances might permit him to take. There is, of course, nothing surprising in this. It is simply the consequence of the firm commitment which the parties may be supposed to have made or which they would make in the general position, together with the fact that they have participated in and accepted the benefits of a practice which they regard as fair.

Now the acknowledgment of this constraint in particular cases, which is manifested in acting fairly or wishing to make amends, feeling ashamed, and the like, when one has evaded it, is one of the forms of conduct by which participants in a common practice exhibit their recognition of each other as persons with similar interests and capacities. In the same way that, failing a special explanation, a criterion for the recognition of suffering is helping one who suffers, acknowledging the duty of fair play is a necessary part of the criterion for recognizing another as a person with interests and feelings similar to one's own.[18] A person who never under any circumstances showed a wish to help others in pain would show, at the same time, that he did not recognize that they were in pain; nor could he have any feelings of affection or friendship for anyone; for having these feelings implies, failing special circumstances, that he comes to their aid when they are suffering. Recognition that another is a person in pain shows itself in sympathetic action; this primitive natural response of compassion is one of those responses upon which the various forms of moral conduct are built.

Similarly, the acceptance of the duty of fair play by participants in a common practice is a reflection in each person of the recognition of the aspirations and interests of the others to be realized by their joint activity. Failing a special explanation, their acceptance of it is a necessary part of the criterion for their recognizing one another as persons with similar interests and capacities, as the conception of their relations in the general position supposes them to be. Otherwise they would show no recognition of one another as persons with similar capacities and interests, and indeed, in some cases, perhaps hypothetical, they would not recognize one another as persons at all, but as complicated objects involved in a complicated activity. To recognize another as a person one must respond to him and act towards him in certain ways; and these ways are intimately connected

---

[18] I am using the concept of criterion here in what I take to be Wittgenstein's sense. See *Philosophical Investigations* (Oxford: B. Blackwell, 1953); and Norman Malcolm's review, "Wittgenstein's *Philosophical Investigations*," *Philosophical Review* 63 (1954), 543–547. That the response of compassion, under appropriate circumstances, is part of the criterion for whether or not a person understands what "pain" means, is, I think, in the *Philosophical Investigations*. The view in the text is simply an extension of this idea.

with the various prima facie duties. Acknowledging these duties in some degree, and so having the elements of morality, is not a matter of choice or of intuiting moral qualities or a matter of the expression of feelings or attitudes (the three interpretations between which philosophical opinion frequently oscillates); it is simply the pursuance of one of the forms of conduct in which the recognition of others as persons is manifested.

The remarks in the last two paragraphs are unhappily somewhat obscure. The thesis they sketch, however, need not be argued here. Their main purpose is simply to forestall, together with the remarks in section 4, a misinterpretation of the view presented, and to indicate in advance the manner in which the concept of justice is connected with human conduct and enters into an explanation of it. If in the conjectural account one emphasizes the condition of equality of power between the parties, it might seem that the argument implied that the acceptance of justice and the acknowledgment of the duty of fair play depends in everyday life solely on their being a de facto balance of forces between the parties. It would indeed be unwise to underestimate the importance of such a balance in securing justice; but it is not the only basis thereof. In the conjectural account it was stated that the condition of equality of power was unnecessary for the argument, and that the procedure expressing the constraints of having a morality could be regarded as simply laid down. The place of the condition of equal power was to indicate circumstances in which such a procedure might be adopted, or, if already in existence, might continue in use. But now one must ask, what is the basis of the procedure beyond that of the condition of equal power? In establishing the fundamental proposition about the concept of justice it may be satisfactory to suppose that it is simply laid down. But the concept of justice is embedded in the thoughts, feelings, and actions of real persons; in studying the concept of justice one is studying something abstracted from a certain form of life. Now what is the basis of the procedure in this form of life? The answer, sketched above, is that the recognition of one another as persons with similar interests and capacities must show itself, failing a special explanation, in the acceptance of the principles of justice and in the acknowledgment of the duty of fair play in particular cases. The procedure is not strictly speaking "imposed" by anything; it is involved in the notion of persons with similar interests and capacities and engagaed in common undertakings. Thus even if a person is in a position to insist that the design of a practice give him an unjust advantage over another, or even if, in a particular situation, he can with impunity reap a gain which is disallowed, he will, failing a special explanation, not do so. This conduct is what expresses his recognition of others as persons with interests and capacities similar to his own. Or put a bit differently: since practices to which fairness applies differ from those to which justice applies in that they allow a certain freedom of choice to the parties of participating or not participating, there is a tendency, other things being equal, for the former practices to be more in accordance with the principle of reciprocity than the latter. The greater freedom of maneuver of the parties tends to pull these practices in line with what this principle requires. (Who can be gotten to play unfair games?) One could say, then, that the recognition of others as persons leads people to view one another as if each always possessed the freedom of choice and maneuver which holds when fairness applies. It leads them to view justice as fairness. It is this recognition of one another as persons, and the conditions of it, which explains the way in which the concept of justice may be worked into an account of human action.

It may be helpful to conclude this section by a brief summary of the conception of justice contained in this and the preceding sections. The conception at which we have arrived is that the principles of justice may be thought of as associated with the concept of justice in virtue of the possibility of their being derived once the constraints of having a morality are imposed upon rational and mutually self-interested parties who are related and situated in a special way. A practice is just or fair (depending on the case) if it is in accordance with the principles which all who participate in it might reasonably be expected to propose or to acknowledge before one another when they are similarly circumstanced and required to make a firm commitment in advance without knowledge of what will be their peculiar condition, and thus when it satisfies the principle of reciprocity and its rules are those which the parties could accept as just should occasion arise for them to debate its merits. Regarding the participants themselves, once persons knowingly engage in a practice which they acknowledge to be just and accept the benefits of doing so, they are bound by the duty of fair play to follow the rules when it comes their turn to do so, and this implies a limitation on their pursuit of self-interest in particular cases.

VI

The argument so far has been excessively abstract. While this is perhaps unavoidable, I should now like to bring out some of the special features of the conception of justice as reciprocity by comparing it with the conception of justice in classical utilitarianism as represented by Bentham and Sidgwick, and with its counterpart in welfare economics.

In order to do this, the following consequence of the conception of justice as reciprocity must first be noted, namely, that where it applies, there is no moral value in the satisfaction of a claim incompatible with it. Such a claim violates the conditions of reciprocity and community amongst persons, and he who presses it, not being willing to acknowledge it when pressed by another, has no grounds for complaint when it is denied; whereas he against whom it is pressed can complain. As it cannot be mutually acknowledged it is a resort to coercion—granting the claim is possible only if one party can compel acceptance of what the other will not admit. But it makes no sense to concede claims the denial of which cannot be complained of in preference to claims the denial of which can be objected to. Thus in deciding on the justice of a practice it is not enough to ascertain that it answers to wants and interests in the fullest and most effective manner. For if any of these conflict with justice, they should not be counted, as their satisfaction is no reason at all for having a practice. It would be irrelevant to say, even if true, that it resulted in the greatest satisfaction of desire. In tallying up the merits of a practice one must toss out the satisfaction of interests the claims of which are incompatible with the principles of justice.

The conception of justice in classical utilitarianism conflicts, then, with the conception of justice as reciprocity. For on the utilitarian view justice is assimilated to benevolence and the latter in turn to the most effective design of institutions to promote the general welfare. Justice is a kind of efficiency.[19] Now it is said occasionally that this form of utilitarianism puts no restrictions on what might be a just assignment of rights and duties in that there might be circumstances which, on utilitarian grounds, would justify institutions highly offensive to our ordinary sense of justice. But the classical utilitarian conception is not totally unprepared for this objection. Beginning with the notion that the general happiness can be represented by a asocial utility function consisting of a sum of individual utility functions with identical weights (this being the meaning of the maxim that each counts for one and no more than one),[20] it is commonly assumed that the utility functions of individuals are similar in all essential respects. Differ-

---

[19] While this assimilation is implicit in Bentham's and Sidgwick's moral theory, explicit statements of it as applied to justice are relatively rare. One clear instance in *The Principles of Morals and Legislation* occurs in ch. X, footnote 2 to section XL: ". . . justice, in the only sense in which it has a meaning, is an imaginary personage, feigned for the convenience of discourse, whose dictates are the dictates of utility, applied to certain particular cases. Justice, then, is nothing more than an imaginary instrument, employed to forward on certain occasions, and by certain means, the purposes of benevolence. The dictates of justice are nothing more than a part of the dictates of benevolence, which, on certain occasions, are applied to certain subjects. . . ." Likewise in *The Limits of Jurisprudence Defined*, ed. by C. W. Everett (New York: Columbia University Press, 1945), pp. 117f., Bentham criticizes Grotius for denying that justice derives from utility; and in *The Theory of Legislation*, ed. by C. K. Ogden (New York: Harcourt, Brace and Co., 1931), p. 3, he says that he uses the words "just" and "unjust" along with other words "simply as collective terms including the ideas of certain pains or pleasures." That Sidgwick's conception of justice is similar to Bentham's is admittedly not evident from his discussion of justice in Book III, ch. V of *Methods of Ethics*. But it follows, I think, from the moral theory he accepts. Hence C. D. Broad's criticisms of Sidgwick in the matter of distributive justice in *Five Types of Ethical Theory* (New York: Harcourt, Brace and Co., 1930), pp. 249–253, do not rest on a misinterpretation.

[20] This maxim is attributed to Bentham by J. S. Mill in *Utilitarianism*, ch. V, par. 36. I have not found it in Bentham's writings, nor seen such a reference. Similarly James Bonar, *Philosophy and Political Economy* (London, 1893), p. 23n. But it accords perfectly with Bentham's ideas. See the hitherto unpublished manuscript in David Baumgardt, *Bentham and the Ethics of Today* (Princeton, N.J.: Princeton University Press, 1952), Appendix IV. For example, "the total value of the stock of pleasure belonging to the whole community is to be obtained by multiplying the number expressing the value of it as respecting any one person, by the number expressing the multitude of such individuals" (p. 556).

ences between individuals are ascribed to accidents of education and up-bringing, and they should not be taken into account. This assumption, coupled with that of diminishing marginal utility, results in a prima facie case for equality, e.g., of equality in the distribution of income during any given period of time, laying aside indirect effects on the future. Equality can easily be seen to follow by reflecting that if one person A has more income than another B, it must be possible, given the assumptions, to increase the total utility shared by A and B by transferring units of income from A to B. For that the utility functions are the same means that x units to A gives the same utility as x units to B; and diminishing marginal utility implies that in general the $(n+1)$ th unit yields less utility than the nth.

Yet even if utilitarianism is interpreted as having such restrictions built into the utility function, and even if it is supposed that these restrictions have in practice much the same result as the application of the principles of justice (and appear perhaps to be ways of expressing these principles in the language of mathematics and psychology), the fundamental idea is very different from the conception of justice as reciprocity. For one thing, that the principles of justice should be accepted is interpreted as the contingent result of a higher order administrative decision. The form of this decision is regarded as being similar to that of an entrepreneur deciding how much to produce of this or that commodity in view of its marginal revenue, or to that of someone distributing goods to needy persons according to the relative urgency of their wants. The choice between practices by a social utility function consisting of a sum of individual utility functions burdens to individuals (these being measured by the present capitalized value of their utility over the full period of the practice's existence), which results from the distribution of rights and duties established by a practice.

Moreover, the individuals receiving these benefits are not conceived as being related in any way: they represent so many different directions in which limited resources may be allocated. The value of assigning resources is thought of as being made on the basis of the allocation of benefits and interests of individuals as individuals. The satisfaction of desire has its value irrespective of the moral relations between persons, say as members of a joint undertaking, and of the claims which, in the name of these interests, they are prepared to make on one another;[21] and it is this value which

---

[21] An idea essential to the classical utilitarian conception of justice. Bentham is firm in his statement of it: "It is only upon that principle [the principle of asceticism], and not from the principle of utility, that the most abominable pleasure which the vilest of malefactors ever reaped from his crime would be reprobated, if it stood alone. The case is, that it never does stand alone; but is necessarily followed by such a quantity of pain (or, what comes to the same thing, such a chance for a certain quantity of pain) that the pleasure in comparison of it, is as nothing: and this is the true and sole, but perfectly sufficient, reason for making it a ground for punishment." (*The Principles of Morals and Legislation*, ch. II, sec. IV. See also ch. X, sec. X, footnote 1.) The same point is made in *The Limits of Jurisprudence Defined*, pp. 115f. Although much recent welfare economics, as found in such important works as I. M. D. Little, *A Critique of Welfare Economics*, 2nd edition (Oxford: The University Press, 1957) and K. J. Arrow, *Social Choice*

is to be taken into account by the (ideal) legislator who is conceived as adjusting the rules of the system from the center so as to maximize the value of the social utility function.[22]

It is thought that the principles of justice will not be violated by a legal system so conceived provided these executive decisions are correctly made. In this fact the principles of justice are said to have their derivation and explanation; they simply express the most important general features of social institutions in which the administrative problem is solved in the best way. These principles have, indeed, a special urgency because, given the facts of human nature, so much depends on them; and this explains the peculiar quality of the moral feelings associated with justice.[23] This assimilation of justice to a higher order executive decision, certainly a striking conception, is central to classical utilitarianism; and it also brings out its profound individualism, in one sense of this ambiguous word. It regards persons as so many separate directions in which benefits and burdens may

---

and Individual Values (New York: Wiley, 1951), dispenses with the idea of cardinal utility and uses instead the theory of ordinal utility as stated by J. R. Hicks, *Value and Capital*, 2nd ed. (Oxford: The University Press, 1946), pt. I, it assumes with utilitarianism that individual preferences have value as such and so accepts the idea being criticized here. The same is true of those writers who, following von Neumann's lead, hold on to the notion of cardinal utility. See, for example, J. C. Harsanyi, "Cardinal Welfare, Individual Ethics, and Interpersonal Comparisons of Utility," *Journal of Political Economy*, 63 (1955), 309–321. Indeed, the same must apply here because the cardinal utility is generated by applying the notion of a probability mixture to a set of preferences having value as they stand. I hasten to add, however, that this is no objection to it as a means of analyzing economic policy, and for that purpose it may, indeed, be a necessary simplifying assumption. Nevertheless it is an assumption which cannot be made in so far as one is trying to analyze moral concepts, especially the concept of justice, as economists would, I think, agree. Justice is usually regarded as a separate and distinct part of any comprehensive criterion of economic policy. See, for example, Tibor Scitovsky, *Welfare and Competition* (London: Unwin University Books, 1963), pp. 59–69, and Little, *Welfare Economics*, ch. VII.

[22] The force of the word "ideal," which I have put in parentheses, is to take account of the fact that Bentham did not, of course, believe that there should be an actual administrator or legislator with full power to adjust the rules of the system from the center. But he did think, as a principle of justification, that one institution is better than another if, in the course of the way in which it could be expected to work, it is reasonable to suppose that on the whole it will have better consequences from the standpoint of an ideal legislator, so defined. Representative institutions are to be preferred to monarchy and aristocracy because human nature being what it is, democracy will in the long run give results more in accord with the principle of utility as an ideal legislator would apply it. See his *Plan of Parliamentary Reform* in *The Works of Jeremy Bentham*, ed. John Bowring (London, 1843), vol. III. One might say, further, in view of the argument in the first two chapters of *The Principles of Morals and Legislation*, that Bentham thought that the principle of utility was the only one that could be consistently recommended and the only one that could be mutually acknowledged. He says, for example: "When a man attempts to combat the principle of utility, it is with reasons drawn without his being aware of it, from the very principle itself." Ch. I, par. 13. In the footnote to par. 14 of ch. II he would appear to say that the principle of utility is the only one by which a man can justify his opinions not only when he reflects within himself, but when he addresses the community. If, however, the argument of the previous sections is correct, these notions properly interpreted require a modification in the conception of the principle of utility as Bentham stated it.

[23] See J. S. Mill's argument in *Utilitarianism*, ch. V, pars. 16–25.

be assigned; and the value of the satisfaction or dissatisfaction of desire is not thought to depend in any way on the moral relations in which individuals stand, or on the kinds of claims which they are willing, in the pursuit of their interests, to press on each other.

VII

Many social decisions are, of course, of an administrative nature. Certainly this is so when it is a matter of social utility in what one may call its ordinary sense: that is, when it is a question of the efficient design of social institutions for the use of common means to achieve common ends. In this case either the benefits and burdens may be assumed to be impartially distributed, or the question of distribution is misplaced, as in the instance of maintaining public order and security or national defense. Nevertheless it is a fundamental mistake to use the notion of a higher order executive decision as the basis for interpreting the principles of justice and their derivation. In this section I shall try to show why classical utilitarianism is wrong in doing so. Throughout I shall use the example of slavery; it has the advantage of being a clear case regarding which men, both unreasonable and reasonable, may be expected to agree.

One may begin by noticing that classical utilitarianism permits one to argue that slavery is unjust on the grounds that the advantages to the slaveholder as slaveholder do not counterbalance the disadvantages to the slave and to society at large, burdened by a comparatively inefficient system of labor. Now the conception of justice as reciprocity, when applied to the practice of slavery with its offices of slaveholder and slave, would not allow one to consider the advantages of the slaveholder in the first place. As that office is not in accordance with principles which could be mutually acknowledged, the gains accruing to the slaveholder, assuming them to exist, cannot be counted as in any way mitigating the injustice of the practice. The question whether these gains outweigh the disadvantages to the slave and to society cannot arise, since in considering the justice of slavery these gains have no weight at all which requires that they be overridden. Where the conception of justice as reciprocity applies, slavery is always unjust.

I am not, of course, suggesting the absurdity that the classical utilitarians approved of slavery.[24] I am only rejecting a type of argument which their view allows them to use in support of their disapproval of it. The conception of justice as derivative from efficiency implies that judging the justice of a practice is always, in principle at least, a matter of weighing up advantages, each having an intrinsic value or disvalue is the satisfaction of interests, irrespective of whether or not these interests necessarily involve

---

[24] To the contrary, Bentham argued very powefully against it. See A *Fragment of Government*, ch. II, par. 34, footnote 2, *The Principles of Morals and Legislation*, ch. XVI, par. 44, footnote, ch. XVII, par. 4 footnote, *The Theory of Legislation*, pt. III, ch. II.

acquiescence in principles which could not mutually be acknowledged. Utilitarianism cannot account for the fact that slavery is always unjust, nor for the fact that it would be recognized as irrelevant in defeating the accusation of injustice for one person to say to another, engaged with him in a common practice and debating its merits, that nevertheless it allowed of the greatest satisfaction of desire. The charge of injustice cannot be rebutted in this way. If justice were derivative from a higher order executive efficiency, this would not be so.

But now, even if it is taken as established that, so far as the ordinary conception of justice goes, slavery is always unjust (that is, slavery by definition violates commonly recognized principles of justice), the classical utilitarian would surely reply that these principles, like other moral principles subordinate to that of utility, are only generally correct. It is simply for the most part true that slavery is less efficient than other institutions; and while common sense may define the concept of justice in such a way that slavery is proved unjust, nevertheless, where slavery would lead to the greatest satisfaction of desire, it is not wrong. Indeed, it is then right, and for the very same reason that justice, as ordinarily understood, is usually right. If, as ordinarily understood, slavery is always unjust, to this extent the utilitarian conception of justice might be admitted to differ from that of moral opinion. Still the utilitarian would want to hold that, as a matter of moral principle, his view is correct in giving no special weight to considerations of justice beyond that allowed for by the general presumption of effectiveness. And this, he claims, is as it should be. The everyday opinion is morally in error, although, indeed, it is a useful error, since it protects rules of generally high utility.

The question, then, relates not simply to the analysis of the concept of justice as common sense defines it, but the analysis of it in the wider sense as to how much weight considerations of justice, as defined, are to have when laid against other kinds of moral considerations. Here again I wish to argue that reasons of justice have a special weight for which only the conception of justice as reciprocity can account. Moreover, it belongs to the concept of justice that they do have this special weight. While Mill recognized that this was so, he thought that it could be accounted for by the special urgency of the moral feelings which naturally support principles of such high utility. But it is a mistake to resort to the urgency of feeling; as with the appeal to intuition, it manifests a failure to pursue the question far enough. The special weight of considerations of justice can be explained from the conception of justice as reciprocity. It is only necessary to elaborate a bit what has already been said, as follows.

If one examines the circumstances in which a certain tolerance of slavery is justified, or perhaps better, excused, it turns out that these are of a rather special sort. Perhaps slavery exists as an inheritance from the past and it proves necessary to dismantle it piece by piece; at times slavery may conceivably be an advance on previous institutions. Now while there may be some excuse for slavery in special conditions, it is never an excuse for it that it is sufficiently advantageous to the slaveholder to outweigh the disadvantages to the slave and to society. A person who argues in this way is not perhaps making a wildly irrelevant remark; but he is guilty of a moral fallacy. There is disorder in his conception of the ranking of moral principles. For the slaveholder, by his own admission, has no moral title to the advantages which he receives as a slaveholder. He is no more prepared than the slave to acknowledge the principle upon which is founded the respective positions in which they both stand. Since slavery does not accord with principles which they could mutually acknowledge, they each may be supposed to agree that it is unjust: it grants claims which it ought not to grant and in doing so denies claims which it ought not to deny. Amongst persons in a general position who are debating the form of their common practices, it cannot, therefore, be offered as a reason for a practice that, in conceding these very claims that ought to be denied, it nevertheless meets existing interests more effectively. By their very nature the satisfaction of these claims is without weight and cannot enter into any tabulation of advantages and disadvantages.

Furthermore, it follows from the concept of morality that, to the extent that the slaveholder recognizes his position vis-à-vis the slave to be unjust, he would not choose to press his claims. His not wanting to receive his special advantages is one of the ways in which he shows that he thinks slavery is unjust. It would be fallacious for the legislator to suppose, then, that it is a ground for having a practice that it brings advantages greater than disadvantages, if those for whom the practice is designed and to whom the advantages flow, acknowledge that they have no moral title to them and do not wish to receive them.

For these reasons the principles of justice have a special weight; and with respect to the principle of the greatest satisfaction of desire, as cited in the general position amongst those discussing the merits of their common practices, the principles of justice have an absolute weight. In this sense they are not contingent; and this is why their force is greater than can be accounted for by the general presumption (assuming that there is one) of the effectiveness, in the utilitarian sense, of practices which in fact satisfy them.

If one wants to continue using the concepts of classical utilitarianism, one will have to say, to meet this criticism, that at least the individual or social utility functions must be so defined that no value is given to the satisfaction of interests the representative claims of which violate the principles of justice. In this way it is no doubt possible to include these principles within the form of the utilitarian conception; but to do so is, of course, to change its inspiration altogether as a moral conception. For it is to incorporate within it principles which cannot be understood on the basis of a higher order executive decision aiming at the greatest satisfaction of desire.

It is worth remarking, perhaps, that this criticism of utilitarianism does not depend on whether or not the two assumptions, that of individuals having similar utility functions and that of diminishing marginal utility, are interpreted as psychological propositions to be supported or refuted by experience or as moral and political principles expressed in a somewhat technical language. There are, certainly, several advantages in taking them in the latter fashion.[25] For one thing, one might say that this is what Bentham and others really meant by them, at least as shown by how they were used in arguments for social reform. More importantly, one could hold that the best way to defend the classical utilitarian view is to interpret these assumptions as moral and political principles. It is doubtful whether, taken as psychological propositions, they are true of men in general as we know them under normal conditions. On the other hand, utilitarians would not have wanted to propose them merely as practical working principles of legislation, or as expedient maxims to guide reform, given the egalitarian sentiments of modern society.[26] When pressed they might well have invoked the idea of a more or less equal capacity of men in relevant respects if given an equal chance in a just society.

If, however, the argument above regarding slavery is correct, granting these assumptions as moral and political principles makes no difference. To view individuals as equally fruitful lines for the allocation of benefits, even as a matter of moral principle, still leaves the mistaken notion that the satisfaction of desire has value in itself irrespective of the relations between persons as members of a common practice, and irrespective of the claims upon one another which the satisfaction of interests represents. To see the error of this idea one must give up the conception of justice as an executive decision altogether and refer to the notion of justice as fairness: that participants in a common practice be regarded as having an original and equal liberty and that their common practices be considered unjust unless they accord with principles which persons so circumstanced and related could freely acknowledge before one another, and so could accept as fair. Once the emphasis is put upon the concept of the mutual recognition of principles by participants in a common practice the rules of which are to define their several relations and give form to their claims on one another, then it is clear that the granting of a claim the principle of which could not be acknowledged by each in the general position (that is, in the position in which the parties propose and acknowledge principles before one another) is not a reason for adopting a practice. Viewed in this way, the

---

[25] See D. G. Ritchie, *Natural Rights* (London, 1894), pp. 95ff., 249ff. Lionel Robbins has insisted on this point on several occasions. See *An Essay on the Nature and Significance of Economic Science*, 2nd ed. (London: Macmillan & Co., 1935), pp. 134–143; "Interpersonal Comparisons of Utility: A Comment," *Economic Journal* 48 (1938), 635–641, and more recently, "The Theory of Economic Policy," in *English Classical Political Economy* (London: Macmillan & Co., 1952), pp. 179ff.

[26] As Sir Henry Maine suggested Bentham may have regarded them. See *The Early History of Institutions* (London, 1875), pp. 398ff.

background of the claim is seen to exclude it from consideration; that it can represent a value in itself arises from the conception of individuals as separate lines for the assignment of benefits, as isolated persons who stand as claimants on an administrative or benevolent largesse. Occasionally persons do so stand to one another; but this is not the general case, nor, more importantly, is it the case when it is a matter of the justice of practices themselves in which participants stand in various relations to be appraised in accordance with standards which they may be expected to acknowledge before one another. Thus, however mistaken the notion of the social contract may be as history, and however far it may overreach itself as a general theory of social and political obligation, it does express, suitably interpreted, an essential part of the concept of justice.[27]

VIII

The framework of the analysis of the concept of justice is now complete, and some of its special features have been brought out by comparing it with the conception of justice in classical utilitarianism. It should be remarked, though, that the original modification of the utilitarian principle (that it require of practices that the offices and positions defined by them be equal unless it is reasonable to suppose that the representative man in every office would find the inequality to his advantage), slight as it may seem at first sight, actually has a different conception of justice behind it. The argument has been intended to show how this is so by developing the concept of justice as reciprocity and by indicating how this notion, which involves the mutual acceptance from a general position of the principles on which a practice is founded, is the common element in the concepts of justice and fairness, and how the conception of justice so framed requires the exclusion from consideration of claims violating the principles of justice. The slight alteration of principle reveals another family of notions, another way of looking at the concept of justice.

Again, I should like to emphasize that I have been dealing with the concept of justice. The analytic construction is directed at setting out the kinds of principles upon which judgments concerning the justice of practices may be said to stand and the manner in which these principles are

[27] Thus Kant took the right step when he interpreted the original contract as an "Idea of Reason," and so in effect, as an ethical principle applicable to social arrangements irrespective of the question of origins. See the second part of the essay, "On the Saying 'That may be right in theory but has no value in practice'" (1793), in *Kant's Principle of Politics,* trans. W. Hastie (Edinburgh, 1891). All the elements of the analysis of justice as reciprocity is stated as the meaning of the second formulation of the categorical imperative in the *Grundlegung.* See *The Groundwork of the Metaphysic of Morals,* trans. H. J. Paton (London, New York: Hutchinson's University Library, 1948), pp. 95ff. I should like to stress this tie with Kant's moral theory as well as that with Hume and utilitarianism generally, for I think it can be shown that the conflict between them is not of the sort often supposed.

associated with the concept of justice in view of its sense. The analysis will be successful to the degree that it expresses the principles involved in these judgments when made by competent persons upon deliberation and reflection, or, more personally, to the extent that it clarifies for any particular individual his reflections about matters of justice. Moreover, the analysis is pointed toward a universal moral idea, for every people may be supposed to have the concept of justice. In the life of every society there must be at least some relations in which the parties consider themselves to be circumstanced and related as the concept of justice as reciprocity requires. Societies will differ from one another not in having or in failing to have this notion but in the range of cases to which they apply it and in the emphasis which they give to it as compared with other moral concepts.

A comprehensive understanding of the concept of justice is necessary if these variations and the reasons for them are to be intelligible. No study of the development of moral ideas and of their influence in society is more sound than an analysis of the fundamental moral concepts upon which it must depend. I have tried, therefore, to give an analysis of the concept of justice which will apply generally, however large a part the concept may have in a given morality, and which can be used in explaining the course of men's thoughts about justice and its relation to other moral concepts.

ECONOMIC INCOME AND SOCIAL JUSTICE [*]

JOEL FEINBERG

The term "distributive justice" traditionally applied to burdens and benefits directly distributed by political authorities, such as appointed offices, welfare doles, taxes, and military conscription, but it has now come to apply also to goods and evils of a nonpolitical kind that can be distributed by private citizens to other private citizens. In fact, in most recent literature, the term is reserved for *economic* distributions, particularly the justice of differences in economic income between classes, and of various schemes of taxation which discriminate in different ways between classes. Further, the phrase can refer not only to acts of distributing but also to de facto states of affairs, such as *the fact that* at present "the five percent at the top get 20 percent [of our national wealth] while the 20 percent at the bottom get about five percent." [1] There is, of course, an ambiguity in the meaning of "distribution." The word may refer to the *process* of dis-

[*] From Joel Feinberg, *Social Philosophy* (Englewood Cliffs: Prentice-Hall, 1973). Reprinted by permission of the publisher.

[1] "T. R. B. from Washington" in *The New Republic,* Vol. CLX, No. 12 (March 22, 1969), p. 4.

tributing, or the *product* of some process of distributing, and either or both of these can be appraised as just or unjust. In addition, a "distribution" can be understood to be a "product" which is *not* the result of any deliberate distributing process, but simply a state of affairs whose production has been too complicated to summarize or to ascribe to any definite group of persons as their deliberate doing. The present "distribution" of American wealth is just such a state of affairs.

Are the 5 percent of Americans "at the top" really different from the 20 percent "at the bottom" in any respect that would justicize the difference between their incomes? It is doubtful that there is any characteristic—relevant or irrelevant—common and peculiar to all members of either group. *Some* injustices, therefore, must surely exist. Perhaps there are some traits, however, that are more or less characteristic of the members of the privileged group, that make the current arrangements at least approximately just. What could (or should) those traits be? The answer will state a standard of relevance and a principle of material justice for questions of economic distributions, at least in relatively affluent societies like that of the United States.

At this point there appears to be no appeal possible except to *basic attitudes,* but even at this level we should avoid premature pessimism about the possibility of rational agreement. Some answers to our question have been generally discredited, and if we can see why those answers are inadequate, we might discover some important clues to the properties any adequate answer must possess. Even philosophical adversaries with strongly opposed initial attitudes may hope to come to eventual agreement if they share *some* relevant beliefs and standards and a common commitment to consistency. Let us consider why we all agree (that is the author's assumption) in rejecting the view that differences in race, sex, IQ, or social "rank" are the grounds of just differences in wealth or income. Part of the answer seems obvious. People cannot by their own voluntary choices determine what skin color, sex, or IQ they shall have, or which hereditary caste they shall enter. To make such properties the basis of discrimination between individuals in the distribution of social benefits would be "to treat people differently in ways that profoundly affect their lives because of differences for which they have no responsibility." [2] Differences in a given respect are *relevant* for the aims of distributive justice, then, only if they are differences for which their possessors can be held responsible; properties can be the grounds of just discrimination between persons only if those persons had a *fair opportunity* to acquire or avoid them. Having rejected a number of material principles that cleaarly fail to satisfy the "fair opportunity" requirement, we are still left with as many as five candidates for our acceptance. (It is in theory open to us to accept two or more of these

[2] W. K. Frankena, "Some Beliefs About Justice," *The Lindley Lecture,* Department of Philosophy Pamphlet (Lawrence: University of Kansas, 1966), p. 10.

five as valid principles, there being no a priori necessity that the list be reduced to one.) These are: (1) the principle of perfect equality; (2) the principle[s] of need; (3) the principles of merit and achievement; (4) the principle of contribution (or due return); (5) the principle of effort (or labor). I shall discuss each of these briefly.

(i) Equality

The principle of perfect equality obviously has a place in any adequate social ethic. Every human being is equally a human being, and . . . that minimal qualification entitles all human beings equally to certain absolute human rights: positive rights to noneconomic "goods" that by their very natures cannot be in short supply, negative rights not to be treated in cruel or inhuman ways, and negative rights not to be exploited or degraded even in "humane" ways. It is quite another thing, however, to make the minimal qualification of humanity the ground for an absolutely equal distribution of a country's *material wealth* among its citizens. A strict equalitarian could argue that he is merely applying Aristotle's formula of proportionate equality (presumably accepted by all parties to the dispute) with a criterion of relevance borrowed from the human rights theorists. Thus, distributive justice is accomplished between A and B when the following ratio is satisfied:

$$\frac{A\text{'s share of } P}{B\text{'s share of } P} = \frac{A\text{'s possession of } Q}{B\text{'s possession of } Q}$$

Where P stands for economic goods, Q must stand simply for "humanity" or "a human nature," and since every human being possesses *that* Q equally, it follows that all should also share a society's economic wealth (the P in question) equally.

The trouble with this argument is that its major premise is no less disputable than its conclusion. The standard of relevance it borrows from other contexts where it seems very little short of self-evident, seems controversial, at best, when applied to purely economic contexts. It seems evident to most of us that merely being human entitles *everyone*—bad men as well as good, lazy as well as industrious, inept as well as skilled—to a fair trial if charged with a crime, to equal protection of the law, to equal consideration of his interests by makers of national policy, to be spared torture or other cruel and inhuman treatment, and to be permanently ineligible for the status of chattel slave. Adding a right to an equal share of the economic pie, however, is to add a benefit of a wholly different order, one whose presence on the list of goods for which mere humanity is the sole qualifying condition is not likely to win wide assent without further argument.

It is far more plausible to posit a human right to the satisfaction of (better: to an opportunity to satisfy) one's *basic* economic needs, that is, to enough food and medicine to remain healthy, to minimal clothing, housing, and so on. As Hume pointed out,[3] even these rights cannot exist under conditions of extreme scarcity. Where there is not enough to go around, it cannot be true that everyone has a right to an equal share. But wherever there is moderate abundance or better—wherever a society produces more than enough to satisfy the *basic needs of everyone*—there it seems more plausible to say that mere possession of basic human needs qualifies a person for the opportunity to satisfy them. It would be a rare and calloused sense of justice that would not be offended by an affluent society, with a large annual agricultural surplus and a great abundance of manufactured goods, which permitted some of its citizens to die of starvation, exposure, or easily curable disease. It would certainly be *unfair* for a nation to produce more than it needs and not permit some of its citizens enough to satisfy their basic biological requirements. Strict equalitarianism, then, is a perfectly plausible material principle of distributive justice when confined to affluent societies and basic biological needs, but it loses plausibility when applied to division of the "surplus" left over after basic needs are met. To be sure, the greater the degree of affluence, the higher the level at which we might draw the line between "basic needs" and merely "wanted" benefits, and insofar as social institutions create "artificial needs," it is only fair that society provide all with the opportunity to satisfy them.[4] But once the line has been drawn between what is needed to live a minimally decent life by the realistic standards of a given time and place and what is only added "gravy," it is far from evident that justice still insists upon absolutely equal shares of the total. And it is evident that justice does *not* require strict equality wherever there is reason to think that unequal distribution causally determines greater production and is therefore in the interests of everyone, even those who receive the relatively smaller shares.

Still, there is no way to *refute* the strict equalitarian who requires exactly equal shares for everyone whenever that can be arranged without discouraging total productivity to the point where everyone loses. No one would insist upon equal distributions that would diminish the size of the total pie and thus leave smaller slices for *everyone;* that would be opposed to reason. John Rawls makes this condition part of his "rational principle" of justice: "Inequalities are arbitrary unless it is reasonable to expect that they will work out to everyone's advantage. . . ."[5] We are left then with a version of strict equalitarianism that is by no means evidently true and yet is impossible to refute. That is the theory that purports to apply not only to basic needs but to the total wealth of a society, and allows departures from

---

[3] David Hume, *Enquiry Concerning the Principles of Morals* Part III (LaSalle, Ill.: The Open Court Publishing Company, 1947). Originally published in 1777.

[4] This point is well made in Katzner, "An Analysis of the Concept of Justice," pp. 173–203.

[5] John Rawls, "Justice as Fairness," *The Philosophical Review*, LXVII (1958), 165.

strict equality when, *but only when,* they will work out to everyone's advantage. Although I am not persuaded by this theory, I think that any adequate material principle will have to attack great importance to keeping differences in wealth within reasonable limits, even after all basic needs have been met. One way of doing this would be to raise the standards for a "basic need" as total wealth goes up, so that differences between the richest and poorest citizens (even when there is no real "poverty") are kept within moderate limits.

(ii) Need

The principle of need is subject to various interpretations, but in most of its forms it is not an independent principle at all, but only a way of mediating the application of the principle of equality. It can, therefore, be grouped with the principle of perfect equality as a member of the equalitarian family and contrasted with the principles of merit, achievement, contribution, and effort, which are all members of the nonequalitarian family. Consider some differences in "needs" as they bear on distributions. Doe is a bachelor with no dependents; Roe has a wife and six children. Roe must satisfy the needs of eight persons out of his paycheck, whereas Doe need satisfy the needs of only one. To give Roe and Doe equal pay would be to treat Doe's interests substantially *more* generously than those of anyone in the Roe family. Similarly, if a small private group is distributing food to its members (say a shipwrecked crew waiting rescue on a desert island), it would not be fair to give precisely the same quantity to a one hundred pounder as to a two hundred pounder, for that might be giving one person all he needs and the other only a fraction of what he needs—a difference in treatment not supported by any relevant difference between them. In short, to distribute goods in proportion to basic needs is not really to depart from a standard of equality, but rather to bring those with some greater initial burden or deficit up to the same level as their fellows.

The concept of a "need" is extremely elastic. In a general sense, to say that S needs X is to say simply that if he doesn't have X he will be harmed. A "basic need" would then be for an X in whose absence a person would be harmed in some crucial and fundamental way, such as suffering injury, malnutrition, illness, madness, or premature death. Thus we all have a basic need for foodstuffs of a certain quantity and variety, fuel to heat our dwellings, a roof over our heads, clothing to keep us warm, and so on. In a different but related sense of need, to say that S needs X is to say that without X he cannot achieve some specific purpose or perform some specific function. If they are to do their work, carpenters need tools, merchants need capital and customers, authors need paper and publishers. Some helpful goods are not strictly needed in the sense: an author with pencil and paper does not really need a typewriter to write a book, but he may need it to write a book speedily, efficiently, and conveniently. We sometimes come to rely upon "merely helpful but unneeded goods" to such a degree that we develop a strong habitual dependence on them, in which case (as it is often said) we have a "psychological" as opposed to a material need for them. If we don't possess that for which we have a strong psychological need, we may be unable to be happy, in which case a merely psychological need for a functional instrument may become a genuine need in the first sense distinguished above, namely, something whose absence is harmful to us. (Cutting across the distinction between material and psychological needs is that between "natural" and "artificial" needs, the former being those that can be expected to develop in any normal person, the latter being those that are manufactured or contrived, and somehow implanted in, or imposed upon, a person.) The more abundant a society's material goods, the higher the level at which we are required (by the force of psychological needs) to fix the distinction between "necessities" and "luxuries"; what *everyone* in a given society regards as "necessary" tends to become an actual, basic need.

(iii) Merit and Achievement

The remaining three candidates for material principles of distributive justice belong to the nonequalitarian family. These three principles would each distribute goods in accordance, not with need, but with *desert;* since persons obviously differ in their deserts, economic goods would be distributed unequally. The three principles differ from one another in their conceptions of the relevant *bases of desert* for economic distributions. The first is the principle of *merit*. Unlike the other principles in the nonequalitarian family, this one focuses not on what a person has *done* to deserve his allotment, but rather on what kind of person he is—what characteristics he has.

Two different types of characteristic might be considered meritorious in the appropriate sense: skills and virtues. Native skills and inherited aptitudes will not be appropriate desert bases, since they are forms of merit ruled out by the fair opportunity requirement. No one deserves credit or blame for his genetic inheritance, since no one has the opportunity to select his own genes. Acquired skills may seem more plausible candidates at first, but upon scrutiny they are little better. First, all acquired skills depend to a large degree on native skills. Nobody is born knowing how to read, so reading is an acquired skill, but actual differences in reading skill are to a large degree accounted for by genetic differences that are beyond anyone's control. Some of the differences are no doubt caused by differences in motivation afforded different children, but again the early conditions contributing to a child's motivation are also largely beyond his control. We may still have some differences in acquired skills that are to be accounetd for solely or primarily by differences in the degree of practice, drill, and perseverance expended by persons with roughly equal opportunities. In respect to these, we can propitiate the requirement of fair opportunity, but only by nullifying the significance of acquired skill as such, for now skill is a relevant basis of desert only to the extent that it is a product of one's own effort. Hence, *effort* becomes the true basis of desert (as claimed by our fifth principle, discussed below), and not simply skill as such.

Those who would propose rewarding personal *virtues* with a larger than average share of the economic pie, and punishing defects of character with a smaller than average share, advocate assigning to the economic system a task normally done (if it is done at all) by noneconomic institutions. What they propose, in effect, is that we use retributive criteria of distributive justice. Our criminal law, for a variety of good reasons, does not purport to punish people for what they are, but only for what they do. A man can be as arrogant, rude, selfish, cruel, insensitive, irresponsible, cowardly, lazy, or disloyal as he wishes; unless he *does* something prohibited by the criminal law, he will not be made to suffer legal punishment. At least one of the legal system's reasons for refusing to penalize character flaws as such would also explain why such defects should not be listed as relevant differences in a material principle of distributive justice. The apparatus for detecting such flaws (a "moral police"?) would be enormously cumbersome and impractical, and its methods so uncertain and fallible that none of us could feel safe in entrusting the determination of our material allotments to it. We could, of course, give roughly equal shares to all except those few who have *outstanding* virtues—gentleness, kindness, courage, diligence, reliability, warmth, charm, considerateness, generosity. Perhaps these are traits that deserve to be rewarded, but it is doubtful that larger economic allotments are the appropriate vehicles of rewarding. As Benn and Peters remind us, "there are some sorts of 'worth' for which rewards in terms of income seem inappropriate. Great courage in battle is recognized by medals, not by increased pay." [6] Indeed, there is something repugnant, as Socrates and the Stoics insisted, in paying a man to be virtuous. Moreover, the rewards would offer a pecuniary motive for certain forms of excellence that require motives of a different kind, and would thus tend to be self-defeating.

The most plausible nonequalitarian theories are those that locate relevance not in meritorious traits and excellences of any kind, but rather in prior doings: not in what one is, but in what one has done. Actions, too, are sometimes called "meritorious," so there is no impropriety in denominating the remaining families of principles in our survey as "meritarian." One type of action-oriented meritarian might cite *achievement* as a relevant desert basis for pecuniary rewards, so that departures from equality in income are to be justicized only by distinguished achievements in science, art, philosophy, music, athletics, and other basic areas of human activity. The attractions and disadvantages of this theory are similar to those of theories which I rejected above that base rewards on skills and virtues. Not all persons have fair opportunity to achieve great things, and economic rewards

---

[6] Benn and Peters, *Social Principles and the Democratic State,* p. 139.

seem inappropriate as vehicles for expressing recognition and admiration of noneconomic achievements.

(iv) Contribution or "Due Return"

When the achievements under consideration are themselves contributions to our general economic well-being, the meritarian principle of distributive justice is much more plausible. Often it is conjoined with an economic theory that purports to determine exactly what percentage of our total economic product a given worker or class has produced. Justice, according to this principle, requires that each worker get back exactly that proportion of the national wealth that he has himself created. This sounds very much like a principle of "commutative justice" directing us to *give back* to every worker what is really his own property, that is, the product of his own labor.

The French socialist writer and precursor of Karl Marx, Pierre Joseph Proudhon (1809–1865), is perhaps the classic example of this kind of theorist. In his book *What Is Property?* (1840), Proudhon rejects the standard socialist slogan, "From each according to his ability, to each according to his needs," [7] in favor of a principle of distributive justice based on contribution, as interpreted by an economic theory that employed a pre-Marxist "theory of surplus value." The famous socialist slogan was not intended, in any case, to express a principle of distributive justice. It was understood to be a rejection of all considerations of "mere" justice for an ethic of human brotherhood. The early socialists thought it unfair, in a way, to give the great contributors to our wealth a disproportionately small share of the product. But in the new socialist society, love of neighbor, community spirit, and absence of avarice would overwhelm such bourgeois notions and put them in their proper (subordinate) place.

Proudhon, on the other hand, based his whole social philosophy not on brotherhood (an ideal he found suitable only for small groups such as families) but on the kind of distributive justice to which even some capitalists gave lip service:

> The key concept was "mutuality" or "reciprocity." "Mutuality, reciprocity exists," he wrote, "when all the workers in an industry, instead of working for an entrepreneur who pays them and keeps their products, work for one another and thus collaborate in the making of a common product whose profits they share among themselves." [8]

Proudhon's celebrated dictum that "property is theft" did not imply that all *possession* of goods is illicit, but rather that the system of rules that per-

---

[7] Traced to Louis Blanc. For a clear brief exposition of Proudhon's view which contrasts it with that of other early socialists and also that of Karl Marx, see Robert Tucker's "Marx and Distributive Justice," in *Nomos VI: Justice*, ed. C. J. Friedrich and J. W. Chapman (New York: Aldine-Atherton Press, 1963), pp. 306–25.

[8] Tucker, "Marx and Distributive Justice," p. 310.

mitted the owner of a factory to hire workers and draw profits ("surplus value") from *their* labor robs the workers of what is rightly theirs. "This profit, consisting of a portion of the proceeds of labor that rightfully belonged to the laborer himself, was 'theft.'" [9] The injustice of capitalism, according to Proudhon, consists in the fact that those who create the wealth (through their labor) get only a small part of what they create, whereas those who "exploit" their labor, like voracious parasites, gather in a greatly disproportionate share. The "return of contribution" principle of distributive justice, then, cannot work in a capitalist system, but requires a *fédération mutualiste* of autonomous producer-cooperatives in which those who create wealth by their work share it in proportion to their real contributions.

Other theorists, employing different notions of what produces or "creates" economic wealth, have used the "return of contribution" principle to support quite opposite conclusions. The contribution principle has even been used to justicize quite unequalitarian capitalistic status quos, for it is said that capital as well as labor creates wealth, as do ingenious ideas, inventions, and adventurous risk-taking. The capitalist who provided the money, the inventor who designed a product to be manufactured, the innovator who thought of a new mode of production and marketing, the advertiser who persuaded millions of customers to buy the finished product, the investor who risked his savings on the success of the enterprise—these are the ones, it is said, who did the most to produce the wealth created by a business, not the workers who contributed only their labor, and of course, these are the ones who tend, on the whole, to receive the largest personal incomes.

Without begging any narrow and technical questions of economics, I should express my general skepticism concerning such facile generalizations about the comparative degrees to which various individuals have contributed to our social wealth. Not only are there impossibly difficult problems of measurement involved, there are also conceptual problems that appear beyond all nonarbitrary solution. I refer to the elements of luck and chance, the social factors not attributable to any assignable individuals, and the contributions of population trends, uncreated natural resources, and the efforts of people now dead, which are often central to the explanation of any given increment of social wealth.

The difficulties of separating out causal factors in the production of social wealth might influence the partisan of the "return of contribution" principle in either or both of two ways. He might become very cautious in his application of the principle, requiring that deviations from average shares be restricted to very clear and demonstrable instances of unusually great or small contributions. But the moral that L. T. Hobhouse [10] drew from these difficulties is that *any* individual contribution will be very small relative to

---

[9] Tucker, "Marx and Distributive Justice," p. 311.
[10] L. T. Hobhouse, *The Elements of Social Justice* (London: George Allen and Unwin Ltd., 1922). See especially pp. 161–63.

the immeasurably great contribution made by political, social, fortuitous, natural, and "inherited" factors. In particular, strict application of the "return of contribution" principle would tend to support a larger claim for the *community* to its own "due return," through taxation and other devices.

In a way, the principle of contribution is not a principle of mere *desert* at all, no matter how applied. As mentioned above, it resembles a principle of commutative justice requiring repayment of debts, return of borrowed items, or compensation for wrongly inflicted damages. If I lend you my car on the understanding that you will take good care of it and soon return it, or if you steal it, or damage it, it will be too *weak* to say that I "deserve" to have my own car, intact, back from you. After all, the car is *mine* or my due, and questions of ownership are not settled by examination of deserts; neither are considerations of ownership and obligation commonly outbalanced by considerations of desert. It is not merely "unfitting" or "inappropriate" that I should not have my own or my due; it is downright *theft* to withhold it from me. So the return of contribution is not merely a matter of merit deserving reward. It is a matter of a maker demanding that which he has created and is thus properly his. The ratio—A's share of X is to B's share of X as A's contribution to X is to B's contribution to X—appears, therefore, to be a very strong and plausible principle of distributive justice, whose main deficiencies, when applied to economic distributions, are of a practical (though severe) kind. If Hobhouse is right in claiming that there are social factors in even the most pronounced individual contributions to social wealth, then the principle of due return serves as a moral basis in support of taxation and other public claims to private goods. In any case, if A's contribution, though apparently much greater than B's, is nevertheless only the tiniest percentage of the total contribution to X (whatever that may mean and however it is to be determined), it may seem like the meanest quibbling to distinguish very seriously between A and B at all.

(v) Effort

The principle of due return, as a material principle of distributive justice, does have some vulnerability to the fair opportunity requirement. Given unavoidable variations in genetic endowments and material circumstances, different persons cannot have precisely the same opportunities to make contributions to the public weal. Our final candidate for the status of a material principle of distributive justice, the *principle of effort*, does much better in this respect, for it would distribute economic products not in proportion to successful achievement but according to the degree of effort exerted. According to the principle of effort, justice decrees that hard-working executives and hard-working laborers receive precisely the same remuneration (although there may be reasons having nothing to do with justice for paying more to the executives), and that freeloaders be penalized by allotments of proportionately lesser shares of the joint products of everyone's labor. The most persuasive argument for this principle is that it is the closest approximation to the intuitively valid principle of due return that can pass the fair opportunity requirement. It is doubtful, however, that even the principle of effort fully satisfies the requirements of fair opportunity, since those who inherit or acquire certain kinds of handicap may have little opportunity to *acquire the motivation* even to do their best. In any event, the principle of effort does seem to have intuitive cogency giving it at least some weight as a factor determining the justice of distributions.

In very tentative conclusion, it seems that the principle of equality (in the version that rests on needs rather than that which requires "perfect equality") and the principles of contribution and effort (where nonarbitrarily applicable, and only *after* everyone's basic needs have been satisfied) have the most weight as determinants of economic justice, whereas all forms of the principle of merit are implausible in that role. The reason for the priority of basic needs is that, where there is economic abundance, the claim to life itself and to minimally decent conditions are, like other human rights, claims that all men make with perfect equality. As economic production increases, these claims are given even greater consideration in the form of rising standards for distinguishing basic needs from other wanted goods. But no matter where that line is drawn, when we go beyond it into the realm of economic surplus or "luxuries," nonequalitarian considerations (especially contribution and effort) come increasingly into play.

10

Privacy

The technological capability for eavesdropping, surveillance, snooping, and spying on nations and individuals is by now proverbial, and techniques are being steadily developed. The will to use these surfaces almost daily, whether it be private detectives, the government, research agencies, health-insurance organizations, credit agencies, or various file keepers and data banks that one may not even have ever heard of or suspected that they existed. Efforts to preserve privacy through legislation and administrative means are difficult to assess, because verification of compliance is often clouded by uncertainty: Have "they" really destroyed the files on me that "they" said they would? Recall that most real international spying is not done by cloak-and-dagger intrigue but by poring over data that are somewhere published, and you can see how easy it is for our personal secrets to leak out.

But what does privacy consist of, and why do we value it so much? Is there a right to privacy, and if so, are some areas of privacy of little importance and others extremely vital? Supreme Court rulings on birth control and abortion have affirmed a right to privacy. (See also our later discussions of sexual behavior and the law.) Charles Fried argues that temptations to keep tabs on parolees by bugging their persons and monitoring their movements and speech take away from them something no government has a right to do. Such relationships as love, friendship, and trust are impossible without privacy. Control over release of information about oneself is the essence of privacy. Release of this to carefully selected persons is the use of "moral capital," for how else could we show intimacy and other cherished qualities or relationships without sharing such secrets? To put a person, even a convicted felon, in an electronic fishbowl strips him or her of these most important relationships and restricts that person to purely secondary associations. Fried holds that some areas of privacy are symbolic of all privacy whatever, and every society must preserve some areas of privacy at least as if they were sacred, for they will stand for one's very life or psyche itself as something of inestimable worth.

Jeffrey Reiman's paper rejects Judith Jarvis Thompson's view that there is no peculiar right called privacy but that so-called right of privacy is simply a broad name for a collection of different rights centering around property. He also criticizes Thomas Scanlon's attempt to remedy this position as uninformative. Reiman argues that while Charles Fried and James Rachels have a better explanation of the right of privacy than these, their account sounds too much like the economics of the marketplace, not personal relations as such. He holds that privacy is itself a right. Unlike Fried, he sees the importance of privacy in caring more than in sharing, even the sharing of secrets as "moral capital." Rachels claims that privacy is a social ritual by which a person's moral title to his or her existence is conferred, and as a precondition to personhood.

PRIVACY: A RATIONAL CONTEXT *

CHARLES FRIED

. . . A rational context may be defined as a context the awareness of which is part of the principle of a rational action. . . . The usefulness of the term is simply that it draws attention to a common aspect of a variety of principles, actions, and ends. Privacy is such a context.

In this chapter I analyze the concept of privacy and attempt to show why it assumes such high significance in our system of values. There is a puzzle here, since we do not feel comfortable about asserting that privacy is intrinsically valuable, an end in itself—privacy is always for or in relation to something or someone. On the other hand, to view privacy as simply instrumental, as one way of getting other goods, seems unsatisfactory too. For we feel that there is a necessary quality, after all, to the importance we ascribe to privacy. This perplexity is displayed when we ask how privacy might be traded off against other values. We wish to ascribe to privacy more than an ordinary priority. My analysis attempts to show why we value privacy highly and why also we do not treat it as an end in itself. Briefly, my argument is that privacy provides the rational context for a number of our most significant ends, such as love, trust and friendship, respect and self-respect. Since it is a necessary element of those ends, it draws its significance from them. And yet since privacy is only an element of those ends, not the whole, we have not felt inclined to attribute to privacy

---

* Reprinted by permission of the publishers from "An Anatomy of Values" by Charles Fried, Cambridge, Massachusetts: Harvard University Press, copyright © 1970 by the President and Fellows of Harvard College.

ultimate significance. In general this analysis of privacy illustrates how the concepts in this essay can provide a rational account for deeply held moral values.

An Immodest Proposal: Electronic Monitoring

There are available today electronic devices to be worn on one's person which emit signals permitting one's exact location to be determined by a monitor some distance away. These devices are so small as to be entirely unobtrusive: other persons cannot tell that a subject is "wired," and even the subject himself—if he could forget the initial installation—need be no more aware of the device than of a small bandage. Moreover, existing technology can produce devices capable of monitoring not only a person's location, but other significant facts about him: his temperature, pulse rate, blood pressure, the alcoholic content of his blood, the sounds in his immediate environment—for example, what he says and what is said to him —and perhaps in the not too distant future even the pattern of his brain waves. The suggestion has been made, and is being actively investigated, that such devices might be employed in the surveillance of persons on probation or parole.

Probation leaves an offender at large in the community as an alternative to imprisonment, and parole is the release of an imprisoned person prior to the time that all justification for supervising him and limiting his liberty has expired. Typically, both probation and parole are granted subject to various restrictions. Most usually the probationer or parolee is not allowed to leave a prescribed area. Also common are restrictions on the kinds of places he may visit—bars, pool halls, brothels, and the like may be forbidden—the persons he may associate with, and the activities he may engage in. The most common restriction on activities is a prohibition on drinking, but sometimes probation and parole have been revoked for "immorality"— that is, intercourse with a person other than a spouse. There are also affirmative conditions, such as a requirement that the subject work regularly in an approved employment, maintain an approved residence, report regularly to correctional, social, or psychiatric personnel. Failure to abide by such conditions is thought to endanger the rehabilitation of the subject and to identify him as a poor risk.

Now the application of personal monitoring to probation and parole is obvious. Violations of any one of the conditions and restrictions could be uncovered immediately by devices using present technology or developments of it; by the same token, a wired subject assured of detection would be much more likely to obey. Although monitoring is admitted to be unusually intrusive, it is argued that this particular use of monitoring is entirely proper, since it justifies the release of persons who would otherwise remain in prison, and since surely there is little that is more intrusive and unprivate than a prison regime. Moreover, no one is obliged to submit to monitoring: an offender may decline and wait in prison until his sentence has expired or until he is judged a proper risk for parole even without monitoring. Proponents of monitoring suggest that seen in this way monitoring of offenders subject to supervision is no more offensive than the monitoring on an entirely voluntary basis of epileptics, diabetics, cardiac patients, and the like.

Much of the discussion about this and similar (though perhaps less futuristic) measures has proceeded in a fragmentary way to catalog the disadvantages they entail: the danger of the information falling into the wrong hands, the opportunity presented for harassment, the inevitable involvement of persons as to whom no basis for supervision exists, the use of the material monitored by the government for unauthorized purposes, the danger to political expression and association, and so on.

Such arguments are often sufficiently compelling, but situations may be envisaged where they are overridden. The monitoring case in some of its aspects is such a situation. And yet one often wants to say the invasion of privacy is wrong, intolerable, although each discrete objection can be met. The reason for this, I submit, is that privacy is much more than just a possible social technique for assuring this or that substantive interest. Such analyses of the value of privacy often lead to the conclusion that the various substantive interests may after all be protected as well by some other means, or that if they cannot be protected quite as well, still those other means will do, given the importance of our reasons for violating privacy. It is just because this instrumental analysis makes privacy so vulnerable that we feel impelled to assign to privacy some intrinsic significance. But to translate privacy to the level of an intrinsic value might seem more a way of cutting off analysis than of carrying it forward.

It is my thesis that privacy is not just one possible means among others to insure some other value, but that it is necessarily related to ends and relations of the most fundamental sort: respect, love, friendship, and trust. Privacy is not merely a good technique for furthering these fundamental relations; rather without privacy they are simply inconceivable. They require a context of privacy or the possibility of privacy for their existence. To make clear the necessity of privacy as a context for respect, love, friendship, and trust is to bring out also why a threat to privacy seems to threaten our very integrity as persons. To respect, love, trust, or feel affection for others and to regard ourselves as the objects of love, trust, and affection is at the heart of our notion of ourselves as persons among persons, and privacy is the necessary atmosphere for these attitudes and actions, as oxygen is for combustion.

Privacy and Personal Relations

Before going further, it is necessary to sharpen the intuitive concept of privacy. As a first approximation, privacy seems to be related to secrecy, to limiting the knowledge of others about oneself. This notion must be refined. It is not true, for instance, that the less that is known about us the more privacy we have. Privacy is not simply an absence of information about us in the minds of others; rather it is the control we have over information about ourselves.

To refer, for instance, to the privacy of a lonely man on a desert island would be to engage in irony. The person who enjoys privacy is able to grant or deny access to others. Even when one considers private situations into which outsiders could not possibly intrude, the context implies some alternative situation where the intrusion is possible. A man's house may be private, for instance, but that is because it is constructed—with doors, windows, window shades—to allow it to be made private, and because the law entitles a man to exclude unauthorized persons. And even the remote vacation hideaway is private just because one resorts to it in order—in part—to preclude access to unauthorized persons.

Privacy, thus, is control over knowledge about oneself. But it is not simply control over the quantity of information abroad; there are modulations in the quality of the knowledge as well. We may not mind that a person knows a general fact about us, and yet feel our privacy invaded if he knows the details. For instance, a casual acquaintance may comfortably know that I am sick, but it would violate my privacy if he knew the nature of the illness. Or a good friend may know what particular illness I am suffering from, but it would violate my privacy if he were actually to witness my suffering from some symptom which he must know is associated with the disease.

Privacy in its dimension of control over information is an aspect of personal liberty. Acts derive their meaning partly from their social context—from how many people know about them and what the knowledge consists of. For instance, a reproof administered out of the hearing of third persons may be an act of kindness, but if administered in public it becomes cruel and degrading. Thus if a man cannot be sure that third persons are not listening—if his privacy is not secure—he is denied the freedom to do what he regards as an act of kindness.

Besides giving us control over the context in which we act, privacy has a more defensive role in protecting our liberty. We may wish to do or say things not forbidden by the restraints of morality but nevertheless unpopular or unconventional. If we thought that our every word and deed were public, fear of disapproval or more tangible retaliation might keep us from doing or saying things which we would do or say if we could be sure of keeping them to ourselves or within a circle of those who we know approve or tolerate our tastes.

These reasons support the familiar arguments for the right of privacy. Yet they leave privacy with less security than we feel it deserves; they leave it vulnerable to arguments that a particular invasion of privacy will secure to us other kinds of liberty which more than compensate for what is lost. To present privacy, then, only as an aspect of or an aid to general liberty is to miss some of its most significant differentiating features. The value of control over information about ourselves is more nearly absolute than that. For privacy is the necessary context for relationships which we would hardly be human if we had to do without—the relationships of love, friendship, and trust.

Love and friendship . . . involve the initial respect for the rights of others which morality requires of everyone. They further involve the voluntary and spontaneous relinquishment of something between friend and friend, lover and lover. The title to information about oneself conferred by privacy provides the necessary something. To be friends or lovers persons must be intimate to some degree with each other. Intimacy is the sharing of information about one's actions, beliefs or emotions which one does not share with all, and which one has the right not to share with anyone. By conferring this right, privacy creates the moral capital which we spend in friendship and love.

The entitlements of privacy are not just one kind of entitlement among many which a lover can surrender to show his love. Love or friendship can be partially expressed by the gift of other rights—gifts of property or of service. But these gifts, without the intimacy of shared private information, cannot alone constitute love or friendship. The man who is generous with his possessions, but not with himself, can hardly be a friend, nor—and this more clearly shows the necessity of privacy for love—can the man who, voluntarily or involuntarily, shares everything about himself with the world indiscriminately.

Privacy is essential to friendship and love in another respect besides providing what I call moral capital. The rights of privacy are among those basic entitlements which men must respect in each other; and mutual respect is the minimal precondition for love and friendship.

Privacy also provides the means for modulating those degrees of friendship which fall short of love. Few persons have the emotional resources to be on the most intimate terms with all their friends. Privacy grants the control over information which enables us to maintain degrees of intimacy. Thus even between friends the restraints of privacy apply; since friendship implies a voluntary relinquishment of private information, one will not wish to know what his friend or lover has not chosen to share with him. The rupture of this balance by a third party—the state perhaps—thrusting information concerning one friend upon another might well destroy the limited degree of intimacy the two have achieved.

Finally, there is a more extreme case where privacy serves not to save something which will be "spent" on a friend, but to keep it from all the world. There are thoughts whose expression to a friend or lover would be a hostile act, though the entertaining of them is completely consistent with friendship or love. That is because these thoughts, prior to being given expression, are mere unratified possibilities for action. Only by expressing them do we adopt them, choose them as part of ourselves, and draw them into our relations with others. Now a sophisticated person knows that a friend or lover must entertain thoughts which if expressed would be wounding, and so—it might be objected—why should he attach any significance to their actual expression? In a sense the objection is well taken. If it were possible to give expression to these thoughts and yet make clear to ourselves and to others that we do not thereby ratify them, adopt them as our own, it might be that in some relations, at least, another could be allowed complete access to us. But this possibility is not a very likely one. Thus the most complete form of privacy is perhaps also the most basic, since it is necessary not only to our freedom to define our relations with others but also to our freedom to define ourselves. To be deprived of this control over what we do and who we are is the ultimate assault on liberty, personality, and self-respect.

Trust is the attitude of expectation that another will behave according to the constraints of morality. Insofar as trust is only instrumental to the more convenient conduct of life, its purposes could be as well served by cheap and efficient surveillance of the person upon whom one depends. One does not trust machines or animals; one takes the fullest economically feasible precautions against their going wrong. Often, however, we choose to trust people where it would be safer to take precautions—to watch them or require a bond from them. This must be because, as I have already argued, we value the relation of trust for its own sake. It is one of those relations, less inspiring than love or friendship but also less tiring, through which we express our humanity.

There can be no trust where there is no possibility of error. More specifically, man cannot know that he is trusted unless he has a right to act without constant surveillance so that he knows he can betray the trust. Privacy confers that essential right. And since, as I have argued, trust in its fullest sense is reciprocal, the man who cannot be trusted cannot himself trust or learn to trust. Without privacy and the possibility of error which it protects that aspect of his humanity is denied to him.

The Concrete Recognition of Privacy

In concrete situations and actual societies, control over information about oneself, like control over one's bodily security or property, can only be relative and qualified. As is true for property or bodily security, the control over privacy must be limited by the rights of others. And as in the cases of property and bodily security, so too with privacy, the more one ventures into the outside, the more one pursues one's other interests with the aid of, in competition with, or even in the presence of others, the more one must risk invasions. As with property and personal security, it is the business of legal and social institutions to define and protect the right of privacy which emerges intact from the hurly-burly of social interactions. Now it would be absurd to argue that these concrete definitions and protections, differing as they do from society to society, are or should be strict derivations from general principles, the only legitimate variables being differing empirical circumstances (such as differing technologies or climatic conditions). The delineation of standards must be left to a political and social process the results of which will accord with justice if two conditions are met: (1) the process itself is just, that is, the interests of all are fairly represented; and (2) the outcome of the process protects basic dignity and provides moral capital for personal relations in the form of absolute title to at least some information about oneself.

The particular areas of life which are protected by privacy will be conventional at least in part, not only because they are the products of political processes, but also because of one of the reasons we value privacy. Insofar as privacy is regarded as moral capital for relations of love, friendship, and trust, there are situations where what kinds of information one is entitled to keep to oneself is not of the first importance. The important thing is that there be *some* information which is protected. Convention may quite properly rule in determining the particular areas which are private.

Convention plays another more important role in fostering privacy and the respect and esteem which it protects; it designates certain areas, intrinsically no more private than other areas, as symbolic of the whole institution of privacy, and thus deserving of protection beyond their particular importance. This apparently exaggerated respect for conventionally protected areas compensates for the inevitable fact that privacy is gravely compromised in any concrete social system: it is compromised by the inevitably and utterly just exercise of rights by others, it is compromised by the questionable but politically sanctioned exercise of rights by others, it is compromised by conduct which society does not condone but which it is unable or unwilling to forbid, and it is compromised by plainly wrongful invasions and aggressions. In all this there is a real danger that privacy might be crushed altogether, or, what would be as bad, that any venture outside the most limited area of activity would mean risking an almost total compromise of privacy.

Given these threats to privacy in general, social systems have given symbolic importance to certain conventionally designated areas of privacy. Thus in our culture the excretory functions are so shielded that situations in which this privacy is violated are experienced as extremely distressing, as detracting from one's dignity and self-esteem. Yet there does not seem to be any reason connected with the principles of respect, esteem, and the like why this would have to be so, and one can imagine other cultures in which it was not so, but where the same symbolic privacy was attached to, say, eating and drinking. There are other more subtly modulated symbolic areas of privacy, some of which merge into what I call substantive privacy (that is, areas where privacy does protect substantial interests). The very complex norms of privacy about matters of sex and health are good examples.

An excellent, very different sort of example of a contingent, symbolic recognition of an area of privacy as an expression of respect for personal integrity is the privilege against self-incrimination and the associated doctrines denying officials the power to compel other kinds of information without some explicit warrant. By according the privilege as fully as it does, our society affirms the extreme value of the individual's control over information about himself. To be sure, prying into a man's personal affairs by asking questions of others or by observing him is not prevented. Rather it is the point of the privilege that a man cannot be forced to make public information about himself. Thereby his sense of control over what others know of him is significantly enhanced, even if other sources of the same information exist. Without his cooperation, the other sources are necessarily incomplete, since he himself is the only ineluctable witness to his own present life, public or private, internal or manifest. And information about himself which others have to give out is in one sense information over which he has already relinquished control.

The privilege is contingent and symbolic. It is part of a whole structure of rules by which there is created an institution of privacy sufficient to the sense of respect, trust, and intimacy. It is contingent in that it cannot, I believe, be shown that some particular set of rules is necessary to the existence of such an institution of privacy. It is symbolic because the exercise of the privilege provides a striking expression of society's willingness to accept constraints on the pursuit of valid, perhaps vital, interests in order to recognize the right of privacy and the respect for the individual that privacy entails. Conversely, a proceeding in which compulsion is brought to bear on an individual to force him to make revelations about himself provides a striking and dramatic instance of a denial of title to control information about oneself, to control the picture we would have others have of us. In this sense such a procedure quite rightly seems profoundly humiliating. Nevertheless it is not clear to me that a system is unjust which sometimes allows such an imposition.

In calling attention to the symbolic aspect of some areas of privacy I do not mean to minimize their importance. On the contrary, they are highly significant as expressions of respect for others in a general situation where much of what we do to each other may signify a lack of respect or at least presents no occasion for expressing respect. That this is so is shown not so much on the occasions where these symbolic constraints are observed, for they are part of our system of expectations, but where they are violated. Not only does a person feel his standing is gravely compromised by such symbolic violations, but also those who wish to degrade and humiliate others often choose just such symbolic aggressions and invasions on the assumed though conventional area of privacy.

The Concept of Privacy Applied to the Problem of Monitoring

Let us return now to the concrete problem of electronic monitoring to see whether the foregoing elucidation of the concept of privacy will help to establish on firmer ground the intuitive objection that monitoring is an intolerable violation of privacy. Let us consider the more intrusive forms of monitoring where not only location but conversations and perhaps other data are monitored.

Obviously such a system of monitoring drastically curtails or eliminates altogether the power to control information about oneself. But, it might be said, this is not a significant objection if we assumed the monitored data will go only to authorized persons—probation or parole officers—and cannot be prejudicial so long as the subject of the monitoring is not violating the conditions under which he is allowed to be at liberty. This retort misses the importance of privacy as a context for all kinds of relations, from the most intense to the most casual. For all of these may require a context of some degree of intimacy, and intimacy is made impossible by monitoring.

It is worth being more precise about this notion of intimacy. Monitoring obviously presents vast opportunities for malice and misunderstanding on the part of authorized personnel. For that reason the subject has reason to be constantly apprehensive and inhibited in what he does. There is always an unseen audience, which is the more threatening because of the possibility that one may forget about it and let down his guard, as one would not with a visible audience. Even assuming the benevolence and understanding of the official audience, there are serious consequences to the fact that no degree of true intimacy is possible for the subject. Privacy is not, as we have seen, just a defensive right. It forms the necessary context for the intimate relations of love and friendship which give our lives much of whatever affirmative value they have. In the role of citizen or fellow worker, one need reveal himself to no greater extent than is necessary to display the attributes of competence and morality appropriate to those roles. In order to be a friend or lover one must reveal far more of himself. Yet where any intimate revelation may be heard by monitoring officials, it loses the quality of exclusive intimacy required of a gesture of love or friendship. Thus monitoring, in depriving one of privacy, destroys the possibility of bestowing the gift of intimacy, and makes impossible the essential dimension of love and friendship.

Monitoring similarly undermines the subject's capacity to enter into relations of trust. As I analyzed trust, it required the possibility of error on the part of the person trusted. The negation of trust is constant surveillance —such as monitoring—which minimizes the possibility of undetected default. The monitored parolee is denied the sense of self-respect inherent in being trusted by the government which has released him. More important, monitoring prevents the parolee from entering into true *relations* of trust with persons in the outside world. An employer, unaware of the monitoring, who entrusts a sum of money to the parolee cannot thereby grant him the sense of responsibility and autonomy which an unmonitored person in the same position would have. The parolee in a real—if special and ironical—sense, cannot be trusted.

Now let us consider the argument that however intrusive monitoring may seem, surely prison life is more so. In part, of course, this will be a matter of fact. It may be that a reasonably secure and well-run prison will allow prisoners occasions for conversation among themselves, with guards, or with visitors, which are quite private. Such a prison regime would in this respect be less intrusive than monitoring. Often prison regimes do not allow even this, and go far toward depriving a prisoner of any sense of privacy: if the cells have doors, these may be equipped with peepholes. But there is still an important difference between this kind of prison and monitoring: the prison environment is overtly, even punitively unprivate. The contexts for relations to others are obviously and drastically different from what they are on the "outside." This itself, it seems to me, protects the prisoner's human orientation where monitoring only assails it. If the prisoner has a reasonably developed capacity for love, trust, and friendship and has in fact experienced ties of this sort, he is likely to be strongly aware (at least for a time) that prison life is a drastically different context from the one in which he enjoyed those relations, and this awareness will militate against his confusing the kinds of relations that can obtain in a "total institution" like a prison with those of freer social settings on the outside.

Monitoring, by contrast, alters only in a subtle and unobtrusive way—though a significant one—the context for relations. The subject appears free to perform the same actions as others and to enter the same relations, but in fact an important element of autonomy, of control over one's environment, is missing: he cannot be private. A prisoner can adopt a stance of withdrawal, of hibernation as it were, and thus preserve his sense of privacy intact to a degree. A person subject to monitoring by virtue of being in a free environment, dealing with people who expect him to have certain responses, capacities, and dispositions, is forced to make at least a show of intimacy to the persons he works closely with, those who would be his friends, and so on. They expect these things of him, because he is assumed to have the capacity and disposition to enter into ordinary relations with them. Yet if he does—if, for instance, he enters into light banter with slight sexual overtones with the waitress at the diner where he eats regularly—he has been forced to violate his own integrity by revealing to his official monitors even so small an aspect of his private personality, the personality he wishes to reserve for persons toward whom he will make some gestures of intimacy and friendship. Theoretically, of course, a monitored parolee might adopt the same attitude of withdrawal that a prisoner does, but in fact that too would be a costly and degrading experience. He would be tempted, as in prison he would not be, to "give himself away" and to act like everyone else, since in every outward respect he seems like everyone else. Moreover, by withdrawing, the person subject to monitoring would risk seeming cold, unnatural, odd, inhuman, to the very people whose esteem and affection he craves. In prison the circumstances dictating a reserved and tentative facade are so apparent to all that adopting such a facade is no reflection on the prisoner's humanity.

The insidiousness of a technique which forces a man to betray himself in this humiliating way or else seem inhuman is compounded when one considers that the subject is also forced to betray others who may become intimate with him. Even persons in the overt oppressiveness of a prison do not labor under the burden of this double betrayal.

As against all of these considerations, there remains the argument that so long as monitoring depends on the consent of the subject, who feels it is preferable to prison, to close off this alternative in the name of a morality so intimately concerned with liberty is absurd. This argument may be decisive; I am not at all confident that the alternative of monitored release should be closed off. My analysis does show, I think, that it involves costs to the prisoner which are easily overlooked, that on inspection it is a less desirable alternative than might at first appear. Moreover, monitoring presents systematic dangers to potential subjects as a class. Its availability as a compromise between conditional release and continued imprisonment may lead officials who are in any doubt whether or not to trust a man on parole or probation to assuage their doubts by resorting to monitoring.

The seductions of monitored release disguise not only a cost to the subject but to society as well. The discussion of trust should make clear that unmonitored release is a very different experience from monitored release, and so the educational and rehabilitative effect of unmonitored release is also different. Unmonitored release affirms in a far more significant way the relations of trust between the convicted criminal and the society which he violated by his crime and which we should now be seeking to re-establish. But trust can only arise, as any parent knows, through the experience of being trusted.

Finally, it must be recognized that more limited monitoring—for instance where only the approximate location of the subject is revealed—lacks the offensive features of total monitoring, and is obviously preferable to prison.

The Role of Law

This evaluation of the proposal for electronic monitoring has depended on the general theoretical framework of this whole essay. It is worth noting the kind of evaluation that framework has permitted. Rather than inviting a fragmentation of the proposal into various pleasant and unpleasant elements and comparing the "net utility" of the proposal with its alternatives, we have been able to evaluate the total situation created by the proposal in another way. We have been able to see it as a system in which certain actions and relations, the pursuit of certain ends, are possible or impossible.

Certain systems of actions, ends, and relations are possible or impossible in different social contexts. Moreover, the social context itself is a system of actions and relations. The social contexts created by monitoring and its alternatives, liberty or imprisonment, are thus evaluated by their conformity to a model system in which are instantiated the principles of morality, justice, friendship, and love. Such a model, which is used as a standard, is of course partially unspecified in that there is perhaps an infinite number of specific systems which conform to those principles. Now actual systems, as we have seen, may vary in respect to how other ends—for example, beauty, knowledge—may be pursued in them, and they may be extremely deficient in allowing for the pursuit of such ends. But those who design, propose, and administer social systems are first of all bound to make them conform to the model of morality and justice, for in so doing they express respect and even friendship—what might be called civic friendship—toward those implicated in the system. If designers and administrators fail to conform to this model, they fail to express that aspect of their humanity which makes them in turn fit subjects for the respect, friendship, and love of others.

Finally, a point should be noted about the relation between legal structures and other social structures in establishing a rational context such as privacy. This context is established in part by rules which guarantee to a person the claim to control certain areas, his home, perhaps his telephone communications, and so forth, and back this guarantee with enforceable sanctions. These norms are, of course, legal norms. Now these legal norms are incomprehensible without some understanding of what kind of a situation one seeks to establish with their aid. Without this understanding we cannot grasp their importance, the vector of development from them in changing circumstances (such as new technology), the consequences of abandoning them, and so on.* What is less obvious is that law is not just an instrument for bringing about a separately identifiable and significant social result: it is a part of the very situation that it helps to bring about. The concept of privacy requires, as we have seen, a sense of control and a justified, acknowledged power to control aspects of one's environment. In most developed societies the only way to give a person the full measure of both the sense and the fact of control is to give him a legal title to control. A legal right to control is control which is the least open to question and argument, it is the kind of control we are most serious about. Consider

---

* It is a tenet of some forms of positivism that this statement is wrong insofar as it suggests that without appreciation of the context we have no understanding of the meaning of legal norms. This tenet seems wrong for a number of reasons. Legal norms are necessarily phrased in open-ended language, and their specification in actual circumstaces needs the aid of the context—that is, the reason for the norm—to determine the appropriate application. This is obviously so when there are changed circumstances and recourse must be had to the principle of the norm. It is less obvious in so-called "central" or "paradigm" cases, but I suggest this is less obvious only because the context is so unproblematic as to require no explicit attention.

the analogy of the power of testamentary disposition. A testator is subject
to all sorts of obligations, pressures, and arguments; certain things are so
outrageous that he would scarcely dare to do them. Yet, within very broad
limits, in the last analysis he is after all free to do the outrageous. And
both the fact that certain dispositions are outrageous, immoral, wrong, and
the fact that the testator is nevertheless free to make them are *together*
important to define the autonomy and personality of a person in the particular situation. In the same way the public and ultimate character of law
is part of the definition of the rational context of privacy.

PRIVACY, INTIMACY, AND PERSONHOOD °

JEFFREY H. REIMAN

The Summer 1975 issue of *Philosophy & Public Affairs* featured three
articles on privacy, one by Judith Jarvis Thomson, one by Thomas Scanlon
in response to Thomson, and one by James Rachels in response to them
both.[1] Thomson starts from the observation that "the most striking thing
about the right to privacy is that nobody seems to have any very clear idea
what it is" (p. 295) and goes on to argue that nobody should have one—a
very clear idea, that is. Her argument is essentially that all the various
protections to which we feel the right to privacy entitles us are already
included under other rights, such as "the cluster of rights which the right
over the person consists in and also . . . the cluster of rights which owning
property consists in" (p. 306). After a romp through some exquisitely fan-
ciful examples, she poses and answers some questions about some of the
kinds of "invasions" we would likely think of as violations of the right to
privacy:

> Someone looks at your pornographic picture in your wall-safe? He violates your
> right that your belongings not be looked at, and you have the right because
> you have ownership rights—and it is because you have them that what he does
> is wrong. Someone uses an X-ray device to look at you through the walls of
> your house? He violates your right not to be looked at, and you have that right

° From Jeffrey Reiman, "Privacy, Intimacy, and Personhood," *Philosophy and Public Affairs*, 6, pp. 26–44, (Fall, 1976). Reprinted by permission of the author and *Philosophy
and Public Affairs*.

I am grateful to the editors of *Philosophy & Public Affairs* for many helpful comments
and suggestions which have aided me in clarifying and communicating the views presented here.

[1] Judith Jarvis Thomson, "The Right to Privacy," Thomas Scanlon, "Thomson on
Privacy," and James Rachels, "Why Privacy is Important," *Philosophy & Public Affairs*,
4, no. 4 (Summer 1975): 295–333. Unless otherwise indicated, page numbers in the
text refer to this issue.

because you have rights over your person analogous to the rights you have over your property—and it is because you have these rights that what he does is wrong [p. 313].

From this she concludes that the right to privacy is "derivative," and therefore that "there is no need to find the that-which-is-in-common to all rights in the right of privacy cluster and no need to settle disputes about its boundaries" (p. 313). In other words, we are right not to have any very clear idea about what the right is, and we ought not spin our wheels trying to locate some unique "something" that is protected by the right to privacy. Now I think Thomson is wrong about this—and, incidentally, so do Scanlon and Rachels, although I am inclined to believe they think so for the wrong reasons.

Thomson's argument is a large non sequitur balanced on a small one. She holds that the right to privacy is "derivative" in the sense that each right in the cluster of rights to privacy can be explained by reference to another right and thus without recourse to the right to privacy. This is the little non sequitur. The easiest way to see this is to recognize that it is quite consistent with the notion that the other rights (that is, the rights over one's person and one's property) are—in whole or in part—expressions of the right to privacy, and thus *they are* "derivative" from *it*. If all the protections we include under the right to privacy were specified in the Fourth and Fifth Amendments, this would hardly prove that the right to privacy is "derivative" from the right to be secure against unreasonable search or seizure and the privilege against self-incrimination. It would be just as plausible to assert that this is evidence that the Fourth and Fifth Amendment protections are "derivative" from the right to privacy.[2]

Now all of this would amount to mere semantics, and Professor Thomson could define "derivative" however she pleased, if she didn't use this as an argument against finding (indeed, against even looking for) the "that-which-is-in-common" to the cluster of rights in the right to privacy. This is the large non sequitur. Even if the right were derivative in the sense urged by Thomson, it would not follow that there is nothing in common to all the protections in the right-to-privacy cluster, or that it would be silly to try to find what they have in common. Criminology is probably derivative from sociology and psychology and law and political science in just the

[2] This reversibility of "derivative"-ness is to be found in Justice Douglas' historic opinion on the right to privacy in Griswold v. State of Connecticut. He states there that "specific guarantees in the Bill of Rights have penumbras, formed by emanations from those guarantees that help give them life and substance." The right of privacy, he goes on to say, is contained in the penumbras of the First, Third, Fourth, Fifth, and Ninth Amendment guarantees. Surely the imagery of penumbral emanations suggests that the right to privacy is "derivative" from the rights protected in these amendments. But later Douglas states that the Court is dealing "with a right of privacy older than the Bill of Rights," which along with other language he uses, suggests that the rights in the Bill of Rights are meant to give reality to an even more fundamenal right, the right to privacy, 381 U.S. 479, 85 S. Ct. 1678 (1965).

way that Thomson holds privacy rights to be derivative from rights to person and property. This hardly amounts to a reason for not trying to define the unifying theme of criminological studies—at least a large number of criminologists do not think so.[3] In other words, even if privacy rights were a grab-bag of property and personal rights, it might still be revealing, as well as helpful, in the resolution of difficult moral conflicts to determine whether there is anything unique that this grab-bag protects that makes it worthy of distinction from the full field of property and personal rights.

I shall argue that there is indeed something unique protected by the right to privacy. And we are likely to miss it if we suppose that what is protected is just a subspecies of the things generally safe-guarded by property rights and personal rights. And if we miss it, there may come a time when we think we are merely limiting some personal or property right in favor of some greater good, when in fact we are really sacrificing something of much greater value.

At this point, I shall leave behind all comments on Thomson's paper, since if I am able to prove that there is something unique and uniquely valuable protected by the right to privacy, I shall take this as refutation of her view. It will serve to clarify my own position, however, to indicate briefly what I take to be the shortcomings of the responses of Scanlon and Rachels to Thomson.

Scanlon feels he has refuted Thomson by finding the "special interests" which are the "common foundation" for the right(s) to privacy. He says:

> I agree with Thomson that the rights whose violation strikes us as invasion of privacy are many and diverse, and that these rights do not derive from any single overarching right to privacy. I hold, however, that these rights have a common foundation in the special interests that we have in being able to be free from certain kinds of intrusions. The most obvious examples of such offensive intrusions involve observation of our bodies, our behavior or our interactions with other people (or overhearings of the last two), but while these are central they do not exhaust the field [p. 315].

Now on first glance, it is certainly hard to dispute this claim. But it is nonetheless misleading. Scanlon's position is arresting and appears true because it rests on a tautology, not unlike the classic "explanation" of the capacity of sedatives to induce sleep by virtue of their "dormative powers." The right to privacy *is* the right "to be free from certain kinds of (offensive) intrusions." Scanlon's position is equivalent to holding that the common foundation of our right to privacy lies in our "privatistic interests."

In sum, Scanlon announces that he has found the common element in rights to privacy: rights to privacy protect our special interest in privacy!

---

[3] See for instance, Herman and Julia Schwendinger, "Defenders of Order or Guardians of Human Rights?" *Issues in Criminology* 5, no. 2 (Summer 1970): 123–157, especially the section entitled "The Thirty-Year-Old Controversy," pp. 123–129.

Thomson could hardly deny this, although I doubt she would find it adequate to answer the questions she raised in her essay. What Scanlon has not told us is *why* we have a special interest in privacy, that is, a special interest in being free from certain kinds of intrusions; and *why* it is a legitimate interest, that is, an interest of sufficient importance to warrant protection by our fellow citizens.[4] I suspect that this is the least that would be necessary to convince Thomson that there is a common foundation to privacy rights.

James Rachels tries to provide it. He tries to answer precisely the questions Scanlon leaves unanswered. He asks, "Why, exactly, is privacy important to us?" (p. 323). He starts his answer by categorizing some of the interests we might have in privacy and finds that they basically have to do with protecting our reputations or the secrecy of our plans or the like. Rachels recognizes, however, that

> reflection on these cases gives us little help in understanding the value which privacy has in *normal* or *ordinary* situations. By this I mean situations in which there is nothing embarrassing or shameful or unpopular in what we are doing, and nothing ominous or threatening connected with its possible disclosure. For example, even married couples whose sex-lives are normal (whatever that is), and so who have nothing to be ashamed of, by even the most conventional standards, and certainly nothing to be blackmailed about, do not want their bedrooms bugged [p. 325].

In other words, Rachels recognizes that if there is a unique interest to be protected by the right(s) to privacy, it must be an interest simply in being able to limit other people's observation of us or access to information about us—even if we have certain knowledge that the observation or information would not be used to our detriment or used at all. Rachels tries to identify such an interest and to point out why it is important.

His argument is this. Different human relationships are marked—indeed, in part, constituted—by different degrees of sharing personal information. One shares more of himself with a friend than with an employer, more with a life-long friend than with a casual friend, more with a lover than an acquaintance. He writes that "however one conceives one's relations with other people, there is inseparable from that conception an idea of how it is appropriate to behave with and around them, and what information about oneself it is appropriate for them to have" (pp. 328–329). It is "an important part of what it means to have a friend that we welcome his company, that we confide in him, *that we tell him things about ourselves, and that we show him sides of our personalities which we would not tell or show to just anyone*" (pp. 327–328, my emphasis). And therefore, Rachels concludes, "because our ability to control who has access to us, and who knows what about

---

[4] I think it is fair to say that Scanlon makes no claim to answer these questions in his essay.

us, allows us to maintain the variety of relationships with other people that we want to have, it is, I think, one of the most important reasons why we value privacy" (p. 329).

Rachels acknowledges that his view is similar to that put forth by Charles Fried in *An Anatomy of Values*. Since, for our purposes, we can regard these views as substantially the same, and since they amount to an extremely compelling argument about the basis of our interest in privacy, it will serve us well to sample Fried's version of the doctrine. He writes that

> privacy is the necessary context for relationships which we would hardly be human if we had to do without—the relationships of love, friendship, and trust.
> Love and friendship . . . involve the voluntary and spontaneous relinquishment of something between friend and friend, lover and lover. The title to information about oneself conferred by privacy provides the necessary something. To be friends or lovers persons must be intimate to some degree with each other. Intimacy is the sharing of information about one's actions, beliefs or emotions, which one does not share with all, and which one has the right not to share with anyone. By conferring this right, privacy creates the moral capital which we spend in friendship and love.[5]

The Rachels-Fried theory is this. Only because we are able to withhold personal information about—and forbid intimate observation of—ourselves from the rest of the world, can we give out the personal information—and allow the intimate observations—to friends and/or lovers, that constitute intimate relationships. On this view, intimacy is both signaled and constituted by the sharing of information and allowing of observation *not shared with or allowed to the rest of the world*. If there were nothing about myself that the rest of the world did not have access to, I simply would not have anything to give that would mark off a relationship as intimate. As Fried says,

> The man who is generous with his possessions, but not with himself, can hardly be a friend, nor—and this more clearly shows the necessity of privacy for love— can the man who, voluntarily or involuntarily, shares everything about himself with the world indiscriminately.[6]

[5] Charles Fried, *An Anatomy of Values: Problems of Personal and Social Choice* (Cambridge, Mass., 1970), p. 142. It might be thought that in lifting Fried's analysis of privacy out of his book, I have lifted it out of context and thus done violence to his theory. Extra weight is added to this objection by the recognition that when Fried speaks about love in his book (though not in the chapter relating privacy to love), he speaks of something very like the caring that I present as a basis for refuting his view. For instance Fried writes that, "There is rather a creation of love, a middle term, which is a new pattern or system of interests which both share and both value, in part at least just because it is shared" (ibid., p. 79). What is in conflict between us then is not recognition of this or something like this as an essential component of the love relationship. The conflict rather lies in the fact that I argue that recognition of this factor undermines Fried's claim that *privacy* is *necessary* for the very existence of love relationships.

[6] Ibid., p. 142.

Presumably such a person cannot enter into a friendship or a love because he has literally squandered the "moral capital" which is neccessary for intimate emotional investment in another.

Now I find this analysis both compelling and hauntingly distasteful. It is compelling first of all because it fits much that we ordinarily experience. For example, it makes jealousy understandable. If the value—indeed, the very reality—of my intimate relation with you lies in your sharing with me what you don't share with others, then if you do share it with another, what I have is literally decreased in value and adulterated in substance. This view is also compelling because it meets the basic requirement for identifying a compelling interest at the heart of privacy. That basic requirement is, as I have already stated, an important interest in simply being able to restrict information about, and observation of, myself regardless of what may be done with that information or the results of that observation.

The view is distasteful, however, because it suggests a market conception of personal intimacy. The value and substance of intimacy—like the value and substance of my income—lies not merely in what I have but essentially in what others do *not* have. The reality of my intimacy with you is constituted not simply by the quality and intensity of what we share, but by its unavailability to others—in other words, by its scarcity. It may be that our personal relations are valuable to us because of their exclusiveness rather than because of their own depth or breadth or beauty. But it is not clear that this is necessary. It may be a function of the historical limits of our capacity for empathy and feeling for others. It may be a function of centuries of acculturation to the nuclear family with its narrow intensities. The Rachels-Fried thesis, however, makes it into a logical necessity by asserting that friendship and love *logically* imply exclusiveness and narrowness of focus.

As compelling as the Rachels-Fried view is then, there is reason to believe it is an example of the high art of ideology: the rendering of aspects of our present possessive market-oriented world into the eternal forms of logical necessity. Perhaps the tip-off lies precisely in the fact that, on their theory, jealousy—the most possessive of emotions—is rendered rational. All of this is not itself an argument against the Rachels-Fried view, but rather an argument for suspicion. However, it does suggest an argument against that view.

I think the fallacy in the Rachels-Fried view of intimacy is that it overlooks the fact that what constitutes intimacy is not merely the sharing of otherwise withheld information, but the context of caring which makes the sharing of personal information significant. One ordinarily reveals information to one's psychoanalyst that one might hesitate to reveal to a friend or lover. That hardly means one has an intimate relationship with the analyst. And this is not simply because of the asymmetry. If two analysts decided to psychoanalyze one another alternately—the evident unwisdom of this arrangement aside—there is no reason to believe that their relationship would necessarily be the most intimate one in their lives, even if they revealed to each other information they withheld from everyone else, lifelong friends and lovers included. And this wouldn't be changed if they cared about each other's well-being. What is missing is that particular kind of caring that makes a relationship not just personal but intimate.

The kind of caring I have in mind is not easily put in words, and so I shall claim no more than to offer an approximation. Necessary to an intimate relationship such as friendship or love is a reciprocal desire to share present and future intense and important experiences together, not merely to swap information. Mutual psychoanalysis is not love or even friendship so long as it is not animated by this kind of caring. This is why it remains localized in the office rather than tending to spread into other shared activities, as do love and friendship. Were mutual psychoanalysis animated by such caring it might indeed be part of a love or friendship—but then the "prime mover" of the relationship would not be the exchange of personal information. It would be the caring itself.

In the context of a reciprocal desire to share present and future intense and important experiences, the revealing of personal information takes on significance. The more one knows about the other, the more one is able to understand how the other experiences things, what they mean to him, how they feel to him. In other words the more each knows about the other, the more they are able to really share an intense experience alongside one another. The revealing of personal information then is not what constitutes or powers the intimacy. Rather it deepens and fills out, invites and nurtures, the caring that powers the intimacy.

On this view—in contrast to the Rachels-Fried view—it is of little importance who has access to personal information about me. What matters is who cares about it and to whom I care to reveal it. Even if all those to whom I am indifferent and who return the compliment were to know the intimate details of my personal history, my capacity to enter into an intimate relationship would remain unhindered. So long as I could find someone who did not just want to collect data about me, but who cared to know about me in order to share my experience with me and to whom I cared to reveal information about myself so that person could share my experience with me, and vice versa, I could enter into a meaningful friendship or love relationship.

On the Rachels-Fried view, it follows that the significance of sexual intimacy lies in the fact that we signal the uniqueness of our love relationships by allowing our bodies to be seen and touched by the loved one in ways that are forbidden to others. But here too, the context of caring that turns physical contact into intimacy is overlooked. A pair of urologists who examine each other are no more lovers than our reciprocating psychoanalysts. What is missing is the desire to share intense and important experiences. And to say this is to see immediately the appropriateness of sexual intimacy to love: in sexual intimacy one is literally and symbolically stripped of the ordinary masks that obstruct true sharing of experience. This happens not merely in the nakedness of lovers but even more so in the giving of themselves over to the physical forces in their bodies. In surrendering the ordinary restraints, lovers allow themselves to be what they truly are—at least as bodies—intensely and together. (Recall Sartre's marvelous description of the *caress*.) [7] If this takes place in the context of caring—in other words if people are making love and not just fucking—their physical intimacy is an expression and a consummation of that caring. It is one form of the authentic speech of loving.

Finally, on this view—in contrast to the Rachels-Fried view—the unsavory market notion of intimacy is avoided. Since the content of intimacy is caring, rather than the revealing of information or the granting of access to the body usually withheld from others, there is no necessary limit to the number of persons one can be intimate with, no logical necessity that friendship or love be exclusive. The limits rather lie in the limits of our capacity to care deeply for others, and of course in the limits of time and energy. In other words it may be a fact—for us at this point in history, or even for all people at all points in history—that we can only enter into a few true friendships and loves in a lifetime. But this is not an inescapable logical necessity. It is only an empirical fact of our capacity, one that might change and might be worth trying to change. It might be a fact that we are unable to disentangle love from jealousy. But this, too, is not an a priori truth. It is rather an empirical fact, one that might change if fortune brought us into a less possessive, less exclusive, less invidious society.

This much is enough, I think, to cast doubt on the relationship between privacy and friendship or love asserted by Rachels and Fried. It should also be enough to refute their theory of the grounds on which the right to privacy rests. For if intimacy *may* be a function of caring and not of the yielding of otherwise withheld information, their claim to have established the *necessity* of privacy for important human relationships must fall. I think, however, that there is another equally fundamental ground for rejecting their position: it makes the right to individual privacy "derivative" from the right to social (that is, interpersonal) relationships. And I mean "derivative" in a much more irreversible way than Thomson does.

On the Rachels-Fried view, my right to parade around naked alone in my house free from observation by human or electronic peeping toms, is not a fundamental right. It is derived from the fact that without this right, I could not meaningfully reveal my body to the loved one in that exclusive

[7] "The Other's flesh did not exist explicitly for me since I grasped the Other's body in situation; neither did it exist for her since she transcended it toward her possibilities and toward the object. The caress causes the Other to be born as flesh for me and for herself . . . , the caress reveals the flesh by stripping the body of its action, by cutting it off from the possibilities which surround it; the caress is designed to uncover the web of inertia beneath the action—i.e., the pure 'being-there'—which sustains it. . . . The caress is designed to cause the Other's body to be born, through pleasure, for the Other—and for myself. . . ." Jean-Paul Sartre, *Being and Nothingness*, trans. Hazel E. Barnes (New York, 1956), p. 390.

way that is necessary to intimacy on the Rachels-Fried view. This strikes me as bizarre. It would imply that a person who had no chance of entering into social relations with others, say a catatonic or a perfectly normal person legitimately sentenced to life imprisonment in solitary confinement, would thereby have no ground for a right to privacy. This must be false, because it seems that if there is a right to privacy it belongs to individuals regardless of whether they are likely to have friends or lovers, regardless of whether they have reason to amass "the moral capital which we spend in friendship and love." What this suggests is that even if the Rachels-Fried theory of the relationship of privacy and intimacy were true, it would not give us a fundamental interest that can provide the foundation for a right to privacy for all human individuals. I believe, however, that such a fundamental interest can be unearthed. Stanley I. Benn's theory of the foundation of privacy comes closer to the view which I think is ultimately defensible.

Benn attempts to base the right to privacy on the principle of respect for persons. He too is aware that utilitarian considerations—for example, prevention of harm that may result from misuse of personal information—while important, are not adequate to ground the right to privacy.

> The underpinning of a claim not to be watched without leave will be more general if it can be grounded in this way on the principle of respect for persons than on a utilitarian duty to avoid inflicting suffering. That duty may, of course, reinforce the claim in particular instances. But respect for persons will sustain an objection even to secret watching, which may do no actual harm at all. Covert observation—spying—is objectionable because it deliberately deceives a person about his world [that is, it transforms the situation he thinks is unobserved into one which is observed], thwarting, for reasons that *cannot* be his reasons, his attempts to make a rational choice. One cannot be said to respect a man as engaged on an enterprise worthy of consideration if one knowingly and deliberately alters his conditions of action, concealing the fact from him. The offense is different in this instance, of course, from A's open intrusion on C's conversation. In that case, A's attentions were liable to affect C's enterprise by changing C's perception of it; he may have felt differently about his conversation with D, even to the extent of not being able to see it as any longer the same activity, knowing that A was now listening.[8]

Benn's view is that the right to privacy rests on the principle of respect for persons as choosers. Covert observation or unwanted overt observation deny this respect because they transform the actual conditions in which the person chooses and acts, and thus make it impossible for him to act in the way he set out to act, or to choose in the way he thinks he is choosing.

This too is a compelling analysis. I shall myself argue that the right to privacy is fundamentally connected to personhood. However, as it stands,

<hr>

[8] Stanley I. Benn, "Privacy, Freedom, and Respect for Persons," in Richard Wasserstrom, ed., *Today's Moral Problems* (New York, 1975), p. 8.

Benn's theory gives us too much—and though he appears to know it, his way of trimming the theory to manageable scale is not very helpful. Benn's theory gives us too much because it appears to establish a person's right never to be observed when he thought he wasn't being observed, and never to be overtly observed when he didn't wish it. This would give us a right not to have people look at us from their front windows as we absent-mindedly stroll along, as well as a right not to be stared in the face. To deal with this, Benn writes,

> it cannot be sufficient that I do not *want* you to observe something; for the principle of respect to be relevant, it must be something about my own person that is in question, otherwise the principle would be so wide that a mere wish of mine would be a prima facie reason for everyone to refrain from observing and reporting on anything at all. I do not make something a part of me merely by having feelings about it. The principle of privacy proposed here is, rather, that any man who desires that he *himself* should not be an object of scrutiny has a reasonable claim to immunity.[9]

Benn goes on to say that what is rightly covered by this immunity are one's body and those things, like possessions, which the conventions of a culture may cause one to think of as part of one's identity.

But this begs the question. Benn has moved from the principle that respect for me as a person dictates that I am entitled not to have the conditions in which I choose altered by unknown or unwanted observation, to the principle that I am entitled to have those things (conventionally) bound up with my identity exempt from unknown or unwanted observation. But the first principle does not entail the second, because the second principle is not merely a practical limitation on the first; it is a moral limitation. It asserts that it is wrong (or at least, significantly worse) to have the conditions in which I choose altered, when things closely bound up with my identity are concerned. But this follows only if the first principle is conjoined with another that holds that the closer something is to my identity, the worse it is for others to tamper with it. But this is after all just an abstract version of the right to privacy itself. And since Benn has not shown that it follows from the principle of respect for persons as choosers, his argument presupposes what he seeks to establish. It is quite strictly a *petitio principii*.

In sum then, though we have moved quite a bit further in the direction of the foundation of privacy, we have still not reached our destination. What we are looking for is a fundamental interest, connected to personhood, which provides a basis for a right to privacy to which all human beings are entitled (even those in solitary confinement) and which does not go so far as to claim a right never to be observed (even on crowded streets). I proceed now to the consideration of a candidate for such a fundamental interest.

Privacy is a social practice. It involves a complex of behaviors that

[9] Ibid., p. 10.

stretches from refraining from asking questions about what is none of one's business to refraining from looking into open windows one passes on the street, from refraining from entering a closed door without knocking to refraining from knocking down a locked door without a warrant.

Privacy can in this sense be looked at as a very complicated social ritual. But what is its point? In response I want to defend the following thesis. *Privacy is a social ritual by means of which an individual's moral title to his existence is conferred.* Privacy is an essential part of the complex social practice by means of which the social group recognizes—and communicates to the individual—that his existence is his own. And this is a precondition of personhood. To be a person, an individual must recognize not just his actual capacity to shape his destiny by his choices. He must also recognize that he has an exclusive moral right to shape his destiny. And this in turn presupposes that he believes that the concrete reality which he is, and through which his destiny is realized, belongs to him in a moral sense.

And if one takes—as I am inclined to—the symbolic interactionist perspective which teaches that "selves" are created in social interaction rather than flowering innately from inborn seeds, to this claim is added an even stronger one: privacy is necessary to the creation of *selves* [10] out of human beings, since a self is at least in part a human being who regards his existence—his thoughts, his body, his actions—as his *own*.

Thus the relationship between privacy and personhood is a twofold one. First, the social ritual of privacy seems to be an essential ingredient in the process by which "persons" are created out of prepersonal infants. It conveys to the developing child the recognition that this body to which he is uniquely "connected" is a body over which he has some exclusive moral rights. Secondly, the social ritual of privacy confirms, and demonstrates respect for, the personhood of already developed persons. I take the notion of "conferring title to one's existence" to cover both dimensions of the relationship of privacy to personhood: the original bestowal of title and the ongoing confirmation. And of course, to the extent that we believe that the creation of "selves" or "persons" is an ongoing social process—not just something which occurs once and for all during childhood—the two dimensions become one: privacy is a condition of the original and continuing creation of "selves" or "persons."

To understand the meaning of this claim, it will be helpful to turn to Erving Goffman's classic study, "On the Characteristics of Total Institutions." [11] Goffman says of total institutions that "each is a natural experi-

---

[10] For purposes of this discussion, we can take "self" and "person" as equivalent. I use them both insofar as they refer to an individual who recognizes that he *owns* his physical and mental reality in the sense that he is morally entitled to realize his destiny through it, and thus that he has at least a strong presumptive moral right not to have others interfere with his self-determination.

[11] Erving Goffman, *Asylums* (New York, 1961), pp. 1–124.

ment on what can be done to the self." [12] The goal of these experiments is *mortification of the self,* and in each case total deprivation of privacy is an essential ingredient in the regimen. I have taken the liberty of quoting Goffman at length, since I think his analysis provides poignant testimony to the role that elimination of privacy plays in destruction of the self. And thus conversely, he shows the degree to which the self *requires* the social rituals of privacy to exist.

> There is another form of mortification in total institutions; beginning with admission a kind of contaminative exposure occurs. On the outside, the individual can hold objects of self-feeling—such as his body, his immediate actions, his thoughts, and some of his possessions—clear of contact with alien and contaminating things. But in total institutions *these territories of the self are violated....*
>
> There is, first, a violation of one's informational preserve regarding self. During admission, facts about the inmate's social statuses and past behavior—especially discreditable facts—are collected and recorded in a dossier available to staff....
>
> New audiences not only learn discreditable facts about oneself that are ordinarily concealed but are also in a position to perceive some of these facts directly. Prisoners and mental patients cannot prevent their visitors from seeing them in humiliating circumstances. Another example is the shoulder-patch of ethnic identification worn by concentration-camp inmates. Medical and security examinations often expose the inmate physically, sometimes to persons of both sexes; a similar exposure follows from collective sleeping arrangements and doorless toilets.... In general, of course, the inmate is never fully alone, he is always within sight and often earshot of someone, if only his fellow inmates. Prison cages with bars for walls fully realize such exposure.[13]

That social practices which penetrate "the private reserve of the individual" [14] are effective means to mortify the inmate's self—that is, literally, to kill if off—suggests (though it doesn't prove) that privacy is essential to the creation and maintenance of selves. My argument for this will admittedly be speculative. However, in view of the fact that it escapes the shortcomings of the views we have already analyzed, fits Goffman's evidence on the effects of deprivation of privacy, fulfills the requirement that it be a fundamental human interest worthy of protection, provides the basis for a right to privacy to which all human beings are entitled, and yet does not claim a right never to be observed, I think it is convincing.

If I am sitting with other people, how do I know this body which is connected to the thoughts I am having is *mine* in the moral sense? That is, how do I know that I have a unique moral right to this body? It is not enough to say that it is connected to my consciousness, since that simply repeats the

[12] Ibid., p. 12.
[13] Ibid., pp. 23–25; my emphasis.
[14] Ibid., p. 29.

question or begs the question of what makes these thoughts *my* consciousness. In any event, connection to my consciousness is a factual link, not a moral one. In itself it accounts for why I am not likely to confuse the events in this body (mine) with events in that body (yours). It does not account for the moral title which gives me a unique right to control the events in this body which I don't have in respect to the events in that body.

Ownership in the moral sense presupposes a social institution. It is based upon a complex social practice. A social order in which bodies were held to belong to others or to the collectivity, and in which individuals grew up believing that their bodies were not theirs from a moral point of view, is conceivable. To imagine such an order does not require that we deny that for each body only one individual is able to feel or move it. Such a social order is precisely what Goffman portrays in his description of total institutions and it might be thought of as displaying the ultimate logic of totalitarianism. Totalitarianism is the political condition that obtains when a state takes on the characteristics of a total institution. For a society to exist in which individuals do not own their bodies, what is necessary is that people not be treated as if entitled to control what the bodies they can feel and move do, or what is done to those bodies—in particular that they not be treated as if entitled to determine when and by whom that body is experienced.[15]

This suggests that there are two essential conditions of moral owership of one's body. The right to do with my body what I wish, and the right to control when and by whom my body is experienced. This in turn reflects the fact that things can be appropriated in two ways: roughly speaking, actively and cognitively. That is, something is "mine" to the extent that I have the power to use it, to dispose of it as I see fit. But additionally there is a way in which something becomes "mine" to the extent that I know it. What I know is "my" knowledge; what I experience is "my" experience. Thus, it follows that if an individual were granted the right to control his bodily movements although always under observation, he might develop some sense of moral ownership of his physical existence.[16] However, that ownership would surely be an impoverished and partial one compared to what we take to be contained in an individual's title to his existence. This is because it would be ownership only in one of the two dimensions of appropriation, the active. Ownership, in the sense we know it, requires control over cognitive appropriation as well. It requires that the individual have control over whether or not his physical existence becomes part of someone

[15] Macabre as it may sound, a world in which the body that I can feel and move *is distinct from* the body that I own *is* conceivable. Imagine, for example, a world of 365 people each born on a different day of the year, in which each person has complete access to the body of the person whose birthday is the day after his.

[16] I am indebted to Professor Phillip H. Schribner for pointing this out to me.

else's experience. That is, it requires that the individual be treated as entitled to determine when and by whom his concrete reality is experienced. Moral ownership in the full sense requires the social ritual of privacy.

As I sit among my friends, I know this body is mine because first of all, unlike any other body present, I believe—and my friends have acted and continue to act as if they believe—that I am entitled to do with this body what I wish. Secondly, but also essential, I know this body is mine because unlike any other body present, I have in the past taken it outside of the range of anyone's experience but my own, I can do so now, and I expect to be able to do so in the future. What's more, I believe—and my friends have acted and continue to act as if they believe—that it would be wrong for anyone to interfere with my capacity to do this. In other words, they have and continue to treat me according to the social ritual of privacy. And since my view of myself is, in important ways, a reflection of how others treat me, I come to view myself as the kind of entity that is entitled to the social ritual of privacy. That is, I come to believe that this body is mine in the moral sense.

I think the same thing can be said about the thoughts of which I am aware. That there are thoughts, images, reveries and memories of which only I am conscious does not make them mine in the moral sense—any more than the cylinders in a car belong to it just because they are in it. This is why ascribing ownership of my body to the mere connection with my consciousness begs the question. Ownership of my thoughts requires a social practice as well. It has to do with learning that I can control when, and by whom, the thoughts in my head will be experienced by someone other than myself and learning that I am entitled to such control—that I will not be forced to reveal the contents of my consciousness, even when I put those contents on paper. The contents of my consciousness become mine because they are treated according to the ritual of privacy.

It may seem that this is to return full circle to Thomson's view that the right to privacy is just a species of the rights over person and property. I would argue that it is more fundamental. The right to privacy is the right to the existence of a social practice which makes it possible for me to think of this existence as *mine*. This means that it is the right to conditions necessary for me to think of myself as the kind of entity for whom it would be meaningful and important to claim personal and property rights. It should also be clear that the ownership of which I am speaking is surely more fundamental than property rights. Indeed, it is only when I can call this physical existence mine that I can call objects somehow connected to this physical existence mine. That is, the transformation of physical possession into ownership presupposes ownership of the physical being I am. Thus the right to privacy protects something that is presupposed by both personal and property rights. Thomson's recognition that there is overlap should come as no surprise. The conclusion she draws from the existence of this overlap is, however, unwarranted. Personal and property rights presuppose an individual with title to his existence—and privacy is the social ritual by which that title is conferred.

The right to privacy, then, protects the individual's interest in becoming, being, and remaining a person. It is thus a right which *all* human individuals possess—even those in solitary confinement. It does not assert a right never to be seen even on a crowded street. It is sufficient that I can control whether and by whom my body is experienced in some significant places and that I have the real possibility of repairing to those places. It is a right which protects my capacity to enter into intimate relations, not because it protects my reserve of generally withheld information, but because it enables me to make the commitment that underlies caring as *my* commitment uniquely conveyed by *my* thoughts and witnessed by *my* actions.

11

Abortion:
A Woman's Right

Abortion was forcibly brought to the attention of Americans during the period in which horribly deformed babies were being born to women who had been given the drug thalidomide during pregnancy. Abortion was illegal and women who had taken the tranquilizer on a physician's advice had to decide whether to abort illegally, risk bearing an armless or legless child, or go abroad for a legal abortion at great expense. In 1973 in *Roe* v. *Wade* the U.S. Supreme Court ruled a Texas woman who filed under the pseudonym "Jane Roe" was deprived of her constitutional rights by state laws forbidding all abortions except those that were needed to save the mother's life. Justice Blackmun wrote the majority opinion (7–2) affirming the woman's right of privacy and due process and the right to an abortion up to the end of the first three months of pregnancy. After the first trimester, the opinion said, states may make laws restricting abortion, if compelling state interest can be demonstrated.

In the dissent, Justices White and Rehnquist held that the Court was overstepping its authority, and creating something that had not before existed, a "right for pregnant mothers" taking precedence over "the right of potential life of the fetus." The abortion controversy was by no means ended. Efforts to secure local laws severely restricting abortions, and to place in the Constitution an amendment forbidding it, have been vigorous and persistent. Some political figures claim that many voters are one-issue voters, and that abortion, like gun control, has made the political fortunes of some senators or representatives who had little claim to office other than their opposition on one or both of these issues, bearing children and bearing arms. Writing before the Supreme Court decision, Judith Jarvis Thomson laid out an argument for woman's right as over against the fetus's right-to-life, so often the rallying ground for abortion foes. Though rejecting the idea that a fetus is a person from the moment of conception and that all abortion is thus taking the life of a person, Thomson defends the right of a pregnant woman to abort herself in many cases in which all might agree, for argument's sake, that the fetus is a person. Generally, this is on the grounds of a kind of self-defense, the most obvious case being pregnancy by rape, in which she is forced to be pregnant by a man who wishes her ill. But mostly the paper rebuts the claims of right-to-life arguments. The fetus's right to life does not give it the right to use her body. That right of occupancy is conditional upon other factors of her choosing, and of her sexual partner's, as in most of the pregnancies that we regard either as being willing or at least accepted by the woman as within the sphere of her responsibilities. Her examples deserve careful study.

Baruch Brody's reply to Thomson offers counterexamples. Thomson would be justified in saying a woman has no duty to offer a zygote conceived in a test tube (Petri dish, actually) her uterus as a place of incubation because it has no other place to live. But a woman cannot get rid of a fetus inside her without killing it. (Of course, we rule out the remote chance of finding another woman to have it implanted in her.) So it isn't merely refusal to save a fetal life but the taking of fetal life that is involved here. I'd not be morally obligated to save your life if it would bankrupt me to do so, but I have no right to take your life to prevent bankruptcy to myself. If a fetus is a person from the moment of conception, not even danger to the woman's life justifies killing it. Generally, then, Brody stresses the distinction between the duty to save a life and the duty not to take a life. But Brody does allow one carefully restricted case where abortion would be morally right.

ROE V. WADE 410 U.S. 113, 93 S.CT. 705 (1973) °

MAJORITY OPINION

❋   ❋   ❋

When most criminal abortion laws were first enacted, the procedure was a hazardous one for the woman. This was particularly true prior to the development of antisepsis. Antiseptic techniques, of course, were based on discoveries by Lister, Pasteur, and others first announced in 1867, but were not generally accepted and employed until about the turn of the century. Abortion mortality was high. Even after 1900, and perhaps until as late as the development of antibiotics in the 1940s, standard modern techniques such as dilation and curettage were not nearly so safe as they are today. Thus it has been argued that a State's real concern in enacting a criminal abortion law

* United States Supreme Court, 1973, majority opinion, by Mr. Justice Blackmun.

was to protect the pregnant woman, that is, to restrain her from submitting to a procedure that placed her life in serious jeopardy.

Modern medical techniques have altered this situation. Appellants and various *amici* refer to medical data indicating that abortion in early pregnancy, that is, prior to the end of first trimester, although not without its risk, is now relatively safe. Mortality rates for women undergoing early abortions, where the procedure is legal, appear to be as low as or lower than the rates for normal childbirth. Consequently, any interest of the State in protecting the woman from an inherently hazardous procedure, except when it would be equally dangerous for her to forgo it, has largely disappeared. Of course, important state interests in the area of health and medical standards do remain. The State has a legitimate interest in seeing to it that abortion, like any other medical procedure, is performed under circumstances that insure maximum safety for the patient. This interest obviously extends at least to the performing physician and his staff, to the facilities involved, to the availability of aftercare, and to adequate provision for any complication or emergency that might arise. The prevalence of high mortality rates at illegal "abortion mills" strengthens, rather than weakens, the State's interest in regulating the conditions under which abortions are performed. Moreover, the risk to the woman increases as her pregnancy continues. Thus the State retains a definite interest in protecting the woman's own health and safety when an abortion is proposed at a late stage of pregnancy.

[Another] reason is the State's interest—some phrase it in terms of duty— in protecting prenatal life. Some of the argument for this justification rests on the theory that a new human life is present from the moment of conception. The State's interest and general obligation to protect life then extends, it is argued, to prenatal life. Only when the life of the pregnant mother herself is at stake, balanced against the life she carries within her, should the interest of the embryo or fetus not prevail. Logically, of course, a legitimate state interest in this area need not stand or fall on acceptance of the belief that life begins at conception or at some other point prior to live birth. In assessing the State's interest, recognition may be given to the less rigid claim that as long as at least *potential* life is involved, the State may assert interests beyond the protection of the pregnant woman alone.

Parties challenging state abortion laws have sharply disputed in some courts the contention that a purpose of these laws, when enacted, was to protect prenatal life. Pointing to the absence of legislative history to support the contention, they claim that most state laws were designed solely to protect the woman. Because medical advances have lessened this concern, at least with respect to abortion in early pregnancy, they argue that with respect to such abortions the laws can no longer be justified by any state interest. There is some scholarly support for this view of original purpose. The few state courts called upon to interpret their laws in the 19th and early 20th centuries did focus on the State's interest in protecting the woman's health rather than in preserving the embryo and fetus. Proponents of this view point out that in many States, including Texas, by statute or judicial interpretation, the pregnant woman herself could not be prosecuted for self-abortion or for cooperating in an abortion performed upon her by another. They claim that adoption of the "quickening" distinction through received common law and state statutes tacitly recognizes the greater health hazards inherent in late abortion and impliedly repudiates the theory that life begins at conception.

It is with these interests, and the weight to be attached to them, that this case is concerned.

The Constitution does not explicitly mention any right of privacy. In a line of decisions, however, going back perhaps as far as Union Pacific R. C. v. Botsford, 141 U.S. 250, 251, 11 S.Ct. 1000, 1001, 35 L.Ed. 734 (1891), the Court has recognized that a right of personal privacy, or a guarantee of certain areas or zones of privacy, does exist under the Constitution. In varying contexts the Court or individual Justices have indeed found at least the roots of that right in the First Amendment . . .; the Fourth and Fifth Amendments, . . . the Bill of Rights, . . . the Ninth Amendment, or in the concept of liberty guaranteed by the first section of the Fourteenth Amendment, . . . These decisions make it clear . . . that the right has some extension to activities relating to marriage, . . . procreation, . . . contraception, . . . family relationships, . . . and child rearing and education, ...

This right of privacy, whether it be founded in the Fourteenth Amendment's concept of personal liberty and restrictions upon state action, as we feel it is, or, as the District Court determined, in the Ninth Amendment's reservation of rights to the people, is broad enough to encompass a woman's decision whether or not to terminate her pregnancy. The detriment that the State would impose upon the pregnant woman by denying this choice altogether is apparent. Specific and direct harm medically diagnosable even in early pregnancy may be involved. Maternity, or additional offspring, may force upon the woman a distressful life and future. Psychological harm may be imminent. Mental and physical health may be taxed by child care. There is also the distress, for all concerned, associated with the unwanted child, and there is the problem of bringing a child into a family already unable, psychologically and otherwise, to care for it. In other cases, as in this one, the additional difficulties and continuing stigma of unwed motherhood may be involved. All these are factors the woman and her responsible physician necessarily will consider in consultation.

On the basis of elements such as these, appellants and some *amici* argue that the woman's right is absolute and that she is entitled to terminate her pregnancy at whatever time, in whatever way, and for whatever reason she alone chooses. With this we do not agree. Appellants' arguments that Texas either has no valid interest at all in regulating the abortion decision, or no interest strong enough to support any limitation upon the woman's sole determination, is unpersuasive. The Court's decisions recognizing a right of privacy also acknowledge that some state regulation in areas protected by that right is appropriate. As noted above, a state may properly assert important interests in safeguarding health, in maintaining medical standards, and in protecting potential life. At some point in pregnancy, these respective interests become sufficiently compelling to sustain regulation of the factors that govern the abortion decision. The privacy right involved, therefore, cannot be said to be absolute. In fact, it is not clear to us that the claim asserted by some *amici* that one has an unlimited right to do with one's body as one pleases bears a close relationship to the right of privacy previously articulated in the Court's decisions. The Court has refused to recognize an unlimited right of this kind in the past. Jacobson v. Massachusetts, 197 U.S. 11, 25 S.Ct. 358, 49 L.Ed. 643 (1905) (vaccination); Buck v. Bell, 274 U.S. 200, 47 S.Ct. 584, 71 L.Ed. 1000 (1927) (sterilization).

We therefore conclude that the right of personal privacy includes the abortion decision, but that this right is not unqualified and must be considered against important state interests in regulation.

We note that those federal and state courts that have recently considered abortion law challenges have reached the same conclusion. A majority, in addition to the District Court in the present case, have held state laws unconstitutional, at least in part, because of vagueness or because of overbreadth and abridgement of rights. . . .

Although the results are divided, most of these courts have agreed that the right of privacy, however based, is broad enough to cover the abortion decision; that the right, nonetheless, is not absolute and is subject to some limitations; and that at some point the state interests as to protection of health, medical standards, and prenatal life, become dominant. We agree with this approach.

Where certain "fundamental rights" are involved, the Court has held that regulation limiting these rights may be justified only by a "compelling state interest," . . . .

In the recent abortion cases, cited above, courts have recognized these principles. Those striking down state laws have generally scrutinized the State's interest in protecting health and potential life and have concluded that neither interest justified broad limitations on the reasons for which a physician and his pregnant patient might decide that she should have an abortion in the early stages of pregnancy. Courts sustaining state laws have held that the State's determinations to protect health or prenatal life are dominant and constitutionally justifiable.

The District Court held that the appellee failed to meet his burden of demonstrating that the Texas statute's infringement upon Roe's rights was necessary to support a compelling state interest, and that, although the defendant presented "several compelling justifications for state presence in the area of abortions," the statutes outstripped these justifications and swept "far beyond any areas of compelling state interest."* . . . Appellant and appellee both contest that holding. Appellant, as has been indicated, claims an absolute right that bars any state imposition of criminal penalties in the area. Appellee argues that the State's determination to recognize and protect prenatal life from and after conception constitutes a compelling state interest. As noted above, we do not agree fully with either formulation.

A. The appellee and certain *amici* argue that the fetus is a "person" within the language and meaning of the Fourteenth Amendment. In support of this they outline at length and in detail the well-known facts of fetal development. If this suggestion of personhood is established, the appellant's case, of course, collapses, for the fetus' right to life is then guaranteed specifically by the Amendment. The appellant conceded as much on reargument. On the other hand, the appellee conceded on reargument that no case could be cited that holds that a fetus is a person within the meaning of the Fourteenth Amendment.

The Constitution does not define "person" in so many words. Section 1 of the Fourteenth Amendment contains three references to "person." The first, in defining "citizens," speaks of "persons born or naturalized in the United States." The word also appears both in the Due Process Clause and in the Equal Protection Clause. "Person" is used in other places in the Constitution: in the listing of qualifications for representatives and senators, Art. I, § 2, cl. 2, and § 3, cl. 3; in the Apportionment Clause, Art. I, § 2, cl. 3; in the Migration and Importation provision, Art. I, § 9, cl. 1; in the Emolument Clause, Art. I, § 9, cl. 8; in the Electors provisions, Art. II, § 1, cl. 2, and the superseded cl. 3; in the provision outlining qualifications for the office of President, Art. II, § 1, cl. 5; in the Extradition provisions, Art. IV, § 2, cl. 2, and the superseded Fugitive Slave cl. 3; and in the Fifth, Twelfth, and Twenty-second Amendments as well as in §§ 2 and 3 of the Fourteenth Amendment. But in nearly all these instances, the use of the word is such that it has application only postnatally. None indicates, with any assurance, that it has any possible pre-natal application.

[12] All this, together with our observation, *supra*, that throughout the major portion of the 19th century prevailing legal abortion practices were far freer than they are today, persuades us that the word "person," as used in the Fourteenth Amendment, does not include the unborn. This is in accord with the results reached in those few cases where the issue has been squarely presented. . . . Indeed, our decision in United States v. Vuitch, 402 U.S. 62, 91 S.Ct. 1294, 28 L.Ed.2d 601 (1971), inferentially is to the same effect, for we there would not have indulged in statutory interpretation favorable to abortion in specified circumstances if the necessary consequence was the termination of life entitled to Fourteenth Amendment protection.

This conclusion, however, does not of itself fully answer the contentions raised by Texas, and we pass on to other considerations.

B. The pregnant woman cannot be isolated in her privacy. She carries an embryo and, later, a fetus, if one accepts the medical definitions of the developing young in the human uterus. See Dorland's *Illustrated Medical Dictionary*, 478–479, 547 (24th ed. 1965). The situation therefore is inherently different from marital intimacy, or bedroom possession of obscene material, or marriage, or procreation, or education, with which *Eisenstadt, Griswold, Stanley, Loving, Skinner, Pierce,* and *Meyer* were respectively concerned. As we have intimated above, it is reasonable and appropriate for a State to decide that at some point in time another interest, that of health of the mother or that of potential human life, becomes significantly involved. The woman's privacy is no longer sole and any right of privacy she possesses must be measured accordingly.

Texas urges that, apart from the Fourteenth Amendment, life begins at conception and is present throughout pregnancy, and that, therefore, the State has a compelling interest in protecting that life from and after conception. We need not resolve the difficult question of when life begins. When those trained in the respective disciplines of medicine, philosophy, and theology are unable to arrive at any consensus, the judiciary, at this point in the development of man's knowledge, is not in a position to speculate as to the answer.

It should be sufficient to note briefly the wide divergence of thinking on this most sensitive and difficult question. There has always been strong support for the view that life does not begin until live birth. This was the belief of the Stoics. It appears to be the predominant, though not the unanimous, attitude of the Jewish faith. It may be taken to represent also the position of a large segment of the Protestant community, insofar as that can be ascertained; organized groups that have taken a formal position on the abortion issue have generally regarded abortion as a matter for the conscience of the individual and her family. As we have noted, the common law found greater significance in quickening. Physicians and their scientific colleagues have regarded that event with less interest and have tended to focus either upon conception or upon live birth or upon the interim point at which the fetus becomes "viable," that is, potentially able to live outside the mother's womb, albeit with artificial aid. Viability is usually placed at about seven months (28 weeks) but may occur earlier, even at 24 weeks. The Aristotelian theory of "mediate animation," that held sway throughout the Middle Ages and the Renaissance in Europe, continued to be official Roman Catholic dogma until the 19th century, despite opposition to this "ensoulment" theory from those in the Church who would recognize the existence of life from the moment of conception. The latter is now, of course, the official belief of the Catholic Church. As one of the briefs *amicus* discloses, this is a view strongly held by many non-Catholics as well, and by many physicians. Substantial problems for precise definition of this view are posed, however, by new embryological data that purport to indicate that conception is a "process" over time, rather than an event, and by new medical techniques such as menstrual extraction, the "morning-after" pill, implantation of embryos, artificial insemination, and even artificial wombs.

In areas other than criminal abortion the law has been reluctant to endorse any theory that life, as we recognize it, begins before live birth or to accord legal rights to the unborn except in narrowly defined situations and except when the rights are contingent upon live birth. For example, the traditional rule of tort law had denied recovery for prenatal injuries even though the child was born alive. That rule has been changed in almost every jurisdiction. In most States recovery is said to be permitted only if the fetus was viable, or at least quick, when the injuries were sustained, though few courts have squarely so held. In a recent development, generally opposed by the commentators, some States permit the parents of a stillborn child to maintain an action for wrongful death because of prenatal injuries. Such an action, however, would appear to be one to vindicate the parents' interest and is thus consistent with the view that the fetus, at most, represents only the potentiality of life. Similarly, unborn children have been recognized as acquiring rights or interests by way of inheritance or other devolution of property, and have been represented by guardians *ad litem*. Perfection of the interests involved, again, has generally been contingent upon live birth. In short, the unborn have never been recognized in the law as persons in the whole sense.

In view of all this, we do not agree that, by adopting one theory of life, Texas may override the rights of the pregnant woman that are at stake. We repeat, however, that the State does have an important and legitimate interest in preserving and protecting the health of the pregnant woman, whether she be a resident of the State or a non-resident who seeks medical consultation and treatment there, and that it has still *another* important and legitimate interest in protecting the potentiality of human life. These interests are separate and distinct. Each grows in substantiality as the woman approaches term and, at a point during pregnancy, each becomes "compelling."

With respect to the State's important and legitimate interest in the health of the mother, the "compelling" point, in the light of present medical knowledge, is at approximately the end of the first trimester. . . . until the end of the first trimester mortality in abortion is less than mortality in normal childbirth. It follows that, from and after this point, a State may regulate the abortion procedure to the extent that the regulation reasonably relates to the preservation and protection of maternal health. Examples of permissible state regulation in this area are requirements as to the qualifications of the person who is to perform the abortion; as to the licensure of that person; as to the facility in which the procedure is to be performed, that is, whether it must be a hospital or may be a clinic or some other place of less-than-hospital status; as to the licensing of the facility; and the life.

This means, on the other hand, that, for the period of pregnancy prior to this "compelling" point, the attending physician, in consultation with his patient, is free to determine, without regulation by the State, that in his medical judgment the patient's pregnancy should be terminated. If that decision is reached, the judgment may be effectuated by an abortion free of interference by the State.

With respect to the State's important and legitimate interest in potential life, the "compelling" point is at viability. This is so because the fetus then presumably has the capability of meaningful life outside the mother's womb. State regulation protective of fetal life after viability thus has both logical and biological justifications. If the State is interested in protecting fetal life after viability, it may go so far as to proscribe abortion during that period except when it is necessary to preserve the life or health of the mother.

Measured against these standards, Art. 1196 of the Texas Penal Code, in restricting legal abortions to those "procured or attempted by medical advice for the purpose of saving the life of the mother," sweeps too broadly. The statute makes no distinction between abortions performed early in pregnancy and those performed later, and it limits to a single reason, "saving" the mother's life, the legal justification for the procedure. The statute, therefore, cannot survive the constitutional attack made upon it here. . . .

*   *   *

CONCURRING OPINION

Mr. Justice Douglas, concurring.*
While I join the opinion of the court, I add a few words.

The questions presented in the present cases go far beyond the issues of vagueness, which we considered in United States v. Vuitch, 402 U.S. 62, 91 S.Ct. 1294, 28 L.Ed.2d 601. They involve the right of privacy, one aspect of which we considered in Griswold v. Connecticut, 381 U.S. 479, 484, 85 S.Ct. 1678, 1681, 14 L.Ed.2d 510, when we held that various guarantees in the Bill of Rights create zones of privacy.

The *Griswold* case involved a law forbidding the use of contraceptives. We held that law as applied to married people unconstitutional:

> We deal with a right of privacy older than the Bill of Rights—older than our political parties, older than our school system. Marriage is a coming together for better or for worse, hopefully enduring and intimate to the degree of being sacred. *Id.*, 486, 85 S.Ct., 1682.

The District Court in *Doe* held that *Griswold* and related cases "establish a Constitutional right to privacy broad enough to encompass the right of a woman to terminate an unwanted pregnancy in its early stages, by obtaining an abortion." . . .

The Supreme Court of California expressed the same view in People v. Belous, 71 Cal.2d 954, 963, 80 Cal.Rptr. 354, 458 P.2d 194.

The Ninth Amendment obviously does not create federally enforceable

---

* ["Doe" refers to Georgia v. Doe, a companion case.]

rights. It merely says, "The enumeration in the Constitution of certain rights, shall not be construed to deny or disparage others retained by the people." But a catalogue of these rights includes customary, traditional, and time-honored rights, amenities, privileges, and immunities that come within the sweep of "the Blessings of Liberty" mentioned in the preamble to the Constitution. Many of them in my view come within the meaning of the term "liberty" as used in the Fourteenth Amendment.

First is the autonomous control over the development and expression on one's intellect, interests, tastes, and personality.

These are rights protected by the First Amendment and in my view they are absolute, permitting of no exceptions. . . . The Free Exercise Clause of the First Amendment is one facet of this constitutional right. The right to remain silent as respects one's own beliefs, . . . is protected by the First and the Fifth. The First Amendment grants the privacy of first-class mail, . . . All of these aspects of the right of privacy are "rights retained by the people" in the meaning of the Ninth Amendment.

Second is freedom of choice in the basic decisions of one's life respecting marriage, divorce, procreation, contraception, and the education and upbringing of children.

These rights, unlike those protected by the First Amendment, are subject to some control by the police power. Thus the Fourth Amendment speaks only of "unreasonable searches and seizures" and of "probable cause." These rights are "fundamental" and we have held that in order to support legislative action the statute must be narrowly and precisely drawn and that a "compelling state interest" must be shown in support of the limitation. . . .
    . . . the right of procreation, . . . and the privacy of the marital relation, . . . are in this category. Only last Term in Eisenstadt v. Baird, 405 U.S. 438, 92 S.Ct. 1029, 31 L.Ed.2d 349, another contraceptive case, we expanded the concept of *Griswold* by saying:

> It is true that in Griswold the right of privacy in question inhered in the marital relationship. Yet the marital couple is not an independent entity with a mind and heart of its own, but an association of two individuals each with a separate intellectual and emotional make up. If the right of privacy means anything, it is the right of the *individual,* married or single, to be free from unwarranted governmental intrusion into matters so fundamentally affecting a person as the decision whether to bear or beget a child.

This right of privacy was called by Mr. Justice Brandeis the right "to be let alone." Olmstead v. United States, 277 U.S. 438, 478, 48 S.Ct. 564, 572, 72 L.Ed. 944. That right includes the privilege of an individual to plan his own affairs, for "outside areas of plainly harmful conduct, every American is left to shape his own life as he thinks best, do what he pleases, go where he pleases." Kent v. Dulles, 357 U.S. 116, 126, 78 S.Ct. 1113, 1118, 2 L.Ed.2d 1204.

Third is the freedom to care for one's health and person, freedom from bodily restraint or compulsion, freedom to walk, stroll, or loaf.

These rights, though fundamental, are likewise subject to regulation on a showing of "compelling state interest." We stated in Papachristou v. City of Jacksonville, 405 U.S. 156, 164, 92 S.Ct. 839, 844, 31 L.Ed.2d 110, that walking, strolling, and wandering "are historically part of the amenities of life, as we have known [them]." As stated in Jacobson v. Massachusetts, 197 U.S. 11, 29, 25 S.Ct. 358, 362, 49 L.Ed. 643:

There is, of course, a sphere within which the individual may assert the supremacy of his own will and rightfully dispute the authority of any human government,—especially of any free government existing under a written constitution, to interfere with the exercise of that will.

In Union Pac. Ry. Co. v. Botsford, 141 U.S. 250, 251, 11 S.Ct. 1000, 1001, 35 L.Ed. 734, the Court said,

The inviolability of the person is as much invaded by a compulsory stripping and exposure as by a blow.

In Terry v. Ohio, 392 U.S. 1, 8–9, 88 S.Ct. 1868, 1873, 20 L.Ed.2d 889, the Court in speaking of the Fourth Amendment stated

This inestimable right of personal security belongs as much to the citizen on the streets of our cities as to the [Governor] closeted in his study to dispose of his secret affairs.

Katz v. United States, 389 U.S. 347, 350, 88 S.Ct. 507, 510, 19 L.Ed.2d 576, emphasizes that the Fourth Amendment

protects individual privacy against certain kinds of governmental intrusion.

In Meyer v. Nebraska, 262 U.S. 390, 399, 43 S.Ct. 625, 626, 67 L.Ed. 1042, the Court said:

Without doubt, it [liberty] denotes not merely freedom from bodily restraint but also the right of the individual to contract, to engage in any of the common occupations of life, to acquire useful knowledge, to marry, establish a home and bring up children, to worship God according to the dictates of his own conscience, and generally to enjoy those privileges long recognized at common law as essential to the orderly pursuit of happiness by free men.

The Georgia statute is at war with the clear message of these cases—that a woman is free to make the basic decision whether to bear an unwanted child. Elaborate argument is hardly necessary to demonstrate that childbirth may deprive a woman of her preferred life style and force upon her a radically different and undesired future. For example, rejected applicants under the Georgia statute are required to endure the discomforts of pregnancy; to incur the pain, higher mortality rate, and aftereffects of childbirth; to abandon educational plans; to sustain loss of income; to forgo the satisfactions of careers; to tax further mental and physical health in providing childcare; and, in some cases, to bear the lifelong stigma of unwed motherhood, a badge which may haunt, if not deter, later legitimate family relationships.

Such a holding is, however, only the beginning of the problem. The State has interests to protect. Vaccinations to prevent epidemics are one example, as *Jacobson* holds. The Court held that compulsory sterilization of imbeciles afflicted with hereditary forms of insanity or imbecility is another. . . . Abortion affects another. While childbirth endangers the lives of some women, voluntary abortion at any time and place regardless of medical standards would impinge on the rightful concern of society. The woman's health is part of that concern; as is the life of the fetus after quickening. These concerns justify the State in treating the procedure as a medical one.

One difficulty is that this statute as construed and applied apparently does not give full sweep to the "psychological as well as physical well-being" of women patients which saved the concept "health" from being void for vagueness in United States v. Vuitch, *supra,* 402 U.S. at 72, 91 S.Ct. at 1299. But apart from that, Georgia's enactment has a constitutional infirmity because, as stated by the District Court, it "limits the number of reasons for which an abortion may be sought." I agree with the holding of the District Court, "This the State may not do, because such action unduly restricts a decision sheltered by the Constitutional right of privacy." . . .

The vicissitudes of life produce pregnancies which may be unwanted, or which may impair "health" in the broad *Vutch* sense of the term, or which may imperil the life of the mother, or which in the full setting of the case may create such suffering, dislocations, misery, or tragedy as to make an early abortion the only civilized step to take. These hardships may be properly embraced in the "health" factor of the mother as appraised by a person of insight. Or they may be part of a broader medical judgment based on what is "appropriate" in a given case, though perhaps not "necessary" in a strict sense.

The "liberty" of the mother, though rooted as it is in the Constitution, may be qualified by the State for the reasons we have stated. But where fundamental personal rights and liberties are involved, the corrective legislation must be "narrowly drawn to prevent the supposed evil," . . . . Unless regulatory measures are so confined and are addressed to the specific areas of compelling legislative concern, the police power would become the great leveller of constitutional rights and liberties.

There is no doubt that the State may require abortions to be performed by qualified medical personnel. The legitimate objective of preserving the mother's health clearly supports such laws. Their impact upon the woman's privacy is minimal. But the Georgia statute outlaws virtually all such operations—even in the earliest stages of pregnancy. In light of modern medical evidence suggesting that an early abortion is safer healthwise than childbirth itself, it cannot be seriously urged that so comprehensive a ban is aimed at protecting the woman's health. Rather, this expansive proscription of all abortions along the temporal spectrum can rest only on a public goal of preserving both embryonic and fetal life.

The present statute has struck a balance between the woman and the State's interests wholly in favor of the latter. I am not prepared to hold that a State may equate, as Georgia has done, all phases of maturation preceding birth. We held in *Griswold* that the States may not preclude spouses from attempting to avoid the joinder of sperm and egg. If this is true, it is difficult to perceive any overriding public necessity which might attach precisely at the moment of conception. As Mr. Justice Clark has said:

> To say that life is present at conception is to give recognition to the potential, rather than the actual. The unfertilized egg has life, and if fertilized, it takes on human proportions. But the law deals in reality, not obscurity—the known rather than the unknown. When sperm meets egg, life may eventually form, but quite often it does not. The law does not deal in speculation. The phenomenon of life takes time to develop, and until it is actually present, it cannot be destroyed. Its interruption prior to formation would hardly be homicide, and as we have seen, society does not regard it as such. The rites of Baptism are not performed and death certificates are not required when a miscarriage occurs. No prosecutor has ever returned a murder indictment charging the taking of the life of a fetus. This would not be the case if the fetus constituted human life.

In summary, the enactment is overbroad. It is not closely correlated to the aim of preserving pre-natal life. In fact, it permits its destruction in several cases, including pregnancies resulting from sex acts in which unmarried females are below the statutory age of consent. At the same time, however, the measure broadly proscribes aborting other pregnancies which may cause severe mental disorders. Additionally, the statute is overbroad because it equates the value of embryonic life immediately after conception with the worth of life immediately before birth.

Under the Georgia Act the mother's physician is not the sole judge as to whether the abortion should be performed. Two other licensed physicians must concur in his judgment. Moreover, the abortion must be performed in a licensed hospital; and the abortion must be approved in advance by a committee of the medical staff of that hospital.

Physicians, who speak to us in *Doe* through an *amicus* brief, complain of the Georgia Act's interference with their practice of their profession.

The right of privacy has no more conspicuous place than in the physician-patient relationship, unless it be in the priest-penitent relation.

It is one thing for a patient to agree that her physician may consult with another physician about her case. It is quite a different matter for the State compulsorily to impose on that physician-patient relationship another layer or, as in this case, still a third layer of physicians. The right of privacy —the right to care for one's health and person and to seek out a physician of one's own choice protected by the Fourteenth Amendment—becomes only a matter of theory not a reality, when a multiple physician approval system is mandated by the State.

The State licenses a physician. If he is derelict or faithless, the procedures available to punish him or to deprive him of his license are well known. He is entitled to procedural due process before professional disciplinary sanctions may be imposed. . . . Crucial here, however, is state-imposed control over the medical decision whether pregnancy should be interrupted. The good-faith decision of the patient's chosen physician is overriden and the final decision passed on to others in whose selection the patient has no part. This is a total destruction of the right of privacy between physician and patient and the intimacy of relation which that entails.

The right to seek advice on one's health and the right to place his reliance on the physician of his choice are basic to Fourteenth Amendment values. We deal with fundamental rights and liberties, which, as already noted, can be contained or controlled only by discretely drawn legislation that preserves the "liberty" and regulates only those phases of the problem of compelling legislative concern. The imposition by the State of group controls over the physician-patient relation is not made on any medical procedure apart from abortion, no matter how dangerous the medical step may be. The oversight imposed on the physician and patient in abortion cases denies them their "liberty," *viz.*, their right of privacy, without any compelling, discernible state interest.

Georgia has constitutional warrant in treating abortion as a medical problem. To protect the woman's right of privacy, however, the control must be through the physician of her choice and the standards set for his performance.

The protection of the fetus when it has acquired life is a legitimate concern of the State. Georgia's law makes no rational, discernible decision on that score. For under the Act the developmental stage of the fetus is irrelevant when pregnancy is the result of rape or when the fetus will very likely be born with a permanent defect or when a continuation of the pregnancy will endanger the life of the mother or permanently injure her health. When life is present is a question we do not try to resolve. While basically a question for medical experts, as stated by Mr. Justice Clark, it is, of course, caught up in matters of religion and morality.

In short, I agree with the Court that endangering the life of the woman or seriously and permanently injuring her health are standards too narrow for the right of privacy that are at stake.

* * *

DISSENTING OPINION

MR. JUSTICE WHITE, with whom MR. JUSTICE RHENQUIST joins, dissenting.

At the heart of the controversy in these cases are those recurring pregnancies that pose no danger whatsoever to the life or health of the mother but are nevertheless unwanted for any one or more of a variety of reasons—convenience, family planning, economics, dislike of children, the embarrassment of illegitimacy, etc. The common claim before us is that for any one of such reasons, or for no reason at all, and without asserting or claiming any threat to life or health, any woman is entitled to an abortion at her request if she is able to find a medical advisor willing to undertake the procedure.

The Court for the most part sustains this position: During the period prior to the time the fetus becomes viable, the Constitution of the United States values the convenience, whim or caprice of the putative mother more than the life or potential life of the fetus; the Constitution, therefore, guarantees the right to an abortion as against any state law or policy seeking to protect the fetus from an abortion not prompted by more compelling reasons of the mother.

With all due respect, I dissent. I find nothing in the language or history of the Constitution to support the Court's judgment. The Court simply fashions and announces a new constitutional right for pregnant mothers and, with scarcely any reason or authority for its action, invests that right with sufficient substance to override most existing state abortion statutes. The upshot is that the people and the legislatures of the 50 States are constitutionally disentitled to weigh the relative importance of the continued existence and development of the fetus on the one hand against a spectrum of possible impacts on the mother on the other hand. As an exercise of raw judicial power, the Court perhaps has authority to do what it does today; but in my view its judgment is an improvident and extravagant exercise of the power of judicial review which the Constitution extends to this Court.

The Court apparently values the convenience of the pregnant mother more than the continued existence and development of the life or potential life which she carries. Whether or not I might agree with that marshalling of values, I can in no event join the Court's judgment because I find no constitutional warrant for imposing such an order of priorities on the people and legislatures of the States. In a sensitive area such as this, involving as it does issues over which reasonable men may easily and heatedly differ, I cannot accept the Court's exercise of its clear power of choice by interposing a constitutional barrier to state efforts to protect human life and by investing mothers and doctors with the constitutionally protected right to exterminate it. This issue, for the most part, should be left with the people and to the political processes the people have devised to govern their affairs.

It is my view, therefore, that the Texas statute is not constitutionally infirm because it denies abortions to those who seek to serve only their convenience rather than to protect their life or health. Nor is this plaintiff, who claims no threat to her mental or physical health, entitled to assert the possible rights of those women whose pregnancy assertedly implicates their health. This, together with United States v. Vuitch, 402 U.S. 62, 91 S.Ct. 1294, 28 L.Ed.2d 601 (1971), dictates reversal of the judgment of the District Court.

Likewise, because Georgia may constitutionally forbid abortions to putative mothers who, like the plaintiff in this case, do not fall within the reach of § 26–1202(a) of its criminal code, I have no occasion, and the District Court had none, to consider the constitutionality of the procedural requirements of the Georgia statute. . . .

A DEFENSE OF ABORTION * 1

JUDITH JARVIS THOMSON

Most opposition to abortion relies on the premise that the fetus is a human being, a person, from the moment of conception. The premise is argued for, but, as I think, not well. Take, for example, the most common argument. We are asked to notice that the development of a human being from conception through birth into childhood is continuous; then it is said that to draw a line, to choose a point in this development and say "before this point the thing is not a person, after this point it is a person" is to make an arbitrary choice, a choice for which in the nature of things no good reason can be given. It is concluded that the fetus is, or anyway that we had better say it is, a person from the moment of conception. But this conclusion does not follow. Similar things might be said about the development of an acorn into an oak tree, and it does not follow that acorns are oak trees, or that we had better say they are. Arguments of this form are sometimes called "slippery slope arguments"—the phrase is perhaps

* From Judith Jarvis Thomson, "A Defense of Abortion" *Philosophy and Public Affairs*, 1, No. 1 (Fall, 1971), pp. 47–66. Reprinted by permission of the author and Princeton University Press.

1 I am very much indebted to James Thomson for discussion, criticism, and many helpful suggestions.

self-explanatory—and it is dismaying that opponents of abortion rely on them so heavily and uncritically.

I am inclined to agree, however, that the prospects for "drawing a line" in the development of the fetus look dim. I am inclined to think also that we shall probably have to agree that the fetus has already become a human person well before birth. Indeed, it comes as a surprise when one first learns how early in its life it begins to acquire human characteristics. By the tenth week, for example, it already has a face, arms and legs, fingers and toes; it has internal organs, and brain activity is detectable.[2] On the other hand, I think that the premise is false, that the fetus is not a person from the moment of conception. A newly fertilized ovum, a newly implanted clump of cells, is no more a person than an acorn is an oak tree. But I shall not discuss any of this. For it seems to me to be of great interest to ask what happens if, for the sake of argument, we allow the premise. How, precisely, are we supposed to get from there to the conclusion that abortion is morally impermissible? Opponents of abortion commonly spend most of their time establishing that the fetus is a person, and hardly any time explaining the step from there to the impermissibility of abortion. Perhaps they think the step too simple and obvious to require much comment. Or perhaps instead they are simply being economical in argument. Many of those who defend abortion rely on the premise that the fetus is not a person, but only a bit of tissue that will become a person at birth; and why pay out more arguments than you have to? Whatever the explanation, I suggest that the step they take is neither easy nor obvious, that it calls for closer examination than it is commonly given, and that when we do give it this closer examination we shall feel inclined to reject it.

I propose, then, that we grant that the fetus is a person from the moment of conception. How does the argument go from here? Something like this, I take it. Every person has a right to life. So the fetus has a right to life. No doubt the mother has a right to decide what shall happen in and to her body; everyone would grant that. But surely a person's right to life is stronger and more stringent than the mother's right to decide what happens in and to her body, and so outweighs it. So the fetus may not be killed; an abortion may not be performed.

It sounds plausible. But now let me ask you to imagine this. You wake up in the morning and find yourself back to back in bed with an unconscious violinist. A famous unconscious violinist. He has been found to have a fatal kidney ailment, and the Society of Music Lovers has canvassed all the available medical records and found that you alone have the right blood

---

[2] Daniel Callahan, *Abortion: Law, Choice and Morality* (New York, 1970), p. 373. This book gives a fascinating survey of the available information on abortion. The Jewish tradition is surveyed in David M. Feldman, *Birth Control in Jewish Law* (New York, 1968), Part 5, the Catholic tradition in John T. Noonan, Jr., "An Almost Absolute Value in History," in *The Morality of Abortion*, ed. John T. Noonan, Jr. (Cambridge, Mass., 1970).

type to help. They have therefore kidnapped you, and last night the violinist's circulatory system was plugged into yours, so that your kidneys can be used to extract poisons from his blood as well as your own. The director of the hospital now tells you, "Look, we're sorry the Society of Music Lovers did this to you—we would never have permitted it if we had known. But still, they did it, and the violinist now is plugged into you. To unplug you would be to kill him. But never mind, it's only for nine months. By then he will have recovered from his ailment, and can safely be unplugged from you." Is it morally incumbent on you to accede to this situation? No doubt it would be very nice of you if you did, a great kindness. But do you *have* to accede to it? What if it were not nine months, but nine years? Or longer still? What if the director of the hospital says, "Tough luck, I agree, but you've now got to stay in bed, with the violinist plugged into you, for the rest of your life. Because remember this. All persons have a right to life, and violinists are persons. Granted you have a right to decide what happens in and to your body, but a person's right to life outweighs your right to decide what happens in and to your body. So you cannot ever be unplugged from him." I imagine you would regard this as outrageous, which suggests that something really is wrong with that plausible-sounding argument I mentioned a moment ago.

In this case, of course, you were kidnapped; you didn't volunteer for the operation that plugged the violinist into your kidneys. Can those who oppose abortion on the ground I mentioned make an exception for a pregnancy due to rape? Certainly. They can say that persons have a right to life only if they didn't come into existence because of rape; or they can say that all persons have a right to life, but that some have less of a right to life than others, in particular, that those who came into existence because of rape have less. But these statements have a rather unpleasant sound. Surely the question of whether you have a right to life at all, or how much of it you have, shouldn't turn on the question of whether or not you are the product of a rape. And in fact the people who oppose abortion on the ground I mentioned do not make this distinction, and hence do not make an exception in case of rape.

Nor do they make an exception for a case in which the mother has to spend the nine months of her pregnancy in bed. They would agree that would be a great pity, and hard on the mother; but all the same, all persons have a right to life, the fetus is a person, and so on. I suspect, in fact, that they would not make an exception for a case in which, miraculously enough, the pregnancy went on for nine years, or even the rest of the mother's life.

Some won't even make an exception for a case in which continuation of the pregnancy is likely to shorten the mother's life; they regard abortion as impermissible even to save the mother's life. Such cases are nowadays very rare, and many opponents of abortion do not accept this extreme view. All the same, it is a good place to begin: a number of points of interest come out in respect to it.

1. Let us call the view that abortion is impermissible even to save the mother's life "the extreme view." I want to suggest first that it does not issue from the argument I mentioned earlier without the addition of some fairly powerful premises. Suppose a woman has become pregnant, and now learns that she has a cardiac condition such that she will die if she carries the baby to term. What may be done for her? The fetus, being a person, has a right to life, but as the mother is a person too, so has she a right to life. Presumably they have an equal right to life. How is it supposed to come out that an abortion may not be performed? If mother and child have an equal right to life, shouldn't we perhaps flip a coin? Or should we add to the mother's right to life her right to decide what happens in and to her body, which everybody seems to be ready to grant—the sum of her rights now outweighing the fetus' right to life?

The most familiar argument here is the following. We are told that performing the abortion would be directly killing [3] the child, whereas doing nothing would not be killing the mother, but only letting her die. Moreover, in killing the child, one would be killing an innocent person, for the child has committed no crime, and is not aiming at his mother's death. And then there are a variety of ways in which this might be continued. (1) But as directly killing an innocent person is always and absolutely impermissible, an abortion may not be performed. Or, (2) as directly killing an innocent person is murder, and murder is always and absolutely impermissible, an abortion may not be performed.[4] Or, (3) as one's duty to refrain from directly killing an innocent person is more stringent than one's duty to keep a person from dying, an abortion may not be performed. Or, (4) if one's only options are directly killing an innocent person or letting a person die, one must prefer letting the person die, and thus an abortion may not be performed.[5]

Some people seem to have thought that these are not further premises which must be added if the conclusion is to be reached, but that they

---

[3] The term "direct" in the arguments I refer to is a technical one. Roughly, what is meant by "direct killing" is either killing as an end in itself, or killing as a means to some end, for example, the end of saving someone else's life. See note 6, below, for an example of its use.

[4] Cf. *Encyclical Letter of Pope Pius XI on Christian Marriage*, St. Paul Editions (Boston, n.d.), p. 32: "however much we may pity the mother whose health and even life is gravely imperiled in the performance of the duty allotted to her by nature, nevertheless what could ever be a sufficient reason for excusing in any way the direct murder of the innocent? This is precisely what we are dealing with here." Noonan (*The Morality of Abortion,* p. 43) reads this as follows: "What cause can ever avail to excuse in any way the direct killing of the innocent? For it is a question of that."

[5] The thesis in (4) is in an interesting way weaker than those in (1), (2), and (3): they rule out abortion even in cases in which both mother *and* child will die if the abortion is not performed. By contrast, one who held the view expressed in (4) could consistently say that one needn't prefer letting two persons die to killing one.

follow from the very fact that an innocent person has a right to life.[6] But this seems to me to be a mistake, and perhaps the simplest way to show this is to bring out that while we must certainly grant that innocent persons have a right to life, the theses in (1) through (4) are all false. Take (2), for example. If directly killing an innocent person is murder, and thus is impermissible, then the mother's directly killing the innocent person inside her is murder, and thus is impermissible. But it cannot seriously be thought to be murder if the mother performs an abortion on herself to save her life. It cannot seriously be said that she *must* refrain, that she *must* sit passively by and wait for her death. Let us look again at the case of you and the violinist. There you are, in bed with the violinist, and the director of the hospital says to you, "It's all most distressing, and I deeply sympathize, but you see this is putting an additional strain on your kidneys, and you'll be dead within the month. But you *have* to stay where you are all the same. Because unplugging you would be directly killing an innocent violinist, and that's murder, and that's impermissible." If anything in the world is true, it is that you do not commit murder, you do not do what is impermissible, if you reach around to your back and unplug yourself from that violinist to save your life.

The main focus of attention in writings on abortion has been on what a third party may or may not do in answer to a request from a woman for an abortion. This is in a way understandable. Things being as they are, there isn't much a woman can safely do to abort herself. So the question asked is what a third party may do, and what the mother may do, if it is mentioned at all, is deduced, almost as an afterthought, from what it is concluded that third parties may do. But it seems to me that to treat the matter in this way is to refuse to grant to the mother that very status of person which is so firmly insisted on for the fetus. For we cannot simply read off what a person may do from what a third party may do. Suppose you find yourself trapped in a tiny house with a growing child. I mean a very tiny house, and a rapidly growing child—you are already up against the wall of the house and in a few minutes you'll be crushed to death. The child on the other hand won't be crushed to death; if nothing is done to stop him from growing he'll be hurt, but in the end he'll simply burst open the house and walk out a free man. Now I could well understand it if a bystander were to say, "There's nothing we can do for you. We cannot choose between your life and his, we cannot be the ones to decide who is

---

[6] Cf. the following from Pius XII, *Address to the Italian Catholic Society of Midwives*: "The baby in the maternal breast has the right to life immediately from God.—Hence there is no man, no human authority, no science, no medical, eugenic, social, economic or moral 'indication' which can establish or grant a valid juridical ground for a direct deliberate disposition of an innocent human life, that is a disposition which looks to its destruction either as an end or as a means to another end perhaps in itself not illicit.—The baby, still not born, is a man in the same degree and for the same reason as the mother" (quoted in Noonan, *The Morality of Abortion*, p. 45).

to live, we cannot intervene." But it cannot be concluded that you too can do nothing, that you cannot attack it to save your life. However innocent the child may be, you do not have to wait passively while it crushes you to death. Perhaps a pregnant woman is vaguely felt to have the status of house, to which we don't allow the right of self-defense. But if the woman houses the child, it should be remembered that she is a person who houses it.

I should perhaps stop to say explicitly that I am not claiming that people have a right to do anything whatever to save their lives. I think, rather, that there are drastic limits to the right of self-defense. If someone threatens you with death unless you torture someone else to death, I think you have not the right, even to save your life, to do so. But the case under consideration here is very different. In our case there are only two people involved, one whose life is threatened, and one who threatens it. Both are innocent: the one who is threatened is not threatened because of any fault, the one who threatens does not threaten because of any fault. For this reason we may feel that we bystanders cannot intervene. But the person threatened can.

In sum, a woman surely can defend her life against the threat to it posed by the unborn child, even if doing so involves its death. And this shows not merely that the theses in (1) through (4) are false; it shows also that the extreme view of abortion is false, and so we need not canvass any other possible ways of arriving at it from the argument I mentioned at the outset.

2. The extreme view could of course be weakened to say that while abortion is permissible to save the mother's life, it may not be performed by a third party, but only by the mother herself. But this cannot be right either. For what we have to keep in mind is that the mother and the unborn child are not like two tenants in a small house which has, by an unfortunate mistake, been rented to both: the mother *owns* the house. The fact that she does adds to the offensiveness of deducing that the mother can do nothing from the supposition that third parties can do nothing. But it does more than this: it casts a bright light on the supposition that third parties can do nothing. Certainly it lets us see that a third party who says "I cannot choose between you" is fooling himself if he thinks this is impartiality. If Jones has found and fastened on a certain coat, which he needs to keep him from freezing, but which Smith also needs to keep him from freezing, then it is not impartiality that says "I cannot choose between you" when Smith owns the coat. Women have said again and again "This body is *my* body!" and they have reason to feel angry, reason to feel that it has been like shouting into the wind. Smith, after all, is hardly likely to bless us if we say to him, "Of course it's your coat, anybody would grant that it is. But no one may choose between you and Jones who is to have it."

We should really ask what it is that says "no one may choose" in the face of the fact that the body that houses the child is the mother's body. It may be simply a failure to appreciate this fact. But it may be something more interesting, namely the sense that one has a right to refuse to lay hands on people, even where it would be just and fair to do so, even where justice seems to require that somebody do so. Thus justice might call for somebody to get Smith's coat back from Jones, and yet you have a right to refuse to be the one to lay hands on Jones, a right to refuse to do physical violence to him. This, I think, must be granted. But then what should be said is not "no one may choose," but only "*I* cannot choose," and indeed not even this, but "*I* will not *act*," leaving it open that somebody else can or should, and in particular that anyone in a position of authority, with the job of securing people's rights, both can and should. So this is no difficulty. I have not been arguing that any given third party must accede to the mother's request that he perform an abortion to save her life, but only that he may.

I suppose that in some views of human life the mother's body is only on loan to her, the loan not being one which gives her any prior claim to it. One who held this view might well think it impartiality to say "I cannot choose." But I shall simply ignore this possibility. My own view is that if a human being has any just, prior claim to anything at all, he has a just, prior claim to his own body. And perhaps this needn't be argued for here anyway, since, as I mentioned, the arguments against abortion we are looking at do grant that the woman has a right to decide what happens in and to her body.

But although they do grant it, I have tried to show that they do not take seriously what is done in granting it. I suggest the same thing will reappear even more clearly when we turn away from cases in which the mother's life is at stake, and attend, as I propose we now do, to the vastly more common cases in which a woman wants an abortion for some less weighty reason than preserving her own life.

3. Where the mother's life is not at stake, the argument I mentioned at the outset seems to have a much stronger pull. "Everyone has a right to life, so the unborn person has a right to life." And isn't the child's right to life weightier than anything other than the mother's own right to life, which she might put forward as ground for an abortion?

This argument treats the right to life as if it were unproblematic. It is not, and this seems to me to be precisely the source of the mistake.

For we should now, at long last, ask what it comes to, to have a right to life. In some views having a right to life includes having a right to be given at least the bare minimum one needs for continued life. But suppose that what in fact *is* the bare minimum a man needs for continued life is something he has no right at all to be given? If I am sick unto death, and the only thing that will save my life is the touch of Henry Fonda's cool hand on my fevered brow, then all the same, I have no right to be given the touch of Henry Fonda's cool hand on my fevered brow. It would be frightfully nice of him to fly in from the West Coast to provide it. It would be less nice, though no doubt well meant, if my friends flew out to the West Coast and carried Henry Fonda back with them. But I have no right at all against anybody that he should do this for me. Or again, to return to the story I told earlier, the fact that for continued life that violinist needs the continued use of your kidneys does not establish that he has a right to be given the continued use of your kidneys. He certainly has no right against you that *you* should give him continued use of your kidneys. For nobody has any right to use your kidneys unless you give him such a right; and nobody has the right against you that you shall give him this right—if you do allow him to go on using your kidneys, this is a kindness on your part, and not something he can claim from you as his due. Nor has he any right against anybody else that *they* should give him continued use of your kidneys. Certainly he had no right against the Society of Music Lovers that they should plug him into you in the first place. And if you now start to unplug yourself, having learned that you will otherwise have to spend nine years in bed with him, there is nobody in the world who must try to prevent you, in order to see to it that he is given something he has a right to be given.

Some people are rather stricter about the right to life. In their view, it does not include the right to be given anything, but amounts to, and only to, the right not to be killed by anybody. But here a related difficulty arises. If everybody is to refrain from killing that violinist, then everybody must refrain from doing a great many different sorts of things. Everybody must refrain from slitting his throat, everybody must refrain from shooting him—and everybody must refrain from unplugging you from him. But does he have a right against everybody that they shall refrain from unplugging you from him? To refrain from doing this is to allow him to continue to use your kidneys. It could be argued that he has a right against us that *we* should allow him to continue to use your kidneys. That is, while he had no right against us that we should give him the use of your kidneys, it might be argued that he anyway has a right against us that we shall not now intervene and deprive him of the use of your kidneys. I shall come back to third-party interventions later. But certainly the violinist has no right against you that *you* shall allow him to continue to use your kidneys. As I said, if you do allow him to use them, it is a kindness on your part, and not something you owe him.

The difficulty I point to here is not peculiar to the right to life. It reappears in connection with all the other natural rights; and it is something which an adequate account of rights must deal with. For present purposes it is enough just to draw attention to it. But I would stress that I am not arguing that people do not have a right to life—quite to the contrary, it seems to me that the primary control we must place on the acceptability of an account of rights is that it should turn out in that account to be a truth that all persons have a right to life. I am arguing only that having a right to life does not guarantee having either a right to be given the use of or a right to be allowed continued use of another person's body—even if one needs it for life itself. So the right to life will not serve the op-

ponents of abortion in the very simple and clear way in which they seem
to have thought it would.

4. There is another way to bring out the difficulty. In the most ordinary
sort of case, to deprive someone of what he has a right to is to treat him
unjustly. Suppose a boy and his small brother are jointly given a box of
chocolates for Christmas. If the older boy takes the box and refuses to give
his brother any of the chocolates, he is unjust to him, for the brother has
been given a right to half of them. But suppose that, having learned that
otherwise it means nine years in bed with that violinist, you unplug yourself from him. You surely are not being unjust to him, for you gave him
no right to use your kidneys, and no one else can have given him any such
right. But we have to notice that in unplugging yourself, you are killing
him; and violinists, like everybody else, have a right to life, and thus in
the view we were considering just now, the right not to be killed. So here
you do what he supposedly has a right you shall not do, but you do not act
unjustly to him in doing it.

The emendation which may be made at this point is this; the right to
life consists not in the right not to be killed, but rather in the right not to
be killed unjustly. This runs a risk of circularity, but never mind: it would
enable us to square the fact that the violinist has a right to life with the
fact that you do not act unjustly toward him in unplugging yourself, thereby
killing him. For if you do not kill him unjustly, you do not violate his right
to life, and so it is no wonder you do him no injustice.

But if this emendation is accepted, the gap in the argument against
abortion stares us plainly in the face: it is by no means enough to show
that the fetus is a person, and to remind us that all persons have a right
to life—we need to be shown also that killing the fetus violates its right
to life, i.e., that abortion is unjust killing. And is it?

I suppose we may take it as a datum that in a case of pregnancy due
to rape the mother has not given the unborn person a right to the use of
her body for food and shelter. Indeed, in what pregnancy could it be
supposed that the mother has given the unborn person such a right? It is
not as if there were unborn persons drifting about the world, to whom a
woman who wants a child says "I invite you in."

But it might be argued that there are other ways one can have acquired
a right to the use of another person's body than by having been invited to
use it by that person. Suppose a woman voluntarily indulges in intercourse,
knowing of the chance it will issue in pregnancy, and then she does become pregnant; is she not in part responsible for the presence, in fact the
very existence, of the unborn person inside her? No doubt she did not
invite it in. But doesn't her partial responsibility for its being there itself
give it a right to the use of her body? [7] If so, then her aborting it would

---

[7] The need for a discussion of this argument was brought home to me by members of
the Society for Ethical and Legal Philosophy, to whom this paper was originally presented.

be more like the boy's taking away the chocolates, and less like your un-plugging yourself from the violinist—doing so would be depriving it of what it does have a right to, and thus would be doing it an injustice.

And then, too, it might be asked whether or not she can kill it even to save her own life: If she voluntarily called it into existence, how can she now kill it, even in self-defense?

The first thing to be said about this is that it is something new. Opponents of abortion have been so concerned to make out the independence of the fetus, in order to establish that it has a right to life, just as its mother does, that they have tended to overlook the possible support they might gain from making out that the fetus is *dependent* on the mother, in order to establish that she has a special kind of responsibility for it, a responsibility that gives it rights against her which are not possessed by any independent person—such as an ailing violinist who is a stranger to her.

On the other hand, this argument would give the unborn person a right to its mother's body only if her pregnancy resulted from a voluntary act, undertaken in full knowledge of the chance a pregnancy might result from it. It would leave out entirely the unborn person whose existence is due to rape. Pending the availability of some further argument, then, we would be left with the conclusion that unborn persons whose existence is due to rape have no right to the use of their mothers' bodies, and thus that aborting them is not depriving them of anything they have a right to and hence is not unjust killing.

And we should also notice that it is not at all plain that this argument really does go even as far as it purports to. For there are cases and cases, and the details make a difference. If the room is stuffy, and I therefore open a window to air it, and a burglar climbs in, it would be absurd to say, "Ah, now he can stay, she's given him a right to the use of her house—for she is partially responsible for his presence there, having voluntarily done what enabled him to get in, in full knowledge that there are such things as burglars, and that burglars burgle." It would be still more absurd to say this if I had had bars installed outside my windows, precisely to prevent burglars from getting in, and a burglar got in only because of a defect in the bars. It remains equally absurd if we imagine it is not a burglar who climbs in, but an innocent person who blunders or falls in. Again, suppose it were like this: people-seeds drift about in the air like pollen, and if you open your windows, one may drift in and take root in your carpets or upholstery. You don't want children, so you fix up your windows with fine mesh screens, the very best you can buy. As can happen, however, and on very, very rare occasions does happen, one of the screens is defective; and a seed drifts in and takes root. Does the person-plant who now develops have a right to the use of your house? Surely not—despite the fact that you voluntarily opened your windows, you knowingly kept carpets and upholstered furniture, and you knew that screens were sometimes defective. Someone may argue that you are responsible for its rooting, that it does have a right to your house, because after all you *could* have lived out your life with bare floors and furniture, or with sealed windows and doors. But this won't do—for by the same token anyone can avoid a pregnancy due to rape by having a hysterectomy, or anyway by never leaving home without a (reliable!) army.

It seems to me that the argument we are looking at can establish at most that there are *some* cases in which the unborn person has a right to the use of its mother's body, and therefore *some* cases in which abortion is unjust killing. There is room for much discussion and argument as to precisely which, if any. But I think we should sidestep this issue and leave it open, for at any rate the argument certainly does not establish that all abortion is unjust killing.

5. There is room for yet another argument here, however. We surely must all grant that there may be cases in which it would be morally indecent to detach a person from your body at the cost of his life. Suppose you learn that what the violinist needs is not nine years of your life, but only one hour: all you need do to save his life is to spend one hour in that bed with him. Suppose also that letting him use your kidneys for that one hour would not affect your health in the slightest. Admittedly you were kidnapped. Admittedly you did not give anyone permission to plug him into you. Nevertheless it seems to me plain you *ought* to allow him to use your kidneys for that hour—it would be indecent to refuse.

Again, suppose pregnancy lasted only an hour, and constituted no threat to life or health. And suppose that a woman becomes pregnant as a result of rape. Admittedly she did not voluntarily do anything to bring about the existence of a child. Admittedly she did nothing at all which would give the unborn person a right to the use of her body. All the same it might well be said, as in the newly emended violinist story, that she *ought* to allow it to remain for that hour—that it would be indecent in her to refuse.

Now some people are inclined to use the term "right" in such a way that it follows from the fact that you ought to allow a person to use your body for the hour he needs, that he has a right to use your body for the hour he needs, even though he has not been given that right by any person or act. They may say that it follows also that if you refuse, you act unjustly toward him. This use of the term is perhaps so common that it cannot be called wrong; nevertheless it seems to me to be an unfortunate loosening of what we would do better to keep a tight rein on. Suppose that box of chocolates I mentioned earlier had not been given to both boys jointly, but was given only to the older boy. There he sits, stolidly eating his way through the box, his small brother watching enviously. Here we are likely to say "You ought not to be so mean. You ought to give your brother some of those chocolates." My own view is that it just does not follow from the truth of this that the brother has any right to any of the chocolates. If the boy refuses to give his brother any, he is greedy, stingy, callous—but not unjust. I suppose that the people I have in mind will say it does follow that the brother has a right to some of the chocolates, and thus that the boy does act unjustly if he refuses to give his brother any. But the effect of saying this is to obscure what we should keep distinct, namely the difference between the boy's refusal in this case and the boy's refusal in the earlier case, in which the box was given to both boys jointly, and in which the small brother thus had what was from any point of view clear title to half.

A further objection to so using the term "right" that from the fact that A ought to do a thing for B, it follows that B has a right against A that A do it for him, is that it is going to make the question of whether or not a man has a right to a thing turn on how easy it is to provide him with it; and this seems not merely unfortunate, but morally unacceptable. Take the case of Henry Fonda again. I said earlier that I had no right to the touch of his cool hand on my fevered brow, even though I needed it to save my life. I said it would be frightfully nice of him to fly in from the West Coast to provide me with it, but that I had no right against him that he should do so. But suppose he isn't on the West Coast. Suppose he has only to walk across the room, place a hand briefly on my brow—and lo, my life is saved. Then surely he ought to do it, it would be indecent to refuse. Is it to be said "Ah, well, it follows that in this case she has a right to the touch of his hand on her brow, and so it would be an injustice in him to refuse"? So that I have a right to it when it is easy for him to provide it, though no right when it's hard? It's rather a shocking idea that anyone's rights should fade away and disappear as it gets harder and harder to accord them to him.

So my own view is that even though you ought to let the violinist use your kidneys for the one hour he needs, we should not conclude that he has a right to do so—we should say that if you refuse, you are, like the boy who owns all the chocolates and will give none away, self-centered and callous, indecent in fact, but not unjust. And similarly, that even supposing a case in which a woman pregnant due to rape ought to allow the unborn person to use her body for the hour he needs, we should not conclude that he has a right to do so; we should conclude that she is self-centered, callous, indecent, but not unjust, if she refuses. The complaints are no less grave; they are just different. However, there is no need to insist on this point. If anyone does wish to deduce "he has a right" from "you ought," then all the same he must surely grant that there are cases in which it is not morally required of you that you allow that violinist to use your kidneys, and in which he does not have a right to use them, and in which you do not do him an injustice if you refuse. And so also for mother and unborn child. Except in such cases as the unborn person has a right to demand it—and we were leaving open the possibility that there may be such cases—nobody is morally *required* to make large sacrifices, of health, of all other interests and concerns, of all other duties and commitments, for nine years, or even for nine months, in order to keep another person alive.

6. We have in fact to distinguish between two kinds of Samaritan: the Good Samaritan and what we might call the Minimally Decent Samaritan. The story of the Good Samaritan, you will remember, goes like this:

> A certain man went down from Jerusalem to Jericho, and fell among thieves, which stripped him of his raiment, and wounded him, and departed, leaving him half dead.
>
> And by chance there came down a certain priest that way; and when he saw him, he passed by on the other side.
>
> And likewise a Levite, when he was at the place, came and looked at him, and passed by on the other side.
>
> But a certain Samaritan, as he journeyed, came where he was; and when he saw him he had compassion on him.
>
> And went to him, and bound up his wounds, pouring in oil and wine, and set him on his own beast, and brought him to an inn, and took care of him.
>
> And on the morrow, when he departed, he took out two pence, and gave them to the host, and said unto him, "Take care of him; and whatsoever thou spendest more, when I come again, I will repay thee."   (Luke 10:30–35)

The Good Samaritan went out of his way, at some cost to himself, to help one in need of it. We are not told what the options were, that is, whether or not the priest and the Levite could have helped by doing less than the Good Samaritan did, but assuming they could have, then the fact they did nothing at all shows they were not even Minimally Decent Samaritans, not because they were not Samaritans, but because they were not minimally decent.

These things are a matter of degree, of course, but there is a difference, and it comes out perhaps most clearly in the story of Kitty Genovese, who, as you will remember, was murdered while thirty-eight people watched or listened, and did nothing at all to help her. A Good Samaritan would have rushed out to give direct assistance against the murderer. Or perhaps we had better allow that it would have been a Splendid Samaritan who did this, on the ground that it would have involved a risk of death for himself. But the thirty-eight not only did not do this, they did not even trouble to pick up a phone to call the police. Minimally Decent Samaritanism would call for doing at least that, and their not having done it was monstrous.

After telling the story of the Good Samaritan, Jesus said "Go, and do thou likewise." Perhaps he meant that we are morally required to act as the Good Samaritan did. Perhaps he was urging people to do more than is morally required of them. At all events it seems plain that it was not morally required of any of the thirty-eight that he rush out to give direct assistance at the risk of his own life, and that it is not morally required of anyone that he give long stretches of his life—nine years or nine months

—to sustaining the life of a person who has no special right (we were leaving open the possibility of this) to demand it.

Indeed, with one rather striking class of exceptions, no one in any country in the world is *legally* required to do anywhere near as much as this for anyone else. The class of exceptions is obvious. My main concern here is not the state of the law in respect to abortion, but it is worth drawing attention to the fact that in no state in this country is any man compelled by law to be even a Minimally Decent Samaritan to any person; there is no law under which charges could be brought against the thirty-eight who stood by while Kitty Genovese died. By contrast, in most states in this country women are compelled by law to be not merely Minimally Decent Samaritans, but Good Samaritans to unborn persons inside them. This doesn't by itself settle anything one way or the other, because it may well be argued that there should be laws in this country—as there are in many European countries—compelling at least Minimally Decent Samaritanism.[8] But it does show that there is a gross injustice in the existing state of the law. And it shows also that the groups currently working against liberalization of abortion laws, in fact working toward having it declared unconstitutional for a state to permit abortion, had better start working for the adoption of Good Samaritan laws generally, or earn the charge that they are acting in bad faith.

I should think, myself, that Minimally Decent Samaritan laws would be one thing, Good Samaritan laws quite another, and in fact highly improper. But we are not here concerned with the law. What we should ask is not whether anybody should be compelled by law to be a Good Samaritan, but whether we must accede to a situation in which somebody is being compelled—by nature, perhaps—to be a Good Samaritan. We have, in other words, to look now at third-party interventions. I have been arguing that no person is morally required to make large sacrifices to sustain the life of another who has no right to demand them, and this even where the sacrifices do not include life itself; we are not morally required to be Good Samaritans or anyway Very Good Samaritans to one another. But what if a man cannot extricate himself from such a situation? What if he appeals to us to extricate him? It seems to me plain that there are cases in which we can, cases in which a Good Samaritan would extricate him. There you are, you were kidnapped, and nine years in bed with that violinist lie ahead of you. You have your own life to lead. You are sorry, but you simply cannot see giving up so much of your life to the sustaining of his. You cannot extricate yourself, and ask us to do so. I should have thought that —in light of his having no right to the use of your body—it was obvious that we do not have to accede to your being forced to give up so much.

---

[8] For a discussion of the difficulties involved, and a survey of the European experience with such laws, see *The Good Samaritan and the Law*, ed. James M. Ratcliffe (New York, 1966).

We can do what you ask. There is no injustice to the violinist in our doing so.

7. Following the lead of the opponents of abortion, I have throughout been speaking of the fetus merely as a person, and what I have been asking is whether or not the argument we began with, which proceeds only from the fetus' being a person, really does establish its conclusion. I have argued that it does not.

But of course there are arguments and arguments, and it may be said that I have simply fastened on the wrong one. It may be said that what is important is not merely the fact that the fetus is a person, but that it is a person for whom the woman has a special kind of responsibility issuing from the fact that she is its mother. And it might be argued that all my analogies are therefore irrelevant—for you do not have that special kind of responsibility for that violinist, Henry Fonda does not have that special kind of responsibility for me. And our attention might be drawn to the fact that men and women both *are* compelled by law to provide support for their children.

I have in effect dealt (briefly) with this argument in section 4 above; but a (still briefer) recapitulation now may be in order. Surely we do not have any such "special responsibility" for a person unless we have assumed it, explicitly or implicitly. If a set of parents do not try to prevent pregnancy, do not obtain an abortion, and then at the time of birth of the child do not put it out for adoption, but rather take it home with them, then they have assumed responsibility for it, they have given it rights, and they cannot *now* withdraw support from it at the cost of its life because they now find it difficult to go on providing for it. But if they have taken all reasonable precautions against having a child, they do not simply by virtue of their biological relationship to the child who comes into existence have a special responsibility for it. They may wish to assume responsibility for it, or they may not wish to. And I am suggesting that if assuming responsibility for it would require large sacrifices, then they may refuse. A Good Samaritan would not refuse—or anyway, a Splendid Samaritan, if the sacrifices that had to be made were enormous. But then so would a Good Samaritan assume responsibility for that violinist; so would Henry Fonda, if he is a Good Samaritan, fly in from the West Coast and assume responsibility for me.

8. My argument will be found unsatisfactory on two counts by many of those who want to regard abortion as morally permissible. First, while I do argue that abortion is not impermissible, I do not argue that it is always permissible. There may well be cases in which carrying the child to term requires only Minimally Decent Samaritanism of the mother, and this is a standard we must not fall below. I am inclined to think it a merit of my account precisely that it does *not* give a general yes or a general no. It allows for and supports our sense that, for example, a sick and des-

perately frightened fourteen-year-old schoolgirl, pregnant due to rape, may *of course* choose abortion, and that any law which rules this out is an insane law. And it also allows for and supports our sense that in other cases resort to abortion is even positively indecent. It would be indecent in the woman to request an abortion, and indecent in a doctor to perform it, if she is in her seventh month, and wants the abortion just to avoid the nuisance of postponing a trip abroad. The very fact that the arguments I have been drawing attention to treat all cases of abortion, or even all cases of abortion in which the mother's life is not at stake, as morally on a par ought to have made them suspect at the outset.

Secondly, while I am arguing for the permissibility of abortion in some cases, I am not arguing for the right to secure the death of the unborn child. It is easy to confuse these two things in that up to a certain point in the life of the fetus it is not able to survive outside the mother's body; hence removing it from her body guarantees its death. But they are importantly different. I have argued that you are not morally required to spend nine months in bed, sustaining the life of that violinist; but to say this is by no means to say that if, when you unplug yourself, there is a miracle and he survives, you then have a right to turn round and slit his throat. You may detach yourself even if this costs him his life; you have no right to be guaranteed his death, by some other means, if unplugging yourself does not kill him. There are some people who will feel dissatisfied by this feature of my argument. A woman may be utterly devastated by the thought of a child, a bit of herself; put out for adoption and never seen or heard of again. She may therefore want not merely that the child be detached from her, but more, that it die. Some opponents of abortion are inclined to regard this as beneath contempt—thereby showing insensitivity to what is surely a powerful source of despair. All the same, I agree that the desire for the child's death is not one which anybody may gratify, should it turn out to be possible to detach the child alive.

At this place, however, it should be remembered that we have only been pretending throughout that the fetus is a human being from the moment of conception. A very early abortion is surely not the killing of a person, and so is not dealt with by anything I have said here.

THOMSON ON ABORTION [*]

BARUCH BRODY

There is a familiar argument that purports to show that it is always wrong for an expectant woman to have an abortion. It runs as follows: (1) from the moment of conception, a foetus is a human being with the same

[*] From Baruch Brody, "Thomson on Abortion," *Philosophy and Public Affairs*, 1: (1972), pp. 335–340. Reprinted by Permission of the author and Princeton University Press.

rights to life as any other human being; (2) it is always wrong to take (directly) the life of an innocent human being; (3) therefore, it is always wrong to have an abortion. Judith Jarvis Thomson, in her recent article,[1] criticized the above argument by challenging (2). More importantly, she argued that (at least in most cases) a woman has the right to secure an abortion even if (1) is true, although there are cases in which it would be positively indecent to exercise this right. It seems to me, however, that her discussions of these points, as interesting as they are, are not entirely convincing. I would like in this note to explain why.

I

Professor Thomson unfortunately offers as her counterexample to (2) her very problematic account of the violinist, a case to which we will return below. There are, however, far more straightforward cases that show that (2) is false. One such case—another will be discussed briefly at the end of this note—is the one in which Y is about to shoot X and X can save his life only by taking Y's life. We would certainly want to say that, as part of his right of self-defense, X has the right to take Y's life, and he has that right even if Y is a perfectly innocent child. So the right of self-defense includes in some cases the taking of innocent lives, (2) is false, and the above argument against abortion collapses.

This point raises important theoretical issues and it is therefore worth elaborating upon. In a normal case of self-defense, the following three factors seem to be involved: (a) the continued existence of Y poses a threat to the life of X, a threat that can be met only by the taking of Y's life; (b) Y is unjustly attempting to take X's life; (c) Y is responsible for his attempt to take X's life and is therefore guilty of attempting to take X's life. There is, moreover, a very plausible argument that would seem to suggest that all three of these factors must be involved if X is to be justified in taking Y's life in self-defense. It runs as follows: Why is X justified in killing Y? Isn't it Y's guilt for his attempt to take X's life together with the threat that Y's continued existence poses for X's life that justifies X's killing Y? Or, to put it another way, Y's guilt makes X's life take precedence over Y's. But if this is the justification for taking a life in self-defense, then conditions (a), (b), and (c) must be satisfied. If (a) is not satisfied, then Y's living is no threat to X, and if (b) and (c) are not satisfied, then there is no relevant guilt on Y's part that makes X's life take precedence over his.

What our example of the child shows is that this plausible argument will not do. Even if conditions (a) and (b), but not (c), are satisfied, X has the right to take Y's life in self-defense. This means that the above justification is not the justification for acts of self-defense. And this raises two

[1] "A Defense of Abortion," *Philosophy & Public Affairs* 1, no. 1 (Fall 1971): 47–66. (Page numbers in the text refer to this article.)

fundamental and interrelated questions: What is the justification for taking a life in self-defense, and what conditions are required for an act of self-defense to be justified? The answers to these questions are not clear.[2] One thing is, however, certain. X is not justified in taking Y's life merely because condition (a) is satisfied, and the justification for acts of self-defense is not simply that one has the right to do anything one has to in order to save one's life. After all, if Z threatens to, and will, kill X unless X kills Y, then Y's continued existence poses a threat to the life of X that can only be met by the taking of Y's life. Nevertheless, X is not therefore justified in killing Y. We would understand X's killing Y, and we might even excuse the action, but he would certainly have killed Y unjustly.

All of this has great relevance to the problem of abortion. While our discussion has shown that Professor Thomson is right in claiming that step (2) of the standard argument against abortion is mistaken, it also casts considerable doubt upon a standard argument for abortion. It is often argued that, no matter what status we ascribe to the foetus, the woman has, as part of her right of self-defense, the right to abort the foetus if the continuation of the pregnancy threatens her life. Now the foetus certainly does not satisfy condition (c), but that, as we have seen, is not required for the woman's being able to destroy it in self-defense. However, the foetus is not even attempting to take her life, and it therefore doesn't even satisfy condition (b). This must therefore cast doubt upon the claim that, no matter what the status of the foetus, abortions can sometimes be justified on grounds of self-defense.

II

Assuming that the foetus is human and that one should look at an abortion as a standard case of self-defense, we have seen that even when the foetus' continued existence poses a threat to the life of the woman, she probably has no right, as an act of self-defense, to an abortion. How then does Professor Thomson defend her claim that even if (1) is true the woman (at least in most cases) has the right to have an abortion, whether or not her life is threatened and whether or not she has consented to the act of intercourse in which the foetus is conceived? At one point, she makes the following strange suggestion: "In our case there are only two people involved, one whose life is threatened and one who threatens it. Both are innocent: the one who is threatened is not threatened because of any fault, the one who threatens does not threaten because of any fault. For this reason we may feel that we bystanders cannot intervene. But the person threatened can". But surely this description is equally applicable to the following case. X and Y are adrift in a lifeboat. Y has a disease which he

---

[2] I have offered partial answers to these questions, and have related them to the problem of abortion, in my "Abortion and the Sanctity of Human Life" (forthcoming).

can survive but which will kill X if he contracts it, and the only way X can avoid that is by killing Y and pushing him overboard. Surely, X has no right to do this. So there must be some other reason why the woman has, if she does, the right to abort the foetus.

There is, however, an important difference between our lifeboat case and an abortion, one that leads us to the heart of Professor Thomson's argument. In the case we envisaged, both X and Y had equal right to be in the lifeboat; but the woman's body is hers, not the foetus', and she has first rights to its use. This is why the woman has a right to an abortion if her life is threatened (and even if it is not). Professor Thomson summarizes this argument, which she illustrates by her violinist example, as follows: "I am arguing only that having a right to life does not guarantee having either a right to be given the use of or a right to be allowed continued use of another person's body—even if one needs it for life itself."

One part of this claim is clearly correct. I have no duty to X to save X's life by giving him the use of my body (or my live savings, my wife, etc.) and X has no right, even to save his life, to any of those things. Thus, if a foetus were conceived in a test tube and would die unless it were implanted in a woman's body, that foetus has no right to any woman's body. But all of this is irrelevant to the abortion issue, for what is at stake there is something else, the right of the woman to kill X to get back the sole use of her body, and that is an entirely different matter.

This point can also be put as follows: we must distinguish the taking of X's life from the saving of X's life, even if we assume that one has a duty not to do the former and to do the latter. Now that second duty, if it exists at all, is much weaker than the first duty; many things will relieve us of it which will not relieve us of the first one. Thus, I am certainly relieved of my duty to save X's life by the fact that fulfilling it means a loss of my life savings. It may be noble for me to save X's life at the cost of everything I have, but I certainly have no duty to do that. And the same thing is true in cases in which I can save X's life by giving him use of my body for an extended period of time. However, I am not relieved of my duty not to take X's life by the fact that fulfilling it means the loss of everything I have and not even by the mere fact that fulfilling it means the loss of my life. As the original example of Y threatening X shows, something more is required before rights like self-defense become applicable. A fortiori, it would seem that I am not relieved of my duty not to take X's life by the fact that its fulfillment means that some other person, who is innocently occupying it, continues to use my body. I cannot see, then, how the woman's right to her body gives her a right to take the life of the foetus.

Perhaps we are missing the point of Professor Thomson's argument. Could we perhaps view her argument as follows: consider the case (and only the case) in which the foetus threatens the life of the woman. Then don't we have a choice between saving the woman and saving the foetus, and doesn't the woman come first because it is her body? I think, once more, that there is a point to such a claim. When one has a choice between using all or part of a woman's body to save her or the foetus, the fact that it is her body gives her precedence. But that is not the choice in the case of an abortion. There one chooses between saving the woman by taking the life of the foetus and not taking the life of the foetus, thereby failing to save the woman. Given that choice, as we have seen, her rights to her body have no relevance.

I conclude, therefore, that Professor Thomson has not established the truth of her claims about abortion, primarily because she has not attended to the distinction between our duty to save X's life and our duty not to take it. Once one attends to that distinction, it would seem that if (1) is true, it is wrong to perform an abortion even to save the life of the woman.

III

What has been said above might seem to suggest that if (1) is true, then it is always wrong for a woman to secure an abortion. I think that this suggestion is a mistake, and I should like, in this final section, to propose [3] that there is at least one case in which, even if (1) is true, the woman has the right to secure an abortion.

The general principle about the taking of human lives that lies behind this case is rather complicated. It can best be stated as follows: it is permissible for X to take Y's life in order to save his own life if Y is going to die anyway in a relatively short time, taking Y's life is the only way to save X's life, and either (i) taking X's life (or doing anything else) will not save Y's life or (ii) there is a way to save Y's life but it has been determined by a fair random method that X's life should be saved rather than Y's. The rationale for this principle is that, in such a case, there is everything to gain by X's taking Y's life and nothing to lose. After all, both X and Y will die soon anyway if nothing is done, so Y loses nothing by X's killing him. Moreover, there is a reason why X should be saved rather than Y; either Y's life cannot be saved or X won over Y in a fair random choice.

It should be noted that this is not a principle of self-defense, for in some of the cases that it covers Y is in no way attempting to take X's life and is doing no action that leads to X's death. It should also be noted that this principle has nothing to do with the objectionable principles that would allow one to save several lives by taking a single innocent life. All such maximization-of-lives-saved principles, but not our principle, fall prey to the same objection that destroys all standard maximization-of-happiness principles, viz., that they fail to insure that no one will be treated unjustly when we maximize the quantity in question.

If we apply this principle to the question of abortion, we see that an

---

[3] This proposal is developed more fully in my "Abortion and the Sanctity of Human Life." [Cambridge, Mass., and London, 1975.]

abortion would be justified if, were the abortion not performed, both the woman and foetus would die soon, and if we either cannot save the foetus or have determined by a fair random procedure that it is the woman that should be saved.

One important point should be noted about this argument. It makes no appeal to any special fact about the foetus, the woman, or their relation. It depends solely upon a general principle about the taking of some human lives to save others. It is for just this reason that there can be no doubt about its conclusion being perfectly compatible with the claim that the foetus is just another human being.

12

Abortion: The Right to Life

Judith Jarvis Thomson advocates a woman's right to her own body. What of the rights of the fetus? The moral issue becomes entwined with the factual question, What is a person, or *when* is a person? (The question, When does human life *end?* we shall see is essential in the debate on euthanasia.)

Wertheimer distinguishes the possible positions on when, if ever, abortion is justified. The question is not whether abortion destroys something living and valuable, but what it destroys. (1) Conservatives hold that abortion is never justified except, perhaps, to save the mother's life. The conservative view, which is hard to dispute, is that the development from conception to birth is continuous and points straight to a human being. (2) Liberals, by contrast, argue that a fetus is not a human being until viability, capability of existence outside the womb. But that capability is a function of the technology at any given time, the state of the art. Presumably, a convinced liberal would hold that abortion isn't killing a human being and that the human being comes into existence at birth. If conservatives stress the continuity of life, the liberal stresses the contrast between the fetus and very young infants and ourselves. (3) Moderates on abortion take an in-between view: A fetus has a moral status for part of its life, like an animal; not any and every kind of treatment is right, but it is impossible to draw a line as to when abortion is killing a human being. Finally, the liberal and conservative present no facts that the other side disputes to support the conclusion that a fetus is or is not a human being, but rather say, "Can't you see that it is (isn't)?" The problem is that we cannot literally see the fetus or interact with it. Such interaction with any living thing is the usual basis on which we develop attitudes and beliefs about its moral status, e.g., its possession of rights and how to treat it.

398

UNDERSTANDING THE ABORTION ARGUMENT °
ROGER WERTHEIMER

I want to understand an argument. By an argument I do not mean a concatenation of deathless propositions, but something with two sides that you have with someone, not present to him; not something with logical relations alone, but something encompassing human relations as well. We need to understand the argument in this fuller sense, for if we don't understand the human relations, we won't understand the logical ones either. For data I use a fair share of the published material plus intensive discussions with some two hundred students.[1] Here too, if we don't understand what people actually say and do, we shall never understand what they ought to say and do.

The argument is over the legalization of abortion. In its moral, as opposed to, say, its political or medical aspects, the issue is statable as a double-barreled question: At what stage of fetal development, if any, and for what reasons, if any, is abortion justifiable? Each part of the question has received diverse answers, which in turn have been combined in various ways. Thus, we have not a single argument but many, so I must subject them to considerable summary and simplification in order to handle the larger issues.

Let me list a few popular positions. According to the liberal, the fetus should be disposable upon the mother's request until it is viable; thereafter it may be destroyed only to save the mother's life. To an extreme liberal the fetus is always merely *pars viscerum matris*, like an appendix, and may be destroyed upon demand anytime before its birth. In effect, this view denies that abortion ever needs any justification at all. A moderate view is that until viability the fetus should be disposable if it is the result of felonious intercourse, or if the mother's or child's physical or mental health would probably be gravely impaired. This position is susceptible to wide variations. For example, it can be liberalized by giving more weight to the reasonably foreseeable consequences of the pregnancy for the family as a whole. The conservative position is that the fetus may be aborted before quickening but not after, unless the mother's life is at stake. For the extreme conservative, the fetus, once conceived, may not be destroyed for any reason short of saving the mother's life.

This last might be called the Catholic view, but note that it, or some

° From Roger Wertheimer, "Understanding the Abortion Argument," *Philosophy and Public Affairs*, 1: 1 (1971), pp. 67–95. Reprinted by permission of the author and Princeton University Press.

[1] My thanks to Mrs. Marilyn Weaver of the Oregon Committee on Legal Termination of Pregnancy for providing much of the literature, and to Portland State University for providing the students.

close variant of it, is shared by numerous Christian sects, and is or was maintained by Jews, by Indians of both hemispheres, by a variety of tribes of diverse geographical location and cultural level, and even by some contemporary atheistical biochemists who are political liberals. Much the same can be said of any of the listed positions. I call attention to such facts for two reasons. First, they suggest that the abortion issue is in some way special, since, given any position on abortion and any position on any other issue, you can probably find a substantial group of people, many of whom are rational and intelligent, who have simultaneously held both. Second, these facts are regularly denied or distorted by the disputants. Thus, liberals habitually argue as though extreme conservatism were an invention of contemporary scholasticism with a mere century of popish heritage behind it. This in the face of the fact that that position has had the force of law in most American states for more than a century, and continues to be law even in states where Catholicism is without influence. But why should liberals want to deny that conservatism can be freed from the peculiarities of Romanist theology and from religious belief altogether? After all, wouldn't the liberal critique be even more devastating if it located the true source of its adversary's beliefs and tore those beliefs up by their roots? We shall see that these two points are not unrelated.

Now, it is commonly said that the crux of the controversy is a disagreement as to the *value* of fetal life in its various stages. But I submit that this subtly but seriously misdescribes the actual arguments, and, further, betrays a questionable understanding of morality and perhaps a questionable morality as well. Instead, I suggest, we had best take the fundamental question to be: When does a human life begin?

First off I should note that the expressions "a human life," "a human being," "a person" are virtually interchangeable in this context. As I use these expressions, except for monstrosities, every member of our species is indubitably a person, a human being, at the very latest at birth. The question is whether we are human lives at any time before birth. Virtually everyone, at least every party to the current controversy, *actually* does agree to this. However, we should be aware that in this area both agreement and disagreement are often merely verbal and therefore only apparent. For example, many people will *say* that it takes a month or perhaps a year or even more after birth for the infant to become a person, and they will explain themselves by saying that a human being must have self-consciousness, or a personality, or be able to recognize and consciously interact with its environment. But upon investigation this disagreement normally turns out to be almost wholly semantic, for we can agree on all the facts about child development, and furthermore we can agree, at least in a general way, in our moral judgments on the care to be accorded the child at various stages. Thus, though they deny that a day-old infant is a person, they admit that its life cannot be forfeited for any reason that would not equally apply to a two-year-old.[2] Still, some substantive disagreements may separate myself from someone who is disinclined to call a neonate a person, but they are subtler than any I can encompass here.

On the other hand, significant disagreements can be masked by a merely verbal agreement. Sometimes a liberal will grant that a previable fetus is a human being, but investigation reveals that he means only that the fetus is a potential human being. Often he will flatly say that he calls it a human being because it would *become* a human being, thereby evidencing an ambiguity in his use of that expression. Or he may call it human to distinguish it from canine and feline fetuses, and call it alive or living in opposition to dead or inert. But this much can be said of any cells of the maternal organism, and the sum of these parts does not equal what he means when he uses the phrase "a human life" in connection with himself and his friends, for in that extended sense he could equally apply that expression to human terata, and, at least in extreme cases, he is inclined to deny that they are human lives, and to dispose of them accordingly.

Implicit in my remarks is the suggestion that one way to find out how someone uses the expression "human being" and related ones is by looking at his moral judgments. I am suggesting that this is a way, sometimes the only way, of learning both what someone means by such expressions and what his conception of a human being is. So, I am tempted to call our concept of a human being a moral concept—but I wouldn't know quite what I meant if I said that. Let me put it in more manageable, if somewhat vague, terms. It seems clear enough, at least in outline, that given that a man has a certain set of desires, we can discern his conception of something, X, by seeing what kinds of behavior he takes to be appropriate regarding X. I am saying that we may have to look at his *moral* beliefs regarding X, especially if X is a human being. And I want to say further that while some moral judgments are involved in determining whether the fetus is a human being, still, the crucial question about the fetus is not "How much is it worth?" but "What is it?" Admittedly, so far this is all horribly obscure. To get some clarity we must start examining the details of the abortion argument.

The defense of the extreme conservative position, as normally stated by Catholics, runs as follows. The key premise is that a human fetus is a human being, not a partial or potential one, but a full-fledged, actualized human life. Given that premise, the entire conservative position unfolds with a simple, relentless logic, every principle of which would be endorsed by any

---

2 Granted, some societies practice infanticide, but their members are not parties to the present abortion dispute. And granted, further, in many of our jurisdictions infanticide, the murder of the young infant by its mother, is not punished as severely as other murders. However, this seems to be a function of our compassionate understanding of the anxiety and trauma attending the first months of motherhood; if a stranger kills the infant, the act is treated simply as murder.

sensible liberal. Suppose human embryos are human beings. Their innocence is beyond question, so nothing could justify our destroying them
except, perhaps, the necessity of saving some other innocent human life.
That is, since similar cases must be treated in similar ways, some consideration would justify the abortion of a prenatal child if and only if a comparable consideration would justify the killing of a postnatal child.[3]

This is a serious and troubling argument posing an objection in principle
to abortion. It is the *only* such argument. Nothing else could possibly justify
the staggering social costs of the present abortion laws. Once the Catholic
premise is granted, a liberal could reasonably dissent on only three side issues, none of which is a necessary or essential feature of conservatism.[4]

It should be unmistakably obvious what the Catholic position is. Yet, and
this deserves heavy emphasis, liberals seem not to understand it, for their
arguments are almost invariably infelicitous. The Catholic defense of the
status quo is left unfazed, even untouched, by the standard liberal critique
that consists of an inventory of the calamitous effects of our abortion laws
on mother and child, on family, and on society in general. Of course, were
it not for those effects we would feel no press to be rid of the laws—nor any
need to retain them. That inventory does present a conclusive rebuttal of
any of the piddling objections conservatives often toss in for good measure.
But still, the precise, scientific tabulations of grief do not add up to an
argument here, for sometimes pain, no matter how considerable and how
undesirable, may not be avoidable, may not stem from some injustice. I do
not intend to understate that pain; the tragedies brought on by unwanted
children are plentiful and serious—but so too are those brought on by
unwanted parents, yet few liberals would legalize parricide as the final solution to the massive social problem of the permanently visiting parent who
drains his children's financial and emotional resources. In the Church's view,
these cases are fully analogous: the fetus is as much a human life as is the

---

[3] For brevity, I use an oversimplification of the principle against killing persons. Further refinements are otiose here, because, whatever they are, the issue remains whether
they are to be applied equally to prenatal and postnatal humans.

[4] The first concerns the Church's use of what is called the principle of double effect,
which, when applied to some special obstetrical circumstances, implies that the doctor
must let the mother die if his only alternative is intentionally killing the unborn child.
Jonathan Bennett ("Whatever the Consequences," *Analysis* 26, no. 3 [1966]: 83–102)
and Philippa Foot ("The Problem of Abortion and the Doctrine of the Double Effect,"
Oxford Review 5 [1967]: 5–15) have, I think, shown the principle to be ultimately indefensible, but in the process they make it seem to be more enlightened and to encapsu-
late many more insights than liberals have credited. At any rate, the principle has ceased
to have much bearing on abortion cases because medical technology usually prevents the
relevant circumstances from arising. Another spot at which a liberal could diverge from
a Catholic is in the particular decisions regarding the degree of deformity required to
warrant the destruction of the offspring. Since the nature of this dispute is much the
same as that concerning the fetus, separate discussion would prove redundant. Lastly, a
liberal could argue that human beings—of whatever age—can be blamelessly killed in
more circumstances than Catholics concede. (Cf. note 3.) But clearly, any conservative
concessions here would lend little comfort to liberals, since even liberals are reluctant to
be very permissive about such principles.

parent; they share the same moral status. Either can be a source of abiding anguish and hardship for the other—and sometimes there may be no escape. In this, our world, some people get stuck with the care of others, and sometimes there may be no way of getting unstuck, at least no just and decent way. Taking the other person's life is not such a way.

The very elegance of the Catholic response is maddening. The ease with which it sweeps into irrelevance the whole catalogue of sorrow has incited many a liberal libel of the Catholic clergy as callous and unfeeling monsters, denied domestic empathy by their celibacy and the simplest human sympathies by their unnatural asceticism. Of course, slander is no substitute for argument—that's what the logic books say—and yet, we cast our aspersions with care, for they must deprive the audience of the *right* to believe the speaker. What wants explanation, then, is why the particular accusation of a *warped sensibility* seems, to the liberal, both just and pertinent. I shall come back to this. For the moment, it suffices to record that the liberal's accusation attests to a misunderstanding of the Catholic defense, for it is singularly inappropriate to label a man heartless who wants only to protect innocent human lives at all costs.

There is a subsidiary approach, a peculiarly liberal one, which seeks to disarm the Catholic position not by disputing it, but by conceding the Catholic's right to believe it and act accordingly. The liberal asks only that Catholics concede him the same freedom, and thus abandon support of abortion laws. To the liberal, the proposal is sweet reasonableness itself; the only demand is that Catholics be liberals—and when his offer is spurned, the depth of his exasperation measures the extent of his misunderstanding of the Catholic defense. The Catholic must retort that the issue is not, as the liberal supposes, one of religious ritual and self-regarding behavior, but of minority rights, the minority being not Catholics but the fetuses of all faiths, and the right being the right of an innocent human being to life itself. The liberal's proposal is predicated on abortion being a crime without a victim, like homosexuality or the use of contraceptives, but in the Catholic view the fetus is a full-scale victim and is so independent of the liberal's recognition of that fact. Catholics can no more think it wrong for themselves but permissible for Protestants to destroy a fetus than liberals can think it wrong for themselves but permissible for racists to victimize blacks. Given his premise, the Catholic is as justified in employing the power of the state to protect embryos as the liberal is to protect blacks. I shall be returning to this analogy, because the favored defense of slavery and discrimination, from Aristotle to the Civil War and beyond, takes the form of a claim that the subjugated creatures are by nature inferior to their masters, that they are *not fully human.*[5]

[5] A further instance of the liberal's befuddlement: for the Catholic, not only must a Catholic—or non-Catholic—doctor refrain from performing an abortion, he must also refuse a patient's request for a referral to a doctor who would perform it. Liberals regularly rage against this as an additional outrage by the Church, but it is an additional

Now, why do liberals, even the cleverest ones, so consistently fail to make contact with the Catholic challenge? [6] After all, as I have made plain, once premised that the fetus is a person, the entire conservative position recites the common sense of any moral man. The liberal's failure is, I suggest, due to that premise, not to some Jesuitical subtlety in the reasoning. It is the liberal's imagination, not his intellect, that is boggled. He doesn't know how to respond to the argument, because he cannot *make sense* of that premise. To him, it is not simply false, but wildly, madly false; it is nonsense, totally unintelligible, literally unbelievable. Just look at an embryo. It is an amorphous speck of apparently coagulated protoplasm. It has no eyes or ears, no head at all. It can't walk or talk; you can't dress it or wash it. Why, it doesn't even qualify as a Barbie doll, and yet millions of people call it a human being, just like one of us. It's as though someone were to look at an acorn and call it an oak tree, or, better, it's as though someone squirted a paint tube at a canvas and called the outcome a painting, a work of art—and people believed him. The whole thing is precisely that mad—and just that sane. The liberal is befuddled by the conservative's argument, just as Giotto would be were he to assess a Pollock production as a *painting*. If the premises make no sense, then neither will the rest of the argument, except as an exercise in abstract logic—and that is, I think, the only way in which liberals do understand the conservative argument.

The Catholic claim would be a joke were it not that millions of people take it seriously, and millions more suffer for their solemnity. Liberals need an explanation of how it is possible for the conservatives to believe what they say, for after all, conservatives are not ignorant or misinformed about the facts here—I mean, for example, the facts of embryology. To be sure, both camps have their complement of the benighted, but then again, neither side has a monopoly on competent doctors. It's not as though the antiabortionists thought embryos were homunculi in the mother's belly, just like us, only much, much smaller. If they thought something like that (and, in fact, at one time some of them did) then perhaps the liberal could understand them and dismiss their ravings with the aid of an electron microscope. So the liberal asks, "How *can* they believe what they say? How *can* they even make sense of it?" The question is forced upon the liberal because his conception of rationality is jeopardized by the possibility that a normal, unbiased observer of the relevant facts could really accept the conservative claim. It is this question, I think, that drives the liberal to attribute the whole antiabortion movement to Catholicism and to the Roman clergy in

---

part of the Church's position only in being distinct, not in being separable, since, if an act constitutes a grave wrong, surely it is wrong to aid and abet that act. If it is wrong to enslave a man, it is wrong to inform a master of the whereabouts of his fugitive slave, and also wrong to refer him to someone who would so inform.

  [6] I think it undeniable that some of the liberals' bungling can be dismissed as the unseemly sputterings and stutterings of a transparently camouflaged anti-Catholic bias—but not all of it can.

particular. For it is comforting to suppose that the conservative beliefs could take root only in a mind that had been carefully cultivated since infancy to support every extravagant dogma of an arcane theology fathered by the victims of unnatural and unhealthy lives.[7] But, discomforting though it may be, people, and not just Catholics, can and sometimes do agree on all the facts about embryos and still disagree as to whether they are persons. Indeed, apparently people can agree on *every* fact and still disagree on whether it is a fact that embryos are human beings. So now one might begin to wonder: What sort of fact is it?

I hasten to add that not only can both parties agree on the scientific facts, they need not disagree on any supernatural facts either. The situation here is *not* comparable to that in which a man stands before what looks for all the world like some fermented grape juice and a biscuit and calls it the blood and body of someone who died and decomposed a couple of millennia ago. The conservative claim does not presuppose that we are invested with a soul, some sort of divine substance, at or shortly after our conception. No doubt it helps to have one's mind befogged by visions of holy hocus-pocus, but it's not necessary, since some unmuddled atheists endorse a demythologized Catholic view. Moreover, since ensoulment is an unverifiable occurrence, the theologian dates it either by means of some revelation—which, by the way, the Church does not (though some of its parishioners may accept the humanity of embryos on the Church's say-so)—or by means of the same scientifically acceptable data by which his atheistical counterpart gauges the emergence of an unbesouled human life (e.g., that at such and such a time the organism is capable of independent life, or is motile, or assumes human form, or possesses its complete genetic makeup).

The religious position derives its plausibility from independent secular considerations. It serves as an expression of them, not as a substitute for them. In brief, here as elsewhere, talk about souls involves an unnecessary shuffle. Yet, though unnecessary, admittedly it is not without effect, for such conceptions color our perceptions and attitudes toward the world and thereby give sense and substance to certain arguments whose secular translations lack appeal. To take a pertinent instance, the official Church position (not the one believed by most of the laity or used against the liberals, but the official position) is that precisely because ensoulment is an unverifiable occurrence, we can't locate it with certainty, and hence abortion at any stage involves the *risk* of destroying a human life. But first

---

[7] Consequently, liberals deprive themselves of any genuine understanding of that theology by overlooking its natural attractions, which are considerable. Not a few liberals have eagerly believed that the Church's population policy was designed by devilishly clever bishops questing after worldly wealth and power via a burgeoning Catholic horde. So, it is left a mystery as perturbing as the Trinity why the wily Romanists insist that the heathen numbers keep pace, and why they persist in their plot in spite of the fact, oft-noted by liberals, that the continuing overpopulation of Catholic countries perpetuates their poverty and impotence.

off, it is doubtful whether this claim can support the practical conclusions the Catholic draws. For even if it is true, is abortion an *unwarrantable* risk? Always? Is it morally indefensible to fire a pistol into an uninspected barrel? After all, a child *might* be hiding in it. Secondly, though this argument has no attractive secular version, still, it derives its appeal from profane considerations. For what is it that so much as makes it seem that a blastocyst *might* be a person? If the conception of being besouled is cut loose from the conception of being human sans soul, then a human soul might reside in anything at all (or at least any living thing), and then the destruction of anything (or any living thing) would involve the risk of killing someone. This picture of the world is quite alien to the rationalist tradition of Catholicism, but some Eastern religions have adopted it, and the course of life appropriate to it. Not surprisingly, that course of life seems madly inefficient and irrational to Western liberals.

I have said that the argument from risk has no secular counterpart. But why not? Well, for example, what sense would it make to the liberal to suppose that an embryo *might* be a person? Are there any discoveries that are really (not just logically) possible which would lead him to admit he was mistaken? It is not a *hypothesis* for the liberal that embryos are not persons; *mutatis mutandis* for the conservative, who might well say of the fetus: "My attitude towards him is an attitude towards a soul. I am not of the *opinion* that he has a soul." [8]

At this juncture of the argument, a liberal with a positivistic background will announce that the whole dispute is not over a matter of fact at all; it's just a matter of definition whether the fetus is a person. If by this the liberal means that the question "Is a fetus a person?" is equivalent to "Is it proper to call a fetus a person?"—that is, "Is it true to say of a fetus, 'It is a person'?"—then the liberal is quite right and quite unhelpful. But he is likely to add that we can define words any way we like. And that is either true and unhelpful or flatly false. For note, both liberals and conservatives think it wrong to kill an innocent person except when other human lives would be lost. So neither party will reform their speech habits regarding the fetus unless that moral principle is reworded in a way that vouchsafes their position on abortion. Any stipulated definition can be recommended only by appealing to the very matters under dispute. Any such definition will therefore fail of universal acceptance and thus only mask the real issues, unless it is a mere systematic symbol switch. In brief, agreement on a definition will be a consequence of, not a substitute for, agreement on the facts.

A more sophisticated liberal may suggest that fetuses are borderline cases. Asking whether fetuses are persons is like asking whether viruses are living creatures: the proper answer is that they are like them in some ways but not in others; the rules of the language don't dictate one way or the other, so

---

[8] Ludwig Wittgenstein, *Philosophical Investigations*, trans. G. E. M. Anscombe (New York, 1953), p. 178e.

you can say what you will. Yet this suggests that we share a single concept of a human being, one with a fuzzy or multifaceted boundary that would make any normal person feel indecision about whether a fetus is a human being, and would enable that person, however he decided, to understand readily how someone else might decide otherwise. But at best this describes only the minds of moderates. Liberals and conservatives suffer little indecision, and, further, they are enigmatic to one another, both intellectually and as whole persons. The liberal can neither understand nor believe in the conservative's horror of abortion, especially when the conservative then so blithely accepts the consequences of prohibiting the operation. In turn, the conservative is baffled by and mistrustful of the liberal who welcomes abortion with an easy equanimity and then agonizes his soul so mightily over the poignant dilemma posed by Ivan Karamazov to Alyosha ("Rebellion"). Each side suspects the other of schizoid derangement or self-serving hypocrisy or both. And finally, precisely because with the virus you can say what you will, it is unlike the fetus. As regards the virus, scientists can manage nicely while totally ignoring the issue. Not so with the fetus, because deciding what to call it is tantamount to a serious and unavoidable moral decision.

This last remark suggests that the fetus' humanity is really a moral issue, not a factual one at all. This suggestion would sit well with the positivistically minded liberals, since for them it would explain how there could be unanimity on every issue except whether a fetus is a person. But I submit that if one insists on using that raggy fact-value distinction, then one ought to say that the dispute is over a matter of fact in the sense in which it is a fact that the Negro slaves were human beings. But it would be better to say that this dispute calls that distinction into question. To see this, let us look at how people actually argue about when a human life begins.

The liberal dates hominization from birth or viability. The choice of either stage is explicable by reference to some obvious considerations. At birth the child leaves its own private space and enters the public world. He becomes an active member of the community, a physically separate and distinct individual. He begins to act and behave like a human being, not just move as he did in the womb. And he can be looked at and acted upon and interacted with. He has needs and wants independent from those of his mother. And so on. On the other hand, someone may say viability is the crucial point, because it is then that the child has the capacity to do all those things it does at birth; the sole difference is a quite inessential one of geography.

Now note about both of these sets of considerations that they are not used as proofs or parts of proofs that human life begins at birth or at viability. What would the major premise of such a proof be? The liberal does not —nor does anyone else—have a rule of the language or a definition of "human life" from which it follows that if the organism has such and such properties, then it is a human life. True, some people, especially some scholastically oriented Catholics, have tried to state the essence of human life and argue from that definition, but the correctness of any such definition must first be tested against our judgments of particular cases, and on some of those judgments people disagree; so the argument using such a definition which tries to settle that disagreement can only beg the question. Thus, it seems more accurate to say simply that the kinds of considerations I have mentioned explain why the liberal chooses to date human life in a certain way. More accurately still, I don't think the liberal chooses or decides at all; rather, he looks at certain facts and he responds in a particular way to those facts: he dates human life from birth or from viability—and he acts and feels accordingly.[9] There is nothing surprising in such behavior, nor anything irrational or illegitimate.

All this can be said of any of the considerations that have been used to mark the beginning of a human life. Quickening—that is, when the mother first *feels* the fetus move—could be used, because that clearly serves as a sign of life. Liberal detractors point out that the fetus moves long before the mother feels it, and biologically it is a living organism long before that. But such objections overlook the connections between our concept of a person and our concept of an agent, something that can act. It's not to be wondered at that quickening should seem a dramatic moment, especially to the mother who receives the fetus' signal that it *can now move on its own.*

Similarly, liberals always misplace the attractions of fertilization as the critical date when they try to argue that if you go back that far, you could just as well call the sperm or the egg a human being. But people call the zygote a human life not just because it contains the DNA blueprint which determines the physical development of the organism from then on, and not just because of the potential inherent in it, but also because it and it alone can claim to be the beginning of the spatio-temporal-causal chain of the physical object that is a human body. And though I think the abortion controversy throws doubt on the claim that bodily continuity is the *sole* criterion of personal identity, I think the attractions of that philosophical thesis are of a piece with the attractions of fertilization as the point marking the start of a person. Given our conceptual framework, one can't go back further. Neither the sperm nor the egg could be, by itself, a human being, any more than an atom of sodium or an atom of chlorine could by itself properly be called salt. One proof of this is that *no one* is in the least inclined to call a sperm or an egg a human life, a fact acknowledged by the liberal's very argument, which has the form of a *reductio ad absurdum.* At one time people were so inclined, but only because they thought the sperm merely triggered the development of the egg and hence the egg was a human being, or they thought that the egg was merely the seedbed for the male seed and thus the sperm was a human being.

---

[9] His response has cognitive, behavioral, and affective aspects. I make no suggestion regarding their temporal or causal relations.

One other dating deserves mention, since, though rarely stated, it is often used, especially by moderates: the period during which the fetus takes on a recognizably human form, the period when it begins to *look* human. The appeal of this is conveyed by Wittgenstein's remark: "The human body is the best picture of the human soul." [10]

These are some of the considerations, but how are they actually presented? What, for example, does the liberal say and do? Note that his arguments are usually formulated as a series of rhetorical questions. He points to certain facts, and then, quite understandably, he expects his listeners to respond in a particular way—and when they don't, he finds their behavior incomprehensible. First he will point to an infant and say, "Look at it! Aren't you inclined to say that it is one of us?" And then he will describe an embryo as I did earlier, and say, "Look at the difference between it and us! Could you call that a human being?" All this is quite legitimate, but notice what the liberal is doing. First, he has us focus our attention on the *earliest stages* of the fetus, where the contrast with us is greatest. He does not have us look at the fetus shortly before viability or birth, where the differences between it and what he is willing to call a human being are quite minimal. Still, this is not an unfair tactic when combating the view that the fertilized egg is a human life. The other side of this maneuver is that he has us compare the embryo with *us adults*. This seems fair in that we are our own best paradigms of a person. If you and I aren't to be called human beings, then what is? And yet the liberal would not say that a young child or a neonate or even a viable fetus is to be called a human life only in an extended sense. He wants to say that the infant at birth or the viable fetus is a one-hundred-percent human being, but, again, the differences between a neonate and a viable fetus or between a viable fetus and a soon-to-be-viable fetus are not impressive.

The liberal has one other arrow in his meager quiver. He will say that if you call an embryo a human life, then presumably you think it is a valuable entity. But, he adds, what does it have that is of any value? Its biochemical potential to become one of us doesn't ensure that it itself is of any real value, especially if neither the mother nor any other interested party wants it to fulfill that potential. Besides, it's not as though zygotes were rare; they're all too plentiful, and normally it's no great hardship to mix another batch. And don't tell me that the zygote is of great worth because it has a divine soul, for you can't even show that such things exist, let alone that *this* entity has one.

When liberals say that an embryo is of no value if no one has a good reason to want to do anything but destroy it, I think they are on firm ground. But the conservative is not saying that the embryo has some really nifty property, so precious that it's a horrid waste to destroy it. No, he is saying that the embryo is a human being and it is wrong to kill human beings, and that is why you must not destroy the embryo. The conservative realizes that, unless he uses religious premises, premises inadmissible in the court of common morality, he has no way of categorically condemning the killing of a fetus except by arguing that a fetus is a person. And he doesn't call it a human being because its properties are valuable. The properties it has which make it a human being may be valuable, but he does not claim that it is their value which makes it a human being. Rather, he argues that it is a human being by turning the liberal's argument inside out.

The conservative points, and keeps pointing, to the similarities between each set of successive stages of fetal development, instead of pointing, as the liberal does, to the gross differences between widely separated stages. Each step of his argument is persuasive, but if this were all there was to it, his total argument would be no more compelling than one which traded on the fuzziness of the boundaries of baldness and the arbitrariness of any sharp line of demarcation to conclude that Richard M. Nixon is glabrous. If this were the whole conservative argument, then it would be open to the liberal's *reductio* argument, which says that if you go back as far as the zygote, the sperm and the egg must also be called persons. But in fact the conservative can stop at the zygote; fertilization does seem to be a nonarbitrary point marking the inception of a particular object, a human body. That is, the conservative has *independent* reasons for picking the date of conception, just like the liberal who picks the date of birth or viability, and unlike the sophist who concludes that Nixon is bald.

But we still don't have the whole conservative argument, for on the basis of what has been said so far the conservative should also call an acorn an oak tree, but he doesn't, and the reason he uses is that, as regards a human life, it would be *morally* arbitrary to use any date other than that of conception. That is, he can ask liberals to name the earliest stage at which they are willing to call the organism a human being, something which may not be killed for any reason short of saving some other human life. The conservative will then take the stage of development immediately preceding the one the liberals choose and challenge them to point to a difference between the two stages, a difference that is a morally relevant difference, a difference that would justify the massive moral and legal difference of allowing us to kill the creature at the earlier stage while prohibiting that same act at the succeeding stage.

Suppose the liberal picks the date of birth. Yet a newborn infant is only a fetus that has suffered a change of address and some physiological changes like respiration. A neonate delivered in its twenty-fifth week lies in an incubator physically less well developed and no more independent than a normal fetus in its thirty-seventh week in the womb. What difference is there that justifies calling that neonate a person, but not that fetus? What difference is there that can be used to justify killing the prenatal child where it would be wrong to kill the postnatal child?

Or suppose the liberal uses the date of viability. But the viability of a fetus is its capacity to survive outside the mother, and *that* is totally relative to the state of the available medical technology. At present the law dates viability from the twenty-eighth week, but so late a date is now without any medical justification. In principle, eventually the fetus may be deliverable at any time, perhaps even at conception. The problems this poses for liberals are obvious, and in fact one finds that either a liberal doesn't understand what viability really is, so that he takes it to be necessarily linked to the later fetal stages; or he is an extreme liberal in disguise, who is playing along with the first kind of liberal for political purposes; or he has abandoned the viability criterion and is madly scurrying about in search of some other factor in the late fetal stages which might serve as a non-arbitrary cutoff point. For example, in recent years some liberals have been purveying pious nonsense about the developing cerebral cortex in the third trimester and its relation to consciousness. But I am inclined to suppose that the conservative is right, that going back stage by stage from the infant to the zygote one will not find any differences between successive stages significant enough to bear the enormous moral burden of allowing wholesale slaughter at the earlier stage while categorically denying that permission at the next stage.

It needs to be stressed here that we are talking about life and death on a colossal scale. It has been estimated that thirty million abortions are performed yearly, one million in the United States alone. So the situation contrasts sharply with that in which a society selects a date like the eighteenth or twenty-first birthday on which to confer certain legal rights, for the social costs of using a less arbitrary measure of maturity can reasonably be held to outweigh any injustices involved in the present system. Even the choice of a birthday for military conscription, a morally ambiguous practice anyway, is not comparable for obvious reasons.

The full power and persuasiveness of the conservative argument is still not revealed until we uncover its similarities to and connections with any of the dialectical devices that have been used to widen a man's recognition of his fellowship with all the members of his biological species, regardless of their race or sex or nationality or religion or lineage or social class. To be sure, not every discriminatory injustice based on such arbitrary and morally irrelevant features as race or sex has been rationalized on the grounds that the victim is not a full-fledged human being. Still, it is a matter of record that men of good will have often failed to recognize that a certain class of fellow creatures were really human beings just like themselves.

To take but one example, the history of Negro slavery includes among the white oppressors men who were, in all other regards, essentially just and decent. Many such men sincerely defended their practice of slavery with the claim that the Negro was not a member of the moral community of men. Not only legally, but also conceptually, for the white master, the Negro was property, livestock. The manor lord could be both benevolent and unjust with a clear Christian conscience because he regarded the slave as some sort of demiperson, a blathering beast of burden. And given the white man's background, we can understand, if not sympathize with, his perception of Negroes. For either he had never seen one before, or he had been reared in a culture in which it was an accepted practice to treat and regard them, to talk about and perceive them in a certain way. That they were full-fledged human beings, the sort of creatures that it is wrong to kill or enslave, was a claim he found incredible. He would be inclined to, and actually did, simply point to the Negroes and say: "Look at them! Can't you see the differences between them and us?" And the fact is that at one time that argument had an undeniable power, as undeniable as the perceptual differences it appealed to. Check your own perceptions. Ask yourself whether you really, in a purely phenomenological sense, *see* a member of another race in the same way you see a member of your own. Why is it that all Chinamen look alike and are so inscrutable? Add to the physiological facts that staggering cultural disparities dividing slave and master, and you may start to sense the force of the master's argument. What has been the rebuttal? We point to the similarities between Negro and white, and then step by step describe the differences and show about each one that it is not a morally relevant difference, not the kind of difference that warrants enslaving or in any way discriminating against a Negro.

The parallels with the abortion controversy are palpable. Let me extend them some more. First, sometimes a disagreement over a creature's humanity does turn on beliefs about subsidiary matters of fact—but it need not. Further, when it does not, when the disagreement develops from differing responses to the same data, the issue is still a factual one and not a matter of taste. It is not that one party prefers or approves of or has a favorable attitude or emotion toward some property, while the other party does not. Our response concerns what the thing is, not whether we like it or whether it is good. And when I say I don't *care* about the color of a man's skin, that it's not *important* to me, I am saying something quite different than when I say I don't care about the color of a woman's hair. I am saying that this property cannot be used to justify discriminatory behavior or social arrangements. It cannot be so used because it is irrelevant; neither black skin nor white skin is, in and of itself, of any value. Skin color has no logical relation to the question of how to treat a man. The slaveholder's response is not that white skin is of intrinsic value. Rather, he replies that people with naturally black skins are niggers, and that is an inferior kind of creature. So, too, the liberal does not claim that infants possess some intrinsically valuable attribute lacked by prenatal children. Rather, he says that a prenatal child is a fetus, not a human being.

In brief, when seen in its totality the conservative's argument *is* the liberal's argument turned completely inside out. While the liberal stresses the differences between disparate stages, the conservative stresses the resemblances between consecutive stages. The liberal asks, "What has a zygote got that is valuable?" and the conservative answers, "Nothing, but it's a human being, so it is wrong to abort it." Then the conservative asks, "What does a fetus lack that an infant has that is so valuable?" and the liberal answers, "Nothing, but it's a fetus, not a human being, so it is all right to abort it." The arguments are equally strong and equally weak, for they are the *same* argument, an argument that can be pointed in either of two directions. The argument does not itself point in either direction: it is *we* who must point it, and *we* who are led by it. If you are led in one direction rather than the other, that is not because of logic, but because you respond in a certain way to certain facts.

Recall that the arguments are usually formulated in the interrogative, not the indicative, mood. Though the answers are supposed to be absolutely obvious, they are not comfortably assertible. Why? Because an assertion is a truth claim which invites a request for a proof, but here any assertible proof presupposes premises which beg the question. If one may speak of proof here, it can lie only in the audience's response, in their acceptance of the answer and of its obviousness. The questions convince by leading us to appreciate familiar facts. The conclusion is validated not through assertible presuppositions, but through our acknowledgment that the questions are *rhetorical.* You might say that the conclusion is our seeing a certain aspect: e.g., we see the embryo as a human being. But this seems an unduly provocative description of the situation, for what is at issue is whether such an aspect is there to be seen.

Evidently, we have here a paradigm of what Wittgenstein had in mind
. when he spoke of the possibility of two people agreeing on the application of a rule for a long period, and then, suddenly and quite inexplicably, diverging in what they call going on in the same way. This possibility led him to insist that linguistic communication presupposes not only agreement in definitions, but also agreement in judgments, in what he called forms of life [11]—something that seems lacking in the case at hand. Apparently, the conclusion to draw is that it is not true that the fetus is a human being, but it is not false either. Without an agreement in judgments, without a common response to the pertinent data, the assertion that the fetus is a human being cannot be assigned a genuine truth-value.

Yet, we surely want to say that Negroes are and always have been full-fledged human beings, no matter what certain segments of mankind may have thought, and no matter how numerous or unanimous those segments were. The humanity of the slaves seems unlike that of the fetus, but not because by now a monolithic majority recognizes—however grudgingly—the full human status of Negroes, whereas no position regarding the fetus commands more than a plurality. The mere fact of disagreement in judgments

---

[11] Caveat lector! The notion of a form of life is a swamp from whose bourn no philosopher has returned. I would fain forgo the well-known conceits of another had I but time and talent enow to conjure with my own.

or forms of life would not render unsettleable statements about the humanity of fetuses, otherwise, the comparable statements about Negroes, or for
that matter whites, would meet a similar fate. What seems special about the
fetus is that, apparently, we have no vantage point from which to criticize
opposing systems of belief.

It will be said by some that a form of life is a "given," "what has to be
accepted," [12] something not really criticizable by or from an opposing form
of life. There are various long answers to that, but a couple of short ones
should suffice here. First, it is also part of our form of life, and every other
one I know of, that rational and justifiable criticisms of opposing forms of
life can be and are made; it seems that that practice "has to be accepted"
at face value as much as any other. Second, in this instance the point is
without practical relevance, since the differences between the disputants
are not so systematic and entire as to block every avenue of rational discussion. Clearly, their communality is very great, their differences relatively
isolated and free-floating. Thus, for example, liberals and conservatives
seem quite capable of understanding this paper. At any rate, it would be
self-indulgent for me to take any disagreements they may have with me to
be evidence to the contrary.

At this stage of the dispute over a creature's humanity, I stand to the
slaveholder in roughly the same relation I stand to the color-blind man
who judges this sheet of paper to be gray. Our differing color judgments
express our differing immediate responses to the same data. But his color
judgment is mistaken because his vision is defective. I criticize his judgment by criticizing him, but showing him to be abnormal, deviant—which is
not the same as being in the minority. In a like manner we criticize those
basic beliefs and attitudes which sanction and are sustained by the slaveholder's form of life. We argue that his form of life is, so to speak, an accident of history, explicable by reference to special socio-psychological circumstances that are inessential to the natures of blacks and whites.[13] The
fact that Negroes *can* and, special circumstances aside, naturally *would* be
regarded and treated no differently than Caucasians is at once a necessary
and a sufficient condition for its being right to so regard and treat them.
Thus, while we may in large measure understand the life-style of the slaveholder and perhaps withhold condemnation of the man, we need not and
should not condone his behavior.

Liberals and conservatives rail at each other with this same canonical
schema. And if, for example, antiabortionism required the perverting of
natural reason and normal sensibilities by a system of superstitions, then
the liberal could discredit it—but it doesn't, so he can't. As things stand,
it is not at all clear what, if anything, is the normal or natural or healthy

---

[12] Wittgenstein, *Philosophical Investigations*, p. 226e.
[13] This point can be overstated. We develop our concept of a human through our relations with those near us and like us, and thus, at least initially, an isolated culture will
generally perceive and describe foreigners as alien, strange, and not foursquare human.

response toward the fetus; it is not clear what is to count as the special historical and social circumstances, which, if removed, would leave us with the appropriate way to regard and treat the fetus.[14] And I think that the unlimited possibility of natural *responses* is simply the other side of the fact of severely limited possibilities of natural *relationships* with the fetus. After all, there isn't much we can do with a fetus; either we let it out or we do it in. I have little hope of seeing a justification for doing one thing or the other unless this situation changes. As things stand, the range of interactions is so minimal that we are not compelled to regard the fetus in any particular way. For example, respect for a fetus cannot be wrung from us as respect for a Negro can be and is, unless we are irretrievably warped or stunted.

No doubt the assumptions behind these remarks are large and complex, but I take the essential points here to be bits of moral common sense, data to be understood, and, at least at the outset, accepted, not philosophical theses to be refuted. Of course, if we discredit certain *basic* beliefs because of their causal history, we may have to redefine the so-called genetic fallacy and reassess the work of Wittgenstein and others who treat as irrelevant to the validity of such basic beliefs the explanation of how and why we come to have them.[15] However that may be, we seem to be stuck with the indeterminateness of the fetus' humanity. This does not mean that, whatever you believe, it is true or true for you if you believe it. Quite the contrary, it means that, whatever you believe, it's not true—but neither is it false. You believe it, and that's the end of the matter.

But obviously that's not the end of the matter; the same urgent moral and political decisions still confront us. But before we run off to make our existential leaps over the liberal-conservative impasse, we might meander through the moderate position. I'll shorten the trip by speaking only of features found throughout the spectrum of moderate views. For the moderate, the fetus is not a human being, but it's not a mere maternal appendage either; it's a human fetus, and it has a separate moral status just

14 I have heard many people say that they believe what they do about the fetus "because that's what I was brought up to believe." Of course this can't justify their belief, but it's also suspect as an explanation. Even if you acquired your belief by *learning*, it does not follow that you were *taught*. Ask yourself when were you taught and by whom that a human life begins at such and such a time—or have you repressed the memory of that terrifying scene? Have you told a child or seen it done? Many people (e.g., Catholics) are instructed on this matter, and many of them accept the teachings, but many people come to reject what they were taught. (Even contemporary Catholic theologians disagree.) How is that to be explained?

15 Incidentally, we might also stop balking at the *structure* of Nietzsche's critique of our morality, and start facing up to the *content* of his argument. One could concede the claim that our morality, our set of basic values is a *cause* of a sick (diseased, unhealthy, unnatural) mind (person, life, culture), for the claim leaves open whether certain values should be sacrificed for certain others. One cannot be so glib with the claim that our values are a *consequence* of our valetudinarian condition, for if the claim is granted the conclusion seems as inescapable as it is terrible. (Nietzsche spoke of "terrible truths.") Nietzsche may have made the first claim; he certainly made the second.

as animals do. A fetus is not an object that we can treat however we wish, but neither is it a person whom we must treat as we would wish to be treated in return. Thus, *some* legal prohibitions on abortions *might* be justified in the name of the fetus qua human fetus, just as we accord some legal protection to animals, not for the sake of the owners, but for the benefit of the animals themselves.

The popularity of this position is, I believe, generally underestimated; ultimately, most liberals and conservatives are, in a sense, only extreme moderates. Few liberals really regard abortion, at least in the later stages, as a bit of elective surgery. Suppose a woman had her fifth-month fetus aborted purely out of curiosity as to what it looked like, and perhaps then had it bronzed. Who among us would not deem both her and her actions reprehensible? Or, to go from the lurid to the ludicrous, suppose a wealthy woman, a Wagner addict, got an abortion in her fourth month because she suddenly realized that she would come to term during the Bayreuth Festival. Only an exceptional liberal would not blanch at such behavior. Of course, in both cases one might refuse to outlaw the behavior, but still, clearly we do not respond to these cases as we would to the removal of an appendix or a tooth. Similarly, in my experience few of even the staunchest conservatives consistently regard the fetus, at least in the earlier stages, in the same way as they do a fellow adult. When the cause of grief is a miscarriage, the object of grief is the mother; rarely does anyone feel pity or sorrow for the embryo itself. So too, it is most unusual for someone to urge the same punishment for a mother who aborts a young fetus as for one who murders her grown child. Nevertheless, enough people give enough substance to the liberal and conservative positions to justify describing them as I have done, as views differing in kind rather than degree.[16]

The moderate position is as problematic as it is popular. (The virtue of compromise is mass appeal; coherence may not be a consideration.) The moderate is driven in two directions, liberalism and conservatism, by the very same question: Why do you make these exceptions and not those? Why, for example, single out incestuous offspring as unworthy of protection? Are they so tainted by a broken taboo, or is the exception based upon a general utilitarian consideration that would equally justify the mass of abortions that are actually desired?

The difficulty here is comparable to that regarding animals. There are dogs, pigs, mosquitoes, worms, bacteria, etc., and we kill them for food, clothing, ornamentation, sport, convenience, and out of simple irritation or unblinking inadvertence. We allow different animals to be killed for different reasons, and there are enormous differences between people on all of this. In general, for most of us, the higher the evolutionary stage of

---

[16] On the other hand, the above considerations suggest that the human status of a fetus is not indeterminate for the *whole* of its gestation.

the species or the later the developmental stage of the fetus, the more restricted our permission to kill; the more a thing is like us—ontogenetically or phylogenetically—the more we are disposed to treat it like a human being. But it is far more complicated than that, and anyone with a fully consistent, let alone principled, system of beliefs on these matters is usually thought fanatical by the rest of us.

To stabilize his position, the moderate would have to *invent* a new set of moral categories and principles. A happy amalgamation of the ones we have won't do, because our principles of justice apply solely to the relations between persons,[17] and our concepts of zygote, embryo, and fetus are biological, not moral, categories. But *how* is one to invent new categories and principles? I'm not sure it can be done, especially with the scanty building materials available. Again, our interactions with fetuses are extremely limited and peripheral, which is why our normative conceptual machinery in this area is so abbreviated, unformed, and up for grabs.

But perhaps this could be otherwise. Close your eyes for a moment and imagine that, due to advances in medical technology or mutation caused by a nuclear war, the relevant cutaneous and membranous shields became transparent from conception to parturition, so that when a mother put aside her modesty and her clothing the developing fetus would be in full public view. Or suppose instead, or in addition, that anyone could at any time pluck a fetus from its womb, air it, observe it, fondle it, and then stick it back in after a few minutes. And we could further suppose that this made for healthier babies, and so maybe laws would be passed requiring that it be done regularly. And we might also imagine that gestation took nine days rather than nine months. What then would we think of aborting a fetus? What would *you* think of aborting it? And what does that say about what you *now* think?

In my experience, when such imaginative exercises are properly presented people are often, not always, moved by them, different people by different stories. They begin to talk about all of it somewhat differently than they had before, and less differently from each other. However, the role of such conjectures in or as arguments is far from clear. I'm not sure whether people find out something about themselves, or change under the impact of their own imaginations, or both—one as a consequence of the other. I don't think we discover the justifications for our beliefs by such a procedure. A liberal who is disturbed by the picture of a transparent womb may be acquiring some self-knowledge; he may come to realize how much power being visible and being hidden have for us and for him, and he may make a connection between this situation and the differing experiences of

---

[17] An oversimplification whose import remains to be gauged. Compare: I stumble in the dark over my sleeping schnauzer; I stumble over my ottoman. To *blame* either nonperson is irrational; to blame the dog is also *unfair,* but to blame the furniture is neither fair nor unfair. So too: by bitch leaves me five pups. Without special reason it would be *unfair* to apportion the food unequally among them.

an infantryman and a bombardier. But surely the fetus' being hidden was not the liberal's *reason* for thinking it expendable.

Nor is it evident that such *Gedanken* experiments reveal the causes of our beliefs. Their results seem too unreliable to provide anything but the grossest projections as to how we would in fact react in the imagined situations. When I present myself with such science fiction fantasies, I am inclined to respond as I do to a question posed by Hilary Putnam: [18] If we build robots with a psychology isomorphic with ours and a physical structure comparable to ours, should we award them civil rights? In contrast to Putnam, who thinks we can now give a more disinterested and hence objective answer to this question, I would say that our present answer, whatever it is, is so disinterested as to count for nothing. It seems to me that such questions about the robot or the fetus can't be answered in advance. This seems so for much the same reason that some things, especially regarding moral matters, can't be told to a child. A child can of course hear the words and operate with them, but he will not really understand them without undergoing certain experiences, and maybe not even then. Odd as it may sound, I want to know exactly what the robot looks like and what it's like to live with it. I want to know how in fact we—how I— look at it, respond to it, and feel toward it. Hypothetical situations of this sort raise questions which seem answerable only when the situation is realized, and perhaps then there is no longer a real question.

I am suggesting that what our natural response to a thing is, how we naturally react to it cognitively, affectively, and behaviorally, is partly definitive of that thing, and is therefore partly definitive of how we ought to respond to that thing. Often only an actual confrontation will tell us what we need to know, and sometimes we may each respond differently, and thus have differing understandings.

Moreover, the relation of such hypothetical situations to our actual situation is problematic. My hunch is that if the fetal condition I described were realized, fewer of us would be liberals and more of us would be conservatives and moderates. But suppose that in fact we would all be hidebound conservatives and that we knew that now. Would a contemporary liberal be irrational, unjustified, or wicked if he remained adamant? Well, if a slaveholder with a conscience were shown why he feels about Negroes as he does, and that he would regard them as his equals if only he had not been reared to think otherwise, he might change his ways, and if he didn't I would unhesitatingly call him irrational and his behavior unjustified and wicked.

But now suppose that dogs or chimps could and did talk, so that they entered our lives in more significant roles than those of experimental tools, friendly playthings, or faithful servants, and we enacted antivivisectionist

---

[18] "Robots: Machines or Artificially Created Life?" *The Journal of Philosophy* 61, no. 21 (1964): 668–691.

legislation. If we discovered all this now, the news might deeply stir us, but would we necessarily be wrong if we still used animals as we do? Here, so I am inclined to think, we might sensibly maintain that in the hypothetical case the animals and their relations with us are essentially and relevantly different from what they now are. The capacities may exist now, but their realization constitutes a crucial change like that from an infant to an adult, and unlike that from a slave to a citizen. We would no more need to revise our treatment of animals than we need to apply the same principles of reciprocity to children and adults, a practice which, even if it weren't unfair, would be pointless and self-defeating—as resentful parents discover too late.

In the abortion case my instincts are similar but shakier. Yet I think that the adamant liberal could reply that what is special about fetuses, what distinguishes them from babies, slaves, animals, robots, and the rest, is that they essentially are and relate to us as bundles of potentialities. So, obviously, if their potentialities were actualized, not singly or partially, but in sufficient number and degree, we would feel differently. But to make them and their situation in respect to us different enough so that we would naturally regard them as human beings, they would have to become what they can become: human beings. In the hypothetical situation, they are babes in a biological incubator, and therefore that situation is irrelevant to our situation. In brief, an argument based on such a situation only restates the conservative's original argument with imaginary changes instead of the actual set of changes which transforms the fetus into a human child.

Does accepting the liberal's reply scotch all further argument? I think not. One obvious candidate for investigation is the principle that it is wrong to kill a human being, a principle to which some participants in the controversy, in particular utilitarians, apparently do not subscribe. Another candidate is the topic of euthanasia, which is part replica and part mirror image of the abortion problem: patients get described as vegetables, but their human status is elided because their capacities are exhausted rather than dormant. But such similarities may be only surface features; the substance of the two issues may lie in separate spaces. Either topic is as large and caliginous as that of abortion itself—discussable, but not here.

Instead, let me tempt you with a summary argument that the present abortion laws are illegitimate. The existence and powers of the state are legitimated through their rational acceptability to the citizenry, and it would be irrational for the citizens to grant the state any coercive power whose exercise *could* not be rationally justified to them. Thus, the state has the burden of proving that its actions are legitimate. Now, without question, the present abortion laws seriously restrict the freedom and diminish the welfare of the citizenry. A law with that effect is not *ipso facto* unjust, but the state has the burden of showing that such a law is necessary to attain the legitimate ends of the state. But the social costs of the present abortion laws are so drastic that only the preservation of human lives could justify them.[19] So to justify those laws the state must demonstrate that the fetus is a human being. But if that can't be done at all, the state can't do it either, so the laws must be deemed an unjustifiable burden and hence an illegitimate exercise of power.

Note carefully how limited this argument is. It does not show that abortions are morally okay; at best it shows that the legal prohibitions are not. Nor does it work against every possible prohibition of abortion; statutes having milder social liabilities might be warranted without arguing for the fetus' humanity. Further, while the laws are illegitimate because unjustifiable, they need not therefore be unjust; they might be just or unjust or neither without being demonstrably so. Finally, it does not follow that a conservative who promotes such prohibitions is reproachable.[20] What I said about the state does not apply to its citizens. If anything, the burden seems on the complaining liberals to show that a conservative is reprehensible when his political or personal behavior is unacceptable to the liberals. And while any constraint of liberty or any harm to others (e.g., an abortion law) is prima facie objectionable, so that the burden of proof is on its perpetrator, it is not evident that the perpetrator is criticizable when his victims are unsatisfied by an argument they cannot refute. So, for a citizen but not a state, to act without demonstrable justification is not to act wrongly.

---

[19] The truth of this claim may be arguable but becomes ever less so as the multiplication of mankind transforms the preservation of each new life into an increasingly direct threat to every human life.

[20] The issue here was brought to my attention by Thomas Nagel.

13

Sex, Morality, and the Law

Questions of the relation of law to morality often center around issues of private conscience, as do those of law and religion. But the private sphere and its relation to those matters that are of concern to the public interest (not merely public curiosity or gossip) are discussed here, especially so-called "victimless crimes" and other issues of the relation of private and public in law and morals.

Sir Patrick Devlin opposed proposals to relax British laws on homosexuality. He said that law and morality are intimately connected, though he did not hold that laws can make people very highly moral. What the average person thinks is immoral is immoral, so far as law is concerned. The Christian morality is the basis of the criminal law, and without the Christian religion moral order would collapse in Christian nations. It is not the purpose of law to protect individuals so much as to protect society, and those institutions and community of ideas that enable people to live together in peace.

H. L. A. Hart replies to Devlin that the latter goes beyond Mill's position in *Liberty* that society's right to interfere in an individual's life is limited to prevention of harm to others and that Devlin wants to say that not only what harms others must be made illegal (Mill) but what offends people also, e.g., homosexuality. Devlin supposes that vice is subversive to society and seems to put it too close to murder in the seriousness of the threat it poses. But Hart says there is no private subversion (though there might be secret subversion); there is private immorality. Homosexuality isn't treason, and removal of the crime from the statutes does not spell the death of society. Unreasoned disgust can lead to witch hunts. To make the moral feelings of the majority the power behind the law gives the majority that tyrannical power against which Mill warned.

MORALS AND THE CRIMINAL LAW *

PATRICK DEVLIN

What is the connexion between crime and sin and to what extent, if at all, should the criminal law of England concern itself with the enforcement of morals and punish sin or immorality as such?

The statements of principle in the Wolfenden Report provide an admirable and modern starting-point for such an inquiry. In the course of my examination of them I shall find matter for criticism. If my criticisms are sound, it must not be imagined that they point to any shortcomings in the Report. Its authors were not, as I am trying to do, composing a paper on the jurisprudence of morality; they were evolving a working formula to use for reaching a number of practical conclusions. I do not intend to express any opinion one way or the other about these; that would be outside the scope of a lecture on jurisprudence. I am concerned only with general principles; the statement of these in the Report illuminates the entry into the subject and I hope that its authors will forgive me if I carry the lamp with me into places where it was not intended to go.

Early in the Report [1] the Committee put forward:

Our own formulation of the function of the criminal law so far as it concerns the subjects of this enquiry. In this field, its function, as we see it, is to preserve public order and decency, to protect the citizen from what is offensive or injurious, and to provide sufficient safeguards against exploitation and corruption of others, particularly those who are specially vulnerable because they are young, weak in body or mind, inexperienced, or in a state of special physical, official or economic dependence.

It is not, in our view, the function of the law to intervene in the private lives of citizens, or to seek to enforce any particular pattern of behaviour, further than is necessary to carry out the purposes we have outlined.

The Committee preface their most important recommendation [2]

that homosexual behavior between consenting adults in private should no longer be a criminal offence, [by stating the argument [3]] which we believe to be decisive, namely, the importance which society and the law ought to give to individual freedom of choice and action in matters of private morality. Unless a deliberate attempt is to be made by society, acting through the agency of the law, to equate the sphere of crime with that of sin, there must remain a realm

---

* Abridged from *The Enforcement of Morals* by Patrick Devlin, © Oxford University Press 1965. By permission of Oxford University Press. Reprinted from Chapter One.

[1] Para. 13.
[2] Para. 62.
[3] Para. 61.

of private morality and immorality which is, in brief and crude terms, not the law's business. To say this is not to condone or encourage private immorality.

Similar statements of principle are set out in the chapters of the Report which deal with prostitution. No case can be sustained, the Report says, for attempting to make prostitution itself illegal.[4] The Committee refer to the general reasons already given and add: 'We are agreed that private immorality should not be the concern of the criminal law except in the special circumstances therein mentioned.' They quote [5] with approval the report of the Street Offences Committee,[6] which says: 'As a general proposition it will be universally accepted that the law is not concerned with private morals or with ethical sanctions.' It will be observed that the emphasis is on *private* immorality. By this is meant immorality which is not offensive or injurious to the public in the ways defined or described in the first passage which I quoted. In other words, no act of immorality should be made a criminal offence unless it is accompanied by some other feature such as indecency, corruption, or exploitation. This is clearly brought out in relation to prostitution: 'It is not the duty of the law to concern itself with immorality as such . . . it should confine itself to those activities which offend against public order and decency or expose the ordinary citizen to what is offensive or injurious.' [7]

* * *

In jurisprudence, as I have said, everything is thrown open to discussion and, in the belief that they cover the whole field, I have framed three interrogatories addressed to myself to answer:

1. Has society the right to pass judgment at all on matters of morals? Ought there, in other words, be a public morality, or are morals always a matter for private judgement?
2. If society has the right to pass judgment, has it also the right to use the weapon of the law to enforce it?
3. If so, ought it to use that weapon in all cases or only in some; and if only in some, on what principles should it distinguish?

I shall begin with the first interrogatory and consider what is meant by the right of society to pass a moral judgement, that is, a judgement about what is good and what is evil. The fact that a majority of people may disapprove of a practice does not of itself make it a matter for society as a whole. Nine men out of ten may disapprove of what the tenth man is

[4] Para. 224.
[5] Para. 227.
[6] Cmd. 3231 (1928).
[7] Para. 257.

doing and still say that it is not their business. There is a case for a collective judgement (as distinct from a large number of individual opinions which sensible people may even refrain from pronouncing at all if it is upon somebody else's private affairs) only if society is affected. Without a collective judgement there can be no case at all for intervention. Let me take as an illustration the Englishman's attitude to religion as it is now and as it has been in the past. His attitude now is that a man's religion is his private affair; he may think of another man's religion that it is right or wrong, true or untrue, but not that it is good or bad. In earlier times that was not so; a man was denied the right to practise what was thought of as heresy, and heresy was thought of as destructive of society.

The language used in the passages I have quoted from the Wolfenden Report suggests the view that there ought not to be a collective judgement about immorality *per se*. Is this what is meant by 'private morality' and 'individual freedom of choice and action'? Some people sincerely believe that homosexuality is neither immoral nor unnatural. Is the 'freedom of choice and action' that is offered to the individual, freedom to decide for himself what is moral or immoral, society remaining neutral; or is it freedom to be immoral if he wants to be? The language of the Report may be open to question, but the conclusions at which the Committee arrive answer this question unambiguously. If society is not prepared to say that homosexuality is morally wrong, there would be no basis for a law protecting youth from 'corruption' or punishing a man for living on the 'immoral' earnings of a homosexual prostitute, as the Report recommends.[8] This attitude the Committee make even clearer when they come to deal with prostitution. In truth, the Report takes it for granted that there is in existence a public morality which condemns homosexuality and prostitution. What the Report seems to mean by private morality might perhaps be better described as private behaviour in matters of morals.

This view—that there is such a thing as public morality—can also be justified by *a priori* argument. What makes a society of any sort is community of ideas, not only political ideas but also ideas about the way its members should behave and govern their lives; these latter ideas are its morals. Every society has a moral structure as well as a political one: or rather, since that might suggest two independent systems, I should say that the structure of every society is made up both of politics and morals. Take, for example, the institution of marriage. Whether a man should be allowed to take more than one wife is something about which every society has to make up its mind one way or the other. In England we believe in the Christian idea of marriage and therefore adopt monogamy as a moral principle. Consequently the Christian institution of marriage has become the basis of family life and so part of the structure of our society. It is there not because it is Christian. It has got there because it is Christian, but it remains there because it is built into the house in which we live and

8 Para. 76.

could not be removed without bringing it down. The great majority of those who live in this country accept it because it is the Christian idea of marriage and for them the only true one. But a non-Christian is bound by it, not because it is part of Christianity but because, rightly or wrongly, it has been adopted by the society in which he lives. It would be useless for him to stage a debate designed to prove that polygamy was theologically more correct and socially preferable; if he wants to live in the house, he must accept it as built in the way in which it is.

We see this more clearly if we think of ideas or institutions that are purely political. Society cannot tolerate rebellion; it will not allow argument about the rightness of the cause. Historians a century later may say that the rebels were right and the Government was wrong and a percipient and conscientious subject of the State may think so at the time. But it is not a matter which can be left to individual judgment.

The institution of marriage is a good example for my purpose because it bridges the division, if there is one, between politics and morals. Marriage is part of the structure of our society and it is also the basis of a moral code which condemns fornication and adultery. The institution of marriage would be gravely threatened if individual judgements were permitted about the morality of adultery; on these points there must be a public morality. But public morality is not to be confined to those moral principles which support institutions such as marriage. People do not think of monogamy as something which has to be supported because our society has chosen to organize itself upon it; they think of it as something that is good in itself and offering a good way of life and that it is for that reason that our society has adopted it. I return to the statement that I have already made, that society means a community of ideas; without shared ideas on politics, morals, and ethics no society can exist. Each one of us has ideas about what is good and what is evil; they cannot be kept private from the society in which we live. If men and women try to create a society in which there is no fundamental agreement about good and evil they will fail; if, having based it on common agreement, the agreement goes, the society will disintegrate. For society is not something that is kept together physically; it is held by the invisible bonds of common thought. If the bonds were too far relaxed the members would drift apart. A common morality is part of the bondage. The bondage is part of the price of society; and mankind, which needs society, must pay its price. . . .

You may think that I have taken far too long in contending that there is such a thing as public morality, a proposition which most people would readily accept, and may have left myself too little time to discuss the next question which to many minds may cause greater difficulty: to what extent should society use the law to enforce its moral judgements? But I believe that the answer to the first question determines the way in which the second should be approached and may indeed very nearly dictate the answer to the second question. If society has no right to make judgements on morals, the law must find some special justification for entering the field of morality: if homosexuality and prostitution are not in themselves wrong, then the onus is very clearly on the lawgiver who wants to frame a law against certain aspects of them to justify the exceptional treatment. But if society has the right to make a judgement and has it on the basis that a recognized morality is as necessary to society as, say, a recognized government, then society may use the law to preserve morality in the same way as it uses it to safeguard anything else that is essential to its existence. If therefore the first proposition is securely established with all its implications, society has a prima facie right to legislate against immorality as such.

The Wolfenden Report, notwithstanding that it seems to admit the right of society to condemn homosexuality and prostitution as immoral, requires special circumstances to be shown to justify the intervention of the law. I think that this is wrong in principle and that any attempt to approach my second interrogatory on these lines is bound to break down. I think that the attempt by the Committee does break down and that this is shown by the fact that it has to define or describe its special circumstances so widely that they can be supported only if it is accepted that the law *is* concerned with immorality as such.

The widest of the special circumstances are described as the provision of 'sufficient safeguards against exploitation and corruption of others, particularly those who are specially vulnerable because they are young, weak in body or mind, inexperienced, or in a state of special physical, official or economic dependence'.[9] The corruption of youth is a well-recognized ground for intervention by the State and for the purpose of any legislation the young can easily be defined. But if similar protection were to be extended to every other citizen, there would be no limit to the reach of the law. The 'corruption and exploitation of others' is so wide that it could be used to cover any sort of immorality which involves, as most do, the co-operation of another person. Even if the phrase is taken as limited to the categories that are particularized as 'specially vulnerable', it is so elastic as to be practically no restriction. This is not merely a matter of words. For if the words used are stretched almost beyond breaking-point, they still are not wide enough to cover the recommendations which the Committee make about prostitution.

Prostitution is not in itself illegal and the Committee do not think that it ought to be made so.[10] If prostitution is private immorality and not the law's business, what concern has the law with the ponce or the brothel-keeper or the householder who permits habitual prostitution? The Report recommends that the laws which make these activities criminal offences should be maintained or strengthened and brings them (so far as it goes into principle; with regard to brothels it says simply that the law rightly

[9] Para. 13.
[10] Paras. 224, 285, and 318.

frowns on them) under the head of exploitation.[11] There may be cases of exploitation in this trade, as there are or used to be in many others, but in general a ponce exploits a prostitute no more than an impresario exploits an actress. The Report finds that 'the great majority of prostitutes are women whose psychological makeup is such that they choose this life because they find in it a style of living which is to them easier, freer and more profitable than would be provided by any other occupation. . . . In the main the association between prostitute and ponce is voluntary and operates to mutual advantage.' [12] The Committee would agree that this could not be called exploitation in the ordinary sense. They say: 'It is in our view an over-simplification to think that those who live on the earnings of prostitution are exploiting the prostitute as such. What they are really exploiting is the whole complex of the relationship between prostitute and customer; they are, in effect, exploiting the human weaknesses which cause the customer to seek the prostitute and the prostitute to meet the demand.' [13]

All sexual immorality involves the exploitation of human weaknesses. The prostitute exploits the lust of her customers and the customer the moral weakness of the prostitute. If the exploitation of human weaknesses is considered to create a special circumstance, there is virtually no field of morality which can be defined in such a way as to exclude the law.

I think, therefore, that it is not possible to set theoretical limits to the power of the State to legislate against immorality. It is not possible to settle in advance exceptions to the general rule or to define inflexibly areas of morality into which the law is in no circumstances to be allowed to enter. Society is entitled by means of its laws to protect itself from dangers, whether from within or without. Here again I think that the political parallel is legitimate. The law of treason is directed against aiding the king's enemies and against sedition from within. The justification for this is that established government is necessary for the existence of society and therefore its safety against violent overthrow must be secured. But an established morality is as necessary as good government to the welfare of society. Societies disintegrate from within more frequently than they are broken up by external pressures. . . . Suppression of vice is as much the law's business as the suppression of subversive activities; it is no more possible to define a sphere of private morality than it is to define one of private subversive activity. It is wrong to talk of private morality or of the law not being concerned with immorality as such or to try to set rigid bounds to the part which the law may play in the suppression of vice. There are no theoretical limits to the power of the State to legislate against treason and sedition, and likewise I think there can be no theoretical limits to legislation against immorality. You may argue that if a man's sins affect

[11] Paras. 302 and 320.
[12] Para. 223.
[13] Para. 306.

only himself it cannot be the concern of society. If he chooses to get drunk every night in the privacy of his own home, is any one except himself the worse for it? But suppose a quarter or a half of the population got drunk every night, what sort of society would it be? You cannot set a theoretical limit to the number of people who can get drunk before society is entitled to legislate against drunkenness.

                                    *   *   *

In what circumstances the State should exercise its power is the third of the interrogatories I have framed. But before I get to it I must raise a point which might have been brought up in any one of the three. How are the moral judgements of society to be ascertained? By leaving it until now, I can ask it in the more limited form that is now sufficient for my purpose. How is the law-maker to ascertain the moral judgements of society? It is surely not enough that they should be reached by the opinion of the majority; it would be too much to require the individual assent of every citizen. English law has evolved and regularly uses a standard which does not depend on the counting of heads. It is that of the reasonable man. He is not to be confused with the rational man. He is not expected to reason about anything and his judgement may be largely a matter of feeling. It is the viewpoint of the man in the street—or to use an archaism familiar to all lawyers—the man in the Clapham omnibus. He might also be called the right-minded man. For my purpose I should like to call him the man in the jury box, for the moral judgement of society must be something about which any twelve men or women drawn at random might after discussion be expected to be unanimous. This was the standard the judges applied in the days before Parliament was as active as it is now and when they laid down rules of public policy. They did not think of themselves as making law but simply as stating principles which every right-minded person would accept as valid. It is what Pollock called 'practical morality', which is based not on theological or philosophical foundations but 'in the mass of continuous experience half-consciously or unconsciously accumulated and embodied in the morality of common sense'. He called it also 'a certain way of thinking on questions of morality which we expect to find in a reasonable civilized man or a reasonable Englishman, taken at random'.[14]

Immorality then, for the purpose of the law, is what every right-minded person is presumed to consider to be immoral. Any immorality is capable of affecting society injuriously and in effect to a greater or lesser extent it usually does; this is what gives the law its *locus standi*. It cannot be shut out. But—and this brings me to the third question—the individual has a *locus standi* too; he cannot be expected to surrender to the judgement of society the whole conduct of his life. It is the old and familiar question

[14] *Essays in Jurisprudence and Ethics* (1882), Macmillan, pp. 278 and 353.

of striking a balance between the rights and interests of society and those of the individual. This is something which the law is constantly doing in matters large and small. To take a very down-to-earth example, let me consider the right of the individual whose house adjoins the highway to have access to it; that means in these days the right to have vehicles stationary in the highway, sometimes for a considerable time if there is a lot of loading or unloading. There are many cases in which the courts have had to balance the private right of access against the public right to use the highway without obstruction. It cannot be done by carving up the highway into public and private areas. It is done by recognizing that each have rights over the whole; that if each were to exercise their rights to the full, they would come into conflict; and therefore that the rights of each must be curtailed so as to ensure as far as possible that the essential needs of each are safeguarded.

I do not think that one can talk sensibly of a public and private morality any more than one can of a public or private highway. Morality is a sphere in which there is a public interest and a private interest, often in conflict, and the problem is to reconcile the two. This does not mean that it is impossible to put forward any general statements about how in our society the balance ought to be struck. Such statements cannot of their nature be rigid or precise; they would not be designed to circumscribe the operation of the law-making power but to guide those who have to apply it. While every decision which a court of law makes when it balances the public against the private interest is an *ad hoc* decision, the cases contain statements of principle to which the court should have regard when it reaches its decision. In the same way it is possible to make general statements of principle which it may be thought the legislature should bear in mind when it is considering the enactment of laws enforcing morals.

I believe that most people would agree upon the chief of these elastic principles. There must be toleration of the maximum individual freedom that is consistent with the integrity of society. It cannot be said that this is a principle that runs all through the criminal law. Much of the criminal law that is regulatory in character—the part of it that deals with *malum probibitum* rather than *malum in se*—is based upon the opposite principle, that is, that the choice of the individual must give way to the convenience of the many. But in all matters of conscience the principle I have stated is generally held to prevail. It is not confined to thought and speech; it extends to action, as is shown by the recognition of the right to conscientious objection in war-time; this example shows also that conscience will be respected even in times of national danger. The principle appears to me to be peculiarly appropriate to all questions of morals. Nothing should be punished by the law that does not lie beyond the limits of tolerance. It is not nearly enough to say that a majority dislike a practice; there must be a real feeling of reprobation. Those who are dissatisfied with the present law on homosexuality often say that the opponents of reform are swayed simply by disgust. If that were so it would be wrong, but I do not think one can ignore disgust if it is deeply felt and not manufactured. Its presence is a good indication that the bounds of toleration are being reached. Not everything is to be tolerated. No society can do without intolerance, indignation, and disgust,[15] they are the forces behind the moral law, and indeed it can be argued that if they or something like them are not present, the feelings of society cannot be weighty enough to deprive the individual of freedom of choice. I suppose that there is hardly anyone nowadays who would not be disgusted by the thought of deliberate cruelty to animals. No one proposes to relegate that or any other form of sadism to the realm of private morality or to allow it to be practised in public or in private. It would be possible no doubt to point out that until a comparatively short while ago nobody thought very much of cruelty to animals and also that pity and kindliness and the unwillingness to inflict pain are virtues more generally esteemed now than they have ever been in the past. But matters of this sort are not determined by rational argument. Every moral judgement, unless it claims a divine source, is simply a feeling that no right-minded man could behave in any other way without admitting that he was doing wrong. It is the power of a common sense and not the power of reason that is behind the judgements of society. But before a society can put a practice beyond the limits of tolerance there must be a deliberate judgement that the practice is injurious to society. There is, for example, a general abhorrence of homosexuality. We should ask ourselves in the first instance whether, looking at it calmly and dispassionately, we regard it as a vice so abominable that its mere presence is an offence. If that is the genuine feeling of the society in which we live, I do not see how society can be denied the right to eradicate it. Our feeling may not be so intense as that. We may feel about it that, if confined, it is tolerable, but that if it spread it might be gravely injurious; it is in this way that most societies look upon fornication, seeing it as a natural weakness which must be kept within bounds but which cannot be rooted out. It becomes then a question of balance, the danger to society in one scale and the extent of the restriction in the other. On this sort of point the value of an investigation by such a body as the Wolfenden Committee and of its conclusions is manifest.

The limits of tolerance shift. This is supplementary to what I have been saying but of sufficient importance in itself to deserve statement as a separate principle which law-makers have to bear in mind. I suppose that moral standards do not shift; so far as they come from divine revelation they do not, and I am willing to assume that the moral judgements made by a society always remain good for that society. But the extent to which society will tolerate—I mean tolerate, not approve—departures from moral standards varies from generation to generation. . . . Especially [laws] which are based

---

[15] These words which have been much criticized, are considered again in the Preface at p. viii.

on morals, are less easily moved. It follows as another good working principle that in any new matter of morals the law should be slow to act. By the next generation the swell of indignation may have abated and the law be left without the strong backing which it needs. But it is then difficult to alter the law without giving the impression that moral judgement is being weakened. This is now one of the factors that is strongly militating against any alteration to the law on homosexuality.

A third elastic principle must be advanced more tentatively. It is that as far as possible privacy should be respected. This is not an idea that has ever been made explicit in the criminal law. Acts or words done or said in public or in private are all brought within its scope without distinction in principle. But there goes with this a strong reluctance on the part of judges and legislators to sanction invasions of privacy in the detection of crime. The police have no more right to trespass than the ordinary citizen has; there is no general right to search; to this extent an Englishman's home is still his castle.

* * *

This indicates a general sentiment that the right to privacy is something to be put in the balance against the enforcement of the law. Ought the same sort of consideration to play any part in the formation of the law? Clearly only in a very limited number of cases. When the help of the law is invoked by an injured citizen, privacy must be irrelevant; the individual cannot ask that his right to privacy should be measured against injury criminally done to another. But when all who are involved in the deed are consenting parties and the injury is done to morals, the public interest in the moral order can be balanced against the claims of privacy. The restriction on police powers of investigation goes further than the affording of a parallel; it means that the detection of crime committed in private and when there is no complaint is bound to be rather haphazard and this is an additional reason for moderation. These considerations do not justify the exclusion of all private immorality from the scope of the law. I think that, as I have already suggested, the test of 'private behaviour' should be substituted for 'private morality' and the influence of the factor should be reduced from that of a definite limitation to that of a matter to be taken into account. Since the gravity of the crime is also a proper consideration, a distinction might well be made in the case of homosexuality between the lesser acts of indecency and the full offence, which on the principles of the Wolfenden Report it would be illogical to do.

The last and the biggest thing to be remembered is that the law is concerned with the minimum and not with the maximum; there is much in the Sermon on the Mount that would be out of place in the Ten Commandments. We all recognize the gap between the moral law and the law of the land. No man is worth much who regulates his conduct with the sole object of escaping punishment, and every worthy society sets for its members standards which are above those of the law. We recognize the existence of such higher standards when we use expressions such as 'moral obligation' and 'morally bound'. The distinction was well put in the judgement of African elders in a family dispute: 'We have power to make you divide the crops, for this is our law, and we will see this is done. But we have not power to make you behave like an upright man.'

It can only be because this point is so obvious that it is so frequently ignored. Discussion among law-makers, both professional and amateur, is too often limited to what is right or wrong and good or bad for society. There is a failure to keep separate the two questions I have earlier posed —the question of society's right to pass a moral judgement and the question of whether the arm of the law should be used to enforce the judgement. The criminal law is not a statement of how people ought to behave; it is a statement of what will happen to them if they do not behave; good citizens are not expected to come within reach of it or to set their sights by it, and every enactment should be framed accordingly.

The arm of the law is an instrument to be used by society, and the decision about what particular cases it should be used in is essentially a practical one.

*   *   *

The part that the jury plays in the enforcement of the criminal law, the fact that no grave offence against morals is punishable without their verdict, these are of great importance in relation to the statements of principle that I have been making. They turn what might otherwise be pure exhortation to the legislature into something like rules that the law-makers cannot safely ignore. The man in the jury box is not just an expression; he is an active reality. It will not in the long run work to make laws about morality that are not acceptable to him.

This then is how I believe my third interrogatory should be answered—not by the formulation of hard and fast rules, but by a judgement in each case taking into account the sort of factors I have been mentioning. The line that divides the criminal law from the moral is not determinable by the application of any clear-cut principle. It is like a line that divides land and sea, a coastline of irregularities and indentations. There are gaps and promontories, such as adultery and fornication, which the law has for centuries left substantially untouched. Adultery of the sort that breaks up marriage seems to me to be just as harmful to the social fabric as homosexuality or bigamy. The only ground for putting it outside the criminal law is that a law which made it a crime would be too difficult to enforce; it is too generally regarded as a human weakness not suitably punished by imprisonment. All that the law can do with fornication is to act against its worst manifestations; there is a general abhorrence of the commercialization of vice, and that sentiment gives strength to the law against brothels and immoral earnings. There is no logic to be found in this. The boundary between the criminal law and the moral law is fixed by balancing in the case of each particular crime the pros and cons of legal enforcement in accordance with the sort of considerations I have been outlining. The fact that adultery, fornication, and lesbianism are untouched by the criminal law does not prove that homosexuality ought not to be touched. The error of jurisprudence in the Wolfenden Report is caused by the search for some single principle to explain the division between crime and sin. The Report finds it in the principle that the criminal law exists for the protection of individuals; on this principle fornication in private between consenting adults is outside the law and thus it becomes logically indefensible to bring homosexuality between consenting adults in private within it. But the true principle is that the law exists for the protection of society. It does not discharge its function by protecting the individual from injury, annoyance, corruption, and exploitation; the law must protect also the institutions and the community of ideas, political and moral, without which people cannot live together. Society cannot ignore the morality of the individual any more than it can his loyalty; it flourishes on both and without either it dies.

*   *   *

I return now to the main thread of my argument and summarize it. Society cannot live without morals. Its morals are those standards of conduct which the reasonable man approves. A rational man, who is also a good man, may have other standards. If he has no standards at all he is not a good man and need not be further considered. If he has standards, they may be very different; he may, for example, not disapprove of homosexuality or abortion. In that case he will not share in the common morality; but that should not make him deny that it is a social necessity. A rebel may be rational in thinking that he is right but he is irrational if he thinks that society can leave him free to rebel.

A man who concedes that morality is necessary to society must support the use of those instruments without which morality cannot be maintained. The two instruments are those of teaching, which is doctrine, and of enforcement, which is the law.

*   *   *

IMMORALITY AND TREASON °

H. L. A. HART

The most remarkable feature of Sir Patrick's lecture is his view of the nature of morality—the morality which the criminal law may enforce. Most previous thinkers who have repudiated the liberal point of view have done

° From *The Listener* (July 30, 1959), pp. 162–163. Reprinted by permission of the author.

so because they thought that morality consisted either of divine commands or of rational principles of human conduct discoverable by human reason. Since morality for them had this elevated divine or rational status as the law of God or reason, it seemed obvious that the state should enforce it, and that the function of human law should not be merely to provide men with the opportunity for leading a good life, but actually to see that they lead it. Sir Patrick does not rest his repudiation of the liberal point of view on these religious or rationalist conceptions. Indeed much that he writes reads like an abjuration of the notion that reasoning or thinking has much to do with morality. English popular morality has no doubt its historical connection with the Christian religion: 'That', says Sir Patrick, 'is how it got there.' But it does not owe its present status or social significance to religion any more than to reason.

What, then, is it? According to Sir Patrick it is primarily a matter of feeling. 'Every moral judgment', he says, 'is a feeling that no right-minded man could act in any other way without admitting that he was doing wrong.' Who then must feel this way if we are to have what Sir Patrick calls a public morality? He tells us that it is 'the man in the street', 'the man in the jury box', or (to use the phrase so familiar to English lawyers) 'the man on the Clapham omnibus'. For the moral judgments of society so far as the law is concerned are to be ascertained by the standards of the reasonable man, and he is not to be confused with the rational man. Indeed, Sir Patrick says 'he is not expected to reason about anything and his judgment may be largely a matter of feeling.'

Intolerance, Indignation, and Disgust

But what precisely are the relevant feelings, the feelings which may justify use of the criminal law? Here the argument becomes a little complex. Widespread dislike of a practice is not enough. There must, says Sir Patrick, be 'a real feeling of reprobation'. Disgust is not enough either. What is crucial is a combination of intolerance, indignation, and disgust. These three are the forces behind the moral law, without which it is not 'weighty enough to deprive the individual of freedom of choice'. Hence there is, in Sir Patrick's outlook, a crucial difference between the mere adverse moral judgment of society and one which is inspired by feeling raised to the concert pitch of intolerance, indignation, and disgust.

This distinction is novel and also very important. For on it depends the weight to be given to the fact that when morality is enforced individual liberty is necessarily cut down. Though Sir Patrick's abstract formulation of his views on this point is hard to follow, his examples make his position fairly clear. We can see it best in the contrasting things he says about fornication and homosexuality. In regard to fornication, public feeling in most societies is not now of the concert-pitch intensity. We may feel that it is tolerable if confined: only its spread might be gravely injurious. In such cases the question whether individual liberty should be restricted is for Sir Patrick a question of balance between the danger to society in the one scale, and the restriction of the individual in the other. But if, as may be the case with homosexuality, public feeling is up to concert pitch, if it expresses a 'deliberate judgment' that a practice as such is injurious to society, if there is 'a genuine feeling that it is a vice so abominable that its mere presence is an offence', then it is beyond the limits of tolerance, and society may eradicate it. In this case, it seems, no further balancing of the claims of individual liberty is to be done, though as a matter of prudence the legislator should remember that the popular limits of tolerance may shift: the concert-pitch feeling may subside. This may produce a dilemma for the law; for the law may then be left without the full moral backing that it needs, yet it cannot be altered without giving the impression that the moral judgment is being weakened.

A Shared Morality

If this is what morality is—a compound of indignation, intolerance, and disgust—we may well ask what justification there is for taking it, and turning it as such, into criminal law with all the misery which criminal punishment entails. Here Sir Patrick's answer is very clear and simple. A collection of individuals is not a society; what makes them into a society is among other things a shared or public morality. This is as necessary to its existence as an organized government. So society may use the law to preserve its morality like anything else essential to it. 'The suppression of vice is as much the law's business as the suppression of subversive activities'. The liberal point of view which denies this is guilty of 'an error in jurisprudence': for it is no more possible to define an area of private morality than an area of private subversive activity. There can be no 'theoretical limits' to legislation against immorality just as there are no such limits to the power of the state to legislate against treason and sedition.

Surely all this, ingenious as it is, is misleading. Mill's formulation of the liberal point of view may well be too simple. The grounds for interfering with human liberty are more various than the single criterion of 'harm to others' suggests: cruelty to animals or organizing prostitution for gain do not, as Mill himself saw, fall easily under the description of harm to others. Conversely, even where there is harm to others in the most literal sense, there may well be other principles limiting the extent to which harmful activities should be repressed by law. So there are multiple criteria, not a single criterion, determining when human liberty may be restricted. Perhaps this is what Sir Patrick means by a curious distinction which he often stresses between theoretical and practical limits. But with all its simplicities the liberal point of view is a better guide than Sir Patrick to clear thought on the proper relation of morality to the criminal law: for it stresses what he obscures—namely, the points at which thought is needed before we turn popular morality into criminal law.

Society and Moral Opinion

No doubt we would all agree that a consensus of moral opinion on certain matters is essential if society is to be worth living in. Laws against murder, theft, and much else would be of little use if they were not supported by a widely diffused conviction that what these laws forbid is also immoral. So much is obvious. But it does not follow that everything to which the moral vetoes of accepted morality attach is of equal importance to society; nor is there the slightest reason for thinking of morality as a seamless web: one which will fall to pieces carrying society with it, unless all its emphatic vetoes are enforced by law. Surely even in the face of the moral feeling that is up to concert pitch—the trio of intolerance, indignation, and disgust—we must pause to think. We must ask a question at two different levels which Sir Patrick never clearly enough identifies or separates. First, we must ask whether a practice which offends moral feeling is harmful, independently of its repercussion on the general moral code. Secondly, what about repercussion on the moral code? Is it really true that failure to translate this item of general morality into criminal law will jeopardize the whole fabric of morality and so of society?

We cannot escape thinking about these two different questions merely by repeating to ourselves the vague nostrum: 'This is part of public morality and public morality must be preserved if society is to exist.' Sometimes Sir Patrick seems to admit this, for he says in words which both Mill and the Wolfenden Report might have used, that there must be the maximum respect for individual liberty consistent with the integrity of society. Yet this, as his contrasting examples of fornication and homosexuality show, turns out to mean only that the immorality which the law may punish must be generally felt to be intolerable. This plainly is no adequate substitute for a reasoned estimate of the damage to the fabric of society likely to ensue if it is not suppressed.

Nothing perhaps shows more clearly the inadequacy of Sir Patrick's approach to this problem than his comparison between the suppression of sexual immorality and the suppression of treason or subversive activity. Private subversive activity is, of course, a contradiction in terms because 'subversion' means overthrowing government, which is a public thing. But it is grotesque, even where moral feeling against homosexuality is up to concert pitch, to think of the homosexual behaviour of two adults in private as in any way like treason or sedition either in intention or effect. We can make it *seem* like treason only if we assume that deviation from a general moral code is bound to affect that code, and to lead not merely to its modification but to its destruction. The analogy could begin to be plausible only if it was clear that offending against this item of morality was likely to jeopardize the whole structure. But we have ample evidence for believing that people will not abandon morality, will not think any better of murder, cruelty, and dishonesty, merely because some private sexual practice which they abominate is not punished by the law.

Because this is so the analogy with treason is absurd. Of course 'No man is an island': what one man does in private, if it is known, may affect others in many different ways. Indeed it may be that deviation from general sexual morality by those whose lives, like the lives of many homosexuals, are noble ones and in all other ways exemplary will lead to what Sir Patrick calls the shifting of the limits of tolerance. But if this has any analogy in the sphere of government it is not the overthrow of ordered government, but a peaceful change in its form. So we may listen to the promptings of common sense and of logic, and say that though there could not logically be a sphere of private treason there is a sphere of private morality and immorality.

Sir Patrick's doctrine is also open to a wider, perhaps a deeper, criticism. In his reaction against a rationalist morality and his stress on feeling, he has I think thrown out the baby and kept the bath water; and the bath water may turn out to be very dirty indeed. When Sir Patrick's lecture was first delivered *The Times* greeted it with these words: 'There is a moving and welcome humility in the conception that society should not be asked to give its reason for refusing to tolerate what in its heart it feels intolerable.' This drew from a correspondent in Cambridge the retort: 'I am afraid that we are less humble than we used to be. We once burnt old women because, without giving our reasons, we felt in our hearts that witchcraft was intolerable.'

This retort is a bitter one, yet its bitterness is salutary. We are not, I suppose, likely, in England, to take again to the burning of old women for witchcraft or to punishing people for associating with those of a different race or colour, or to punishing people again for adultery. Yet if these things were viewed with intolerance, indignation, and disgust, as the second of them still is in some countries, it seems that on Sir Patrick's principles no rational criticism could be opposed to the claim that they should be punished by law. We could only pray, in his words, that the limits of tolerance might shift.

Curious Logic

It is impossible to see what curious logic has led Sir Patrick to this result. For him a practice is immoral if the thought of it makes the man on the Clapham omnibus sick. So be it. Still, why should we not summon all the resources of our reason, sympathetic understanding, as well as critical intelligence, and insist that before general moral feeling is turned into criminal law it is submitted to scrutiny of a different kind from Sir Patrick's? Surely, the legislator should ask whether the general morality is based on ignorance, superstition, or misunderstanding; whether there is a false conception that those who practise what it condemns are in other ways dangerous or hostile to society; and whether the misery to many parties, the blackmail and the other evil consequences of criminal punishment, especially for sexual offences, are well understood. It is surely extraordinary that among the things which Sir Patrick says are to be considered before we legislate against immorality these appear nowhere; not even as 'practical considerations', let alone 'theoretical limits'. To any theory which, like this one, asserts that the criminal law may be used on the vague ground that the preservation of morality is essential to society and yet omits to stress the need for critical scrutiny, our reply should be: 'Morality, what crimes may be committed in thy name!'

As Mill saw, and de Tocqueville showed in detail long ago in his critical but sympathetic study of democracy, it is fatally easy to confuse the democratic principle that power should be in the hands of the majority with the utterly different claim that the majority with power in their hands need respect no limits. Certainly there is a special risk in a democracy that the majority may dictate how all should live. This is the risk we run, and should gladly run; for it is the price of all that is so good in democratic rule. But loyalty to democratic principles does not require us to maximize this risk: yet this is what we shall do if we mount the man in the street on the top of the Clapham omnibus and tell him that if only he feels sick enough about what other people do in private to demand its suppression by law no theoretical criticism can be made of his demand.

14

Sexual Perversion

Devlin and Hart have debated the relationship between what people feel is disgusting in human behavior and their attempts to control the behavior of other people by law. Homosexuality was a frequent example. Many consider homosexuality, whether in men or women, as sexual perversion. What makes sex perverse? Let us look at a reading that may provide a bit of an interlude, more or less psychological in nature, between bouts of fairly solid grappling with moral problems. While not exactly dealing with the subject as a moral problem, the discussion of "perversion" has a definite tinge of values about it. Sex is very definitely a value! But its nature is often a puzzle. Love is surely a value, and, likewise, its nature is elusive. Thomas Nagel manages to discuss both in a way that is reminiscent of the late Jean-Paul Sartre and which yet is more palatable to the perhaps mythical "average American."

Nagel addresses the issue of what sexual perversion consists of. He sees it as a way of clarifying what sex is. For Nagel, sex is not primarily a physiological or sociological but a psychological category. Perversion in sex consists of an incompleteness in the relations between minds and bodies, e.g., making a mere object of another with no awareness that he or she is also a subject, a person. But Nagel does not say that all deviance is perverse sex, including the usual psychological description of the homosexual relation.

SEXUAL PERVERSION [*]

THOMAS NAGEL

There is something to be learned about sex from the fact that we possess a concept of sexual perversion. I wish to examine the concept, defending it against the charge of unintelligibility and trying to say exactly what about human sexuality qualifies it to admit of perversions. Let me make some preliminary comments about the problem before embarking on its solution.

Some people do not believe that the notion of sexual perversion makes sense, and even those who do disagree over its application. Nevertheless I think it will be widely conceded that, if the concept is viable at all, it must meet certain general conditions. First, if there are any sexual perversions, they will have to be sexual desires or practices that can be plausibly described as in some sense unnatural, though the explanation of this natural/ unnatural distinction is of course the main problem. Second, certain practices will be perversions if anything is, such as shoe fetishism, bestiality, and sadism; other practices, such as unadorned sexual intercourse, will not be; about still others there is controversy. Third, if there are perversions, they will be unnatural sexual *inclinations* rather than merely unnatural practices adopted not from inclination but for other reasons. I realize that this is at variance with the view, maintained by some Roman Catholics, that contraception is a sexual perversion. But although contraception may qualify as a deliberate perversion of the sexual and reproductive functions, it cannot be significantly described as a *sexual* perversion. A sexual perversion must reveal itself in conduct that expresses an unnatural *sexual* preference. And although there might be a form of fetishism focused on the employment of contraceptive devices, that is not the usual explanation for their use.

I wish to declare at the outset my belief that the connection between sex and reproduction has no bearing on sexual perversion. The latter is a concept of psychological, not physiological interest, and it is a concept that we do not apply to the lower animals, let alone to plants, all of which have reproductive functions that can go astray in various ways. (Think of seedless oranges.) Insofar as we are prepared to regard higher animals as perverted, it is because of their psychological, not their anatomical similarity to humans. Furthermore, we do not regard as a perversion every deviation from the reproductive function of sex in humans: sterility, miscarriage, contraception, abortion.

Another matter that I believe has no bearing on the concept of sexual perversion is social disapprobation or custom. Anyone inclined to think that in each society the perversions are those sexual practices of which the community disapproves, should consider all the societies that have frowned upon adultery and fornication. These have not been regarded as unnatural prac-

[*] From Thomas Nagel, "Sexual Perversion," *The Journal of Philosophy*, **66** (1969). Reprinted by permission of the author and *The Journal of Philosophy*.

tices, but have been thought objectionable in other ways. What is regarded as unnatural admittedly varies from culture to culture, but the classification is not a pure expression of disapproval or distaste. In fact it is often regarded as a *ground* for disapproval, and that suggests that the classification has an independent content.

I am going to attempt a psychological account of sexual perversion, which will depend on a specific psychological theory of sexual desire and human sexual interactions. To approach this solution I wish first to consider a contrary position, one which provides a basis for skepticism about the existence of any sexual perversions at all, and perhaps about the very significance of the term. The skeptical argument runs as follows:

"Sexual desire is simply one of the appetites, like hunger and thirst. As such it may have various objects, some more common than others perhaps, but none in any sense 'natural'. An appetite is identified as sexual by means of the organs and erogenous zones in which its satisfaction can be to some extent localized, and the special sensory pleasures which form the core of that satisfaction. This enables us to recognize widely divergent goals, activities, and desires as sexual, since it is conceivable in principle that anything should produce sexual pleasure and that a nondeliberate, sexually charged desire for it should arise (as a result of conditioning, if nothing else). We may fail to empathize with some of these desires, and some of them, like sadism, may be objectionable on extraneous grounds, but once we have observed that they meet the criteria for being sexual, there is nothing more to be said on *that* score. Either they are sexual or they are not: sexuality does not admit of imperfection, or perversion, or any other such qualification—it is not that sort of affection."

This is probably the received radical position. It suggests that the cost of defending a psychological account may be to deny that sexual desire is an appetite. But insofar as that line of defense is plausible, it should make us suspicious of the simple picture of appetites on which the skepticism depends. Perhaps the standard appetites, like hunger, cannot be classed as pure appetites in that sense either, at least in their human versions.

Let us approach the matter by asking whether we can imagine anything that would qualify as a gastronomical perversion. Hunger and eating are importantly like sex in that they serve a biological function and also play a significant role in our inner lives. It is noteworthy that there is little temptation to describe as perverted an appetite for substances that are not nourishing. We should probably not consider someone's appetites as *perverted* if he liked to eat paper, sand, wood, or cotton. Those are merely rather odd and very unhealthy tastes: they lack the psychological complexity that we expect of perversions. (Coprophilia, being already a sexual perversion, may be disregarded.) If on the other hand someone liked to eat cookbooks, or magazines with pictures of food in them, and preferred these to ordinary food—or if when hungry he sought satisfaction by fondling a napkin or ashtray from his favorite restaurant—then the concept of perversion might seem appropriate (in fact it would be natural to describe this as a case of gastronomical fetishism). It would be natural to describe as gastronomically perverted someone who could eat only by having food forced down his throat through a funnel, or only if the meal were a living animal. What helps in such cases is the peculiarity of the desire itself, rather than the inappropriateness of its object to the biological function that the desire serves. Even an appetite, it would seem, can have perversions if in addition to its biological function it has a significant psychological structure.

In the case of hunger, psychological complexity is provided by the activities that give it expression. Hunger is not merely a disturbing sensation that can be quelled by eating; it is an attitude toward edible portions of the external world, a desire to relate to them in rather special ways. The method of ingestion; chewing, savoring, swallowing, appreciating the texture and smell, all are important components of the relation, as is the passivity and controllability of the food (the only animals we eat live are helpless mollusks). Our relation to food depends also on our size: we do not live upon it or burrow into it like aphids or worms. Some of these features are more central than others, but any adequate phenomenology of eating would have to treat it as a relation to the external world and a way of appropriating bits of that world, with characteristic affection. Displacements or serious restrictions of the desire to eat could then be described as perversions, if they undermined that direct relation between man and food which is the natural expression of hunger. This explains why it is easy to imagine gastronomical fetishism, voyeurism, exhibitionism, or even gastronomical sadism and masochism. Indeed some of these perversions are fairly common.

If we can imagine perversions of an appetite like hunger, it should be possible to make sense of the concept of sexual perversion. I do not wish to imply that sexual desire is an appetite—only that being an appetite is no bar to admitting of perversions. Like hunger, sexual desire has as its characteristic object a certain relation with something in the external world; only in this case it is usually a person rather than an omelet, and the relation is considerably more complicated. This added complication allows scope for correspondingly complicated perversions.

The fact that sexual desire is a feeling about other persons may tempt us to take a pious view of its psychological content. There are those who believe that sexual desire is properly the expression of some other attitude, like love, and that when it occurs by itself it is incomplete and unhealthy— or at any rate subhuman. (The extreme Platonic version of such a view is that sexual practices are all vain attempts to express something they cannot in principle achieve: this makes them all perversions, in a sense.) I do not believe that any such view is correct. Sexual desire is complicated enough without having to be linked to anything else as a condition for phenomenological analysis. It cannot be denied that sex may serve various functions—

economic, social, altruistic—but it also has its own content as a relation between persons, and it is only by analyzing that relation that we can understand the conditions of sexual perversion.

I believe it is very important that the object of sexual attraction is a particular individual, who transcends the properties that make him attractive. When different persons are attracted to a single person for different reasons: eyes, hair, figure, laugh, intelligence—we feel that the object of their desire is nevertheless the same, namely that person. There is even an inclination to feel that this is so if the lovers have different sexual aims, if they include both men and women, for example. Different specific attractive characteristics seem to provide enabling conditions for the operation of a single basic feeling, and the different aims all provide expressions of it. We approach the sexual attitude toward the person through the features that we find attractive, but these features are not the objects of that attitude.

This is very different from the case of an omelet. Various people may desire it for different reasons, one for its fluffiness, another for its mushrooms, another for its unique combination of aroma and visual aspect; yet we do not enshrine the transcendental omelet as the true common object of their affections. Instead we might say that several desires have accidentally converged on the same object: any omelet with the crucial characteristics would do as well. It is not similarly true that any person with the same flesh distribution and way of smoking can be substituted as object for a particular sexual desire that has been elicited by those characteristics. It may be that they will arouse attraction whenever they recur, but it will be a new sexual attraction with a new particular object, not merely a transfer of the old desire to someone else. (I believe this is true even in cases where the new object is unconsciously identified with a former one.)

The importance of this point will emerge when we see how complex a psychological interchange constitutes the natural development of sexual attraction. This would be incomprehensible if its object were not a particular person, but rather a person of a certain *kind*. Attraction is only the beginning, and fulfillment does not consist merely of behavior and contact expressing this attraction, but involves much more.

The best discussion of these matters that I have seen appears in part III of Sartre's *Being and Nothingness*.[1] Since it has influenced my own views, I shall say a few things about it now. Sartre's treatment of sexual desire and of love, hate, sadism, masochism, and further attitudes toward others, depends on a general theory of consciousness and the body which we can neither expound nor assume here. He does not discuss perversion, and this is partly because he regards sexual desire as one form of the perpetual attempt of an embodied consciousness to come to terms with the existence of others, an attempt that is as doomed to fail in this form as it is in any of

[1] Translated by Hazel E. Barnes (New York: Philosophical Library: 1956).

the others, which include sadism and masochism (if not certain of the more impersonal deviations) as well as several nonsexual attitudes. According to Sartre, all attempts to incorporate that other into my world as another subject, i.e., to apprehend him at once as an object for me and as a subject for whom I am an object, are unstable and doomed to collapse into one or other of the two aspects. Either I reduce him entirely to an object, in which case his subjectivity escapes the possession or appropriation I can extend to that object; or I become merely an object for him, in which case I am no longer in a position to appropriate his subjectivity. Moreover, neither of these aspects is stable; each is continually in danger of giving way to the other. This has the consequence that there can be no such thing as a *successful* sexual relation, since the deep aim of sexual desire cannot in principle be accomplished. It seems likely, therefore, that the view will not permit a basic distinction between successful or complete and unsuccessful or incomplete sex, and therefore cannot admit the concept of perversion.

I do not adopt this aspect of the theory, nor many of its metaphysical underpinnings. What interests me is Sartre's picture of the attempt. He says that the type of possession that is the object of sexual desire is carried out by "a double reciprocal incarnation" and that this is accomplished, typically in the form of a caress, in the following way: "I make myself flesh in order to impel the Other to realize *for-herself* and *for me* her own flesh, and my caresses cause my flesh to be born for me in so far as it is for the Other *flesh causing her to be born as flesh*" (391; italics Sartre's). The incarnation in question is described variously as a clogging or troubling of consciousness, which is inundated by the flesh in which it is embodied.

The view I am going to suggest, I hope in less obscure language, is related to this one, but it differs from Sartre's in allowing sexuality to achieve its goal on occasion and thus in providing the concept of perversion with a foothold.

Sexual desire involves a kind of perception, but not merely a single perception of its object, for in the paradigm case of mutual desire there is a complex system of superimposed mutual perceptions—not only perceptions of the sexual object, but perceptions of oneself. Moreover, sexual awareness of another involves considerable self-awareness to begin with—more than is involved in ordinary sensory perception. The experience is felt as an assault on oneself by the view (or touch, or whatever) of the sexual object.

Let us consider a case in which the elements can be separated. For clarity we will restrict ourselves initially to the somewhat artificial case of desire at a distance. Suppose a man and a woman, whom we may call Romeo and Juliet, are at opposite ends of a cocktail lounge, with many mirrors on the walls which permit unobserved observation, and even mutual unobserved observation. Each of them is sipping a martini and studying other people in the mirrors. At some point Romeo notices Juliet. He is moved, somehow, by the softness of her hair and the diffidence with which she sips her martini, and this arouses him sexually. Let us say that X *senses* Y whenever X regards Y with sexual desire. (Y need not be a person, and X's apprehension of Y can be visual, tactile, olfactory, etc., or purely imaginary; in the present example we shall concentrate on vision.) So Romeo senses Juliet, rather than merely noticing her. At this stage he is aroused by an unaroused object, so he is more in the sexual grip of his body than she of hers.

Let us suppose, however, that Juliet now senses Romeo in another mirror on the opposite wall, though neither of them yet knows that he is seen by the other (the mirror angles provide three-quarter views). Romeo then begins to notice in Juliet the subtle signs of sexual arousal: heavy-lidded stare, dilating pupils, faint flush, et cetera. This of course renders her much more bodily, and he not only notices but senses this as well. His arousal is nevertheless still solitary. But now, cleverly calculating the line of her stare without actually looking her in the eyes, he realizes that it is directed at him through the mirror on the opposite wall. That is, he notices, and moreover senses, Juliet sensing him. This is definitely a new development, for it gives him a sense of embodiment not only through his own reactions but through the eyes and reactions of another. Moreover, it is separable from the initial sensing of Juliet; for sexual arousal might begin with a person's sensing that he is sensed and being assailed by the perception of the other person's desire rather than merely by the perception of the person.

But there is a further step. Let us suppose that Juliet, who is a little slower than Romeo, now senses that he senses her. This puts Romeo in a position to notice, and be aroused by, her arousal at being sensed by him. He senses that she senses that he senses her. This is still another level of arousal, for he becomes conscious of his sexuality through his awareness of its effect on her and of her awareness that this effect is due to him. Once she takes the same step and senses that he senses her sensing him, it becomes difficult to state, let alone imagine, further iterations, though they may be logically distinct. If both are alone, they will presumably turn to look at each other directly, and the proceedings will continue on another plane. Physical contact and intercourse are perfectly natural extensions of this complicated visual exchange, and mutual touch can involve all the complexities of awareness present in the visual case, but with a far greater range of subtlety and acuteness.

Ordinarily, of course, things happen in a less orderly fashion—sometimes in a great rush—but I believe that some version of this overlapping system of distinct sexual perceptions and interactions is the basic framework of any full-fledged sexual relation and that relations involving only part of the complex are significantly incomplete. The account is only schematic, as it must be to achieve generality. Every real sexual act will be psychologically far more specific and detailed, in ways that depend not only on the physical techniques employed and on anatomical details, but also on countless features of the participants' conceptions of themselves and of each other, which become embodied in the act. (It is a familiar enough fact, for example, that people often take their social roles and the social roles of their partners to bed with them.)

The general schema is important, however, and the proliferation of levels of mutual awareness it involves is an example of a type of complexity that typifies human interactions. Consider aggression, for example. If I am angry with someone, I want to make him feel it, either to produce self-reproach by getting him to see himself through the eyes of my anger, and to dislike what he sees—or else to produce reciprocal anger or fear, by getting him to perceive my anger as a threat of attack. What I want will depend on the details of my anger, but in either case it will involve a desire that the object of that anger be aroused. This accomplishment constitutes the fulfillment of my emotion, through domination of the object's feelings.

Another example of such reflexive mutual recognition is to be found in the phenomenon of meaning, which appears to involve an intention to produce a belief or other effect in another by bringing about his recognition of one's intention to produce that effect. (That result is due to H. P. Grice,[2] whose position I shall not attempt to reproduce in detail.) Sex has a related structure: it involves a desire that one's partner be aroused by the recognition of one's desire that he or she be aroused.

It is not easy to define the basic types of awareness and arousal of which these complexes are composed, and that remains a lacuna in this discussion. I believe that the object of awareness is the same in one's own case as it is in one's sexual awareness of another, although the two awarenesses will not be the same, the difference being as great as that between feeling angry and experiencing the anger of another. All stages of sexual perception are varieties of identification of a person with his body. What is perceived is one's own or another's *subjection* to or *immersion* in his body, a phenomenon which has been recognized with loathing by St. Paul and St. Augustine, both of whom regarded "the law of sin which is in my members" as a grave threat to the dominion of the holy will.[3] In sexual desire and its expression the blending of involuntary response with deliberate control is extremely important. For Augustine, the revolution launched against him by his body is symbolized by erection and the other involuntary physical components of arousal. Sartre too stresses the fact that the penis is not a prehensile organ. But mere involuntariness characterizes other bodily processes as well. In sexual desire the involuntary responses are combined with submission to spontaneous impulses: not only one's pulse and secretions but one's actions are taken over by the body; ideally, deliberate control is needed only to guide the expression of those impulses. This is to some extent also true of an appetite like hunger, but the takeover there is more localized, less perva-

---

[2] "Meaning," *Philosophical Review,* LXVI, 3 (July 1957): 377–388.
[3] See Romans, VII, 23; and the *Confessions, Book* 8, v.

sive, less extreme. One's whole body does not become saturated with hunger as it can with desire. But the most characteristic feature of a specifically sexual immersion in the body is its ability to fit into the complex of mutual perceptions that we have described. Hunger leads to spontaneous interactions with food; sexual desire leads to spontaneous interactions with other persons, whose bodies are asserting their sovereignty in the same way, producing involuntary reactions and spontaneous impulses in *them*. These reactions are perceived, and the perception of them is perceived, and that perception is in turn perceived; at each step the domination of the person by his body is reinforced, and the sexual partner becomes more possessible by physical contact, penetration, and envelopment.

Desire is therefore not merely the perception of a preexisting embodiment of the other, but ideally a contribution to his further embodiment which in turn enhances the original subject's sense of himself. This explains why it is important that the partner be aroused, and not merely aroused, but aroused by the awareness of one's desrie. It also explains the sense in which desire has unity and possession as its object: physical possession must eventuate in creation of the sexual object in the image of one's desire, and not merely in the object's recognition of that desire, or in his or her own private arousal. (This may reveal a male bias: I shall say something about that later.)

To return, finally, to the topic of perversion: I believe that various familiar deviations constitute truncated or incomplete versions of the complete configuration, and may therefore be regarded as perversions of the central impulse.

In particular, narcissistic practices and intercourse with animals, infants, and inanimate objects seem to be stuck at some primitive version of the first stage. If the object is not alive, the experience is reduced entirely to an awareness of one's own sexual embodiment. small children and animals permit awareness of the embodiment of the other, but present obstacles to reciprocity, to the recognition by the sexual object of the subject's desire as the source of his (the object's) sexual self-awareness.

Sadism concentrates on the evocation of passive self-awareness in others, but the sadist's engagement is itself active and requires a retention of deliberate control which impedes awareness of himself as a bodily subject of passion in the required sense. The victim must recognize him as the source of his own sexual passivity, but only as the active source. De Sade claimed that the object of sexual desire was to evoke involuntary responses from one's partner, especially audible ones. The infliction of pain is no doubt the most efficient way to accomplish this, but it requires a certain abrogation of one's own exposed spontaneity. All this, incidentally, helps to explain why it is tempting to regard as sadistic an excessive preoccupation with sexual technique, which does not permit one to abandon the role of agent at any stage of the sexual act. Ideally one should be able to surmount one's technique at some point.

A masochist on the other hand imposes the same disability on his partner as the sadist imposes on himself. The masochist cannot find a satisfactory embodiment as the object of another's sexual desire, but only as the object of his control. He is passive not in relation to his partner's passion but in relation to his nonpassive agency. In addition, the subjection to one's body characteristic of pain and physical restraint is of a very different kind from that of sexual excitement: pain causes people to contract rather than dissolve.

Both of these disorders have to do with the second stage, which involves the awareness of oneself as an object of desire. In straightforward sadism and masochism other attentions are substituted for desire as a source of the object's self-awareness. But it is also possible for nothing of that sort to be substituted, as in the case of a masochist who is satisfied with self-inflicted pain or of a sadist who does not insist on playing a role in the suffering that arouses him. Greater difficulties of classification are presented by three other categories of sexual activity: elaborations of the sexual act; intercourse of more than two persons; and homosexuality.

If we apply our model to the various forms that may be taken by two-party heterosexual intercourse, none of them seem clearly to qualify as perversions. Hardly anyone can be found these days to inveigh against oral-genital contact, and the merits of buggery are urged by such respectable figures as D. H. Lawrence and Norman Mailer. There may be something vaguely sadistic about the latter technique (in Mailer's writings it seems to be a method of introducing an element of rape), but is not obvious that this has to be so. In general, it would appear that any bodily contact between a man and a woman that gives them sexual pleasure, is a possible vehicle for the system of multi-level interpersonal awareness that I have claimed is the basic psychological content of sexual interaction. Thus a liberal platitude about sex is upheld.

About multiple combinations, the least that can be said is that they are bound to be complicated. If one considers how difficult it is to carry on two conversations simultaneously, one may appreciate the problems of multiple simultaneous interpersonal perception that can arise in even a small-scale orgy. It may be inevitable that some of the component relations should degenerate into mutual epidermal stimulation by participants otherwise isolated from each other. There may also be a tendency toward voyeurism and exhibitionism, both of which are incomplete relations. The exhibitionist wishes to display his desire without needing to be desired in return; he may even fear the sexual attentions of others. A voyeur, on the other hand, need not require any recognition by his object at all: certainly not a recognition of the voyeur's arousal.

It is not clear whether homosexuality is a perversion if that is measured by the standard of the described configuration, but it seems unlikely. For such a classification would have to depend on the possibility of extracting from the system a distinction between male and female sexuality; and much that has been said so far applies equally to men and women. Moreover, it would have to be maintained that there was a natural tie between the type of sexuality and the sex of the body, and also that two sexualities of the same type could not interact properly.

Certainly there is much support for an aggressive-passive distinction between male and female sexuality. In our culture the male's arousal tends to initiate the perceptual exchange, he usually makes the sexual approach, largely controls the course of the act, and of course penetrates whereas the woman receives. When two men or two women engage in intercourse they cannot both adhere to these sexual roles. The question is how essential the roles are to an adequate sexual relation. One relevant observation is that a good deal of deviation from these roles occurs in heterosexual intercourse. Women can be sexually aggressive and men passive, and temporary reversals of role are not uncommon in heterosexual exchanges of reasonable length. If such conditions are set aside, it may be urged that there is something irreducibly perverted in attraction to a body anatomically like one's own. But alarming as some people in our culture may find such attraction, it remains psychologically unilluminating to class it as perverted. Certainly if homosexuality is a perversion, it is so in a very different sense from that in which shoe-fetishism is a perversion, for some version of the full range of interpersonal perceptions seems perfectly possible between two persons of the same sex.

In any case, even if the proposed model is correct, it remains implausible to describe as perverted every deviation from it. For example, if the partners in heterosexual intercourse indulge in private heterosexual fantasies, that obscures the recognition of the real partner and so, on the theory, constitutes a defective sexual relation. It is not, however, generally regarded as a perversion. Such examples suggest that a simple dichotomy between perverted and unperverted sex is too crude to organize the phenomena adequately.

I should like to close with some remarks about the relation of perversion to good, bad, and morality. The concept of perversion can hardly fail to be evaluative in some sense, for it appears to involve the notion of an ideal or at least adequate sexuality which the perversions in some way fail to achieve. So, if the concept is viable, the judgment that a person or practice or desire is perverted will constitute a sexual evaluation, implying that better sex, or a better specimen of sex, is possible. This in itself is a very weak claim, since the evaluation might be in a dimension that is of little interest to us. (Though, if my account is correct, that will not be true.)

Whether it is a moral evaluation, however, is another question entirely— one whose answer would require more understanding of both morality and perversion than can be deployed here. Moral evaluation of acts and of persons is a rather special and very complicated matter, and by no means all our evaluations of persons and their activities are moral evaluations. We make judgments about people's beauty or health or intelligence which are evaluative without being moral. Assessments of their sexuality may be similar in that respect.

Furthermore, moral issues aside, it is not clear that unperverted sex is necessarily *preferable* to the perversions. It may be that sex which receives the highest marks for perfection *as sex* is less enjoyable than certain perversions; and if enjoyment is considered very important, that might outweigh considerations of sexual perfection in determining rational preference.

That raises the question of the relation between the evaluative content of judgments of perversions and the rather common *general* distinction between good and bad sex. The latter distinction is usually confined to sexual acts, and it would seem, within limits, to cut across the other: even someone who believed, for example, that homosexuality was a perversion could admit a distinction between better and worse homosexual sex, and might even allow that good homosexual sex could be better *sex* than not very good unperverted sex. If this is correct, it supports the position that, if judgments of perversion are viable at all, they represent only one aspect of the possible evaluation of sex, even *qua sex*. Moreover it is not the only important aspect: certainly sexual deficiencies that evidently do not constitute perversions can be the object of great concern.

Finally, even if perverted sex is to that extent not so good as it might be, bad sex is generally better than none at all. This should not be controversial: it seems to hold for other important matters, like food, music, literature, and society. In the end, one must choose from among the available alternatives, whether their availability depends on the environment or on one's own constitution. And the alternatives have to be fairly grim before it becomes rational to opt for nothing.

15
Suicide and Euthanasia

Is human life an absolute value? Is it ever right, even a duty, to take one's own life? Suicide ranks high as the cause of death among the young. Are most people merely driven to it, or is it ever a rational decision? Also, biomedical technology makes it possible to keep the terminally ill "alive" long after they have lapsed into coma. If a person could decide the issue before becoming terminally ill and say, "If I'm ever in that condition, pull the plug," could you do it? Since voluntary euthanasia is a kind of suicide, the issues of suicide and euthanasia are taken up together.

R. B. Brandt stands against those views that condemn suicide under all conditions, those of some deontologists such as Kant, for example. He argues that Kant slices matters thin when he approves of giving one's life in battle, facing certain death, and refuses to accept the morality of suicide as such. Why not give your life to save your loved ones the crushing expense and emotional ordeal of watching you go to slow, painful, and certain death? Also Brandt considers the question of the divine command, "Thou shalt not kill" as applicable to suicide. But he warns against complacent attitudes: A person who is depressed has primitivized reactions, or overreactions, and suffers other deficiencies in the ability to think the issues of "to be or not to be" through clearly and realistically. As for helping another person to commit suicide, Brandt thinks there are cases in which we are obliged to supply such assistance, but we should never suppose that a person who is found unconscious in suicidelike circumstances should be allowed to die without very clear evidence that they have so desired it after thinking it through.

Joseph Fletcher advocates voluntary euthanasia on the grounds that when there is no hope of recovery and slow death is dehumanizing, the request for help out of this life is one that we are at least sometimes obliged to honor. It is not that the pain in itself is to be shunned, but that it is demoralizing. Fletcher takes up ten objections

451

to euthanasia and notes the inconsistencies and twisting of facts and interpretations to maintain the taboo against it, no matter what.

One of the main issues in biomedical ethics is the distinction between killing and letting die. James Rachels challenges the doctrine that letting die is sometimes right, while killing is always wrong; the American Medical Association's adoption of this view is mistaken, be-because, he claims, it introduces irrelevant or morally unimportant grounds into the medical decision-making process.

Tom Beauchamp (pronounced "Beechum") replies to Rachels in defense of the A.M.A. position. The mere distinction between active and passive euthanasia (killing and letting die) is morally insignificant, he says, but more is involved than a technicality, and we ought to ponder the difference in making up our minds. On grounds that could be called utilitarian, he argues that society might be best served by rejecting active euthanasia but permitting the practice of passive euthanasia. The active/passive distinction cannot yet be thrown out, and society will have to live with the question of whether or when to abandon it for some time to come.

Arthur Dyck opposes two papers of Marvin Kohl (not reprinted) that he regards as impressive on the use of euthanasia in cases of painfully prolonged terminal cancer. He tries to rebut three objections Kohl made to opponents of active euthanasia. Dyck does not think the "edge-of-the-wedge" or "slippery-slope" reasoning of opponents of active euthanasia ("Where will you draw the line, once you start killing people?") is entirely mistaken, for, once legalized, active euthanasia would be administered by many persons, and would be carried out in the name of many differing, even though sincere, ideas of what is merciful and what is a death with dignity. Nor does he agree with Kohl that opposition to active euthanasia offers no positive viewpoint, only that of playing it safe and avoiding evil, for, he says, the ideal of saving life rather than taking it is positive. Dyck favors mercy, but not mercy killing, saying that the latter is what the word "euthanasia" (from the Greek) has come mostly to mean. He proposes that a word derived from Latin, "benemortasia," with the same root meaning is needed to convey what "euthanasia" used to mean: a good death. Mercy, yes; mercy killing, no—this seems to be his idea. Mercy includes relief of pain and the isolation from others that pain often brings, respect for a person's right to refuse extraordinary lifesaving measures, and helping the poor, whose deaths are often unnecessarily hastened by their inability to buy medical care. As to dignity, that is respected in allowing a patient to choose not to be treated beyond a certain level of care; it is respected in regarding all life as having worth, and saying that God alone knows when life is not worth preserving.

THE MORALITY AND RATIONALITY OF SUICIDE *

R. B. BRANDT

From the point of view of contemporary philosophy, suicide raises the following distinct questions: whether a person who commits suicide (assuming that there is suicide if and only if there is intentional termination of one's own life) is morally blameworthy, reprehensible, sinful in all circumstances; whether suicide is objectively right or wrong, and in what circumstances it is right or wrong, from a moral point of view; and whether, or in which circumstances, suicide is the best or the rational thing to do from the point of view of the agent's personal welfare.

The Moral Blameworthiness of Suicide

In former times the question of whether suicide is sinful was of great interest because the answer to it was considered relevant to how the agent would spend eternity. At present the practical issue is not as great, although a normal funeral service may be denied a person judged to have committed suicide sinfully. The chief practical issue now seems to be that persons may disapprove of a decedent for having committed suicide, and his friends or relatives may wish to defend his memory against moral charges.

The question of whether an act of suicide was sinful or morally blameworthy is not apt to arise unless it is already believed that the agent morally ought not to have done it: for instance, if he really had very poor reason for doing so, and his act foreseeably had catastrophic consequences for his wife and children. But, even if a given suicide is morally wrong, it does not follow that it is morally reprehensible. For, while asserting that a given act of suicide was wrong, we may still think that the act was hardly morally blameworthy or sinful if, say, the agent was in a state of great emotional turmoil at the time. We might then say that, although what he did was wrong, his action is *excusable*, just as in the criminal law it may be decided that, although a person broke the law, he should not be punished because he was *not responsible*, that is, was temporarily insane, did what he did inadvertently, and so on.

The foregoing remarks assume that to be morally blameworthy (or sinful) on account of an act is one thing, and for the act to be wrong is another. But, if we say this, what after all does it *mean* to say that a person is morally blameworthy on account of an action? We cannot say there is agreement among philosophers on this matter, but I suggest the following account as being safe from serious objection: "X is morally blameworthy on account of an action A" may be taken to mean "X did A, and X would not have done A had not his character been in some respect below standard; and in view of this it is fitting or justified for X to have some disapproving attitudes including remorse toward himself, and for some other persons Y to have some disapproving attitudes toward X and to express them in behavior." Traditional thought would include God as one of the "other persons" who might have and express disapproving attitudes.

In case the foregoing definition does not seem obviously correct, it is worthwhile pointing out that it is usually thought that an agent is not blameworthy or sinful for an action unless it is a *reflection on him;* the definition brings this fact out and makes clear why.

If someone charges that a suicide was sinful, we may now properly ask, "What defect of character did it show?" Some writers have claimed that suicide is blameworthy because it is *cowardly,* and since being cowardly is generally conceded to be a defect of character, if an act of suicide is admitted to be both objectively wrong and also cowardly, the claim to blameworthiness might be warranted in terms of the above definition. Of course, many people would hesitate to call taking one's own life a cowardly act, and there will certainly be controversy about which acts are cowardly and which are not. But at least we can see part of what has to be done to make a charge of blameworthiness valid.

The most interesting question is the general one: which types of suicide in general are ones that, even if objectively wrong (in a sense to be explained below), are not sinful or blameworthy? Or, in other words, when is a suicide *morally excused* even if it is objectively wrong? We can at least identify some types that are morally excusable.

1. Suppose I *think* I am morally bound to commit suicide because I have a terminal illness and continued medical care will ruin my family financially. Suppose, however, that I am mistaken in this belief, and that suicide in such circumstances is not right. But surely I am not morally blameworthy; for I may be doing, out of a sense of duty to my family, what I would personally prefer not to do and is hard for me to do. What defect of character might my action show? Suicide from a genuine sense of duty is not blameworthy, even when the moral conviction in question is mistaken.

2. Suppose that I commit suicide when I am temporarily of unsound mind, either in the sense of the M'Naghten rule that I do not know that what I am doing is wrong, or of the Durham rule that, owing to a mental defect, I am substantially unable to do what is right. Surely, any suicide in an unsound state of mind is morally excused.

3. Suppose I commit suicide when I could not be said to be temporarily of unsound mind, but simply because I am not myself. For instance, I may be in an extremely depressed mood. Now a person may be in a very depressed mood, and commit suicide on account of being in that mood, when there is nothing the matter with his character—or, in other words, his character is not in any relevant way below standard. What are other examples of being "not myself," of emotional states that might be responsible for a per-

son's committing suicide, and that might render the suicide excusable even if wrong? Being frightened; being distraught; being in almost any highly emotional frame of mind (anger, frustration, disappointment in love); perhaps just being terribly fatigued.

So there are at least three types of suicide which can be morally excused even if they are objectively wrong. The main point is this: Mr. X may commit suicide and it may be conceded that he ought not to have done so, but it is another step to show that he is sinful, or morally blameworthy, for having done so. To make out that further point, it must be shown that his act is attributable to some substandard trait of character. So, Mrs. X after the suicide can concede that her husband ought not to have done what he did, but she can also point out that it is no reflection on his character. The distinction, unfortunately, is often overlooked. St. Thomas Aquinas, who recognizes the distinction in other places, seems blind to it in his discussion of suicide.

The Moral Reasons for and Against Suicide

Persons who say suicide is morally wrong must be asked which of two positions they are affirming: Are they saying that *every* act of suicide is wrong, *everything considered;* or are they merely saying that there is always *some* moral obligation—doubtless of serious weight—not to commit suicide, so that very often suicide is wrong, although it is possible that there are *countervailing considerations* which in particular situations make it right or even a moral duty? It is quite evident that the first position is absurd; only the second has a chance of being defensible.

In order to make clear what is wrong with the first view, we may begin with an example. Suppose an army pilot's single-seater plane goes out of control over a heavily populated area; he has the choice of staying in the plane and bringing it down where it will do little damage but at the cost of certain death for himself, and of bailing out and letting the plane fall where it will, very possibly killing a good many civilians. Suppose he chooses to do the former, and so, by our definition, commits suicide. Does anyone want to say that his action is morally wrong? Even Immanuel Kant, who opposed suicide in all circumstances, apparently would not wish to say that it is; he would, in fact, judge that this act is not one of suicide, for he says, "It is no suicide to risk one's life against one's enemies, and even to sacrifice it, in order to preserve one's duties toward oneself." [1] St. Thomas Aquinas, in his discussion of suicide, may seem to take the position that such an act would be wrong, for he says, "It is altogether unlawful to kill oneself," admitting as an exception only the case of being under special command of God. But I believe St. Thomas would, in fact, have concluded that the act is right because the basic intention of the pilot was to save the lives of civilians, and whether an act is right or wrong is a matter of basic intention. [2]

In general, we have to admit that there are things with some moral obligation to avoid which, on account of other morally relevant considerations, it is sometimes right or even morally obligatory to do. There may be some obligation to tell the truth on every occasion, but surely in many cases the consequences of telling the truth would be so dire that one is obligated to lie. The same goes for promises. There is some moral obligation to do what one has promised (with a few exceptions); but, if one can keep a trivial promise only at serious cost to another person (i.e., keep an appointment only by failing to give aid to someone injured in an accident), it is surely obligatory to break the promise.

The most that the moral critic of suicide could hold, then, is that there is *some* moral obligation not to do what one knows will cause one's death; but he surely cannot deny that circumstances exist in which there are obligations to do things which, in fact, will result in one's death. If so, then in principle it would be possible to argue, for instance, that in order to meet my obligation to my family, it might be right for me to take my own life as the only way to avoid catastrophic hospital expenses in a terminal illness. Possibly the main point that critics of suicide on moral grounds would wish to make is that it is never right to take one's own life *for reasons of one's own personal welfare,* of any kind whatsoever. Some of the arguments used to support the immorality of suicide, however, are so framed that if they were supportable at all, they would prove that suicide is *never* moral.

One well-known type of argument against suicide may be classified as *theological.* St. Augustine and others urged that the Sixth Commandment ("Thou shalt not kill") prohibits suicide, and that we are bound to obey a divine commandment. To this reasoning one might first reply that it is arbitrary exegesis of the Sixth Commandment to assert that it was intended to prohibit suicide. The second reply is that if there is not some consideration which shows on the merits of the case that suicide is morally wrong, God had no business prohibiting it. It is true that some will object to this point, and I must refer them elsewhere for my detailed comments on the divine-will theory of morality.[3]

Another theological argument with wide support was accepted by John Locke, who wrote: ". . . Men being all the workmanship of one omnipotent and infinitely wise Maker; all the servants of one sovereign Master, sent into the world by His order and about His business; they are His property, whose workmanship they are made to last during His, not one another's pleasure. . . . Every one . . . is bound to preserve himself, and not to quit his station wilfully. . . ."[4] And Kant: "We have been placed in this world under certain conditions and for specific purposes. But a suicide opposes the purpose of his Creator; he arrives in the other world as one who has deserted his post; he must be looked upon as a rebel against God. So long as we remember the truth that it is God's intention to preserve life, we are bound to regulate our activities in conformity with it. This duty is upon us until the time comes when God expressly commands us to leave this life. Human beings are sentinels on earth and may not leave their posts until relieved by another beneficent hand." [5] Unfortunately, however, even if we grant that it is the duty of human beings to do what God commands or intends them to do, more argument is required to show that God does *not* permit human beings to quit this life when their own personal welfare would be maximized by so doing. How does one draw the requisite inference about the intentions of God? The difficulties and contradictions in arguments to reach such a conclusion are discussed at length and perspicaciously by David Hume in his essay "On Suicide," and in view of the unlikelihood that readers will need to be persuaded about these, I shall merely refer those interested to that essay. [6]

A second group of arguments may be classed as arguments *from natural law*. St. Thomas says: "It is altogether unlawful to kill oneself, for three reasons. First, because everything naturally loves itself, the result being that everything naturally keeps itself in being, and resists corruptions so far as it can. Wherefore suicide is contrary to the inclination of nature, and to charity whereby every man should love himself. Hence suicide is always a mortal sin, as being contrary to the natural law and to charity." [7] Here St. Thomas ignores two obvious points. First, it is not obvious why a human being is morally bound to do what he or she has some inclination to do. (St. Thomas did not criticize chastity.) Second, while it is true that most human beings do feel a strong urge to live, the human being who commits suicide obviously feels a stronger inclination to do something else. It is as natural for a human being to dislike, and to take steps to avoid, say, great pain, as it is to cling to life.

A somewhat similar argument by Immanuel Kant may seem better. In a famous passage Kant writes that the maxim of a person who commits suicide is "From self-love I make it my principle to shorten my life if its continuance threatens more evil than it promises pleasure. The only further question to ask is whether this principle of self-love can become a universal law of nature. It is then seen at once that a system of nature by whose law the very same feeling whose function is to stimulate the furtherance of life should actually destroy life would contradict itself and consequently could not subsist as a system of nature. Hence this maxim cannot possibly hold as a universal law of nature and is therefore entirely opposed to the supreme principle of all duty." [8] What Kant finds contradictory is that the motive of self-love (interest in one's own long-range welfare) should sometimes lead one to struggle to preserve one's life, but at other times to end it. But where is the contradiction? One's circumstances change, and, if the argument of the following section in this chapter is correct, one sometimes maximizes one's own long-range welfare by trying to stay alive, but at other times by bringing about one's demise.

A third group of arguments, a form of which goes back at least to Aristotle, has a more modern and convincing ring. These are arguments to show that, in one way or another, a suicide necessarily does harm to other persons, or to society at large. Aristotle says that the suicide treats the *state* unjustly.[9] Partly following Aristotle, St. Thomas says: "Every man is part of the community, and so, as such, he belongs to the community. Hence by killing himself he injures the community." [10] Blackstone held that a suicide is an offense against the king "who hath an interest in the preservation of all his subjects," perhaps following Judge Brown in 1563, who argued that suicide cost the king a subject—"he being the head has lost one of his mystical members." [11] The premise of such arguments is, as Hume pointed out, obviously mistaken in many instances. It is true that Freud would perhaps have injured society had he, instead of finishing his last book, committed suicide to escape the pain of throat cancer. But surely there have been many suicides whose demise was not a noticeable loss to society; an honest man could only say that in some instances society was better off without them.

It need not be denied that suicide is often injurious to other persons, especially the family of a suicide. Clearly it sometimes is. But, we should notice what this fact establishes. Suppose we admit, as generally would be done, that there is some obligation not to perform any action which will probably or certainly be injurious to other people, the strength of the obligation being dependent on various factors, notably the seriousness of the expected injury. Then there is *some* obligation not to commit suicide, when that act would probably or certainly be injurious to other people. But, as we have already seen, many cases of *some* obligation to do something nevertheless are *not* cases of a duty to do that thing, *everything considered*. So it could sometimes be morally justified to commit suicide, even if the act will harm someone. Must a man with a terminal illness undergo excruciating pain because his death will cause his wife sorrow—when she will be caused sorrow a month later anyway, when he is dead of natural causes? Moreover, to repeat, the fact that an individual has some obligation not to commit suicide when that act will probably injure other persons does not imply that, everything considered, it is wrong for him to do it, namely, that in all circumstances suicide *as such* is something there is some obligation to avoid.

Is there any sound argument, convincing to the modern mind, to establish that there is (or is not) *some moral obligation* to avoid suicide *as* such, an obligation, of course, which might be overridden by other obligations in some or many cases? (Captain Oates may have had a moral obligation not to commit suicide as such, but his obligation not to stand in the way of his comrades getting to safety might have been so strong that, everything considered, he was justified in leaving the polar camp and allowing himself to freeze to death.)

To present all the arguments necessary to answer this question convincingly would take a great deal of space. I shall, therefore, simply state one answer to it which seems plausible to some contemporary philosophers. Suppose it could be shown that it would maximize the long-run welfare of everybody affected if people were taught that there is a moral obligation to avoid suicide—so that people would be motivated to avoid suicide just because they thought it wrong (would have anticipatory guilt feelings at the very idea), and so that other people would be inclined to disapprove of persons who commit suicide unless there were some excuse (such as those mentioned in the first section). One might ask: how could it maximize utility to mold the conceptual and motivational structure of persons in this way? To which the answer might be: feeling in this way might make persons who are impulsively inclined to commit suicide in a bad mood, or a fit of anger or jealousy, take more time to deliberate; hence, some suicides that have bad effects generally might be prevented. In other words, it might be a good thing in its effects for people to feel about suicide in the way they feel about breach of promise or injuring others, just as it might be a good thing for people to feel a moral obligation not to smoke, or to wear seat belts. However, it might be that negative moral feelings about suicide as such would stand in the way of action by those persons whose welfare really is best served by suicide and whose suicide is the best thing for everybody concerned.

When a Decision to Commit Suicide Is Rational from the Person's Point of View

The person who is contemplating suicide is obviously making a choice between future world-courses; the world-course that includes his demise, say, an hour from now, and several possible ones that contain his demise at a later point. One cannot have precise knowledge about many features of the latter group of world-courses, but it is certain that they will all end with death some (possibly short) finite time from now.

Why do I say the choice is between *world*-courses and not just a choice between future life-courses of the prospective suicide, the one shorter than the other? The reason is that one's suicide has some impact on the world (and one's continued life has some impact on the world), and that conditions in the rest of the world will often make a difference in one's evaluation of the possibilities. One *is* interested in things in the world other than just oneself and one's own happiness.

The basic question a person must answer, in order to determine which world-course is best or rational for him to choose, is which he *would* choose under conditions of optimal use of information, when *all* of his desires are taken into account. It is not just a question of what we prefer *now*, with some clarification of all the possibilities being considered. Our preferences change, and the preferences of tomorrow (assuming we can know something about them) are just as legitimately taken into account in deciding what to do now as the preferences of today. Since any reason that can be given today for weighting heavily today's preference can be given tomorrow for weighting heavily tomorrow's preference, the preferences of any time-stretch have a rational claim to an equal vote. Now the importance of that fact is this: we often know quite well that our desires, aversions, and preferences may change after a short while. When a person is in a state of despair—perhaps brought about by a rejection in love or discharge from a long-held position—nothing but the thing he cannot have seems desirable; everything else is turned to ashes. Yet we know quite well that the passage of time is likely to reverse all this; replacements may be found or other types of things that are available to us may begin to look attractive. So, if we were to act on the preferences of today alone, when the emotion of despair seems more than we can stand, we might find death preferable to life; but, if we allow for the preferences of the weeks and years ahead, when many goals will be enjoyable and attractive, we might find life much preferable to death. So, if a choice of what is best is to be determined by what we want not only now but later (and later desires on an equal basis with the present ones)—as it should be—then what is the best or preferable world-course will often be quite different from what it would be if the choice, or what is best for one, were fixed by one's desires and preferences now.

Of course, if one commits suicide there are no future desires or aversions that may be compared with present ones and that should be allowed an equal vote in deciding what is best. In that respect the course of action that results in death is different from any other course of action we may undertake. I do not wish to suggest the rosy possibility that it is often or always reasonable to believe that next week "I shall be more interested in living than I am today, if today I take a dim view of continued existence." On the contrary, when a person is seriously ill, for instance, he may have no reason to think that the preference-order will be reversed—it may be that tomorrow he will prefer death to life more strongly.

The argument is often used that one can never be *certain* what is going to happen, and hence one is never rationally justified in doing anything as drastic as committing suicide. But we always have to live by probabilities and make our estimates as best we can. As soon as it is clear beyond reasonable doubt not only that death is now preferable to life, but also that it will be every day from now until the end, the rational thing is to act promptly.

Let us not pursue the question of whether it is rational for a person with a painful terminal illness to commit suicide; it is. However, the issue seldom arises, and few terminally ill patients do commit suicide. With such patients matters usually get worse slowly so that no particular time seems to call for action. They are often so heavily sedated that it is impossible for the mental processes of decision leading to action to occur; or else they are incapacitated in a hospital and the very physical possibility of ending their lives is not available. Let us leave this grim topic and turn to a practically more important problem: whether it is rational for persons to commit suicide for some reason other than painful terminal physical illness. Most persons who commit suicide do so, apparently, because they face a non-physical problem that depresses them beyond their ability to bear.

Among the problems that have been regarded as good and sufficient reasons for ending life, we find (in addition to serious illness) the following: some event that has made a person feel ashamed or lose his prestige and status; reduction from affluence to poverty; the loss of a limb or of physical beauty; the loss of sexual capacity; some event that makes it seem impossible to achieve things by which one sets store; loss of a loved one; disappointment in love; the infirmities of increasing age. It is not to be denied that such things can be serious blows to a person's prospects of happiness.

Whatever the nature of an individual's problem, there are various plain errors to be avoided—errors to which a person is especially prone when he is depressed—in deciding whether, everything considered, he prefers a world-course containing his early demise to one in which his life continues to its natural terminus. Let us forget for a moment the relevance to the decision of preferences that he may have tomorrow, and concentrate on some errors that may infect his preference as of today, and for which correction or allowance must be made.

In the first place, depression, like any severe emotional experience, tends to primitivize one's intellectual processes. It restricts the range of one's survey of the possibilities. One thing that a rational person would do is compare the world-course containing his suicide with his *best* alternative. But his best alternative is precisely a possibility he may overlook if, in a depressed mood, he thinks only of how badly off he is and cannot imagine any way of improving his situation. If a person is disappointed in love, it is possible to adopt a vigorous plan of action that carries a good chance of acquainting him with someone he likes at least as well; and if old age prevents a person from continuing the tennis game with his favorite partner, it is possible to learn some other game that provides the joys of competition without the physical demands.

Depression has another insidious influence on one's planning; it seriously affects one's judgment about probabilities. A person disappointed in love is very likely to take a dim view of himself, his prospects, and his attractiveness; he thinks that because he has been rejected by one person he will probably be rejected by anyone who looks desirable to him. In a less gloomy frame of mind he would make different estimates. Part of the reason for such gloomy probability estimates is that depression tends to repress one's memory of evidence that supports a nongloomy prediction. Thus, a rejected lover tends to forget any cases in which he has elicited enthusiastic response from ladies in relation to whom he has been the one who has done the rejecting. Thus his pessimistic self-image is based upon a highly selected, and pessimistically selected, set of data. Even when he is reminded of the data, moreover, he is apt to resist an optimistic inference.

Another kind of distortion of the look of future prospects is not a result of depression, but is quite normal. Events distant in the future feel small, just as objects distant in space look small. Their prospect does not have the effect on motivational processes that it would have if it were of an event in the immediate future. Psychologists call this the "goal-gradient" phenomenon; a rat, for instance, will run faster toward a perceived food box than a distant unseen one. In the case of a person who has suffered some misfortune, and whose situation now is an unpleasant one, this reduction of the motivational influence of events distant in time has the effect that present unpleasant states weigh far more heavily than probable future pleasant ones in any choice of world-courses.

If we are trying to determine whether we now prefer, or shall later prefer, the outcome of one world-course to that of another (and this is leaving aside the questions of the weight of the votes of preferences at a later date), we must take into account these and other infirmities of our "sensing" machinery. Since knowing that the machinery is out of order will not tell us what results it would give if it were working, the best recourse might be to refrain from making any decision in a stressful frame of mind. If decisions have to be made, one must recall past reactions, in a normal frame of mind, to outcomes like those under assessment. But many suicides seem to occur in moments of despair. What should be clear from the above is that a moment of despair, if one is seriously contemplating suicide, ought to be a moment of reassessment of one's goals and values, a reassessment which the individual must realize is very difficult to make objectively, because of the very quality of his depressed frame of mind.

A decision to commit suicide may in certain circumstances be a rational one. But a person who wants to act rationally must take into account the various possible "errors" and make appropriate rectification of his initial evaluations.

The Role of Other Persons

What is the moral obligation of other persons toward those who are contemplating suicide? The question of their moral blameworthiness may be ignored and what is rational for them to do from the point of view of personal welfare may be considered as being of secondary concern. Laws make it dangerous to aid or encourage a suicide. The risk of running afoul of the law may partly determine moral obligation, since moral obligation to do something may be reduced by the fact that it is personally dangerous.

The moral obligation of other persons toward one who is contemplating suicide is an instance of a general obligation to render aid to those in serious distress, at least when this can be done at no great cost to one's self. I do not think this general principle is seriously questioned by anyone, whatever his moral theory; so I feel free to assume it as a premise. Obviously the person contemplating suicide is in great distress of some sort; if he were not, he would not be seriously considering terminating his life.

How great a person's obligation is to one in distress depends on a number of factors. Obviously family and friends have special obligations to devote time to helping the prospective suicide—which others do not have.

But anyone in this kind of distress has a moral claim on the time of any person who knows the situation (unless there are others more responsible who are already doing what should be done).

What is the obligation? It depends, of course, on the situation, and how much the second person knows about the situation. If the individual has decided to terminate his life if he can, and it is clear that he is right in this decision, then, if he needs help in executing the decision, there is a moral obligation to give him help. On this matter a patient's physician has a special obligation, from which any talk about the Hippocratic oath does not absolve him. It is true that there are some damages one cannot be expected to absorb, and some risks which one cannot be expected to take, on account of the obligation to render aid.

On the other hand, if it is clear that the individual should not commit suicide, from the point of view of his own welfare, or if there is a presumption that he should not (when the only evidence is that a person is discovered unconscious, with the gas turned on), it would seem to be the individual's obligation to intervene, prevent the successful execution of the decision, and see to the availability of competent psychiatric advice and temporary hospitalization, if necessary. Whether one has a right to take such steps when a clearly sane person, after careful reflection over a period of time, comes to the conclusion that an end to his life is what is best for him and what he wants, is very doubtful, even when one thinks his conclusion a mistaken one; it would seem that a man's own considered decision about whether he wants to live must command respect, although one must concede that this could be debated.

The more interesting role in which a person may be cast, however, is that of adviser. It is often important to one who is contemplating suicide to go over his thinking with another, and to feel that a conclusion, one way or the other, has the support of a respected mind. One thing one can obviously do, in rendering the service of advice, is to discuss with the person the various types of issues discussed above, made more specific by the concrete circumstances of his case, and help him find whether, in view, say, of the damage his suicide would do to others, he has a moral obligation to refrain, and whether it is rational or best for him, from the point of view of his own welfare, to take this step or adopt some other plan instead.

To get a person to see what is the rational thing to do is no small job. Even to get a person, in a frame of mind when he is seriously contemplating (or perhaps has already unsuccessfully attempted) suicide, to recognize a plain truth of fact may be a major operation. If a man insists, "I am a complete failure," when it is obvious that by any reasonable standard he is far from that, it may be tremendously difficult to get him to see the fact. But there is another job beyond that of getting a person to see what is the rational thing to do; that is to help him *act* rationally, or *be* rational, when he has conceded what would be the rational thing.

How either of these tasks may be accomplished effectively may be discussed more competently by an experienced psychiatrist than by a philosopher. Loneliness and the absence of human affection are states which exacerbate any other problems; disappointment, reduction to poverty, and so forth, seem less impossible to bear in the presence of the affection of another. Hence simply to be a friend, or to find someone a friend, may be the largest contribution one can make either to helping a person be rational or see clearly what is rational for him to do; this service may make one who was contemplating suicide feel that there is a future for him which it is possible to face.

NOTES AND REFERENCES

1. Immanuel Kant, *Lectures on Ethics*, New York: Harper Torchbook (1963), p. 150.

2. See St. Thomas Aquinas, *Summa Theologica*, Second Part of the Second Part, Q. 64, Art. 5. In Article 7, he says: "Nothing hinders one act from having two effects, only one of which is intended, while the other is beside the intention. Now moral acts take their species according to what is intended, and not according to what is beside the intention, since this is accidental as explained above" (Q. 43, Art. 3: I-II, Q. 1, Art. 3, as 3). Mr. Norman St. John-Stevas, the most articulate contemporary defender of the Catholic view, writes as follows: "Christian thought allows certain exceptions to its general condemnation of suicide. That covered by a particular divine inspiration has already been noted. Another exception arises where suicide is the method imposed by the State for the execution of a just death penalty. A third exception is *altruistic* suicide, of which the best known example is Captain Oates. Such suicides are justified by invoking the principles of double effect. The act from which death results must be good or at least morally indifferent; some other good effect must result: The death must not be directly intended or the real means to the good effect: and a grave reason must exist for adopting the course of action" [*Life, Death and the Law*, Bloomington, Ind.: Indiana University Press (1961), pp. 250–51]. Presumably the Catholic doctrine is intended to allow suicide when this is required for meeting strong moral obligations; whether it can do so consistently depends partly on the interpretation given to "real means to the good effect." Readers interested in pursuing further the Catholic doctrine of double effect and its implications for our problem should read Philippa Foot, "The Problem of Abortion and the Doctrine of Double Effect," *The Oxford Review*, 5:5–15 (Trinity 1967).

3. R. B. Brandt, *Ethical Theory*, Englewood Cliffs, N.J.: Prentice-Hall (1959), pp. 61–82.

4. John Locke, *Two Treatises of Government*, Ch. 2.

5. Kant, *Lectures on Ethics*, p. 154.

6. This essays appears in collections of Hume's works.

7. For an argument similar to Kant's, see also St. Thomas Aquinas, *Summa Theologica*, II, II, Q. 64, Art. 5.

8. Immanuel Kant, *The Fundamental Principles of the Metaphysic of Morals*, trans H. J. Paton, London: The Hutchinson Group (1948), Ch. 2.

EUTHANASIA: OUR RIGHT TO DIE °

JOSEPH FLETCHER

Euthanasia, the deliberate easing into death of a patient suffering from a painful and fatal disease, has long been a troubling problem of conscience in medical care. For us in the Western world the problem arises, *pro forma*, out of a logical contradiction at the heart of the Hippocratic Oath. Our physicians all subscribe to that oath as the standard of their professional ethics. The contradiction is there because the oath promises two things: first, to relieve suffering, and second, to prolong and protect life. When the patient is in the grip of an agonizing and fatal disease, these two promises are incompatible. Two duties come into conflict. To prolong life is to violate the promise to relieve pain. To relieve the pain is to violate the promise to prolong and protect life.

Ordinarily an attempt is made to escape the dilemma by relieving the pain with an analgesic that does not induce death. But this attempt to evade the issue fails in many cases for the simple reason that the law of diminishing returns operates in narcosis. Patients grow semi-immune to its effects, for example in some forms of osteomyelitis, and a dose which first produces four hours of relief soon gives only three, then two, then almost none. The dilemma still stands: the choice between euthanasia or suffering. Euthanasia may be described, in its broadest terms, as a "theory that in certain circumstances, when owing to disease, senility or the like, a person's life has permanently ceased to be either agreeable or useful, the sufferer should be painlessly killed, either by himself or by another." [1] More simply, we may call euthanasia merciful release from incurable suffering.

Our task in this book is to put the practice under examination in its strictly medical form, carefully limiting ourselves to cases in which the patient himself chooses euthanasia and the physician advises against any reasonable hope of recovery or of relief by other means. Yet even in so narrowly defined an application as this, there are conscientious objections, of the sort applied to broader concepts or usages. In the first place it is claimed that the practice of euthanasia might be taken as an encouragement of suicide or of the wholesale murder of the aged and infirm. Again, weak or unbalanced people may more easily throw away their lives if medical euthanasia has approval. Still another objection raised is that the practice would raise grave problems for the public authority. Government would have to overcome the resistance of time-honored religious beliefs, the universal feeling that human life is too sacred to be tampered with, and the

---

° From Joseph Fletcher, *Morals and Medicine* with a foreword by Karl Menninger, © 1954 by Princeton University Press (Princeton), pp. 172–176, and 189–210. Reprinted by permission of Princeton University.

[1] H. J. Rose, "Euthanasia," *Encyc. of Rel. and Ethics*, v, 598–601.

problem of giving euthanasia legal endorsement as another form of justifiable homicide. All of this could lead to an appalling increase of crimes such as infanticide and geronticide. In short, in this problem as in others which we have been analyzing there is a common tendency to cry abuse and to ignore *abusus non tollit usum*. [Abuse doesn't refute proper use.]

Prudential and expedient objections to euthanasia quickly jump to mind among many people confronted with the issue. There are few, presumably, who would not be moved by such protests as this one from the *Linacre Quarterly*: "Legalized euthanasia would be a confession of despair in the medical profession; it would be the denial of hope for further progress against presently incurable maladies. It would destroy all confidence in physicians, and introduce a reign of terror. . . . [Patients] would turn in dread from the man on whose wall the Hippocratic Oath proclaims, 'If any shall ask of me a drug to produce death I will not give it, nor will I suggest such counsel.' " [2]

However, it is the objection that euthanasia is inherently wrong, that the disposition of life is too sacred to be entrusted to human control, which calls for our closest analysis. As in preceding chapters, here too we shall be dealing with the *personal* dimensions of morality in medical care. The social ethics of medical care, as it is posed to conscience by proposals to use euthanasia for eugenic reasons, population control, and the like, have to be left for another time and place.

Not infrequently the newspapers carry stories of the crime of a spouse, or a member of the family or a friend, of a hopelessly stricken and relentlessly tortured victim of, let us say, advanced cancer. Desperate people will sometimes take the law into their own hands and administer some lethal dose to end it all. Sometimes the euthanasiast then commits suicide, thus making two deaths instead of one. Sometimes he is tried for murder in a court of law, amid great scandal and notoriety. But even if he is caught and indicted, the judgment never ends in conviction, perhaps because the legalism of the charge can never stand up in the tested conscience of a sympathetic jury.

For the sake of avoiding offense to any contemporaries, we might turn to literary history for a typical example of our problem. Jonathan Swift, the satirist and Irish clergyman, after a life of highly creative letters ended it all in a horrible and degrading death. It was a death degrading to himself and to those close to him. His mind crumbled to pieces. It took him eight years to die while his brain rotted. He read the third chapter of Job on his birthday as long as he could see. "And Job spake, and said, Let the day perish when I was born, and the night in which it was said, There is a man child conceived." The pain in Swift's eye was so acute that it took five men to hold him down, to keep him from tearing out his eye with his own hands. For the last three years he sat and drooled. Knives had

[2] Hilary R. Wertz, S.J., in April 1947, 19.2, p. 33.

to be kept entirely out of his reach. When the end came, finally, his fits of convulsion lasted thirty-six hours.[3] Now, whatever may be the theological meaning of St. Paul's question, "O death, where is thy sting?"[4] the moral meaning—in a word, the evil—of a death like that is only too plain.

We can imagine the almost daily scene preceding Swift's death. (Some will say we should not imagine such things, that it is not fair to appeal to emotion. Many good people cannot willingly accept the horrendous aspects of reality as a factor of reasoning, especially when reality cuts across their customs and commitments. The relative success with which we have repressed the reality of atomic warfare and its dreadful prospects is an example on a wider scale.) We can easily conceive of Dean Swift grabbing wildly, madly, for a knife or a deadly drug. He was *demoralized*, without a vestige of true self-possession left in him. He wanted to commit what the law calls suicide and what vitalistic ethics calls sin. Standing by was some good doctor of physick, trembling with sympathy and frustration. Secretly, perhaps, he wanted to commit what the law calls murder. Both had full knowledge of the way out, which is half the foundation of moral integrity, but unlike his patient the physician felt he had no freedom to act, which is the other half of moral integrity. And so, meanwhile, necessity, blind and unmoral, irrational physiology and pathology, made the decision. It was in reality no decision at all, no moral behavior in the least, unless submission to physical ruin and spiritual disorganization can be called a decision and a moral choice. For let us not forget that in such tragic affairs there is a moral destruction, a spiritual disorder, as well as a physical degeneration. As Swift himself wrote to his niece fully five years before the end: "I am so stupid and confounded that I cannot express the mortification I am under both of body and soul."[5]

The story of this man's death points us directly to the broad problem of suicide, as well as to the more particular problem of euthanasia. We get a glimpse of this paradox in our present customary morality, that it sometimes condemns us to live or, to put it another way, destroys our moral being for the sake of just *being*. This aspect of suicide makes it important for us to distinguish from the outset between voluntary and involuntary euthanasia. They are by no means the same, either in policy or ethical meaning. Those who condemn euthanasia of both kinds would call the involuntary form murder and the voluntary form a compounded crime of murder and suicide if administered by the physician, and suicide alone if administered by the patient himself. As far as voluntary euthanasia goes, it is impossible to separate it from suicide as a moral category; it is, indeed, a form of suicide. In a very proper sense, the case for medical euthanasia depends upon the case for the righteousness of suicide, given the necessary

---

[3] Virginia Moore, *Ho for Heaven,* New York, 1946, pp. 180–182.
[4] I Cor. 15:55.
[5] Quoted by Richard Garnett, "Jonathan Swift" in *Encyc. Brit.,* 11th ed.

circumstances. And the justification of its administration by an attending physician is therefore dependent upon it too, under the time-honored rule that what one may lawfully do another may help him to do. . . .

Pro and Con

It is at this point that we can turn to the definitely moral arguments for and against euthanasia. Our aim here is to be as orderly as possible in the discussion, and to forsake any *argumentum ad miserciordiam*. We must try to avoid the penny-dreadful type of treatment Richard Cabot had in mind when he spoke of euthanasia as "that ancient and reliable novelty . . . which the newspapers trick out afresh each year in August when politics are dull and there is a dearth of copy." [6] In a limited space, perhaps the best procedure will be to speak directly to the ten most common and most important objections. Therefore, suppose we deal with them as if they stood one by one in a bill of particulars.

1. It is objected that euthanasia, when voluntary, is really suicide. If this is true, and it would seem to be obviously true, then the proper question is: have we ever a right to commit suicide? Among Catholic moralists the most common ruling is that "it is never permitted to kill oneself intentionally, without explicit divine inspiration to do." [7] Humility requires us to assume that divine inspiration cannot reasonably be expected to occur either often or explicitly enough to meet the requirements of medical euthanasia. A plea for legal recognition of "man's inalienable right to die" is placed at the head of the physicians' petition to the New York State Assembly. Now, has man any such right, however limited and imperfect it may be? Surely he has, for otherwise the hero or martyr and all those who deliberately give their lives are morally at fault. It might be replied that there is a difference between the suicide, who is directly seeking to end his life, and the hero or martyr, who is seeking directly some other end entirely, death being only an undesired by-product. But to make this point is only to raise a question as to what purposes are sufficient to justify the loss of one's life. If altruistic values, such as defense of the innocent, are enough to justify the loss of one's life (and we will all agree that they are), then it may be argued that personal integrity is a value worth the loss of life, especially since, by definition, there is no hope of relief from the demoralizing pain and no further possibility of serving others. To call euthanasia egoistic or self-regarding makes no sense, since in the nature of the case the patient is not choosing his own good rather than the good of others.

Furthermore, it is important to recognize that there is no ground, in a

[6] *Adventures on the Borderlands of Ethics, op. cit.*, p. 34.

[7] Henry Davis, S.J., *Moral and, Pastoral Theology*, New York, 1943, II, 142. This author explains that Jerome and Lessius excused suicide in defense of chastity, but that Aquinas opposed even this exception to the prohibition.

rational or Christian outlook, for regarding life itself as the *summum bonum*. As a ministers' petition to buttress the New York bill puts it, "We believe in the sacredness of *personality*, but not in the worth of mere existence or 'length of days.' . . . We believe that such a sufferer has the right to die, and that society should grant this right, showing the same mercy to human beings as to the sub-human animal kingdom." (The point might be made validly in criticism of this statement that society can only recognize an "inalienable right," it cannot confer it. Persons are not mere creatures of the community, even though it is ultimately meaningless to claim integrity for them unless their lives are integrated into the community.) In the personalistic view of man and morals, asserted throughout these pages, personality is supreme over mere life. To prolong life uselessly, while the personal qualities of freedom, knowledge, self-possession and control, and responsibility are sacrificed is to attack the moral status of a person. It actually denies morality in order to submit to fatality. And in addition, to insist upon mere "life" invades religious interests as well as moral values. For to use analgesic agents to the point of depriving sufferers of consciousness is, by all apparent logic, inconsistent even with the practices of sacramentalist Christians. The point of death for a human person *in extremis* is surely by their own account a time when the use of reason and conscious self-commitment is most meritorious; it is the time when a responsible competence in receiving such rites as the viaticum and extreme unction would be most necessary and its consequences most invested with finality.

2. It is objected that euthanasia, when involuntary, is murder. This is really an objection directed against the physician's role in medical euthanasia, assuming it is administered by him rather than by the patient on his own behalf. We might add to what has been said above about the word "murder" in law and legal definition by explaining that people with a moral rather than a legal interest—doctors, pastors, patients, and their friends— will never concede that malice means only premeditation, entirely divorced from the motive and the end sought. These factors are entirely different in euthanasia from the motive and the end in murder, even though the means—taking life—happens to be the same. If we can make no moral distinction between acts involving the same means, then the thrifty parent who saves in order to educate his children is no higher in the scale of merit than the miser who saves for the sake of hoarding. But, as far as medical care is concerned, there is an even more striking example of the contradictions which arise from refusing to allow for anything but the consequences of a human act. There is a dilemma in medication for terminal diseases which is just as real as the dilemma posed by the doctor's oath to relieve pain while he also promises to prolong life. As medical experts frequently point out, morphine, which is commonly used to ease pain, also shortens life, i.e., it induces death. Here we see that the two promises of the Hippocratic Oath actually conflict at the level of means as well as the level of motive and intention.

3. What of the common religious opinion that God reserves for himself the right to decide at what moment a life shall cease? Koch-Preuss says euthanasia is the destruction of "the temple of God and a violation of the property rights of Jesus Christ." [8] As to this doctrine, it seems more than enough just to answer that if such a divine-monopoly theory is valid, then it follows with equal force that it is immoral to lengthen life. Is medical care, after all, only a form of human self-assertion or a demonic pretension, by which men, especially physicians, try to put themselves in God's place? Prolonging life, on this divine-monopoly view, when a life appears to be ending through natural or physical causes, is just as much an interference with natural determinism as mercifully ending a life before physiology does it in its own amoral way.

This argument that we must not tamper with life also assumes that physiological life is sacrosanct. But as we have pointed out repeatedly, this doctrine is a form of vitalism or naturalistic determinism. Dean Sperry of the Harvard Divinity School, who is usually a little more sensitive to the scent of anti-humane attitudes, wrote recently in the *New England Journal of Medicine* that Albert Schweitzer's doctrine of "reverence for life," which is often thought to entail an absolute prohibition against taking life, has strong claims upon men of conscience.[9] Perhaps so, but men of conscience will surely reject the doctrine if it is left unqualified and absolute. In actual fact, even Schweitzer has suggested that the principle is subject to qualification. He has, with apparent approval, explained that Gandhi "took it upon himself to go beyond the letter of the law against killing. . . . He ended the sufferings of a calf in its prolonged death-agony by giving it poison." [10] It seems unimaginable that either Schweitzer or Gandhi would deny to a human being what they would render, with however heavy a heart, to a calf. Gandhi did what he did in spite of the special sanctity of kine in Hindu discipline. In any case Dr. Schweitzer in his African hospital at Lambaréné is even now at work administering death-inducing-because-pain-relieving drugs. As William Temple once pointed out, "The notion that life is absolutely sacred is Hindu or Buddhist, not Christian." He neglected to remark that even those Oriental religionists forget their doctrine when it comes to *suttee* and *hara-kiri*. He said further that the argument that it cannot ever be right to kill a fellow human being will not stand up because "such a plea can only rest upon a belief that life, physiological life, is sacrosanct. This is not a Christian idea at all; for, if it were, the martyrs would be wrong. If the sanctity is *in* life, it must be wrong to give your life for a noble cause as well as to take another's. But the Christian must be ready to give life gladly for his faith, as for a noble cause. Of course, this implies that, *as compared with some things,* the loss of life

[8] Koch, Antony and Preuss, *Handbook of Moral Theology* St. Louis, 1925, II, 76.
[9] Dec. 23, 1948. Incorporated in Willard Sperry, *The Ethical Basis of Medical Care,* New York, 1950, p. 160 sq.
[10] *Indian Thought and Its Development,* London, 1930, pp. 225–238.

is a small evil; and if so, then, *as compared with some other things,* the taking of life is a small injury.[11]

Parenthetically we should explain, if it is not evident in these quotations themselves, that Dr. Temple's purpose was to justify military service. Unfortunately for his aim, he failed to take account of the ethical factor of free choice as a right of the person who thus loses his life at the hands of the warrior. We cannot put upon the same ethical footing the ethical right to take our own lives, in which case our freedom is not invaded, and taking the lives of others in those cases in which the act is done against the victim's will and choice. The true parallel is between self-sacrifice and a merciful death provided at the person's request; there is none between self-sacrifice and violent or coercive killing. But the relevance of what Dr. Temple has to say and its importance for euthanasia is perfectly clear. The non-theological statement of the case agrees with Temple: "Are we not allowing ourselves to be deceived by our self-preservative tendency to rationalize a merely instinctive urge and to attribute spiritual and ethical significance to phenomena appertaining to the realm of crude, biological utility?"[12]

4. It is also objected by religious moralists that euthanasia violates the Biblical command, "Thou shalt not kill." It is doubtful whether this kind of Biblicism is any more valid than the vitalism we reject. Indeed, it is a form of fundamentalism, common to both Catholics and reactionary Protestants. An outspoken religious opponent of euthanasia is a former chancellor to Cardinal Spellman as military vicar to the armed forces, Monsignor Robert McCormick. As presiding judge of the Archdiocesan Ecclesiastical Tribunal of New York, he warned the General Assembly of that state in 1947 not to "set aside the commandment 'Thou shalt not kill.'"[13] In the same vein, the general secretary of the American Council of Christian Churches, an organization of fundamentalist Protestants, denounced the fifty-four clergymen who supported the euthanasia bill, claiming that their action was "an evidence that the modernistic clergy have made further departure from the eternal moral law."[14]

Certainly those who justify war and capital punishment, as most Christians do, cannot condemn euthanasia on this ground. We might point out to the fundamentalists in the two major divisions of Western Christianity that the beatitude "Blessed are the merciful" has the force of a commandment too! The medical profession lives by it, has its whole *ethos* in it. But the simplest way to deal with this Christian text-proof objection might be to point out that the translation "Thou shalt not kill" is incorrect. It should be rendered, as in the responsive decalogue of the *Book of Common Prayer*, "Thou shalt do no murder," i.e., unlawful killing. It is sufficient just to

---

11 *Thoughts in War Time*, London, 1940, pp. 31–32. Italics in original.
12 H. Roberts, "Two Essays on Medicine," in *Living Age*, Oct. 1934, 347.159–162.
13 Quoted H. N. Oliphant, *Redbook Magazine*, Sep. 1948.
14 *Ibid.*

remember that the ancient Jews fully allowed warfare and capital punishment. Lawful killing was also for hunger-satisfaction and sacrifice. Hence, a variety of Hebrew terms such as *shachat, harag, tabach,* but *ratsach* in the Decalogue (both Exodus 20:13 and Deut. 5:17), clearly means *unlawful* killing, treacherously, for private vendetta or gain. Thus it is laid down in Leviticus 24:17 that "he who kills a man shall be put to death," showing that the lawful forms of killing may even be used to punish the unlawful! In the New Testament references to the prohibition against killing (e.g., Matt. 5:21, Luke 18:20, Rom. 13:9) are an endorsement of the commandments in the Jewish law. Each time, the verb *phoneuo* is used and the connotation is *unlawful* killing, as in the Decalogue. Other verbs connote simply the fact of killing, as *apokteino* (Luke 12:4, "Be not afraid of them that kill the body") and *thuo* which is used interchangeably for slaughter of animals for food and for sacrifice. We might also remind the Bible-bound moralists that there was no condemnation either of Abimelech, who chose to die, or of his faithful sword-bearer who carried out his wish for him.[15]

5. Another common objection in religious quarters is that suffering is a part of the divine plan for the good of man's soul, and must therefore be accepted. Does this mean that the physicians' Hippocratic Oath is opposed to Christian virtue and doctrine? If this simple and naive idea of suffering were a valid one, then we should not be able to give our moral approval to anesthetics or to provide any medical relief of human suffering. Such has been the objection of many religionists at every stage of medical conquest, as we pointed out in the first chapter in the case of anesthetics at childbirth. Here is still another anomaly in our mores of life and death, that we are, after much struggle, now fairly secure in the righteousness of easing suffering at birth but we still feel it is wrong to ease suffering at death! Life may be begun without suffering, but it may not be ended without it, if it happens that nature combines death and suffering.

Those who have some acquaintance with the theological habit of mind can understand how even the question of euthanasia may be colored by the vision of the Cross as a symbol of redemptive suffering in Christian doctrine. As Emil Brunner has said of the crucifix, "it is not without its significance that the picture of a dying man is the sacred sign of Christendom." [16] But when it is applied to suffering in general it becomes, of course, a rather uncritical exemplarism which ignores the unique theological claims of the doctrine of the Atonement and the saving power of the Cross as a singular event. It is, at least, difficult to see how any theological basis for the suffering argument against medical euthanasia would be any different or any more compelling for keeping childbirth natural and "as God hath provided it."

It is much more realistic and humble to take as our regulative principle

---

[15] Judges 9:54.
[16] *Man in Revolt,* New York, 1939, pp. 388–389.

the rule that "Blessed are the merciful, for they shall see mercy," since this moral standard gives more recognition in actual fact to the motive of compassion, which, according to the theology of Atonement, lies behind the crucifixion of Jesus and gave it its power and its *ethos*. "All things whatsoever you would that men should do unto you, do you even so unto them." Mercy to the suffering is certainly the point of Psalm 102, vs. 12: "As a father hath compassion on his children, so hath the Lord compassion on them that fear him: for he knoweth our frame." Let the Biblicist take his position on the story of Job! Job explored the problem of human suffering and left it a mystery for the man of faith. Some have tried to find a recommendation of suicide in Job's wife's advice, but it is hardly more than a warning that he must not curse God.[17] In Job 7:15 there may be a thought of suicide, but nothing more than that. Our point here is that even Job never hinted that euthanasia was wrong; he only wondered, as we all do sometimes, why such a thing is ever needed or desired. The patience of Job is proverbial, but this is the Job of the prose part of the book. The poetry has another Job, a most rebellious and morally disturbed one. He could come to no other conclusion but that suffering is a mystery, as far as God's will and power are concerned. He did not give much attention to man's part in its control, nor to its particular aspect in incurable illness.

6. It is frequently pointed out, as an objection to euthanasia, that patients pronounced incurable might recover after all, for doctors can and do make mistakes. This seems, frankly, like a fundamentally obstructionist argument. It takes us back to the evasion based on fallibility with which we had to deal in the question of truth-telling. Doctors are indeed finite creatures. So they may also err in recommending and carrying out operations, or in other forms of treatment. As far as the accuracy of their advice is concerned, we have to trust them, although it is always our right to doubt their advice and to change doctors. If reluctance to trust them were a common attitude pervading medical relationships generally, it would spell the doom of medical care. Also, it is sometimes added that if we will just hang on something may turn up, perhaps a new discovery which will save us after all. Although this objection really evades the point at issue, it has a very great importance when seen in its own perspective. We always have ground for hope that many of the conditions which have called for euthanasia in the past will no longer do so. Not long ago crippling arthritis was thought almost hopeless, but cortisone and ACTH have offered new hope and success. Medical science is also continuously making discoveries which narrow the range of cases in which the conditions of justifiable euthanasia are apt to occur. Improved narcosis, new healing drugs and treatments, surgical relief of pain by new techniques of chordotomy and labotomy—these things make news constantly.

And there are, of course, occasional incidents of totally unexpected, last-

---

[17] Job 2:9–10.

minute recovery from "hopeless" illnesses. An actual case would be that of the hospital chaplain who once stood by at a "certain" death and a horrible one from pemphigus. The doctors had even advised that the patient's family be called in for a last visit. Then, at the last moment, a new penicillin drug was flown in from another city, and the patient was saved. Such things happen, yes. But all we need to say to this objection to euthanasia is that by no stretch of the imagination, in a typical situation, can we foresee a discovery that will restore health to a life already running out. A patient dying of metastatic cancer may be considered already dead, though still breathing. In advanced cases, even if a cure was to be found, toxemia has in all likelihood damaged the tissues and organs fatally.

7. It is said, with some truth, that patients racked by pain might make impulsive and ill-considered requests for euthanasia, if it were morally and legally approved. To this there are two rejoinders: first, that a careful law, such as that of the Euthanasia Society, would provide that there must be medical advice that death is certain, which rules out any hasty euthanasia in non-fatal illnesses; and, second, that the law would provide an interval between application and administration. The law should not permit euthanasia to be done on the spur of the moment, and the patient should be free to withdraw his request at any time. The requirement that the disease must be of a fatal character is needed to guard against unconscious wishes for destruction which are to be seen sometimes, although rarely, in patients. The confirmation of the patient's and the attending physician's decisions by disinterested parties is a sufficient bulwark against impulsive action. This might also be the place to emphasize that a doctor is always free to refuse to administer medical euthanasia, as a patient ought to be free to request it. In a wide search of the literature, incidentally, only one really *medical* objection to the practice was found, although there are frequent moral objections. Dr. A. A. Brill, of the International Psychoanalytical Association, has declared that *although doctors are actually doing it they should stop,* because for reasons of depth psychology the practice will demoralize both patients and doctors, fill them with fear that inhibits healing relationships and lowers vitality.[18] As we have already seen, Dr. Brill's colleague in the Association, Dr. Ernest Jones, does not regard this as a real objection to euthanasia, if we may draw that conclusion from his support of it before the United Nations.

Connected with this is this further objection: what if the patient can no longer speak or even gesture intelligibly? Can we be sure we always understand the patient's real desire, his choice for or against death, especially in cases where his condition is nearly unconscious or comatose? We all know that communication is not solely verbal. The provision that the request must come from the patient in a documentary form is introduced in proposals like that of the Euthanasia Society out of great caution, presum-

---

[18] *Journ. of Nervous and Mental Diseases,* July 1936, p. 84.

ably in the fear that a gesture or other sign might be misinterpreted. A restriction like this will also exclude the possibility of a doctor's carrying out euthanasia when the patient had expressed a desire for it but the formalities could not be fulfilled before his physical powers to apply had failed. This would be tragic, but perhaps it is the necessary price exacted for legalization. There is also, of course, the reverse possibility that a patient might make the proper application, then change his mind after his powers of communication had failed. But these seem unreal problems, purely logical in character, if it is held, as we indeed do hold, that a patient who has completely lost the power to communicate has passed into a submoral state, outside the forum of conscience and beyond moral being. Being no longer responsive, he is no longer responsible.

Conscience and consciousness are inseparable and presuppose each other. Their interdependence has always been recognized, since the Stoics first explored the cognitive aspect of conscience as distinct from the judicial, and recognized that to act with *conscientia,* with knowledge, requires consciousness. The Stoics predicated awareness or consciousness of Natural Law insight; the Christians have predicated Natural Law insight plus communion with God and the voice of the Holy Spirit. Some have held that the moral factor in consciousness is innate; others, acquired. Some have thought it to be reason; others, intuition; still others, emotion. In any case, these faculties are parts of consciousness, without which personality is gone and there is no longer a "person" to fulfill even the minimum requirements of moral status, i.e., freedom and knowledge.

8. Sometimes we hear it said that the moral and legal approval of euthanasia would weaken our moral fiber, tend to encourage us to minimize the importance of life. Hence such well-known witticisms as G. K. Chesterton's, that the proponents of euthanasia now seek only the death of those who are a nuisance to themselves; but soon it will be broadened to include those who are a nuisance to others.[19] It is very hard to find any real hope of taking hold of an objection like this, with its broad value-terms such as "moral fiber" and "the importance of life." It could just as easily be reasoned that to ask for euthanasia, to leave voluntarily for the unknown, would call for courage and resolution and faith, and would encourage us to live with faith and without fear of the unknown. There is great wisdom and moral assurance in the decision of Charlotte Perkins Gilman, one of America's greatest women, who chose self-euthanasia rather than endure a degenerative death by cancer. These were her last words, typed by her own hand: "A last duty. Human life consists in mutual service. No grief, no pain, misfortune or 'broken heart' is excuse for cutting off one's life while any power of service remains. But when all usefulness is over, when one is assured of an imminent and unavoidable death, it is the simplest of human rights to choose a quick and easy death in place of a slow and

---

[19] Symposium, "Pro and Con," in *The Digest,* Oct. 23, 1937, 124.22–23.

horrible one. Public opinion is changing on this subject. The time is approaching when we shall consider it abhorrent to our civilization to allow a human being to lie in prolonged agony which we should mercifully end in any other creature. Believing this choice to be of social service in promoting wider views on this question, I have preferred chloroform to cancer." [20]

Our attention should be given particularly to one sentence here: "No grief, no pain, no misfortune or 'broken heart' is excuse for cutting off one's life while any power of service remains." It is a cause for joy that many avenues of service are open, or could be opened, to properly diagnosed terminal patients. Because of its psychological effects, genuine service, or being needed, will postpone the unendurable stages of pain or collapse. Enlightened hospital procedure is making great advances in this respect. One of the most significant services open to terminal patients is willingness to submit to drugs and cures and narcotics of an experimental kind, aimed at eliminating *the very pain and demoralization which is a major justification for euthanasia.* This consideration is certainly a welcome one to the advocates of euthanasia, and is always kept in mind by them. For them the best possible news would be that medicine has at last deprived euthanasia of its *raison d'être.*

Sometimes it is suggested by advocates of euthanasia that those who insist that the suffering go on are unconscious sadists, moved by the wish to make others suffer, or in a voyeurist version actually eager to see them suffer. This is an extremely problematical ground upon which to enter in the discussion, and it tends to "psychologize" all ethical reason out of the picture. It is true, theoretically, that the idea of noble suffering may be, deep down, a reaction-formation to rationalize sadistic or masochistic sentiments. But on the other hand, opponents of euthanasia could charge that the advocates are the victims of a death instinct or destruction-wishes; or even a sado-masochist syndrome, sadist in the friends of the patient, masochist in the patient. To this, in their turn, the advocates could reply that if they were sadistic in their drives they would *want* the suffering to go on. There are hardly any limits to the kind of wool-gathering that could develop along these lines, with little or no possibility of contributing to a solution ethically.

9. It is objected that the ethics of a physician forbids him to take life. We have already recognized that fact *as a fact,* but the issue is raised precisely because there are cases when the doctor's duty to prolong and protect life is in conflict with his equal duty to relieve suffering. As a matter of fact, this dilemma is actually inescapable and inherent in the medical care of many terminal illnesses anyway, at the technical as well as the moral level. If the physician's obligation is both to relieve pain and prolong life, how then can he use analgesics, which bring relief but have the neces-

<hr>

[20] Quoted by A. L. Woolbarst, *Medical Record,* May 17, 1939.

sary effect of hastening death? Great strides in non-toxemic medications are being made, but it remains true that, for example, prolonged morphine has a lethal effect, especially when finally there is a failure of natural functions such as breathing, salivation, and heat regulation, and when it no longer works intravenously because circulation is ceasing and it has to be injected directly into the heart. Everyone concerned in the care of the sick knows quite well that the medication itself is euthanasia. We hear constantly of overdoses somehow or other taken in terminal cases. There are many cases indeed in which actions are carried out by patients or attendants in the spirit of Socrates, drinking the cup of hemlock, who cried to Crito, "We owe a cock to Aesculapius. . . . Pay the debt and do not forget it." [21]

The dilemma of the physician who takes a contradictory oath could hardly be more evident than in the words of an article in *The New England Journal of Medicine* entitled "The Theology [sic] of Medicine." The author, a physician, declared, "I feel as Dr. Woodward did when he said, 'I have no sympathy with the man who would shorten the death agony of a dog but prolong that of a human being.'" [22] Dr. Woodward had himself advised a class of medical students, "I hold it to be your duty to smooth as much as possible the pathway to the grave even if life is somewhat shortened. Nor is it necessary to talk it over with friends and relatives, nor need you expect them to formally countenance either neglect or expedition. Let that be your affair, settled with your own conscience." [23] It is a dilemma. The only real problem in conscience is not whether the mystique of vitalism or an ethic of mercifulness should reign, but whether the decision should rest upon the lonely conscience of the doctor without honest approval or responsibility shared fully with patient and family. Dr. Woodward is correct ethically to show mercy, but he is not justified in being so god-like about it. He should be man-like about it, and so should the students to whom he was giving his advice. As long as doctors continue, as at present, making unilateral decisions, they are in the position of needing something stronger than a Rule of Double Effect of their own, whereby they can convince themselves that it is right to do a good thing if they do not intend the evil consequences. Under these circumstances, can they sort out their emotions and motives, and make sure that they do not *want* the luckless patient to reach an end to his sufferings? Under these circumstances, what of the Hippocratic Oath?

Our defense of the right to die, with the doctor's aid, is not made in any kind of illness except the fatal and demoralizing ones. Besides, as we have seen in other questions already discussed, there are common exceptions to the rule against medical homicide. If one can be made at the beginning of life (abortion) why not also at the end of life (euthanasia)?

[21] *Phaedo*, conclusion.
[22] R. E. Osgood, M.D., 210.4, 182–192, Jan. 25, 1934.
[23] *Ibid.*, 202.18, 843–853.

The one situation is no more absolute than the other. There is no more stigma in the one than in the other. On personalistic grounds we could say that there is less question morally in euthanasia, for in euthanasia a merciful death is chosen in cooperation with a person whose integrity is threatened by disintegration, whereas an embryo in therapeutic abortion has no personal value or development at stake and cannot exercise the moral qualities of freedom and knowledge.

10. Finally, it is objected that doctors do not want euthanasia made legal.[24] It is not at all uncommon to hear doctors admit that they generally engage in the practice, in one way or another. Lest any reader be skeptical, he should examine the Cumulative Book Index and the index of periodicals for medical opinion on the subject, and he will find several places in which the admission is candidly made.[25] From time to time there are reports, undocumentable but from usually reliable sources, of medical meetings such as one recently in the Middle West at which a speaker asked for a show of hands from those who have never administered euthanasia. Not a hand was raised.[26] In 1935 great excitement was caused by a doctor's public confession in a London newspaper that he had been practicing euthanasia, and in *Time Magazine* an article reported, "Pungent, voluble Dr. Morris Fishbein, editor of the American Medical Association's *Journal*, observed that the average doctor frequently faces the problem, that when it is a matter between him and his patient he may decide it in his own way without interference." [27] Many are the uses which we may be sure are made of drugs such as bichloride of mercury, potassium cyanide, and some of the barbiturates. In 1947, when an English doctor publicly announced he too engaged in medical euthanasia, a spokesman for the British Medical Association, in a very oblique but patent *non dixit*, said, "I think a good many doctors feel as Dr. Barton does, that euthanasia ought to be legalized. The association has no objection to doctors saying what they think about law." [28]

There are three other objections closely allied to these we have examined. They may deserve just a word or two. First, it is said that medical euthanasia would weaken medical research, that it would take away the incentive to find cures for painful maladies. This is nonsense because doctors are already practicing euthanasia and yet their fight against fatal diseases is mounting, not flagging. As cancer and malignant tumors, for example, increase (nearly 200,000 Americans will die of them this year) the

[24] Cf. G. E. Byers, *Ohio Med. Journ.*, 1936, 32.342; J. S. Manson, *Brit. Med. Journ.*, 1936, 1.86; W. W. Gregg, *North Amer. Rev.*, 1934, 237.239; J. J. Walsh, *The Forum*, Dec. 1935, 333–334. The Council of the World Medical Association, at Copenhagen, Apr. 24–28, 1950, *recommended* that "the practice of euthanasia be condemned." Cf. *Journal of the Amer. Med. Assoc.*, June 10, 1950, 143–6, p. 561.
[25] E.g., cf. Frank Hinman, M.D., *Journ. of Nervous and Mental Diseases*, 99, 1944.
[26] Cf. H. N. Oliphant, *op. cit.*
[27] Nov. 18, 1935, 26.21, pp. 53–54.
[28] *New York Herald Tribune*, May 23, 1947.

research in that field increases too. The motive behind medical research is the elimination or control of disease, not merely the avoidance of suffering.[29] Second, it is objected that the heirs or enemies of an invalid might use euthanasia to hasten his death. To this we reply that the legal requirement of a written application by the sufferer, and of both legal and medical investigations, would be a safeguard. He would have far more protection than is provided for many patients now committed for treatment of mental disorders. He would, indeed, have a great deal more protection than he now receives under the present system of clandestine euthanasia being widely practiced. Third, it is claimed that once we legalize mercy deaths the application of the principle will be widened disastrously to cover non-fatal illnesses. But why is it, then, that although legal killing by capital punishment has been in vogue a long time, yet it has been narrowed rather than extended in scope? In fact it has been narrowed a great deal from the days when people were hanged for stealing a few shillings. This alarmist objection is the old red herring against which we have had to aim the rule of *abusus non tollit usum* time and again. It is drawn across many ethical trails.

A Time to Plant, a Time to Pluck

To draw our thinking together, we ought to repeat that there are three schools of thought favoring euthanasia. First, there are those who favor voluntary euthanasia, a personalistic ethical position. Second, there are those who favor involuntary euthanasia for monstrosities at birth and mental defectives, a partly personalistic and partly eugenic position.[30] Third, there are those who favor involuntary euthanasia for all who are a burden upon the community, a purely eugenic position. It should be perfectly obvious that we do not have to endorse the third school of thought just because we favor either the first or the second, or both. Our discussion has covered only the first one—voluntary medical euthanasia—as a means of ending a human life enmeshed in incurable and fatal physical suffering. The principles of right based upon selfhood and moral being favor it.

Defense of voluntary medical euthanasia, it should be made plain, does not depend upon the superficial system of values in which physical evil (pain) is regarded as worse than moral evil (sin) or intellectual evil (error). On the contrary, unless we are careful to see that pain is the least of evils, then our values would tie us back into that old attitude of taking

[29] See the thrilling story of vigorous medical progress in an account by the Secretary of the American Medical Association, Stephen M. Spencer, *Wonders of Modern Medicine*, New York, 1953. Between 1900 and 1952 the average life span of Americans has risen from 49 to 69 years, and Louis I. Dublin of the Metropolitan Life Insurance Company estimates it will be 73 within this generation, thus exceeding the threescore and ten allotted in the Bible.

[30] It has always been a quite common practice of midwives and, in modern times, doctors, simply to fail to respirate monstrous babies at birth.

the material or physical aspects of reality so seriously that we put nature or things as they are *out there* in a determinant place, subordinating the ethical and spiritual values of freedom and knowledge and upholding, in effect, a kind of naturalism. C. S. Lewis has described it by saying that, "Of all evils, pain only is sterilized or disinfected evil." [31] Pain cannot create moral evil, such as a disintegration or demoralization of personality would be, unless it is submitted to in brute fashion as opponents of euthanasia insist we should do.

We repeat, the issue is not one of life or death. The issue is which kind of death, an agonized or peaceful one. Shall we meet death in personal integrity or in personal disintegration? Should there be a moral or a demoralized end to mortal life? Surely, . . . we are not as persons of moral stature to be ruled by ruthless and unreasoning physiology, but rather by reason and self-control. Those who face the issues of euthanasia with a religious faith will not, if they think twice, submit to the materialistic and animistic doctrine that God's will is revealed by what nature does, and that life, qua life, is absolutely sacred and untouchable. All of us can agree with Reinhold Niebuhr that "the ending of our life would not threaten us if we had not falsely made ourselves the center of life's meaning." [32] One of the pathetic immaturities we all recognize around us is stated bluntly by Sigmund Freud in his *Reflections on War and Death*: "In the subconscious every one of us is convinced of his immortality." Our frantic hold upon life can only cease to be a snare and delusion when we objectify it in some religious doctrine of salvation, or, alternatively, agree with Sidney Hook that "the romantic pessimism which mourns man's finitude is a vain lament that we are not gods." [33] At least, the principles of personal morality warn us not to make physical phenomena, unmitigated by human freedom, the center of life's meaning. There is an impressive wisdom in the words of Dr. Logan Clendenning: "Death itself is not unpleasant. I have seen a good many people die. To a few death comes as a friend, as a relief from pain, from intolerable loneliness or loss, or from disappointment. To even fewer it comes as a horror. To most it hardly comes at all, so gradual is its approach, so long have the senses been benumbed, so little do they realize what is taking place. As I think it over, death seems to me one of the few evidences in nature of the operation of a creative intelligence exhibiting qualities which I recognize as mind stuff. To have blundered onto the form of energy called life showed a sort of malignant power. After having blundered on life, to have conceived of death was a real stroke of genius." [34]

As Ecclesiastes the Preacher kept saying in first one way and then another, "The living know that they shall die" and there is "a time to be born and a time to die, a time to plant and a time to pluck up that which

[31] *The Problem of Pain*, London, 1943, p. 104.
[32] *Human Destiny*, New York, 1943, II, 293.
[33] Quoted by Corliss Lamont, *The Illusion of Immortality*, New York, 1950, p. 191.
[34] *The Human Body*, New York, 1941, 3rd ed., pp. 442–443.

is planted." [35] And in the New Covenant we read that "all flesh is as grass" and "the grass withereth, and the flower thereof falleth away." Nevertheless, "who is he that will harm you, if ye be followers of that which is good?" [36]

Medicine contributes too much to the moral stature of men to persist indefinitely in denying the ultimate claims of its own supreme virtue and ethical inspiration, mercy. With Maeterlinck, we may be sure that "there will come a day when Science will protest its errors and will shorten our sufferings." [37]

[35] Eccl. 9:5 and 3:2.
[36] I Pet. 1:24 and 3:13.
[37] Quoted by G. W. Jacoby, *Physician, Pastor and Patient,* New York, 1936, p. 206.

ACTIVE AND PASSIVE EUTHANASIA [*]

JAMES RACHELS

The distinction between active and passive euthanasia is thought to be crucial for medical ethics. The idea is that it is permissible, at least in some cases, to withhold treatment and allow a patient to die, but it is never permissible to take any direct action designed to kill the patient. This doctrine seems to be accepted by most doctors, and it is endorsed in a statement adopted by the House of Delegates of the American Medical Association on December 4, 1973:

> The intentional termination of the life of one human being by another—mercy killing—is contrary to that for which the medical profession stands and is contrary to the policy of the American Medical Association.
>
> The cessation of the employment of extraordinary means to prolong the life of the body when there is irrefutable evidence that biological death is imminent is the decision of the patient and/or his immediate family. The advice and judgment of the physician should be freely available to the patient and/or his immediate family.

However, a strong case can be made against this doctrine. In what follows I will set out some of the relevant arguments, and urge doctors to reconsider their views on this matter.

To begin with a familiar type of situation, a patient who is dying of incurable cancer of the throat is in terrible pain, which can no longer be satisfactorily alleviated. He is certain to die within a few days, even if

[*] From James Rachels, "Active and Passive Euthanasia," *The New England Journal of Medicine,* **292**: 2 (January 9, 1975), pp. 78–80. Reprinted by permission of the author and *The New England Journal of Medicine.*

present treatment is continued, but he does not want to go on living for those days since the pain is unbearable. So he asks the doctor for an end to it, and his family joins in the request.

Suppose the doctor agrees to withhold treatment, as the conventional doctrine says he may. The justification for his doing so is that the patient is in terrible agony, and since he is going to die anyway, it would be wrong to prolong his suffering needlessly. But now notice this. If one simply withholds treatment, it may take the patient longer to die, and so he may suffer more than he would if more direct action were taken and a lethal injection given. This fact provides strong reason for thinking that, once the initial decision not to prolong his agony has been made, active euthanasia is actually preferable to passive euthanasia, rather than the reverse. To say otherwise is to endorse the option that leads to more suffering rather than less, and is contrary to the humanitarian impulse that prompts the decision not to prolong his life in the first place.

Part of my point is that the process of being "allowed to die" can be relatively slow and painful, whereas being given a lethal injection is relatively quick and painless. Let me give a different sort of example. In the United States about one in 600 babies is born with Down's syndrome. Most of these babies are otherwise healthy—that is, with only the usual pediatric care, they will proceed to an otherwise normal infancy. Some, however, are born with congenital defects such as intestinal obstructions that require operations if they are to live. Sometimes, the parents and the doctor will decide not to operate, and let the infant die. Anthony Shaw describes what happens then:

> . . . When surgery is denied [the doctor] must try to keep the infant from suffering while natural forces sap the baby's life away. As a surgeon whose natural inclination is to use the scalpel to fight off death, standing by and watching a salvageable baby die is the most emotionally exhausting experience I know. It is easy at a conference, in a theoretical discussion, to decide that such infants should be allowed to die. It is altogether different to stand by in the nursery and watch as dehydration and infection wither a tiny being over hours and days. This is a terrible ordeal for me and the hospital staff—much more so than for the parents who never set foot in the nursery.†

I can understand why some people are opposed to all euthanasia, and insist that such infants must be allowed to live. I think I can also understand why other people favor destroying these babies quickly and painlessly. But why should anyone favor letting "dehydration and infection wither a tiny being over hours and days?" The doctrine that says that a baby may be allowed to dehydrate and wither, but may not be given an injection that would end its life without suffering, seems so patently cruel

† Shaw A: 'Doctor, Do We Have a Choice?' The New York Times Magazine, January 30, 1972, p. 54.

as to require no further refutation. The strong language is not intended to offend, but only to put the point in the clearest possible way.

My second argument is that the conventional doctrine leads to decisions concerning life and death made on irrelevant grounds.

Consider again the case of the infants with Down's syndrome who need operations for congenital defects unrelated to the syndrome to live. Sometimes, there is no operation, and the baby dies, but when there is no such defect, the baby lives on. Now, an operation such as that to remove an intestinal obstruction is not prohibitively difficult. The reason why such operations are not performed in these cases is, clearly, that the child has Down's syndrome and the parents and doctor judge that because of that fact it is better for the child to die.

But notice that this situation is absurd, no matter what view one takes of the lives and potentials of such babies. If the life of such an infant is worth preserving, what does it matter if it needs a simple operation? Or, if one thinks it better that such a baby should not live on, what difference does it make that it happens to have an unobstructed intestinal tract? In either case, the matter of life and death is being decided on irrelevant grounds. It is the Down's syndrome, and not the intestines, that is the issue. The matter should be decided, if at all, on that basis, and not be allowed to depend on the essentially irrelevant question of whether the intestinal tract is blocked.

What makes this situation possible, of course, is the idea that when there is an intestinal blockage, one can "let the baby die," but when there is no such defect there is nothing that can be done, for one must not "kill" it. The fact that this idea leads to such results as deciding life or death on irrelevant grounds is another good reason why the doctrine should be rejected.

One reason why so many people think that there is an important moral difference between active and passive euthanasia is that they think killing someone is morally worse than letting someone die. But is it? Is killing, in itself, worse than letting die? To investigate this issue, two cases may be considered that are exactly alike except that one involves killing whereas the other involves letting someone die. Then, it can be asked whether this difference makes any difference to the moral assessments. It is important that the cases be exactly alike, except for this one difference, since otherwise one cannot be confident that it is this difference and not some other that accounts for any variation in the assessments of the two cases. So, let us consider this pair of cases:

In the first, Smith stands to gain a large inheritance if anything should happen to his six-year-old cousin. One evening while the child is taking his bath, Smith sneaks into the bathroom and drowns the child, and then arranges things so that it will look like an accident.

In the second, Jones also stands to gain if anything should happen to his six-year-old cousin. Like Smith, Jones sneaks in planning to drown the child in his bath. However, just as he enters the bathroom Jones sees the child slip and hit his head, and fall face down in the water. Jones is delighted; he stands by, ready to push the child's head back under if it is necessary, but it is not necessary. With only a little thrashing about, the child drowns all by himself, "accidentally," as Jones watches and does nothing.

Now Smith killed the child, whereas Jones "merely" let the child die. That is the only difference between them. Did either man behave better, from a moral point of view? If the difference between killing and letting die were in itself a morally important matter, one should say that Jones's behavior was less reprehensible than Smith's. But does one really want to say that? I think not. In the first place, both men acted from the same motive, personal gain, and both had exactly the same end in view when they acted. It may be inferred from Smith's conduct that he is a bad man, although that judgment may be withdrawn or modified if certain further facts are learned about him—for example, that he is mentally deranged. But would not the very same thing be inferred about Jones from his conduct? And would not the same further considerations also be relevant to any modification of this judgment? Moreover, suppose Jones pleaded, in his own defense, "After all, I didn't do anything except just stand there and watch the child drown. I didn't kill him; I only let him die." Again, if letting die were in itself less bad than killing, this defense should have at least some weight. But it does not. Such a "defense" can only be regarded as a grotesque perversion of moral reasoning. Morally speaking, it is no defense at all.

Now, it may be pointed out, quite properly, that the cases of euthanasia with which doctors are concerned are not like this at all. They do not involve personal gain or the destruction of normal healthy children. Doctors are concerned only with cases in which the patient's life is of no further use to him, or in which the patient's life has become or will soon become a terrible burden. However, the point is the same in these cases: the bare difference between killing and letting die does not, in itself, make a moral difference. If a doctor lets a patient die, for humane reasons, he is in the same moral position as if he had given the patient a lethal injection for humane reasons. If his decision was wrong—if, for example, the patient's illness was in fact curable—the decision would be equally regrettable no matter which method was used to carry it out. And if the doctor's decision was the right one, the method used is not in itself important.

The AMA policy statement isolates the crucial issue very well; the crucial issue is "the intentional termination of the life of one human being by another." But after identifying this issue, and forbidding "mercy killing," the statement goes on to deny that the cessation of treatment is the intentional termination of a life. This is where the mistake comes in, for what is the cessation of treatment, in these circumstances, if it is not "the intentional termination of the life of one human being by another?" Of course it is exactly that, and if it were not, there would be no point to it.

Many people will find this judgment hard to accept. One reason, I think, is that it is very easy to conflate the question of whether killing is, in itself, worse than letting die, with the very different question of whether most actual cases of killing are more reprehensible than most actual cases of letting die. Most actual cases of killing are clearly terrible (think, for example, of all the murders reported in the newspapers), and one hears of such cases every day. On the other hand, one hardly ever hears of a case of letting die, except for the actions of doctors who are motivated by humanitarian reasons. So one learns to think of killing in a much worse light than of letting die. But this does not mean that there is something about killing that makes it in itself worse than letting die, for it is not the bare difference between killing and letting die that makes the difference in these cases. Rather, the other factors—the murderer's motive of personal gain, for example, contrasted with the doctor's humanitarian motivation—account for different reactions to the different cases.

I have argued that killing is not in itself any worse than letting die; if my contention is right, it follows that active euthanasia is not any worse than passive euthanasia. What arguments can be given on the other side? The most common, I believe, is the following:

"The important difference between active and passive euthanasia is that, in passive euthanasia, the doctor does not do anything to bring about the patient's death. The doctor does nothing, and the patient dies of whatever ills already afflict him. In active euthanasia, however, the doctor does something to bring about the patient's death: he kills him. The doctor who gives the patient with cancer a lethal injection has himself caused his patient's death; whereas if he merely ceases treatment, the cancer is the cause of the death."

A number of points need to be made here. The first is that it is not exactly correct to say that in passive euthanasia the doctor does nothing, for he does do one thing that is very important: he lets the patient die. "Letting someone die" is certainly different, in some respects, from other types of action—mainly in that it is a kind of action that one may perform by way of not performing certain other actions. For example, one may let a patient die by way of not giving medication, just as one may insult someone by way of not shaking his hand. But for any purpose of moral assessment, it is a type of action nonetheless. The decision to let a patient die is subject to moral appraisal in the same way that a decision to kill him would be subject to moral appraisal: it may be assessed as wise or unwise, compassionate or sadistic, right or wrong. If a doctor deliberately let a patient die who was suffering from a routinely curable illness, the doctor would certainly be to blame for what he had done, just as he would be to blame if he had needlessly killed the patient. Charges against him would then be appropriate. If so, it would be no defense at all for him to insist that he didn't "do anything." He would have done something very serious indeed, for he let his patient die.

Fixing the cause of death may be very important from a legal point of view, for it may determine whether criminal charges are brought against the doctor. But I do not think that this notion can be used to show a moral difference between active and passive euthanasia. The reason why it is considered bad to be the cause of someone's death is that death is regarded as a great evil—and so it is. However, if it has been decided that euthanasia —even passive euthanasia—is desirable in a given case, it has also been decided that in this instance death is no greater an evil than the patient's continued existence. And if this is true, the usual reason for not wanting to be the cause of someone's death simply does not apply.

Finally, doctors may think that all of this is only of academic interest— the sort of thing that philosophers may worry about but that has no practical bearing on their own work. After all, doctors must be concerned about the legal consequences of what they do, and active euthanasia is clearly forbidden by the law. But even so, doctors should also be concerned with the fact that the law is forcing upon them a moral doctrine that may well be indefensible, and has a considerable effect on their practices. Of course, most doctors are not now in the position of being coerced in this matter, for they do not regard themselves as merely going along with what the law requires. Rather, in statements such as the AMA policy statement that I have quoted, they are endorsing this doctrine as a central point of medical ethics. In that statement, active euthanasia is condemned not merely as illegal but as "contrary to that for which the medical profession stands," whereas passive euthanasia is approved. However, the preceding considerations suggest that there is really no moral difference between the two, considered in themselves (there may be important moral differences in some cases in their *consequences*, but, as I pointed out, these differences may make active euthanasia, and not passive euthanasia, the morally preferable option). So, whereas doctors may have to discriminate between active and passive euthanasia to satisfy the law, they should not do any more than that. In particular, they should not give the distinction any added authority and weight by writing it into official statements of medical ethics.

A REPLY TO RACHELS ON ACTIVE AND PASSIVE EUTHANASIA * †

TOM L. BEAUCHAMP

James Rachels has recently argued that the distinction between active and passive euthanasia is neither appropriately used by the American Medical Association nor generally useful for the resolution of moral problems of euthanasia.[1] Indeed he believes this distinction—which he equates with the killing/letting die distinction—does not in itself have any moral importance. The chief object of his attack is the following statement adopted by the House of Delegates of the American Medical Association in 1973:

> The intentional termination of the life of one human being by another—mercy killing—is contrary to that for which the medical profession stands and is contrary to the policy of the American Medical Association.
> The cessation of the employment of extraordinary means to prolong the life of the body when there is irrefutable evidence that biological death is imminent is the decision of the patient and/or his immediate family. The advice and judgment of the physician should be freely available to the patient and/or his immediate family [481].

Rachels constructs a powerful and interesting set of arguments against this statement. In this paper I attempt the following: (1) to challenge his views on the grounds that he does not appreciate the moral reasons which give weight to the active/passive distinction; and (2) to provide a constructive account of the moral relevance of the active/passive distinction; and (3) to offer reasons showing that Rachels may nonetheless be correct in urging that we *ought* to abandon the active/passive distinction for purposes of moral reasoning.

I

I would concede that the active/passive distinction is *sometimes* morally irrelevant. Of this Rachels convinces me. But it does not follow that it is *always* morally irrelevant. What we need, then, is a case where the distinction is a morally relevant one and an explanation why it is so. Rachels himself uses the method of examining two cases which are exactly alike except that "one involves killing whereas the other involves letting die"

* From Tom L. Beauchamp, "A Reply to Rachels on Active and Passive Euthanasia," *Ethical Issues in Death and Dying*, ed. by Beauchamp and Seymour Perlin (Englewood Cliffs: Prentice-Hall, 1978). Reprinted by permission.

† This paper is a heavily revised version of an article by the same title first published in T. Mappes and J. Zembaty, eds. *Social Ethics* (N.Y.: McGraw-Hill, 1976). Copyright © 1975, 1977 by Tom L. Beauchamp.

[483]. We may profitably begin by comparing the kinds of cases governed by the AMA's doctrine with the kinds of cases adduced by Rachels in order to assess the adequacy and fairness of his cases.

The second paragraph of the AMA statement is confined to a narrowly restricted range of passive euthanasia cases, viz., those (a) where the patients are on extraordinary means, (b) where irrefutable evidence of imminent death is available, and (c) where patient or family consent is available. Rachels' two cases involve conditions notably different from these:

> In the first, Smith stands to gain a large inheritance if anything should happen to his six-year-old cousin. One evening while the child is taking his bath, Smith sneaks into the bathroom and drowns the child, and then arranges things so that it will look like an accident.
>
> In the second, Jones also stands to gain if anything should happen to his six-year-old cousin. Like Smith, Jones sneaks in planning to drown the child in his bath. However, just as he enters the bathroom Jones sees the child slip and hit his head, and fall face down in the water. Jones is delighted; he stands by, ready to push the child's head back under if it is necessary, but it is not necessary. With only a little thrashing about, the child drowns all by himself, "accidentally," as Jones watches and does nothing.
>
> Now Smith killed the child, whereas Jones "merely" let the child die. That is the only difference between them [484].

Rachels say there is no moral difference between the cases in terms of our moral assessments of Smith and Jones' behavior. This assessment seems fair enough, but what can Rachels' cases be said to prove, as they are so markedly disanalogous to the sorts of cases envisioned by the AMA proposal? Rachels concedes important disanalogies, but thinks them irrelevant:

> The point is the same in these cases: the bare difference between killing and letting die does not, in itself, make a moral difference. If a doctor lets a patient die, for humane reasons, he is in the same moral position as if he had given the patient a lethal injection for humane reasons [op. cit.].

Three observations are immediately in order. First, Rachels seems to infer that from such cases we can conclude that the distinction between killing and letting die is *always* morally irrelevant. This conclusion is fallaciously derived. What the argument in fact shows, being an analogical argument, is only that in all *relatively similar* cases the distinction does not in itself make a moral difference. Since Rachels concedes that other cases are disanalogous, he seems thereby to concede that his argument is as weak as the analogy itself. Second, Rachels' cases involve two *unjustified* actions, one of killing and the other of letting die. The AMA statement distinguishes one set of cases of unjustified killing and another of *justified* cases of allowing to die. Nowhere is it claimed by the AMA that what makes the difference in these cases is the active/passive distinction itself. It is only implied that one set of cases, the justified set, *involves* (passive) letting die while the unjustified set *involves* (active) killing. While it is said that justified euthanasia cases are passive ones and unjustified ones active, it is not said either that what makes some acts justified is the fact of their being passive or that what makes others unjustified is the fact of their being active. This fact will prove to be of vital importance.

The third point is that in both of Rachels' cases the respective moral agents—Smith and Jones—are morally responsible for the death of the child and are morally blameworthy—even though Jones is presumably not causally responsible. In the first case death is caused by the agent, while in the second it is not; yet the second agent is no less morally responsible. While the law might find only the first homicidal, morality condemns the motives in each case as equally wrong, and it holds that the duty to save life in such cases is as compelling as the duty not to take life. I suggest that it is largely because of this equal degree of moral responsibility that there is no morally relegant difference in Rachels' cases. In the cases envisioned by the AMA, however, an agent is held to be responsible for taking life by actively killing but is not held to be morally required to preserve life, and so not responsible for death, when removing the patient from extraordinary means (under conditions a–c above). I shall elaborate this latter point momentarily. My only conclusion thus far is the negative one that Rachels' arguments rest on weak foundations. His cases are not relevantly similar to euthanasia cases and do not support his apparent conclusion that the active/passive distinction is *always* morally irrelevant.

II

I wish first to consider an argument that I believe has powerful intuitive appeal and probably is widely accepted as stating the main reason for rejecting Rachels' view. I will maintain that this argument fails, and so leaves Rachels' contentions untouched.

I begin with an actual case, the celebrated Quinlan case.[2] Karen Quinlan was in a coma, and was on a mechanical respirator which artificially sustained her vital processes and which her parents wished to cease. At least some physicians believed there was irrefutable evidence that biological death was imminent and the coma irreversible. This case, under this description, closely conforms to the passive cases envisioned by the AMA. During an interview the father, Mr. Quinlan, asserted that he did not wish to kill his daughter, but only to remove her from the machines in order to see whether she would live or would die a natural death.[3] Suppose he had said—to envision now a second and hypothetical, but parallel case—that he wished only to see her die painlessly and therefore wished that the doctor could induce death by an overdose of morphine. Most of us would think the second act, which involves active killing, morally unjustified in these circumstances, while many of us would think the first act morally justified. (This is not the place to consider whether in fact it is justified, and if so under what conditions.) What accounts for the apparent morally relevant difference?

I have considered these two cases together in order to follow Rachels' method of entertaining parallel cases where the only difference is that the one case involves killing and the other letting die. However, there is a further difference, which crops up in the euthanasia context. The difference rests in our judgments of medical fallibility and moral responsibility. Mr. Quinlan seems to think that, after all, the doctors might be wrong. There is a remote possibility that she might live without the aid of a machine. But whether or not the medical prediction of death turns out to be accurate, if she dies then no one is morally responsible for directly bringing about or causing her death, as they would be if they caused her death by killing her. Rachels finds explanations which appeal to causal conditions unsatisfactory; but perhaps this is only because he fails to see the nature of the causal link. To bring about her death is by that act to preempt the possibility of life. To "allow her to die" by removing artificial equipment is to allow for the possibility of wrong diagnosis or incorrect prediction and hence to absolve oneself of moral responsibility for the taking of life under false assumptions. There may, of course, be utterly no empirical possibility of recovery in some cases since recovery would violate a law of nature. However, judgments of empirical impossibility in medicine are notoriously problematic—the reason for emphasizing medical fallibility. And in all the hard cases we do not *know* that recovery is empirically impossible, even if good *evidence* is available.

The above reason for invoking the active/passive distinction can now be generalized: Active termination of life removes all possibility of life for the patient, while passively ceasing extraordinary means may not. This is not trivial since patients have survived in several celebrated cases where, in knowledgeable physicians' judgments, there was "irrefutable" evidence that death was imminent.[4]

One may, of course, be entirely responsible and culpable for another's death either by killing him or by letting him die. In such cases, of which Rachels' are examples, there is no morally significant difference between killing and letting die precisely because whatever one does, omits, or refrains from doing does not absolve one of responsibility. Either active or passive involvement renders one responsible for the death of another, and both involvements are equally wrong for the same principled moral reason: it is (prima facie) morally wrong to bring about the death of an innocent person capable of living whenever the causal intervention or negligence is intentional. (I use causal terms here because causal involvement need not be active, as when by one's negligence one is nonetheless causally responsible.) But not all cases of killing and letting die fall under this same moral principle. One is sometimes culpable for killing, because morally responsible as the agent for death, as when one pulls the plug on a respirator sustaining a recovering patient (a murder). But one is sometimes not culpable for letting die because not morally responsible as agent, as when one pulls the plug on a respirator sustaining an irreversibly comatose and unrecoverable patient (a routine procedure, where one is *merely* causally responsible).[5] Different degrees and means of involvement assess different degrees of responsibility, and our assessments of culpability can become intricately complex. The only point which now concerns us, however, is that because different moral principles may govern very similar circumstances, we are sometimes morally culpable for killing but not for letting die. And to many people it will seem that in passive cases we are not morally responsible for causing death, though we are responsible in active cases.

This argument is powerfully attractive. Although I was once inclined to accept it in virtually the identical form just developed,[6] I now think that, despite its intuitive appeal, it cannot be correct. It is true that different degrees and means of involvement entail different degrees of responsibility, but it does not follow that we are *not* responsible and therefore are absolved of possible culpability in *any* case of intentionally allowing to die. We are responsible and *perhaps* culpable in either active or passive cases. Here Rachels' argument is entirely to the point: It is not primarily a question of greater or lesser responsibility by an active or a passive means that should determine culpability. Rather, the question of culpability is decided by the moral *justification* for choosing either a passive or an active means. What the argument in the previous paragraph overlooks is that one might be unjustified in using an active means or unjustified in using a passive means, and hence be culpable in the use of either; yet one might be justified in using an active means or justified in using a passive means, and hence not be culpable in using either. Fallibility might just as well be present in a judgment to use one means as in a judgment to use another. (A judgment to allow to die is just as subject to being based on *knowledge which is fallible* as a judgment to kill.) Moreover, in either case, it is a matter of what one knows and believes, and not a matter of a particular kind of causal connection or causal chain. If we kill the patient, then we are certainly causally responsible for his death. But, similarly, if we cease treatment, and the patient dies, the patient might have recovered if treatment had been continued. The patient might have been saved in either case, and hence there is no morally relevant difference between the two cases. It is, therefore, simply beside the point that "one is sometimes culpable for killing . . . but one is sometimes not culpable for letting die"— as the above argument concludes.

Accordingly, despite its great intuitive appeal and frequent mention, this argument from responsibility fails.

III

There may, however, be more compelling arguments against Rachels, and I wish now to provide what I believe is the most significant argument that can be adduced in defense of the active/passive distinction. I shall develop this argument by combining (1) so-called wedge or slippery slope arguments with (2) recent arguments in defense of rule utilitarianism. I shall explain each in turn and show how in combination they may be used to defend the active/passive distinction.

(1) *Wedge arguments* proceed as follows: if killing were allowed, even under the guise of a merciful extinction of life, a dangerous wedge would be introduced which places all "undesirable" or "unworthy" human life in a precarious condition. Proponents of wedge arguments believe the initial wedge places us on a slippery slope for at least one of two reasons: (i) It is said that our justifying principles leave us with no principled way to avoid the slide into saying that all sorts of killings would be justified under similar conditions. Here it is thought that once killing is allowed, a firm line between justified and unjustified killings cannot be securely drawn. It is thought best not to redraw the line in the first place, for redrawing it will inevitably lead to a downhill slide. It is then often pointed out that as a matter of historical record this is precisely what has occurred in the darker regions of human history, including the Nazi era, where euthanasia began with the best intentions for horribly ill, non-Jewish Germans and gradually spread to anyone deemed an enemy of the people. (ii) Second, it is said that our basic principles against killing will be gradually eroded once some form of killing is legitimated. For example, it is said that permitting voluntary euthanasia will lead to permitting involuntary euthanasia, which will in turn lead to permitting euthanasia for those who are a nuisance to society (idiots, recidivist criminals, defective newborns, and the insane, e.g.). Gradually other principles which instill respect for human life will be eroded or abandoned in the process.

I am not inclined to accept the first reason (i).[7] If our justifying principles are themselves justified, then any action they warrant would be justified. Accordingly, I shall only be concerned with the second approach (ii).

(2) *Rule utilitarianism* is the position that a society ought to adopt a rule if its acceptance would have better consequences for the common good (greater social utility) than any comparable rule could have in that society. Any action is right if it conforms to a valid rule and wrong if it violates the rule. Sometimes it is said that alternative rules should be measured against one another, while it has also been suggested that whole moral *codes* (complete sets of rules) rather than individual rules should be compared. While I prefer the latter formulation (Brandt's), this internal dispute need not detain us here. The important point is that a particular rule or a particular code of rules is morally justified if and only if there is no other

competing rule or moral code whose acceptance would have a higher utility value for society, and where a rule's acceptability is contingent upon the consequences which would result if the rule were made current.

Wedge arguments, when conjoined with rule utilitarian arguments, may be applied to euthanasia issues in the following way. We presently subscribe to a no-active-euthanasia rule (which the AMA suggests we retain). Imagine now that in our society we make current a restricted-active-euthanasia rule (as Rachels seems to urge). Which of these two moral rules would, if enacted, have the consequence of maximizing social utility? Clearly a restricted-active-euthanasia rule would have *some* utility value, as Rachels notes, since some intense and uncontrollable suffering would be eliminated. However, it may not have the highest utility value in the structure of our present code or in any imaginable code which could be made current, and therefore may not be a component in the ideal code for our society. If wedge arguments raise any serious questions at all, as I think they do, they rest in this area of whether a code would be weakened or strengthened by the addition of active euthanasia principles. For the disutility of introducing legitimate killing into one's moral code (in the form of active euthanasia rules) may, in the long run, outweigh the utility of doing so, as a result of the eroding effect such a relaxation would have on rules in the code which demand respect for human life. If, for example, rules permitting active killing were introduced, it is not implausible to suppose that destroying defective newborns (a form of involuntary euthanasia) would become an accepted and common practice, that as population increases occur the aged will be even more neglectable and neglected than they now are, that capital punishment for a wide variety of crimes would be increasingly tempting, that some doctors would have appreciably reduced fears of actively injecting fatal doses whenever it seemed to them propitious to do so, and that laws of war against killing would erode in efficacy even beyond their already abysmal level.

A hundred such possible consequences might easily be imagined. But these few are sufficient to make the larger point that such rules permitting killing could lead to a general reduction of respect for human life. Rules against killing in a moral code are not *isolated* moral principles; they are pieces of a web of rules against killing which forms the code. The more threads one removes, the weaker the fabric becomes. And if, as I believe, moral principles against active killing have the deep and continuously civilizing effect of promoting respect for life, and if principles which allow passively letting die (as envisioned in the AMA statement) do not themselves cut against this effect, then this seems an important reason for the maintenance of the active/passive distinction. (By the logic of the above argument passively letting die would also have to be prohibited if a rule permitting it had the serious adverse consequence of eroding acceptance of rules protective of respect for life. While this prospect seems to me improbable, I can hardly claim to have refuted those conservatives who would claim that even rules which sanction letting die place us on a precarious slippery slope.)

A troublesome problem, however, confronts my use of utilitarian and wedge arguments. Most all of us would agree that both killing and letting die are justified under some conditions. Killings in self-defense and in "just" wars are widely accepted as justified because the conditions excuse the killing. If society can withstand these exceptions to moral rules prohibiting killing, then why is it not plausible to suppose society can accept another excusing exception in the form of justified active euthanasia? This is an important and worthy objection, but not a decisive one. The defenseless and the dying are significantly different classes of persons from aggressors who attack individuals and/or nations. In the case of aggressors, one does not confront the question whether their lives are no longer *worth living*. Rather, we reach the judgment that the aggressors' morally blameworthy actions justify counteractions. But in the case of the dying and the otherwise ill, there is no morally blameworthy action to justify our own. Here we are required to accept the judgment that their lives are no longer *worth living* in order to believe that the termination of their lives is justified. It is the latter sort of judgment which is feared by those who take the wedge argument seriously. We do not now permit and never have permitted the taking of morally blameless lives. I think this is the key to understanding why recent cases of intentionally allowing the death of defective newborns (as in the now famous case at the Johns Hopkins Hospital) have generated such protracted controversy. Even if such newborns could not have led meaningful lives (a matter of some controversy), it is the wedged foot in the door which creates the most intense worries. For if we once take a decision to allow a restricted infanticide justification or any justification at all on grounds that a life is not meaningful or not worth living, we have qualified our moral rules against killing. That this qualification is a matter of the utmost seriousness needs no argument. I mention it here only to show why the wedge argument may have moral force even though we *already* allow some very different conditions to justify intentional killing.

There is one final utilitarian reason favoring the preservation of the active/passive distinction.[8] Suppose we distinguish the following two types of cases of wrongly diagnosed patients:

1. Patients wrongly diagnosed as hopeless, and who will survive even if a treatment *is* ceased (in order to allow a natural death).
2. Patients wrongly diagnosed as hopeless, and who will survive only if the treatment is *not ceased* (in order to allow a natural death).

If a social rule permitting only passive euthanasia were in effect, then doctors and families who "allowed death" would lose only patients in class 2, not those in class 1; whereas if active euthanasia were permitted, at least some patients in class 1 would be needlessly lost. Thus, the consequence of a no-active-euthanasia rule would be to save some lives which could not be saved if both forms of euthanasia were allowed. This reason is not a *decisive* reason for favoring a policy of passive euthanasia, since these classes (1 and 2) are likely to be very small and since there might be counterbalancing reasons (extreme pain, autonomous expression of the patient, etc.) in favor of active euthanasia. But certainly it is *a* reason favoring only passive euthanasia and one which is morally relevant and ought to be considered along with other moral reasons.

IV

It may still be insisted that my case has not touched Rachels' leading claim, for I have not shown, as Rachels puts it, that it is "the bare difference between killing and letting die that makes the difference in these cases" [484]. True, I have not shown this, and in my judgment it cannot be shown. But this concession does not require capitulation to Rachels' argument. I adduced a case which is at the center of our moral intuition that killing is morally different (in at least some cases) from letting die; and I then attempted to account for at least part of the grounds for this belief. The grounds turn out to be other than the *bare* difference, but nevertheless *make* the distinction morally relevant. The identical point can be made regarding the voluntary/involuntary distinction, as it is commonly applied to euthanasia. It is not the bare difference between voluntary euthanasia (i.e., euthanasia with patient consent) and involuntary euthanasia (i.e., without patient consent) that makes one justifiable and one not. Independent moral grounds based on, for example, respect for autonomy or beneficence, or perhaps justice will alone make the moral difference.

In order to illustrate this general claim, let us presume that it is sometimes justified to kill another person and sometimes justified to allow another to die. Suppose, for example, that one may kill in self-defense and may allow to die when a promise has been made to someone that he would be allowed to die. Here conditions of self-defense and promising justify actions. But suppose now that someone A promises in exactly similar circumstances to kill someone B at B's request, and also that someone C allows someone D to die in an act of self-defense. Surely A is obliged equally to kill or to let die if he promised; and surely C is permitted to let D die if it is a matter of defending C's life. If this analysis is correct, then it follows that killing is sometimes right, sometimes wrong, depending on the circumstances, and the same is true of letting die. It is the justifying reasons which make the difference whether an action is right, not merely the kind of action it is.

Now, *if* letting die led to disastrous conclusions but killing did not, then letting die but not killing would be wrong. Consider, for example, a possible world in which dying would be indefinitely prolongable even if all extraordinary therapy were removed and the patient were allowed to die. Suppose that it costs over one million dollars to let each patient die, that nurses consistently commit suicide from caring for those being "allowed to die," that physicians are constantly being successfully sued for malpractice for allowing death by cruel and wrongful means, and that hospitals are uncontrollably overcrowded and their wards filled with communicable diseases which afflict only the dying. Now suppose further that killing in this possible world is quick, painless, and easily monitored. I submit that in this world we would believe that *killing is morally acceptable but that allowing to die is morally unacceptable.* The point of this example is again that it is the circumstances that make the difference, not the bare difference between killing and letting die.

It is, however, worth noticing that there is nothing in the AMA statement which says that the bare difference between killing and letting die itself and alone makes the difference in our differing moral assessments of rightness and wrongness. Rachels forces this interpretation on the statement. Some philosophers may have thought bare difference makes the difference, but there is scant evidence that the AMA or any thoughtful ethicist *must* believe it in order to defend the relevance and importance of the active/passive distinction. When this conclusion is coupled with my earlier argument that from Rachels' paradigm cases it follows only that the active/passive distinction is sometimes, but not always, morally irrelevant, it would seem that his case against the AMA is rendered highly questionable.

V

There remains, however, the important question as to whether we *ought* to accept the distinction between active and passive euthanasia, now that we are clear about (at least one way of drawing) the moral grounds for its invocation. That is, should we employ the distinction in order to judge some acts of euthanasia justified and others not justified? Here, as the hesitant previous paragraph indicates, I am uncertain. This problem is a substantive moral issues—not merely a conceptual one—and would require at a minimum a lengthy assessment of wedge arguments and related utilitarian considerations. In important respects empirical questions are involved in this assessment. We should like to know, and yet have hardly any evidence to indicate, what the consequences would be for our society if we were to allow the use of active means to produce death. The best hope for making such an assessment has seemed to some to rest in analogies to suicide and capital punishment statutes. Here it may reasonably be asked whether recent liberalizations of laws limiting these forms of killing have served as the thin end of a wedge leading to a breakdown of principles protecting life or to widespread violations of moral principles. Nonetheless, such analogies do not seem to me promising, since they are still fairly remote from the pertinent issue of the consequences of allowing active humanitarian killing of one person by another.

It is interesting to notice the outcome of the Kamisar-Williams debate on euthanasia—which is almost exclusively cast by both writers in a consequential, utilitarian framework.[9] At one crucial point in the debate, where possible consequences of laws permitting euthanasia are under discussion, they exchange "perhaps" judgments:

> I [Williams] will return Kamisar the compliment and say: "Perhaps." We are certainly in an area where no solution is going to make things quite easy and happy for everybody, and all sorts of embarrassments may be conjectured. But these embarrassments are not avoided by keeping to the present law: we suffer from them already.[10]

Because of the grave difficulties which stand in the way of making accurate predictions about the impact of liberalized euthanasia laws—especially those that would permit active killing—it is not surprising that those who debate the subject would reach a point of exchanging such "perhaps" judgments. And that is why, so it seems to me, we are uncertain whether to perpetuate or to abandon the active-passive distinction in our moral thinking about euthanasia. I think we *do* perpetuate it in medicine, law, and ethics because we are still somewhat uncertain about the conditions under which *passive* euthanasia should be permitted by law (which is one form of social *rule*). We are unsure about what the consequences will be of the California "Natural Death Act" and all those similar acts passed by other states which have followed in its path. If no untoward results occur, and the balance of the results seems favorable, then we will perhaps be less concerned about further liberalizations of euthanasia laws. If untoward results do occur (on a widespread scale), then we would be most reluctant to accept further liberalizations and might even abolish natural death acts.

In short, I have argued in this section that euthanasia in its active and its passive forms presents us with a dilemma which can be developed by using powerful consequentialist arguments on each side, yet there is little clarity concerning the proper resolution of the dilemma precisely because of our uncertainty regarding proclaimed consequences.

VI

I reach two conclusions at the end of these several arguments. First, I think Rachels is incorrect in arguing that the distinction between active and passive is (always) morally irrelevant. It may well be relevant, and for moral reasons—the reasons adduced in section III above. Second, I think nonetheless that Rachels may ultimately be shown correct in his contention that we ought to dispense with the active-passive distinction—for reasons adduced in sections IV–V. But if he is ultimately judged correct, it will be because we have come to see that some forms of active killing have generally acceptable social consequences, and not primarily because of the arguments he adduces in his paper—even though *something* may be said for each of these arguments. Of course, in one respect I have conceded a great deal to Rachels. The bare difference argument is vital to his position, and I have fully agreed to it. On the other hand, I do not see that the bare difference argument does play or need play a major role in our moral thinking—or in that of the AMA.

NOTES

1. "Active and Passive Euthanasia," *New England Journal of Medicine* 292 (January 9, 1975), 78–80. [All page references in parentheses refer to Rachels's article as reprinted above.]
2. As recorded in the Opinion of Judge Robert Muir, Jr., Docket No. C-201-75 of the Superior Court of New Jersey, Chancery Division, Morris County (November 10, 1975).
3. See Judge Muir's Opinion, p. 18—a slightly different statement but on the subject.
4. This problem of the strength of evidence also emerged in the Quinlin trial, as physicians disagreed whether the evidence was "irrefutable." Such disagreement, when added to the problems of medical fallibility and causal responsibility just outlined, provides in the eyes of some one important argument against the *legalization* of active euthanasia, as perhaps the AMA would agree. Cf. Kamisar's arguments. . . .
5. Among the moral reasons why one is held to be responsible in the first sort of case and not responsible in the second sort are, I believe, the moral grounds for the active/passive distinction under discussion in this section.
6. In *Social Ethics,* as cited in the permission note [i.e., Beauchamp's] to this article.
7. An argument of this form, which I find unacceptable for reasons given below, is Arthur Dyck, "Beneficent Euthanasia and Benemortasia: Alternative Views of Mercy," in M. Kohl, ed., *Beneficent Euthanasia* (Buffalo: Prometheus Books, 1975), pp. 120f. [Reprinted below.]
8. I owe most of this argument to James Rachels, whose comments on an earlier draft of this paper led to several significant alterations.
9. Williams bases his pro-euthanasia argument on the prevention of two consequences: (1) loss of liberty and (2) cruelty. Kamisar bases his anti-euthanasia position on three projected consequences of euthanasia laws: (1) mistaken diagnosis, (2) pressured decisions by seriously ill patients, and (3) the wedge of the laws will lead to legalized involuntary euthanasia. Kamisar admits that individual acts of euthanasia are sometimes justified. It is the rule that he opposes. He is thus clearly a rule-utilitarian, and I believe Williams is as well (cf. his views on children and the senile). Their assessments of wedge arguments are, however, radically different.
10. Glanville Williams, "Mercy-Killing Legislation—A Rejoinder," *Minnesota Law Review,* 43, no. 1 (1958), 5.

BENEFICENT EUTHANASIA AND BENEMORTASIA: ALTERNATIVE VIEWS OF MERCY °

ARTHUR DYCK

Debates about the rightness or wrongness of mercy killing generate heated displays of emotion. There are those who consider it so cruel deliberately to end the lives of relatively powerless individuals who are dying that they tend to imagine that only people who are merciless, like the prototypical Nazi agent, could sanction such acts. At the same time, there are others who find it so cruel to wait for death if a dying person is suffering that they tend to regard opponents of mercy killing as insensitive moral legalists, willing to be inhuman for the sake of obedience to absolute rules. Both the proponents and opponents of mercy killing think of themselves as merciful, but each finds it virtually impossible to think of the other as merciful. Perhaps the reader holds the view that moral debates generally engage our deepest emotions. Regardless of our views on that topic, I would like to examine some of the reasons for the strong disagreements that exist between proponents and opponents of mercy killing.

The debate over mercy killing involves different understandings of what it means to show mercy. Indeed, *Webster's New World Dictionary* [1] attaches at least two quite different meanings to the word *mercy*. On the one hand, mercy refers to a constraint against acting in certain ways. Mercy defined in this way is "a refraining from harming or punishing offenders, enemies, persons in one's power, etc." To kill someone is a commonly recognized form of harm, so that refraining from killing someone, particularly someone in one's power, can be seen as being merciful. The association of "mercy" and "failing to kill or be killed" is rendered explicit when the dictionary further defines mercy as "a fortunate thing; thing to be grateful for; blessing (a *mercy* he wasn't killed)."

On the other hand, the dictionary defines mercy as "a disposition to forgive, pity, or be kind" and as "kind or compassionate treatment; relief of suffering." Those who advocate mercy killing under certain circumstances emphasize this meaning of mercy. For them, killing can be justified when it is done out of kindness for the relief of suffering. Because proponents of mercy killing wish to observe and uphold the general prohibition against killing, they limit relief of suffering to instances where suffering can no longer be seen as serving any useful purpose. They speak, therefore, of needless or unnecessary suffering.

So far I have used the term *mercy killing* where many now use the word *euthanasia*. Originally the Greek word *euthanasia* meant painless, happy death. This meaning still appears as one definition of the term.

° This article first appeared in the book: BENEFICENT EUTHANASIA, edited by Marvin Kohl, 1975, published by Prometheus Books, Buffalo, N.Y., and is reprinted by permission.

However, a second meaning is now usually added that specifies euthanasia as an "act or method of causing death painlessly, so as to end suffering: advocated by some as a way to deal with persons dying of incurable, painful diseases."[2] Increasingly, euthanasia has come to be equated with mercy killing. For the purposes of this essay, therefore, I will use *mercy killing* and *euthanasia* as synonyms referring to the deliberate inducement of a quick, painless death.

The problem I wish to pose in this essay is whether or not the desire and obligation to be merciful or kind commits us to a policy of euthanasia. Some have claimed that there is a moral obligation to be kind or beneficent and that beneficent euthanasia is, therefore, not only morally justified but morally obligatory. This is a claim that deserves the careful scrutiny of any morally conscientious person. Having examined the arguments for beneficent euthanasia, I will then consider the possibility of an alternative notion of what mercy or kindness requires in those situations where mercy killing would appear to be morally justified or even obligatory.

The Ethics of Beneficent Euthanasia

One of the most compelling cases for beneficent euthanasia has been offered by Marvin Kohl.[3] According to Kohl, all of us have a prima facie obligation to act kindly. For the purposes of indicating when euthanasia would be an act of kindness, he specifies the following sense in which an act can be described as kind: ". . . an act is kind if it (a) is intended to be helpful; (b) is done so that, if there be any expectation of receiving remuneration (or the like), the individual would nonetheless act even if it became apparent that there was little chance of his expectation being realized; and (c) results in beneficial treatment for the intended recipient. The Boy or Girl Scout helping an elderly man or woman cross the street, or the proverbial Good Samaritan, are paradigm cases of kindness."[4] From this definition of kindness, Kohl argues that "the necessary, and perhaps sufficient, conditions for beneficent euthanasia are that the act must involve a painless inducement to a quick death; that the act must result in beneficial treatment for the intended recipient; and that, aside from the desire to help the recipient, no other considerations are relevant [a combination of conditions a and b]."[5]

To further clarify what he means by beneficent euthanasia, Kohl offers the reader two paradigm cases. The first case involves a patient (1) who is suffering from an irremediable condition such as cancer (disseminated carcinoma metastasis); (2) who has severe pain; (3) who has to die as a result of his or her condition; (4) who voluntarily favors some means of "easy death"; and (5) no other relevant circumstances, apart from the desire to help the patient. Kohl cites another case as a paradigm, that of a child severely handicapped, but who is not suffering pain and for whom death is not imminent. These two cases are quite different in Kohl's mind, except insofar as they both involve serious and irremediable physical conditions as well as the arousal in others of a wish to help. However, the most important feature that they share in Kohl's thinking is that induced death would probably be considered an act of kindness by most persons. Kohl underlines the importance of this claim because "if true it means that considerations of free choice, the imminence of death, and/or the existence of pain are not always relevant, at least not to judgments of kindness." [6]

With these paradigms in mind and on the assumption that societies and their individual members have a prima facie obligation to treat one another kindly, Kohl infers quite logically that beneficent euthanasia, because it is a species of kindness, is a prima facie obligation. This conclusion seems so obvious to Kohl that he believes that, were it not for some of the objections that have been raised against euthanasia, no further argument on behalf of beneficent euthanasia would be needed. Kohl, however, is concerned with the possible cogency of objections to his arguments for beneficent euthanasia and therefore adds three more arguments on behalf of it. (1) Over against "edge of the wedge" arguments, he asserts that a policy of beneficent euthanasia will result in minimizing suffering and maximizing kindly treatment. (2) Over against those who claim that homicide is intrinsically unjust, he argues that beneficent euthanasia satisfies a fundamental need for human dignity. And (3) over against those who argue that we are not obligated to kill, even out of kindness, he argues that failure to give help in the form of beneficent euthanasia is a failure to live up to the Good Samaritan ideal.

1. *The "Wedge" Argument.* Kohl interprets the "wedge" as claiming that if beneficent euthanasia is morally justified, then euthanasia that cannot be considered to be beneficent will come to be practiced and justified. He sees wedge arguments as based upon two assumptions: first, that all theories of euthanasia ultimately rest upon a principle of utility, and second, that all theories of utility are the same as those held by the Nazis, the implication being that great cruelties rather than kindness will result from such theories.

Kohl disassociates himself from any view that would advocate euthanasia for economic reasons. He distinguishes utility from beneficence. The duty of beneficence is in his view the duty to minimize suffering and to maximize kindly treatment. If there is a "slippery slide" that results from policies of beneficent euthanasia, it will be in the direction of minimizing suffering and maximizing kindly treatment. Secondly, he distinguishes between the kindest way of doing X and the kindest way of treating a human being as a human being. Beneficent euthanasia has for its objective not merely death with dignity but living and dying with dignity. Again the goal is to minimize suffering and to maximize kindness.

In dealing with the wedge argument, Kohl has not yet confronted it in its most powerful form. A wedge argument does not have to predict that certain practices will follow from another. A wedge argument is concerned with the form or logic of moral justifications.

Consider, for example, Kohl's point that it is morally justifiable and obligatory to practice beneficent euthanasia in some cases where the person to be killed does not choose death, is not dying, and is not in pain. It is difficult to see why this would not justify involuntary euthanasia. Suppose, however, that Kohl is not bothered by this, as indeed he should not be. The next question is that of procuring agreement on the narrowness or broadness of the categories of persons to be appropriate candidates for mercy killing. Presumably the criterion that would for Kohl keep the category of cases narrowly defined is that of preserving the dignity of human beings. A child born without limbs, sight, hearing, or a functioning cerebral cortex, while not in pain and not dying, is for Kohl lacking in dignity, or in any event, will be treated with dignity if painlessly put to death.

Some people have argued that mongoloids, however happy or educable, are also lacking in dignity, so that their lives need not always be sustained, even when they could be. What the wedge argument is saying is that there is no logical or easily agreed upon reason why the range of cases should be restricted to Kohl's paradigm or why it would not be beneficial to extend the range even beyond the retarded. For example, we have instances where quadriplegics who are fully conscious and rational are not asked whether they wish to live but are drugged and deprived of life support so that they die. The justification for this is logically the same as the justification for beneficent euthanasia in the case of the severely retarded. The physician considers the life of a quadriplegic to be undignified or one of suffering or, at least, a life not worth living. Such physicians certainly see themselves as acting out of kindness.

The point of the wedge argument is very simple. Since killing is generally wrong, it should be kept to as narrow a range of exceptions as possible. But the argument for beneficent euthanasia, unlike arguments for killing in self-defense, applies logically to a wide range of cases, and the reasons for keeping the range of cases narrow are not reasons on which people will easily agree. In short, arguments for beneficent euthanasia apply logically to either a narrow or a wide range of cases. Whether beneficent euthanasia will be applied to a narrow range of cases does not depend simply on how kind a society is. It will depend also on the various notions that are held about what constitutes a dignified or meaningful human life. About this there will be widespread differences of opinion, many of them based on implicit or explicit theological assumptions.

Furthermore, the wedge argument warns against adopting a principle of minimizing suffering and maximizing kindness. It sounds right, but its logical implications go far beyond the intentions of a Marvin Kohl. If minimizing suffering is linked with killing, we have the unfortunate implication that killing is a quicker, more painless way to alleviate suffering than is the provision of companionship for the lonely and long-term care for those who are either dying or recuperating from illnesses.

Clearly, Kohl does not want to minimize suffering by resort to killing, but only by resort to killing out of kindness. The question remains, then, whether killing out of kindness can be maximized without involving a much wider range of cases than Kohl envisages. I shall come back to the question about whether mercy killing restricted to a narrow range of cases in accord with Kohl's paradigms is something that should be justified despite the very telling difficulties raised by the wedge argument.

2. *Euthanasia as Unjust.* Kohl argues that beneficent euthanasia is consistent with justice because it meets a basic need for dignity and self-respect. Such dignity is clearly exercised when people ask for a quick and painless death in circumstances where they see only pain and suffering as their lot. But Kohl does not want to restrict euthanasia to instances where consent can be obtained. Sometimes, he contends, neither justice nor dignity is served when the misery of an individual increases and consent is not possible.

Here again we see that there are instances in which Kohl would claim the inducement of a painless, quick death confers dignity where otherwise there is none. As was noted previously, however, it is difficult to know how wide a range of cases should be included among those where dignity is obtained through a nonvoluntarily induced, painless death. Those who induce this death will no doubt have varying notions as to what kind of misery and how much of it renders a life undignified. This is precisely the problem that the wedge argument points to. If euthanasia were practiced on others by someone like Kohl, it would be used as a last resort. If, however, there were a general policy of considering beneficent euthanasia a moral obligation and accompanying laws that permitted people to live up to that obligation, its practice might be quite different from what Kohl envisages and sanctions. This would be true not because killing is contagious (Kohl has quite properly objected to that argument) but because the notion of dignity is open to a wide range of meanings. It is also true, as was noted previously, that agreement on what confers dignity is difficult to obtain. In any event, those who advocate beneficent euthanasia should clearly specify what they mean by dignity and how they justify their invocation of that term.

3. *The Obligation to Avoid Killing.* Kohl recognizes that there are some who argue that one is not obligated to help the suffering in every way possible, particularly if such help entails killing. On Kohl's view an important assumption in that argument is that cruelty is to be avoided. Kohl contends that beneficent euthanasia also seeks to avoid cruelty. The difference between opponents and proponents of euthanasia here is over the meaning of what constitutes cruelty and whether or not avoidance of

cruelty is morally sufficient. Kohl argues that those who oppose euthanasia on grounds that it is cruel interpret cruelty in a narrow sense to mean deliberately causing unnecessary pain or harm. They do not use the broader sense of the term, which refers to deliberately causing or allowing needless pain or harm. As a consequence, Kohl maintains, these opponents of euthanasia are too prone to tolerate or excuse human misery.

Kohl calls this desire to avoid cruelty a "taboo" morality, it tells us what not to do, but not what to do. A society that avoids cruelty is admittedly better than one that does not. However, this "taboo" morality is contrary to the ideal of the Good Samaritan, who unlike those who walk past the injured or the sick, seeks to help. Aversion to cruelty may not harm anyone, but it is not, he argues, a sufficient principle of action if it does not include the obligation to help and be beneficent to others.

These arguments by Kohl are not consistent with his usual fairness to opponents. Those who oppose euthanasia because it is an act of killing, and as such is cruel, are trying to prevent death where possible. Those who share with the Good Samaritan the concern to keep somebody from dying do substitute care for killing or letting die. That is surely one of the major reasons for opposing euthanasia, namely, to help people stay alive even when that may not appear to be something they devoutly wish. Kohl would seem to qualify the ideal of the Good Samaritan, so that if the dying man on the road to Jericho had asked the Good Samaritan to help him by making his death painless and quick, presumably the Good Samaritan would have had the obligation to do so, depending upon whether he felt that the injured man was indeed dying.

We see then how we have come full circle. In effect, Kohl is taking the position that only proponents of euthanasia wish positively to exercise mercy, whereas opponents of euthanasia are simply trying to avoid doing something wrong and are so bent on that that they are not willing or able to be merciful. Whether or not one favors euthanasia and whether or not it is considered an obligation would seem, then, to depend on one's notion of what is merciful. Another significant ground for differences between proponents and opponents of euthanasia lies in opposing or sometimes unexamined notions of human dignity.

An Ethic of Benemortasia

It is not possible here to do more than sketch some of the main contours of a policy that accepts mercy as a moral obligation but rejects beneficent euthanasia or mercy killing. Such a sketch will, however, clarify the different conceptions of mercy and human dignity that distinguish an ethic of benemortasia from an ethic of beneficent euthanasia.

Because euthanasia no longer functions as a merely descriptive term for a happy or good death, it is necessary to invent another term for this purpose. I have chosen the word "benemortasia," which is derived from two familiar Latin words, *bene* (good) and *mors* (death). What *bene* in bene-mortasia means depends upon the ethical framework that one adopts in order to interpret what it is to experience a good death, or at least what would be the most morally responsible way to behave in the face of death, either one's own or that of others. The ethic of benemortasia suggested in this essay is concerned with how we ought to behave toward those who are dying or whose death would appear to be a merciful event. It is not neces-sarily the only ethic one might or should adopt, nor is it complete in scope as presented here.

The ethic of benemortasia that I wish to argue for recognizes mercy or kindness as a moral obligation. Mercy is understood in at least two ways: first, it is merciful not to kill; second, it is merciful to provide care for the dying and the irremediably handicapped where consent is obtained without coercion. (Instances where voluntary consent to care being offered cannot be obtained from its intended recipients, as in cases of comatose or severely retarded patients, raise special issues that will be discussed later.)

The injunction not to kill is part of a total effort to prevent the destruc-tion of human beings and of the human community. It is an absolute pro-hibition in the sense that no society can be indifferent about the taking of human life. Any act, insofar as it is an act of taking a human life, is wrong; that is to say, taking a human life is a wrong-making characteristic of actions.

To say, however, that killing is prima facie wrong does not mean that an act of killing may never be justified.[7] For example, a person's effort to prevent someone's death may lead to the death of the attacker. However, we can morally justify that act of intervention because it is an act of saving a life, but not because it is an act of taking a life. If it were simply an act of taking a life, it would be wrong.

Advocates of beneficent euthanasia would generally agree that one should not kill innocent people, particularly those who are as powerless to defend themselves as the dying and the handicapped. However, restraint against harming people is not enough. What about positive actions to relieve pain and suffering?

For our ethic of benemortasia, at least the following kind of care can be given to patients who are considered to be imminently dying: (1) relief of pain, (2) relief of suffering, (3) respect for a patient's right to refuse treatment, and (4) universal provision of health care.

1. *Relief of Pain.* There is widespread agreement among those who oppose beneficent euthanasia but who believe in mercy that pain relief can be offered to patients even when it means shortening the dying process. This is not considered killing or assisting in a killing because the cause of death is the terminal illness of the patient, and the shortening of the dying process has to do with a choice on the part of a patient to live with less pain during his last days. All of us make choices about whether we will seek

pain relief. When we are not terminally ill we also make choices about the kind of care we do or do not seek. There is no reason to deny such freedom to someone who is dying. Indeed, there is every reason to be especially solicitous of a person who is terminally ill. There is no legal or moral objection to the administration of pain relief provided it is for that purpose and not for the purpose of killing someone. This means that one does not knowingly give an overdose of a pain reliever, but rather concentrates on dosages that are sufficient for relief of pain, knowing that at some point the dose administered will be final. Indeed the official regulations of Roman Catholic hospitals in this country explicitly permit hastening the dying process through the administration of pain relief.

2. *Relief of Suffering.* Suffering is not the same as pain, although in instances where pain is extremely excruciating, it is virtually impossible to avoid suffering. We know, for example, that physicians can relieve suffering in a variety of ways. There is some evidence that patients who know they are dying generally suffer less and are less inclined to ask for pain relief than those who do not know that they are dying. We know also that one of the major sources of suffering for dying people is loneliness and lack of companionship. Our ethic of benemortasia would consider it not only merciful but part of good care in the strictest medical sense to make provision for companionship, whether with medical, paramedical, or other kinds of persons brought to the hospital expressly for this purpose. Churches and other voluntary organizations often assist in this way. Note also the splendid care provided by someone like Elisabeth Kubler-Ross, who is an opponent of beneficent euthanasia but a staunch proponent and practitioner of mercy in the form of relief of suffering.[8]

3. *A Patient's Right to Refuse Treatment.* Dying patients are also living patients. They retain the same right as everyone else voluntarily to leave the hospital or to refuse specific kinds of care. Indeed, the right to refuse care is legally recognized. No new law is required to allow patients to exercise their rights. One of the important good effects of the whole discussion of euthanasia is that all of us, including health professionals, are becoming more sensitive to this right to refuse care. Given the concern not to kill, one would continue to expect that physicians who hold out some hope of saving a life would usually presuppose consent to try to save patients, who in a desperate state may be expressing a wish to die.

Those who are irreversibly comatose or those who, as in Kohl's paradigm, have no functioning of the cerebral cortex, no use of muscles, and so forth, pose special difficulties, both for an ethic of beneficent euthanasia and an ethic of benemortasia. In such instances we are dealing with very tragic circumstances. No decision we make is totally satisfactory from a moral point of view. From the standpoint of our ethic of benemortasia, there is a strong presumption to continue supporting the irreversibly comatose and the severely brain-damaged until there is virtually no reasonable hope of sustaining life, apart from measures that go far beyond ordinary care. There comes a point when the decision to let die can be made out of mercy and also out of the recognition that for the irreversibly comatose death is inevitable and that for the severely brain-damaged child it would be merciful to withhold more than ordinary care in the face of the next serious bout of illness, recognizing also that such episodes of illness will be frequent and devastating. The difference between beneficent euthanasia and our ethic of benemortasia is that, whereas the former would deliberately induce death, the latter, as a last resort after making every effort to save and repair life, mercifully retreats in the face of death's inevitability.

4. *Universal Health Care.* In order to be merciful as well as just in the provision of care for dying and severely handicapped people, no single person or family should have to bear alone the burden of extensive medical costs. It is notorious that poor people are more often and much sooner let go as dying persons than those who have ample financial resources. Those concerned with mercy should also bear in mind that the much higher rates of maternal and infant death suffered by blacks is one of the more subtle, systematic ways in which a society can permit euthanasia. It is difficult to imagine that anyone could call such subtle forms of euthanasia in any sense merciful or beneficent. Discussions of beneficent euthanasia should not overlook these subtle forms of injustice to people in need of care.

So far, in discussing an ethic of benemortasia, I have stressed the ways in which mercy can be extended to patients without inducing death. However, the proponents of beneficent euthanasia would not be completely satisfied in all cases with the form that mercy takes in our ethic of benemortasia. Kohl emphasizes a quick, painless death. Our ethic of benemortasia emphasizes erring on the side of the protection of life, while still minimizing suffering. In order to understand this remaining difference between beneficent euthanasia and our ethic of benemortasia, it is necessary to see that they differ with respect to their notions of what constitutes human dignity.

Proponents of beneficent euthanasia, including Kohl, tend to rest their case on the following kinds of presuppositions: (1) that the dignity that attaches to personhood by reason of the freedom to make moral choices demands also the freedom to take one's own life or to have it taken when this freedom is absent or lost; (2) that there is such a thing as a life not worth living, a life that lacks dignity, whether by reason of distress, illness, physical or mental handicaps, or even sheer despair for whatever reason; (3) that what is sacred or supreme in value is the "human dignity" that resides in the rational capacity to choose and control life and death.

Our ethic of benemortasia as outlined here rests on the following kinds of presuppositions about human dignity: (1) that the dignity that attaches to personhood by reason of the freedom to make moral choices includes the freedom to refuse noncurative, life-prolonging interventions when one is dying, but does not extend to taking one's life or causing the death of someone who is dying, because that would be unjustified killing (2) that every life has some worth; (3) that notions of dignity are judged on the basis of what is right, merciful, and just, obligations that the dying and those who care for them share. Being less than perfect, humans require constraints on their decisions regarding the dying. No human being or human community can presume to know who deserves to live or die. From a religious perspective, some would leave that kind of decision to God.[9]

There are two critical differences between these two sets of presuppositions. Whereas in the ethic of beneficent euthanasia, life of a certain kind, or life having dignity, is what has value, in our ethic of benemortasia, life as such retains some value whatever form it takes. This does not mean that an opponent of beneficent euthanasia cannot let die or administer pain relief that may hasten death. What it means is that life as a value is always a consideration; that is one reason why the onus is on those who believe a person should be allowed to die to give stringent and compelling reasons for their belief.

Another critical difference between these two ethical views is that the notion of mercy in our ethic of benemortasia is controlled by what is considered right, particularly the injunction not to kill, on which a wide moral and social consensus exists. The notion of mercy in an ethic of beneficent euthanasia as depicted, for example, by Kohl and Joseph Fletcher [10] is controlled by the conception of human dignity. One of the reasons that Kohl and Fletcher insist upon including quick death is their belief that certain lives are quite undignified and only become dignified in death. It is for this reason that Fletcher can speak of a right to die.

It is precisely this appeal to some notion of dignity to justify killing that evokes "wedge" arguments. As I indicated previously, there are serious and widespread differences among people about what constitutes human dignity. If who shall live and who shall die is made contingent upon these widely divergent views of human dignity, moral and legal policies that justify mercy killing can in principle justify a very narrow and/or a very wide range of instances in which it will be claimed that we as a society are obligated to kill someone. No one using "wedge" arguments against beneficent euthanasia need predict whether at a given moment in history a country like the United States will or will not, if euthanasia becomes lawful, use such laws to indulge in widespread killing of helpless people. The point of the wedge argument is that logically and actually there is no provision made by proponents of beneficent euthanasia for limiting in principle the notion of human dignity and for guaranteeing some kind of consensus about what constitutes human dignity. In the absence of such a consensus, it is understandable that some people having certain notions of human dignity will welcome a policy of beneficent euthanasia, whereas others will be fearful of their lives should euthanasia be legalized.

The debate concerning what constitutes human dignity cannot be easily resolved. There are deep philosophical and religious differences that divide people on that issue. However, the injunction not to kill is not divisive in this way. Much of the emotion generated by the debate over euthanasia finds its source precisely in the understandable and deep uneasiness that many individuals feel when they are asked to move away from a stringent notion of refraining from acts of killing, regarding which there is widespread agreement, and to make judgments about who shall live and who shall die on the basis of conceptions of human dignity, regarding which there are deep religious, ethnic, philosophical, and other differences. Anyone who would argue for beneficent euthanasia needs to confront this difficult and divisive aspect of his proposal. Kohl and those who share his point of view will either have to present a notion of human dignity on which widespread agreement can be obtained or make a case for beneficent euthanasia that does not depend on such a complex set of assumptions about human dignity. Until one or the other of these cases is rendered plausible by proponents of beneficent euthanasia, many of us will continue to work out and try to refine an ethic of benemortasia.

NOTES

1. *Webster's New World Dictionary* (Second College Edition), ed. David B. Guralnik (Englewood Cliffs, N.J.: Prentice-Hall, and New York: World Publishing Co., 1970), p. 889.

2. *Ibid.*, p. 484.

3. See Marvin Kohl, "Understanding the Case for Beneficent Euthanasia," *Science, Medicine and Man*, 1 (1973), pp. 111–121; and "Beneficent Euthanasia," *The Humanist* (July/August 1974), pp. 9–11.

4. Marvin Kohl, "Understanding the Case for Beneficent Euthanasia," p. 112.

5. *Ibid.*, pp. 112–113.

6. *Ibid.*, p. 113.

7. W. D. Ross, *The Right and the Good* (London: Oxford Univ. Press, 1930).

8. Elisabeth Kubler-Ross, *On Death and Dying* (New York: Macmillan, 1970).

9. See Arthur J. Dyck, "An Alternative to the Ethic of Euthanasia," in R. H. Williams, ed., *To Live and To Die: When, Why and How?* (New York: Springer-Verlag, 1973), pp. 98–112, for a fuller discussion of the way in which these presuppositions emerge.

10. See the articles by Marvin Kohl listed in note 3 and Joseph Fletcher, "The Patient's Right To Die," in A. B. Downing, ed., *Euthanasia and the Right to Death* (New York: Humanities Press, 1971).

16
Modification of Human Life by Biomedical Research

Homo sapiens is the great intervener, the ingenious modifier. We not only learn the secrets of how we were modified by natural processes over millions of years, we also learn how to become the main element in our own modification. Leon Kass takes up the theme of Francis Bacon written in the Renaissance period: Power over nature is "for the relief of man's estate." He does not share the optimism of Bacon and others that such power will be wisely used, or have the hoped-for results. He recites the dangers of directing our own evolution, or changing the material on which we work, ourselves. The twenty-first century may see an addition of from twenty to forty years in the human life span. Those who would have died and not reproduced may now live to make their contribution to the gene pool. Cloning of amphibians has been accomplished, and human and non-human cells have been fused experimentally. But if we would abort all carriers of defective genes we would undertake a staggering program, as each person carries four to eight recessive, lethal genes.

Behavior modification is a big item on the horizon; already electronic stimulation of the brain enables each person to carry around his or her own do-it-yourself pleasure kit.

Decisions as to whether to develop and use biomedical technology are based on value judgments. Science gives means, not ends. Utilitarian computation of costs and benefits needs light shone upon their value assumptions and, above all, the inclusion of social costs, not merely economic. And the usual question of "Who decides?" is the wrong one, for it should be: "How shall the costs and benefits be distributed?"

Every new human power is power over other human beings. Population control, for instance, an abstract good, will probably be forced. Given control over reproduction, on what basis will this couple be allowed to reproduce and that one not? What will it do to us when

510

someone, perhaps ourselves included, knows to what crimes or fol-
lies or genius our genes incline us?

People can and do dehumanize and demoralize themselves by tools
that medicine has placed in their hands: adding years to life, and
finding old age lonely; lying comatose indefinitely while the machinery works its mindless magic; seeking and finding Huxley's frightful
"brave new world."

Kass believes that the lessons of the past are that what can be
done will be done, that someone usually finds profit, power, or satisfaction of some desire in making the technologically possible actual.
Official and public *laissez faire* does not avoid controls over research
and its applications, it only delays them. Nor will those controls that
are inevitable be adequate if confined to one's own national boundaries, for science and technology are international in their effects. He
closes with a plea that he who proposes a change bears the burden
of proof that the change is needed and is beneficial, and for an educated and alert public.

THE NEW BIOLOGY: WHAT PRICE
RELIEVING MAN'S ESTATE? *

LEON R. KASS

Recent advances in biology and medicine suggest that we may be rapidly acquiring the power to modify and control the capacities and activities of men by direct intervention and manipulation of their bodies and
minds. Certain means are already in use or at hand, others await the solution of relatively minor technical problems, while yet others, those offering
perhaps the most precise kind of control, depend upon further basic research. Biologists who have considered these matters disagree on the question of how much how soon, but all agree that the power for "human engineering," to borrow from the jargon, is coming and that it will probably
have profound social consequences.

These developments have been viewed both with enthusiasm and with
alarm; they are only just beginning to receive serious attention. Several biologists have undertaken to inform the public about the technical possibilities,
present and future. Practitioners of social science "futurology" are attempting to predict and describe the likely social consequences of and public responses to the new technologies. Lawyers and legislators are exploring institutional innovations for assessing new technologies. All of these activities

* From Leon R. Kass, "The New Biology: What Price Relieving Man's Estate?" *Science*
(Nov. 19, 1971), pp. 779–788. Reprinted by permission of the author and *Science*.
Copyright 1971, by the American Association for the Advancement of Science.

are based upon the hope that we can harness the new technology of man for the betterment of mankind.

Yet this commendable aspiration points to another set of questions, which are, in my view, sorely neglected—questions that inquire into the meaning of phrases such as the "betterment of mankind." A *full* understanding of the new technology of man requires an exploration of ends, values, standards. What ends will or should the new techniques serve? What values should guide society's adjustments? By what standards should the assessment agencies assess? Behind these questions lie others: what is a good man, what is a good life for man, what is a good community? This article is an attempt to provoke discussion of these neglected and important questions.

While these questions about ends and ultimate ends are never unimportant or irrelevant, they have rarely been more important or more relevant. That this is so can be seen once we recognize that we are dealing here with a group of technologies that are in a decisive respect unique: the object upon which they operate is man himself. The technologies of energy or food production, of communication, of manufacture, and of motion greatly alter the implements available to man and the conditions in which he uses them. In contrast, the biomedical technology works to change the user himself. To be sure, the printing press, the automobile, the television, and the jet airplane have greatly altered the conditions under which and the way in which men live; but men as biological beings have remained largely unchanged. They have been, and remain, able to accept or reject, to use and abuse these technologies; they choose, whether wisely or foolishly, the ends to which these technologies are means. Biomedical technology may make it possible to change the inherent capacity for choice itself. Indeed, both those who welcome and those who fear the advent of "human engineering" ground their hopes and fears in the same prospect: *that man can for the first time recreate himself.*

Engineering the engineer seems to differ in kind from engineering his engine. Some have argued, however, that biomedical engineering does not differ qualitatively from toilet training, education, and moral teachings—all of which are forms of so-called "social engineering," which has man as its object, and is used by one generation to mold the next. In reply, it must at least be said that the techniques which have hitherto been employed are feeble and inefficient when compared to those on the horizon. This quantitative difference rests in part on a qualitative difference in the means of intervention. The traditional influences operate by speech or by symbolic deeds. They pay tribute to man as the animal who lives by speech and who understands the meanings of actions. Also, their effects are, in general, reversible, or at least subject to attempts at reversal. Each person has greater or lesser power to accept or reject or abandon them. In contrast, biomedical engineering circumvents the human context of speech and meaning, bypasses choice, and goes directly to work to modify the human material itself. Moreover, the changes wrought may be irreversible.

In addition, there is an important practical reason for considering the biomedical technology apart from other technologies. The advances we shall examine are fruits of a large, humane project dedicated to the conquest of disease and the relief of human suffering. The biologist and physician, regardless of their private motives, are seen, with justification, to be the well-wishers and benefactors of mankind. Thus, in a time in which technological advance is more carefully scrutinized and increasingly criticized, biomedical developments are still viewed by most people as benefits largely without qualification. The price we pay for these developments is thus more likely to go unrecognized. For this reason, I shall consider only the dangers and costs of biomedical advance. As the benefits are well known, there is no need to dwell upon them here. My discussion is deliberately partial.

I begin with a survey of the pertinent technologies. Next, I will consider some of the basic ethical and social problems in the use of these technologies. Then, I will briefly raise some fundamental questions to which these problems point. Finally, I shall offer some very general reflections on what is to be done.

The Biomedical Technologies

The biomedical technologies can be usefully organized into three groups, according to their major purpose: (i) control of death and life, (ii) control of human potentialities, and (iii) control of human achievement. The corresponding technologies are (i) medicine, especially the arts of prolonging life and of controlling reproduction, (ii) genetic engineering, and (iii) neurological and psychological manipulation. I shall briefly summarize each group of techniques.

1) *Control of death and life.* Previous medical triumphs have greatly increased average life expectancy. Yet other developments, such as organ transplantation or replacement and research into aging, hold for the promise of increasing not just the average, but also the maximum life expectancy. Indeed, medicine seems to be sharpening its tools to do battle with death itself, as if death were just one more disease.

More immediately and concretely, available tchniques of prolonging life —respirators, cardiac pacemakers, artificial kidneys—are already in the lists against death. Ironically, the success of these devices in forestalling death has introduced confusion in determining that death has, in fact, occurred. The traditional signs of life—heartbeat and respiration—can now be maintained entirely by machines. Some physicians are now busily trying to devise so-called "new definitions of death," while others maintain that the technical advances show that death is not a concrete event at all, but rather a gradual process, like twilight, incapable of precise temporal localization.

The real challenge to death will come from research into aging and senescence, a field just entering puberty. Recent studies suggest that aging is a genetically controlled process, distinct from disease, but one that can be manipulated and altered by diet or drugs. Extrapolating from animal studies, some scientists have suggested that a decrease in the rate of aging might also be achieved simply by effecting a very small decrease in human body temperature. According to some estimates, by the year 2000 it may be technically possible to add from 20 to 40 useful years to the period of middle life.

Medicine's success in extending life is already a major cause of excessive population growth: death control points to birth control. Although we are already technically competent, new techniques for lowering fertility and chemical agents for inducing abortion will greatly enhance our powers over conception and gestation. Problems of definition have been raised here as well. The need to determine when individuals acquire enforceable legal rights gives society an interest in the definition of human life and of the time when it begins. These matters are too familiar to need elaboration.

Technologies to conquer infertility proceed alongside those to promote it. The first successful laboratory fertilization of human egg by human sperm was reported in 1969 (1). In 1970, British scientists learned how to grow human embryos in the laboratory up to at least the blastocyst stage [that is, to the age of 1 week (2)]. We may soon hear about the next stage, the successful reimplantation of such an embryo into a woman previously infertile because of oviduct disease. The development of an artificial placenta, now under investigation, will make possible full laboratory control of fertilization and gestation. In addition, sophisticated biochemical and cytological techniques of monitoring the "quality" of the fetus have been and are being developed and used. These developments not only give us more power over the generation of human life, but make it possible to manipulate and to modify the quality of the human material.

2) *Control of human potentialities.* Genetic engineering, when fully developed, will wield two powers not shared by ordinary medical practice. Medicine treats existing individuals and seeks to correct deviations from a norm of health. Genetic engineering, in contrast, will be able to make changes that can be transmitted to succeeding generations and will be able to create new capacities, and hence to establish new norms of health and fitness.

Nevertheless, one of the major interests in genetic manipulation is strictly medical: to develop treatments for individuals with inherited diseases. Genetic disease is prevalent and increasing, thanks partly to medical advances that enable those affected to survive and perpetuate their mutant genes. The hope is that normal copies of the appropriate gene, obtained biologically or synthesized chemically, can be introduced into defective individuals to correct their deficiencies. This *therapeutic* use of genetic technology appears to be far in the future. Moreover, there is some doubt that it will ever be practical, since the same end could be more easily achieved by transplanting cells or organs that could compensate for the missing or defective gene product.

Far less remote are technologies that could serve *eugenic* ends. Their development has been endorsed by those concerned about a general deterioration of the human gene pool and by others who believe that even an undeteriorated human gene pool needs upgrading. Artificial insemination with selected donors, the eugenic proposal of Herman Muller (3), has been possible for several years because of the perfection of methods for long-term storage of human spermatozoa. The successful maturation of human oocytes in the laboratory and their subsequent fertilization now make it possible to select donors of ova as well. But a far more suitable technique for eugenic purposes will soon be upon us—namely, nuclear transplantation, or cloning. Bypassing the lottery of sexual recombination, nuclear transplantation permits the asexual reproduction or copying of an already developed individual. The nucleus of a mature but unfertilized egg is replaced by a nucleus obtained from a specialized cell of an adult organism or embryo (for example, a cell from the intestines or the skin). The egg with its transplanted nucleus develops as if it had been fertilized and, barring complications, will give rise to a normal adult organism. Since almost all the hereditary material (DNA) of a cell is contained within its nucleus, the renucleated egg and the individual into which it develops are genetically identical to the adult organism that was the source of the donor nucleus. Cloning could be used to produce sets of unlimited numbers of genetically identical individuals, each set derived from a single parent. Cloning has been successful in amphibians and is now being tried in mice; its extension to man merely requires the solution of certain technical problems.

Production of man-animal chimeras by the introduction of selected nonhuman material into developing human embryos is also expected. Fusion of human and nonhuman cells in tissue culture has already been achieved.

Other, less direct means for influencing the gene pool are already available, thanks to our increasing ability to identify and diagnose genetic diseases. Genetic counselors can now detect biochemically and cytologically a variety of severe genetic defects (for example, Mongolism, Tay-Sachs disease) while the fetus is still in utero. Since treatments are at present largely unavailable, diagnosis is often followed by abortion of the affected fetus. In the future, more sensitive tests will also permit the detection of heterozygote carriers, the unaffected individuals who carry but a single dose of a given deleterious gene. The eradication of a given genetic disease might then be attempted by aborting all such carriers. In fact, it was recently suggested that the fairly common disease cystic fibrosis could be completely eliminated over the next 40 years by screening all pregnancies and aborting the 17,000,000 unaffected fetuses that will carry a single gene for this disease. Such zealots need to be reminded of the consequences should each geneticist be allowed an equal assault on his favorite genetic disorder, given that each human being is a carrier for some four to eight such recessive, lethal genetic diseases.

3) *Control of human achievement.* Although human achievement depends at least in part upon genetic endowment, heredity determines only

the material upon which experience and education impose the form. The limits of many capacities and powers of an individual are indeed genetically determined, but the nurturing and perfection of these capacities depend upon other influences. Neurological and psychological maniipulation hold forth the promise of controlling the development of human capacities, particularly those long considered most distinctively human: speech, thought, choice, emotion, memory, and imagination.

These techniques are now in a rather primitive state because we understand so little about the brain and mind. Nevertheless, we have already seen the use of electrical stimulation of the human brain to produce sensations of intense pleasure and to control rage, the use of brain surgery (for example, frontal lobotomy) for the relief of severe anxiety, and the use of aversive conditioning with electric shock to treat sexual perversion. Operant-conditioning techniques are widely used, apparently with success, in schools and mental hospitals. The use of so-called consciousness-expanding and hallucinogenic drugs is widespread, to say nothing of tranquilizers and stimulants. We are promised drugs to modify memory, intelligence, libido, and aggressiveness.

The following passages from a recent book by Yale neurophysiologist José Delgado—a book instructively entitled *Physical Control of the Mind: Toward a Psychocivilized Society*—should serve to make this discussion more concrete. In the early 1950's, it was discovered that, with electrodes placed in certain discrete regions of their brains, animals would repeatedly and indefatigably press levers to stimulate their own brains, with obvious resultant enjoyment. Even starving animals preferred stimulating these so-called pleasure centers to eating. Delgado comments on the electrical stimulation of a similar center in a human subject (4, p. 185).

> [T]he patient reported a pleasant tingling sensation in the left side of her body 'from my face down to the bottom of my legs.' She started giggling and making funny comments, stating that she enjoyed the sensation 'very much.' Repetition of these stimulations made the patient more communicative and flirtatious, and she ended by openly expressing her desire to marry the therapist.

And one further quotation from Delgado (4, p. 88).

> Leaving wires inside of a thinking brain may appear unpleasant or dangerous, but actually the many patients who have undergone this experience have not been concerned about the fact of being wired, nor have they felt any discomfort due to the presence of conductors in their heads. Some women have shown their feminine adaptability to circumstances by wearing attractive hats or wigs to conceal their electrical headgear, and many people have been able to enjoy a normal life as out-patients, returning to the clinic periodically for examination and stimulation. In a few cases in which contacts were located in pleasurable areas, patients have had the opportunity to stimulate their own brains by pressing the button of a portable instrument, and this procedure is reported to have therapeutic benefits.

It bears repeating that the sciences of neurophysiology and psychophar-macology are in their infancy. The techniques that are now available are crude, imprecise, weak, and unpredictable, compared to those that may flow from a more mature neurobiology.

Basic Ethical and Social Problems in the Use of Biomedical Technology

After this cursory review of the powers now and soon to be at our dis-posal, I turn to the questions concerning the use of these powers. First, we must recognize that questions of use of science and technology are always moral and political questions, never simply technical ones. All private or public decisions to develop or to use biomedical technology—and decisions *not* to do so—inevitably contain judgments about value. This is true even if the values guiding those decisions are not articulated or made clear, as in-deed they often are not. Secondly, the value judgments cannot be derived from biomedical science. This is true even if scientists themselves make the decisions.

These important points are often overlooked for at least three reasons.

1) They are obscured by those who like to speak of "the control of nature by science." It is men who control, not that abstraction "science." Science may provide the means, but men choose the ends; the choice of ends comes from beyond science.

2) Introduction of new technologies often appears to be the result of no decision whatsoever, or of the culmination of decisions too small or uncon-scious to be recognized as such. What can be done is done. However, some-one is deciding on the basis of some notions of desirability, no matter how self-serving or altruistic.

3) Desires to gain or keep money and power no doubt influence much of what happens, but these desires can also be formulated as reasons and then discussed and debated.

Insofar as our society has tried to deliberate about questions of use, how has it done so? Pragmatists that we are, we prefer a utilitarian calculus: we weigh "benefits" against "risks," and we weigh them for both the individual and "society." We often ignore the fact that the very definitions of "a benefit" and "a risk" are themselves based upon judgments about value. In the bio-medical areas just reviewed, the benefits are considered to be self-evident: prolongation of life, control of fertility and of population size, treatment and prevention of genetic disease, the reduction of anxiety and aggressiveness, and the enhancement of memory, intelligence, and pleasure. The assessment of risk is, in general, simply pragmatic—will the technique work effectively and reliably, how much will it cost, will it do detectable bodily harm, and who will complain if we proceed with development? As these questions are familiar and congenial, there is no need to belabor them.

The very pragmatism that makes us sensitive to considerations of economic cost often blinds us to the larger social costs exacted by biomedical advances. For one thing, we seem to be unaware that we may not be able to maximize all the benefits, that several of the goals we are promoting conflict with each other. On the one hand, we seek to control population growth by lowering fertility; on the other hand, we develop techniques to enable every infertile woman to bear a child. On the one hand, we try to extend the lives of individuals with genetic disease; on the other, we wish to eliminate deleterious genes from the human population. I am not urging that we resolve these conflicts in favor of one side or the other, but simply that we recognize that such conflicts exist. Once we do, we are more likely to appreciate that most "progress" is heavily paid for in terms not generally included in the simple utilitarian calculus.

To become sensitive to the larger costs of biomedical progress, we must attend to several serious ethical and social questions. I will briefly discuss three of them: (i) questions of distributive justice, (ii) questions of the use and abuse of power, and (iii) questions of self-degradation and dehumanization.

Distributive Justice

The introduction of any biomedical technology presents a new instance of an old problem—how to distribute scarce resources justly. We should assume that demand will usually exceed supply. Which people should receive a kidney transplant or an artificial heart? Who should get the benefits of genetic therapy or of brain stimulation? Is "first-come, first served" the fairest principle? Or are certain people "more worthy," and if so, on what grounds?

It is unlikely that we will arrive at answers to these questions in the form of deliberate decisions. More likely, the problem of distribution will continue to be decided ad hoc and locally. If so, the consequence will probably be a sharp increase in the already far too great inequality of medical care. The extreme case will be longevity, which will probably be, at first, obtainable only at great expense. Who is likely to be able to buy it? Do conscience and prudence permit us to enlarge the gap between rich and poor, especially with respect to something as fundamental as life itself?

Questions of distributive justice also arise in the earlier decisions to acquire new knowledge and to develop new techniques. Personnel and facilities for medical research and treatment are scarce resources. Is the development of a new technology the best use of the limited resources, given current circumstances? How should we balance efforts aimed at prevention against those aimed at cure, or either of these against efforts to redesign the species? How should we balance the delivery of available levels of care against further basic research? More fundamentally, how should we balance efforts in biology and medicine against efforts to eliminate poverty, pollution, urban decay, discrimination, and poor education? This last question about distribution is perhaps the most profound. We should reflect upon the social consequences of seducing many of our brightest young people to spend their lives locating the biochemical defects in rare genetic diseases, while our more serious problems go begging. The current squeeze on money for research provides us with an opportunity to rethink and reorder our priorities.

Problems of distributive justice are frequently mentioned and discussed, but they are hard to resolve in a rational manner. We find them especially difficult because of the enormous range of conflicting values and interests that characterizes our pluralistic society. We cannot agree—unfortunately, we often do not even try to agree—on standards for just distribution. Rather, decisions tend to be made largely out of a clash of competing interests. Thus, regrettably, the question of how to distribute justly often gets reduced to who shall decide how to distribute. The question about justice has led us to the question about power.

Use and Abuse of Power

We have difficulty recognizing the problems of the exercise of power in the biomedical enterprise because of our delight with the wondrous fruits it has yielded. This is ironic because the notion of power is absolutely central to the modern conception of science. The ancients conceived of science as the *understanding* of nature, pursued for its own sake. We moderns view science as power, as *control* over nature; the conquest of nature "for the relief of man's estate" was the charge issued by Francis Bacon, one of the leading architects of the modern scientific project (5).

Another source of difficulty is our fondness for speaking of the abstraction "Man." I suspect that we prefer to speak figuratively about "Man's power over Nature" because it obscures an unpleasant reality about human affairs. It is in fact particular men who wield power, not Man. What we really mean by "Man's power over Nature" is a power exercised by some men over other men, with a knowledge of nature as their instrument.

While applicable to technology in general, these reflections are especially pertinent to the technologies of human engineering, with which men deliberately exercise power over future generations. An excellent discussion of this question is found in *The Abolition of Man*, by C. S. Lewis (6).

> It is, of course, a commonplace to complain that men have hitherto used badly, and against their fellows, the powers that science has given them. But that is not the point I am trying to make. I am not speaking of particular corruptions and abuses which an increase of moral virtue would cure: I am considering what the thing called "Man's power over Nature" must always and essentially be. . . .
> In reality, of course, if any one age really attains, by eugenics and scientific education, the power to make its descendants what it pleases, all men who live after it are the patients of that power. They are weaker, not stronger: for though we may have put wonderful machines in their hands, we have pre-

ordained how they are to use them. . . . The real picture is that of one dominant age . . . which resists all previous ages most successfully and dominates all subsequent ages most irresistibly, and thus is the real master of the human species. But even within this master generation (itself an infinitesimal minority of the species) the power will be exercised by a minority smaller still. Man's conquest of Nature, if the dreams of some scientific planners are realized, means the rule of a few hundreds of men over billions upon billions of men. There neither is nor can be any simple increase of power on Man's side. Each new power won *by* man is a power *over* man as well. Each advance leaves him weaker as well as stronger. In every victory, besides being the general who triumphs, he is also the prisoner who follows the triumphal car.

Please note that I am not yet speaking about the problem of the misuse or abuse of power. The point is rather that the power which grows is unavoidably the power of only some men, and that the number of powerful men decreases as power increases.

Specific problems of abuse and misuse of specific powers must not, however, be overlooked. Some have voiced the fear that the technologies of genetic engineering and behavior control, though developed for good purposes, will be put to evil uses. These fears are perhaps somewhat exaggerated, if only because biomedical technologies would add very little to our highly developed arsenal for mischief, destruction, and stultification. Nevertheless, any proposal for large-scale human engineering should make us wary. Consider a program of positive eugenics based upon the widespread practice of asexual reproduction. Who shall decide what constitutes a superior individual worthy of replication? Who shall decide which individuals may or must reproduce, and by which method? These are questions easily answered only for a tyrannical regime.

Concern about the use of power is equally necessary in the selection of means for desirable or agreed-upon ends. Consider the desired end of limiting population growth. An effective program of fertility control is likely to be coercive. Who should decide the choice of means? Will the program penalize "conscientious objectors"?

Serious problems arise simply from obtaining and disseminating information, as in the mass screening programs now being proposed for detection of genetic disease. For what kinds of disorders is compulsory screening justified? Who shall have access to the data obtained, and for what purposes? To whom does information about a person's genotype belong? In ordinary medical practice, the patient's privacy is protected by the doctor's adherence to the principle of confidentiality. What will protect his privacy under conditions of mass screening?

More than privacy is at stake if screening is undertaken to detect psychological or behavioral abnormalities. A recent proposal, tendered and supported high in government, called for the psychological testing of all 6-year-olds to detect future criminals and misfits. The proposal was rejected; current tests lack the requisite predictive powers. But will such a proposal be rejected if reliable tests become available? What if certain genetic disorders, diagnosable in childhood, can be shown to correlate with subsequent antisocial behavior? For what degree of correlation and for what kinds of behavior can mandatory screening be justified? What use should be made of the data? Might not the dissemination of the information itself undermine the individual's chance for a worthy life and contribute to his so-called antisocial tendencies?

Consider the seemingly harmless effort to redefine clinical death. If the need for organs for transplantation is the stimulus for redefining death, might not this concern influence the definition at the expense of the dying? One physician, in fact, refers in writing to the revised criteria for declaring a patient dead as a "new definition of heart donor eligibility" (7, p. 526).

Problems of abuse of power arise even in the acquisition of basic knowledge. The securing of a voluntary and informed consent is an abiding problem in the use of human subjects in experimentation. Gross coercion and deception are now rarely a problem; the pressures are generally subtle, often related to an intrinsic power imbalance in favor of the experimentalist.

A special problem arises in experiments on or manipulations of the unborn. Here it is impossible to obtain the consent of the human subject. If the purpose of the intervention is therapeutic—to correct a known genetic abnormality, for example—consent can reasonably be implied. But can anyone ethically consent to nontherapeutic interventions in which parents or scientists work their wills or their eugenic visions on the child-to-be? Would not such manipulation represent in itself an abuse of power, independent of consequences?

There are many clinical situations which already permit, if not invite, the manipulative or arbitrary use of powers provided by biomedical technology: obtaining organs for transplantation, refusing to let a person die with dignity, giving genetic counselling to a frightened couple, recommending eugenic sterilization for a mental retardate, ordering electric shock for a homosexual. In each situation, there is an opportunity to violate the will of the patient or subject. Such opportunities have generally existed in medical practice, but the dangers are becoming increasingly serious. With the growing complexity of the technologies, the technician gains in authority, since he alone can understand what he is doing. The patient's lack of knowledge makes him deferential and often inhibits him from speaking up when he feels threatened. Physicians *are* sometimes troubled by their increasing power, yet they feel they cannot avoid its exercise. "Reluctantly," one commented to me, "we shall have to play God." With what guidance and to what ends I shall consider later. For the moment, I merely ask: "By whose authority?"

While these questions about power are pertinent and important, they are in one sense misleading. They imply an inherent conflict of purpose between physician and patient, between scientist and citizen. The discussion conjures up images of master and slave, of oppressor and oppressed. Yet it must be remembered that conflict of purpose is largely absent, especially with regard to general goals. To be sure, the purposes of medical scientists are not always the same as those of the subjects experimented on. Nevertheless, basic sponsors and partisans of biomedical technology are precisely those upon whom the technology will operate. The will of the scientist and physician is happily married to (rather, is the offspring of) the desire of all of us for better health, longer life, and peace of mind.

Most future biomedical technologies will probably be welcomed, as have those of the past. Their use will require little or no coercion. Some developments, such as pills to improve memory, control mood, or induce pleasure, are likely to need no promotion. Thus, even if we should escape from the dangers of coercive manipulation, we shall still face large problems posed by the voluntary use of biomedical technology, problems to which I now turn.

Voluntary Self-Degradation and Dehumanization

Modern opinion is sensitive to problems of restriction of freedom and abuse of power. Indeed, many hold that a man can be injured only by violating his will. But this view is much too narrow. It fails to recognize the great dangers we shall face in the use of biomedical technology, dangers that stem from an excess of freedom, from the uninhibited exercises of will. In my view, our greatest problem will increasingly be one of voluntary self-degradation, or willing dehumanization.

Certain desired and perfected medical technologies have already had some dehumanizing consequences. Improved methods of resuscitation have made possible heroic efforts to "save" the severely ill and injured. Yet these efforts are sometimes only partly successful; they may succeed in salvaging individuals with severe brain damage, capable of only a less-than-human, vegetating existence. Such patients, increasingly found in the intensive care units of university hospitals, have been denied a death with dignity. Families are forced to suffer seeing their loved ones so reduced, and are made to bear the burdens of a protracted death watch.

Even the ordinary methods of treating disease and prolonging life have impoverished the context in which men die. Fewer and fewer people die in the familiar surroundings of home or in the company of family and friends. At that time of life when there is perhaps the greatest need for human warmth and comfort, the dying patient is kept company by cardiac pacemakers and defibrillators, respirators, aspirators, oxygenators, catheters, and his intravenous drip.

But the loneliness is not confined to the dying patient in the hospital bed. Consider the increasing number of old people who are still alive, thanks to medical progress. As a group, the elderly are the most alienated members of our society. Not yet ready for the world of the dead, not deemed fit for the world of the living, they are shunted aside. More and more of them spend the extra years medicine has given them in "homes for senior citizens," in chronic hospitals, in nursing homes—waiting for the end. We have learned how to increase their years, but we have not learned how to help them enjoy their days. And yet, we bravely and relentlessly push back the frontiers against death.

Paradoxically, even the young and vigorous may be suffering because of medicine's success in removing death from their personal experience. Those born since penicillin represent the first generation ever to grow up without the experience or fear of probable unexpected death at an early age. They look around and see that virtually all of their friends are alive. A thoughtful physician, Eric Cassell, has remarked on this in "Death and the Physician" (8, p. 76):

> [W]hile the gift of time must surely be marked as a great blessing, the *perception* of time, as stretching out endlessly before us, is somewhat threatening. Many of us function best under deadlines, and tend to procrastinate when time limits are not set. . . . Thus, this unquestioned boon, the extension of life, and the removal of the threat of premature death, carries with it an unexpected anxiety: the anxiety of an unlimited future.
>
> In the young, the sense of limitless time has apparently imparted not a feeling of limitless opportunity, but increased stress and anxiety, in addition to the anxiety which results from other modern freedoms: personal mobility, a wide range of occupational choice, and independence from the limitations of class and familial patterns of work. . . . A certain aimlessness (often ringed around with great social consciousness) characterizes discussions about their own aspirations. The future is endless, and their inner demands seem minimal. Although it may appear uncharitable to say so, they seem to be acting in a way best described as "childish"—particularly in their lack of a time sense. They behave as though there were no tomorrow, or as though the time limits imposed by the biological facts of life had become so vague for them as to be nonexistent.

Consider next the coming power over reproduction and genotype. We endorse the project that will enable us to control numbers and to treat individuals with genetic disease. But our desires outrun these defensible goals. Many would welcome the chance to become parents without the inconvenience of pregnancy; others would wish to know in advance the characteristics of their offspring (sex, height, eye color, intelligence); still others would wish to design these characteristics to suit their tastes. Some scientists have called for the use of the new technologies to assure the "quality" of all new babies (9). As one obstetrician put it: "The business of obstetrics is to produce *optimum* babies." But the price to be paid for the "optimum baby" is the transfer of procreation from the home to the laboratory and its coincident transformation into manufacture. Increasing control over the product is purchased by the increasing depersonalization of the process. The complete depersonalization of procreation (possible with the development of an artificial placenta) shall be, in itself, seriously dehumanizing, no matter how optimum the product. It should not be forgotten that human procreation not only issues new human beings, but is itself a human activity.

Procreation is not simply an activity of the rational will. It is a more complete human activity precisely because it engages us bodily and spiritually, as well as rationally. Is there perhaps some wisdom in that mystery of nature which joins the pleasure of sex, the communication of love, and the desire for children in the very activity by which we continue the chain of human existence? Is not biological parenthood a built-in "mechanism," selected because it fosters and supports in parents an adequate concern for and commitment to their children? Would not the laboratory production of human beings no longer be *human* procreation? Could it keep human parenthood human?

The dehumanizing consequences of programmed reproduction extend beyond the mere acts and processes of life-giving. Transfer of procreation to the laboratory will no doubt weaken what is presently for many people the best remaining justification and support for the existence of marriage and the family. Sex is now comfortably at home outside of marriage; child-rearing is progressively being given over to the state, the schools, the mass media, and the child-care centers. Some have argued that the family, long the nursery of humanity, has outlived its usefulness. To be sure, laboratory and governmental alternatives might be designed for procreation and child-rearing, but at what cost?

This is not the place to conduct a full evaluation of the biological family. Nevertheless, some of its important virtues are, nowadays, too often overlooked. The family is rapidly becoming the only institution in an increasingly impersonal world where each person is loved not for what he does or makes, but simply because he is. The family is also the institution where most of us, both as children and as parents, acquire a sense of continuity with the past and a sense of commitment to the future. Without the family, we would have little incentive to take an interest in anything after our own deaths. These observations suggest that the elimination of the family would weaken ties to past and future, and would throw us, even more than we are now, to the mercy of an impersonal, lonely present.

Neurobiology and psychobiology probe most directly into the distinctively human. The technological fruit of these sciences is likely to be both more tempting than Eve's apple and more "catastrophic" in its result (10). One need only consider contemporary drug use to see what people are willing to risk or sacrifice for novel experiences, heightened perceptions, or just "kicks." The possibility of drug-induced, instant, and effortless gratification will be welcomed. Recall the possibilities of voluntary self-stimulation of the brain to reduce anxiety, to heighten pleasure, or to create visual and auditory sensation unavailable through the peripheral sense organs. Once these techniques are perfected and safe, is there much doubt that they will be desired, demanded, and used?

What ends will these techniques serve? Most likely, only the most elemental, those most tied to the bodily pleasures. What will happent to thought, to love, to friendship, to art, to judgment, to public-spiritedness in a society with a perfected technology of pleasure? What kinds of creatures will we become if we obtain our pleasure by drug or electrical stimulation without the usual kind of human efforts and frustrations? What kind of society will we have?

We need only consult Aldous Huxley's prophetic novel *Brave New World* for a likely answer to these questions. There we encounter a society dedicated to homogeneity and stability, administered by means of instant gratifications and peopled by creatures of human shape but of stunted humanity. They consume, fornicate, take "soma," and operate the machinery that makes it all possible. They do not read, write, think, love, or govern themselves. Creativity and curiosity, reason and passion, exist only in a rudimentary and mutilated form. In short, they are not men at all.

True, our techniques, like theirs, may in fact enable us to treat schizophrenia, to alleviate anxiety, to curb aggressiveness. We, like they, may indeed be able to save mankind from itself, but probably only at the cost of its humanness. In the end, the price of relieving man's estate might well be the abolition of man (*11*).

There are, of course, many other routes leading to the abolition of man. There are many other and better known causes of dehumanization. Disease, starvation, mental retardation, slavery, and brutality—to name just a few—have long prevented many, if not most, people from living a fully human life. We should work to reduce and eventually to eliminate these evils. But the existence of these evils should not prevent us from appreciating that the use of the technology of man, uninformed by wisdom concerning proper human ends, and untempered by an appropriate humility and awe, can unwittingly render us all irreversibly less than human. For, unlike the man reduced by disease or slavery, the people dehumanized à la *Brave New World* are not miserable, do not know that they are dehumanized, and, what is worse, would not care if they knew. They are, indeed, happy slaves, with a slavish happiness.

Some Fundamental Questions

The practical problems of distributing scarce resources, of curbing the abuses of power, and of preventing voluntary dehumanization point beyond themselves to some large, enduring, and most difficult questions: the nature of justice and the good community, the nature of man and the good for man. My appreciation of the profundity of these questions and my own ignorance before them makes me hesitant to say any more about them. Nevertheless, previous failures to find a shortcut around them have led me to believe that these questions must be faced if we are to have any hope of understanding where biology is taking us. Therefore, I shall try to show in outline how I think some of the larger questions arise from my discussion of dehumanization and self-degradation.

My remarks on dehumanization can hardly fail to arouse argument. It might be said, correctly, that to speak about dehumanization presupposes a concept of "the distinctively human." It might also be said, correctly, that to speak about wisdom concerning proper human ends presupposes that such ends do in fact exist and that they may be more or less accessible to human understanding, or at least to human understanding, or at least to rational inquiry. It is true that neither presupposition is at home in modern thought.

The notion of the "distinctively human" has been seriously challenged by modern scientists. Darwinists hold that man is, at least in origin, tied to the subhuman; his seeming distinctiveness is an illusion or, at most, not very important. Biochemists and molecular biologists extend the challenge by blurring the distinction between the living and the nonliving. The laws of physics and chemistry are found to be valid and are held to be sufficient for explaining biological systems. Man is a collection of molecules, an accident on the stage of evolution, endowed by chance with the power to change himself, but only along determined lines.

Psychoanalysts have also debunked the "distinctly human." The essence of man is seen to be located in those drives he shares with other animals—pursuit of pleasure and avoidance of pain. The so-called "higher functions" are understood to be servants of the more elementary, the more base. Any distinctiveness or "dignity" that man has consists of his superior capacity for gratifying his animal needs.

The idea of "human good" fares no better. In the social sciences, historicists and existentialists have helped drive this question underground. The former hold all notions of human good to be culturally and historically bound, and hence mutable. The latter hold that values are subjective: each man makes his own, and ethics becomes simply the cataloging of personal tastes.

Such appear to be the prevailing opinions. Yet there is nothing novel about reductionism, hedonism, and relativism; these are doctrines with which Socrates contended. What is new is that these doctrines seem to be vindicated by scientific advance. Not only do the scientific notions of nature and of man flower into verifiable predictions, but they yield marvelous fruit. The technological triumphs are held to validate their scientific foundations. Here, perhaps, is the most pernicious result of technological progress—more dehumanizing than any actual manipulation or technique, present or future. We are witnessing the erosion, perhaps the final erosion, of the idea of man as something splendid or divine, and its replacement with a view that sees man, no less than nature, as simply more raw material for manipulation and homogenization. Hence, our peculiar moral crisis. We are in turbulent seas without a landmark precisely because we adhere more and more to a view of nature and of man which both gives us enormous power and, at the same time, denies all possibility of standards to guide its use. Though well-equipped, we know not who we are nor where we are going. We are left to the accidents of our hasty, biased, and ephemeral judgments.

Let us not fail to note a painful irony: our conquest of nature has made us the slaves of blind chance. We triumph over nature's unpredictabilities only to subject ourselves to the still greater unpredictability of our capricious wills and our fickle opinions. That we have a method is no proof against our madness. Thus, engineering the engineer as well as the engine, we race our train we know not where (12).

While the disastrous consequences of ethical nihilism are insufficient to refute it, they invite and make urgent a reinvestigation of the ancient and enduring questions of what is a proper life for a human being, what is a good community, and how are they achieved (13). We must not be deterred from these questions simply because the best minds in human history have failed to settle them. Should we not rather be encouraged by the fact that they considered them to be the most important questions?

As I have hinted before, our ethical dilemma is caused by the victory of modern natural science with its nonteleological view of man. We ought therefore to reexamine with great care the modern notions of nature and of man, which undermine those earlier notions that provide a basis for ethics. If we consult our common experience, we are likely to discover some grounds for believing that the questions about man and human good are far from closed. Our common experience suggests many difficulties for the modern "scintific view of man." For example, this view fails to account for the concern for justice and freedom that appears to be characteristic of all human societies (14). It also fails to account for or to explain the fact that men have speech and not merely voice, that men can choose and act and not merely move or react. It fails to explain why men engage in moral discourse, or, for that matter, why they speak at all. Finally, the "scientific view of man" cannot account for scientific inquiry itself, for why men seek to know. Might there not be something the matter with a knowledge of man that does not explain or take account of his most distinctive activities, aspirations, and concerns (15)?

Having gone this far, let me offer one suggestion as to where the difficulty might lie: in the modern understanding of knowledge. Since Bacon, as I have mentioned earlier, technology has increasingly come to be the basic justification for scientific inquiry. The end is power, not knowledge for its own sake. But power is not only the end. It is also an important *validation* of knowledge. One definitely knows that one knows only if one can make. Synthesis is held to be the ultimate proof of understanding (16). A more radical formulation holds that one knows only what one makes: knowing *equals* making.

Yet therein lies a difficulty. If truth be the power to change or to make the object studied, then of what do we have knowledge? If there are no fixed realities, but only material upon which we may work our wills, will not "science" be merely the "knowledge" of the transient and the manipulatable? We might indeed have knowledge of the laws by which things change and the rules for their manipulation, but no knowledge of the things themselves. Can such a view of "science" yield any knowledge about the nature of man, or indeed, about the nature of anything? Our questions appear to lead back to the most basic of questions: What does it mean to know? What is it that is knowable (*17*)?

We have seen that the practical problems point toward and make urgent certain enduring, fundamental questions. Yet while pursuing these questions, we cannot afford to neglect the practical problems as such. Let us not forget Delgado and the "psychocivilized society." The philosophical inquiry could be rendered moot by our blind, confident efforts to dissect and redesign ourselves. While awaiting a reconstruction of theory, we must act as best we can.

What Is to Be Done?

First, we sorely need to recover some humility in the face of our awesome powers. The arguments I have presented should make apparent the folly of arrogance, of the presumption that we are wise enough to remake ourselves. Because we lack wisdom, caution is our urgent need. Or to put it another way, in the absence of that "ultimate wisdom," we can be wise enough to know that we are not wise enough. When we lack sufficient wisdom to do, wisdom consists in not doing. Caution, restraint, delay, abstention are what this second-best (and, perhaps, only) wisdom dictates with respect to the technology for human engineering.

If we can recognize that biomedical advances carry significant social costs, we may be willing to adopt a less permissive, more critical stance toward new developments. We need to reexamine our prejudice not only that all biomedical innovation is progress, but also that it is inevitable. Precedent certainly favors the view that what can be done will be done, but is this necessarily so? Ought we not to be suspicious when technologists speak of coming developments as automatic, not subject to human control? Is there not something contradictory in the notion that we have the power to control all the untoward consequences of a technology, but lack the power to determine whether it should be developed in the first place?

What will be the likely consequences of the perpetuation of our permissive and fatalistic attitude toward human engineering? How will the large decisions be made? Technocratically and self-servingly, if our experience with previous technologies is any guide. Under conditions of laissez-faire, most technologists will pursue techniques, and most private industries will pursue profits. We are fortunate that, apart from the drug manufacturers, there are at present in the biomedical area few large industries that influence public policy. Once these appear, the voice of "the public interest" will have to shout very loudly to be heard above their whisperings in the halls of Congress. These reflections point to the need for institutional controls.

Scientists understandably balk at the notion of the regulation of science and technology. Censorship is ugly and often based upon ignorant fear; bureaucratic regulation is often stupid and inefficient. Yet there is something disingenuous about a scientist who professes concern about the social consequences of science, but who responds to every suggestion of regulation with one or both of the following: "No retrictions on scientific research," and "Technological progress should not be curtailed." Surely, to suggest that *certain* technologies ought to be regulated or forestalled is not to call for the halt of *all* technological progress (and says nothing at all about basic research). Each development should be considered on its own merits. Although the dangers of regulation cannot be dismissed, who, for example, would still object to efforts to obtain an effective, complete, global prohibition on the development, testing, and use of biological and nuclear weapons?

The proponents of laissez-faire ignore two fundamental points. They ignore the fact that not to regulate is as much a policy decision as the opposite, and that it merely postpones the time of regulation. Controls will eventually be called for—as they are now being demanded to end environmental pollution. If attempts are not made early to detect and diminish the social costs of biomedical advances by intelligent institutional regulation, the society is likely to react later with more sweeping, immoderate, and throttling controls.

The proponents of laissez-faire also ignore the fact that much of technology is already regulated. The federal government is already deep in research and development (for example, space, electronics, and weapons) and is the principal sponsor of biomedical research. One may well question the wisdom of the direction given, but one would be wrong in arguing that technology cannot survive social control. Clearly, the question is not control versus no control, but rather what kind of control, when, by whom, and for what purpose.

Means for achieving international regulation and control need to be devised. Biomedical technology can be no nation's monopoly. The need for international agreements and supervision can readily be understood if we consider the likely American response to the successful asexual reproduction of 10,000 Mao Tse-tungs.

To repeat, the basic short-term need is caution. Practically, this means that we should shift the burden of proof to the *proponents* of a new biomedical technology. Concepts of "risk" and "cost" need to be broadened to include some of the social and ethical consequences discussed earlier. The probable or possible harmful effects of the widespread use of a new technique should be anticipated and introduced as "costs" to be weighed in deciding about the *first* use. The regulatory institutions should be encouraged to exercise restraint and to formulate the grounds for saying "no." We must all get used to the idea that biomedical technology makes possible many things we should never do.

But caution is not enough. Nor are clever institutional arrangements. Institutions can be little better than the people who make them work. However worthy our intentions, we are deficient in understanding. In the *long* run, our hope can only lie in education: in a public educated about the meanings and limits of science and enlightened in its use of technology; in scientists better educated to understand the relationships between science and technology on the one hand, and ethics and politics on the other; in human beings who are as wise in the latter as they are clever in the former.

REFERENCES AND NOTES

1. R. G. Edwards, B. D. Bavister, P. C. Steptoe, *Nature* **221**, 632 (1969).

2. R. G. Edwards, P. C. Steptoe, J. M. Purdy, *ibid.* **227**, 1307 (1970). [Steptoe achieved the first "test tube" baby in 1978.—C.L.R.]

3. H. J. Muller, *Science* **134**, 643 (1961).

4. J. M. R. Delgado, *Physical Control of the Mind: Toward a Psychocivilized Society* (Harper & Row, New York, 1969).

5. F. Bacon, *The Advancement of Learning, Book I*, H. G. Dick, Ed. (Random House, New York, 1955), p. 193.

6. C. S. Lewis, *The Abolition of Man* (Macmillan, New York, 1965), pp. 69–71.

7. D. D. Rutstein, *Daedalus* (Spring 1969), p. 523.

8. E. J. Cassell, *Commentary* (June 1969), p. 73.

9. B. Glass, *Science* **171**, 23 (1971).

10. It is, of course, a long-debated question as to whether the fall of Adam and Eve ought to be considered "catastrophic," or more precisely, whether the Hebrew tradition considered it so. I do not mean here to be taking sides in this quarrel by my use of the term "catastrophic," and, in fact, tend to line up on the negative side of the questions, as put above. Curiously, as Aldous Huxley's *Brave New World* [(Harper & Row, New York, 1969)] suggests, the implicit goal of the biomedical technology could well be said to be the reversal of the Fall and a return of man to the hedonic and immortal existence of the Garden of Eden. Yet I can point to at least two problems. First, the new Garden of Eden will probably have no gardens; the received, splendid world of nature will be buried beneath asphalt, concrete, and other human fabrications, a transformation that is already far along. (Recall that in *Brave New World* elaborate consumption-oriented, mechanical amusement parks—featuring, for example, centrifugal bumble-puppy—had supplanted wilderness and even ordinary gardens.) Second, the new inhabitant of the new "Garden" will have to be a creature for whom we have no precedent, a creature as difficult to imagine as to bring into existence. He will have to be simultaneously an innocent like Adam and a technological wizard who keeps the "Garden" running. (I am indebted to Dean Robert Goldwin, St. John's College, for this last insight.)

11. Some scientists naively believe that an engineered increase in human intelligence will steer us in the right direction. Surely we have learned by now that intelligence, whatever it is and however measured, is not synonymous with wisdom and that, if harnessed to the wrong ends, it can cleverly perpetrate great folly and evil. Given the activities in which many, if not most, of our best minds are now engaged, we should not simply rejoice in the prospect of enchancing IQ. On what would this increased intelligence operate? At best, the programming of further increases in IQ. It would design and operate techniques for prolonging life, for engineering reproduction, for delivering gratifications. With no gain in wisdom, our gain in intelligence can only enhance the rate of our dehumanization.

12. The philosopher Hans Jonas has made the identical point: "Thus the slow-working accidents of nature, which by the very patience of their small increments, large numbers, and gradual decisions, may well cease to be 'accident' in outcome, are to be replaced by the fast-working accidents of man's hasty and biased decisions, not exposed to the long test of the ages. His uncertain ideas are to set the goals of generations, with a certainty borrowed from the presumptive certainty of the means. The latter presumption is doubtful enough, but this doubtfulness becomes secondary to the prime question that arises when man indeed undertakes to 'make himself': in what image of his own devising shall he do so, even granted that he can be sure of the means? In fact, of course, he can be sure of neither, not of the end, nor of the means, once he enters the realm where he plays with the roots of life. Of one thing only can he be sure: of his power to move the foundations and to cause incalculable and irreversible consequences. Never was so much power coupled with so little guidance for its use." [*J. Cent. Conf. Rabbis* (January 1968), p. 27.] These remarks demonstrate that, contrary to popular belief, we are not even on the right road toward a rational understanding of and rational control over human nature and human life. It is indeed the height of irrationality triumphantly to pursue rationalized technique, while at the same time insisting that questions of ends, values, and purposes lie beyond rational discourse.

13. It is encouraging to note that these questions are seriously being raised in other quarters—for example, by persons concerned with the decay of cities or the pollution of nature. There is a growing dissatisfaction with ethical nihilism. In fact, its tenets are unwittingly abandoned, by even its staunchest adherents, in any discussion of "what to do." For example, in the biomedical area, everyone, including the most unreconstructed and technocratic reductionist, finds himself speaking about the use of powers for "human betterment." He has wandered unawares onto ethical ground. One cannot speak of "human betterment" without considering what is meant by *the human* and by the related notion of *the good for man*. These questions can be avoided only by asserting that practical matters reduce to tastes and power, and by confessing that the use of the phrase "human betterment" is a deception to cloak one's own will to power. In other words, these questions can be avoided only by ceasing to discuss.

14. Consider, for example, the widespread acceptance, in the legal systems of very different societies and cultures, of the principle and the practice of third-party adjudication of disputes. And consider why, although many societies have practiced slavery, no slaveholder has preferred his own enslavement to his own freedom. It would seem that some notions of justice and freedom, as well as right and truthfulness, are constitutive for any society, and that a concern for these values may be a fundamental characteristic of "human nature."

15. Scientists may, of course, continue to believe in righteousness or justice or truth, but these beliefs are not grounded in their "scientific knowledge" of man. They rest instead upon the receding wisdom of an earlier age.

16. This belief, silently shared by many contemporary biologists, has recently been given the following clear expression: "One of the acid tests of understanding an object is the ability to put it together from its component parts. Ultimately, molecular biologists will attempt to subject their understanding of all structure and function to this sort of test by trying to synthesize a cell. It is of some interest to see how close we are to this goal." [P. Handler, Ed, *Biology and the Future of Man* (Oxford Univ. Press, New York, 1970), p. 55.]

17. When an earlier version of this article was presented publicly, it was criticized by one questioner as being "antiscientific." He suggested that my remarks "were the kind that gave science a bad name." He went on to argue that, far from being the enemy of morality, the pursuit of truth was itself a highly moral activity, perhaps the highest. The relation of science and morals is a long and difficult question with an illustrious history, and it deserves a more extensive discussion than space permits. However, because some readers may share the questioner's response, I offer a brief reply. First, on the matter of reputation, we should recall that the pursuit of truth may be in tension with keeping a good name (witness Oedipus, Socrates, Galileo, Spinoza, Solzhenitsyn). For most of human history, the pursuit of truth (including "science") was not a reputable activity among the many, and was, in fact, highly suspect. Even today, it is doubtful whether more than a few appreciate knowledge as an end in itself. Science has acquired a "good name" in recent times largely because of its technological fruit; it is therefore to be expected that a disenchantment with technology will reflect badly upon science. Second, my own attack has not been directed against science, but against the use of *some* technologies and, even more, against the unexamined belief—indeed, I would say, superstition—that all biomedical technology is an unmixed blessing. I share the questioner's belief that the pursuit of truth is a highly moral activity. In fact, I am inviting him and others to join in a pursuit of the truth about whether all these new technologies are really good for us. This is a question that merits and is susceptible of serious intellectual inquiry. Finally, we must ask whether what we call "science" has a monopoly on the pursuit of truth. What is "truth"? What is knowable, and what does it mean to know? Surely, these are also questions that can be examined. Unless we do so, we shall remain ignorant about what "science" is and about what it discovers. Yet "science"—that is, modern natural science—cannot begin to answer them; they are philosophical questions, the very ones I am trying to raise at this point in the text.

INDEX

533